D1823614

THE SECULAR CLERGY IN ENGLAND, 1066–1216

The Secular Clergy in England, 1066–1216

HUGH M. THOMAS

OXFORD

UNIVERSITY PRESS

OXFORD

UNIVERSITY PRESS

Great Clarendon Street, Oxford, OX2 6DP,
United Kingdom

Oxford University Press is a department of the University of Oxford.
It furthers the University's objective of excellence in research, scholarship,
and education by publishing worldwide. Oxford is a registered trade mark of
Oxford University Press in the UK and in certain other countries

© Hugh M. Thomas 2014

The moral rights of the author have been asserted

First Edition published in 2014

Impression: 1

All rights reserved. No part of this publication may be reproduced, stored in
a retrieval system, or transmitted, in any form or by any means, without the
prior permission in writing of Oxford University Press, or as expressly permitted
by law, by licence or under terms agreed with the appropriate reprographics
rights organization. Enquiries concerning reproduction outside the scope of the
above should be sent to the Rights Department, Oxford University Press, at the
address above

You must not circulate this work in any other form
and you must impose this same condition on any acquirer

Published in the United States of America by Oxford University Press
198 Madison Avenue, New York, NY 10016, United States of America

British Library Cataloguing in Publication Data
Data available

Library of Congress Control Number: 2014931569

ISBN 978–0–19–870256–6

Printed and bound by
CPI Group (UK) Ltd, Croydon, CR0 4YY

Links to third party websites are provided by Oxford in good faith and
for information only. Oxford disclaims any responsibility for the materials
contained in any third party website referenced in this work.

To my daughter, Julia

Acknowledgments

It is a great pleasure to acknowledge the many organizations and people who have helped me throughout the extended process of researching and writing this book. I have spent so long on it that the University of Miami has provided me with two sabbatical leaves, the second of which was particularly useful because it allowed me to take an outside fellowship. The university has also provided the funds for a number of short research trips to do research on the project at various archives and libraries, and the College of Arts and Sciences helped pay for the inclusion of plates in the work. The Center for the Humanities, which is a wonderful addition to scholarly life at the University of Miami, provided additional leave time to begin writing, and its head, Mihoko Suzuki, and the other fellows created a stimulating intellectual atmosphere in which to work. Over the years, the university as a whole has invested many resources in my research, for which I owe a large debt of gratitude. A term as a Visiting Fellow at All Souls College, Oxford, provided two months of access to the extraordinary resources of Oxford University and much convivial and absorbing interaction with other scholars. Much of the first draft was written during a fellowship at the Shelby Cullom Davis Center for Historical Studies at Princeton University. There, Dan Rodgers, then director, Yair Mintzker, then executive secretary, the other fellows, and the Princeton faculty created yet another delightful environment in which to work.

This book has benefited from work in many libraries and archives, and I would like to thank the staff of the Richter Library at the University of Miami, the Firestone Library at Princeton (particularly Elizabeth Bennett), the Bodleian Library, the British Library, the Cambridge University Library, the All Souls and Corpus Christi College libraries in Oxford, the Corpus Christi, Sidney Sussex, and Trinity College libraries in Cambridge, the Hereford and Lincoln Cathedral libraries, the Exeter Cathedral archive, the Lambeth Palace library, the West Sussex Record Office, and the Westminster Abbey archives. In addition, I would like to thank the Master and Fellows of Trinity College, Cambridge, the Lincoln Cathedral Library, the Bodleian Libraries at the University of Oxford, the Bibliothèque de Valenciennes, and the Universitäts- und Landesbibliothek, Darmstadt, for permission to reproduce images from their collections. I regret that one important book, Everett Crosby's *The King's Bishops: The Politics of Patronage in England and Normandy, 1066–1216* (New York, 2013), came to my attention too late for its findings to be incorporated into my work.

Many scholars have helped me in a variety of ways. My colleagues in the history department at the University of Miami have provided a supportive atmosphere. Michael Clanchy, John Gillingham, Ruth Karras, Mary Lindemann, Bill Jordan, and Guido Ruggiero have generously supported my career in various ways in the last decade. Karl Gunther helped me think about the issue of reform for this book, and Helen Deeming sent me notes on some manuscripts. The audiences of a number of scholarly talks that I have given over the years have provided me with valuable feedback on specific parts of the book, and scholars too numerous to name have helped me to think about the project in informal discussions. Dominique Reill helped me to deal with the vagaries of my reference software and Hermann Beck helped me with obtaining one of my images. Julia Barrow, Monica Green, Ruth Karras, Frédérique Lachaud, Cary Nederman, Jennifer Thibodeaux, and Elisabeth van Houts all sent me useful books or articles they had written, in some cases in advance of publication. Paul Brand, Ruth Karras, Guido Ruggiero, Rod Thomson, Jennifer Thibodeaux, Ralph Turner, and Elisabeth van Houts all read chapters of the book and provided excellent feedback. Michael Clanchy and an anonymous scholar read the whole work for Oxford University Press and provided many probing comments and useful suggestions for the final revisions. At Oxford University Press, Christopher Wheeler, now retired, got the submissions underway, and Cathryn Steele, Emma Slaughter, Gillian Northcott Liles, and Francis Eaves provided much help along the way. Thanks to all this help, the book is much better than it would otherwise have been, and for this I am profoundly grateful.

Contents

List of Plates   xiii

I. MODELS OF CLERICAL BEHAVIOR

1. Introduction   3

2. The Model Priest and his Antithesis   17
  1. The exalted status of priests and clerics   20
  2. The critique of the clergy   24

3. The Aristocratic Cleric   37
  1. The aristocratic status of elite clerics   38
  2. Clerics and aristocratic culture   42
  3. Social, moral, and religious tensions   48

II. THE CLERGY AND THE WORLD

4. The Wealth of the Secular Clergy   55
  1. Ecclesiastical incomes   56
  2. Secular sources of clerical income   71
  3. Clerics and economic development   75
  4. Religious anxiety about clerical wealth   81

5. Patronage and Advancement   87
  1. The competition for benefices   88
  2. Acquiring benefices: simony, inheritance, and nepotism   90
  3. Acquiring benefices: lordship, service, and friendship   99
  4. Acquiring benefices: morals and education   109
  5. Patronage, tension, and anxiety   114

6. Courtiers, Bureaucrats, and Hell   117
  1. Service to ecclesiastical magnates, secular lords, and the king 118
  2. Lay and clerical administrators   122
  3. Literacy, numeracy, education, and bureaucracy   125
  4. The religious critique of courts and clerical courtiers   139

7. Clerical Marriage and Clerical Celibacy   154
  1. The campaign for clerical celibacy   155
  2. Resistance to the campaign for clerical celibacy   164
  3. Exhortation and the impact on priests' partners and children   178

4. How successful was the drive for clerical celibacy?   183
5. Same-sex relationships and the secular clergy   186

8. **Kinship, Household, Hospitality, and Friendship**   190
1. Kinship   191
2. Household and hospitality   196
3. Friendship   199

9. **Violence, Clerical Status, and the Issue of Criminous Clerks**   209
1. Clerics, violence, and taboos   210
2. Clerical violence and the Becket dispute   214
3. Causes and motives of clerical violence   222

III. THE CULTURAL AND INTELLECTUAL IMPACT OF THE CLERGY

10. **English Secular Clerics and the Growth of European Intellectual Life in the Twelfth-Century Renaissance**   227
1. English clerics and continental centers of learning   228
2. England and the Twelfth-Century Renaissance   238
3. The proliferation of intellectuals among the secular clergy   239

11. **Secular Clerics as Collectors and Donors of Books**   246
1. Numbers of books owned by secular clerics   248
2. Types of books owned by secular clerics   254
3. The impact of book ownership by secular clerics   260

12. **Secular Clerics as Authors and Intellectuals**   266
1. The varieties of intellectual work by secular clerics   267
2. Secular clerics and "practical" knowledge   277
3. Controversies over learning   289

13. **Secular Clerics as Cultural Patrons and Performers**   298
1. Secular clerics and the "performing arts"   299
2. Secular clerics as patrons of art   307
3. Secular clerics, architecture, architectural sculpture, and wall painting   313
4. Intellectuals and art   318

IV. THE RELIGIOUS LIFE OF THE CLERGY

14. **Clerics and Religious Life**   323
1. Efforts to improve pastoral care   324
2. Sacraments, worship, intercession, and the Christian habitus 331
3. The pious activities of secular clerics   335
4. Skepticism and intolerance   338

15. The War against the Monks 343
    1. The rivalry and its causes 344
    2. Competition over authority and morality 353
    3. Peacemaking, cooperation, and ambivalence 357
    4. The secular clergy as second best 360

Conclusion 365

Bibliography 373
Index 413

List of Plates

1. Jordan Fantosme as a student of Gilbert de la Porrée (Bibliothèque Municipale de Valenciennes, MS 197, fol. 4v)

2. Master Adam of Balsham, Socrates, Plato, and Aristotle surrounding Lady Dialectic (Universitäts- und Landesbibliothek Darmstadt, MS 2282, fol. 1v)

3. Musical composition of Ralph Niger (Lincoln Cathedral Library, MS 15, fol. 38)

4. King David playing the harp in a manuscript donated by Hamo the Chancellor (Lincoln Cathedral Library, MS 174, fol. 51v)

5. Judith in a bible donated by Nicholas, archdeacon of Huntingdon (Lincoln Cathedral Library, MS 1, fol. 70r)

6. Initial in the form of a dragon in a manuscript donated by Jordan the Treasurer (Lincoln Cathedral Library, MS 171, fol. 139r)

7. Illuminated initials in a manuscript donated to Exeter by Robert de Hanc (Bodleian Libraries, University of Oxford, MS Bodl. 725, fol. 226r)

8. Illuminated initials from Herbert of Bosham's psalter (Trinity College, Cambridge, MS B.5.4, fol. 71r)

PART I
MODELS OF CLERICAL BEHAVIOR

1

Introduction

Thomas Becket is best known as an archbishop who became a martyr as a result of his dispute with Henry II. Even before Becket became archbishop, however, he was one of the most important men in England. Despite being from an urban rather than a noble background, he was arguably King Henry II's most influential confidant. As a chancellor who also carried out a wide variety of miscellaneous tasks for Henry, he was a dominant figure in the royal government. So important was he that in 1158 he headed a lavish embassy to Paris to arrange a wedding between Henry II's heir and a daughter of the king of France. In the following year, he led a large military contingent in Henry's expedition against the counts of Toulouse. Thomas, in short, was a very powerful man. He was also a member of an extremely influential group that has been surprisingly neglected in the scholarship: the secular clergy beneath the level of bishop.

Any reader interested in the lay nobility or in monks and nuns in England in the central Middle Ages can find a number of books on those subjects.[1] However, no book exists on the English secular clergy below the level of bishop for any period before 1495.[2] The English historiography is by no means unique. Francis Rapp, in

---

[1] For example, David Knowles, *The Monastic Order in England: A History of its Development from the Times of St. Dunstan to the Fourth Lateran Council, 940–1216* (Cambridge, 1963); Barbara F. Harvey, *Living and Dying in England, 1100–1540: The Monastic Experience* (Oxford, 1993); Brian Golding, *Gilbert of Sempringham and the Gilbertine Order, c.1130–c.1300* (Oxford, 1995); Emma Mason, *Westminster Abbey and its People, c.1050–c.1216* (Woodbridge, 1996); Janet E. Burton, *The Monastic Order in Yorkshire, 1069–1215* (Cambridge, 1999); Antonia Gransden, *A History of the Abbey of Bury St Edmunds, 1182–1256: Samson of Tottington to Edmund of Walpole* (Woodbridge, 2007); Janet E. Burton and Karen Stöber, eds., *Monasteries and Society in the British Isles in the Later Middle Ages* (Woodbridge, 2008); Janet Burton, *Monastic and Religious Orders in Britain, 1000–1300* (Cambridge, 1994); Sharon K. Elkins, *Holy Women of Twelfth-Century England* (Chapel Hill, 1988); Sally Thompson, *Women Religious: The Founding of English Nunneries after the Norman Conquest* (Oxford, 1991); David Crouch, *The Image of Aristocracy in Britain, 1000–1300* (London, 1993); Peter R. Coss, *The Knight in Medieval England, 1000–1400* (Stroud, 1993); Hugh M. Thomas, *Vassals, Heiresses, Crusaders, and Thugs: The Gentry of Angevin Yorkshire, 1154–1216* (Philadelphia, 1993); Judith A. Green, *The Aristocracy of Norman England* (Cambridge, 1997); David Crouch, *The Birth of Nobility: Constructing Aristocracy in England and France, 900–1300* (Harlow, 2005); David Crouch, *The English Aristocracy, 1070–1272: A Social Transformation* (New Haven, 2011). Henry Mayr-Harting recently described the period 1066–1216 in England as the "monastic century": Henry Mayr-Harting, *Religion, Politics and Society in Britain, 1066–1272* (Harlow, 2011), 130–82.

[2] Margaret Bowker, *The Secular Clergy in the Diocese of Lincoln, 1495–1520* (Cambridge, 1968). A. Hamilton Thompson's book on the English clergy obviously devoted space to them, but most of it was on bishops, diocesan organization, and monks: A. Hamilton Thompson, *The English Clergy and their Organization in the Later Middle Ages* (Oxford, 1947). Two books on the late Middle Ages are devoted to important subsections among the secular clergy: Peter Heath, *The English Parish Clergy on*

the introduction to *Le clerc séculier au moyen âge*, noted that no earlier books had been devoted to the subject, and even that book, though it contains admirable essays on a variety of subjects, provides no general overview.[3] There is, of course, plenty to learn about the English secular clergy from overviews of the English Church or from works on specific aspects of ecclesiastical history.[4] In addition, Robert Bartlett, Michael Richter, and John Cotts have written biographies of Gerald of Wales and Peter of Blois, two prominent secular clerics who spent substantial portions of their careers in England, and Diana Greenway and Julia Barrow have done invaluable prosopographical work on the cathedral clergy in the *Fasti Ecclesiae Anglicanae*.[5] Yet the only scholar who has focused on the English secular clergy in the period as a distinct group or topic is Julia Barrow, who has written some excellent articles dealing with various aspects of the lives of secular clerics, particularly cathedral canons.[6] This scholarly neglect is remarkable, given that the secular clergy formed one of the most influential religious, cultural, political, and even economic groups in medieval society, even when one excludes those clerics who had become bishops.

The first major goal of this work is to rectify the neglect of the secular clergy, at least for England in the long twelfth century, by providing a comprehensive picture of their lives and activities drawn from as many angles as possible. The approach will be prosopographical: the study of collective biography. Some of the angles or topics from which to view the clergy, such as their religious duties or intellectual contributions, will come as no surprise to the reader. Others, including wealth, kinship and friendship networks, artistic patronage, and rivalry with the regular clergy, may be more unexpected. A fully rounded portrait of the secular clergy is

---

the Eve of the Reformation (London, 1969); David Lepine, *A Brotherhood of Canons Serving God: English Secular Cathedrals in the Later Middle Ages* (Woodbridge, 1995). Moorman devoted a good amount of space to the parish clergy in his work on the English Church in the thirteenth century: John R. H. Moorman, *Church Life in England in the Thirteenth Century* (Cambridge, 1946), 1–153, 210–41. See also Nicholas Bennett, "Pastors and Masters: The Beneficed Clergy of North-East Lincolnshire, 1290-1340," in Philippa M. Hoskin, Christopher Brooke, and Barry Dobson, eds., *The Foundations of Medieval English Ecclesiastical History: Studies Presented to David Smith* (Woodbridge, 2005), 40–62.

[3] Francis Rapp, "Rapport introductif," *Le clerc séculier au moyen âge* (Paris, 1993), 9–25, at 9.

[4] Frank Barlow, *The English Church, 1066–1154: A History of the Anglo-Norman Church* (London, 1979); C. R. Cheney, *From Becket to Langton* (Manchester, 1956); H. R. Loyn, *The English Church, 940–1154* (Harlow, 2000).

[5] Michael Richter, *Giraldus Cambrensis: The Growth of the Welsh Nation* (Aberystwyth, 1972); Robert Bartlett, *Gerald of Wales, 1146–1223* (Oxford, 1982); John D. Cotts, *The Clerical Dilemma: Peter of Blois and Literate Culture in the Twelfth Century* (Washington, D.C., 2009); Diana E. Greenway and Julia Barrow, eds., *Fasti Ecclesiae Anglicanae*, vols. 1–8, 10 (London, 1968–2005).

[6] See particularly Julia Barrow, "Cathedrals, Provosts, and Prebends: A Comparison of Twelfth-Century German and English Practice," *Journal of Ecclesiastical History* 37 (1986), 536–64; Julia Barrow, "Hereford Bishops and Married Clergy, c.1130–1240," *Historical Research* 60 (1987), 1–8; Julia Barrow, "Education and the Recruitment of Cathedral Canons in England and Germany, 1100–1225," *Viator* 20 (1989), 117–38; Julia Barrow, "Vicars Choral and Chaplains in Northern European Cathedrals, 1100–1250," in W. J. Sheils and Diana Wood, eds., *The Ministry: Clerical and Lay* (Oxford, 1989), 87–97; Julia Barrow, "The Canons and Citizens of Hereford, c.1160–c.1240," *Midland History* 24 (1999), 1–23; Julia Barrow, "Origins and Careers of Cathedral Clergy in Twelfth-Century England," *Medieval Prosopography* 21 (2000), 23–40.

useful simply for its own sake. In addition, the various facets of their lives intersected in crucial ways. For instance, the great wealth potentially available to secular clerics through acquiring benefices explains the competitiveness of their search for patronage and posts, which in turn helps explain the increasing demand for education among them, since learning gave them an edge in winning appointments. By viewing the secular clergy from a variety of angles, this study sheds more light on each individual aspect of their lives. Many of the subjects in this work will naturally be religious in nature. However, I am a social historian and this will be primarily a social history, albeit one of special interest to historians of religion. In some respects this social history approach is particularly fitting to the subject. The secular clergy, after all, got their name from the Latin *saeculum*, in this context meaning "the world." The secular clergy operated out in the world, rather than within monastic confines, and one major complaint about them was that they were too worldly. Their liminal status, the fact that they had one foot in the religious sphere and one in the worldly, is probably one of the reasons for their neglect in the scholarly literature. Religiously minded scholars are more interested in those groups such as saints, monks, and nuns who were most thoroughly ensconced in a religious environment and most likely to be thoroughly committed to their religion. For more secularly minded scholars like me, in contrast, the secular clergy have perhaps been considered too much in the religious sphere. Yet it is precisely this dual religious and worldly status that makes the secular clergy particularly interesting.

It also made them important, and the second major goal of this work is to show just *how* important the secular clergy were to their society and to historical change within the long twelfth century. Much of their importance, naturally, lay in the religious sphere. Not only were the secular clergy responsible for the lion's share of pastoral care, but they were also crucial to the development of ecclesiastical institutions and to the rise of the schools and universities, which were then primarily religious in purpose. However, their importance extended far beyond religion. Even the economic growth and innovation of the period owed something to the secular clergy. More important, in England, as elsewhere, the secular clergy made possible what Michael Clanchy has called the shift "from memory to written record," in which writing gained an important place in what had formerly been a primarily oral society.[7] England was a pioneer in the growth of royal government in this period, which would have been impossible without the skills provided by secular clerics and the incomes provided by ecclesiastical benefices. Not surprisingly, secular clerics dominated the study of canon law, but they also participated in the creation of the English common law. Even in warfare, governments depended heavily on secular clerics. Though scholars associate chivalry and courtly love almost exclusively with the lay aristocracy, secular clerics participated in, propagated, and above all recorded these phenomena, and the secular clergy played a vital role in cultural developments more generally. In keeping with my broad prosopographical approach, I will not focus simply on the contributions of unusually

---

[7] M. T. Clanchy, *From Memory to Written Record, England 1066–1307* (Oxford, 1993).

influential figures such as Thomas Becket or John of Salisbury. I certainly won't ignore such figures, but one of the points I wish to make is the collective importance of such figures as ordinary intellectuals, minor bureaucrats, or parish priests.

Specialists are, of course, aware of the importance of the secular clergy in some areas, such as government and the rise of the schools, but they have tended not to look at the specific and sometimes unique roles of the secular clergy in these developments. Moreover, I intend to offer the results of extensive research in the English sources to help expand and improve our understanding of these developments. More generally, no one has systematically studied the overall importance of the secular clergy, and the tendency has therefore been to overlook their collective impact. R. I. Moore, it is true, does ascribe an extraordinary importance to *clerici* in the period, specifically in the increasing persecution of certain groups, but more generally in a fundamental reorganization of Western society. However, his somewhat abstract category of *clerici*, which seems to consist primarily of administrators, including lay ones, is different from mine, and his discussion of the specific mechanisms by which they influenced society is limited.[8] I intend to provide a more concrete discussion of the extensive impact of the secular clergy.

My claims, while not perhaps as sweeping as Moore's, will nonetheless be far-reaching, for I will argue that secular clerics contributed more than any other group to that set of intellectual, cultural, political, and economic changes that scholars call the Twelfth-Century Renaissance. The concept of a Twelfth-Century Renaissance and its root paradigm of renaissance are of course both problematic. The term arose as a riposte to the marginalization of the Middle Ages caused by the glorification of the Italian Renaissance, and was most effectively disseminated by Charles Homer Haskins's influential book, provocatively entitled *The Renaissance of the Twelfth Century*, which focused on the intellectual and literary developments of the period.[9] The idea of a Twelfth-Century Renaissance has long had its critics but has come under increasing fire in recent years for various reasons. Scholars have noted that it was a period marked as much by pessimism and anxiety as by optimism and triumphalism; that the twelfth century was as important for the rise of intolerance as for more positive cultural achievements; and that by its nature the concept of renaissance tends to devalue the achievements of preceding periods, often unfairly. Other terms have emerged to characterize the period: renewal, revolution, crisis, transformations.[10] I cannot but acknowledge the problems raised by the critics,

---

[8] R. I. Moore, *The First European Revolution, c.970–1215* (Oxford, 2000), 6, 160–98; R. I. Moore, *The Formation of a Persecuting Society: Authority and Deviance in Western Europe, 950–1250* (Oxford, 2007), 128–47, 165–71.

[9] Charles Homer Haskins, *The Renaissance of the Twelfth Century* (Cambridge, Mass., 1927).

[10] For works on the Twelfth-Century Renaissance, and attempts to define it, see Erwin Panofsky, *Renaissance and Renascences in Western Art* (New York, 1972), 42–113; Robert Louis Benson and Giles Constable, eds., *Renaissance and Renewal in the Twelfth Century* (Cambridge, Mass., 1982), xxix–xxx; R. N. Swanson, *The Twelfth-Century Renaissance* (Manchester, 1999), 207–13; Jacques Le Goff, "What did the Twelfth-Century Renaissance Mean?," in Peter Linehan and Janet L. Nelson, eds., *The Medieval World* (London, 2001), 635–47; Marcia L. Colish, "Haskins's *Renaissance* Seventy Years Later: Beyond Anti-Burckhardtianism," *Haskins Society Journal* 11 (2003), 1–15; C. Stephen Jaeger,

above all the implicit denigration of the developments of the preceding period. Nonetheless, for all its flaws, the concept of the Twelfth-Century Renaissance still has utility. It captures the dynamism and historical importance of the period and is well known even beyond the ranks of medievalists.[11] None of the other terms used to capture the essence of the twelfth century has yet caught on, and some are likely to be just as controversial. To my mind, the Twelfth-Century Renaissance is still a useful descriptor for the myriad developments of the period.

One advantage of thinking in terms of a renaissance in the context of this specific project is that it focuses attention on intellectual and cultural change, arenas in which the secular clergy had particular impact. Nonetheless, as a social historian, I think of the Twelfth-Century Renaissance in broader terms, including social, political, and economic developments. The cultural achievements of the long twelfth century, which no one denies, are best understood in the context of broader social change, including economic growth, the development in some lands of stronger governments, and the growing institutional power of the Church. Obviously, all social groups, including nobles, peasants, townspeople, monks, and nuns, made crucial contributions to historical change in the long twelfth century, and one's assignment of relative importance to various groups will depend partly on whether one believes, for instance, that economic change or developments in learning made a greater difference. Nonetheless, by the end of the book I hope to have convinced readers that my claim that the secular clergy were the most important single group in creating the Twelfth-Century Renaissance is at least defensible.

The third major goal of this book is to explore the dramatic tensions that arose because clerics were religious figures operating in the world, often in very secular settings and functions. Cotts gave the title *The Clerical Dilemma* to his biography of Peter of Blois, and it is a fitting one. He described Peter's dilemma as "the balancing of professional, educational, and spiritual concerns in an uneasy synthesis."[12] This was a dilemma that many other clerics faced, and was but one of the many tensions clerics experienced as a result of the extraordinarily high expectations moralists placed upon them, the more worldly expectations patrons and relatives had for them, and the temptations of worldly power and wealth. To some degree these were tensions that religious figures, especially those working outside the shelter and

---

"Pessimism in the Twelfth-Century 'Renaissance'," *Speculum* 78 (2003), 1151–83; Moore, *First European Revolution*; Leidulf Melve, "'The Revolt of the Medievalists.' Directions in Recent Research on the Twelfth-Century Renaissance," *Journal of Medieval History* 32 (2006), 231–52; Thomas F. X. Noble, "Introduction," in Thomas F. X. Noble and John H. Van Engen, eds., *European Transformations: The Long Twelfth Century* (Notre Dame, 2012), 1–16; John H. Van Engen, "The Twelfth-Century: Reading, Reason, and Revolt in a World of Custom," in Thomas F. X. Noble and John H. Van Engen, eds., *European Transformations: The Long Twelfth Century* (Notre Dame, 2012), 17–44, at 17–20; John D. Cotts, *Europe's Long Twelfth Century: Order, Anxiety and Adaptation, 1095–1229* (Basingstoke, 2013), 3–9.

[11] For an overview of the remarkable amount of change in England, see John Gillingham, "A Historian of the Twelfth-Century Renaissance and the Transformation of English Society, 1066–ca. 1200," in Thomas F. X. Noble and John H. Van Engen, eds., *European Transformations: The Long Twelfth Century* (Notre Dame, 2012), 45–74.

[12] Cotts, *Clerical Dilemma*, 15.

restrictions of monastic walls, inevitably faced within medieval Christianity. However, this was a period in which secular clerics faced some important new moral and religious dilemmas. On the one hand, the Gregorian Reform, which sought to uniformly enforce earlier ideals such as clerical celibacy, created new tensions by placing important and, for all practical purposes, new demands on their behavior. On the other hand, the worldly opportunities available to secular clerics increased, particularly because of their growing employment in secular and ecclesiastical administration, thus creating new temptations and adding urgency to questions about the proper role of the cleric working in the world. No cleric could escape the moral, religious, and practical tensions that resulted from a clerical yet worldly status. Even the spiritually lukewarm faced a juggling act in trying to conform to competing expectations while fulfilling their own desires, and spiritually committed clerics experienced profound moral struggles in trying to live as moralists believed they should.

In studying the secular clergy of England in the long twelfth century one is blessed with an unusual abundance of sources. As with so many subjects, the extensive records of the royal government provide a rich body of evidence. So too do charters and other documents. However, the fact that so many secular clerics were active writers is particularly helpful. The works of Gerald of Wales alone take up eight volumes in the Rolls Series, and even so a couple of his works were left out or only partially printed there.[13] Secular clerics produced chronicles, letter collections, and writings in a host of other genres. Sermons form an especially significant source for this project. Most of the works used in this book are published and many are well known, but some informative treatises and sermon collections remain unpublished and little explored by the scholarly community. Overall, the plentiful evidence allows an unusually full reconstruction of the lives of secular clerics and of their influence on society in the period.

Before turning to the main subjects of the book it is necessary to discuss its temporal and geographic parameters and to describe the definition, nature, and membership of the secular clergy. The temporal parameters are fairly straightforward: the Norman Conquest and the death of King John in 1216, just one year after the Fourth Lateran Council. The dates were picked to give full scope to the long twelfth century, but the latter date was also chosen to end the study before the coming of the friars to England in the 1220s, which altered certain religious dynamics by introducing orders of regular clergy who operated outside the cloister. Both of these dates are nonetheless largely ones of convenience and therefore I have not hesitated to use a few sources from early in Henry III's reign which can shed light backwards and for which comparable sources do not exist earlier. Because of the exponential growth in surviving writing over the long twelfth century, far more

---

[13] Gerald of Wales, *Giraldi Cambrensis Opera*, ed. J. S. Brewer, James F. Dimock, and George F. Warner, 8 vols. (London, 1861–91); W. S. Davies, "Giraldus Cambrensis: *De Invectionibus*," *Y Cymmrodor* 30 (1920), 1–248; Gerald of Wales, *Speculum Duorum, or A Mirror of Two Men*, ed. Brian Dawson et al. (Cardiff, 1974). See also Gerald of Wales, *Expugnatio Hibernica: The Conquest of Ireland*, ed. A. B. Scott and F. X. Martin (Dublin, 1978).

of the evidence will come from the later decades of the period than from the early ones. Because of the temporal imbalance in the evidence and because of the large scope of the project, the analysis tends to be synchronic, evaluating the role of the clergy in various contexts throughout the period rather than trying to systematically chart change in each area of clerical life. There will be exceptions, however, such as a review of the slow rise of clerical celibacy in England, and it is my expectation that future scholars, perhaps drawing on sources from beyond England, will be able to more closely chart temporal change in many of the areas studied here.

The geographic parameters are complicated by the fact that elite secular clerics often had careers that took them back and forth across England's boundaries, partly because of political ties with other lands after 1066, but also because this was a period in which clerics throughout Europe could have international careers.[14] The focus will be on clerical careers within England, whatever the origins of the clerics in question, but I will also be studying the intellectual activities of English students and scholars working outside of England. In selecting to study clerics in England I am *not* making any claims about their distinctiveness compared to clerics else-where. Instead, I am focusing on England for purely pragmatic reasons: it is the region whose history and sources I know thoroughly. There were, of course, differences as well as similarities between the social and religious situations of the clergy in different parts of Europe: for instance, Julia Barrow has explored some specific differences between cathedral canons in England and Germany.[15] How-ever, at this point the work on the secular clergy is so limited that systematic comparison of English secular clerics and those of other areas is not yet possible.

What did it mean in this period to be a secular cleric? I will address this question on two levels. The first concerns a broader set of characteristics and behaviors that were meant to set the secular clergy apart as a radically distinctive group with a fundamentally important religious role. The second level is a narrower, technical discussion of what precisely made an individual a secular cleric and entitled him to acquire a benefice or enjoy the legal privileges of the clergy. The importance of the first level is clear, and indeed in setting out the characteristics and behaviors that were supposed to distinguish the clergy I will start the process of showing their importance and interest. The second level is crucial because it determines which individuals fit into the study even when they did not embrace the characteristics expected of the clergy and live their lives as clerics were supposed to.

From the standpoint of contemporary writers, as the next chapter will show, possibly the most important distinguishing mark of the clergy, and above all of priests, was their regular and intimate contact with God through the performance of the Eucharist. Though this was only one of their many ritual and pastoral duties, it was particularly important because, in the eyes of religious writers, it conferred an extraordinary religious significance on them and meant that they *had* to set themselves apart as a distinctive group and follow certain behaviors to avoid

---

[14] See Chapter 10, section 1.
[15] Barrow, "Cathedrals, Provosts, and Prebends," 536–64; Barrow, "Education and Recruitment," 117–38.

pollution when handling God. Though the history of ordination and women is complex, by this time women had been firmly excluded from any hope of membership in the clergy, partly on the basis of pollution fears.[16] Clerics, moreover, were not just supposed to be males, but a special and unusual category of men. They were expected to live an unusually moral life according to the dictates of church morality. More particularly, they were supposed to renounce violence, and though demands for clerical celibacy were hotly disputed, the belief that clerics of the status of subdeacon and higher should remain celibate was winning the day. More generally, secular clerics were supposed to remove themselves from worldly entanglements as much as possible, and this prohibition was in fact quite far-reaching: for instance, they were also supposed to avoid service at court and many kinds of economic activity. Finally, clerics were expected to be distinguished for their learning and command of Latin. Thus, the theoretical distinctiveness of the clergy entailed a range of factors: religion, with an emphasis on sacramental functions, pastoral care, and holy behavior; a closely associated stress on unworldliness; a rejection of sexuality and violence, with the rethinking of gender norms that this entailed; and literacy and learning.

Even in theory, not all these attributes were unique to the secular clergy. They shared several with monks, regular canons, and nuns, and especially with those males in religious orders who were ordained. The main theoretical difference, particularly between regular and secular clerics, was that the former remained cloistered and the latter operated out in the world, which in particular limited the ability of the former to perform pastoral care. Secular clerics were supposed to be much more sharply distinguished from the laity, but there could be similarities even with them. A small minority of laypeople were literate, and all were encouraged to emulate some aspects of unworldliness and enjoined to accept limited restrictions on violence and sexuality. Even so, secular clerics were supposed to lead a radically different life from the laypeople among whom they lived. Maureen Miller, in an article on clerical and lay culture in northern Italy, suggests that one should treat religion, in this case meaning attachment to the clergy rather than adherence to a specific religion, as a category of difference comparable to race, class, and gender.[17] Religious writers of the central Middle Ages, had they been exposed to this kind of modern historical thinking, might well have agreed, and have argued that clerics should be at least as different from the laity as women were from men and nobles were from peasants.

They would also, no doubt, have gone on to lament that the secular clergy did not distinguish themselves from the laity nearly as much as they should have. Of course, monks and nuns too were susceptible to temptations and various aspects of worldliness but, as I shall argue, secular clerics did tend to be much worldlier than the regular clergy for reasons both practical and ideological. They had families,

---

[16] For women and ordination, see Gary Macy, *The Hidden History of Women's Ordination: Female Clergy in the Medieval West* (Oxford, 2008).

[17] Maureen Miller, "Religion Makes a Difference: Clerical and Lay Cultures in the Courts of Northern Italy, 1000–1300," *American Historical Review* 105 (2000), 1095–130, at 1129–30.

employed violence, and lived lavish lifestyles. They accumulated wealth through secular as well as religious activities and enthusiastically served kings and secular magnates. Indeed, their learning, one of their key distinguishing attributes, only made them more attractive as royal officials and baronial advisors. One should not, of course, go to the opposite extreme and treat the secular clergy as no different from the laity; the difference was, as Miller urges, quite important. The secular clergy were distinguished by their religious functions and many did try to live up to the ideal of being quite different from the laity. Many of the tensions discussed in this book arose precisely from the problems of secular clerics trying to live up to the exalted distinctiveness expected of them. Nonetheless, the fact that secular clerics could not escape extensive involvement in the secular world and that some were quite worldly only makes the more technical factors that defined membership in the clergy all the more important.

So what were the more technical aspects? A secular cleric was, first of all, a man who had been ordained by a proper authority. A hierarchy of seven clerical orders, from doorkeeper to priest, had been defined in earlier centuries. By the long twelfth century the lowest three orders had fallen out of practical use, and clerics in the so-called minor orders were classified either as acolytes or merely as clerics. Above acolytes were subdeacons, deacons, and, most importantly, priests.[18] Very occasionally, writers seem to have associated mere clerics with the laity. Thus, in a Thorney Abbey charter of 1127, which was attested by abbots, monks, priests, and a deacon among others, two clerics were placed within the category of *laici*.[19] Normally, however, even ordinary clerics were held to be a category quite distinct from the laity. They had specific privileges, particularly in the legal arena, and in theory they distinguished themselves from the laity by having their hair tonsured and by wearing distinctive clerical garb.

What defined a *secular* cleric? As Cotts has noted, secular clerics were defined first and foremost in opposition to monks.[20] In the earliest centuries of monasticism, most monks were laypeople, and thus distinct from the ordained clergy. As the Middle Ages advanced, however, more and more monks were ordained, thus blurring lines. Indeed, some scholars have argued that there was little distinction between monks and the clergy in England in the early Anglo-Saxon period, though this remains a subject of debate.[21] In any case, by 1066 monks clearly formed a distinct group, and can be defined as part of the regular clergy, a term drawn from the Latin *regula*, which indicates that monks were distinguished by following a rule. Many eleventh-century reformers, however, felt that all clerics, or at least as many as possible (and particularly those associated with a cathedral or other large church), should be encouraged or required to live a common life, like monks. This effort had some success in various regions of Europe. Ultimately, however, it mainly resulted

---

[18] Julia Barrow, "Grades of Ordination and Clerical Careers, *c.*900–*c.*1200," *Anglo-Norman Studies* 30 (2007), 41–61.

[19] Cambridge University Library, Add. MS 3020, fos. 145r–v.

[20] Cotts, *Clerical Dilemma*, 12.

[21] For a recent overview that argues that the distinction *was* clear, see Catherine Cubitt, "The Clergy in Early Anglo-Saxon England," *Historical Research* 78 (2005), 273–87.

in the creation of a new type of regular clergy, the regular canons, rather than causing most clerics to follow a rule or adopt a common life.[22] As a result, the secular clergy began to be defined against regular canons as well as against monks. Indeed, the creation of separate prebends at most non-monastic English cathedrals, based most immediately on Norman models, can presumably be seen as a rejection of the drive for a common life for clerics, and it helped to distinguish secular canons more sharply.[23] Admittedly, monks sometimes lumped the regular canons in with the secular clergy.[24] Moreover, the categories of regular canons and secular clergy were new enough that the terminology was sometimes treated as unfamiliar or novel.[25] Indeed, as late as the 1160s, John of Salisbury could speak of those whom the "public (*vulgus*) called seculars" in describing how Pope Eugenius had had to reassure the canons of St. Paul's that when he commanded that they elect someone in religious habit, he did not just mean monks and regular canons, but anyone tonsured.[26] Part of the reluctance to embrace the terminology of regular and secular clergy had to do with the implied judgment values. Godwin, precentor of Salisbury, felt it necessary to insist that clerics who did not live the common life should not be called "irregular," and the monastic satirist Nigel of Whiteacre could not resist stating that secular clerics earned their title from their worldliness.[27] Many authors continued to refer to secular clerics simply as clerics, but as the twelfth century advanced, writers began more frequently to use the terminology of monks, regular canons, and the secular clergy.[28] The terminology eventually became common because several factors clearly *did* distinguish secular clerics from regular canons and

[22] J. C. Dickinson, *The Origins of the Austin Canons and their Introduction into England* (London, 1950), 26–58; Johannes Laudage, *Priesterbild und Reformpapsttum im 11. Jahrhundert* (Cologne, 1984), 44–7, 90–2, 119–21, 199–202, 236–42, 285–303; Uta-Renate Blumenthal, *The Investiture Controversy: Church and Monarchy from the Ninth to the Twelfth Century* (Philadelphia, 1988), 68–9. Bishop Leofric's adoption of the rule of Chrodegang at Exeter probably took place in the context of this drive to "regularize" the clergy, but did not set a trend, though the organization of the Exeter chapter remained distinctive as a result: Diana E. Greenway, *Fasti Ecclesiae Anglicanae, 1066–1300. 10. Exeter* (London, 2005), xvii–xviii; David Blake, "The Development of the Chapter of the Diocese of Exeter, 1050–1161," *Journal of Medieval History* 8 (1982), 1–11.

[23] C. N. L. Brooke, *The Medieval Idea of Marriage* (Oxford, 1989), 78–82.

[24] Orderic Vitalis, *The Ecclesiastical History of Orderic Vitalis*, ed. Marjorie Chibnall, 6 vols. (Oxford, 1969–80), 6:318–21; Gerald of Wales, *Opera*, 4:82.

[25] Dickinson, *Austin Canons*, 51–3; Alain Boureau, "Hypothèses sur l'émergence lexicale et théorique de la catégorie de séculier au XIIe siècle," *Le clerc séculier au moyen âge* (Paris, 1993), 35–43; Giles Constable, *The Reformation of the Twelfth Century* (Cambridge, 1996), 11–12.

[26] John of Salisbury, *The Historia Pontificalis of John of Salisbury*, ed. Marjorie Chibnall (Oxford, 1986), 88.

[27] Bodleian Library, Digby MS 96, fos. 20v–21r; Nigel of Whiteacre, *Nigel de Longchamps: Speculum Stultorum*, ed. John H. Mozley and Robert R. Raymo (Berkeley, 1960), 82–3. See also Giles Constable and Bernard Smith, eds., *Libellus de Diversis Ordinibus et Professionibus qui sunt in Aecclesia* (Oxford, 1972), 98–9.

[28] For example, E. O. Blake, ed., *Liber Eliensis*, Camden Society, 3rd ser., 92 (London, 1962), 295; Gervase of Canterbury, *The Historical Works of Gervase of Canterbury*, ed. William Stubbs, 2 vols. (London, 1879–80), 1:260–1, 332, 540; Ralph of Diceto, *Radulfi de Diceto Decani Lundoniensis Opera Historica*, ed. William Stubbs, 2 vols. (London, 1876), 1:420; Adam of Eynsham, *Magna Vita Sancti Hugonis: The Life of St. Hugh of Lincoln*, ed. Decima L. Douie and David Hugh Farmer, 2 vols. (Oxford, 1985), 1:123; William Dugdale, *Monasticon Anglicanum*, 6 in 8 vols. (London, 1846), 6:63–4.

monks: they did not have to follow a specific rule; they could own property; and above all they were not expected to live common lives, even when serving a church with other clerics or canons.

In theory, ordination should have made the distinction between the secular clergy and the laity even sharper than that between clerics and monks, and to a large degree it did, but several factors served to blur the distinction in practice. One simple matter was fraud. Papal documents reveal the case of one man who received a church without being a tonsured cleric.[29] In Lincolnshire, in 1202, a man accused of taking unwarranted tolls from ships had himself tonsured after being released to pledges, presumably in hopes of invoking clerical privilege.[30] A bigger factor in blurring the lines, and also one that helped make fraud possible, was the ability of those in minor orders to leave the clergy. This was not always viewed favorably: one miracle of the hermit Godric involved him detecting and rebuking a former cleric who was serving as a squire in a noble household; from Godric's perspective the youth was still a cleric.[31] Nonetheless, canon law allowed departure from clerical status and it may have been fairly common. There was, however, no formal process of disavowing clerical status; one simply abandoned the tonsure and clerical dress. This lack of a formal process made it easier for some individuals to maintain clerical positions while essentially abandoning the clergy. One of the miracles attributed to Thomas Becket after his death involved a former deacon who "lived secularly off of ecclesiastical revenues."[32] Clerics of elite status sometimes adopted knighthood to make clear their abandonment of clerical status, but others tried to alternate between the two statuses in the pursuit of their own interests.[33] Thus one papal decretal referred to a man who had adopted knightly arms but continued to hold a church from Cirencester Abbey, and one case in the royal courts referred to a chaplain who sometimes claimed to be a knight and sometimes a priest.[34] Other figures abandoned clerical status only to try to resume it when they thought it might be beneficial. According to the later chronicler Matthew Paris, Stephen of Segrave, who had a highly successful career in royal government under John and Henry III, had been a cleric in his youth, abandoned the clergy, and then tried to claim privilege of clergy at a politically dangerous moment in his

[29] Walther Holtzmann, Stanley Chodorow, and Charles Duggan, eds., *Decretales Ineditae Saeculi XII*, Monumenta Iuris Canonici. Series B, Corpus Collectionum, 4 (Vatican City, 1982), 129–30; Mary G. Cheney, *Roger, Bishop of Worcester, 1164–1179: An English Bishop of the Age of Becket* (Oxford, 1980), 343, 359.

[30] Doris M. Stenton, ed., *The Earliest Lincolnshire Assize Rolls, A. D. 1202–1209*, Publications of the Lincoln Record Society, vol. 22 (Lincoln, 1926), 107, 160.

[31] Reginald of Durham, *Libellus de Vita et Miraculis Sancti Godrici, Heremitae de Finchale*, ed. Joseph Stevenson, Surtees Society, vol. 20 (London, 1847), 226–8.

[32] James Craigie Robertson and J. B. Sheppard, eds., *Materials for the History of Thomas Becket, Archbishop of Canterbury*, 7 vols. (London, 1875–85), 1:358.

[33] Jean Dunbabin, "From Clerk to Knight: Changing Orders," in Christopher Harper-Bill and Ruth Harvey, eds., *The Ideals and Practice of Medieval Knighthood, II: Papers from the Third Strawberry Hill Conference* (Woodbridge, 1988), 26–39.

[34] Walther Holtzmann, ed., *Papsturkunden in England*, 3 vols. (Berlin, 1930–52), 3:162; *Curia Regis Rolls*, 7 vols. (London, 1922–35), 6:146.

career.[35] Both ecclesiastical and church officials tried to police the boundaries between lay and clerical status, but some individuals treated those boundaries as permeable.

This permeability creates minor problems of determining who should be included among the secular clergy. By and large I have simply followed contemporary designations of individuals as clerics or holders of some more specific office such as deacon, priest, chaplain, or archdeacon. Someone like Stephen of Segrave, who did not hold church office and was never identified as currently being a cleric, is therefore not included. A couple of problems remain, however. Titles sometimes became bynames or family names. One twelfth-century document decribes a sale to a Ralph *Clericus*, "called thus not by office but as a cognomen."[36] It is unlikely, however, that such cases were common. More important, Clanchy and other scholars have noted a tendency among some writers to equate learning and clerical status. *Clericus/litteratus* became a pair to contrast with *laicus/illitteratus* and even someone of clearly clerical status like Hubert Walter, in succession dean of York, bishop of Salisbury, and archbishop of Canterbury, could be described as *laicus et illitteratus*. If clerics could be described as *laici* because of a lack of learning, it is at least possible that learned laymen might occasionally have been described as *clerici*. However, most of the writers Clanchy quotes were stressing that clerics *ought* to be learned, or were abusing enemies, as in the case of Hubert Walter, so it is not at all clear that writers outside of polemical contexts would have been likely to ascribe clerical status or lack thereof simply on the basis of learning.[37] In a later period, it is true, those who wanted to claim clerical privilege simply had to pass a reading test, thus making any male with minimal literacy a cleric if he chose to claim the status, but the reading test did not appear until Edward I's reign and did not become common until the fourteenth century.[38] There is no evidence that the acquisition of learning routinely caused laypeople to be labeled as clerics, and in any case most of the important figures discussed in this book were in higher orders or held specific church positions that place their clerical status beyond doubt. Though the occasional blurring of learned and clerical status *is* an issue when it comes to discussing the topic of the clergy, the laity, and literacy, a subject I will take up in Chapter 6, otherwise it does not constitute a major problem.

It is true, of course, that some individuals who were technically clerics might reasonably be described as clerics in name only. William of Wrotham, as will be seen in Chapter 6, was a prominent royal official in the reigns of Richard I and John. He received church offices in Richard's reign but also a surprising amount of

[35] Ralph V. Turner, *Men Raised from the Dust: Administrative Service and Upward Mobility in Angevin England* (Philadelphia, 1988), 125.

[36] Emma Mason, ed., *Westminster Abbey Charters, 1066–c.1214*, London Record Society Publications, vol. 25 (London, 1988), 246.

[37] Clanchy, *From Memory to Written Record*, 226–30. See also Ralph V. Turner, *Judges, Administrators and the Common Law in Angevin England* (London, 1994), 121–2; Constable, *Reformation of the Twelfth Century*, 9–10.

[38] Leona C. Gabel, *Benefit of Clergy in England in the Later Middle Ages*, 2nd edn. (New York, 1969), 65–74.

land. Possibly he was keeping the option of leaving the clergy and becoming a landed layman open early in his clerical career, before he became an archdeacon *c*.1204. In a letter of that same year concerning a dispute over a prebend at Wells, Pope Innocent described him as a royal sergeant, normally a title reserved for the laity, and said that he had formerly lived as a layman, though the pope may well have been relying primarily on hostile testimony. During the hearing of the case, one witness testified about lending vestments to William when he was installed at Wells, and another about seeing him perform in the choir there. Their testimony was designed to show that he was in fact a properly installed canon at Wells, but William's need for such testimony suggests that he was very much an absentee (which was quite common), and the fact that he had to borrow vestments for his own installation suggests that he was not strongly committed to clerical life.[39] Nonetheless, there is no doubt that William was technically a cleric, and that is what matters for inclusion here. Indeed, because one of the main arguments is that the secular clergy straddled the worldly and the religious, the fact that William tended strongly towards the worldly only makes his example all the more useful as an illustration of one possible type of clerical life.

I am not including in the study bishops who were secular clerics, once they had been promoted to that rank, except in passing. If one included them, the arguments for the importance of the secular clergy would be even stronger. However, once clerics became bishops, they became magnates, and thus part of a very different social category. Sometimes the jump in riches and power was smaller than one might expect.[40] Nonetheless, bishops as a group were quite different in authority, wealth, and influence from most clerics, and the distinction between the regular and secular clergy became less important at the episcopal level. Moreover, bishops have been studied much more fully than lesser secular clerics, though there is certainly room for more work, especially since the *English Episcopal Acta* have made so much evidence available in a well-edited format.[41] Among the rest of the secular clergy, I will be paying more attention to the clerical elites, for instance archdeacons, cathedral canons, royal clerics, and *magistri*, than to the parish priesthood or to local clerics in minor orders. To a large degree this choice is a matter of the available evidence. Collectively, of course, the parish clergy was tremendously important, particularly when it came to pastoral care, and I will certainly not ignore them, but unfortunately it is not always possible to say much about this group. Moreover, in certain key respects such as intellectual change or the building of royal government, the clerical elite were far more important in effecting change.

The remainder of the book is divided into four sections. The first, containing Chapters 2 and 3, concerns models of clerical behavior. Chapter 2 describes the extraordinary, even cosmological, status accorded to clerics, and above all priests,

---

[39] C. R. Cheney and Mary G. Cheney, eds., *The Letters of Pope Innocent III (1198–1216) Concerning England and Wales* (Oxford, 1967), 87, 106, 110; Norma Adams and Charles Donahue, eds., *Select Cases from the Ecclesiastical Courts of the Province of Canterbury, c.1200–1301*, Publications of the Selden Society, vol. 95 (London, 1981), 11–14. For William's service, see Chapter 6, section 2.
[40] See Chapter 4, section 1.   [41] British Academy, 42 volumes published to date.

and explores the expectations of behavior that moralists laid out for the clergy. Chapter 3 discusses the comparison contemporaries often made between elite clerics and knights, and describes a loose model of an aristocratic clerical lifestyle. The second section investigates the economic, political, and social situation of the secular clergy. Chapter 4 looks at the remarkable collective wealth of the clergy and their resulting economic influence. Chapter 5 studies the patronage system and social mobility among the clergy. Chapter 6 demonstrates the fundamental importance of clerical service to ecclesiastical and secular lords and above all to the crown. Chapter 7 is about clerical families, the drive to enforce clerical celibacy, and the widespread resistance to that drive. Chapter 8 investigates other kinds of kinship relationships, clerical households, hospitality, and friendship among the clergy. Chapter 9 studies the use of violence among the clergy, with particular emphasis on the dispute between Henry II and Thomas Becket over criminous clerks. The third section focuses on the intellectual and cultural influence of the secular clergy. Chapter 10 investigates the contributions of the English clergy to international centers of learning, notes the rise of a new class of learned *magistri*, and comments on models of England's place in the Twelfth-Century Renaissance. Chapter 11 looks at clerics as owners and donors of books, stressing the collective importance of their small private libraries and the role of the clergy in the development of the book trade. Chapter 12 concerns clerics as intellectuals and particularly as authors, showing their extensive intellectual productivity in a wide range of areas. Chapter 13 investigates the cultural and artistic influence of the secular clergy both as performers and patrons. The last section focuses more narrowly on religious matters. Chapter 14 investigates the religious lives of the secular clergy, exploring what little can be known of their performance of routine religious duties, demonstrating a reasonably widespread commitment to the improvement of pastoral care, revealing that clerics frequently performed acts of private piety, and demonstrating that some could even be pioneers in practices more often associated with lay piety. Chapter 15 describes the extraordinarily bitter rivalry between monks and secular clerics. Altogether, the book strives to bring to life the world of the secular clergy in England in the long twelfth century and to show their great social and historical importance. My hope is that by showing how fascinating and how influential a group of clerics could be, I will help spark a wave of future research on the secular clergy in places and periods throughout Catholic Europe and throughout the Middle Ages, which will in turn greatly enhance our understanding of medieval history and society.

2

The Model Priest and his Antithesis

In a sermon to priests in a synod, the scholar Peter of Blois informed his audience that they were angels and gods.[1] To a modern audience such comparisons might seem ridiculously pretentious, bordering on the blasphemous, but twelfth-century religious writers often accorded priests an extraordinarily high cosmological status and authority. Gervase of Chichester, canon of Chichester Cathedral and one of Thomas Becket's circle of learned men, systematically compared priests to kings, angels, and gods in a commentary on Malachi, and various influential scholars and preachers, such as Baldwin of Ford, Gerald of Wales, Alexander Neckam, and Thomas Agnellus, made similar if less systematic comparisons, all drawing on biblical language.[2] Yet religious thinkers also frequently described priests as morally delinquent. Thus, Peter of Blois wrote that "The priest is often considered the worst among all people. . . .Those who ought to be a light of heaven and splendor of the firmament are made an obscenity."[3] William de Montibus, chancellor of Lincoln Cathedral and an important writer of practical works for preachers, expressed a similar view in an *exemplum* concerning two priestly friends who made a pact that the first to die would report back. When one died, he duly returned, gave his friend a taste of the torments of the damned, and showed the following written on his left hand: "Satan and all demons give thanks to archbishops, bishops, archdeacons, deacons, and parish priests because by their examples Christians are entirely turned to evil so that daily and without any impediment they are seized for the confinements of hell."[4]

Writers and preachers in the long twelfth century set out a demanding model of angelic, godlike behavior for clerics and especially for priests, but they largely defined what they expected negatively, by describing how contemporary clerics

---

[1] Peter of Blois, *Opera*, ed. J. P. Migne, *Patrologia Latina*, vol. 207 (Paris, 1855), 735–6.

[2] British Library, Royal MS 3 B X, fos. 34v–39r; Gerald of Wales, *Opera*, 2:190, 357; Baldwin of Ford, *Opera*, ed. David N. Bell (Turnhout, 1991), 85–7; Bodleian Library, Wood empt. MS 13, fo. 32r; Bodleian Library, Laud. Misc. MS 71, fos. 6r, 10r, 88r. Gervase's work is discussed in Beryl Smalley, *The Becket Conflict and the Schools: A Study of Intellectuals in Politics* (Totowa, 1973), 221–8. For Alexander Neckam, who was probably still a secular cleric when he composed his sermons, see R. W. Hunt and Margaret T. Gibson, *The Schools and the Cloister: The Life and Writings of Alexander Nequam (1157–1217)* (Oxford, 1984). For a brief overview of the career of Thomas Agnellus, see Frances M. R. Ramsey, ed., *English Episcopal Acta. 10, Bath and Wells, 1061–1205* (Oxford, 1995), 218.

[3] Peter of Blois, *Opera*, 737.

[4] British Library, Cotton MS Vespasian E X, fos. 183r–v. For William and his work, see Joseph Goering, *William de Montibus (c.1140–1213): The Schools and the Literature of Pastoral Care* (Toronto, 1992).

fell short of their expectations.[5] This chapter explores their model with two main goals in mind: to show why twelfth-century thinkers accorded such extraordinary religious authority and importance to the clergy; and to reveal the extremely rigorous moral demands they made of priests and other clerics with few concessions or none to human frailty or to the conflicting demands society made on the clergy. Many themes familiar to students of medieval religion will appear in this chapter, including concerns about the quality of pastoral care, demands for worthier appointments to benefices, and condemnations of clerical vice. However, as the comparisons of priests to gods and angels underscores, medieval thinkers could have a radically different perspective on religious matters from modern people, and historians need to pay close attention to exactly what medieval writers argued about these issues and to the rhetoric they employed. At times, admittedly, I will read against the grain, in order to emphasize ways in which moralists, who generally strove to focus on individual choice and vice, ignored, glossed over, or implicitly grappled with social realities that made it difficult for even the most zealous to live up to the model of the ideal priest. However, an exploration of the precise logic and the harsh rhetoric of the moralists will illuminate discussions in subsequent chapters of how the demands of reformers over matters such as pastoral care and clerical celibacy played out in society as a whole. In particular, exploration of the works of contemporary reformers will reveal just how wide the gap was between expectations of clerics and the ways they actually behaved, thus underscoring the tension between ideal and reality that forms an important theme of this work.[6]

Before turning to the substance of the chapter, it is important to consider the terms "reform," "reformation," and "reformer," the last of which I will be using frequently. The paradigm of reform, of course, comes from the Protestant Reformation, but medievalists have long spoken of the Gregorian or Papal Reform and other reform movements. As Giles Constable notes, in discussing monastic reform movements in *The Reformation of the Twelfth Century*, terms such as *reformare* do appear in medieval writing.[7] However, scholars often think of movements with systematic agendas when they use terms such as reformation. In contrast, the writers and preachers I discuss, though heavily influenced by the Gregorian Reform movement, did not plan systematic change, even on a local scale. Instead, they were calling on the individual clerics in their audiences to repent their shortcomings and improve their behavior and their performance of their duties. Given the general pessimism that Stephen Jaeger has stressed was so strong in the period, they may have been as concerned to prevent decline as to encourage improvement.[8] Instead of

---

[5] Most of these writings focused on the priesthood, but some writers also discuss other clerical orders; Bodleian Library, Laud. Misc. MS 71, fos. 58v–62v; Robert Pullen, "Sententiarum Libri Octo," in J.-P. Migne, ed., *Patrologia Latina*, vol. 186 (Paris, 1854), 639–1010, at 922–3.

[6] For a recent discussion of priests with some similar arguments, see Mayr-Harting, *Religion, Politics and Society*, 119–24.

[7] Constable, *Reformation of the Twelfth Century*. For a shrewd assessment of the limitations of the terminology and even concept of reform for the period up to *c.*1100, see Julia Barrow, "Ideas and Applications of Reform," in Thomas F. X. Noble and Julia M. H. Smith, eds., *The Cambridge History of Christianity. Vol. 3, Early Medieval Christianities, c.600–c.1100* (Cambridge, 2008), 345–62.

[8] Jaeger, "Pessimism," 1151–83.

an exciting movement designed to bring rapid and profound improvement, one must speak here of an ongoing slog designed to maintain and *perhaps* improve the discipline and quality of the clergy. I am therefore using the term "reformer" in a loose sense, though I think there is good precedent for this usage, and throughout the chapter I use it interchangeably with the term "moralist."[9] Even though one cannot speak of a movement, however, the phenomenon of ongoing even if unorganized efforts to improve or at least maintain the quality of the clergy is an important one, and it provided the impetus for continually promulgating a model of the ideal cleric.

In reconstructing models of clerical status and behavior, I am relying chiefly on treatises written as guides for priests and on a genre of sermon addressed to clerics, priests, or synods, all of them composed by writers, mainly secular clerics, associated with England in the period.[10] Many of the views of the reformers working in England that are discussed in this chapter can be found in works from other periods and places, and indeed the writers I employ drew heavily on sources from earlier periods and from outside England.[11] However, the English writers and preachers were the ones most likely to have had an impact in England and to represent the precise currents of thought there. Most of the sources were written in Latin, and thus restricted to a clerical audience, but I have also drawn upon a French "estates" poem written for Countess Cecilia of Hereford by Etienne de Fougères, a continental bishop who had earlier served at the court of Henry II, and on anonymous sermons in English, which show that the views of the clergy discussed in the chapter were conveyed to laypeople as well.[12]

[9] For a similar use of the term "reformer," see, for instance, Moorman, *Church Life*, 210–41.

[10] For some unpublished sermons to synods and priests by Stephen Langton, I rely on the discussion in Franco Morenzoni, "Pastorale et ecclésiologie dans la prédication d'Étienne Langton," in Louis J. Bataillon et al., eds., *Étienne Langton: prédicateur, bibliste, théologien* (Turnhout, 2010), 449–66. See also Phyllis Barzillay Roberts, *Studies in the Sermons of Stephen Langton* (Toronto, 1968), 117–21.

[11] For instance, Gerald of Wales borrowed heavily from the Parisian master, Peter the Chanter, in one of his treatises: John W. Baldwin, *Masters, Princes, and Merchants: The Social Views of Peter the Chanter and his Circle* (Princeton, 1970), 1:42–3. For examples of the discussion of similar themes in other times and places, see Carine van Rhijn, *Shepherds of the Lord: Priests and Episcopal Statutes in the Carolingian Period* (Turnhout, 2007); D. Whitelock, M. Brett, and C. N. L. Brooke, eds., *Councils and Synods: With Other Documents Relating to the English Church. Vol. 1, Part 1, 871–1066* (Oxford, 1981), 191–226, 255–302, 313–38; Rosamond McKitterick, *The Frankish Church and the Carolingian Reforms, 789–895* (London, 1977), 44–79; Laudage, *Priesterbild*, 55, 65–8, 72–4, 79–81, 88, 198–9, 244, 274–8; Adam J. Davis, *The Holy Bureaucrat: Eudes Rigaud and Religious Reform in Thirteenth-Century Normandy* (Ithaca, 2006), 25, 125–9; Moorman, *Church Life*, 213–16; Gerald Robert Owst, *Preaching in Medieval England: An Introduction to Sermon Manuscripts of the Period, c.1350–1450* (Cambridge, 1926), 249–53; Siegfried Wenzel, *Latin Sermon Collections from Later Medieval England: Orthodox Preaching in the Age of Wyclif* (Cambridge, 2005), 266–77. Franco Morenzoni discusses critiques of the clergy by Gerald of Wales, Thomas of Chobham, and continental contemporaries: Franco Morenzoni, *Des écoles aux paroisses: Thomas de Chobham et la promotion de la prédication au début du XIIIe siècle* (Paris, 1995), 137–44. A particularly useful comparison may be made with the themes of the synodal sermons of Geoffrey Babion: Jean-Hervé Foulon, "Le clerc et son image dans le prédication synodale de Geoffroy Babion, archevêque de Bourdeaux (1135-1158)," *Le clerc séculier au moyen âge* (Paris, 1993), 45–60. For discussion of synodal preaching generally, see Nicole Bériou, "La prédication synodale au XIIIe siècle d'après l'exemple cambrésien," *Le clerc séculier au moyen âge* (Paris, 1993), 229–47.

[12] Etienne de Fougères, *Le livre des manières*, ed. R. Anthony Lodge (Geneva, 1979); R. Morris, ed., *Old English Homilies of the Twelfth Century*, Early English Text Society, vol. 53 (London, 1873), 160–5, 214–15.

1. THE EXALTED STATUS OF PRIESTS AND CLERICS

Why did writers make such exalted claims for priests being comparable to gods, angels, and kings? Generally they claimed biblical warrant, however tenuous, but in practice the comparisons were linked to the Eucharist and to the pastoral duties of priests. The presence of Christ in the Eucharist was fundamentally important in the theology of the time, an importance underscored by such Eucharistic controversies as the one between Berengar of Tours and more conservative scholars such as Lanfranc, the first archbishop of Canterbury appointed after the Norman Conquest.[13] For religious writers of the time, performance of the Eucharist gave even the most ordinary priest a truly cosmological significance. The Latin verb *conficio* in this context is generally translated as "to consecrate," but had a broader sense of making, accomplishing, or producing. In consecrating the wine and bread, priests in a sense produced the divine. Thomas Agnellus preached that priests were greater than angels because they "confected" God, that their voices at the Eucharist opened and closed heaven, that angels assisted them at mass, and that at the altar they "shared the table" with angels, in a sense recreating the Last Supper with them.[14] That priests "confected" God, touched and handled God, ate and drank God on a daily basis gave them a powerful contact with the divine. According to a sermon of a priest named Peter Maude, which links the Eucharist, Easter, and the resurrection, "no rejoicing compares to the rejoicing [of the priest who] makes Easter daily, daily chews the body of the lord."[15] Alexander Neckam preached that not even angels could touch God, only priests.[16] Performance of the Eucharist theoretically allowed priests to breach the boundaries between the worldly and the divine in a way that no other humans could and gave them a close, tactile relationship with God.

Writers also attributed an exalted status to priests because of their importance to their flocks, often called their *subditi* or subjects. William de Montibus described priests as the kings of souls.[17] Gervase of Chichester wrote of the priest as the head that ought to rule the body.[18] The great intellectual John of Salisbury, in his influential elaboration of the metaphor of the body politic, extended the leading role of the clergy to society as a whole. Though unlike Gervase he depicted the ruler as the head of this body, he compared the clergy to the soul, and argued that they

---

[13] H. E. J. Cowdrey, *Lanfranc: Scholar, Monk, and Archbishop* (Oxford, 2003), 59–74. For an overview of the importance of the Eucharist in the central and later Middle Ages, see Miri Rubin, *Corpus Christi: The Eucharist in Late Medieval Culture* (Cambridge, 1991). For its importance for priestly authority, see R. N. Swanson, "Problems of the Priesthood in Pre-Reformation England," *English Historical Review* 105 (1990), 845–69, at 855–7.

[14] Bodleian Library, Laud. Misc. MS 71, fos. 6r, 51r.

[15] Trinity College, Cambridge, MS B.14.8, fo. 21v. Peter was an otherwise unknown author of a set of twelfth-century sermons, said in an inscription in the manuscript to have lived in the time of Henry II.

[16] Bodleian Library, Wood empt. MS 13, fo. 33v. See also 3v.

[17] British Library, Royal MS 8 G II, fo. 68v. William referred to prelates, but this was a term often used for priests in the period.

[18] British Library, Royal MS 3 B X, fo. 24v.

ought therefore to have *principatus*, pre-eminence in or command over, the state.[19] Individually and collectively, priests were responsible for providing the guidance and leadership that might get their "subjects" into heaven. However, if priests had great power to do good for their flock, many writers, like William de Montibus, also feared that bad priests had tremendous power to do them harm. As Bartholomew, bishop of Exeter, preached: "Evil priests are the ruin of the people."[20]

The well-known emphasis by the Gregorian reformers and their successors on distinguishing and separating the clergy from the laity was strongly linked to the exalted status claimed for clerics. Thomas Agnellus, in a sermon specifically dealing with clerical status and drawing on a New Testament passage in which the writer addressed his audience as a "chosen people, a royal priesthood," described the clerical tonsure as a sign of kingship.[21] For Alexander Neckam, the tonsure was a sign of the rejection of terrestrial vanities, but was also a crown that could be linked to the crown of thorns. The clergy were meant to be separate but superior. In reality, not all clerics considered the tonsure a positive sign of distinction. Alexander Neckam implied as much by saying that it was never shameful to bear the mark, and Godwin, precentor of Salisbury Cathedral in the early twelfth century, wrote that some clerics preferred not to be distinguished from the laity.[22] Whatever the social status of the clergy, however, writers, in comparing priests to gods, angels, and kings, made implicit but very strong claims for their religious authority and their place in Christian society and indeed in the universe.

Moralists, however, emphasized the awe-inspiring authority of priests not primarily to raise their status but to jolt them out of any sense of complacency and to impress upon them the weight of their sacramental and pastoral responsibilities. Writers and preachers frequently told their audiences that the exalted office of priests demanded extremely high standards of them. As Peter of Blois preached, "the more worthy the order of priests, the greater the lapse and the more dangerous the ruin."[23] Reformers therefore placed high expectations on priests and other clerics.

Modern historians tend to focus on the pastoral duties of the medieval clergy, but for medieval writers failures in the performance of the Eucharist and of other rites were as damning as pastoral neglect. Gervase of Chichester compared priests who read, chanted psalms, or celebrated masses badly, whether through neglect or lack of learning, to the two priestly sons of Aaron whom God, in the Bible,

---

[19] John of Salisbury, *Policraticus sive de Nugis Curialium et de Vestigiis Philosophorum*, ed. Clement C. J. Webb, 2 vols. (Oxford, 1909), 1:282–3. For discussion of this metaphor, see Tilman Struve, "The Importance of the Organism in the Political Theory of John of Salisbury," in Michael Wilks, ed., *The World of John of Salisbury* (Oxford, 1984), 303–17; Frédérique Lachaud, *L'éthique du pouvoir au Moyen Âge: l'office dans la culture politique (Angleterre, vers 1150–vers 1330)* (Paris, 2010), 177–216.

[20] Bodleian Library, Bodleian MS 449, fo. 25r. For Bartholomew's life and work, see Adrian Morey, *Bartholomew of Exeter, Bishop and Canonist: A Study in the Twelfth Century* (Cambridge, 1937).

[21] Bodleian Library, Laud. Misc. MS 71, fo. 59r.

[22] 1st Peter, 2:9; Bodleian Library, Wood empt. MS 13, fo. 35v; Bodleian Library, Digby MS 96, fo. 23r.

[23] Peter of Blois, *Opera*, 733.

consumed with fire for botching a ritual.[24] Beyond the mechanics, many writers stressed the importance of performing rituals, particularly the Eucharist, with the proper mindset, including inward focus on the ceremony and the appropriate attitudes.[25] For Herbert of Bosham, a learned cleric in Thomas Becket's circle, one of the characteristics that made Thomas a saint was the way in which he celebrated mass with contrition, humility, and tears, serving as an example for other priests.[26] Above all, moralists made an urgent demand, stemming particularly from the daily contact with God through the Eucharist, for ritual purity. All aspects of the Eucharist theoretically demanded great care for purity, as shown by the space Thomas of Chobham, subdean of Salisbury, devoted in his influential manual for confessors to advising clerical readers how to deal with practical matters that might affect the sacrality of the Eucharist, such as a spider dropping into the wine.[27] Gervase of Chichester, however, used such concerns to stress the need for corporal purity by priests, describing their bodies as the vessels of sacrifice. The Eucharist was not affected by the quality of the priest, he noted (that would have been a heretical position), but it was far better for the priest to be pure.[28] Alexander Neckam drew a striking comparison with Simeon holding Jesus at Mary's purification to emphasize that the body of the priest needed to be pure because he held God. Alexander and others also emphasized purity of heart or mind, but the stress on purity of body allowed moralists to focus on behavior.[29] This was particularly true of sexual behavior, a point I shall develop later in the chapter. However, Neckam could also urge priests to keep their mouths pure for the Eucharist by avoiding obscene words, and Baldwin of Ford could extend this injunction to lies, perjury, and scurrilous words.[30] Exhortations to purity were partly a means to an end. As Mary Douglas wrote in her classic work, *Purity and Danger*, "pollution rules can have another socially useful function—that of marshalling moral disapproval when it lags."[31] Purity, however, was very much an end in itself, for to moralists it showed proper respect to God and to the exalted priestly office.

Writers did, of course, also stress the duties of priests to their flocks.[32] To some degree moralists depicted this duty as a matter of reciprocity, arguing that the tithes

---

[24] British Library, Royal MS 3 B X, fo. 40r. The death of the sons of Aaron is in Leviticus 10:1–3 and Numbers 3:4 and 26:61.

[25] Peter of Blois, *Opera*, 727; British Library, Royal MS 3 B X, fos. 7r–8r, 9v, 40r–v; Bodleian Library, Laud. Misc. MS 71, fo. 51r; Morenzoni, "Pastorale et ecclésiologie dans la prédication d'Étienne Langton," 456.

[26] Robertson and Sheppard, eds., *Materials*, 3:209–12. For Herbert's life and work, see Deborah L. Goodwin, *Take Hold of the Robe of a Jew: Herbert of Bosham's Christian Hebraism* (Leiden, 2006).

[27] Thomas of Chobham, *Thomae de Chobham Summa Confessorum*, ed. F. Broomfield (Louvain, 1968), 136–43.

[28] British Library, Royal MS 3 B X, fo. 3v. See also Morenzoni, "Pastorale et ecclésiologie dans la prédication d'Étienne Langton," 452.

[29] Bodleian Library, Wood empt. MS 13, fos. 15r–v, 33v–34r, 46r; Bodleian Library, Laud. Misc. MS 71, fo. 51r; British Library, Royal MS 3 B X, fo. 7r.

[30] Bodleian Library, Wood empt. MS 13, fo. 46r; Baldwin of Ford, *Opera*, 96.

[31] Mary Douglas, *Purity and Danger: An Analysis of the Concepts of Pollution and Taboo* (London, 1984), 131–2.

[32] Victoria Thompson has found similar arguments made in late Anglo-Saxon sermons; Victoria Thompson, *Dying and Death in Later Anglo-Saxon England* (Woodbridge, 2004), 86–7; Victoria

priests received placed them under great obligation. As Baldwin of Ford put it, the lands of the priest's "subjects" owed tithes, and in return the priest owed himself and everything he owned to his flock.[33] Far more important was the matter of salvation, and reformers emphasized that priests would have to account for any souls in their flock damned through their negligence, sometimes using the image that God would demand the blood of their parishioners from priests on Judgment Day.[34] In this context, moralists placed particular emphasis on preaching and the correction of sin. For instance, Gervase of Chichester wrote that those with pastoral care must burn in zeal against delinquents.[35] The emphasis on preaching helps explain why preachers and writers put so much emphasis on learning, which they considered to be essential to the adequate handling of the duties of the priest. Herbert of Bosham depicted clerical ignorance as ludicrous by comparing a priest in a church without proper understanding of scriptures to an ape in a great hall.[36] Other writers spelled out the consequences of ignorance. Gervase of Chichester wrote that without learning, priests would only teach heresy and profane novelties.[37] Alexander of Ashby, a regular canon who composed a treatise on preaching, after sarcastically attacking priests who learned the names of trees and birds but did not even know what such basic books for priests as the computus and the penitential were, wrote that the ignorance of many priests condemned both themselves *and* others to hell.[38]

Moralists, however, constantly emphasized that learning must be linked with good morals, for priests had to teach both by word and by example. Caroline Bynum has written of this as an ideology characteristic of regular canons in the period, but it was at least as prominent among the secular clergy.[39] The necessity of both learning and a good life (*scientia et vita*, *scientia et mores*, or some variation thereof) is a theme that appears repeatedly, and sometimes writers developed elaborate metaphors to stress its importance. Peter Maude preached that one wheel in a cart was insufficient without the other, that one foot was not enough for walking, and that the wisdom of a priest without purity of life was like fire which vanishes into smoke, while purity without wisdom was like food without salt.[40] Thomas Agnellus preached that there were two books of the Church, the

---

Thompson, "The Pastoral Contract in Late Anglo-Saxon England: Priest and Parishioner in Oxford, Bodleian Library, MS Laud Miscellaneous 482," in Francesca Tinti, ed., *Pastoral Care in Late Anglo-Saxon England* (Woodbridge, 2005), 106–20, at 112–16.

[33] Baldwin of Ford, *Opera*, 90.

[34] Thomas of Chobham, *Summa de Arte Praedicandi*, ed. Franco Morenzoni (Turnhout, 1988), 137; British Library, Royal MS 3 B X, fo. 111r; Baldwin of Ford, *Opera*, 101; Lambeth Palace, MS 458 part 2, fo. 129v.

[35] British Library, Royal MS 3 B X, fo. 75r.

[36] Robertson and Sheppard, eds., *Materials*, 3:204.

[37] British Library, Royal MS 3 B X, fos. 34r–v.

[38] Alexander of Ashby, "De Artificioso Modo Predicandi," in Franco Morenzoni, ed., *Alexandri Essebiensis Opera Omnia* (Turnhout, 2004), 2 vols. 1:1–104, at 65.

[39] Caroline Walker Bynum, *Docere Verbo et Exemplo: An Aspect of Twelfth-Century Spirituality* (Missoula, 1979); Caroline Walker Bynum, *Jesus as Mother: Studies in the Spirituality of the High Middle Ages* (Berkeley, 1982), 36–40.

[40] Trinity College, Cambridge, MS B.14.8, fos. 18v–19r.

scripture and the clergy. Clerics read the scriptures, but the laity read the lives of the clergy to learn how they ought to conduct their lives.[41] An ideal priest would therefore lead a spotless life, and so Alexander of Ashby wrote of the need for a preacher to have perfection of virtue.[42]

Few clerics, of course, could live up to such a demand, but as with clerical ignorance, reformers vividly stressed the dire consequences of clerical immorality. Thomas Agnellus lamented the kind of preacher who nourished his flock with good doctrine but because of carnal desires set a bad example and "killed" (i.e. damned) parishioners as a result, comparing him to a prostitute who nursed her baby during the day but rolled over and crushed it while sleeping at night.[43] Alexander of Ashby imagined laypeople saying of their priest:

> This [priest] praises hospitality, blames avarice, but does not extend hospitality to travelers, rarely hosts them, no one hates them more. He extols sobriety, damns gluttony and drunkenness, but goes to feasts and taverns with the first and leaves with the last; when he ought to say vespers, he is so drunk he cannot put two words together [. . .]. He condemns fornication, but does not cease from it; one is not enough, he has two or three of the more beautiful young girls from his flock.

In his view, widespread hypocrisy and bad behavior by priests caused laypeople not to take sin seriously. To emphasize how serious this was he wrote that priests drew the world into peril by their silence as preachers and by their example, and he compared bad priests to the dragon of the apocalypse or the serpent in the Garden of Eden.[44]

2. THE CRITIQUE OF THE CLERGY

Because moralists like Alexander usually defined the proper behavior of priests by its opposite, much of the remainder of the chapter will be focused on discussing criticisms about the moral failings of the clergy, but in addition to providing an overview of such criticisms, I will attempt to move beyond the tendency of moralists to attribute all lapses to sin and personal failings.[45] Though clerics, of course, were as subject to lust, greed, and other temptations as anyone else, their perceived failings often emerged from a variety of social ties and emotional needs that moralists tended to downplay. Clerics often faced choices between competing social and religious demands rather than clear-cut even if difficult choices between proper and sinful behavior. Partly because of such complications, society allowed

---

[41] Bodleian Library, Laud. Misc. MS 71, fos. 54r, 93v. Jacques de Vitry and Thomas of Chobham also described the clergy as the book of the laity; Stephen C. Ferruolo, *The Origins of the University: The Schools of Paris and their Critics, 1100–1215* (Stanford, 1985), 266; Claire M. Waters, *Angels and Earthly Creatures: Preaching, Performance, and Gender in the Later Middle Ages* (Philadelphia, 2004), 41.
[42] Alexander of Ashby, "De Artificioso Modo Predicandi," 59.
[43] Bodleian Library, Laud. Misc. MS 71, fo. 10v.
[44] Alexander of Ashby, "De Artificioso Modo Predicandi," 59, 68–69.
[45] Morenzoni, "Pastorale et ecclésiologie dans la prédication d'Étienne Langton," 457–8.

priests and other clerics wide latitude in their behavior, as later chapters will show. That, however, only makes it worth emphasizing how uncompromising the demands of moralists remained in theory and what harsh rhetoric they applied to what were in fact fairly common lapses.

One major problem, according to moralists, was that the whole system of appointments was shot through with corruption. They naturally condemned simony; for instance, Etienne de Fougères wrote, "If a cleric is of good reputation but does not have a fistful of coins, he will not have a church near or far, unless he greases the palm."[46] Reformers also described many other distortions in the patronage system. John of Salisbury wrote that churchmen relied on noble birth, power, or obsequious service to get ahead in the Church.[47] Nigel of Whiteacre, in a treatise against clerics of the court, provided a particularly full picture of the various ways in which the Church's endowment, which he (and others) evocatively called the "patrimony of the Crucified One," was put up for sale "and transferred to depraved and detestable uses." Nigel's attack covered a range of subjects, including simony, nepotism, and rewards for secular service, and was so detailed that he even covered such clever ruses as clerics granting interest-free loans to bishops and then demanding a benefice when it became vacant, making clear that immediate repayment would otherwise be required. "Benefices today," he lamented, "are conferred to no one by grace or merit, but all are granted venally and shamefully by price, though under a veil of shadow and with dissimulation of iniquity."[48] What such fulminations ignored is that meritocratic religious ideals faced severe competition from secular values that placed a heavy premium on kinship and lordship. Clerics and patrons were not only forced to choose between greed or ambition and religious responsibility, but also between social and religious duties. In sermons and treatises (though not in their own actions) reformers glossed over clashes of competing values, and fiercely denounced any deviation from meritocratic norms.

Accompanying this concern about appointments, moralists sometimes worried that many entered the clergy for purely economic reasons and harshly condemned those who did so. In a poem, the historian Henry, archdeacon of Huntingdon, compared clerics who entered office mainly for gain to shepherds who never loved their flocks but only the fleeces, likened such clerics to thieves, and accused them of simony, presumably because financial concerns lay at the heart of their ministry.[49] Gervase of Chichester wrote that priests who had sought ordination for their own ends rather than God's were crucifying Christ anew when using his patrimony for their own purposes.[50] In a society in which many men faced limited economic prospects outside the Church, the prospect of an ecclesiastical income was undoubtedly an important practical incentive for many to enter the clergy, but in the

---

[46] Etienne de Fougères, *Le livre des manières*, 71.   [47] John of Salisbury, *Policraticus*, 2:163.
[48] Nigel of Whiteacre, *Nigellus de Longchamp dit Wireker. Vol. 1 Introduction, Tractatus Contra Curiales et Officiales Clericos*, ed. André Boutemy (Paris, 1959), 156–64.
[49] Henry of Huntingdon, *Historia Anglorum: The History of the English People*, ed. Diana E. Greenway (Oxford, 1996), 780–1.
[50] British Library, Royal MS 3 B X, fo. 86r.

rhetoric of reformers it was an utterly wicked motive, and moralists did not distinguish between economic necessity and greed.

Not surprisingly, pluralism, and the resulting practice of absenteeism, which could also arise from other causes, came in for attack as well. Nigel of Whiteacre satirized the cleric for whom fifteen or twenty churches did not suffice and who sought to acquire one prebend in every cathedral church of the realm while trying to add a deanship and ultimately to become a bishop.[51] Thomas of Chobham lamented that some clerics had many churches which they rarely saw, never preaching and giving alms, nor setting any example except the bad one of neglecting their religious duties through their absence.[52] Pluralism and absenteeism did not attract the same outrage for contemporaries as other practices did; in some ways they are a greater target for some modern scholars concerned about the quality of ministry in the parishes and inequities within the medieval Church.[53] Moreover, pluralism was sometimes made necessary by the poverty of benefices (though the definition of poverty was sometimes quite generous[54]) and absenteeism could be prompted by legitimate purposes such as study or service to ecclesiastical superiors. Nonetheless, moralists tended to reduce such practices to expressions of greed.

The problems created by simony, nepotism, pluralism, and absenteeism seem obvious to a modern audience; more foreign is the strong condemnation of involvement in secular business, which, like many of the practices discussed so far, was generally attributed simply to greed. In this context "business" generally involved trade. Thus, Thomas of Chobham defined business as buying cheap and selling dear.[55] Such condemnations could be surprisingly strong. Peter of Blois attacked an anonymous clerical correspondent who engaged in trading, saying that any cleric who did so was "an idolater of money, a slave of mammon," and even claiming that commerce was a species of usury, rejecting his correspondent's argument that he was simply reaping the fruits of his labor.[56] Above all, reformers seem to have been wary of the cash nexus. Lester Little and Alexander Murray have linked both concerns about simony and an increasing emphasis on avarice in the period to the process of commercialization.[57] After all, what was simony, in its purest form, if not a commercial transaction? For reformers, there seems to have been something problematic about money itself.[58] William de Montibus

[51] Nigel of Whiteacre, *Tractatus Contra Curiales*, 168.

[52] Thomas of Chobham, *Summa de Arte Praedicandi*, 55.

[53] A. D. M. Barrell, "Abuse or Expediency? Pluralism and Non-residence in Northern England in the Late Middle Ages," in John T. Appleby and Paul Dalton, eds., *Government, Religion, and Society in Northern England, 1000–1700* (Stroud, 1997), 117–30, at 117.

[54] See Chapter 4, section 4.

[55] Thomas of Chobham, *Summa Confessorum*, 301.

[56] Peter of Blois, *Opera*, 63. Usury was still in the process of being defined during Peter's lifetime, but this was an unusually broad application of the term: Baldwin, *Masters, Princes, and Merchants*, 1:270–95.

[57] Lester K. Little, *Religious Poverty and the Profit Economy in Medieval Europe* (Ithaca, 1978), 31; Alexander Murray, *Reason and Society in the Middle Ages* (Oxford, 1978), 59–61, 63–7.

[58] Little, *Religious Poverty*, 34–5; Amy G. Remensnyder, "Pollution, Purity, and Peace: An Aspect of Social Reform between the Late Tenth Century and 1076," in Thomas Head and Richard Landes, eds., *The Peace of God: Social Violence and Religious Response around the Year 1000* (Ithaca, 1992),

condemned the blessing of gifts made to the priest because it smacked of greed or of flattery towards the giver, but he put it as follows: money should not be blessed like the host or a farthing like a chalice.[59] There was therefore something of a double standard when it came to commerce and other economic activities. Robert Pullen, an important intellectual and later cardinal, wrote that tithes were justified largely because clerics put aside secular business.[60] However, priests with glebes must often have occupied much of their time farming or managing them. The real issue was not time but commerce.

In a commercializing economy, however, condemnations of involvement in secular business created practical dilemmas for clerics. One might imagine a priest in a self-sufficient parish simply living off tithes and the produce of the glebe, getting items he could not produce himself from the tithes of artisans. If such a situation had ever existed, however, it was unlikely in the increasingly commercialized England of the long twelfth century. One can see Thomas of Chobham, in a treatise designed to deliver practical advice as well as reform rhetoric, wrestling with the necessary involvement of priests and other clerics in the marketplace. He specifically permitted the exercise of crafts by poor clergy. He also allowed certain transactions by priests farming glebes, such as selling pasture, though he did not permit others, such as buying young animals and raising them for later sale, which seemed too much like "business." He prohibited selling the right to collect tithes but stated that clerics *could* sell products they had collected as tithes.[61] Secular clerics were supposed to avoid the marketplace, but inevitably they could not completely do so.

Not surprisingly, moralists were especially harsh in condemning priests who mixed commerce with their performance of the sacraments, especially the mass. Peter of Blois lamented that sacraments were turned into merchandise and the priceless was sold.[62] Gerald of Wales could write that while the upper clergy sold holy orders, benefices, and consecrations, the minor clergy sold weddings, burials, and even baptisms. Gerald was particularly concerned about priests who included certain readings or performed certain masses to get extra offerings, or who said extra masses for profit. Thomas of Chobham had similar worries about masses for the dead, and prohibited the deceased from being named in the mass, lest priests be perceived as seeking donations from relatives and friends. For Gerald the multiplication of masses devalued them; for Thomas, saying frequent masses for the dead in return for gifts made the mass seem venal. Neither pulled punches, for both made comparisons between such practices and Judas's betrayal of Jesus. Indeed, Thomas wrote that laypeople believed a mass cost one silver penny, whereas Judas had

280–307; Megan McLaughlin, *Sex, Gender, and Episcopal Authority in an Age of Reform, 1000–1122* (Cambridge, 2010), 70–80.

[59] Goering, *William de Montibus*, 145.
[60] Robert Pullen, "Sententiarum," 918–19. For Pullen's life and work, see F. Courtney, *Cardinal Robert Pullen: An English Theologian of the Twelfth Century* (Rome, 1954).
[61] Thomas of Chobham, *Summa Confessorum*, 301–3, 533.
[62] Peter of Blois, *Opera*, 736–7.

received thirty; selling the Eucharist was like selling out Christ once more, only at a sharp discount.[63]

As usual, matters were complicated when one moved from rhetoric to reality. Gifts in return for baptism and other services were so customary that they could hardly be distinguished from payments, which made the line between gift giving and commerce very thin.[64] The reciprocal exchange of gifts and favors is a social glue common to many traditional societies, and as the laity increasingly adopted new vehicles of piety, such as masses for the dead, it must have seemed natural to make gifts to priests, including gifts of money, for the trouble they took. Moreover, the kinds of entrepreneurial clerical practices condemned by Gerald of Wales and Thomas of Chobham helped lay the groundwork for the flourishing lay piety of the later Middle Ages, and indeed many unbeneficed priests later came to make their living providing religious services for pay in what Katharine Zieman has called contractual liturgy.[65] Already, moralists were wrestling with just what was acceptable and what was not. Thomas of Chobham condemned priests who enjoined penitents to seek masses for the dead, since the priests could profit thereby, but Gerald of Wales thought that remuneration for prayers, psalms, and even masses enjoined on penitents was acceptable, although perhaps indirectly, through donations to the Church. Thomas himself thought giving money to the poor for saying prayers for the dead was licit, since it was their friendship that was being bought, which would lead to them saying the prayers. On one level, this was a piece of hairsplitting logic, but it also recognized that money could play a role in ties of reciprocity.[66] Specialists in canon law were also struggling to come to grips with new religious practices in a commercialized atmosphere. The English canonist Honorius discussed whether payment for anniversary masses or even candles was simoniacal.[67] In the meantime, priests who participated in new forms of piety risked being identified with Judas.

Another important target of moralists was what they considered the misuse of tithes and church funds for sinful purposes. Thus, Thomas Agnellus admonished his priestly audience that "the patrimony of the Crucified One," which had been "bought with the precious blood of Christ," was for necessities and helping the poor, not for luxuries and the desires of the flesh.[68] Thomas of Chobham lamented the tendency of churchmen to expend the goods of the Church on worldly vanities,

[63] Gerald of Wales, *Opera*, 2:126–38, 281–93; Thomas of Chobham, *Summa Confessorum*, 12, 322–3. See also Bodleian Library, Laud. Misc. MS 71, fo. 68v; Phyllis Roberts, "Master Stephen Langton Preaches to the People and Clergy: Sermon Texts from Twelfth-Century Paris," *Traditio* 36 (1980), 237–68, at 262, 264.

[64] For offerings, their role in church incomes, and the element of reciprocity, see Susan Wood, *The Proprietary Church in the Medieval West* (Oxford, 2006), 459, 478–86.

[65] Katherine Zieman, *Singing the New Song: Literacy and Liturgy in Late Medieval England* (Philadelphia, 2008), 92–100. For lay piety in this period, see Hugh M. Thomas, "Lay Piety in England from 1066 to 1215," *Anglo-Norman Studies* 29 (2007), 179–92.

[66] Thomas of Chobham, *Summa Confessorum*, 12–13, 526, 322–3; Gerald of Wales, *Opera*, 2:19. See also Gerald of Wales, *Opera*, 2:129, 134–5.

[67] Honorius, *Magistri Honorii Summa "De Iure Canonico Tractaturus,"* ed. Rudolf Weigand, Peter Landau, and Waltraud Kozur (Vatican City, 2004), 310–11, 313.

[68] Bodleian Library, Laud. Misc. MS 71, fo. 3r. See also British Library, Royal MS 3 B X, fo. 87v.

jewelry, entertainers, and prostitutes, or on seeking advancement at court.[69] However the dividing lines between luxury and necessity and between acceptable and sinful uses of money must often have been tricky to identify, as subsequent chapters will show.

As one might expect, reformers and preachers also blasted away at what they considered bad personal behavior, including vices such as gluttony. Drunkenness was a particularly important target, partly because it was seen as leading to other bad behaviors, such as fornication, but also because it could threaten proper performance of rituals and ritual purity itself. Gervase of Chichester attacked priests who performed the rites while drunk, linking them to Bacchus as part of an extended metaphor on priests acting like gods, only in all the wrong ways.[70] The monastic author of the *Liber Eliensis* attacked a priest who was so drunk that he could not walk in a straight line, but nonetheless performed mass, during which he both vomited and defecated in front of a congregation, defiling his vestments.[71] This priest was an enemy of the monks of Ely, but the penitential of Bishop Bartholomew of Exeter included a penance for drunken priests who vomited up the Eucharist.[72]

Criticisms of drunkenness and gluttony might seem unproblematic, but even these attacks created moral ambiguities for clerics in a society that valued conviviality. Church synods frequently legislated against priests going to taverns or public drinking parties and a moralist like Gerald of Wales could strongly condemn priests for attending feasts.[73] Yet feasting and drinking formed another important kind of social glue and clerical participation could therefore be seen in a quite different light. The monk Reginald of Durham, in his collection of miracles of St. Cuthbert, favorably portrayed a prosperous priest at Arden in Nottinghamshire who held an annual feast in honor of the saint, in which he fed many poor but also hosted more "respectable" people, both lay and clerical.[74] More striking still, Gerald of Wales's account makes clear that the feasts he was criticizing were sometimes what would later be called church ales, hosted by religious fraternities to raise money for their churches.[75] A synodal decree late in the period did allow clerics to go to feasts if invited by "good people," though it stated that they should leave, sober, after dinner, and that if anything shameful were sung or spoken which they could not prohibit, they should pretend to ignore it.[76] In this case reforming legislators acknowledged the delicate balancing act that religious figures who lived in the secular world had to manage, and it is worth noting that even Gerald was forgiving

---

[69] Thomas of Chobham, *Summa Confessorum*, 300.

[70] British Library, Royal MS 3 B X, fo. 42v.   [71] Blake, ed., *Liber Eliensis*, 370–1.

[72] Morey, *Bartholomew of Exeter*, 270. See also D. Whitelock, M. Brett, and C. N. L. Brooke, eds., *Councils and Synods: With Other Documents Relating to the English Church. Vol. 1, Part 2, 1066–1204* (Oxford, 1981), 676, 979, 984, 1051, 1067, 1073.

[73] Gerald of Wales, *Opera*, 2:255–62.

[74] Reginald of Durham, *Libellus de Admirandis Beati Cuthberti Virtutibus*, Surtees Society, vol. 1 (London, 1835), 127.

[75] Gerald of Wales, *Opera*, 2:258–9.

[76] F. M. Powicke and C. R. Cheney, eds., *Councils and Synods: With Other Documents Relating to the English Church. Vol. 2, Part 1, 1205–1265* (Oxford, 1964), 26.

of those who became drunk while exercising the duty of hospitality.[77] Nonetheless, the fact remains that priests could be condemned for pursuing even social activities that had a religious aspect.

Moralists also condemned the pursuit of certain aristocratic pastimes by clerics. Robert Pullen criticized clerics "who chant, celebrate mass, and say hours, then mount horses, hunt, and play with birds of the sky, or spend the day playing chess, which are not vices to laypeople but to priests, and in every way prohibited."[78] The prohibitions against hunting and falconry were particularly well established.[79] A synod late in the period also banned clerics from attending jousts, tournaments, and other such "vain spectacles," a prohibition that was hardly surprising since the Church tried to ban tournaments themselves.[80] Such prohibitions emerged from a general condemnation of frivolous pleasures, from concerns about clerical association with violence, and from discomfort with aristocratic behavior by clerics. Many elite clerics, however, were essentially aristocrats, and such prohibitions prevented them from participating in some of the key activities that created social networks among the elites. As usual, moralists nonetheless focused on personal shortcomings rather than social pressures.

The greatest target of reformers was sexual misbehavior by clerics. Though the finer points of church law on the subject of celibacy were still being worked out in the long twelfth century, the essential (though widely ignored) rules were that clerics in minor orders could marry, with restrictions, but that subdeacons, deacons, and priests had to remain celibate. The efforts to encourage and enforce clerical celibacy have received increasing scholarly attention, and will receive further attention here in Chapter 7, but it is important to place the demands of moralists for sexual abstinence within their overall efforts to improve the clergy.[81] With one

---

[77] Gerald of Wales, *Opera*, 2:260–1.   [78] Lambeth Palace, MS 458 part 2, fo. 130v.

[79] For example, Whitelock, Brett, and Brooke, eds., *Councils and Synods, 1066–1204*, 606; John of Salisbury, *Policraticus*, 1:34; Peter of Blois, *Opera*, 169–71, 181–4. See also Lachaud, *L'éthique du pouvoir*, 299–316.

[80] Whitelock, Brett, and Brooke, eds., *Councils and Synods, 1066–1204*, 1073.

[81] C. N. L. Brooke, "Gregorian Reform in Action: Clerical Marriage in England, 1050–1200," *Medieval Church and Society: Collected Essays* (London, 1971), 69–99; Barrow, "Hereford Bishops and Married Clergy," 1–8; James A. Brundage, *Law, Sex, and Christian Society in Medieval Europe* (Chicago, 1987), 150–2, 214–23, 251–3, 314–19, 342–3, 401–5; Ross Balzaretti, "Men and Sex in Tenth-Century Italy," in D. M. Hadley, ed., *Masculinity in Medieval Europe* (London, 1999), 143–59; Anne Llewellyn Barstow, *Married Priests and the Reforming Papacy: The Eleventh-Century Debates* (New York, 1982); Dyan Elliott, *Fallen Bodies: Pollution, Sexuality, and Demonology in the Middle Ages* (Philadelphia, 1999), 81–126; Michael Frassetto, ed., *Medieval Purity and Piety: Essays on Medieval Clerical Celibacy and Religious Reform* (New York, 1998); C. A. Frazee, "The Origins of Clerical Celibacy in the Western Church," *Church History* 41 (1972), 149–67; Jo Ann McNamara, "Chaste Marriage and Clerical Celibacy," in Vern L. Bullough and James A. Brundage, eds., *Sexual Practices and the Medieval Church* (Buffalo, 1982), 22–33; Helen L. Parish, *Clerical Celibacy in the West, c.1100–1700* (Farnham, 2009); Jean Gaudemet, "Le célibat ecclésiastique," *Zeitschrift der Savigny Stiftung für Rechtsgeschichte, Kanonistische Abteilung* 68 (1982), 1–31; Monique Vleeschouwers-Van Melkebeek, "Mandatory Celibacy and Priestly Ministry in the Diocese of Tournai at the End of the Middle Ages," in Jean Marie Duvosquel and Erik Thoen, eds., *Peasants & Townsmen in Medieval Europe* (Ghent, 1995), 681–92; M. A. Kelleher, "'Like Man and Wife': Clerics' Concubines in the Diocese of Barcelona," *Journal of Medieval History* 28 (2002), 349–60; Michelle Armstrong-Partida, "Priestly Marriage: The Tradition of Clerical Concubinage in the Spanish Church," *Viator* 40 (2009), 221–53; Elisabeth van

major exception, the attacks of reformers on clerical sex followed the same lines as attacks on other "bad" behaviors. The exception comes with priests setting a bad example. After all, the laity could get married.[82] Fornication, however, was fair game, and during the reform period marriages by priests, deacons, and subdeacons came to be, by definition, no marriages at all, particularly after the Second Lateran Council of 1139.[83] As a result any sexual activity by members of the affected ranks was automatically fornication (or adultery, if with a married woman). Thus, Alexander of Ashby described a cleric saying to a woman, "love me, be my girlfriend (*amica*), you will have no work, sorrow, difficulties, or sadness in all your days," and shortly thereafter he described fornication as one way in which priests could set a bad example.[84] However, this line of attack was rarely used in condemnations of clerical sex.

Above all, when English reformers attacked sex by priests, they stressed the purity needed for the Eucharist, what many scholars have called cultic purity. This was a standard line of attack by reformers throughout Europe, including such influential figures as Peter Damian.[85] Strikingly, moralists used it even though it did not apply particularly well to deacons and subdeacons, who only assisted at mass but were also bound by vows of celibacy. Robert Pullen did write, in discussing the celibacy of subdeacons, that the nearer one was to the altar, the more continent one should be, though this awkwardly suggests a sliding scale of sexual activity rather than a strict abstinence once one had achieved a specific

Houts, "The Fate of Priests' Sons in Normandy with Special Reference to Serlo of Bayeux," *Haskins Society Journal* 25 (2013), forthcoming.

[82] The prohibitions on practices like hunting formed a similar exception.

[83] Gaudemet, "Le celibate ecclésiastique," 16–24.

[84] Alexander of Ashby, "De Artificioso Modo Predicandi," 58–9.

[85] Barstow, *Married Priests*, 58–64, 69–73, 93; Elliott, *Fallen Bodies*, 83, 103–8, 116–18; Phyllis G. Jestice, "Why Celibacy? Odo of Cluny and the Development of a New Sexual Morality," in Michael Frassetto, ed., *Medieval Purity and Piety: Essays on Medieval Clerical Celibacy and Religious Reform* (New York, 1998), 81–115, at 95–108; Michael Frassetto, "Heresy, Celibacy, and Reform in the Sermons of Ademar of Chabannes," in Michael Frassetto, ed., *Medieval Purity and Piety: Essays on Medieval Clerical Celibacy and Religious Reform* (New York, 1998), 131–48, at 138–41; H. E. J. Cowdrey, "Pope Gregory VII and the Chastity of the Clergy," in Michael Frassetto, ed., *Medieval Purity and Piety: Essays on Medieval Clerical Celibacy and Religious Reform* (New York, 1998), 269–302, at 270–1; Ruth Mazo Karras, *Sexuality in Medieval Europe: Doing unto Others* (New York, 2005), 43–4; Ruth Mazo Karras, "Thomas Aquinas's Chastity Belt: Clerical Masculinity in Medieval Europe," in Lisa M. Bitel and Felice Lifshitz, eds., *Gender and Christianity in Medieval Europe: New Perspectives* (Philadelphia, 2008), 52–67, at 60; R. I. Moore, "Family, Community and Cult on the Eve of the Gregorian Reform," *Transactions of the Royal Historical Society* 5th ser., 30 (1980), 49–69, at 66–8; Remensnyder, "Pollution, Purity, and Peace," 280–307; Pauline Stafford, "Queens, Nunneries, and Reforming Churchmen: Gender, Religious States and Reform in Tenth- and Eleventh-Century England," *Past and Present* 163 (1999), 3–35, at 7–10; R. N. Swanson, "Angels Incarnate: Clergy and Reform from Gregorian Reform to Reformation," in D. M. Hadley, ed., *Masculinity in Medieval Europe* (London, 1999), 160–77, at 162, 165; Kathleen G. Cushing, *Reform and the Papacy in the Eleventh Century: Spirituality and Social Change* (Manchester, 2005), 111–17, 120–8; Morenzoni, "Pastorale et ecclésiologie dans la prédication d'Étienne Langton," 451–2. The polemical emphasis on cultic purity, with its concomitant stress on filth, had its roots in a late antique discourse of disgust that was also used in the Middle Ages to attack those of other religions: Alexandra Cuffel, *Gendering Disgust in Medieval Religious Polemic* (Notre Dame, 2007).

rank.[86] In any case, preachers and writers stressed again and again, in the harshest of terms, that sexual activity by priests and particularly contact with the bodies of women polluted them and thereby made them unfit to celebrate the Eucharist. The image of priests going from touching the bodies of "whores" (in some cases women whom the priests still considered their wives) to touching God was an especially common trope for moralists attacking sexual activity.[87] A sermon of Thomas Agnellus provides a particularly full example. He attacked priests who dared to go "from a whore's bed to the table of the lord, from a place of pollution to a place of sanctification, from shameful contact with women to consecrating the sacrament of the flesh and blood of God." He continued, "Whose soul could withstand such insults, whose mind is not confounded at such injury? [. . .] Anyone who is of sane mind blushes to touch material bread, ordinary bread, with sordid hands and a polluted mouth, but the priest, in the impurity of his contamination, does not shudder to chew the bread of angels, the bread that descended from heaven."[88]

When it came to clerical sex, moral disapproval often lagged, and moralists used the purity that handling and consuming God demanded as a stick to beat the wayward with. However, the belief that daily contact with God made purity fundamental to the exercise of the priestly office meant that the demand for cultic purity was not merely a tool for achieving moral reform but one of the key reasons for demanding celibacy. Modern Western norms generally resist the idea of sexual activity as polluting or disgusting. However, a comparison between the attacks on sexual pollution and the anecdote about the priest vomiting and defecating at mass provides a parallel to the visceral disgust some reformers clearly felt about the conjunction of sexual activity and the Eucharist, and to the feelings they hoped to inspire in their audiences. For such reformers, the idea that hands that touched women should touch the body of Christ, or that men who had had sex should have physical and ritual contact with God, was simply disgusting. Dedication to cultic purity was a crucial motivator for reformers, not just a cover for more material concerns.

Nonetheless, concerns about church property also prompted attacks on clerical marriage and concubinage. Moralists criticized the inheritance of benefices surprisingly rarely, given the importance of that phenomenon and the practical measures taken to eliminate it, but one monastic writer complained that married priests thought only of heritable succession. More commonly, reformers stressed the misuse of tithes and revenues on women. The same monastic writer also complained of priests spending their money to decorate their women instead of their churches, and another monk wrote that nearly all priests had whores, complained of money spent on adorning the wives and daughters of priests, and condemned the use of tithes to support "priestesses."[89] An anonymous sermon in English included

[86] Robert Pullen, "Sententiarum" 923.
[87] Gerald of Wales, *Opera*, 2:190–1; 4: 314; Robert Pullen, "Sententiarum" 923–4; Peter of Blois, *Opera*, 361.
[88] Bodleian Library, Laud. Misc. MS 71, fos. 54v–55r.
[89] Frank Barlow, ed., *English Episcopal Acta. 11, Exeter, 1046–1184* (Oxford, 1996), xxxiv, note 9; R. Foreville and J. Leclercq, "Un débat sur le sacerdoce des moines au XIIe siècle," in Raymonde Foreville, et al., eds., *Analecta Monastica* (Rome, 1957), 8–118, at 99, 101–2, 105–7. For this theme in

a typical set of contrasts made by moralists; the priest adorned his "whore" rather than his church; the altar cloths were coarse and soiled, but her clothing was fine and white; and the chalice for the Eucharist was made of tin, but she had a fine wooden cup and a gold ring.[90]

Though moralists generally focused on lust, impurity, and the frivolous waste of money to adorn women, in keeping with the general tendency of reformers to blame all clerical shortcomings on personal sin, some moralists did approach clerical sexuality with an implicit recognition of the attractions not just of sex but also of family life. Since marriage and family were considered unproblematic and even virtuous for the laity, condemning priests for wanting a family posed a particular challenge. Some reformers tried to counteract the attraction by arguing that the economic and social demands of families inevitably drew priests with partners and children into sin. Gerald of Wales, for instance, asked how a priest who lived a "secular" life, with a concubine and a house crammed with infants, cradles, midwives, and nurses, could avoid the greedy accumulation of wealth, and he also noted the expenses of educating and marrying children. In addition, Gerald used misogynistic stereotypes to argue that priests with female partners would suffer from the greed of their women, who would extort from them, say, a fancy garment every market day or a horse and a saddle decorated with pictures, carvings, and gold engravings.[91]

Thomas Agnellus elaborated at length on the disadvantages and moral dangers of having to provide for a family in one striking sermon that fully acknowledged the temptations of family life while trying to undermine them. He echoed some of the themes of Gerald of Wales, though he also placed the adornment of women and subsequent neglect of churches in the context of social competition, thus acknowledging social forces as well as personal sin. Thomas then painted a picture of a dying priest surrounded by a crowd of weeping children, "devoting all his attention to what to leave for the firstborn and what share was for the one in the crib, and what dower to leave to his daughter and what to leave to the concubine who survived him." As a result, the priest dispersed all the goods of the church for his (naturally ungrateful) family, leaving nothing for good works that might aid his salvation. "From the words of my soul," Thomas wrote, "I say there is scarcely a priest who can die securely who leaves surviving children." Yet with slight adjustments, Thomas Agnellus's picture of the dying priest surrounded by his weeping relatives could have been quite positive; a dying husband and father in the bosom of his grieving family. Indeed, Thomas took the unusual step of *explicitly* acknowledging the temptations of family life, but linked them with carnal temptation, cleverly exploiting the idea of marriage creating one flesh, but treating the priest or

---

the Anglo-Saxon period, see Barstow, *Married Priests*, 38; Stafford, "Queens, Nunneries, and Reforming Churchmen," 8–9. See also Elliott, *Fallen Bodies*, 121–2; Karras, *Sexuality in Medieval Europe*, 100–1.

[90] Morris, ed., *Old English Homilies*, 162–3. For a similar set of contrasts in Latin, see British Library, Cotton MS Vespasian E X, fos. 182v–183r.

[91] Gerald of Wales, *Opera*, 2:277–81. See also Trinity College, Cambridge, MS B.14.8, fo. 25r.

his soul as being married (badly) to his own flesh. Thomas wrote that "The flesh with which one is joined, as if with a domestic enemy," might suggest that "it is better to marry a wife to have children than to spend life like an arid limb without fruit." In the face of such emotional temptation, Thomas invoked images of masculine self-control, urging priests to resist such "wifely frivolities" and let "virile dignity" coerce "womanly presumption."[92]

One strategy to counteract the strong attractions of family life was to depict the Church and the flock as an alternative family that would bear greater fruit than marriage and sex. Thomas urged priests to make heirs through spiritual means, and argued that "virginal sterility [was] more fecund than conjugal fecundity."[93] Similarly, Gervase of Chichester wrote of the acquisition of a church or benefice as a kind of marriage through which one produced sons and daughters by acquiring them for the Creator "by word or example."[94] No doubt for many pious priests, pastoral work did provide a satisfying, even preferable alternative to family life. Yet the strategy itself indicates that resistance to clerical celibacy stemmed as much from a desire for emotional bonds as for sex.

Although moralists usually strove to present clerical behavior as a set of clear-cut choices between good and evil rather than acknowledging the many ambiguities clerics faced, they also concentrated on moral gray areas where clerics were most likely to resist claims that specific behaviors were particularly sinful. The notable silence of reformers on clerical violence underscores this. One of the major issues during Henry II's reign, particularly in the Becket controversy, concerned "criminous clerks," especially those who committed violent acts.[95] Yet condemnations of such acts barely appear in the sources I have discussed here. This may reflect a desire of churchmen to close ranks over the issue, but a stronger factor was probably that such behavior was so obviously wrong. Ending violence by clerics was a matter of enforcement, not persuasion. In contrast, reformers had to direct much more energy toward persuading clerics that nepotism, feasting, sexual relations, and the formation of families were clearly and thoroughly wrong and likely to lead to damnation. Their efforts suggest how much resistance they faced.

The focus of reformers on areas where their claims might be disputed rather than on all areas of clerical misbehavior, however, also serves as a reminder that the vigorously expressed concerns of moralists cannot be neatly mapped onto the behaviors of those they criticized. Mayke de Jong has colorfully warned against reading the reforming decrees of Carolingian bishops as showing a fight against a Wild West of whoring and drunken rural priests, and similar caution is needed for the sources discussed here.[96] Medieval rhetoric was not noted for restraint: reformers were aiming for effect, to make their points as vividly as possible, and were happy to employ stereotypes and generalizations. As Kathleen Cushing has noted,

---

[92] Bodleian Library, Laud. Misc. MS 71, fos. 87r–88r, 89v.
[93] Bodleian Library, Laud. Misc. MS 71, fos. 88r–v, 89v.
[94] British Library, Royal MS 3 B X, fo. 59v.   [95] See Chapter 9, section 2.
[96] Mayke de Jong, "Charlemagne's Church," in Joanna Story, ed., *Charlemagne: Empire and Society* (Manchester, 2005), 103–35, at 123.

"The reformers had to marshal public opinion so that actions that had previously failed to provoke a general moral indignation within society would come to be regarded as serious moral offences with untold consequences."[97] Strikingly, when Master Vacarius, an Italian legal scholar who settled in England, saw how a former friend, the Italian heretic Speroni, used claims about the widespread pollution and corruption of the priesthood to challenge the validity of clerical sacraments, he responded not only with theological arguments about the validity of sacramental powers even when exercised by unworthy priests, but also with a denial of Speroni's claims about how widespread clerical misbehavior was.[98] Obviously, when the instrumental purposes of negative depictions of clerical behavior turned threatening, moralists could change their tunes. Moreover, there is obviously a certain literary quality to the sermons and writings, and Claire Waters has discussed the connection between sermons and literature in later medieval England.[99] Already in the long twelfth century, satirical poetry attacked many of the same targets as sermons, and indeed Nigel of Whiteacre, who was quoted earlier, was one of the most noted satirists in the period.[100] The rhetorical and literary qualities of the works discussed in this chapter should put us on guard; they were clearly not intended as objective overviews of clerical behavior.

That said, the opinions described in this chapter and the gap moralists stressed between ideal models and actual behavior need to be taken seriously for several reasons. First, though reformers may have exaggerated the sinfulness of the clergy, later chapters will show ample evidence for much of the behavior criticized by moralists. Second, the harshness of the rhetoric of moralists emerged partly because the perceived stakes were so high: the eternal salvation or damnation not only of priests and clerics but also of laypeople. Third, to a large degree the unyielding rhetoric of preachers and writers represented an unyielding theoretical attitude to the shortcomings of the clergy. Obviously, the medieval Church accepted sin as a fact of life and moralists on some level viewed models of godlike or angelic behavior as no more than aspirations. In practice, even reformers accepted a huge gap between theoretically uncompromising demands and actual behavior, and some of the writers discussed here fell short of the standards they themselves advocated. Even so, the moralizing and didactic works of the time clearly made few allowances either for human frailty or for the complexities of human life, which moralists tended simply to dismiss as worldly entanglements that the clergy should avoid. Indeed, the concept of worldly entanglements was designed partly to brush aside as unworthy of consideration those social values and ties that competed with purely religious ones. Inevitably, any idealistic movement or organization will face a gap between ideal and reality, but for the medieval clergy there was a particularly strong

---

[97] Cushing, *Reform and the Papacy*, 112.

[98] Jason Taliadoros, *Law and Theology in Twelfth-Century England: The Works of Master Vacarius (c.1115/1120–c.1200)* (Turnhout, 2006), 228–9.

[99] Waters, *Angels and Earthly Creatures*, 143–58.

[100] Nigel of Whiteacre, *Speculum Stultorum*; A. G. Rigg, *A History of Anglo-Latin Literature, 1066–1422* (Cambridge, 1992), 141–2.

disconnect between what was presented as acceptable behavior and the behaviors that were actually accepted.

This disconnect inevitably created severe tensions, as all too human clerics were faced with harsh and uncompromising demands for godlike, angelic behavior.[101] For priests and other clerics who took the demands of reformers seriously, life would have been a constant struggle fraught with failure. Peter of Blois, in a letter to an archdeacon of York, criticized him for excessive confidence in his own virtue and wrote that "we scarcely pass one day in which we do not offend God or a neighbor by anger, detracting, murmuring, envy, spreading scandal, desiring, chattering, gluttony, embracing the flesh, contradicting the spirit, or wishing for the things of world."[102] Peter was speaking of challenges facing all Christians, but the expectations facing clerics such as Peter and his correspondent only made the stakes higher. One cannot speak of any concrete, general "crisis of the clergy" in England in the long twelfth century, but clearly many individuals faced their own spiritual crises and the clergy as a whole faced severe moral and religious tensions throughout the period.

---

[101] R. N. Swanson and Claire Waters have also noted this dilemma: Swanson, "Angels Incarnate," 161; Waters, *Angels and Earthly Creatures*.

[102] Peter of Blois, *Opera*, 349.

3

The Aristocratic Cleric

Sources from the long twelfth century often presented clerics and knights as distinct but equally high status social groups. In his courtesy manual, Daniel of Beccles wrote that a polite host should go out to greet a visiting *miles* or *clericus*, and that when a lord sat, members of those two groups could also sit without being commanded.[1] In regulations for King Richard's army during the Third Crusade, clerics and knights received specific privileges such as the right to move from the service of one lord to another and, surprisingly but tellingly, to gamble.[2] A discussion of proper salutations for different social ranks in a treatise on letter writing attributed to Peter of Blois placed *clerici* and *milites* together in a single rank. It also stated that laypeople should defer to clerics in the same rank out of courtesy, even if the latter were inferior in power or nobility, so that magnates should write to priests as superiors.[3] More generally, clerics and knights were often linked as a paired grouping in descriptions of retinues in both vernacular and Latin sources.[4]

This frequent pairing of knights and clerics in the sources powerfully illustrates the main arguments of this chapter. First, the clerical elite, including not just bishops but also the wealthiest and most powerful figures below that level, formed an important part of the social elite in this period. Though clerics formed a *distinct* segment within that elite, the clerical elite arguably had as much prestige as the emerging order of knighthood. Second, the ability of clerics to aspire to a high status created an alternative, informal model of the lordly cleric that competed strongly with the reforming model described in the previous chapter. Though joining the clergy theoretically involved aiming for a practically saintly status, in practice many clerics hoped to become members of a clerical aristocracy. Peter of

---

[1] Daniel of Beccles, *Urbanus Magnus Danielis Becclesiensis*, ed. J. Gilbart Smyly (Dublin, 1939), 42, 77.

[2] Roger of Howden, *Chronica Magistri Rogeri de Houedene*, ed. William Stubbs, 4 vols. (London, 1868–71), 3:59.

[3] Martin Camargo, ed., *Medieval Rhetorics of Prose Composition: Five English* Artes Dictandi *and their Tradition* (Binghamton, 1995), 52. Similar equivalencies can be found in other treatises on letter writing: Giles Constable, "The Structure of Medieval Society According to the *Dictatores* of the Twelfth Century," in Kenneth Pennington and Robert Somerville, eds., *Law, Church, and Society: Essays in Honor of Stephan Kuttner* (Philadelphia, 1977), 253–67.

[4] Walter Map, *De Nugis Curialium: Courtiers' Trifles*, ed. M. R. James, C. N. L. Brooke, and R. A. B. Mynors (Oxford, 1983), 102–3; Jocelin of Brakelond, *The Chronicle of Jocelin of Brakelond*, ed. H. E. Butler (London, 1949), 25, 73; F. M. Stenton, *The First Century of English Feudalism, 1066–1166* (Oxford, 1961), 37–9; Wace, *The Roman de Rou*, ed. A. J. Holden, Glyn S. Burgess, and Elisabeth van Houts (St Helier, 2002), 112–14, 120–1.

Blois, in the letter to the archdeacon of York discussed in the last chapter, criticized his self-satisfied correspondent for his ambition and for his concern for fine furnishings, delicate food, fashionable dress, fat rents, big buildings, and a large retinue.[5] Clearly, this archdeacon of York was trying to cut an impressive, aristocratic figure in the world. Certainly most clerics could not entertain practical aspirations to aristocratic status, but a sizable minority *did* belong to the social elite and, conversely, a sizable percentage of the social elite was made up of clerics. Secular aristocrats sometimes contested aristocratic aspirations by clerics, especially those who were not of high birth. However, the clerical elite overall had a secure position within the upper reaches of society. In the next chapter I will discuss the economic basis for high clerical social status. In this chapter, I will focus on lifestyle and prestige.

1. THE ARISTOCRATIC STATUS OF ELITE CLERICS

Most medieval historians pay little attention to the clerical presence among the social elite of the Middle Ages. Michael Clanchy does discuss Abelard, who came from a knightly family, as being the clerical equivalent of a knight.[6] The arguments of Stephen Jaeger and Martin Aurell about the influence of the clergy on the development of courtliness and other aspects of lay aristocratic culture, to which I will return, presuppose that the upper clergy were intimately involved in aristocratic culture.[7] Indeed, few scholars would deny that bishops and royal clerical favorites formed part of the power elite. Nonetheless, investigations of the social elites in the central Middle Ages almost inevitably focus on the secular aristocracy.

In the Anglophone world at least, the near invisibility to historians of clerics within the social elite may partly stem from a trick of the language. *Miles* and *clericus* in the twelfth century had a different semantic range than knight and clerk, their most frequent modern translations. *Clericus* or its vernacular equivalents could refer to figures ranging from the archbishop of Canterbury to peasant boys who had been tonsured. However, *miles* had also had a broad social range, since it had meant soldier in classical Latin and was only slowly becoming associated with the secular aristocracy during the long twelfth century. The old English *cniht*, whence our term knight comes, had originally meant boy and later follower, which gives some sense of how the English had first viewed the mounted warriors accompanying William the Conqueror.[8] However, knightly status became ever more socially restricted as

---

[5] Peter of Blois, *Opera*, 349.

[6] M. T. Clanchy, *Abelard: A Medieval Life* (Oxford, 1997), 130–48.

[7] C. Stephen Jaeger, *The Origins of Courtliness: Civilizing Trends and the Formation of Courtly Ideals, 939–1210* (Philadelphia, 1985); C. Stephen Jaeger, *The Envy of Angels: Cathedral Schools and Social Ideals in Medieval Europe, 950–1200* (Philadelphia, 1994); Martin Aurell, *Le chevalier lettré: savoir et conduite de l'aristocratie aux XIIe et XIIIe siècles* (Paris, 2011). See also Aldo D. Scaglione, *Knights at Court: Courtliness, Chivalry, and Courtesy from Ottonian Germany to the Italian Renaissance* (Berkeley, 1991), 21–86.

[8] Stenton, *First Century*, 132–6.

the Middle Ages progressed and, as a result, knighthood is associated with exalted social rank even today. In contrast, being a clerk is not now a sign of high social status. When we see the term *clericus*, we are most likely to think of the humble lower orders of the clergy. However, in the pairings I have noted above, the writers were using *clericus* to refer to the clerical elite, just as they were using *miles* to refer to the military elite. We must be wary of letting the later trajectory of these terms influence our reading of twelfth-century sources.

More important, our sources tend to give us a misleading impression. In a society that stressed ideals of poverty, humility, and self-denial for the clergy, celebrating the power, status, and aristocratic lifestyles of the clerical elite was inevitably problematic. As a result, in narrative sources the aristocratic tendencies of many clerics tended to be downplayed, attacked, or filtered through the problematic lens of satire. Moreover, much of the modern image of the aristocratic world of the Middle Ages comes from epics and romances. Occasionally the religious, particularly hermits or prelates, had a minor role in such works. For instance, the hero of the Anglo-Norman *Boeve de Haumpton* had an uncle who was bishop of Cologne and appeared at intervals to help the hero out, baptize his Muslim beloved, and eventually marry the couple.[9] In general, however, the religious were noteworthy largely by their absence in epics and romances, even though the authors of these works were often clerics. This absence largely stems from genre, subject matter, and views of proper clerical behavior; clerics were not supposed to be warriors or adventurers. Assessing the structure of medieval elites from such sources is somewhat like trying to reconstruct the nature of modern governments from spy novels. Because we have so few other narrative sources for elite life, literary works necessarily play a crucial role in shaping our views of the medieval aristocracy, but when it comes to the importance of clerics in the social elite, they are misleading.

Fortunately, we have a set of sources that illustrate the aristocratic lifestyle of one particularly powerful cleric quite well: the lives of Thomas Becket.[10] Before his elevation to the archbishopric of Canterbury and his conversion to a more pious form of life, Thomas was a wildly successful and notably worldly cleric.[11] As Michael Staunton has emphasized, Thomas was initially controversial enough for his biographers to have to make a case for his sanctity, and their subject's early worldliness proved an awkward problem.[12] However, Thomas's history was familiar to the extent that they could not simply ignore his status and behavior as royal chancellor. Moreover, one biographer, William fitz Stephen, seems to have positively reveled in Thomas's worldly success.[13] Though Thomas's history is well known, it is worth lingering over his lifestyle and actions as chancellor, both

---

[9] Albert Stimming, ed., *Der anglonormannische Boeve de Haumtone* (Halle, 1899), 71–2, 85.

[10] The Latin lives are found in Robertson and Sheppard, eds., *Materials*. For the vernacular lives, see Guernes de Pont-Sainte-Maxence, *La vie de saint Thomas Becket*, ed. Emmanuel Walberg (Paris, 1936); Börje Schlyter, ed., *La vie de Thomas Becket par Beneit* (Lund, 1941).

[11] For good recent biographies, see Frank Barlow, *Thomas Becket* (London, 1986); Anne Duggan, *Thomas Becket* (London, 2004).

[12] Michael Staunton, *Thomas Becket and his Biographers* (Woodbridge, 2006), 13.

[13] Robertson and Sheppard, eds., *Materials*, 3:15–35.

because of the contrast with the expectations described in the previous chapter and because he was the very model of the aristocratic cleric despite his urban origins.

Thomas was a pluralist on a grand scale, as archdeacon of Canterbury, provost of Beverley, dean of Hastings, and the holder of various prebends and churches. He controlled castles and managed rich honors for Henry II, collecting huge sums of money. He pursued such aristocratic pastimes as hawking, hunting, and chess. He kept a rich table, filled with gold and silver dishes and lavish food and drink. His household was enormous, with the sons of magnates and of the king himself entrusted to his care and with fifty-two clerics in his service. His retinue could require six ships to cross the English Channel. When Thomas traveled as Henry's emissary to the king of France, he was accompanied by a vast train, which was described in loving detail by William fitz Stephen. It was led by 250 footmen and included many other servitors and followers, of whom 200 were mounted, some of them young nobles. Hunting dogs, hawks, and even apes accompanied the train, and at its end clerics and knights rode two by two (note the assumed equivalency between the two groups) followed by the chancellor with a few familiars. Thomas took twenty-four sets of clothing on the trip, including much silk and many rich furs. Less luxurious but even more impressive was Thomas's following during Henry's war against the count of Toulouse. If William fitz Stephen can be believed, Thomas led 700 knights from his own following as well as 1200 mercenary knights and 4000 foot soldiers. Thomas apparently took Cahors and several castles and on one occasion even unhorsed an enemy knight. The fact that he knighted the Flemish noble, Baldwin, son of Count Arnulf of Guines, attests to his military prestige. It is no wonder that when he was a candidate to be archbishop some Canterbury monks described him as more a knight than a cleric.[14]

Thomas Becket was, of course, extraordinary in the level of success he achieved, and though his benefices would have made him a wealthy man, the lavishness described above depended on access to royal wealth. Nevertheless, lesser figures could have impressive lifestyles. In order to limit the burdens of hospitality on local churches, ecclesiastical law limited the size of the traveling retinues of archdeacons by stating that they could use no more than seven horses during visitations of churches in their territory (bishops could have thirty and archbishops fifty). On one occasion, however, the Augustinian house of Bridlington complained to Pope Innocent III that an archdeacon of Richmond had visited one of their parish churches with ninety-seven horses, twenty-one hounds, and three hawks.[15]

Moreover, contemporaries viewed elite members of the secular clergy as powerful and imposing figures. Two successive archbishops of Canterbury, Baldwin and Hubert Walter, tried to create a college of secular canons to serve as a base for their clerical followers and to provide patronage for other powerful clerics. The cathedral

---

[14] Robertson and Sheppard, eds., *Materials*, 1:5; 2:304–5, 363–4; 3:15–35, 163–77, 183; 4:12–14, 82–6; Barlow, *Thomas Becket*, 24–63; John D. Hosler, "The Brief Military Career of Thomas Becket," *Haskins Society Journal* 15 (2006), 88–100; Jaeger, *Envy of Angels*, 297–308.

[15] William Farrer and Charles T. Clay, eds., *Early Yorkshire Charters*, 13 vols., Yorkshire Archaeological Society Record Series, Extra Series (Edinburgh and Wakefield, 1914–65), 5:347.

monks feared that the canons of this house would siphon resources away from them and perhaps even supplant them. In advertising their fears, they emphasized the power and influence that important secular canons could have, stressing their wealth, legal expertise, ties with ecclesiastical prelates, kinship to kings, nobles, or even popes, participation in royal government, and influence with the king. The monks may have exaggerated the potential threat posed by the canons, but their fear of the power and influence of elite clerics was clearly genuine.[16] In a less hostile though still critical vein, the biographer of Hugh of Avalon, bishop of Lincoln, described the canons at Lincoln as being heavily involved in royal government, prominent in worldly affairs, and excelling in both learning and wealth. He even claimed that some were wealthier than bishops.[17] Vernacular works sometimes described clerics in terms one would normally associate with nobles. Earl William Marshal's biographer described the earl's third son, Gilbert, still a cleric when the biography was composed, as "franz et gentilz et debonaire."[18] Gilbert was of noble origin, but the cleric Philippe de Thaon, in his translation of the Latin computus into French, could call Turchil, a royal cleric and earlier author, "le vaillant," (worthy or valiant), and another writer, Adgar, could likewise describe Master Alberic, a canon of St. Paul's, as "mult vaillant."[19] Thomas Becket was unusual in the heights to which he rose, but other clerics had the lifestyles, wealth, power, and status normally associated with secular aristocrats.

Besides bishops, it was archdeacons, cathedral dignitaries and canons, royal clerics, and clerics in the households of secular and ecclesiastical magnates who were most likely to gain elevated status and power, but parish priests, particularly if they were rectors, could have a high social position locally. I have noted Reginald of Durham's account of the priest of Arden in Nottinghamshire who hosted both the poor and the well-to-do of the area at a yearly feast. On one occasion when raiders attacked his village during Stephen's reign, this priest organized a successful counterattack, at least if Reginald's miracle story is to be believed.[20] Obviously, he was a prominent figure in the neighborhood. Wulfric of Haselbury gained widespread prominence as a saintly hermit, but earlier in his life he had been a worldly parish priest who devoted time to hawking and hunting and who was of sufficient social standing to dine frequently with the lord of the manor.[21] Other priests and clerics can be found holding feasts and socializing with nobles and knights as well.[22] Compared to nobles, most parish priests were minor figures, but at least some could achieve high status locally, even if, like Wulfric, they came from

[16] William Stubbs, ed., *Epistolæ Cantuarienses, the Letters of the Prior and Convent of Christ Church, Canterbury* (London, 1865), 63, 72–3, 380, 533–4.

[17] Adam of Eynsham, *Magna Vita Sancti Hugonis*, 1:92–3.

[18] Anthony J. Holden, Stewart Gregory, and David Crouch, eds., *History of William Marshal*, 3 vols. (London, 2002–6), 2:246–9.

[19] Philippe de Thaon, *Comput (MS BL Cotton Nero A. V)*, ed. Ian Short (London, 1984), 28; Adgar, *Le gracial*, ed. Pierre Kunstmann (Ottawa, 1982), 327.

[20] See Chapter 2, section 2: Reginald of Durham, *Libellus de Cuthberti Virtutibus*, 127–34.

[21] John of Ford, *Wulfric of Haselbury*, ed. Maurice Bell, Somerset Record Society, vol. 47 (Frome, 1933), 13–14.

[22] Robertson and Sheppard, eds., *Materials*, 1:247, 349; 2:163; Gerald of Wales, *Opera*, 7:119.

lowly origins, and Henry Mayr-Harting has argued convincingly that they were influential members of local society.[23]

2. CLERICS AND ARISTOCRATIC CULTURE

A noteworthy aspect of clerical lifestyles was the frequent adoption of forbidden aristocratic pursuits. The prohibition on clerics hunting and practicing falconry may have been widely flouted, as suggested by the examples of Wulfric of Haselbury, the archdeacon of Richmond, and, of course, Thomas Becket. Indeed, the monks of Canterbury also complained that Thomas seemed more of a hunter and falconer than a cleric.[24] The fierce complaints of Roger of Howden and Ralph of Diceto about the royal government amercing clerics for hunting indicates that sporting interests were common among clerics. The complaints, interestingly, were about the royal government, not about the clerics, though Ralph claimed that many were accused on the basis of rumor alone.[25] When one turns to the pipe rolls, one can indeed see amercements of clerics for taking deer or having hunting dogs.[26] Strikingly, one cleric, Thomas de Neville, made sure that hunting rights would be included when he made an offer to King John for the right to farm a manor for life.[27]

Even more striking is the participation of clerics both in the description and in the real or imagined practice of what modern scholars call courtly love. It is easy to focus primarily on the secular aristocracy in this context, yet one of the key texts on the subject was the Latin work of a continental cleric, Andreas Capellanus, ostensibly a guidebook to love, though the last part contains a fierce repudiation of the earlier sections. In the earlier sections, Andreas made only a perfunctory objection to clerical participation in the pursuit of love, and in his eighth dialogue the man involved was explicitly described as a cleric and made arguments for the superiority of clerical lovers. Much of Andreas's discussion of love revolved around status, with an utter rejection of peasants as lovers, and the clerical lover of dialogue eight was a representative of the highest nobility. Partly in light of Andreas's condemnation of love in his last section, many scholars treat his guide to love as ironic, and if so, the impropriety of clerical involvement was no doubt part of the irony. Even so, however, the work did clearly depict elite clerics participating in aristocratic practices of love.[28]

---

[23] Mayr-Harting, *Religion, Politics and Society*, 108–12. See also Michael Burger, *Bishops, Clerks, and Diocesan Governance in Thirteenth-Century England: Reward and Punishment* (Cambridge, 2012), 36–9.

[24] Robertson and Sheppard, eds., *Materials*, 3:183.

[25] [Roger of Howden], *Gesta Regis Henrici Secundi Benedicti Abbatis*, ed. William Stubbs, 2 vols. (London, 1867), 1:99, 105; Ralph of Diceto, *Opera Historica*, 1:402.

[26] See, for instance, *Pipe Roll 33 Henry II*, 3, 169; *Pipe Roll 10 Richard I*, 72, 104–6, 164.

[27] Thomas Duffus Hardy, ed., *Rotuli de Oblatis et Finibus in Turri Londinensi Asservati, Tempore Regis Johannis* (London, 1835), 245. See also Thomas Duffus Hardy, ed., *Rotuli Chartarum in Turri Londinensi Asservati* (London, 1837), 48a, 75b.

[28] P. G. Walsh, ed., *Andreas Capellanus on Love* (London, 1982), 182–9, 208–11, 296–7. For discussion of Andreas, class, and the clergy, see John W. Baldwin, *The Language of Sex: Five Voices from*

Two continental Latin poems from the twelfth century and two Anglo-Norman poems from later in the thirteenth century involved a comparison of knights and clerics as lovers, showing once more the tendency, albeit clearly in a satirical context, to treat the two groups as distinct but equally prestigious.[29] One of the continental poems concerned a council of nuns at Remiremont which ended with a female cardinal excommunicating those "rebels" who had the bad taste to prefer knights as lovers.[30] The other poems described debates between pairs of women over the question, with clerics winning two out of the three. The champions of the clerics in these comic debates described various advantages of clerical lovers, including their wealth and leisure. In one of the Anglo-Norman poems, the debater favoring clerics said that from them came all "good, wisdom, courtesy, valor, love, and druerie," the last term being a synonym for love sometimes translated as "courtly love." She also claimed that they had mastery of "fin amur."[31]

The texts noted so far fall outside either the geographical or temporal framework of this project, but English clerics from the long twelfth century wrote about love in Latin and French. The strong tradition of Latin poetry associated with the Twelfth-Century Renaissance included remarkable love poetry. Much of the best of this poetry came from the continent, but was nonetheless available in England.[32] As for English poets, Henry of Huntingdon and Peter of Blois both confessed to writing love poetry in their youth, though the former's love poetry is lost, so far as we know, and there is debate about whether any of the latter's survives.[33] Gerald of Wales, despite his stance as a strict moralist, preserved several of his poems on themes of love, including one on the effects of being suddenly enamored on seeing a naked girl in a pool.[34] More important, Serlo of Wilton was one of the more accomplished poets of love in the period.[35] It is true that some of these poems may have been as

Northern France around 1200 (Chicago, 1994), 20, 58–9; Don Alfred Monson, *Andreas Capellanus, Scholasticism, and the Courtly Tradition* (Washington, D.C., 2005), 51, 238–86, 326–32. Monson (122–66) also provides a good but skeptical overview of arguments for treating Andreas's work as ironic.

[29] For a recent discussion of such debates, see Aurell, *Le chevalier lettré*, 390–9.

[30] Paul Pascal, ed., *Concilium Romarici Montis*, Bryn Mawr Latin Commentaries (Bryn Mawr, 1993).

[31] P. G. Walsh, *Love Lyrics from the Carmina Burana* (Chapel Hill, 1993), 101–25; P. Meyer, "Notice du MS. 25970 de la bibliothèque Phillipps (Cheltenham)," *Romania* 37 (1908), 209–35, at 221–34; P. Meyer, "Melior et Ydoine," *Romania* 37 (1908), 235–44. For discussion of the Anglo-Norman debate poems, see M. Dominica Legge, *Anglo-Norman Literature and its Background* (Oxford, 1963), 334–6.

[32] Peter Dronke, *Medieval Latin and the Rise of European Love-Lyric*, 2 vols. (Oxford, 1968); Gerald A. Bond, *The Loving Subject: Desire, Eloquence, and Power in Romanesque France* (Philadelphia, 1995); Rigg, *History of Anglo-Latin Literature*, 63–4, 67–8, 149, 153, 155–6; Thomas C. Moser, *A Cosmos of Desire: The Medieval Latin Erotic Lyric in English Manuscripts* (Ann Arbor, 2004).

[33] Henry of Huntingdon, *Historia Anglorum*, cxii–cxiv, 584–5, 618–19, 804–5; Peter of Blois, *Opera*, 234. For an edition and discussion of Peter of Blois's poetry, including poems that may or may not be his, see C. Wollin, ed., *Petri Blesensis Carmina* (Turnhout, 1998). For the uneasiness of writers over erotic love poetry, see Moser, *Cosmos of Desire*, 10–11.

[34] Gerald of Wales, *Opera*, 1:349–54, 356–7. For discussion of his works, see Moser, *Cosmos of Desire*, 173–92.

[35] Moser, *Cosmos of Desire*, 152–7; Dronke, *Medieval Latin*, 1:239–43; 2:493–512.

much about learning as love. Thomas Moser has linked Gerald's poems to Neo-platonic interests of the time, and described them as examples of classicizing school poetry.[36] Serlo of Wilton was certainly, as Dronke describes him, "a virtuoso delighting in language for its own sake, delighting in finding new similarities of sound, making many-sidedness of thought simply an extension of the many-sidedness of language," and Dronke's doubts about the literal truth of some of Serlo's "libertine" claims are reasonable.[37] Nonetheless, Gerald and Serlo were clearly drawing on themes of love and sexuality that resonated within their cultures, and their works should not be considered entirely apart from the traditions of aristo-cratic lovemaking we call courtly love. For instance, the sudden onset of love in Gerald of Wales's poem followed a common theme in that tradition. Indeed, various scholars have argued for the importance of clerics in shaping that tradition, partly through preserving and disseminating Ovid, partly by imparting various religious ideas about love into the secular sphere.[38] Strikingly, Flora, the clerical champion in one of the continental debate poems, claimed that clerics learned and taught what Venus and the God of Love valued, and that knights only became followers of Venus through clerics, which may be an allusion to clerical access to pagan works on love and may point to an awareness of the role of the clergy in shaping medieval ideas about love.[39] In any case, through their literary works, many clerics, even those who came to eschew worldly love, staked a claim to participation in an elite culture of lovemaking.

Indeed, though clerics generally only appear as minor characters in romances, the clerics who wrote them implicitly claimed expertise in the nature of love, and also of chivalry for that matter. One English writer of French, Adgar, though his own subject was the miracles of the Virgin Mary, argued that accounts of amorous delights or battle or other adventures could teach courtesy and other useful knowledge.[40] Moreover, Hue de Roteland, who was almost certainly a cleric, slyly injected a clerical element into his romance, *Ipomedon*. When the eponymous hero remained unmoved by the advances of a queen, Hue commented, using medical terminology appropriate to the learned, that he would have known how to spare her the resulting pain. He then said that Hugh de Hungrie, a contemporary canon at Hereford Cathedral, could have handled the situation even better, for "he knows the gloss on that text." At the end of the romance, Hue wrote that there "was never a knight or learned cleric" who loved like Ipomedon, but then went on, in an obscure but probably obscene passage, to claim that he himself had a charter of absolution for anyone excommunicated for giving up love too soon, and offered to demonstrate this to any woman who came to his house at Credenhill, near Hereford. Hue thus followed convention by treating princes and nobles as the morally appropriate practioners of love and adventure, but then subverted it by inserting clerical

---

[36] Moser, *Cosmos of Desire*, 174–92.
[37] Dronke, *Medieval Latin*, 1:240–1. See also Moser, *Cosmos of Desire*, 153–4.
[38] Aurell, *Le chevalier lettré*, 382–9.
[39] Walsh, *Love Lyrics from the Carmina Burana*, 106.   [40] Adgar, *Le gracial*, 123.

lovers like himself.[41] More straightforwardly, the author of a late twelfth-century Anglo-Norman poem, "Le donnei des amants," spoke of seeing a youth court a lady, but being unwilling to say if he was "cleric or knight, valet of the court or squire." Since the lover in the poem cited the Bible, classical works, and Petrus Alfonsus's *Disciplina Clericalis*, Gaston Paris, the editor of the text, suggested that he must be a cleric, but since the woman being courted cited the example of Dido, such references cannot be treated as conclusive in the imagined world of the poem. Nonetheless, these citations and others do make it likely that the anonymous poet was a cleric, and at the very least the *possibility* of a courtly clerical lover appears in the poem.[42]

Writers also placed actual clerics in the cultural context of courtly love, albeit generally in far-fetched stories. The Cistercian chronicler Ralph of Coggeshall included a story told to him by Gervase of Tilbury in which the latter, as a cleric working in Rheims for the archbishop there, tried to seduce a peasant girl. Her negative reaction convinced him that she was a heretic, which led to her arrest and execution. However, the text described Gervase as having addressed her about "lascivious" love "curialiter" and Edward Peters has drawn parallels between the beginning of this horrific tale and the genre of the pastourelle. Parts of the story, such as the rescue of the girl's *magistra* in heresy by demons, are entirely unbelievable. Apparently, however, there was no incongruity in depicting Gervase as a courtly seducer.[43] One of the conventions of medieval love was lovesickness, marked by sighs and changes in appearance, particularly paleness. Walter Map claimed to have seen such signs in a friend of "philosophical life" (therefore a learned man and thus almost certainly a cleric) and to have detected "the delirium of Venus," using this encounter as a pretext to introduce a misogynistic tract against marriage into his *De Nugis Curialium*.[44] Similarly, a collection of miracle stories from Beverley told how a school- and choirmaster there fell in love and grew increasingly pale and thin until miraculously cured of his infatuation.[45] Another convention of courtly love involved the courtship of powerful, married women. One story from an early thirteenth-century collection of anecdotes, many of them

---

[41] Hue de Rotelande, *Ipomedon: poème de Hue de Rotelande, fin du XIIe siècle*, ed. A. J. Holden (Paris, 1979), 310, 516–17. For comments on these passages, see Legge, *Anglo-Norman Literature*, 94; Susan Crane, *Insular Romance: Politics, Faith, and Culture in Anglo-Norman and Middle English Literature* (Berkeley, 1986), 146–7, 172. Hue never explicitly described himself as a cleric or priest, and he attested one charter (along with another inhabitant of Credenhill) without a title: C. D. Ross and Mary Devine, eds., *The Cartulary of Cirencester Abbey, Gloucestershire*, 3 vols. (London, 1964–77), 1:244. However, clerics with bynames did not always have their titles noted, and Hue's learning and familiarity with clerics such as Hugh de Hungrie strongly suggest that the traditional view that he was a cleric is correct.

[42] Gaston Paris, "Le donnei des amants," *Romania* 25 (1896), 497–541. For commentary on this work, see Legge, *Anglo-Norman Literature*, 128–32.

[43] Ralph of Coggeshall, *Radulphi de Coggeshall Chronicon Anglicanum*, ed. Joseph Stevenson (London, 1875), 122–4; Edward Peters, *The Magician, the Witch, and the Law* (Philadelphia, 1978), 35–9.

[44] Walter also depicted Gerbert of Aurillac, the future pope, as a lovesick youth; Walter Map, *De Nugis Curialium*, 286–9, 350–3.

[45] James Raine, ed., *The Historians of the Church of York and its Archbishops*, 3 vols. (London, 1879–94), 1:281–4.

told by or involving English clerics, turned this convention on its head. In this account, Eleanor of Aquitaine, while queen of France, heard of a beautiful cleric named Gerard la Pucelle, and summoned him to her presence. Seeing his well-formed hands, she exclaimed "what fitting hands for caressing the thighs of a beautiful woman," thighs being a common euphemism for female genitalia. Gerard replied that he would use his hands to handle his Porreta, probably referring to the works of the noted scholar Gilbert de la Porrée.[46] Like Eleanor of Aquitaine, Gerard (whose nickname meant "the maiden") was a historical figure: a noted scholar and later bishop of Coventry. One may well doubt the historicity of this story, which took advantage of Eleanor's scandalous reputation to create a moral *exemplum*, but it did link an actual cleric with one of the most famous figures associated with courtly love.[47]

The evidence for clerical involvement in courtly love admittedly tends to be problematic, though the same could be said of most of the evidence for lay involvement as well. Even as stories, the individual works and anecdotes discussed above can be read in various and often quite complicated ways. Indeed, the degree to which courtly love existed as actual practice, as opposed to fictions, ideals, and discourse, is hard to know.[48] Nonetheless, collectively these sources strongly indicate that contemporaries viewed members of the clerical elite as socially though not morally appropriate lovers (however imaginary) in a largely aristocratic context.

Other arenas in which successful clerics can be seen as part of the elite, similar in many respects to the secular aristocracy, will be discussed in later chapters. Besides the rich incomes of many clerics, examples include their lavish expenditures on expensive housing; their patronage of art, manuscripts, and entertainers; their participation in powerful patronage networks; and their involvement in court life. Contemporaries had an image of secular and clerical elites that were distinct in functions though alike in status, but in fact the groups were more similar than either medieval commentators or modern historians have generally admitted.

Indeed, the overlap was such that clerics, particularly those of noble birth, might shift between the clergy and the laity depending on the opportunities involved. Gilbert Marshal, William Marshal's third son, was originally destined for the Church but his clerical status did not prevent him from becoming earl of Pembroke when his older brothers died. The Walden chronicle described a son of a royal chancellor who passed from being the incumbent of a church to serving as a knight in Stephen's reign and subsequently returned to the clergy and resumed his benefices.[49] An important attorney in the royal courts, Matthew of Bigstrup, held the title of master, indicating that he had received academic training and was a

---

[46] It is possible that a homoerotic joke is intended, but that seems out of character for this collection.

[47] Corpus Christi College, Oxford, MS 32, fo. 99v. For a short biography of Gerard, see M. J. Franklin, ed., *English Episcopal Acta. 17, Coventry and Lichfield, 1183–1208* (Oxford, 1998), xxiii–xxv. For the use of thighs as a euphemism, see Baldwin, *Language of Sex*, 103–4.

[48] For some thoughtful comments on this matter, see Aurell, *Le chevalier lettré*, 399–401.

[49] Diana E. Greenway and Leslie Watkiss, eds., *The Book of the Foundation of Walden Monastery* (Oxford, 1999), 20–1.

cleric. When he inherited his father's lands, however, he gave up the title master and became a knight, though he remained active as an attorney.[50]

There were, of course, important differences between the two groups.[51] The secular aristocracy was a military elite but clerics were supposed to avoid warfare. Despite scattered examples such as Thomas Becket's career as a general, clerics generally did not act as warriors, leading to major practical and cultural distinctions between the two groups. The other great divide had to do with celibacy, marriage, and inheritance. Clerics did continue to marry or take concubines, to have families, and to try to pass on their possessions and offices to children throughout the period. Nonetheless, the success of reformers in limiting these practices was sufficient to prevent the possibility of any hereditary priestly caste that could pass churches and benefices on from generation to generation as secular aristocrats did with their land. In certain specific but important respects, then, the ideal of elite clerics and the military elite as quite different groups remained intact.

The presence of secular clerics among the social elites helps buttress the arguments of Jaeger and Aurell about the impact of the clergy on aristocratic culture.[52] Both scholars draw on and react against the influential ideas of Norbert Elias, who argued that starting in the central Middle Ages, but proceeding largely in the early modern period under powerful rulers, the lay elites experienced a civilizing process involving restraint of violence, increasing self-control, the adoption of polite manners, and other habits and practices that in a sense tamed them.[53] Jaeger and Aurell both contend that much of this process occurred in the central Middle Ages, particularly in the context of the court. Jaeger argues that the clergy, especially bishops, were largely responsible for the origins of courtliness, which only subsequently passed to the secular elites. Though he focuses on Germany and starts in an earlier period than is considered here, he does include such twelfth-century English figures as Peter of Blois, John of Salisbury, and Thomas Becket. Aurell's work, which covers all of Europe in the twelfth and thirteenth centuries, focuses on an increasingly learned secular aristocracy. Nonetheless, he too sees an important role for the clergy, both directly and indirectly (through the spread of "clergie" or learning) on aristocratic culture. In his view, the clergy helped foster aristocratic control of violence and allegiance to the state, partly through the development of chivalry, the rise of manners and self-control, the creation of courtly love, and the growth of aristocratic piety. By their nature, such cultural shifts are hard to chart with precision and their causes are even harder to pin down. Moreover, one must be wary of the possible bias introduced by the clerical origins of so many of our sources. Nonetheless, many of the arguments of Jaeger and Aurell are convincing,

---

[50] Doris M. Stenton, ed., *Pleas before the King or his Justices*, 4 vols., Publications of the Selden Society, vols. 67–8, 83–4 (London, 1953–67), 3:xxxvii–xxxviii.

[51] Despite endorsing Miller's overall emphasis on the distinctiveness of the clergy, I do not see as big a difference as she does between elite secular and elite clerical culture, at least based on the English evidence: Miller, "Religion Makes a Difference," 1095–130.

[52] Jaeger, *Origins of Courtliness*; Jaeger, *Envy of Angels*; Aurell, *Le chevalier lettré*.

[53] Norbert Elias, *The Civilizing Process* (New York, 1978); Norbert Elias, *Power & Civility. The Civilizing Process: Volume II* (New York, 1982).

and the impact they argue that the clergy had was only possible because prominent clerics were so firmly ensconced within the elites.

3. SOCIAL, MORAL, AND RELIGIOUS TENSIONS

The participation of clerics in elite culture, however, brought tensions. Though clerics could be quite worldly and laypeople could be deeply pious, the tensions were sometimes ideological in nature. As noted in the previous chapter, priests were supposed to correct their flocks fiercely. Laypeople did not always suffer this willingly and aristocrats were no doubt particularly unused to being chastised. In a famous episode in the *Poem of William Marshal*, Philip, one of the dying Marshal's clerics, urged him to sell eighty new cloaks in return for money which he could use to expiate his sins. In response, the Marshal said "shut up, you evildoer," berated him for being a bad counselor and having "a heart that had never been good," and directed that the cloaks be distributed among his followers.[54] Philip was acting precisely as moralists would have wished him to, but as a result received only abuse from a lord who placed aristocratic values over perfectly standard religious ones. David Crouch has suggested that this episode reflected antagonism between household clerics and knights.[55] It certainly represented the potential for cultural clashes between clerics and secular aristocrats.

There appears to have been a more general group rivalry between clerics and knights. This could play out comically, as in the debates over the superiority of clerical or knightly lovers. It appears more seriously in a letter of Peter of Blois complaining to an archdeacon about the recipient's nephews, who were knights. "I cannot tolerate the fatuous vainglory of your nephews, who, boasting of the eminence of the military life, slander the order of clerics with many slurs, holding their life and work in opprobrium and contempt." Peter then went on to discuss in detail the shortcomings in warfare and morals of contemporary knights.[56] Knights, then, may sometimes have contested the equality to them of clerics. Based on the surviving sources, however, the rivalry does not seem to have been a major concern to secular clerics, certainly nothing compared to the rivalry between secular and regular clerics. This general lack of defensiveness suggests that what rivalry existed posed no serious threat to the status of the elite clergy.

A more important tension came from the presence within the clerical elite of men who were not of aristocratic birth, though at times this tension existed among clerics as well as between them and secular aristocrats. Ralph Turner has discussed the frequent criticism of courtiers, many of them clerics, for being improperly "raised from the dust," by kings.[57] A classic example was Ranulf Flambard,

---

[54] Holden, Gregory, and Crouch, eds., *History of William Marshal*, 2:436–7.

[55] David Crouch, *William Marshal: Knighthood, War and Chivalry, 1147–1219* (London, 2002), 145.

[56] Peter of Blois, *Opera*, 293–7.

[57] Turner, *Judges, Administrators*, 225–49. See also Crouch, *Birth of Nobility*, 220–1.

described by Orderic Vitalis as the son of a plebeian priest who was raised above his station to the detriment of many.[58] I will address the difficult question of how common such upward mobility was in Chapter 5, but certainly there was a widespread perception that it frequently occurred. Thomas of Chobham, stating that it was appropriate for clerics to retaliate for insults only when the Church as an institution was attacked or the clergy as a whole were unfairly impugned, advised against reacting to attacks concerning social origins. "If someone calls a bishop a son of a peasant or of a serf or says that before he became bishop he was poor or a beggar, this is not shameful to the Church because there are many such individuals who often make good bishops." In a different passage he stated that for similar reasons no vengeance should be taken if someone said a rector was a son of a whore or of a peasant.[59] When Ranulf de Glanville, Henry II's justiciar, asked why clerics in royal service were more oppressive than lay officials, Walter Map replied that the secular elites neglected to give their children education, whereas serfs or peasants struggled to have their "ignoble and degenerate" offspring educated for the sake of riches.[60] Thomas Becket's spectacular rise from the London elite to a more powerful position than that of most nobles became an issue during his dispute with the king, though mainly because of his perceived ingratitude. "Were you not the son of one of my peasants?" one biography has Henry say to Thomas, after reminding the archbishop that he had raised him from humble poverty to the greatest heights. In one account of the royal outburst that led to Thomas's death, Henry referred to Thomas as a low-born (*plebeus*) cleric.[61]

Thomas and others struggled to grapple with the social disabilities low (or relatively low) birth could bring to even the most successful cleric. Thomas acknowledged the king's generosity and defended the status conferred by his London origins in an exchange of letters with Gilbert Foliot, a bishop of aristocratic background, and in other letters was careful to acknowledge the exalted birth of episcopal colleagues such as Henry of Blois, brother of King Stephen, and Roger of Worcester, grandson of Henry I. On the other hand, after defending his own status in his letter to Gilbert Foliot, he used quotes from Paul and Juvenal to downplay the importance of birth.[62] Similarly, John of Salisbury, in his *Policraticus*, which was dedicated to Thomas as chancellor, deprecated relying too heavily on birth and wealth in judging people and stressed that the worth conveyed by noble origins had its limits.[63] Peter of Blois, in one of his letters, criticized a nobleman for reproaching his chaplain for being of low birth. Reminding his correspondent of Christ's poverty and stressing humanity's

---

[58] Orderic Vitalis, *Ecclesiastical History*, 4:170–1.

[59] Whore, in this context, may refer mainly to the concubines of priests: Thomas of Chobham, *Summa Confessorum*, 307, 441.

[60] Walter Map, *De Nugis Curialium*, 12–15.

[61] Robertson and Sheppard, eds., *Materials*, 2:429; 4:27–8.

[62] Anne Duggan, ed., *The Correspondence of Thomas Becket, Archbishop of Canterbury, 1162–1170*, 2 vols. (Oxford, 2000), 1:376–7, 430–3, 682–3; 2:928–9, 1126–7, 1218–21.

[63] John of Salisbury, *Policraticus*, 2:84–5, 335–8. For John's complex attitudes about nobility, see Frédérique Lachaud, "L'idée de noblesse dans le *Policraticus* de Jean de Salisbury (1159)," *Cahiers de recherches médiévales et humanistes* 13 (2006), 3–19.

common descent from Adam, Peter described how the chaplain had wept and sighed on telling Peter about the noble's abuse. He wrote, "What glory did you gain, I ask, by abusing that honest and commendable man for the baseness of his genus? Why do you boast of yours?"[64]

Indeed, issues of class origin may sometimes have fed into the rivalry between clerics and knights. A rare cleric who identified himself with the peasantry and defended them as a class certainly attacked knights with unusual vehemence. This author, who is unfortunately anonymous but was probably English, compared knights unfavorably to clerics and criticized them for drinking, boasting of fighting without actually engaging in combat, and lying about their wealth. Adding a touch of misogyny, he linked knights to women in their concern for clothing and care of the body, thus undermining any claims of knights to superior masculinity. "Let knights," he exclaimed, "cease impudently and proudly to assert themselves to be good."[65] One wonders if this cleric's attitude towards knights was not partly a reaction to aristocratic snobbery about his own origins.

How much issues of birth affected the status of elite clerics is uncertain, but clearly individual clerics found their place among the social elites contested. Christian ideals about the superiority of the religious could only provide limited help, since such ideals suggested clerics should embrace poverty and humility rather than aiming for a high social status. The biblical story of common descent from Adam could only do so much to combat entrenched class prejudices. Nevertheless, such prejudices would only have affected clerics born outside the elites. Moreover, the prestige of clerical status and the wealth and power provided by many church offices still gave even those of low birth a strong claim to elite status. Overall, the attacks on lowborn clerics do not seem to have substantially affected the inclusion of the clerical elite among the broader social elite.

The elite status and comfortable lifestyle of clerics could provoke their own reactions and create social tensions. The miracles of St. Erkenwald of London, written by Arcoid, a canon of St. Paul's, include the account of a laborer's reaction when a cathedral cleric criticized him for working on the saint's feast day. "You clerics have so much time on your hands that you neglect your own business and meddle with what doesn't concern you. You people, honestly, you're free to keep every day as a holiday, and you get to grow soft with idleness and to eat others folks' food. You can sing without care both day and night, for no necessity compels you to work. Your life should be thought of as more a game or stage play than a real occupation. If someone would feed me every day for free, and clothe me, damn me if I wouldn't strain myself for him, no matter if he wanted me to sing high or low." The laborer then went on to attack clerics for despising the lifestyles and work of people like him. As one might expect in a miracle story, this tirade proved to be a mistake. Almost immediately after his angry speech, the laborer tripped over a

---

[64] Peter of Blois, *Opera*, 7–11.
[65] Marvin L. Colker, ed., *Analecta Dublinensia: Three Medieval Latin Texts in the Library of Trinity College, Dublin* (Cambridge, Mass., 1975), 181–2, 231–5.

half-buried human skull, fell, and died.[66] Though dubious, the story surely reflects the kind of criticism that the clergy, and especially the clerical elite, might face. It is unclear how widespread such criticism was, since the voices of lower class lay-people rarely appear in sources, even in the kind of hostile presentation seen here. Nonetheless, this anecdote suggests that class resentments may have been directed against the clerical as well as the secular elites.

Not surprisingly, however, religion and morality were the greatest sources of tension arising from the high status and great power of the upper echelons of the secular clergy. The model of the aristocratic cleric outlined in this chapter clashed in multiple ways with the model of the ideal priest laid out in the previous chapter. Striving for success and wealth demanded the very qualities of ambition and avarice that moralists condemned. A luxurious lifestyle clearly involved the misuse of "the patrimony of the Crucified One." Imitating aristocratic behavior in lavish feasting, hunting, falconry, and gaming violated the norms demanded of the clergy. Courtly love was closely linked to sexual activity, which reformers described as repellent for those handling God in the Eucharist. No doubt hypocrisy, human weakness, and covert rejection of reform ideals help explain why so many clerics pursued an aristocratic life that contradicted the moral demands of their order. Yet, as with many of the behaviors condemned by moralists, clerics were faced not simply with good as opposed to bad behavior but with competing ideas of proper conduct. According to Gerald of Wales, even Bishop Hugh of Lincoln, noted for his personal asceticism and the high demands he made of his cathedral clergy, expected his *familia*, including the clergy, to be well dressed and to be served splendidly and abundantly at the table.[67] Clearly, elite clerics were expected to conform to upper-class expectations. Moreover, social prestige could give clerics the kind of authority they needed to advance the interests and ideals of the Church. Even for a deeply religious cleric, at least some aspects of the aristocratic model may have seemed perfectly acceptable or even laudable.

The aristocratic model was never as clearly formulated as the religious model of priestly behavior. Whereas reformers had a broadly unified outline of how a priest should think and behave, which they disseminated through sermons and treatises, no one was explicitly describing or urging a model of aristocratic behavior for clerics, though William fitz Stephen's laudatory portrait of Becket's early career came close.[68] Some of the subversive or humorous literature of the time, particularly Goliardic poetry, might be described as setting out an anti-model which challenged and played with, but perhaps also reinforced (through satire and a carnivalesque venting of steam), the religious model. The model I have described here, in contrast, was one created by example rather than theory. Yet, as the very fulminations of moralists make clear, and as evidence throughout this book reinforces, this secular model was all too attractive. For many a young man, the

---

[66] E. Gordon Whatley, ed., *The Saint of London: The Life and Miracles of St. Erkenwald* (Binghamton, 1989), 112–15. The translation is Whatley's.
[67] Gerald of Wales, *Opera*, 7:106.   [68] Robertson and Sheppard, eds., *Materials*, 3:15–35.

path of Thomas Becket the successful worldly cleric may have been more inspiring, or at least more tempting, than that of Thomas Becket the saint.

In any case, the most successful among the secular clergy clearly formed part of the social elite in England in the long twelfth century, though this elite status could be contested, sometimes for the clergy as a whole, more often for individuals rising from families of low status. Within the clergy, it is hard to draw any precise dividing line between elite and non-elite; the boundary must often have been relative or subjective, and depended on circumstances. As in later periods, there was clearly an extensive clerical proletariat who earned little while the revenues of the churches they served went elsewhere. Nonetheless, clerics also formed a sizable portion of the male elite in the kingdom. The high status of the clergy stemmed partly from their religious authority, but it also derived from their wealth, their participation in influential patronage networks, and their service to secular and ecclesiastical lords. It is to these subjects that the next three chapters are devoted.

PART II

THE CLERGY AND THE WORLD

4

The Wealth of the Secular Clergy

Shortly after the death of Henry II, Richard the Lionhearted dispatched Gerald of Wales, who had traveled to the continent with the previous king, as an emissary to Wales to try to keep calm along the borders. After Gerald's regular servants had fallen sick during his trip back through France, he had to hire a stranger to replace them. The new servant got separated from Gerald for some days, along with a packhorse carrying Gerald's letters of authority from Richard, a draft of Gerald's *Itinerarium Cambriae*, and over forty marks of gold and silver in money, spoons, and cups. Though all ended well, Gerald was naturally anxious. He stressed that he was most worried about his rough draft and the royal letters of authority (in that order) but noted that the gold and silver was no small matter. Indeed not: Gerald's packhorse was carrying a sum that equaled the annual income of a prosperous knight.[1]

Historians often emphasize the overall wealth of the Church and analyze the incomes of bishops or of institutions such as monasteries or cathedrals, but though they frequently refer in passing to "fat benefices" or wealthy pluralists, the control of vast riches by secular clerics remains a neglected topic.[2] This chapter investigates the wealth of the secular clergy and thereby demonstrates a number of points that are crucial to understanding both their great influence and the many religious and social tensions that affected them. In the first place, many clerics had incomes equivalent to those of knights or even barons. Such incomes provided the material basis for the aristocratic lifestyles described in the previous chapter. Clerics with such high incomes would have been a minority, but many others would have been relatively well off by twelfth-century standards, though others would have been poor. Together, the incomes available to rich and well-to-do clerics provided the leisure, wealth, and often the incentive to carry out a variety of important religious, bureaucratic, intellectual, and cultural functions and practices. In addition, the collective wealth of the secular clergy, from richest to poorest, meant that clerics had an important role in the economic changes that characterized the period. Finally, the possession of wealth in a religion that emphasized poverty prompted much defensiveness and soul searching among the secular clergy.

---

[1] Gerald mentions no concern about losing money belonging to the royal government, so presumably the money was his. Gerald of Wales, *Opera*, 1:81–2.
[2] See, however, Burger, *Bishops, Clerks, and Diocesan Governance*, 30–3.

1. ECCLESIASTICAL INCOMES

Inevitably, the sources to study clerical incomes in the long twelfth-century are not entirely adequate. The systematic though deeply flawed valuations of churches from later periods are missing for the period before 1215 and trying to project backwards from any but the earliest of these surveys is problematic because of varying rates of economic development. The sharp inflationary spike in the first few years of the thirteenth century, in which prices more than doubled, combined with the impact of economic growth, makes comparison of figures even within the period problematic.[3] Conclusions about the numbers of wealthy clerics and comparisons with the wealth of the secular elite can therefore only be impressionistic. Sufficient evidence survives, however, to demonstrate the points outlined above.

It is worth starting with some information on the incomes of the secular elites to provide a basis for comparison. Sidney Painter drew on the pipe rolls to estimate the regular incomes of fifty-four barons between 1160 and 1220. The average income for these barons was £202 and the median income was £115. Seven barons had incomes over £400, the highest being £700 and £800. His findings do not cover all great nobles, and they include on tenurial grounds some relatively unimportant landowners, thus bringing down the median and the average somewhat. Moreover, the figures do not include periodic but potentially substantial income from wardships, tallages, and reliefs. Overall, however, his figures do give a rough basis of comparison. For knights, with whom elite clerics were equated in social terms, there is not such good comparable evidence. At the time of *Domesday Book*, some knights were very poor indeed, but there was a group of more established knights who held five hides or more, producing roughly £1 of income per hide. By the reign of Henry II, development and perhaps some inflation, combined with the continuing social elevation of knighthood, had produced expectations of higher income. In the Assize of Arms of 1181, Henry commanded those with at least sixteen marks (£10 13s 4d) of income to possess the equipment of a knight. In the pipe rolls of Henry II's reign, pay for knights was normally 8d per day but sometimes 12d per day in wartime, which would indicate yearly incomes of just over £12 and £18. Painter suggested a range of £10 to £20 as necessary to support a knight in this period, though since knighthood was still relatively widespread until the 1220s, I suspect that some landowners who qualified as knights in legal terms were poorer. Annual pay of £12 probably reflected normal expectations of knightly living standards, and sixteen marks may not have been the minimum for knighthood, as Painter believed, but the level of income at which a landowner had no excuse for avoiding knightly equipage. I would suggest a bottom range in Henry II's reign more on the order of £7 or £8. By the end of John's reign, standard wages seem to have been 24d per day, or £36 10s a year. However, in 1241, the royal

---

[3] P. D. A. Harvey, "The English Inflation of 1180–1220," *Past and Present* 61 (1973), 3–30; Paul Latimer, "Early Thirteenth-Century Prices," in S. D. Church, ed., *King John: New Interpretations* (Woodbridge, 1999), 41–73.

government demanded that landowners with only £20 become knights and in 1256 set the sum at £15, thus providing a good comparison with the sixteen marks of Henry II's reign.[4]

Though this book focuses on clerics below episcopal rank, it is also worth noting episcopal incomes, since that was a status to which many elite secular clerics aspired and which some achieved. Approximately three-quarters of bishops appointed by kings from William I to John were from the secular clergy, and in the reigns of Henry II and his sons that figure was around 89 percent.[5] Drawing on the same kinds of sources as Painter and using the earlier work of Margaret Howell, Everett Crosby calculated the average incomes of bishoprics in the late twelfth century. These ranged from £50 for Carlisle to £1400 for York, and perhaps £4000 for Durham, depending on how one counts, with a median of £400 and an average of £700. In 1212, the king held ten bishoprics, ranging in value from £157 to £2650 with a median of about £809 and an average of £927.[6] These figures are not exactly comparable to Painter's in that they include the incidental but valuable sources of income that he excluded. Nonetheless, bishops were clearly among the baronage, and the greatest bishops were extremely rich magnates. Given the income available, Ralph of Diceto's claim that one long-tenured archbishop of York had accumulated by his death £11,000 in silver and £300 in gold (not counting his gold and silver plate) may possibly be true.[7] Gaining a bishopric in England in the long twelfth century was something like becoming CEO of a major investment bank in today's world, and the possibility was therefore a powerful motivation for ambitious men at this time.

Secular clerics who did not become bishops could still acquire wealthy incomes from a variety of sources. Cathedral chapters provided one set of potentially lucrative benefices. Monks, however, had gained control of many cathedral chapters in England in the tenth and eleventh centuries, leaving only seven of the seventeen English bishoprics, Chichester, Exeter, Hereford, Lincoln, London, Salisbury, and York, to the secular clergy, though two bishoprics (Bath and Wells,[8] Coventry and Lichfield) had a secular as well as a monastic seat.

---

[4] Sidney Painter, *Studies in the History of the English Feudal Barony* (Baltimore, 1943), 170–2; Sally Harvey, "The Knight and the Knight's Fee in England," *Past and Present* 49 (1970), 3–43; Paul Latimer, "Wages in Late Twelfth- and Early Thirteenth-Century England," *The Haskins Society Journal* 9 (2001), 185–205, at 202–4; Thomas, *Vassals, Heiresses, Crusaders, and Thugs*, 9–10; Michael R. Powicke, "Distraint of Knighthood and Military Obligation under Henry III," *Speculum* 25 (1950), 457–70, at 460, 466; Michael Prestwich, *Plantagenet England, 1225–1360* (Oxford, 2005), 402. For the remarkable drop in the number of knights shortly after John's reign, see Kathryn Faulkner, "The Transformation of Knighthood in Early Thirteenth-Century England," *English Historical Review* 111 (1996), 1–23.

[5] Robert Bartlett, *England under the Norman and Angevin Kings, 1075–1225* (Oxford, 2000), 397.

[6] Everett U. Crosby, *Bishop and Chapter in Twelfth-Century England: A Study of the Mensa Episcopalis* (Cambridge, 1994), 369–70; Margaret Howell, *Regalian Right in Medieval England* (London, 1962), 212–33; *Pipe Roll 14 John*, xxviii.

[7] Ralph of Diceto, *Opera Historica*, 2:12.

[8] Wells was not technically a cathedral from 1090 to 1245, but nonetheless functioned basically in that capacity for most of the period: Diana E. Greenway, "Jocelin of Wells and his Cathedral Chapter," in Robert W. Dunning, ed., *Jocelin of Wells: Bishop, Builder, Courtier* (Woodbridge, 2010), 53–66, at 53–4.

Nonetheless, the cathedrals with secular chapters channeled much wealth to secular clerics serving as dignitaries and canons. By the end of the period most secular cathedrals had four major dignitaries, and over three hundred cathedral prebends existed throughout England.[9] A system also emerged in which canons could appoint vicars to take over their liturgical functions, allowing them to be absent. Thus, cathedrals provided many positions offering both income and a flexibility about residence requirements that was useful to pluralists.

Later evidence shows that the income from prebends and cathedral offices varied immensely but could be very high, particularly in the case of the major dignitaries.[10] The fragmentary evidence for the long twelfth century suggests the same pattern. The pipe rolls provide some figures, though mostly concerning an atypical type of prebend paid as money by the bishop rather than being attached to specific properties or churches. Some payments were quite small, but a sum of £5 was reasonably common. Larger prebends of up to £10 are also recorded.[11] Other evidence also suggests that prebends often had incomes in this range. When Bishop Robert of Bath and Wells set up a prebendary system at Wells in 1136, those prebends with specified values each produced £5, though some later prebends were established there at ten marks (£6 13s 4d).[12] Exeter, which was unusual in creating prebends of entirely uniform monetary value, paid each canon £4 a year.[13] However, there is also evidence indicating that prebends and the incomes of dignitaries could be much more lucrative. A survey of incomes from Salisbury Cathedral from 1226 to 1227, just outside the period, reveals some poor prebends, but it also reveals many wealthy ones. Thirteen canons had incomes of £10 or less (in one case 32s); seventeen had incomes from £10 to £20; twelve had incomes from £20 to £40; and five (mainly dignitaries) had incomes from £40 to £60. Thus, even accounting for inflation, Salisbury provided at least seventeen clerics with income equivalent to that of a prosperous knight, and a handful of these would have had an income equivalent to a minor baron. Overall, Salisbury provided about £900 income to secular clerics.[14] Other cathedrals also included extremely wealthy benefices. In 1190–1 Hubert Walter, having been promoted from dean of York to bishop of Salisbury, offered the king £133 13s 4d for having his grain from Yorkshire, suggesting how large his income from tithes or estates must have been (in 1291 the deanery of York was valued at £373).[15]

---

[9] Bartlett, *England under the Norman and Angevin Kings*, 390. Lists of known occupants of prebends in all the cathedrals but Lichfield can be found in Diana E. Greenway and Julia Barrow, eds., *Fasti Ecclesiae Anglicanae*, vols. 1–8, 10 (London, 1968–2005).

[10] Lepine, *A Brotherhood of Canons*, 3–4, 121–3.

[11] *Pipe Roll 13 Henry II*, 58; *Pipe Roll 14 Henry II*, 168; *Pipe Roll 28 Henry II*, 60; *Pipe Roll 31 Henry II*, 125, 204–5; *Pipe Roll 32 Henry II*, 83, 167.

[12] Ramsey, ed., *English Episcopal Acta 10*, 34–6; William Henry Benbow Bird, *Calendar of the Manuscripts of the Dean and Chapter of Wells. Vol. 1. Register Books* (London, 1907), 58.

[13] Greenway, *Fasti. 10. Exeter*, xix.

[14] W. H. Rich Jones, ed., *The Register of S. Osmund*, 2 vols. (London, 1883), 2:70–5. These figures do not include a prebend held by the bishop and four held by abbots.

[15] *Pipe Roll 2 Richard I*, 121; Diana E. Greenway, *Fasti Ecclesiae Anglicanae, 1066–1300. 6. York* (London, 1999), 7.

The evidence indicates that most prebends provided insufficient income to place a cleric on equal footing with any but the poorest knights. However, canons did not have to pay for armor, weaponry, and war horses. In the *Dialogue of the Exchequer*, the justification for paying knights 8*d* a day rather than the 5*d* their clerical and scribal counterparts received was the need for them to maintain horses and arms.[16] Moreover, canons in residence often received various distributions of food, drink, and money, which may have raised living standards considerably for those who received them. Thus, even a fairly average prebend probably allowed its holder to come close to an aristocratic lifestyle, and richer prebends and dignities clearly provided aristocratic levels of wealth.

Two types of church official, archdeacons and rural deans, warrant special consideration. Territorial archdeacons, in charge of ecclesiastical justice and discipline in specific parts of bishoprics, were introduced after the Norman Conquest, and there were nearly fifty of them by the end of the period. These archdeaconries were divided up in turn into deaneries. Archdeacons sometimes had specific sources of income attached to their offices, such as churches, and rural deans were generally rectors of a church, but both groups also drew various revenues, such as the profits of justice, from the exercise of their office.[17] Some of this income was licit, but archdeacons and rural deans gained a reputation for abusing their office for gain. According to William fitz Stephen, Henry II claimed that the archdeacons and rural deans of the kingdom extorted more money than he received as king.[18] This was almost certainly an exaggeration, but the post of archdeacon could certainly be lucrative. One of Thomas Becket's biographers wrote that before Thomas became archbishop he received £100 a year as archdeacon of Canterbury, providing him close to the median baronial income in the period from what was only one of his many benefices.[19] One pipe roll entry suggests that the archdeaconry of Barnstable produced only £10, but another entry indicates an income of £144 for one archdeacon of Northampton.[20] In Richard's reign a dispute over an appointment to the archdeaconry of York ended with one claimant being appointed deputy to the other and paying a pension of £40, suggesting (when one takes the deputy's income into account) a much larger revenue for the archdeaconry.[21] Similarly, proffers to King Richard and King John of £200 each during disputes over the archdeaconries of Nottingham and Richmond suggest the potential value of these benefices.[22] It is likely that most archdeaconries provided incomes equivalent to

---

[16] Richard fitzNigel, *Dialogus de Scaccario and Constitutio Domus Regis*, ed. Emilie Amt and S. D. Church (Oxford, 2007), 18–19.

[17] See, for instance Avrom Saltman, *Theobald, Archbishop of Canterbury* (London, 1956), 453; C. R. Cheney and Bridgett E. A. Jones, eds., *English Episcopal Acta. 2, Canterbury, 1162–1190* (Oxford, 1986), 54–5.

[18] Robertson and Sheppard, eds., *Materials*, 3:44.

[19] Robertson and Sheppard, eds., *Materials*, 3:17.

[20] *Pipe Roll 29 Henry II*, xxvii, 72; *Pipe Roll 32 Henry II*, 157.

[21] Roger of Howden, *Chronica*, 4:8–9.

[22] *Pipe Roll 9 Richard I*, 154; Hardy, ed., *Rotuli de Oblatis*, 118, 169; Hardy, ed., *Rotuli Chartarum*, 101b–102b.

those of prosperous knights or lesser barons. With the profits of office added to the incomes of their churches, many rural deans were no doubt also well off.

Another source of income for secular clerics consisted of prebends in collegiate churches.[23] A range of such foundations existed, including a number connected with bishoprics, such as the archbishopric of York's wealthy foundations at Ripon, Beverley, and Southwell, others founded by lay donors before and after the conquest, such as Harold Godwineson's richly endowed foundation at Waltham, and some that emerged from old mother churches during the decline of the old minster system. The possessions of collegiate churches varied quite widely, but some were quite affluent, though none equaled cathedrals or the greatest Benedictine monasteries in wealth.[24] Unfortunately for the secular clergy, the great enthusiasm for the new orders of regular clergy, especially regular canons, in the early twelfth century deprived them of many of these churches, for the long twelfth century was a low point in the history of the medieval collegiate church.[25] New foundations of such churches almost ceased fifty years after the Conquest, and many collegiate churches, including ones founded after the Conquest, were converted to monasteries or priories. Brooke counted sixty-six collegiate churches in 1066 and noted that nearly half of those were gone by 1200.[26] Collegiate churches eventually gained favor once again, but Blair has noted that of some 170 collegiate churches existing in 1535, only a quarter existed in 1120 and few of the rest were founded before 1250.[27]

Even so, such churches collectively provided a fair amount of wealth to the secular clergy.[28] Most had only a small number of prebends and offices, usually between three or four and a dozen. However, there were probably never fewer than forty such foundations and even at a conservative estimate of an average of five positions in each church they would have provided 200 incomes. As in cathedrals, the incomes could make their holders prosperous or even rich. One prebend of St. Martin-le-Grand in London consisted of £5 rent from property in

---

[23] For collegiate churches in this period, see John Blair, "Secular Minster Churches in Domesday Book," in Peter Sawyer, ed., *Domesday Book: A Reassessment* (London, 1985), 104–42; Emma Cownie, *Religious Patronage in Anglo-Norman England, 1066–1135* (Woodbridge, 1998), 26–33; Jeffrey H. Denton, *English Royal Free Chapels, 1100–1300: A Constitutional Study* (Manchester, 1970); C. R. Fonge, "Patriarchy and Patrimony: Investing in the Medieval College," in Philippa M. Hoskin, Christopher Brooke, and Barry Dobson, eds., *The Foundations of Medieval English Ecclesiastical History: Studies Presented to David Smith* (Woodbridge, 2005), 77–93. For a later period, see Clive Burgess and Martin Heale, eds., *The Late Medieval English College and its Context* (Woodbridge, 2008).

[24] For the resources available to some collegiate churches, see Charles Fonge, ed., *The Cartulary of St Mary's Collegiate Church, Warwick* (Woodbridge, 2004), lxxv; Joyce Godber, ed., *The Cartulary of Newnham Priory*, 2 vols., Bedford Historical Record Society Publications, vol. 43 (Bedford, 1963–4), 1:9–11; Rosalind Ransford, ed., *The Early Charters of the Augustinian Canons of Waltham Abbey, Essex, 1062–1230* (Woodbridge, 1989), xxxii–lv.

[25] John Blair, *Early Medieval Surrey: Landholding, Church, and Settlement before 1300* (Stroud, 1991), 94–103; Cownie, *Religious Patronage*, 30–3; David Crouch, *The Beaumont Twins: The Roots and Branches of Power in the Twelfth Century* (Cambridge, 1986), 196–204; Reginald Lennard, *Rural England, 1086–1135: A Study of Social and Agrarian Conditions* (Oxford, 1959), 396–404.

[26] Brooke, "Gregorian Reform in Action," 79.

[27] Blair, "Secular Minster Churches," 137.   [28] Moorman, *Church Life*, 19–20.

the city, an income equivalent to many cathedral prebends.[29] When Archbishop Roger of York created one of the few new collegiate foundations in the second half of the twelfth century, he specified that four priests serving there would receive ten marks each (£6 13s 4d), four deacons would get £5, and four subdeacons £4.[30] After Waltham was converted to an Augustinian house, the former dean received in compensation yearly revenues of nearly £40 and after the collegiate church at Dover had passed to the regular clergy its former head claimed he had received £70 in revenue.[31] As with cathedrals, canons who were resident might receive generous distributions of goods and money as well as their prebendal income.[32]

Ultimately, however, the vast majority of income for clerics came directly or indirectly from parish churches. The development of the parish system was a slow process that began long before the Norman Conquest and was largely completed by the end of twelfth century.[33] In the papal taxation of 1291, over 8000 parish churches appear, but this tally was incomplete and John Moorman argued that there were about 9500 parishes.[34] In addition, there were many chapels. Churches derived their revenues from various sources. Almost every church had an agricultural holding called a glebe attached to it. Often glebes were equivalent to peasant holdings, but they could range in size from a few acres to the equivalent of a manor.[35] Even more important were tithes, theoretically a 10 percent levy on the gross income of everyone in the parish. One advantage the English Church had, compared to many areas on the continent, was that lay aristocrats had rarely gained ownership of tithes. Only a few exceptions can be found, and English writers associated the practice with foreign lands, particularly France.[36] Offerings, theoretically voluntary but often in practice obligatory, formed another source of income. Moralists also complained about priests deliberately charging for services,

---

[29] M. J. Franklin, ed., *English Episcopal Acta. 8, Winchester, 1070–1204* (Oxford, 1993), 52–3.

[30] Marie Lovatt, ed., *English Episcopal Acta. 20, York, 1154–1181* (Oxford, 2000), 142–4.

[31] *Pipe Roll 28 Henry II*, 65; John of Salisbury, *The Letters of John of Salisbury*, ed. W. J. Millor, H. E. Butler, and C. N. L. Brooke, 2 vols. (Oxford, 1979–86), 1:100.

[32] A particularly full description of such distributions may be found in Leslie Watkiss and Marjorie Chibnall, eds., *The Waltham Chronicle* (Oxford, 1994), 28–31.

[33] Blair, *Early Medieval Surrey*, 109–33; Bartlett, *England under the Norman and Angevin Kings*, 378–87; M. Brett, *The English Church under Henry I* (London, 1975), 216–33; John Blair, *The Church in Anglo-Saxon Society* (Oxford, 2005), 368–504.

[34] Moorman, *Church Life*, 4–5.

[35] H. C. Darby, *Domesday England* (Cambridge, 1977), 75; Lennard, *Rural England*, 306–16, 327–8.

[36] For the examples of laypeople holding tithes, see Giles Constable, *Monastic Tithes from their Origins to the Twelfth Century* (Cambridge, 1964), 110; John Hudson, ed., *Historia Ecclesie Abbendonensis: The History of the Church of Abingdon*, 2 vols. (Oxford, 2002–7), 2:280–1; Hardy, ed., *Rotuli de Oblatis*, 90, 396. For comments on lay holding of tithes being common elsewhere, see British Library, Royal MS 3 B X, fos. 86r–v; Gerald of Wales, *Opera*, 2:186; Peter of Blois, *Opera*, 253; Stephan Kuttner and Eleanor Rathbone, "Anglo-Norman Canonists of the Twelfth Century," *Traditio* 7 (1949–51), 279–358, at 347. Some scholars have left the possibility of widespread lay exploitation of tithes or churches open: Brett, *English Church*, 229–30; B. R. Kemp, "Monastic Possession of Parish Churches in England in the Twelfth Century," *Journal of Ecclesiastical History* 31 (1980), 133–60, at 141–3. However, the paucity of evidence combined with the statements that this was a foreign practice seems conclusive. Susan Wood sees the possibility of some lay exploitation of church income in England, but sees it as far rarer than in France: Wood, *Proprietary Church*, 501, 510–13.

and evidence for this can sometimes be found, for instance for burials. Indeed, later evidence showed that mortuary fees, by then more standardized, were a valuable source of income for clerics.[37] Overall, parish churches brought enormous wealth to the Church.

Fortunately, for churches we have systematic valuations for taxation, either from 1217 or 1229, for the archdeaconries of Leicester and Ely. Such valuations are inevitably problematic, for they represent estimates which the assessors might have had reason to skew one way or the other, and incomes would have varied from year to year. Nonetheless, they can at least provide broad insights into the revenues of churches. The taxation records of the archdeaconry of Leicester record 202 churches with total revenues of £1190, or just under £6 per church. Some of these churches had reported incomes of as little as 5*s*, but thirty had incomes of more than £10, and one church, Melton Mowbray, had an income of over £41. The archdeaconry (and diocese) of Ely had richer churches or more demanding assessors. The 150 churches there had a total income of about £1740, or about £11 12*s* a church. The smallest income was £1 10*s*, but eighty-nine churches had incomes above £10 and of these nineteen were worth more than £20 a year.[38] In principle, then, these churches from only two archdeaconries could have provided hundreds of priests with a decent living and a smaller number with wealth comparable to knights.

However, as with cathedrals and collegiate churches, much of the wealth from parish churches ended up in the hands of the regular clergy. In the generations after the Conquest lords often transferred portions of a church's tithes from their own property to religious houses, and though this practice basically disappeared in the later twelfth century, much income had already been diverted.[39] Regular houses also resisted paying tithes, and though this was eventually restricted to lands brought newly into cultivation, the practice deprived parish churches of important potential revenue.[40] More important was the granting of parish churches to religious houses.[41] Many churches were already in the hands of monastic houses before 1066, but the enthusiasm of the laity for monasteries, the fact that giving churches did not deprive lords of revenues they could exploit directly, and the desire of reformers to move patronage of churches into the hands of the regulars, led to a flood of donations of churches in the generations following the Conquest. In Surrey, about two-thirds of churches were controlled by monastic houses by 1200, in the diocese of Durham, at least half, and in Northamptonshire slightly over half by the end of the thirteenth century.[42]

---

[37] Robert C. Palmer, *Selling the Church: The English Parish in Law, Commerce, and Religion, 1350–1550* (Chapel Hill, 2002), 42–7; Robertson and Sheppard, eds., *Materials*, 2:90; W. D. Peckham, ed., *The Chartulary of the High Church of Chichester*, Sussex Record Society, vol. 46 (Lewes, 1946), 7; West Sussex Record Office, Chichester Cathedral MS Liber Y, fo. 67r.

[38] William E. Lunt, ed., *The Valuation of Norwich* (Oxford, 1926), 526–39.

[39] For this practice throughout Europe, see Constable, *Monastic Tithes*, 57–136.

[40] Constable, *Monastic Tithes*, 220–306.

[41] Kemp, "Monastic Possession of Parish Churches," 133–60; Janet E. Burton, "Monasteries and Parish Churches in Eleventh- and Twelfth-Century Yorkshire," *Northern History* 23 (1987), 39–50.

[42] Blair, *Early Medieval Surrey*, 150; G. V. Scammell, *Hugh du Puiset, Bishop of Durham* (Cambridge, 1956), 97; C. H. Lawrence, "The English Parish and its Clergy in the Thirteenth Century," in Peter Linehan and Janet L. Nelson, eds., *The Medieval World* (London, 2001), 648–70, at 654.

With few exceptions, secular clerics continued to staff these churches; even Augustinian canons only occasionally served in parishes in this period.[43] Nonetheless, unlike lay patrons, monastic houses could licitly divert a portion of a parish church's revenues to their own ends, and frequently enough they viewed parish churches chiefly as sources of income.[44] For much of the period such transfers occurred through the payment by parish clergy of pensions which could range from a mere token to a major part of a church's revenue. As time went on, a system of appropriations emerged, whereby monastic houses would appoint a vicar who received only a portion of the church's revenues, leaving the remaining income to the religious house. Ulrich Rasche, in an important study of appropriation in England, argues that the practice was rare before the 1150s, picked up in the 1160s and 1170s, and became common from the 1180s on. Monastic houses did not appropriate all the churches they held, partly because heads of religious houses wanted to keep some highly valuable parish benefices for the purposes of patronage. Even in the late thirteenth century only 28 percent of churches in the diocese of Lincoln were appropriated. Nonetheless, the practice was widespread.[45] Between the various practices discussed here, a large percentage of the collective income of parish churches was diverted from the secular to the regular clergy.

However, the overall impact of monastic ownership of churches on the wealth of the secular clergy should not be exaggerated. Thousands of churches remained in the hands of lay patrons and a smaller but significant number were controlled by secular cathedrals and collegiate churches. Indeed, several cathedrals were adept at attracting donations of churches to build up their endowments.[46] Moreover, secular clerics continued to share in a significant portion of the revenues from parish churches controlled by monastic houses. It is true that fewer really rich churches were available to elite clerics than might otherwise have been the case, but certainly some were. The pipe rolls show that the chapelry of Tickhill (which included several churches), produced between £46 and £80 a year.[47] William of Rule, hereditary parson of Rule and of Cottingham in Yorkshire, clearly had a rich income: he funded the building of a refectory for the monks of Meaux, brought

---

[43] Dickinson, *Austin Canons*, 214–41; Moorman, *Church Life*, 48–9. See, however, Mayr-Harting, *Religion, Politics and Society*, 170–4.

[44] Christopher Harper-Bill, "The Struggle for Benefices in Twelfth-Century East Anglia," *Anglo-Norman Studies* 11 (1989), 113–32.

[45] Ulrich Rasche, "The Early Phase of Appropriation of Parish Churches in Medieval England," *Journal of Medieval History* 26 (2000), 213–37. For other work on appropriation, see Kemp, "Monastic Possession of Parish Churches," 147–60; Christopher Harper-Bill, "Battle Abbey and its East Anglian Churches," in Christopher Harper-Bill, Christopher J. Holdsworth, and Janet L. Nelson, eds., *Studies in Medieval History Presented to R. Allen Brown* (Woodbridge, 1989), 159–72; R. A. R. Hartridge, *A History of Vicarages in the Middle Ages* (Cambridge, 1930), 23–76. For the impact of appropriation on the incomes of priests, see Bennett, "Pastors and Masters," 45–6.

[46] Richard Morris, *Churches in the Landscape* (London, 1989), 138; Julia Barrow, "A Lotharingian in Hereford: Bishop Robert's Reorganisation of the Church of Hereford 1079–95," in David Whitehead, ed., *Medieval Art, Architecture, and Archaeology at Hereford* ([London], 1995), 29–49, at 41; Blair, "Secular Minster Churches," 126.

[47] *Pipe Roll 31 Henry II*, 80; *Pipe Roll 32 Henry II*, 85; *Pipe Roll 34 Henry II*, 9; *Pipe Roll 1 Richard I*, 91; Denton, *English Royal Free Chapels*, 115.

them more than £200 when he entered the monastery in his last illness, and, along with his brother, gave them property in Beverley that subsequently sold for £100.[48] Strikingly, some of the most important writers and intellectuals from the period held very profitable parish churches. John of Salisbury and Walter Map each held churches worth forty marks (£26 13s 4d) a year and a successor of Roger of Howden offered King John £200 in grain to enjoy the income of Howden church.[49] Priests in appropriated churches would have been poorer, but bishops increasingly tried to protect their incomes, and few were abysmally poor, a point to which I will return. Moreover, even if most parish clergy were not particularly rich, their collective yearly revenue must have been considerable, in the tens of thousands of pounds even at conservative estimates. Collectively, therefore, parish churches still placed a huge amount of wealth into the hands of the secular clergy.

A final important ecclesiastical source of income consisted of yearly pensions paid to clerics, and since these often came from monasteries they did a little to balance the effects of monastic control of many parish churches.[50] Given that such pensions only appear in the sources incidentally, since there was no reason to preserve records of them for the long term, the surprising number for which evidence survives indicates the practice was widespread. Indeed, it was sufficiently popular for two such grants to warrant inclusion in a formulary from around 1200 of the kinds of letters an ecclesiastical scribe might need to write.[51] Sometimes the pensions were granted for services or perhaps for the help of powerful clerics on behalf of an abbey, as suggested by a pension granted by the abbot of Mont Saint-Michel to the chancellor of Wells which refers to the chancellor's devotion to the abbey.[52] Sometimes such pensions were extorted, as Matthew de Cigogné, one of King John's hated foreign followers, was alleged to have done during the interdict.[53] Often such pensions were granted in anticipation of being replaced later by a benefice. Most pensions were fairly small, from 6s to a few pounds.[54] However, some could be quite lucrative. For instance, Bishop Philip demanded from the priory of Durham pensions of forty marks for one of his clerics, of £10 for a nephew (until they found a benefice worth £20), and of ten marks for another cleric.[55]

---

[48] Thomas de Burton, *Chronica Monasterii de Melsa*, ed. Edward Augustus Bond, 3 vols. (London, 1866–8), 1:217, 233, 314.

[49] John of Salisbury, *Letters*, 2:716–17; Walter Map, *De Nugis Curialium*, 496–7; *Pipe Roll 4 John*, 65.

[50] For pensions from bishops in the thirteenth century, see Burger, *Bishops, Clerks, and Diocesan Governance*, 80–109.

[51] Lambeth Palace, MS 105, fo. 271v.

[52] Frank Barlow, ed., *English Episcopal Acta. 12, Exeter, 1186–1257* (Oxford, 1996), 187–8.

[53] Kathleen Major, ed., *Acta Stephani Langton Cantuariensis Archiepiscopi A. D. 1207–1228*, Canterbury and York Record Series, vol. 50 (Oxford, 1950), 12–13.

[54] For some examples, see Thomas Duffus Hardy, ed., *Rotuli Litterarum Clausarum in Turri Londinensi Asservati* (London, 1833), 83b, 92a, 106a, 190b, 263a; Franklin, ed., *English Episcopal Acta 8*, 117, 120–1; Barlow, ed., *English Episcopal Acta 11*, 118–20; Holtzmann, ed., *Papsturkunden*, 1:424; Mason, ed., *Westminster Abbey Charters*, 160; British Library, Cotton MS Claudius D XIII, fos. 126v–127r; *Pipe Roll 7 Richard I*, 57.

[55] M. G. Snape, ed., *English Episcopal Acta. 25, Durham, 1196–1237* (Oxford, 2002), 206–7.

Though less important than the other sources of income described so far, pensions certainly raised the income of many clerics.

The most important factor in creating a wealthy clerical elite, however, was the practice of pluralism. For the secular clergy as a whole, pluralism redistributed income rather than increasing it, but it concentrated wealth in a way that allowed some clerics to have extremely high incomes. Only a minority of benefices provided enough income for a cleric to have a knightly or baronial lifestyle, but the ability to combine incomes from more than one benefice made the accumulation of large incomes much easier. Pluralism can already be found at the beginning of the period, as *Domesday Book* shows. For instance, Regenbald the Priest, a royal chaplain (and possibly chancellor) of Edward the Confessor who also served William I, held a number of rich churches.[56] Royal and baronial favorites, members of wealthy families, and other clerics continued the practice in the twelfth century. The baron Robert fitz Hamo gave his chaplain Robert thirty churches, which the latter subsequently donated to Tewkesbury. The magnate Nigel d'Aubigny granted nine churches to his chaplain and nephew Samson, several of which subsequently funded the hugely rich benefice of Masham at York Cathedral, the first holder of which was Samson's son Roger.[57] Gunnar Stollberg and Ralph Turner have shown that clerics in royal service tended to be pluralists. A notable example is Henry of London who, before he became archbishop of Dublin, held an archdeaconry, the deanship of two collegiate churches, nine churches, and prebends in two cathedrals.[58] In this context, Nigel of Whiteacre's complaints about clerics for whom fifteen or twenty churches did not suffice, and who wanted a prebend in every cathedral, do not look quite so exaggerated as they might seem at first glance.[59]

How much wealth could pluralism provide? During their dispute with Archbishop Baldwin of Canterbury over his plans to found a collegiate church, the monks claimed, perhaps disingenuously, that he would then be able to reward his clerics with only a single prebend, whereas before he could grant each of them various benefices totaling £50, £60, £100, or even £200 in revenue a year.[60] Any claim in this heated dispute must be taken with a grain of salt, but given the worth of many individual benefices, claims about cumulative incomes of that magnitude are plausible. More concretely, Gerald of Wales stated that he himself had revenues of 100 marks or more from his various benefices in England and Wales.[61] Roger of

[56] Simon Keynes, "Regenbald the Chancellor [*sic*]," *Anglo-Norman Studies* 10 (1988), 185–222, at 194–7.

[57] Robert B. Patterson, ed., *Earldom of Gloucester Charters; The Charters and Scribes of the Earls and Countesses of Gloucester to A.D. 1217* (Oxford, 1973), 161–2; Brett, *English Church*, 217–18; Diana E. Greenway, ed., *Charters of the Honour of Mowbray, 1107–1191* (London, 1972), lxvi.

[58] Gunnar Stollberg, *Die soziale Stellung der intellektuellen Oberschicht im England des 12. Jahrhunderts* (Lubeck, 1973), 172–84; Turner, *Men Raised from the Dust*, 24–5, 95–6; Ralph V. Turner, *The English Judiciary in the Age of Glanvill and Bracton, c.1176–1239* (Cambridge, 1985), 57, 175–7, 297.

[59] Nigel of Whiteacre, *Tractatus Contra Curiales*, 168. For pluralism in the later thirteenth century, including the astonishingly wealthy Bogo of Clare, see Moorman, *Church Life*, 26–8.

[60] Stubbs, ed., *Epistolæ Cantuarienses*, 63.

[61] Gerald of Wales, *Opera*, 3:133; Davies, "Giraldus Cambrensis: *De Invectionibus*," 87.

Howden recorded that Godfrey de Lucy, whom we know from other sources was dean of St. Martin-le-Grand, held two archdeaconries, prebends in four cathedrals, and vicarages in two churches, turned down the bishopric of Exeter, which had an average annual income of £400 in the late twelfth century, because its revenues were insufficient to meet his expenses.[62] Adam of Eynsham's claim that some members of the chapter of Lincoln had accumulated more revenues than bishops had may not have been as hyperbolic as it seems.[63]

It is easy to miss just how rich some clerics, including intellectuals, could be, partly because many felt that they should have been richer. For instance, Gerald of Wales could complain about the lack of reward for his copious writings even though his income equaled that of a very wealthy knight or minor baron.[64] Peter of Blois complained to the dean and chapter of Salisbury that his prebend of five marks at Salisbury was not sufficient to pay for his travel and residence there, and to Pope Innocent III that his archdeaconry of London did not bring in sufficient revenue. Peter may well have had reason to complain in relation to other prebends and archdeaconries, and he may well have had money troubles at times; in one letter, drawing on the vicious anti-Semitism of the time, he complained of being crucified by the Jews. However, he held various lucrative benefices over the course of his lifetime, including the deanery of Wolverhampton, and by the end of his life he had at least one archdeaconry and five prebends, and was able to bequeath luxurious vestments, replete with many gems, to St. Paul's.[65] Peter may have been poor compared to bishops or some other pluralists, but by the general standards of his society he was a wealthy man. Abbot Samson of Bury St Edmunds, who had been a schoolmaster before joining the monastery, once said that if he had had an income of five or six marks to support him in the schools he would never have become a monk. Apparently he felt such an income would have provided him a comfortable lifestyle.[66] Thus, claims about poverty must be assessed in context.

How common was pluralism? Turner has noted that nearly all royal clerics who served as justices were pluralists and Scammell saw pluralism as common in the diocese of Durham.[67] A study of appointments by King John in the patent, close, and charter rolls confirms that pluralism was frequent among royal clerics. The majority of clerics involved, admittedly, received only one benefice from the king, but over sixty held two or three benefices, and another seventeen had between four and twelve appointments based on those sources alone, the champion being Henry of London.[68] To look beyond the royal court, I compiled a list of over 800

---

[62] [Roger of Howden], *Gesta Regis Henrici Secundi*, 1:346; Turner, *English Judiciary*, 57; Crosby, *Bishop and Chapter*, 370.

[63] Adam of Eynsham, *Magna Vita Sancti Hugonis*, 1:92–3.

[64] Gerald of Wales, *Opera*, 6:7; Gerald of Wales, *Expugnatio Hibernica*, 264–5; Bartlett, *Gerald of Wales*, 17, 58–61; Egbert Türk, *Nugae curialium: Le règne d'Henri II Plantegenêt (1154–1189) et l'éthique politique* (Geneva, 1977), 100–1.

[65] Peter of Blois, *Opera*, 395–6, 442–3, 450; Cotts, *Clerical Dilemma*, 45–6, 48.

[66] Jocelin of Brakelond, *Chronicle*, 36.

[67] Turner, *English Judiciary*, 297; Scammell, *Hugh du Puiset*, 100.

[68] Thomas Duffus Hardy, ed., *Rotuli Litterarum Patentium in Turri Londinensi Asservati* (London, 1835); Hardy, ed., *Rotuli Litterarum Clausarum*; Hardy, ed., *Rotuli Chartarum*. Because of problems of

cases of clerics distinguishable as individuals (usually because of a byname though sometimes by a title) who held or were appointed to benefices in parish churches. This list comes mostly from charters but in some cases from legal records where the claim to a benefice was settled or not in doubt. It is drawn from throughout England and from the whole period, though naturally it is weighted to the later decades when sources were more plentiful and surnames more common. Twenty-four of the churches were held by seventeen clerics who also appeared in the records of King John, where most of them can already be identified as pluralists. An additional sixty-two clerics held more than one church on this list alone. Most of them held only two churches from this sample, but some held three or four. A number of archdeacons and cathedral dignitaries also appear on the list holding churches that were not part of their prebends. This list is not a random sample of appointments: clerics with titles or surnames were generally unusually important and therefore more likely to be pluralists. Moreover, about a third of the cases of pluralism here are recorded in single documents or transactions. Nonetheless, the rest are recorded in distinct and often quite disparate records, and the number of pluralists recorded in a relatively small list covering all of England and a broad time period suggests that pluralism was very common among the clerical elite.

Beneath the level of rich, often pluralist clerics, there would have been a much larger layer of prosperous clerics holding individual benefices. Some scholars, it is true, have argued that most parish priests of *Domesday Book* were little different from peasants, partly because of the size of glebes and partly because priests were sometimes lumped in with the village population.[69] I am skeptical at least as far as rectors go, however, for such arguments ignore income from tithes and offerings and the fact that lesser knights were sometimes also lumped in with the village population. Moorman suggested that the average living in England in the thirteenth century was about £10, but perhaps only £6 after expenses were deducted, an income he considered poor.[70] However, the figures for aristocratic wealth noted earlier indicate that such incomes were not that poor, even when one takes inflation into account. Christopher Dyer, using fuller later records, suggests that there were thousands of rectors and vicars with incomes equivalent to members of the gentry, though mainly the lesser gentry.[71] One should of course be wary about extrapolating from later figures, but the figures noted earlier for the values of churches in the archdeaconries of Ely and Leicester indicate that Dyer's picture may apply to the twelfth and thirteenth centuries as well.

identity, these figures must be seen as approximate. Not all royal appointments were recorded here, but it should also be noted that royal rights to appoint might sometimes be successfully contested. The figures also include some incidental mentions of benefices.

[69] Blair, *Church in Anglo-Saxon Society*, 492; C. J. Bond, "Church and Parish in Norman Worcestershire," in John Blair, ed., *Minsters and Parish Churches: The Local Church in Transition, 950–1200* (Oxford, 1988), 119–58, at 134; Lennard, *Rural England*, 329. See, however, Loyn, *English Church*, 95–6, 117.

[70] Moorman, *Church Life*, 154.

[71] Christopher Dyer, *Standards of Living in the Later Middle Ages: Social Change in England, c.1200–1500* (Cambridge, 1989), 20–2, 30–2.

Of course, there were many parish priests who were less prosperous, either because they held poor churches or because they were vicars or stipendiary priests staffing churches from which substantial income was siphoned off to a monastic house, rich pluralist, or absentee rector. Pope Alexander III, obviously responding to a complaint, wrote to the dean and canons of Lincoln forbidding them to increase payments from their churches in the archdiocese of York so much that the clerics ministering there could not pay dues owed diocesan officials, maintain the buildings and ornaments of their churches, and support themselves.[72] The same pope received a complaint from Ralph, vicar of Salford Priors, that Kenilworth Priory was trying to assign him a portion of the revenues on which he could not live decently.[73] In addition to financial pressures, many parish priests had little security of tenure, being appointed on a yearly basis. In 1203, Bishop Herbert of Salisbury wrote to Archbishop Hubert Walter that he was having trouble getting a synod to agree to raise money for the king and for the poor because so few clerics showed up, and many that did were "annual" vicars rather than perpetual vicars or rectors.[74] When the vicar of Salford Priors could not reach an agreement with Kenilworth on his income, the prior asserted that he was only an "annual" rather than a perpetual vicar and tried to eject him. Obviously such vicars could face downward pressure on their incomes and end up losing their positions if they resisted.[75]

By the end of the period, various bishops, prompted by papal urging and reacting to the increasing appropriation of parish churches, were trying to stabilize the situation for resident priests by establishing perpetual vicarages with fixed revenues.[76] Though most such vicarages set aside certain types of income for vicars, some specified a fixed yearly income. In the volumes of *English Episcopal Acta* and similar works published to date I have found thirty-six vicarages up through 1216 (the great majority from the 1190s on) establishing a set income, ranging from two marks (£1 6s 8d) to twenty marks (£13 6s 8d) with an average of approximately £4 9s, but eleven consisting of £2 or less.[77] Hugh of Wells, bishop of Lincoln from 1209 to 1235, established hundreds of vicarages and recorded the terms. Some 133

---

[72] Walther Holtzmann and Eric Waldram Kemp, eds., *Papal Decretals Relating to the Diocese of Lincoln in the Twelfth Century*, Publications of the Lincoln Record Society, vol. 47 (Hereford, 1954), 4–5.

[73] Cheney, *Roger, Bishop of Worcester*, 342.

[74] B. R. Kemp, ed., *English Episcopal Acta. 18, Salisbury, 1078–1217* (Oxford, 1999), 210–11.

[75] Cheney, *Roger, Bishop of Worcester*, 342. See also John of Salisbury, *Letters*, 1:104–5.

[76] Cheney, *From Becket to Langton*, 131–6.

[77] C. R. Cheney and E. John, eds., *English Episcopal Acta. 3, Canterbury, 1193–1205* (Oxford, 1986), 57–8, 201–2, 208–9, 217–23; David M. Smith, ed., *English Episcopal Acta. 4, Lincoln, 1186–1206* (Oxford, 1986), 22–3, 101–2; Christopher Harper-Bill, ed., *English Episcopal Acta. 6, Norwich, 1070–1214* (Oxford, 1990), 203–4, 263–4, 266–7, 346–7; Franklin, ed., *English Episcopal Acta 8*, 83, 113, 187–8, 200; Ramsey, ed., *English Episcopal Acta 10*, 175–6; Barlow, ed., *English Episcopal Acta 12*, 174–5; Franklin, ed., *English Episcopal Acta 17*, 75–6; D. P. Johnson, ed., *English Episcopal Acta. 26, London, 1189–1228* (Oxford, 2003), 14–16, 41–2, 53–4, 68, 115–16; Marie Lovatt, ed., *English Episcopal Acta. 27, York, 1189–1212* (Oxford, 2004), 44–5, 84–5; David M. Smith, ed., *English Episcopal Acta. 30, Carlisle, 1133–1292* (Oxford, 2005), 16–17, 23; Nicholas Karn, ed., *English Episcopal Acta. 42, Ely, 1198–1256* (Oxford, 2013), 13, 45–6; Major, ed., *Acta Stephani Langton*, 51–2; David M. Smith, ed., *The Acta of Hugh of Wells, Bishop of Lincoln, 1209–1235*, Publications of the Lincoln Record Society, vol. 88 (Woodbridge, 2000), 22.

of these specified a yearly income for the vicar, and the sums ranged from £2 to seventeen marks (£11 6s 8d) with nearly half being of five marks (£3 6s 8d) and the average being just over £3 10s.[78] Some vicarages would have allowed their holder to approach knightly status in wealth, and most would have made them much more prosperous than the average peasant. However, even some vicarages were held by absentee clergy, with the work being done by paid chaplains. Moreover, few perpetual vicarages were established until late in the period, and annual vicars or stipendiary chaplains may not have enjoyed the same incomes as perpetual vicars. As a result some parish priests may have been poor even by village standards, though how common this was must remain speculative.

Other groups of clerics with only moderate incomes included chaplains in royal castles, vicars for cathedral prebends, and chantry priests. In the late twelfth century, chaplains in royal chapels were paid 1d a day, or £1 10s 5d a year, though the yearly pay went up to £2 10s early in John's reign. This rate was the same as watchmen and porters in royal castles and for foot soldiers, but less than skilled workers such as carpenters and masons, though free lodging and board probably made up for much of the difference.[79] Remuneration of vicars choral, the substitutes for cathedral canons, started becoming systematized in the late twelfth century. Around 1200, Bishop Henry of Exeter took steps to supplement the income of the vicars there, who already received £1 a year from the canons they served. The dean and chapter of Salisbury in 1214 determined that their vicars would receive 1d most days, but 2d on certain feasts.[80] Chantry priests began appearing late in the period and were remunerated along roughly the same lines. For instance, Bishop Savaric of Bath and Wells arranged that two priests who would say masses for his soul were to be paid two and a half marks (£1 13s 4d) along with the distributions of bread that vicars received.[81] From the standpoint of ordinary peasants and townspeople, these would all have been well-compensating jobs, but nothing beyond the reach of skilled laypeople.

Another group of ordinary clergy consisted of village clerics who aided priests in services, but very little can be learned about their incomes. Some were boys being raised to be priests, such as Osbern, son and future successor of the priest Brictric, who served the hermit Wulfric and probably his own father during mass.[82] Others were adults, and very occasionally formal provision was made for such clerics.[83]

---

[78] A. Gibbons, ed., *Liber Antiquus de Ordinationibus Vicariarum Tempore Hugonis Wells, Lincolniensis Episcopi, 1209–1235* (Lincoln, 1888), 1–71.

[79] *Pipe Roll 34 Henry II*, 4; Latimer, "Wages," 189–90, 192–3, 196–9. See also Simon Townley, "Unbeneficed Clergy in the Thirteenth Century: Two English Dioceses," in David M. Smith, ed., *Studies in Clergy and Ministry in Medieval England* (York, 1991), 38–64, at 42.

[80] Jones, ed., *Register of S. Osmund*, 1:378; Barlow, ed., *English Episcopal Acta 12*, 178–9. For the development of the system of vicars choral, see Barrow, "Vicars Choral and Chaplains," 87–97.

[81] Ramsey, ed., *English Episcopal Acta 10*, 191–2. For the early development of chantries in England, see David Crouch, "The Origin of Chantries: Some Further Anglo-Norman Evidence," *Journal of Medieval History* 27 (2001), 159–80.

[82] John of Ford, *Wulfric of Haselbury*, 52, 102–3.

[83] Barlow, ed., *English Episcopal Acta 12*, 178–9; Farrer and Clay, eds., *Early Yorkshire Charters*, 3:264–5.

Many probably lived in the household of the vicar or rector. Others, however, seem to have supported themselves primarily by secular employment, such as the poor craftsmen who Thomas of Chobham wrote could licitly engage in business.[84] Manorial surveys show that priests and clerics often held private parcels of land varying in size from an acre or a small house to impressive holdings (by village standards) of as much as a hide. It is normally impossible to tell whether such holdings formed investments or additional sources of revenue for priests and clerics whose income came largely from the church, or if they represented the main source of income for clerics who made additional money or satisfied spiritual needs by also serving in the church. However, the surprising number of holdings that were standard sized for a given village suggests that some village clerics were ordinary peasants who had been ordained. In some cases, such clerical agriculturalists may have been of very low status. Thomas Chobham warned that a landlord who knowingly let a serf be ordained could not force him to do "sordid" work such as carrying manure to a field. A couple of clerics in surveys performed the kind of weekly work on the demesnes of lords associated with servile status, and very occasionally one finds lords granting clerics away as though they were serfs. However, the overwhelming majority of landholding clerics paid rents and did the occasional boon service characteristic of free peasants, even when they held villein lands. Such clerics were therefore normally members of the free peasantry, though their prosperity, like that of peasants in general, probably varied widely. [85]

In later periods there was generally a large group of clerics seeking benefices but ending up unemployed, and there are indications that the problem already existed in the long twelfth century. Presumably clerics who had sufficient land to support themselves or could make a living as craftsmen were not at issue, though some of the latter may simply have given up on the search for a benefice and sought a new profession. In some cases, unemployed clerics may have lacked the training to find a position. Thomas of Chobham urged schoolmasters to take care in training their students, because those who did not learn enough to make a living in the Church often became thieves, robbers, or sorcerers.[86] In a largely vain effort to prevent

---

[84] Thomas of Chobham, *Summa Confessorum*, 302–3.

[85] Thomas of Chobham, *Summa Confessorum*, 113; Townley, "Unbeneficed Clergy," 42–3; William Henry Hart and Ponsonby A. Lyons, eds., *Cartularium Monasterii de Rameseia*, 3 vols. (London, 1884–93), 3:244, 248, 257–8, 262–4, 266, 268–9, 274, 276, 279, 282–3, 287, 297, 302, 304, 308–9, 312; D. C. Douglas, ed., *Feudal Documents from the Abbey of Bury St. Edmunds* (London, 1932), 26, 28–32, 35–6, 38–40, 43–4; R. H. C. Davis, ed., *The Kalendar of Abbot Samson of Bury St. Edmunds and Related Documents*, Camden Society, 3rd ser., vol. 84 (London, 1954), 7–8, 11–13, 15, 18, 28, 30, 37, 40, 42, 46–8; N. E. Stacy, ed., *Surveys of the Estates of Glastonbury Abbey c.1135–1201* (Oxford, 2001), 61, 85, 110, 113, 124, 130–1, 136, 146, 149–50, 152, 161, 164, 166, 179, 191, 200, 208–9, 211, 213, 224, 226, 231; Beatrice A. Lees, ed., *Records of the Templars in England in the Twelfth Century* (London, 1935), 2–5, 7, 10, 24, 27, 38–9, 42, 50, 54, 58, 63, 65–8, 70, 77, 83–8, 90–3, 100, 102–4, 106–7, 109–12, 114, 116–17, 124, 130; Marjory Hollings, ed., *The Red Book of Worcester*, 4 vols. (London, 1934–50), 1: 33, 83–4, 167, 232; 2:260, 315–16; 3:351, 406. For grants of clerics, see British Library, Harley MS 3650, fo. 45v; Greenway, ed., *Charters of the Honour of Mowbray*, 69. Greenway suggests in the latter case that *clericus* was a surname, which is of course possible. For a priest clearly on the edge of being a serf, see *Curia Regis Rolls*, 5:94–5.

[86] Thomas of Chobham, *Summa Confessorum*, 298.

excess ordinations, the Church would increasingly demand that bishops not ordain men without a benefice or means of support. Two letters by Pope Innocent III commanding the archbishop of Canterbury to provide benefices for men he had ordained illustrate this effort in the early thirteenth century.[87] It is hard to estimate how large the problem of unbeneficed and impoverished clergy was in the long twelfth century, but the empress Matilda, during the Becket dispute, complained that bishops were ordaining too many clerics without title to churches and that many were falling into "shameful acts" through poverty and idleness.[88]

Work on later periods shows a wide range of incomes within the Church, including a sizable clerical "proletariat."[89] Despite the tendency of twelfth-century writers to equate clerics (meaning elite clerics) with knights (meaning elite soldiers), most clerics would have been less prosperous than knights and many would have been no wealthier than ordinary peasants or townspeople. One should not forget, however, that livelihoods that would have seemed contemptible to the clerical or secular elites would have been welcomed by many clerics of peasant background. More important, the many small incomes of local clergy still added up to a sizable sum, and added to the economic clout of the clergy as a whole.

Moreover, it is still worth stressing that the Church supported surprising numbers of wealthy and even fabulously rich clerics. In a society in which wealth was generally inherited, the Church therefore provided extraordinary opportunities for acquiring riches. Among the laity, a figure like William Marshal, the landless younger son of a baron who became an earl through royal service and marriage, was fairly rare. On average, about one bishopric became vacant a year, creating new ecclesiastical magnates on a regular basis. Far more individuals could gain incomes equivalent to those of knights or even barons. A younger son from the secular elites could conceivably end up better off than his older brother, and for clerics of ordinary background the possibilities must have been astonishing. There were certainly routes to wealth for the laity, such as trade or service to the king or a magnate. Even so, the Church remained the most important path to worldly success, other than birth, that existed in England in the long twelfth century.

2. SECULAR SOURCES OF CLERICAL INCOME

So far I have focused on ecclesiastical income, but clerics often had revenues beyond those provided by the Church. Though collectively far less important to the clergy than the proceeds of ecclesiastical office, such revenues could be significant. Moreover, their acquisition often involved clerics in worldly endeavors, thus increasing the gulf between religious expectations and actual practice. Chief

---

[87] Cheney and Cheney, eds., *Letters of Pope Innocent III*, 64, 106–7.
[88] Duggan, ed., *Correspondence of Thomas Becket*, 1:166–7.
[89] Moorman, *Church Life*, 52–8; A. K. McHardy, "Careers and Disappointments in the Late-Medieval Church: Some English Evidence," in W. J. Sheils and Diana Wood, eds., *The Ministry: Clerical and Lay* (Oxford, 1989), 111–30; R. N. Swanson, *Church and Society in Late Medieval England* (Oxford, 1989), 46–50, 62; Townley, "Unbeneficed Clergy," 38–64.

among the secular sources of income was private ownership of land. I have noted the clerical ownership of many small parcels, but in some cases clerics held much larger estates. Barrow has noted a number of clerics who held over forty hides in *Domesday Book*, including Ingelric, who held over 120. Much of these clerics' landholdings consisted of ecclesiastical holdings, for instance estates attached to minster churches, but some at least seem to have been personal.[90] For subsequent periods, one might note the existence of wealthy landlords such as Herbert the Chamberlain, in Henry I's reign, who were clerics but had essentially become laymen.[91] Even if one focuses on men who remained clerics, however, one can find several holders of knights' fees or fractions thereof in Henry II's *cartae baronum* of 1166.[92] Clerics or their heirs can also sometimes be found contesting large estates, including entire manors, in the records of the royal courts.[93] The secular clergy were particularly active as landowners in towns, and though many only held their own dwellings, others received rents from their property. Barrow has noted that cathedral canons could be urban landholders on a large scale and other clerics frequently owned urban property as well.[94] For instance, the Winchester surveys reveal such clerical landlords as Robert of Inglesham, likely the later archdeacon of Surrey of that name, who was the largest private landowner in 1148, with over £8 rent from thirteen properties, and Thurstin the cleric, who was the third greatest private landlord and received over £5 in rents.[95] Sources are less good for other cities, but the charters of Lincoln Cathedral reveal canons and others with individual properties producing yearly incomes ranging from 1s to 30s.[96] Even for clerics with rich benefices, private property could provide a valuable supplement to ecclesiastical income.

Much of the land held by clerics was doubtlessly inherited. Though the surviving evidence gives the impression that sons who entered the Church could not generally count on receiving family land, there were no doubt exceptions. Moreover, younger sons who were clerics sometimes came into inheritances unexpectedly but remained in the Church. Thus, Hugh and Richard Barre, who came from an important aristocratic family on the honor of Leicester, and both of whom became archdeacons, successively held three manors, and Master Roger Arundel

---

[90] Julia Barrow, *Who Served the Altar at Brixworth?: Clergy in English Minsters c.800–c.1100* (Brixworth, 2013), 22–3.

[91] Christopher Norton, *St. William of York* (Woodbridge, 2006), 7–10.

[92] Hubert Hall, ed., *The Red Book of the Exchequer*, 3 vols. (London, 1896), 1:220, 310, 320–1, 323, 347, 379, 382, 385, 391, 402.

[93] Frederic William Maitland, ed., *Three Rolls of the King's Court in the Reign of King Richard the First, A. D. 1194–1195*, Publications of the Pipe Roll Society, vol. 14 (London, 1891), 125–6; Francis Palgrave, ed., *Rotuli Curiæ Regis. Rolls and Records of the Court Held Before the King's Justiciars or Justices*, 2 vols. (London, 1835), 1:14; *Curia Regis Rolls*, 1:241; 2:23; 3:19; 4:144; 5:136; 6:103–4.

[94] Barrow, "Cathedrals, Provosts, and Prebends," 562; Barrow, "Canons and Citizens of Hereford," 8.

[95] Martin Biddle et al., *Winchester in the Early Middle Ages: An Edition and Discussion of the Winton Domesday* (Oxford, 1976), 372, 392–6.

[96] C. W. Foster and Kathleen Major, eds., *The Registrum Antiquissimum of the Cathedral Church of Lincoln*, 10 vols., Publications of the Lincoln Record Society, vols. 27–9, 32, 34, 41, 46, 51, 62, 67 (Hereford, 1931–73), 8:54–5; 9:66–7, 239–42; 10:92–3, 137–8.

ended up inheriting his family's valuable estates in Yorkshire.[97] However, clerics were also active in the land market, particularly in towns, investing money from their clerical incomes in residences or sources of rent. Charters recording clerics purchasing land are scattered through cartularies and document collections. For instance, Westminster Abbey documents record six purchases by clerics ranging in price from a token 2s to the ten marks (£6 13s 4d) paid by the great royal cleric, Richard of Ilchester, for a house.[98] Similarly, Lincoln Cathedral documents reveal various purchases by clerics of urban or rural land ranging from £2 to twenty marks (£13 6s 8d).[99] Some investments were very large. Walter, Archdeacon of Cornwall, paid £40 for land and houses in Exeter and Robert of Arden, archdeacon of Lisieux, paid approximately the same price for half a knight's fee in Hampton in Arden.[100] Hubert Walter, before being advanced to the episcopacy, paid 220 marks (£146 13s 4d) for the estate of West Dereham, which he then used to endow a monastery he founded.[101] One should not exaggerate the importance of the clergy as private landholders. Only a tiny percentage of manors were held privately by clerics, and estate surveys indicate that clerics generally held only a small percentage of village land. Even in towns clerical landlords would have been far outmatched by institutional and lay landlords. Nonetheless, private property provided another noteworthy source of revenue and economic clout for the secular clergy.

Many clerics also earned income as farmers, or lessors, of estates. Some held estates in fee farm, a form of heritable tenure. For instance, Henry of Huntingdon held two estates at farm from Ramsey Abbey which subsequently passed to his son, grandson, and great-grandson, all of them clerics.[102] More commonly, clerics managed estates for their lifetimes or for shorter terms of years. Thus, St. Paul's Cathedral often used clerics, frequently cathedral canons or other prominent figures, to farm its manors.[103] Monasteries such as St. Benet of Holme could also employ clerics as farmers.[104] Large amounts of land could sometimes be involved. Robert de Béthune, a continental magnate, granted three manors in Gloucestershire at farm for life to his cleric, Walter of Haselton.[105] Robert of Inglesham, the wealthy Winchester landlord, farmed eleven estates for a continental abbey.[106] No

[97] Crouch, *Beaumont Twins*, 82; Farrer and Clay, eds., *Early Yorkshire Charters*, 11:198–9.

[98] Mason, ed., *Westminster Abbey Charters*, 137–8, 239–41, 245–6, 273–4, 282–3.

[99] Foster and Major, eds., *Registrum Antiquissimum*, 2:309–10; 4:115; 6:66–7; 7:87–8; 9:79–80; 10:20, 67–70, 233.

[100] Exeter Cathedral Archives, Dean & Chapter Charter 289; Greenway, ed., *Charters of the Honour of Mowbray*, 212–13, 215–16.

[101] C. R. Cheney, *Hubert Walter* (London, 1967), 29.

[102] Henry of Huntingdon, *Historia Anglorum*, xxvii–xxviii; Charles T. Clay, "Master Aristotle," *English Historical Review* 76 (1961), 303–8, at 305–6.

[103] Ralph of Diceto, *Opera Historica*, 1:lvii–lix; William Hale, ed., *The Domesday of St. Paul's*, Camden Society, vol. 69 (London, 1858), 109–12, 123–39.

[104] J. R. West, ed., *St. Benet of Holme, 1020–1210*, 2 vols., Norfolk Record Society, vols. 2–3 (Norwich, 1932), 1: 84, 106, 112.

[105] Royce, ed., *Landboc sive Registrum Monasterii Beatae Mariae Virginis et Sancti Cenhelmi de Winchelcumba*, 2 vols. (Exeter, 1892–1903), 2:308–9.

[106] R. Allen Brown, ed., *The Memoranda Roll for the Tenth Year of the Reign of King John, 1207–8*, Publications of the Pipe Roll Society, n.s. vol. 31 (London, 1957), 109.

evidence survives of the exact incomes clerics drew from farming, but for manors and collections of manors they must have been considerable. Farming also gave clerics delegated authority over land and many peasants, thus providing them with more economic influence.

Clerics also profited from serving lords, in particular the king. The rewards of service came most frequently in the form of benefices, as the next chapter will show. However, the king and other lords had other forms of reward, including salaries. The pay of castle chaplains and of clerics and scribes in the exchequer has already been noted. In Henry I's reign, the chancellor, inevitably a cleric, received pay of 5*s* a day, amounting to £91 5*s* on a yearly basis, plus provisions.[107] Very occasionally, clerics got yearly pensions from secular sources, such as the £7 12*s* 1d (5*d* per day) Gerald of Wales began receiving, probably as emissary to the Welsh, in Richard's reign.[108] The exercise of many royal offices brought their own revenues, such as the profits of farming estates due to custodians of vacancies, or fees such as those charged by the chancery. The amount of money would-be chancellors offered for the position, £3000 and £4000 in Richard's reign and 5000 marks (£3333 6*s* 8*d*) in John's reign, show just how lucrative royal office could be.[109] Occasionally, kings sold or gave land to royal clerics. For instance, John granted the important royal manor of Cheddar, with the town of Axbridge, to Hugh of Wells, future bishop of Lincoln, and William of Wrotham, archdeacon of Taunton, acquired from Richard and John a collection of estates that could have supported a prosperous knight at the least.[110] Secular magnates gave land to their clerics surprisingly often. For instance, Earl Ranulf of Chester granted various properties to one of his most important clerics, Peter, who also acquired the village of Thornton, presumably with money or other assistance from the earl.[111] In addition, important royal clerics had the connections to purchase expensive but potentially lucrative wardships and marriages from the king. Though less interested than laymen in such investments, perhaps because they had fewer dynastic concerns, clerics can nonetheless be found offering £100 or more for marriages and wardships.[112] Indeed, William de Sainte-Mère-Eglise purchased four wardships in England and one in Normandy for a total of 975 marks (£650) and Hubert Walter, previous to becoming a bishop, purchased three wardships for 800 marks (£533 6*s* 8*d*).[113] Though the secular rewards of service for clerics paled beside the ecclesiastical ones,

---

[107] Anonymous, "Constitutio Domus Regis," in Emilie Amt and S. D. Church, eds., *Dialogus de Scaccario and Constitutio Domus Regis* (Oxford, 2007), 195–215, at 196–7.

[108] *Pipe Roll 5 Richard I*, xiii, 88.

[109] Richard of Devizes, *The Chronicle of Richard of Devizes of the Time of King Richard the First*, ed. John T. Appleby (London, 1963), 7; Hardy, ed., *Rotuli de Oblatis*, 368.

[110] For these and other grants or confirmations by King John, see Hardy, ed., *Rotuli Chartarum*, 29a, 48a–49b, 51b–52a, 88a, 113a–b, 114b, 123b, 129b, 130a–b, 137b, 144a–b, 160a. For these specific grants, see also Bird, *Manuscripts of Wells*, 146; *Pipe Roll 9 Richard I*, 139; Hardy, ed., *Rotuli Litterarum Clausarum*, 18b; Hardy, ed., *Rotuli de Oblatis*, 36, 299–300.

[111] Geoffrey Barraclough, ed., *The Charters of the Anglo-Norman Earls of Chester, c.1071–1237*, Record Society of Lancashire and Cheshire, vol. 126 (Chester, 1988), 236, 279–86.

[112] *Pipe Roll 4 Richard I*, 305; *Pipe Roll 10 Richard I*, 43; Hardy, ed., *Rotuli de Oblatis*, 467–8, 522.

[113] Turner, *Men Raised from the Dust*, 26; Cheney, *Hubert Walter*, 30.

they provided much additional wealth for the clerical elite and added to the enormous collective riches of the secular clergy.

3. CLERICS AND ECONOMIC DEVELOPMENT

The two great economic developments that provided the wealth undergirding the Twelfth-Century Renaissance were increased agricultural production and commercialization.[114] The secular clergy were by no means the primary engineers of the first process, but they nonetheless made a contribution. Presumably they played only a limited role in demographic expansion, one of the main factors driving increasing production, though no doubt far more than moralists would have preferred. More important was the role of clerics as landholders and estate managers in developing the lands they held or oversaw. According to the York historian, Hugh the Chanter, the first Norman archbishop of York, finding the cathedral lands devastated, developed the prebendal system there partly to encourage his canons to redevelop and build on the estates they now held, and a charter of King Stephen indicates they were still clearing land and building in the middle of the twelfth century.[115] On a smaller scale, a document of 1116 reveals the monks of Worcester Cathedral leasing a nearly deserted hamlet to a local priest for development.[116] Little evidence survives of the management of church glebes, but an unusual charter of Archbishop Richard of Canterbury to the rector of a parish church confirmed that his church would profit from any improvements he or his vicar made in the glebe land, particularly from assarting.[117] Other clerics can be found assarting land as well, including Robert of Inglesham, Henry of Huntingdon's grandson Master Aristotle, and Thomas of Chobham.[118] Clerics also occasionally built mills, in two cases windmills, an invention of the period.[119] Clerics

---

[114] For commercialization, see Richard H. Britnell, *The Commercialisation of English Society, 1000–1500* (Manchester, 1996); James Masschaele, *Peasants, Merchants, and Markets: Inland Trade in Medieval England, 1150–1350* (Basingstoke, 1997); John Langdon and James Masschaele, "Commercial Activity and Population Growth in Medieval England," *Past and Present* 190 (2006), 35–81.

[115] Hugh the Chanter, *The History of the Church of York, 1066–1127*, ed. Charles Johnson et al. (Oxford, 1990), 18–19; Diana E. Greenway, "The False *Institutio* of St Osmund," in Diana Greenway, Christopher Holdsworth, and Jane Sayers, eds., *Tradition and Change: Essays in Honour of Marjorie Chibnall* (Cambridge, 1985), 77–101, at 89–90; H. W. Davis et al., eds., *Regesta Regum Anglo-Normannorum, 1066–1154* (Oxford, 1913–69), 3:361–2.

[116] Mary Cheney et al., eds., *English Episcopal Acta. 33, Worcester, 1062–1185* (Oxford, 2007), 30–1.

[117] Cheney and Jones, eds., *English Episcopal Acta 2*, 51–2.

[118] *Pipe Roll 13 Henry II*, 8; Doris M. Stenton, ed., *The Earliest Northamptonshire Assize Rolls, A. D. 1202 and 1203*, The Publications of the Northamptonshire Record Society, vol. 5 (Lincoln 1930), 117; Hardy, ed., *Rotuli Litterarum Clausarum*, 159a. For a particularly large clerical assart of 240 acres, see Davis et al., eds., *Regesta Regum*, 3:207.

[119] *Pipe Roll 12 Henry II*, 47; Vivien Brown, ed., *Eye Priory Cartulary and Charters*, 2 vols., Suffolk Charters, vols. 12–13 (Woodbridge, 1992–94), 1:229; Jocelin of Brakelond, *Chronicle*, 59–60. For the early history of the windmill in England, see Edward J. Kealey, *Harvesting the Air: Windmill Pioneers in Twelfth-Century England* (Berkeley, 1987).

could be as eager as any other landlords to increase their revenues, and in doing so they helped build the economy.

Clerics also contributed to the development of managerial expertise among the English elites, especially those connected to the royal court. Frequent employment as farmers and officials of the king or of magnates, as well as landholding in their own right, gave many powerful clerics extensive experience in managing land and other economic resources. For instance, H. G. Richardson showed that the cleric and royal treasurer William of Ely was an active and able manager of the estates he farmed from St. Paul's, marling land for greater productivity, assarting, and improving buildings.[120] The royal records show clerics overseeing and conducting a surprisingly broad range of economic activities. Clerics were often custodians of vacant bishoprics and abbeys, and less frequently of secular honors, a task that involved supervising the running of extensive estates. For instance, Thomas Becket, as chancellor, had charge of a large assortment of custodies and vacant honors, and William fitz Stephen wrote that he employed many of the fifty-two clerics in his retinue to oversee them.[121] Similarly, in Richard's reign, William de Sainte-Mère-Eglise oversaw escheats for much of the kingdom, sometimes with the help of other prominent royal clerics, and J. E. A. Jolliffe noted several royal clerics who frequently held custodies late in the period.[122] Clerics naturally farmed estates for the king, as for other lords.[123] They can also be found overseeing work on such miscellaneous economic assets as fish ponds and quays or supervising tasks such as enclosing wetlands for farming.[124] Clerics were particularly important in managing royal interests in mining operations. Most notably, William of Wrotham oversaw the king's interests in tin mining in the southwest from 1197 to 1215, in which capacity he helped develop new regulations for the mines, participated in the creation of a new tax that greatly increased royal revenues, and bought and sold tin for the king's profit.[125] Even clerics involved in primarily non-economic functions might end up dealing with economic issues, such as the clerical justices in eyre who also made judgments about the stocking of royal manors.[126]

Extensive experience no doubt prompted some clerics to consider themselves experts in the management of estates. Turner has described one royal cleric, Thomas of Hurstbourne, as nearly making a profession of overseeing vacancies of

---

[120] H. G. Richardson, "William of Ely, the King's Treasurer (? 1195–1215)," *Transactions of the Royal Historical Society* 4th series, 15 (1932), 45–90, at 60–1.

[121] Robertson and Sheppard, eds., *Materials*, 3:29; Barlow, *Thomas Becket*, 52–4.

[122] Turner, *Men Raised from the Dust*, 20; J. E. A. Jolliffe, *Angevin Kingship* (London, 1955), 278, 284–5. For the clerics aiding Sainte-Mère-Eglise, see *Pipe Roll 8 Richard I*, 193–4, 196, 210.

[123] For some examples, see *Pipe Roll 7 Henry II*, 7; *Pipe Roll 27 Henry II*, 107; *Pipe Roll 32 Henry II*, 107.

[124] *Pipe Roll 15 Henry II*, 137; *Pipe Roll 17 Henry II*, 4; *Pipe Roll 5 Richard I*, 158.

[125] For Wrotham, see W. R. Powell, "The Administration of the Navy and the Stannaries, 1189–1216," *English Historical Review* 71 (1956), 177–88. For other clerics, see *Pipe Roll 6 Richard I*, xxxiv, 141; *Pipe Roll 7 Richard I*, 126, 132–4, 182; *Pipe Roll 9 Richard I*, 15–16.

[126] *Pipe Roll 4 Richard I*, 268; *Pipe Roll 7 Richard I*, xxii, 38.

abbeys and bishoprics for Henry II and Richard I.[127] In 1185, Thomas took charge of the affairs of Abingdon Abbey during a vacancy, and in that capacity he reported back to the justiciar, Ranulf de Glanville, with suggestions for changes in the abbey's management practices. Among these, he urged that the monks produce their own oats, rather than relying on selling wheat to buy oats, a practice the monks defended by reference to the example of their founder, Æthelwold. It is odd to see an expert advising against reliance on the market in this period of commercialization, and even odder to see the practice defended as traditional, but there is no doubt that Thomas believed his experience made him qualified to improve the management of Abingdon's affairs by trying to change its customary practices.[128]

Systematic thinking about ways to improve management of estates seems to have been a feature of the period. The best work on this for royal government is Robert Stacey's study of Henry III's government, unfortunately after our period, but Stacey noted evidence that such concerns already existed in the reigns of Henry II and Richard I.[129] More important, the management of estates by various sorts of landlords underwent a major change in England between the 1180s and 1220s with the shift to direct management rather than leasing.[130] The reasons for this shift are not entirely clear, but it must reflect communication among wealthy landlords and the experts they employed. The secular clergy would of course have formed only one part of the equation; lay farmers and officials and above all the great landowners themselves would have played important roles. However, the parallel between systematic thinking about estate management and the systematic analysis of various learned subjects by clerical intellectuals in the schools is striking. It is therefore at least possible that the education clerics received and the resulting habits of mind they passed on to their patrons and to their lay counterparts in administration might have helped trigger the discarding of received wisdom and the rethinking of estate management.

More specifically, though still quite speculatively, learned clerics might even have been inspired by Roman examples to think systematically about estate management. Master Peter of Waltham, archdeacon of London, owned a copy of the late Roman agricultural treatise of Palladius, which has much to say about estate management, and which Peter may have seen as a source of useful information rather than an antiquarian curiosity. Since Peter was in the service of Richard fitz Nigel, royal treasurer, author of *The Dialogue of the Exchequer*, and later bishop of London, Peter would have been part of the circle of experts around the royal court and the households of great lords. He would therefore have been in a position to

---

[127] Turner, *English Judiciary*, 87. For Thomas's various custodies, see *Pipe Roll 30 Henry II*, 24; *Pipe Roll 31 Henry II*, 29; *Pipe Roll 32 Henry II*, 116–17; *Pipe Roll 1 Richard I*, 5–6; *Pipe Roll 6 Richard I*, 256; *Pipe Roll 7 Richard I*, 29–32.

[128] Hudson, ed., *Historia Ecclesie Abbendonensis*, 2:lvi, 368–71.

[129] Robert C. Stacey, *Politics, Policy, and Finance under Henry III, 1216–1245* (Oxford, 1987), 66–91.

[130] Edward Miller, "England in the 12th and 13th Century: An Economic Contrast?" *Economic History Review* 2nd ser. 24 (1971), 1–14; P. D. A. Harvey, "The Pipe Rolls and the Adoption of Demesne Farming in England," *Economic History Review* 2nd ser. 27 (1974), 345–59; Stacey, *Politics, Policy, and Finance*, 68–73.

pass on anything useful he learned from that text, or perhaps even just the general idea of discussing and teaching estate management that it incorporated.[131]

Secular clerics also contributed to the growing use of the written word for estate management, though here they generally lagged behind the regular clergy and the royal government. Ralph of Diceto, dean of St. Paul's, along with other members of the chapter, organized a survey of the estates and churches of the cathedral, but only in 1181, long after various monasteries had carried out similar undertakings.[132] On the other hand, it was Thomas of Hurstbourne who first organized the recording of payments in money and kind to abbey officials and servants at Abingdon.[133] These are only minor instances of the secular clergy's role in the growing use of writing for administration, but such practices, when combined with the managerial expertise of many clerics, helps set the background to the writing of agricultural treatises later in the thirteenth century. In particular, one may mention Robert Grosseteste's *Rules of Estate and Household Management*, since Robert was an ordinary cleric late in the period covered in this work, though a bishop when he wrote the treatise.[134]

The secular clergy were even more important for commercialization than for economic development and management. Here again their contributions must be placed alongside those of other groups, particularly merchants. However, Robert Palmer has convincingly argued that parishes in the late Middle Ages were commercial entities and were crucial to the gathering of agricultural surplus and its entry into the marketplace.[135] Commercialization had obviously not advanced as far in England in the long twelfth century, but its slow development stretched far back into the Anglo-Saxon period. That the monks of Abingdon could see participation in the marketplace as deeply customary shows how entrenched the use of money had become. Moralists may have been troubled by the cash nexus and pushed back against it, but unfortunately for them, clerics could hardly avoid involvement in the slow process of commercialization and instead contributed to its further development.

Clerics participated in commercialization in a variety of ways. The condemnation of trade or business by moralists and occasional scraps of evidence such as amercements for selling wine against the assize show that clerics could be directly involved in commerce.[136] As farmers of estates, clerics must often have sold

---

[131] For Peter's career, see Johnson, ed., *English Episcopal Acta 26*, xlix; Nicholas Karn, ed., *English Episcopal Acta. 31, Ely, 1109–1197* (Oxford, 2005), 136–7. Peter's copy of Palladius is in Bodleian Library, Rawlinson MS G 62. Palladius was unusually popular in England and other copies were owned by religious houses, so any influence it had could also have spread through other routes; Rodney M. Thomson, "Where were the Latin Classics in Twelfth-Century England?," *England and the Twelfth-Century Renaissance* (Aldershot, 1998), 25–40, at 25.

[132] Hale, ed., *Domesday of St. Paul's*, 109–17, 140–52.

[133] Hudson, ed., *Historia Ecclesie Abbendonensis*, 2:358–69.

[134] Dorothea Oschinsky, ed., *Walter of Henley and other Treatises on Estate Management and Accounting* (Oxford, 1971), 191–9, 387–415; Michael Burger, "The Date and Authorship of Robert Grosseteste's *Rules for Household and Estate Management*," *Historical Research* 74 (2001), 106–16; R. W. Southern, *Robert Grosseteste: The Growth of an English Mind in Medieval Europe* (Oxford, 1986), 63–9.

[135] Palmer, *Selling the Church*, 30–47, 247–9. See also Swanson, *Church and Society*, 228–42.

[136] For instance, *Pipe Roll 7 Richard I*, 19; Stenton, ed., *Earliest Lincolnshire Assize Rolls*, 152, 157.

produce for cash, which they could then use for rent, and evidence survives of royal clerics selling large amounts of grain for export.[137] Those clerics who held estates privately or as parts of their benefices must also sometimes have been involved in the market. A particularly striking example comes from the efforts of William of Ely, the royal treasurer, to procure from King John the right to have a fair and a market in his prebend at Lincoln Cathedral.[138] As seen earlier, clerics participated actively in the land market, and in Chapter 2, I noted that moralists complained about priests commercializing religious rituals by performing or altering the Eucharist and other services for money, showing their involvement in the cash nexus even with their most important ritual duties.[139]

Based on Palmer's work on the later Middle Ages, however, the main contribution of clerics to commercialization is likely to have come from turning tithes and the produce of glebes into cash which was then used to purchase goods. Even rectors who were resident in their parish must have sold produce that was not needed for household consumption to pay pensions they owed to religious houses or to buy goods that might not be produced locally, either for their own use or for furnishing their churches. This is presumably why Thomas of Chobham considered certain kinds of sales by clerics as licit.[140] However, it was the siphoning of income away from parishes to pluralists and absentee clerics (as well as to monasteries) that would have done most to draw income from churches into the marketplace. Though goods could have been transferred in kind, coins were easier to transport and there is plentiful evidence of church incomes being turned into cash. One method was by leasing churches, for which documentation can occasionally be found even though short term leases were unlikely to be preserved in cartularies.[141] It is unclear how widespread leasing was, but the complaint of Hugh of Avalon, bishop of Lincoln, about priests who "often farm their churches to others and they in their turn to others . . . so that churches, like vile taverns, are placed at lease for an annual rent for the sake of money," suggests that the practice was common.[142] Reference to the sale by the "custodian" of one rich Yorkshire parish church of grain for £35 provides a specific glimpse of a lessee selling produce.[143] Evidence also survives for the leasing of tithes and offerings, though this practice too was viewed as problematic. Pope Alexander III vacillated on the complaint of a cleric who had bought half a year's offerings and tithes of a church from the rector but then not obtained them. Alexander stated that it seemed dishonest to buy and sell tithes and offerings yet sided with the plaintiff on the grounds that the sale of a single year's production was licit.[144] Clerics could also act

---

[137] Hardy, ed., *Rotuli Litterarum Patentium*, 78b–79a, 108b.

[138] Hardy, ed., *Rotuli Chartarum*, 183b.   [139] See Chapter 2, section 2.

[140] Thomas of Chobham, *Summa Confessorum*, 303, 533.

[141] British Library, Add. MS 35296, fos. 300r–v; Ross and Devine, eds., *Cartulary of Cirencester*, 2:500, 524–5.

[142] Adam of Eynsham, *Magna Vita Sancti Hugonis*, 2:87. See also Thomas of Chobham, *Summa Confessorum*, 299.

[143] Hardy, ed., *Rotuli de Oblatis*, 409.

[144] Farrer and Clay, eds., *Early Yorkshire Charters*, 10:59–60.

as lessees of tithes, and it was not uncommon for religious houses to grant such leases to them.[145] Obviously, there was initially deep discomfort with treating churches, tithes, and offerings as commercial objects, but by the late Middle Ages the leasing of tithes and parishes had become commonplace and entirely acceptable.[146] The willingness of clerics in the long twelfth century to insert their church incomes into the marketplace or to act as lessees made this possible and thereby gave parishes the profound commercial importance they had in the late medieval period.

Clerics also participated in the expansion of credit markets in this period. The strong and frequent condemnation of clerical usurers indicates that clerics sometimes acted as lenders, though direct evidence is hard to find, perhaps because the stigma was so strong that such practices were carefully concealed.[147] It is easier to find clerics borrowing money. Over two dozen clerics owed sums ranging up to £25 to the Jewish financier Aaron of Lincoln when he died.[148] Twelfth-century credit markets did not foster investment in economic enterprise as modern ones sometimes do, but they did facilitate spending and thus promoted commercialization. Clerics also borrowed money to sustain their studies abroad.[149] Sometimes, this was simply because money from England had not arrived, and the needs of students and other clerics traveling or living abroad also helped create a demand for moving money internationally. Admittedly, the sources mainly show how little international financial infrastructure existed in the period; the papacy had to get involved in one case in which Peter of Blois and another cleric borrowed money in Bologna, and the latter defaulted, leaving their surety there in the lurch.[150] Nonetheless, the slow development in the Middle Ages of mechanisms to move money doubtlessly arose not just to meet the needs of merchants, but also those of clerics.

However, the greatest contribution clerics made to commercialization was as consumers. Some of the best evidence for their consumer activities will appear in later chapters, which will show clerics buying or building luxurious dwellings, patronizing the production, exchange, and sale of luxury items such as elaborate textiles, and even playing a key role in the development of an entirely new trade in

---

[145] For some examples, see H. E. Salter, ed., *Newington Longeville Charters*, Oxfordshire Record Society Record Series, vol. 3 (Oxford, 1921), 36–7, 42–5, 48–52, 54, 59–61, 65, 93; G. Herbert Fowler, ed., *A Digest of the Charters Preserved in the Cartulary of the Priory of Dunstable*, Bedfordshire Historical Record Society Publications, vol. 10 (Aspley Guise, 1926), 99; H. E. Salter, ed., *Cartulary of Oseney Abbey*, 6 vols., Oxford Historical Society Record Series, vols. 89–91, 97–8, 101 (Oxford, 1929–36), 4:451.

[146] Palmer, *Selling the Church*, 75–142.

[147] Baldwin, *Masters, Princes, and Merchants*, 1:296, 299–300; Whitelock, Brett, and Brooke, eds., *Councils and Synods, 1066–1204*, 741, 776, 1073; Thomas of Chobham, *Summa de Arte Praedicandi*, 141–2; Morey, *Bartholomew of Exeter*, 257–8; Richard fitzNigel, *Dialogus de Scaccario*, 148–9.

[148] *Pipe Roll 3 Richard I*, 18–23, 32, 50–1, 55, 131, 159.

[149] See Chapter 10, section 1.

[150] Holtzmann, Chodorow, and Duggan, eds., *Decretales Ineditae*, 113–14; Charles Duggan, "Papal Judges Delegate and the Making of the 'New Law' in the Twelfth Century," in Thomas N. Bisson, ed., *Cultures of Power: Lordship, Status, and Process in Twelfth-Century Europe* (Philadelphia, 1995), 172–99, at 191–2. For accounts of the difficulties of other clerics, see Francesco Liverani, ed., *Spicilegium Liberianum* (Florence, 1863), 621–4, 626–8; John of Salisbury, *Letters*, 2:12–15; Gerald of Wales, *Opera*, 1:49; 3:286–91, 297.

books. However, clerics would generally have purchased goods on a more routine, mundane basis, and this is best illustrated by one of the earliest surviving English household accounts, which recorded the expenses of a secular cleric. Based on internal evidence, the account, which has been edited by C. M. Woolgar, comes from 1213, 1219, or 1224.[151] The cleric is not named, but was almost certainly a canon of St. Paul's holding a prebend with lands in Wellesdon, who was clearly also custodian of two vacant monasteries, since he paid their scutage. The account gives a total expenditure of £87 15s 10d over the course of three to four months, an outlay on a baronial scale. The cleric's household may well have received goods for consumption directly from Wellesdon, but even his possession of land involved participation in the market with payments for seed corn and laborers. The account records the purchase of a tun of wine, almost certainly imported from the continent, and of such luxury items as fur for the cleric's cape, pepper to enliven his meals, and, surprisingly enough, swords. However, the household can also be found purchasing such basic items of consumption as grain and ale. Altogether, this record reveals a rich cleric thoroughly enmeshed in the marketplace and carefully managing that involvement through precise record keeping.

Other scholars such as R. N. Swanson and R. I. Moore have noted the impact of the Church on the economy.[152] The importance of the Church, and more specifically of the secular clergy, on economic development should not, of course, be exaggerated. All social groups, including peasants, merchants, lay aristocrats, monks, and nuns, were crucial to economic development in the period, and clearly some of these groups played a larger role in specific economic changes than the secular clergy. Even so, the collective wealth and economic clout of clerics inevitably meant they were important participants in the growth of agricultural production and of commercialization, whether as landlords, farmers of estates, managers of glebes, or consumers. It is possible that their education made them particularly important to the development of systematic thinking about estate management. Even if the secular clergy did not form the main engine driving economic growth in the long twelfth century, they had an important role to play.

4. RELIGIOUS ANXIETY ABOUT CLERICAL WEALTH

The findings of this chapter help explain the laments of moralists about clerics and also illustrate the gap between the models of the ideal priest and of the aristocratic cleric. Despite a strong ideal of poverty in the medieval Church, there were many clerics who had the incomes and lifestyles of aristocrats. Pluralism played a major role in the creation of large incomes, as did corruption at times. Ambition was clearly widespread. Clerics were also involved heavily in the cash nexus that moralists condemned. The contrast between ideal and reality was stark.

[151] C. M. Woolgar, ed., *Household Accounts from Medieval England*, 2 vols. (Oxford, 1992), 1:117–26.
[152] Swanson, *Church and Society*, 191–251; Moore, *First European Revolution*, 37–8.

Because the issue of pluralism provides a particularly good illustration of how messy things could become when the ideals of reformers met reality, it merits further consideration. As noted in Chapter 2, moralists tended to criticize pluralism, though not as strongly as other practices such as simony or concubinage. Others also attacked the practice: the empress Matilda complained that "four or seven churches or prebends are conferred on one cleric" when canon law manifestly prohibited clerics from having even two.[153] Reformers themselves were divided and conflicted on how seriously to attack pluralism. Robert de Courson, a cleric of English origin who spent most of his career outside of England and eventually became a cardinal, waffled on the issue, suggesting it might have some benefits for rewarding scholars but worrying about the bad example it could set and forbidding it as a papal legate. Innocent III, in a decree associated with the Fourth Lateran Council, once again renewed the prohibition of pluralism, but made exceptions for learned or "sublime" clerics.[154] An important distinction was made between benefices with care of souls and those without, which could much more easily be held in plurality, though even for these there was clearly an expectation of moderation.

For illicit types of pluralism, dispensations could be granted (in this period by bishops as well as the pope), and another justification besides the quality of individual clerics was that some benefices were too poor.[155] Making exceptions for poverty was obviously reasonable, but in practice the various exceptions and loopholes made it hard to have any limitations at all. In 1213, Pope Innocent III forbade the bishop of Hereford from admitting to his churches anyone who was "adequately beneficed," but of course an adequate income was very much in the eyes of the beholder.[156] Peter of Blois, like other reformers, sometimes condemned pluralism. For instance, as dean of the collegiate church of Wolverhampton, Peter responded indignantly to a bishop of Bangor who had expected Peter to give a benefice to him instead of a poor but learned cleric. Yet when the custodian of Peter's prebend at Rouen stopped sending Peter his income from that benefice, partly on the grounds that Peter had many other rich benefices, Peter reacted with equal indignation in a letter to the archbishop of Rouen. Many who were considered rich, Peter argued, were actually poor, and riches were perfectly acceptable in any case, if not spent for luxury but for the demands of "moderate necessity."[157] Peter's idea of moderate necessity undoubtedly differed from that of a poor parish priest, but he was not alone. Two papal decisions in disputes about benefices depended partly on the revenues of one of the parties. In one case, Alexander III

[153] Duggan, ed., *Correspondence of Thomas Becket*, 1:168–9.

[154] Baldwin, *Masters, Princes, and Merchants*, 119–20; Ferruolo, *Origins of the University*, 304; Kenneth Pennington, *Pope and Bishops: The Papal Monarchy in the Twelfth and Thirteenth Centuries* (Philadelphia, 1984), 135–6.

[155] The decree of Innocent III, just mentioned, led to the power of such dispensations being restricted to the pope; Pennington, *Pope and Bishops*, 135–48.

[156] C. R. Cheney and W. H. Semple, eds., *Selected Letters of Pope Innocent III Concerning England (1198–1216)* (London, 1953), 143.

[157] Peter of Blois, *Opera*, 422–4, 434–6, 800.

commanded that the plaintiff receive the church if the defendant held one or more churches with an income of at least twenty marks (£13 6s 8d). The other case involved Wimer the chaplain, a royal cleric, sheriff of Norfolk and Suffolk for many years, and custodian of various estates and ecclesiastical vacancies, who was said, at this relatively early stage of his career, to have revenues of at least forty marks (£26 13s 4d) from various churches and benefices. Pope Alexander decreed that if he did have such revenues, he should stop seeking the church in question. Apparently the pope, like Peter of Blois, set a fairly high bar for what constituted an excessive rather than moderate income.[158] With a reforming pope expressing such views, it would hardly be surprising if many clerics felt there was nothing wrong with accumulating benefices in order to acquire at least a moderately aristocratic income. Even clerics who had high incomes, moreover, could presumably claim that their learning and sublimity merited unusual reward.

The papal decisions above also suggest that popes generally did not seek to rigorously enforce rules on pluralism but at most to limit it and exert moral pressure. Other evidence reinforces this impression. In a complicated case in which a dean of Lincoln complained about being deprived of a prebend at Hereford, Alexander III did factor in the wealth of the dean's office at Lincoln, but that was only one of several considerations. Lucius III, responding to a complaint that deans, archdeacons, and others neglected to include their titles in letters requesting benefices, thus concealing that they already had lucrative office, condemned the practice, writing that it was not his will that persons with many rich benefices should vex poor clerics over minor benefices.[159] Yet in neither of these cases did the pope direct bishops or others to deal with more than the issue at hand, for instance by depriving pluralists of anything except possibly the benefice in question. In the case of the dean of Lincoln, it was actually the pluralist dean who initiated the complaint, obviously not thinking that the pope would react badly to him holding more than one benefice. Admittedly, dispensations may have been at work in some cases, but in fact there is remarkably little reference to dispensations in the evidence, and one has to wonder if pluralists in this period even felt it necessary to obtain them very often.[160] In any case, the popes were obviously reacting to specific situations rather than taking a proactive stance against pluralism, and there is no clear evidence that any local archbishops or bishops were acting systematically against pluralism. In practice, the canons against pluralism served largely as another form of moral suasion rather than an effective legal barrier.

There is some evidence that the moral suasion of reformers and of canon law did have an impact. Peter of Blois emphasized that his income from Rouen was being stolen, but he had clearly been placed on the defensive by his custodian's reference

[158] Charles Duggan, "Decretals of Alexander III to England," in Filippo Liotta, ed., *Miscellanea Rolando Bandinelli, Papa Alessandro III* (Siena, 1986), 85–151, at 121; Holtzmann, Chodorow, and Duggan, eds., *Decretales Ineditae*, 81, 94.
[159] Holtzmann and Kemp, eds., *Papal Decretals Relating to Lincoln*, 28–9, 52–3.
[160] One does find the legate Guala Bicchieri granting them right at the end of our period: Nicholas Vincent, ed., *The Letters and Charters of Cardinal Guala Bicchieri, Papal Legate in England, 1216–1218*, The Canterbury and York Society, 83 (Woodbridge, 1996), lxxvii–lxxix.

to his wealth from other benefices. Moreover, there is at least one case in which a cleric took the concerns about pluralism seriously enough to act: a charter of Bishop William of Norwich announced that Robert of Scottow had voluntarily resigned one of his churches because he had three and because his needs were modest.[161] In contrast, however, Gerald of Wales, though a reformer in most respects, seems to have been quite unabashed about his pluralism. Thomas Becket actually defended himself against Gilbert Foliot's charge of ingratitude to Henry II by referring to his possession of the archdeaconry of Canterbury, the provostship of Beverley, and "many churches and several prebends" before entering the king's service.[162] Pluralism seems to have provoked remarkably little embarrassment. In the end, however, the most successful clerics found themselves operating in a system that routinely provided the greatest material rewards short of a bishopric through a practice condemned explicitly by reformers and canon law.

More broadly, successful clerics had to wrestle with the moral and religious dilemmas of being wealthy officials of a religion championing poverty, particularly in an age when new monastic movements emphasizing apostolic poverty, such as the Cistercians, quickly gained remarkable success and influence. However, some clerics tried to offer guidance on how wealth could coexist with a life devoted to the Christian ministry. One answer was that clerics should simply use any wealth beyond that needed to satisfy "modest necessities" (however one defined those) for other proper purposes such as the upkeep and adornment of their churches and charity to the poor. Later chapters will show that priests did in fact spend money on their churches and the poor, though the evidence is insufficient to reveal how much clerical wealth this absorbed.[163]

One writer, Godwin, precentor of Salisbury Cathedral, who was clearly writing partly in response to claims of superiority for the monastic life, tried to defend clerical wealth in a more abstract and sophisticated manner.[164] Godwin echoed other writers in emphasizing that the income of the church should be used for the proper purposes, and made the standard condemnations of greed and involvement in business. However, his chief concern was to combat the belief that the voluntary poverty adopted by monks, nuns, and regular canons was the only path to heaven and that wealth was necessarily a bar to salvation. He admitted that voluntary poverty was admirable, and that key biblical passages suggested that the wealthy faced the danger of damnation. In particular he focused on a biblical story often considered crucial to the monastic embrace of poverty. This was the account of the young rich man who asked Jesus how to gain eternal life and was told to sell all his possessions, give to the poor, and follow Jesus. The story continued with the young

---

[161] Harper-Bill, ed., *English Episcopal Acta 6*, 82; West, ed., *St. Benet of Holme*, 1:52–3.

[162] Duggan, ed., *Correspondence of Thomas Becket*, 1:430–1.

[163] See Chapter 13, sections 2–3 and Chapter 14, section 3.

[164] Bodleian Library, Digby MS 96, fos. 8r–10v, 13r–v, 21r–22v, 28v–29v. Not all of Godwin's discussion of wealth concerned clerical wealth alone, but an important part of it took place in the context of discussions about clerical and monastic life: Bodleian Library, Digby MS 96, fos. 18v–30r. For further discussion, see Teresa Webber, *Scribes and Scholars at Salisbury Cathedral, c.1075–c.1125* (Oxford, 1992), 124–8.

man going away sad, whereupon Jesus uttered the famous statement that it was harder for a camel to pass through the eye of a needle than for the rich to enter the kingdom of heaven.[165] According to the monastic interpretation, though no one could physically follow Jesus after the crucifixion one could obey this command by giving up the right to personal property and devoting oneself to the religious life. Godwin did not dispute this interpretation, but did not see it as the only way for the rich to achieve salvation. According to Godwin, Jesus did not at all intend to exclude all the wealthy from the kingdom of heaven. "Absit!" Instead, he intended to terrify the rich about the difficulty of getting into the kingdom of heaven. However, Godwin continued, Jesus immediately offered hope, saying that although such a feat was impossible for men, all things were possible for God. What of the description of the young rich man going away sad, hardly an encouraging sign for his salvation? For Godwin this was a warning not against failure to obey Jesus's command, but against trusting in wealth and giving in to despair. Yet how could the wealthy, and in particular wealthy clerics, achieve salvation?

Godwin's argument followed various tracks. One was that different rules applied to different orders, and that what was illicit for monks was licit for clerics, partly because of their pastoral duties. The second, related argument was that just as monks held property in common, so too did secular clerics, in their case with the poor. The third argument was that even those who could not, for whatever reason, abandon material wealth, could hold it in contempt. The fourth argument involved a focus on virtues and vices. For Godwin, a key problem of wealth was that it encouraged vice, above all pride. Clerical wealth was licit only so long as the cleric used it with humility and justice. Ultimately, for Godwin, wealth or lack thereof was less important than one's inner state, and the key for those rich in wealth was to become poor *in spirit*. Wealth made following Christian ideals more difficult, but certainly not impossible.

There was, however, an apologetic note to Godwin's defense of clerical wealth. For the pious cleric, there was simply no easy way to ignore or cope with the gap between medieval Christian ideals of poverty and clerical wealth. More than a few clerics solved this dilemma by entering monasteries. Others, however, acknowledged and lived with the tension. On one of the two occasions in which Bishop Herbert of Salisbury was stripped of his property and forced into exile, Peter of Blois wrote him a consoling letter.[166] Peter sympathized with the bishop for his loss, but urged him to see it as a form of divine correction and warning. Bishops, he cautioned, should abhor wealth, and use it only for such proper ends as hospitality and charity to the poor. Riches were of no use when one died and could be quite dangerous—poverty was better. These points were commonplaces of the time, even clichés, and given Peter's concerns about his own income the letter may at first glance seem merely hypocritical. Yet Peter was a pious man who suffered his own share of religious anxieties.[167] He was also a writer whose letters were widely

---

[165] Matthew 19:16–26; Mark 10:17–27; Luke 18:18–27.
[166] Peter of Blois, *The Later Letters of Peter of Blois*, ed. Elizabeth Revell (Oxford, 1993), 79–84.
[167] Cotts, *Clerical Dilemma*, 214–62.

admired because of his ability to express commonplace sentiments elegantly. This one could resonate not only because of its style but also because it probed such a sensitive subject for the elite clergy: the battle between the desire for wealth and the fear that it could lead to damnation.

Henry of Huntingdon was also a sophisticated writer who wrestled not so much with wealth as with the worldly pleasures it could bring. Nancy Partner ended her sensitive study of Henry's writings by stressing how he reacted to such struggles by focusing on contempt for the world. Henry acknowledged his own attraction to and joy in the world, embracing this characteristic but viewing it as a weakness, and emphasized the hollowness of worldly joys compared to heavenly ones. Partner finished off her discussion with a poem in which Henry (playing with the various meanings of the adjective *cultus*) praised the cultivation or elegance of his own verses, his home, his land, his bedchamber (or marriage bed), and his orchard. He wrote that his garden (in the metaphorical as well as literal sense) gleamed with a hundredfold cultivation—only Henry himself was uncultivated. Henry had the good life, but in the end the good life was insufficient.[168] However, Henry wrote another set of verses that expressed the futility of the worldly pleasure that wealth could provide even more sharply. In a poem devoted to urging contempt for the world, Henry used the common trope of human flesh ending up as the food of worms to uncommon effect in a warning to the kind of rich, worldly people who enjoyed a variety of rich foods. Having praised the beauty of cultivated land, proud landholder that he was, he wrote: "You grain fields, gardens, orchards, meadows, now make [men] fat; worms like fatty food. You, forest, send game; sea, send fish; India, send pepper: worms like food flavored with these dishes."[169] How better to express a worldly yet pious cleric's anxiety about wealth and the pleasures it provided?

---

[168] Nancy F. Partner, *Serious Entertainments: The Writing of History in Twelfth-Century England* (Chicago, 1977), 47–8; Henry of Huntingdon, *Historia Anglorum*, 802–3.

[169] Henry of Huntingdon, *Historia Anglorum*, 798–801.

5

Patronage and Advancement

Nigel of Whiteacre, in his tract against clerical courtiers, told the story of an unnamed clerical favorite of Henry II who was accompanying the king on a military expedition in Wales when news came that a wealthy rector had died. The dead man had held many rich churches, and the royal favorite promptly obtained letters from the king to the abbot who held the advowson of the richest one, requesting his appointment. Even with the royal letters, the cleric knew he had to hurry to get to the abbot before the latter had granted the church to someone else. For eight days he traveled relentlessly, changing horses frequently, killing some under him, and leaving less robust companions behind. On the evening of the eighth day, he was ten miles from the abbot, but was so weary that he had to stop to rest. Then he heard that another had received the church. Exhausted and frustrated at his thwarted desire, he turned to the wall and died.[1]

One may reasonably doubt the historicity of this moralizing story with its sensational denouement, but it does vividly capture the competitive scramble that often marked the search for benefices. This chapter explores patronage networks and ecclesiastical appointments of secular clerics. Of necessity, it devotes much attention to the wishes and motives of patrons, but as Nigel's story makes clear, clerics themselves were active participants in patronage networks, often working the system in every way they could. The first section explores the competitive nature of the process more fully. The bulk of the chapter, however, consists of an overview of the factors that led to appointments: simony; inheritance and kinship; patronage by kings, prelates, and secular magnates; friendship networks; and finally the qualities of moral character and learning that were in theory the main qualifications for any candidate. The last part of the chapter describes the social stresses and moral tensions created by patronage practices in the period.[2]

---

[1] Nigel of Whiteacre, *Tractatus Contra Curiales*, 166.

[2] For a good discussion of patronage in East Anglia that focuses primarily on the value of benefices for patrons, see Harper-Bill, "Struggle for Benefices," 113–32. A useful comparison with English patronage, though limited to cathedral chapters, is David Spear, "Power, Patronage and Personality in the Norman Cathedral Chapters, 911–1204," *Anglo-Norman Studies* 20 (1998), 205–21. For overviews of patronage in a later period, see Bowker, *Secular Clergy of Lincoln*, 74–84; Lepine, *A Brotherhood of Canons*, 19–40, 75–86; Swanson, *Church and Society*, 64–82; Heath, *English Parish Clergy*, 27–36.

1. THE COMPETITION FOR BENEFICES

Though aspects of Nigel of Whiteacre's story are far-fetched, competition between clerics seeking the same benefice and demands for appointments by powerful people seeking to provide for their clerical followers were not. *The Chronicle of Battle Abbey* records how Abbot Odo, when trying to find a good priest for the parish church of Battle, had to fend off requests or anticipated requests for the post on behalf of an archdeacon, the chaplain of a local official, and a cleric of Archbishop Richard of Canterbury.[3] Papal documents suggest that multiple requests, often for less than ideal candidates, were commonplace. For instance, Pope Clement III, in a letter on behalf of Ramsey Abbey, wrote of the problems the abbey faced because of the many requests for appointments it received, often for unworthy candidates.[4] Similarly, Alexander III noted a complaint from the abbey of Chester that the monks were frequently forced by the rich and powerful to concede churches to clerics who did not serve them and to assign churches to unworthy rectors at rent.[5] The popes themselves, however, added to the problem. Jocelin of Brakelond records an occasion in which a cleric asked Abbot Samson of Bury St Edmunds for a benefice, whereupon the abbot pulled out seven letters from various popes requesting benefices for other clerics.[6] Even the need for hurry recorded in Nigel's story probably reflected reality: Gilbert Foliot, bishop of London, wrote to another bishop urging him to quickly institute one of Gilbert's relatives to whom he had granted a church, citing the problems often caused by delay.[7] England had thousands of benefices, but the competition for them was clearly stiff, and the drive to secure a benefice was obviously an anxious business.

So fierce was the competition that clerics often maneuvered for specified or unspecified benefices even before they became open. Another story from Nigel of Whiteacre, though once again probably too good to be true, illustrates some of the practices. Nigel recounted how "a noble and honest man," who for over forty years had been rector of a church in the king's gift worth forty or fifty marks, gained the friendship of royal clerics through gifts and hospitality. One of them mendaciously offered to request a favor from the king for the rector, whereupon the rector asked for his learned nephew to be appointed to succeed him. The royal cleric later returned, saying that the king had granted this wish, but when the two went before the bishop (who was in cahoots with the royal cleric), the prelate demanded the rector resign before appointing the nephew. As soon as he had resigned, the royal cleric whipped out a promise of the first vacant benefice in royal control, whereupon he received the church.[8]

---

[3] Eleanor Searle, ed., *The Chronicle of Battle Abbey* (Oxford, 1980), 312–19.

[4] Hart and Lyons, eds., *Cartularium Monasterii de Rameseia*, 2:153–4.

[5] Holtzmann, ed., *Papsturkunden*, 1:421.   [6] Jocelin of Brakelond, *Chronicle*, 56.

[7] Gilbert Foliot, *The Letters and Charters of Gilbert Foliot, Abbot of Gloucester (1139–48), Bishop of Hereford (1148–63), and London (1163–87)*, ed. Z. N. Brooke, Adrian Morey, and C. N. L. Brooke (Cambridge, 1967), 325–6.

[8] Nigel of Whiteacre, *Tractatus Contra Curiales*, 164–5.

Elements of this story clearly mimicked reality. Sometimes arrangements were made for succession to benefices while the rector was still alive.[9] Patrons (and particularly the king, as we shall see) sometimes made promises of the next available benefice, often with pensions provided in the meantime.[10] The papacy conflated the two practices, viewing even promises of undetermined benefices as breaking the rule against appointments to churches with living rectors, and strongly opposed both. Reformers no doubt worried that arranged successions could easily lead to *de facto* inheritance, but they probably also worried that both practices were particularly susceptible to manipulation by the rich and powerful, since pressure could be applied at any time, not just when a benefice was vacant. Thus John of Salisbury wrote of bishops being pressured to promise the next available benefice and then incumbents being pressured to resign.[11] Powerful patrons and clerics did often apply pressure. Alexander III issued one of his condemnations of promises of first benefices in response to a complaint that clerics with 100 or 200 marks in ecclesiastical benefices were claiming churches on the basis of such promises and appealing against other candidates. Innocent III wrote on behalf of St. Augustine's, Canterbury, against the practice of "princes and other powerful men" seeking pensions and first vacancies from the monastery by prayers and threats.[12] In addition to such general statements, specific instances of pressure can be found. For instance, the Yorkshire magnate Adam de Brus issued a charter to his family foundation of Guisborough lamenting that he had extorted from them, by force and fear, uncanonically and at peril to his soul, a pension of £10 for one of his chaplains until the church of Skelton was vacant.[13] Even popes, for all their condemnations, were involved in the practices of promising specified or unspecified benefices. On one occasion Alexander III, forgetting that he had provided letters promising one cleric the first vacant archdeaconry in the diocese of Coventry, provided another cleric with letters to succeed to one of those archdeaconries upon the resignation of his uncle.[14]

The fullest evidence of the fierce competition for church office, however, comes from the frequency and occasional nastiness of disputes over appointments and rights of patronage. Even the reforming preacher Thomas Agnellus was accused of usurping a benefice at Wells.[15] Issues of patronage were so important to kings that they worked hard to ensure that they were heard in royal courts. Indeed, Henry II

---

[9] Farrer and Clay, eds., *Early Yorkshire Charters*, 2:363; 12:39–40; Reginald Thomas Timson, ed., *The Cartulary of Blyth Priory*, 2 vols., Thoroton Society of Nottinghamshire, record series, nos. 27–28 (London, 1973), 145; Lovatt, ed., *English Episcopal Acta 20*, 63–4.

[10] See section 3 within this chapter. For grants that did not involve a pension and did not come from the king, see British Library, Cotton MS Claudius D XIII, fos. 127r–v; Cambridge University Library, Peterborough Dean and Chapter MS 1, fos. 113r–v. For discussion of the practice, see Cheney, *From Becket to Langton*, 76–8.

[11] John of Salisbury, *Policraticus*, 2:165–6.

[12] For these and other condemnations, see Duggan, "Decretals of Alexander III," 140–1; Holtzmann and Kemp, eds., *Papal Decretals Relating to Lincoln*, 54–5; Cheney and Cheney, eds., *Letters of Pope Innocent III*, 103, 133, 166, 246–7, 270.

[13] Farrer and Clay, eds., *Early Yorkshire Charters*, 2:20.

[14] Duggan, "Decretals of Alexander III," 128.

[15] Ramsey, ed., *English Episcopal Acta 10*, xlv.

and his legal advisors developed one of their key assizes, darrein presentment, to expedite patronage disputes. Though cases continued to be heard in church courts on occasion, the kings were largely successful, and the earliest surviving records of the royal courts, from the reigns of Richard I and John, are littered with disputes over ecclesiastical patronage.[16] Information from other sources shows the extremes to which people sometimes went to control patronage. One noblewoman even stole an actual church in an attempt to gain its patronage: she had her followers move it across the church cemetery to land that was on her estate.[17] In other cases, one reads of forced entry into churches, intimidation, and even death threats.[18] Disputes, of course, are more likely to appear in our sources than uncontroversial appointments. Nonetheless, the number of confrontations and legal cases over rights of patronage and individual appointments shows how much importance patrons and clerics both placed on their ability to grant and receive benefices.

2. ACQUIRING BENEFICES: SIMONY, INHERITANCE, AND NEPOTISM

How did ambitious or needy clerics acquire benefices? What factors governed the distribution of patronage? Unfortunately, there is no way to systematically evaluate the relative weight of various factors. Although I have gathered information on hundreds of appointments, these represent only a fraction of the tens of thousands of appointments made during the long twelfth century. Documents rarely reveal why an appointment was made, and narrative sources, though sometimes quite informative, are not plentiful. Even when one knows the identity of the patron and the recipient, moreover, one may not know the whole story. As Nigel of Whiteacre's first story reveals, the cleric's patron, in this case the king, might not have been the actual patron of the benefice, which a record of the appointment would probably not reveal. One also has to be careful about inferring motive from relationships, a point to which I will return. Nonetheless, even if the evidence is woefully insufficient to give a meaningful statistical breakdown of the importance of various factors in prompting appointments, there is certainly enough for a rough overview of the major relationships and qualifications involved.

The practice of simony apparently survived the efforts of reformers to stamp it out, though in fact these attempts provide some of the best evidence of its continuing existence. Though the moralists discussed in Chapter 2 devoted less space to the purchase of church office than to other issues, perhaps because its sinfulness was so well established, they often expressed concerns about it, and

---

[16] For the continuance of advowson cases in church courts, see Cheney, *Roger, Bishop of Worcester*, 142–8. For the assize of darrein presentment, see G. D. G. Hall, ed., *The Treatise on the Laws and Customs of the Realm of England, Commonly called Glanvill* (Oxford, 1993), 160–2.

[17] Saltman, *Theobald, Archbishop of Canterbury*, 350–3; Harper-Bill, "Struggle for Benefices," 120.

[18] Gilbert Foliot, *Letters and Charters*, 319–20; John of Salisbury, *Letters*, 1:162–3; Cheney and Semple, eds., *Selected Letters of Innocent III*, 15; Hardy, ed., *Rotuli de Oblatis*, 105.

prohibitions against the practice appeared repeatedly in English councils and synods.[19] Moreover, Innocent III issued letters to two English bishops urging or authorizing them to act strongly against simony and in one case describing the practice as widespread.[20] Given the frequent condemnations of simony, it is surprisingly hard to find specific cases or accusations, but some examples do survive. Pope Lucius III heard from the bishop of Evreux that the bishop's brother, Earl Roger of Warwick, frequently sold the church of Warwick (probably the collegiate church of St. Mary) to various clerics, which presumably referred to the sale of office rather than the church itself. Two other papal documents, from 1144 and 1189, concern clear and specific accusations of simony, and a few other instances can be found in scattered sources.[21] It is possible that simony in its purest form had become less common than in earlier periods and that the repeated admonitions of reformers represented exaggerated fears. It is also possible, however, that simony was common but carefully concealed, and that it remained an important tool in the acquisition of church office.

Much more evidence survives for the influence of kinship ties, which can be broken into three categories: direct inheritance of office; patronage by powerful clerical relatives; and patronage by powerful lay relatives, particularly those who owned churches or, as canon law became more precise, the advowsons of churches. Of the three categories, the first was most heavily targeted by reformers, and church synods in England, as elsewhere, often legislated against the inheritance of benefices.[22] Nonetheless, the practice was common in the early twelfth century, as earlier historians have noted. Most notably, C. N. L. Brooke has shown that prebends at St. Paul's, London, where the sources are unusually good, were often heritable through the first quarter of the twelfth century.[23] Indeed, some priests, particularly in towns, may have felt churches were simply their own property, and therefore perfectly heritable. In the more common situation, where priests or other clerics were clearly appointees, the analogy to feudal tenancies may still have created expectations of inheritance or succession, especially since patrons tended to treat churches much like fiefs well into the twelfth century, using similar language for the bestowal of churches and of land. Both types of holding were conditional and in both cases an overlord had interests in the property, so it would not be surprising if

[19] Whitelock, Brett, and Brooke, eds., *Councils and Synods, 1066–1204*, 575, 580, 606, 674–6, 738, 747, 981, 987; Powicke and Cheney, eds., *Councils and Synods, 1205–1265*, 25.

[20] Cheney and Cheney, eds., *Letters of Pope Innocent III*, 14–15; Cheney and Semple, eds., *Selected Letters of Innocent III*, 9.

[21] Holtzmann, ed., *Papsturkunden*, 1:256; 2:187–8; Thomas of Marlborough, *History of the Abbey of Evesham*, ed. Jane E. Sayers and Leslie Watkiss (Oxford, 2003), 448–9; Robert Easting, ed., *The Revelation of the Monk of Eynsham*, Early English Text Society, 318 (Oxford, 2002), 138; Gerald of Wales, *Speculum Duorum*, 80–1.

[22] Whitelock, Brett, and Brooke, eds., *Councils and Synods, 1066–1204*, 675, 739, 775–6, 979, 983–4.

[23] C. N. L. Brooke, "The Composition of the Chapter of St. Paul's, 1086–1163," *Cambridge Historical Journal* 10 (1951), 111–32, at 125; Barlow, *English Church, 1066–1154*, 131–2; Brett, *English Church*, 219–20.

priestly families, like families holding fiefs, might feel that they had at least a strong claim to succession.[24]

Two developments slowly undermined any rights of inheritance or expectations about automatic succession to benefices. One was the gradual success of reformers and canon lawyers in undermining the idea of churches as just another form of property.[25] The other, of course, was the targeting of clerical succession as a byproduct of the campaign for clerical celibacy. These changes took time to have effect, however. In the 1180s the son of a priest of a church belonging to Waltham tried to put in a claim to succession.[26] As late as 1194, a jury in a darrein presentment case reported that they could not say who had made the last appointment, because the church had passed "from rector to rector and from father to son," until the death of the most recent incumbent.[27] Nonetheless, change did come. In the Waltham case, the priest's son withdrew his claim "upon mature counsel." In a case from 1207, the jurors referred to hereditary ownership of a church by priests as an outmoded custom and a local one at that.[28] Clearly, reform views of the non-proprietary and non-heritable nature of churches were slowly sinking in.

The gradual destruction of any rights or customary expectations of inheritance to benefices did not prevent sons from trying to succeed their fathers on a *de facto* basis. According to a letter of Peter of Blois, writing as dean of the collegiate church of Wolverhampton, whenever a good man was appointed to a benefice there, the son or *nepos* (nephew or grandson) of the previous prebendary would resist violently.[29] A less confrontational tactic was for fathers to make deals with the holders of advowsons for the succession of their sons. Sometimes, such arrangements were even made with the permission of the papacy.[30] More often, popes issued prohibitions against the practice of appointing sons to their father's churches, even by agreement, at least as long as there was no intervening priest.[31] As the repeated prohibitions suggest, priests continued to succeed to benefices. Around 1217, for instance, the dean of Salisbury cathedral could casually record, in a case involving land attached to a chapel, that the chapel had passed from father to son and brother to brother through five members and three generations of the same family.[32] Henry of Huntingdon's great-grandson Nicholas, who was active until

---

[24] For ownership of churches by priests, priestly tenure, and the similarities between churches and lay fiefs, see Wood, *Proprietary Church*, 551–5, 674–80, 911–18; F. M. Stenton, ed., *Documents Illustrative of the Social and Economic History of the Danelaw* (London, 1920), lxxiv; Lennard, *Rural England*, 320–1; Kemp, "Monastic Possession of Parish Churches," 135–40; B. R. Kemp, "Towards Admission and Institution: English Episcopal Formulae for the Appointment of Parochial Incumbents in the Twelfth Century," *Anglo-Norman Studies* 16 (1994), 155–76, at 158–9.

[25] Wood, *Proprietary Church*, 851–933.

[26] Ransford, ed., *Early Charters of Waltham Abbey*, 154.

[27] Palgrave, ed., *Rotuli Curiæ Regis*, 1:37–8.

[28] *Curia Regis Rolls*, 5:39.   [29] Peter of Blois, *Later Letters*, 28.

[30] Cheney, *Roger, Bishop of Worcester*, 265; Holtzmann, ed., *Papsturkunden*, 1:510.

[31] Holtzmann, ed., *Papsturkunden*, 1:486–7; 3:440–1, 506–7; Cheney and Semple, eds., *Selected Letters of Innocent III*, 82; Cheney and Cheney, eds., *Letters of Pope Innocent III*, 69; Barrow, "Hereford Bishops and Married Clergy," 6.

[32] Jones, ed., *Register of S. Osmund*, 1:359.

*c.*1230, held the rectory of King's Walden, which his father, grandfather, and possibly Henry himself had held.[33]

Nonetheless, the efforts of reformers and church administrators clearly had effect. Whereas secular tenants of fiefs saw expectations and legal rights to inheritance solidify over the long twelfth century, clerics who hoped to succeed to church offices were increasingly thrown on the whims of patrons who often had good reason to favor other supplicants. Would-be clerical heirs also had to avoid ecclesiastical sanction. It is therefore not surprising that, as Brooke showed, succession to prebends at St. Paul's slowed to a trickle after *c.*1125, with the last taking place in 1167.[34] Though C. R. Cheney found evidence for hereditary succession into the thirteenth century, he argued that during that century it became an only occasional practice.[35] Inheritance was an important factor in appointments to church office at the beginning of our period but became much less important as time went on, opening up more and more benefices to the free exercise of patronage.

In contrast to the decline of hereditary succession, the practice of nepotism flourished unchecked into the thirteenth century and beyond. According to Gerald of Wales, Pope Alexander III quipped that God had taken sons away from bishops (or from "us" in another version) but the devil had given them nephews.[36] Reformers could attack nepotism all they wanted, but the importance of family ties was a powerful cultural counterweight, a point to which I will return in Chapter 8. In some cases, clerics carried out nepotism in the same manner as arranged succession of sons to churches: as in the second of Nigel of Whiteacre's anecdotes noted earlier, a relative, usually an uncle, would resign a benefice in anticipation of having his kinsman succeed. Gerald of Wales managed the succession of his nephew, also named Gerald, to his archdeaconry and prebend by resigning these posts, arranging for the younger Gerald to be appointed in his place, and then having himself appointed as administrator, paying a pension to his nephew out of the revenues.[37] Similarly, in the late twelfth century a canon of the collegiate church of St. Mary, Warwick, conveyed his prebend, with its church, to the son of his niece.[38] However, a far more common pattern was for powerful churchmen either to use any benefice at their disposal to support relatives or to use their influence to persuade others to appoint their kin.

As Pope Alexander's quip indicates, the ecclesiastical figures best placed to dispense patronage were bishops, many of whom were secular clerics themselves and most of whom had relatives in the clergy. Throughout the period, bishops regularly used their office to advance relatives; even the saintly Bishop Hugh of Lincoln promoted three clerical relatives to important posts in his diocese.[39]

---

[33] Henry of Huntingdon, *Historia Anglorum*, xxviii; Clay, "Master Aristotle," 304–5, 307–8. See also Wood, *Proprietary Church*, 678–9.

[34] Brooke, "Composition of St. Paul's," 125.   [35] Cheney, *From Becket to Langton*, 126–9.

[36] Gerald of Wales, *Opera*, 2:304; Gerald of Wales, *Speculum Duorum*, 148–9.

[37] Gerald of Wales, *Opera*, 3:325–6; Gerald of Wales, *Speculum Duorum*, 116–19.

[38] Fonge, ed., *Cartulary of St Mary's*, 278.

[39] Smith, ed., *English Episcopal Acta 4*, xxv–xxvi; David M. Smith, "Hugh's Administration of the Diocese of Lincoln," in Henry Mayr-Harting, ed., *St. Hugh of Lincoln* (Oxford, 1987), 19–47, at 29–30.

Bishops sometimes made kinsmen archdeacons.[40] Where they presided over secular chapters, they often appointed relatives as canons.[41] Kinsmen of bishops sometimes held parish churches in their dioceses, and one suspects this was no coincidence.[42] Indeed, Pope Alexander III complained, on behalf of St. Albans, of bishops putting undue pressure on monasteries to obtain benefices for their relatives and clerics.[43] Abbots could also provide for their relatives. Jocelin of Brakelond remarked sardonically on the number of "new" kinsmen who approached Abbot Samson of Bury St Edmunds when he became abbot, and though Samson generally rejected their requests, other abbots were more accommodating.[44] Even powerful clerics who were not ecclesiastical magnates could sometimes gain benefices for their relatives. Thus Godfrey de Lucy, before he became bishop, obtained one for his nephew Richard.[45]

Some clerical kin groups, especially those with royal ties, managed to maintain their wealth and status over several generations through the continual acquisition of new benefices and posts. The most noteworthy of these families did so at the episcopal level. For instance, Archbishop Thomas II of York had a grandfather who had been a Norman priest, an uncle who had been his predecessor as archbishop, and a father and brother who had also been bishops. That Richard of Hexham, in describing these connections, could state that Thomas was famous for the great nobility of his kin suggests that such kin groups were not only tolerated but accepted into the elites.[46] Henry I's favorite, Roger of Salisbury, his nephews Nigel and Alexander, and Nigel's son Richard all became bishops, and another relative, William, continued the family success story into the thirteenth century as a royal official and rich pluralist.[47] Other families were not so successful, but used the presence of one or two bishops in their ranks to establish longstanding ties with individual dioceses: for instance, the Turbe family at Norwich, the Peche family at Coventry, the Foliot family at Hereford (where thirteen members held posts over several generations), and above all the Belmeis family at London.[48]

[40] For instance, Blake, ed., *Liber Eliensis*, 276–7; Franklin, ed., *English Episcopal Acta 17*, lvi; Kemp, ed., *English Episcopal Acta 18*, xlvii, lxv.

[41] Barrow, "Origins and Careers," 35–7; Crosby, *Bishop and Chapter*, 298, 339.

[42] Franklin, ed., *English Episcopal Acta 8*, 168–9; Lovatt, ed., *English Episcopal Acta 20*, 50–2, 154–5; Lovatt, ed., *English Episcopal Acta 27*, 20–1.

[43] Holtzmann, ed., *Papsturkunden*, 3:440–1.

[44] The one kinsman Samson accepted into service was a knight, but it is likely that others were clerics; Jocelin of Brakelond, *Chronicle*, 24. For examples of abbots appointing relatives, see West, ed., *St. Benet of Holme*, 1:52; 2:240–1; H. E. Salter, ed., *Eynsham Cartulary*, 2 vols., Oxford Historical Society Record Series, vols. 49, 51 (Oxford, 1907–8), 1:135; Cheney and John, eds., *English Episcopal Acta 3*, 62–3.

[45] Foster and Major, eds., *Registrum Antiquissimum*, 3:265.

[46] Richard of Hexham, "The History of the Founding of the Church of Hexham," in James Raine, ed., *The Priory of Hexham*, Surtees Society, vol. 44 (Durham, 1864), 1–62, at 50–1.

[47] Stollberg, *Soziale Stellung*, 82–109.

[48] Harper-Bill, ed., *English Episcopal Acta 6*, xxxi–xxxii, xliii; M. J. Franklin, ed., *English Episcopal Acta. 16, Coventry and Lichfield, 1160–1182* (Oxford, 1998), xxvi–xxvii; Barrow, "Origins and Careers," 36–7; Ralph of Diceto, *Opera Historica*, 1:xx–xxix; Crosby, *Bishop and Chapter*, 321–5; Brooke, "Composition of St. Paul's," 126–7. For comparable families in Normandy, see Spear, "Power, Patronage and Personality," 216–20.

How did these kin groups work, beyond the obvious practice of bishops and other notables appointing relatives to benefices directly in their gift? The letters of Gilbert Foliot, abbot of Gloucester, bishop of Hereford and then London, can provide good insight into how his kin network functioned and can illustrate some of the more subtle aspects of patronage networks. Gilbert had plenty of patronage of his own to offer, but his letters show him frequently asking other patrons for benefices for kinsmen or requesting that powerful people provide support for relatives seeking benefices or involved in disputes over benefices. He also promoted the careers of kinsmen by other methods such as seeking a place for one in the household of a bishop. In supporting relatives, he often made use of existing kin ties: he asked several of these favors from his relative, Bishop Robert Chesney of Lincoln, in one case stating that Robert's brother William had initiated the request. Most notably, however, Gilbert used his own standing to help ensure the greater power of his broad kin group by writing letters to popes on behalf of four relatives seeking bishoprics: Robert Chesney, Richard Belmeis II, Robert Foliot, and Richard of Ilchester.[49] Gilbert's letters suggest that we might think as much about kinship networks extending outward from individuals as about discrete families. Richard Belmeis and Robert Chesney had their own kin networks and in some sense Richard of Ilchester created his own lineage, since his sons Herbert and Richard ended up as bishops of Salisbury and Chichester. Nonetheless, their networks clearly intersected with Gilbert's.

However constructed, clerical kin groups could act as an effective unit, and Ralph of Diceto provided some glimpses of the Belmeis family, all close relatives of the founder, Richard Belmeis I, exercising its clout at St. Paul's after Richard's death in 1127. For instance they blocked a candidate for the bishopric whom they disliked (despite an earlier family disagreement about his election) and protected the interests of a family member through sending a delegation to Rome in 1138.[50] In the following decades, they managed to retain several offices in the family, particularly the deanship, and to get Richard Belmeis II elected as bishop in 1152 against the wishes of King Stephen. Working in concert within the cathedral chapter, they were obviously able to exercise a good deal of power. Overall, kinship among clerics mattered a great deal, and even a single highly successful clerical relative could help a young cleric in quest of a career and benefices. Thus, even Thomas Becket, though he ultimately rose largely through his abilities as an administrator, benefited from kinship with Archbishop Theobald of Canterbury, at least according to William fitz Stephen.[51]

For all the success of some families, nepotism and kinship networks did not bring the security or stability that hereditary succession of benefices would have provided or that inheritance of lands afforded to heirs among the laity. Even having a relative who was a bishop, abbot, or abbess provided no guarantee of advancement; after all,

---

[49] Gilbert Foliot, *Letters and Charters*, 38–9, 68–9, 117, 137–8, 144–6, 245–7, 298–9, 321–2, 325–7.
[50] Ralph of Diceto, *Opera Historica*, 1:249–52.
[51] Robertson and Sheppard, eds., *Materials*, 3:15.

Abbot Samson, who admittedly had no close relatives, turned down the requests of his "new" kin. Relatives had a strong head start in winning the favor of a kinsman with patronage, but they still had to gain it, and might have to compete with other relatives. Success through clerical kinship was certainly most likely when a family member was an ecclesiastical magnate, but that in itself depended on the favor of non-relatives, almost always the king, for the election of Richard II Belmeis was an extremely atypical event. Thus, although kinship provided key advantages to some clerics, and though to some degree the elite clergy was a self-reproducing group, each clerical family had to struggle to maintain its influence in every generation. Though some favored clerical scions may have had benefices handed to them, many others would still have had to exert themselves strongly in the competitive search for benefices, particularly if they aimed for the great wealth and power that a truly successful clerical career could provide.

Another privileged group were the offspring of landholding families, particularly those families that controlled the patronage of one or more churches or even, in some cases, cathedral prebends.[52] Landholders in twelfth-century England, as later, often granted benefices to sons, brothers, or other close relatives.[53] I noted a couple of particularly impressive aristocratic pluralists in the previous chapter and examples of members of landholding families receiving one or two churches can be found scattered throughout the sources.[54] Secular aristocrats, like powerful churchmen, could also use their connections to persuade others to make appointments. For instance, Earl Hamelin of Warenne solicited a Yorkshire church for his wife's half-brother, Philip, son of Earl Patrick, from an influential churchman.[55] Monasteries would sometimes appoint a member of the family that had earlier given a church to hold that church, perhaps as a way of settling a dispute over an advowson.[56] A lesser aristocrat in the service of a powerful lord might get his patron to provide a benefice for a relative, as the Wigmore Chronicle reports Hugh Mortimer did for the son of his steward, Oliver de Merlimont.[57] Members of aristocratic lineages gained appointments outside of family churches frequently enough to indicate that powerful secular families, like successful clerical kin groups,

---

[52] For prebends, see Brett, *English Church*, 188–9.

[53] For the diocese of Durham in the late twelfth century, see Scammell, *Hugh du Puiset*, 100. For later periods, see Lawrence, "English Parish," 654–5; Heath, *English Parish Clergy*, 135–7.

[54] See Chapter 4, section 1. For examples from the records of the royal courts and from the published volumes of episcopal acta, see Palgrave, ed., *Rotuli Curiæ Regis*, 2:175–6; *Curia Regis Rolls*, 2:305–6; 3:231; 4:49, 72–3, 185; 5:13; Cheney and Jones, eds., *English Episcopal Acta 2*, 75, 97; Cheney and John, eds., *English Episcopal Acta 3*, 252–3; Harper-Bill, ed., *English Episcopal Acta 6*, 163–4, 180–1, 346–7; Julia Barrow, ed., *English Episcopal Acta. 7, Hereford, 1079–1234* (Oxford, 1993), 26–7, 220–1; Falko Neininger, ed., *English Episcopal Acta. 15, London, 1076–1187* (Oxford, 1999), 115–16; Franklin, ed., *English Episcopal Acta 16*, 14–15; Franklin, ed., *English Episcopal Acta 17*, 41–3, 81–2; Joseph A. Gribbin and Martin Brett, eds., *English Episcopal Acta. 28, Canterbury, 1070–1136* (Oxford, 2004), 47.

[55] Farrer and Clay, eds., *Early Yorkshire Charters*, 8:103–4.

[56] Smith, ed., *English Episcopal Acta 4*, 8; M. G. Snape, ed., *English Episcopal Acta. 24, Durham, 1153–1195* (Oxford, 2002), 22–3, 52.

[57] J. C. Dickinson and P. T. Ricketts, "The Anglo-Norman Chronicle of Wigmore Abbey," *Transactions of the Woolhope Naturalists' Field Club* 39 (1969), 413–46, at 422–3. See also Barraclough, ed., *Charters of the Anglo-Norman Earls of Chester*, 357–9.

often used networks of influence to provide for their clerical members. Indeed, noble family ties could help one gain high rank in the Church. The poetic history of William Marshal made clear, in approving tones, that Richard I arranged for William's brother Henry to become bishop of Exeter as a favor to William.[58] Further down the clerical hierarchy, Julia Barrow has noted that members of prominent local landholding families could be found in the Hereford cathedral chapter.[59] The same was true at York, where several of the deans (Robert de Gant, Robert Butevilain, Hubert Walter, and Henry Marshal) came from landholding families, as did a number of canons.[60]

In fact, one aristocratic strategy for providing for family members was to place sons in the Church, as was common in many places and periods. Despite primogeniture, younger sons of landholding families generally ended up with some land if they remained among the laity, but Nigel of Whiteacre wrote of men giving up their claims to a stake in the family inheritance in return for receiving one and a half times the income they would otherwise have received through clerical benefices. Nigel even spoke of landholders granting benefices as a form of marriage portion for their daughters by appointing their sons-in-law to churches![61] Remarkably, the records of the royal courts reveal a couple of cases in which the advowson of a church was described as the "caput" or head of a family estate, in other words, its chief resource, and in one case the *eldest* son became the rector.[62] Aristocratic families placed sons in the church frequently enough to have a noticeable impact on patronage practices in the period.

The secular aristocracy, however, by no means dominated the Church. As David Crouch and Claire de Trafford have pointed out, bishops from comital or baronial families were rare in England in this period.[63] Barrow also pointed out that only a small minority of important families in the diocese of Hereford were represented in the cathedral chapter there and the same was true of the archdiocese of York. Conversely, canons of known aristocratic origin made up only a small percentage of those chapters.[64] Moreover, high birth might be only one factor in creating a successful clerical career: among the aristocratic deans of York both Robert de Gant

---

[58] Holden, Gregory, and Crouch, eds., *History of William Marshal*, 1:508–9; Crouch, *William Marshal*, 75, 80.

[59] Barrow, "Canons and Citizens of Hereford," 4–7.

[60] Other dignitaries and canons from landholding families included Reginald Arundel, Ralph de Kyme, Roger d'Aubigny, Nicholas de Trailli, Thomas de Reineville, Hamo de Valognes, Hasculf Paynel, Hugh de Gant, Lisiard de Musters, Roger de Cundi, probably both Williams of Bayeux I and II, and William de Percy: Greenway, *Fasti. 6. York*, 8–9, 14, 87, 99, 107, 121–2, 124, 128, 130, 132. No doubt I have missed some, particularly those coming from outside of Yorkshire.

[61] Nigel of Whiteacre, *Tractatus Contra Curiales*, 161–2. For younger sons receiving land, see David Crouch and Claire de Trafford, "The Forgotten Family in Twelfth-Century England," *Haskins Society Journal* 13 (2004), 41–63, at 42–53; Thomas, *Vassals, Heiresses, Crusaders, and Thugs*, 119–24.

[62] *Curia Regis Rolls*, 7:138, 322–4.

[63] Crouch and de Trafford, "Forgotten Family," 47.

[64] Barrow, "Canons and Citizens of Hereford," 6. Landholding families apparently had a greater presence in cathedral chapters later in the Middle Ages: Lepine, *A Brotherhood of Canons*, 48–54.

and Hubert Walter were also important royal clerics.[65] The scion of a powerful family could certainly expect to join the clerical elite but had no guarantee of rising to the greatest heights. For instance, few clerics could have been better placed by birth than Henry, a son of Geoffrey fitz Peter, earl of Essex and justiciar of England. Henry did become dean of Wolverhampton and a canon of Lincoln, and also received a church from Cirencester Abbey.[66] Quite likely he had other benefices as well. Even so, judging by the surviving evidence, he had a less successful career than another dean of Wolverhampton, Peter of Blois. Peter boasted of a noble Breton background, but his father had been an impoverished exile and Peter came at best from the fringes of the aristocracy. Indeed, in a letter he spoke of raising one of his sister's sons from "vile servitude to the title of liberty," which if taken literally would indicate marriage ties to a servile family.[67] Yet in the end Peter's clerical career outstripped that of his much better connected successor at Wolverhampton. Neither Henry nor Peter, of course, could remotely compete with the success of Thomas Becket, who may have had a kinship link with Archbishop Theobald, but rose from a prosperous urban family to become one of the richest and most powerful men in England. High birth was certainly not the only factor in determining the success or failure of a career, and though a fairly substantial minority of appointments probably went to clerics on the basis of birth alone, there were still plenty of appointments, including most of the greatest ones, that depended on other factors.

The clerical elite was therefore neither an entirely open nor an entirely closed group. Though many important clerics came either from the aristocracy or from elite clerical families, there was a perception that social mobility among the clergy was common, as noted in Chapter 3, and one can point to specific examples of highly successful clerics who may even have come from the peasantry. For instance, William of Wrotham, one of the great royal servants of John's reign, at one point claimed a half yoke of land in Kent held by his father, Godwin, in gavelkind tenure, suggesting that he came from the prosperous free peasantry.[68] Moorman has noted a number of examples of men of humble origin who became bishops later in the thirteenth century.[69]

How common were such success stories? Ralph Turner has argued that the phenomenon of kings raising their followers, whether laymen or clerics, "from the dust," to use Orderic Vitalis's phrase, was exaggerated by writers of the period, at least insofar as it implies that many originated as serfs or peasants.[70] No doubt critics did exaggerate the low birth of successful clerics of whom they disapproved,

[65] Richard Mylius Sherman, "Robert de Gant (c.1086–c.1158): Dean of York and King's Chancellor," *Haskins Society Journal* 13 (2004), 99–110; Cheney, *Hubert Walter*, 16–30; Charles R. Young, *Hubert Walter, Lord of Canterbury and Lord of England* (Durham, N.C., 1968), 11–22.

[66] Turner, *Men Raised from the Dust*, 68; Ross and Devine, eds., *Cartulary of Cirencester*, 2:339.

[67] Cotts, *Clerical Dilemma*, 17, 20; Stollberg, *Soziale Stellung*, 38–9; Peter of Blois, *Later Letters*, 39.

[68] *Curia Regis Rolls*, 6:75–6. Anglo-Saxon names such as Godwin were generally an indicator of low status by the generation of William's father.

[69] Moorman, *Church Life*, 25, 158–9.

[70] Turner, *Judges, Administrators*, 225–49; Turner, *English Judiciary*, 25–8, 93, 138, 141–2.

just as Henry II could allegedly describe Thomas Becket as the son of one of his peasants.[71] However, there were plenty of clerics among the clerical elites whose origins cannot be traced. What percentage of these might have been peasants is unclear, since even for knightly families genealogies are often fragmentary.[72] However, peasant origins would be the hardest to trace, meaning that there is a likely bias toward upper-class birth in what the surviving documentary sources reveal to us, and it may well be that complaints about the rise of peasants were not entirely propagandistic. Moreover, Turner would be the first to stress that clerics of bourgeois or minor knightly families could prosper dramatically in royal service.[73] Thus, clerical careers allowed for some movement into the elites and a good deal of movement within existing elites, and Barrow's comparative work suggests that the English clerical elite may have been more open than its German counterpart.[74] For all the benefits of good birth, there were therefore other routes to successful clerical careers.

3. ACQUIRING BENEFICES: LORDSHIP, SERVICE, AND FRIENDSHIP

Lordship and service were among the most obvious of these routes and the history of ecclesiastical patronage in the long twelfth century was closely connected to the development of secular and ecclesiastical institutions and bureaucracies. Lordship was, of course, already an important factor in patronage before the Norman Conquest, as shown by the success of the great pluralist Regenbald.[75] However, the demand for literate, skilled clerical followers grew strongly throughout the long twelfth century, and the needs of patrons ensured that to some degree the Church would be a meritocracy, although not always involving the precise merits reformers would have preferred. Bishops, abbots and abbesses, popes, secular magnates, and above all kings depended on ecclesiastical patronage to build up clerical followings, and the following pages will look at each sort of patron in turn.

The writings of C. R. Cheney and others on individual bishops, work on cathedral chapters, and the introductions of the *English Episcopal Acta* series have given us an increasingly detailed picture of episcopal households, which tended to

---

[71] Robertson and Sheppard, eds., *Materials*, 4:27–8.

[72] For instance, Richard of Ilchester's precise ancestry is uncertain, but a review of the fragmentary evidence suggests that he came from a prosperous knightly family: Virginia Darrow Oggins and Robin S. Oggins, "Richard of Ilchester's Inheritance: An Extended Family in Twelfth-Century England," *Medieval Prosopography* 12 (1991), 57–128.

[73] Turner, *Men Raised from the Dust*, 8. For the likely urban origin of some canons, see Barrow, "Canons and Citizens of Hereford," 5.

[74] Barrow, "Cathedrals, Provosts, and Prebends," 562, 564; Barrow, "Education and Recruitment," 117–38. For the high number of German bishops of aristocratic background, see Paul B. Pixton, *The German Episcopacy and the Implementation of the Decrees of the Fourth Lateran Council, 1216–1245: Watchmen on the Tower* (Leiden, 1995), 194–202.

[75] Keynes, "Regenbald the Chancellor [*sic*]," 194–7.

grow in size and sophistication over the course of the period and were generally dominated by clerics.[76] Bishops had various sources of patronage which they could use to attract and reward followers, including archdeaconries, rectories and vicarages, and in some cases cathedral prebends or prebends in collegiate churches.[77] Bishops' households were also attractive because bishops were themselves enmeshed in useful networks, from which their clerical followers, like their clerical kin, could benefit. For instance, service in the household of a bishop could occasionally be a stepping stone to a bishopric and more often provided an entrée into royal service.[78] Followers of bishops frequently held churches from monasteries, and though religious houses no doubt granted these voluntarily sometimes, since it paid to be on good terms with the bishop and his household, monastic complaints make it clear that bishops could apply pressure. Indeed, Thomas of Marlborough, chronicler and later abbot of Evesham, objected to visitations by bishops and archdeacons partly because, he claimed, they often involved the grants

---

[76] For episcopal households, see David M. Smith, ed., *English Episcopal Acta. 1, Lincoln, 1067–1185* (Oxford, 1980), xxxix–xlvii; Cheney and Jones, eds., *English Episcopal Acta 2*, xxiv–xxxii, lxxvii–lxxviii; Smith, ed., *English Episcopal Acta 4*, xxiii–xxviii; Janet E. Burton, ed., *English Episcopal Acta. 5, York, 1070–1154* (Oxford, 1988), xxxii–xxxvii; Harper-Bill, ed., *English Episcopal Acta 6*, xxxiv, xxxix–xlix; Barrow, ed., *English Episcopal Acta 7*, l–lx; Franklin, ed., *English Episcopal Acta 8*, lviii–lix; Nicholas Vincent, ed., *English Episcopal Acta. 9, Winchester, 1205–1238* (Oxford, 1994), xxxviii–xliii, 163–215; Ramsey, ed., *English Episcopal Acta 10*, xxxvii–lviii; Barlow, ed., *English Episcopal Acta 11*, lviii–lxx; M. J. Franklin, ed., *English Episcopal Acta. 14, Coventry and Lichfield, 1072–1159* (Oxford, 1997), lii–liii; Neininger, ed., *English Episcopal Acta 15*, l–li, lvii, lx; Franklin, ed., *English Episcopal Acta 16*, xxxv–xxxix; Franklin, ed., *English Episcopal Acta 17*, liii–lx; Kemp, ed., *English Episcopal Acta 18*, lxii–lxxxviii; Lovatt, ed., *English Episcopal Acta 20*, xxxiv–liv; Snape, ed., *English Episcopal Acta 24*, xxxix–xlviii; Johnson, ed., *English Episcopal Acta 26*, xxxix–lix; Lovatt, ed., *English Episcopal Acta 27*, xcvi–cxii; Gribbin and Brett, eds., *English Episcopal Acta 28*, xxxvii–xxix, xlvi–xlviii, lvi–lvii, lxxxi; Karn, ed., *English Episcopal Acta 31*, cvii–cxxii; Karn, ed., *English Episcopal Acta 42*, lxxiv–lxxviii; Cheney et al., eds., *English Episcopal Acta 33*, lvi–lxiii; Mary Cheney et al., eds., *English Episcopal Acta. 34, Worcester, 1186–1218* (Oxford, 2008), xliv–xlviii; Henry Mayr-Harting, ed., *The Acta of the Bishops of Chichester, 1075–1207*, Canterbury and York Record Series, 130 (Oxford, 1964), 6–25; Smith, ed., *Acta of Hugh of Wells*, xxxii; Barlow, *Thomas Becket*, 29–32, 77–9; Brett, *English Church*, 173–85; C. R. Cheney, *English Bishops' Chanceries, 1100–1250* (Manchester, 1950), 1–21; Cheney, *Hubert Walter*, 158–71; Cheney, *Roger, Bishop of Worcester*, 99–107; Kathleen Major, "The 'Familia' of Archbishop Stephen Langton," *English Historical Review* 48 (1933), 529–53; Scammell, *Hugh du Puiset*, 222–39; Burger, *Bishops, Clerks, and Diocesan Governance*.

[77] For rewards provided by bishops, see Cheney, *Hubert Walter*, 160–1, 165, 167; Barrow, "Canons and Citizens of Hereford," 7; Barrow, "Origins and Careers," 37–40; Cheney, *Roger, Bishop of Worcester*, 105–6; Crosby, *Bishop and Chapter*, 264, 298, 309; Scammell, *Hugh du Puiset*, 100, 145–6, 235–7; Smith, "Hugh's Administration," 31; Young, *Hubert Walter*, 64, 78–9; Smith, ed., *English Episcopal Acta 1*, xlvi–xlvii; Smith, ed., *English Episcopal Acta 4*, xxv; Harper-Bill, ed., *English Episcopal Acta 6*, xxxix, xlviii–xlix; Barrow, ed., *English Episcopal Acta 7*, li–lx; Ramsey, ed., *English Episcopal Acta 10*, xliv–xlv, li, lvi–lviii; Barlow, ed., *English Episcopal Acta 11*, lviii, lxvii–lxviii; Franklin, ed., *English Episcopal Acta 16*, xxxix; Kemp, ed., *English Episcopal Acta 18*, lxviii, lxxi, lxiv; Johnson, ed., *English Episcopal Acta 26*, xliv; Cheney et al., eds., *English Episcopal Acta 34*, xlv; Smith, ed., *Acta of Hugh of Wells*, xxxii–xxxiii; Major, "Familia," 534; Burger, *Bishops, Clerks, and Diocesan Governance*, 23–135.

[78] Bartlett, *England under the Norman and Angevin Kings*, 396–400; Brett, *English Church*, 181–2; Judith A. Green, *The Government of England under Henry I* (Cambridge, 1986), 168; Saltman, *Theobald, Archbishop of Canterbury*, 165.

of revenues, including benefices.[79] Episcopal households would obviously have been magnets for ambitious clerics.

As the administration of the greatest monasteries and nunneries became more complex, abbots, abbesses, and even obedientiaries also employed increasing numbers of clerics. Great monasteries tended to have an enormous amount of patronage over parish churches, and despite their efforts to divert parish income to their own support, and their need to share the fruits of their patronage with other powerful figures, they still had plenty of rich benefices to support clerics of their own. Abbot Samson, for instance, gathered a number of learned masters around him, judging by their attestations of his charters: Masters Stephen, Ranulf, Gilbert of Walsham, Hervey of St. Edmund, Osbert, and Roger of Walsingham. Masters Stephen and Roger of Walsingham both received vicarages from Bury. Master Ranulf was almost certainly the parson of Westley (a Bury church) to whom Samson also gave land.[80] Similarly, Abbot William of St. Benet of Holme appointed Thomas of Ludham to three churches and Abbot Ralph appointed Thomas of Walton to one church; the two men were among the most assiduous witnesses to abbey charters and were also members of a clerical family that had had longstanding ties to the monastery.[81] Emma Mason has provided a good discussion of Westminster's clerical households, but more work needs to be done on the clerical households of heads of religious houses.[82] Nonetheless, service to powerful abbots and abbesses was clearly another route to success for ambitious clerics.

Judging by the surviving evidence, the use of papal provisions to support papal relatives and followers with English resources was only a minor aspect of twelfth-century English patronage, though it became more common during Innocent III's papacy and expanded thereafter.[83] Admittedly, the evidence is somewhat contradictory: Abbot Samson's seven papal letters for benefices, for instance, would suggest a stronger papal influence earlier on.[84] However, this might be explained by the fact that popes sometimes wrote on behalf of English clerics who had impressed them, but were not their own officials. Thus, Alexander III unsuccessfully sought a prebend at Lincoln for Master David of London.[85] Strikingly, when

---

[79] Thomas of Marlborough, *History of Evesham*, 258–9. See also Burger, *Bishops, Clerks, and Diocesan Governance*, 175–81.

[80] All these masters attested at least five of the abbot's charters: Davis, ed., *Kalendar of Abbot Samson*, 95–6, 113; Harper-Bill, ed., *English Episcopal Acta 6*, 138–9; Jocelin of Brakelond, *Chronicle*, 79–80.

[81] West, ed., *St. Benet of Holme*, 1:56, 66, 102; 2:229, 240.

[82] Mason, *Westminster Abbey and its People*, 98–9, 105–10. Clerics may have been particularly important in the households of abbesses. At Shaftesbury, Abbess Maria had a number of chaplains and other clerics who attested her charters regularly; N. E. Stacy, ed., *Charters and Custumals of Shaftesbury Abbey, 1089–1216* (Oxford, 2006), 20–1, 43–59.

[83] For the development of papal provisions and their early use in England, see Pennington, *Pope and Bishops*, 115–53; Cheney, *From Becket to Langton*, 78–82, 178–81. The papal legates Pandulf and Guala, who took up duties in England in 1211 and 1216 respectively, seem to have expanded the use of papal provisions: Harper-Bill, "Struggle for Benefices," 128; Vincent, ed., *Letters and Charters of Cardinal Guala Bicchieri*, lxvii–lxxiv. Ralph Turner has suggested to me, in a personal communication, that John's submission to papal overlordship may have been important in encouraging papal provisions.

[84] Gransden, *History of Bury St Edmunds*, 81–2.

[85] Liverani, ed., *Spicilegium Liberianum*, 545–6.

Robert Pullen became a cardinal in the 1140s, his archdeaconry of Rochester and several churches passed to his nephew, suggesting that the use of English benefices to support even an English cardinal still seemed inappropriate or impractical.[86] Under Alexander III, one does begin to see papal notaries and relatives receiving English revenues, but only a handful of cases can be found in the surviving evidence.[87] Innocent III was more insistent.[88] Indeed, during his reign the chapter at York became a favored source of benefices for the papal court, so much so that King John, in order to increase pressure against the papacy during his struggle over the archbishopric of Canterbury, had the revenues of the "Romans and Lombards" at York confiscated well before he began confiscating other church revenues.[89] Elsewhere, however, papal favorites hardly make an appearance in English chapters even in the early thirteenth century.[90] Service to the papacy was never a likely option for most English clerics, so from their perspective the most important point about papal patronage was that it should not crowd them out from benefices they might otherwise have acquired.

Studies of individual secular magnates or families and their documents have shed light on the clerical patronage of great lords.[91] Though lay households generally had a smaller clerical component than episcopal households, as one would expect, most great lords had a few chaplains and clerics in their service. Secular magnates gave land to their clerics more frequently, as a percentage of their gifts, than ecclesiastical magnates and the king did, but they naturally made heavy use of ecclesiastical patronage. Thus, clerics of the earls of Chester, including William Barbedavril, a member of their favorite clerical family, and Patrick, son of one of the most important comital clerics, Peter, held churches from the earls or from St. Werburgh's, Chester, which had been founded by the earls.[92] Few clerics can have received anything like the thirty churches Robert fitz Hamo gave his cleric Robert early in the twelfth century, but service to great secular lords must often have been a route

[86] Adams and Donahue, eds., *Select Cases*, 43–4.

[87] Cheney and Jones, eds., *English Episcopal Acta 2*, 64–7; Holtzmann, ed., *Papsturkunden*, 3:301–2; Holtzmann and Kemp, eds., *Papal Decretals Relating to Lincoln*, 50–1.

[88] This apparent shift, however, may owe something to an increase in records. For requests and other references to clerics with papal connections holding benefices in England, see Cheney and Cheney, eds., *Letters of Pope Innocent III*, 13–14, 36, 50, 57, 74–5, 82, 86, 101–4, 107, 111, 119, 133, 152.

[89] Greenway, *Fasti. 6. York*, 34, 85, 89–90; Hardy, ed., *Rotuli Litterarum Clausarum*, 90a; Lovatt, ed., *English Episcopal Acta 27*, lxvii n. 208.

[90] For some exceptions, see Diana E. Greenway, *Fasti Ecclesiae Anglicanae, 1066–1300. 3. Lincoln* (London, 1977), 65, 122–3; Diana E. Greenway, *Fasti Ecclesiae Anglicanae, 1066–1300. 5. Chichester* (London, 1996), 60–1; Diana E. Greenway, *Fasti Ecclesiae Anglicanae, 1066–1300. 7. Bath and Wells* (London, 2001), 71; Julia Barrow, *Fasti Ecclesiae Anglicanae, 1066–1300. 8. Hereford* (London, 2002), 96.

[91] Crouch, *Beaumont Twins*, 82, 148–55; Crouch, *William Marshal*, 155–7; K. J. Stringer, *Earl David of Huntingdon, 1152–1219: A Study in Anglo-Scottish History* (Edinburgh, 1985), 151–3; Patterson, ed., *Earldom of Gloucester Charters*, 9–16; Greenway, ed., *Charters of the Honour of Mowbray*, lxv–lxvii; Robert Bearman, ed., *Charters of the Redvers Family and the Earldom of Devon, 1090–1217*, Devon and Cornwall Record Society, n.s. vol. 37 (Exeter, 1994), 37, 39; J. F. A. Mason, "The Officers and Clerks of the Norman Earls of Shropshire," *Transactions of the Shropshire Archaeological Society* 56 (1957–60), 244–57.

[92] Barraclough, ed., *Charters of the Anglo-Norman Earls of Chester*, 174, 179, 200, 218–19, 232–3, 283–4, 357–61.

to obtaining one or more rich churches.[93] Some of the greatest magnates could also make appointments to the secular colleges founded by their families: as late as John's reign a cleric of the count of Eu held a prebend at the collegiate church of Hastings.[94] As with the households of ecclesiastical magnates, those of secular magnates could serve as a gateway to greater things. Thus, Richard de Belmeis I passed from the household of the earl of Shropshire to that of Henry I through a timely change of allegiance during the earl's failed revolt, and gained the bishopric of London from the king.[95] Similarly, Hugh de Mapenor served in the household of William de Braose, became dean of Hereford after King John made Giles de Braose bishop there, and then succeeded Giles in the bishopric.[96]

Over the course of the early and mid-twelfth century, secular magnates surrendered much of their ecclesiastical patronage by converting collegiate churches into religious houses and granting churches to monasteries. However, many magnate lineages continued to value patronage, and others gained a renewed appreciation for it. The chronicle of Walden Abbey reveals that Earl William de Mandeville, after inheriting the earldom in 1166, complained that because his father had granted all of the family's nearly twenty churches to Walden, he had no benefices for his own clerics. However, as the result of a deal with the monastery, he gained the right to make appointments to seven churches, and his successor, the justiciar Geoffrey fitz Peter, obtained rights to make appointments at nine churches.[97] Frequent advowson cases between magnates and their family monasteries may reflect similar regrets, probably prompted partly by a growing recognition of the utility of educated clerics within baronial administrations. Despite the early shift of patronage rights away from magnates, great secular households remained a locus for clerical advancement.

That the greatest single patronage machine belonged to the king will come as no surprise; many scholars have studied royal appointments and the rewards royal clerics received.[98] Above all, kings controlled the vast majority of appointments to

---

[93] Patterson, ed., *Earldom of Gloucester Charters*, 161–2; Brett, *English Church*, 217–18.

[94] Crouch, *Beaumont Twins*, 197; Mason, "Officers and Clerks," 252–3; Fonge, ed., *Cartulary of St Mary's*, xxix–xxx, 11–12, 425–6, 455; Hardy, ed., *Rotuli Litterarum Patentium*, 59.

[95] Mason, "Officers and Clerks," 253–5; Green, *Government of England*, 135, 168.

[96] Barrow, ed., *English Episcopal Acta 7*, xlv–xlvii.

[97] Greenway and Watkiss, eds., *Foundation of Walden Monastery*, xxv, xxxi–xxxii, 46–7, 50–1, 184–6. For the dismay of a lesser lord at the loss of patronage, despite his own confirmation, see B. R. Kemp, ed., *Reading Abbey Cartularies: British Library Manuscripts, Egerton 3031, Harley 1708, and Cotton Vespasian E XXV*, 2 vols., Camden Society, 4th ser., vols. 31, 33 (London, 1986–7), 2:90–1.

[98] Barlow, *English Church, 1066–1154*, 54–103; Bartlett, *England under the Norman and Angevin Kings*, 396–7; Brett, *English Church*, 106–12, 201, 217; Stephanie Mooers Christelow, "Chancellors and Curial Bishops: Ecclesiastical Promotions and Power in Anglo-Norman England," *Anglo-Norman Studies* 22 (2000), 49–69; Green, *Government of England*, 166–7, 173–6; Sidney Painter, *The Reign of King John* (Baltimore, 1949), 62–6, 80, 199–200, 205; Stollberg, *Soziale Stellung*, 73–110; Türk, *Nugae curialium*, 26–9, 40–51; Turner, *Judges, Administrators*, 192–3; Turner, *Men Raised from the Dust*, 7–8, 24–5, 95–6; Turner, *English Judiciary*, 51–64, 107–21, 171–80, 297. For the careers of some particularly successful royal clerics, see Edward J. Kealey, *Roger of Salisbury, Viceroy of England* (Berkeley, 1972); Cheney, *Hubert Walter*; Charles Duggan, "Richard of Ilchester, Royal Servant and Bishop," in *Canon Law in Medieval England: The Becket Dispute and Decretal Collections* (London, 1982), 1–21; R. W. Southern, *Medieval Humanism and Other Studies* (Oxford, 1970), 183–205; Young,

bishoprics, which they often used to reward their clerical followers, who could in turn reward their own clerical subordinates with the benefices that came into their gift. Kings also used appointments to various collegiate churches, most notably St. Martin-le-Grand in London, to support royal clerics.[99] Though kings, like magnates, gave away many of the churches on their lands, even in the thirteenth century King John still had many parish churches and chapels in his gift. Custody of the heirs of secular magnates and vacancies in bishoprics and abbeys also brought in a flood of appointments to churches, offices, and prebends. For instance, the lucrative benefice worth forty marks that Walter Map received from Henry II was actually a Westminster church.[100] Moreover, kings had even greater opportunities than most powerful people did to persuade or pressure other patrons to accept their candidates, and various sources refer to benefices being granted at a royal request.[101] In particular, the judicial power of the kings enhanced royal influence; King John settled one dispute over an advowson between a monastery and magnate by persuading both to accept his own nominee and then used the justices of the bench to make a hesitant archdeacon push the process through.[102] The biographer of Hugh of Avalon, bishop of Lincoln, emphasized that he at least resisted royal requests for benefices for the king's favorites, but the courage and steadfastness required was seen as one of the characteristics that made Hugh a saint.[103] A couple of legal cases even refer to clerics resigning benefices out of fear of the king, in at least one instance almost certainly to make way for a royal favorite.[104] Thus kings had many avenues by which to reward their clerical favorites using ecclesiastical revenues.

For most kings, as for other patrons, one can only patch together a rough picture of ecclesiastical patronage, but new forms of royal record keeping allow a somewhat more systematic exploration of the subject for King John's reign. The patent rolls recorded many grants of benefices to clerics, with the charter rolls adding a smaller number to the total and the close rolls adding a handful of appointments to prebends.[105] Together, these rolls record presentations to roughly 325 posts in

---

Hubert Walter, Richardson, "William of Ely," 45–90; Nicholas Vincent, *Peter des Roches: An Alien in English Politics, 1205–1238* (Cambridge, 1996); Barrow, *Who Served the Altar at Brixworth?*, 15–26.

[99] For the early history of some of the royal collegiate churches, later called royal free chapels, see Denton, *English Royal Free Chapels*. For St. Martin-le-Grand, see Caroline M. Barron and Matthew Davies, eds., *The Religious Houses of London and Middlesex* (London, 2007), 196–206. For the use of prebends in collegiate churches for royal officials, see A. Hamilton Thompson, "The Deans and Canons of Bridgnorth," *Archaeological Journal* 84 (1927), 24–87, at 25–30; W. R. Jones, "Patronage and Administration: The King's Free Chapels in Medieval England," *Journal of British Studies* 9 (1969), 1–23.

[100] *Curia Regis Rolls*, 6:93.

[101] For instance, Greenway and Watkiss, eds., *Foundation of Walden Monastery*, 26–7; Cheney, *Roger, Bishop of Worcester*, 355–6; Brown, ed., *Eye Priory Cartulary and Charters*, 1:19; Hardy, ed., *Rotuli Litterarum Clausarum*, 84b; Hardy, ed., *Rotuli Litterarum Patentium*, 1a, 64a; Mason, *Westminster Abbey and its People*, 57, 337–8, 340; Türk, *Nugae curialium*, 45.

[102] *Curia Regis Rolls*, 2:191.

[103] Adam of Eynsham, *Magna Vita Sancti Hugonis*, 1:114–15.

[104] Cheney, *Roger, Bishop of Worcester*, 351; Cheney and Semple, eds., *Selected Letters of Innocent III*, 15.

[105] Hardy, ed., *Rotuli Litterarum Patentium*; Hardy, ed., *Rotuli Litterarum Clausarum*; Hardy, ed., *Rotuli Chartarum*.

parish churches, with at least 175 of these appointments being in the king's gift because of vacancies, custodies, escheats, and seizures of estates.[106] In addition, they record John as making appointments to thirty-nine prebends and three deaneries in collegiate churches. Finally, vacancies of bishoprics allowed John to make appointments to twenty-eight cathedral prebends, five cathedral offices, and nine archdeaconries. Of course, these figures represent only a small percentage of the thousands of benefices that would have come open in John's reign, and not all of the appointments necessarily survived legal challenges from competing patrons. Moreover, the interdict meant that John may had more appointments due to vacancies than usual. However, the records of royal appointments are clearly incomplete. The patent rolls only began in the third year of John's reign, and the rolls for three later years are missing. The charter rolls include many duplicate records of appointments made in the patent rolls but some that were not, showing gaps even in the surviving patent rolls. Moreover, John sometimes assigned his patronage to others. For instance, no appointments to St. Martin-le-Grand appear in the surviving rolls, probably because when John made Richard Briger dean, he granted him the right to appoint to the prebends.[107] Most important, these figures do not factor in the informal ways in which kings could exploit patronage belonging to other figures. Thus, no other figure in the kingdom could have come close to matching the king's ecclesiastical patronage network, even if one were to set aside his crucial ability to make appointments to bishoprics.

Unfortunately, the value of benefices granted by the king was rarely recorded. One church was worth only three marks, though the fact that King John forgot whether he had granted it or not suggests he was more accustomed to dealing with richer prizes.[108] Fortunately, the patent and charter rolls also contain promises of unspecified benefices or collections of benefices worth certain amounts, sometimes with an anticipatory pension, which may provide a good idea of the kinds of incomes the king and his officials expected to be able to provide. Thirty-four such promises were made, of which three were for benefices of less than ten marks, nineteen for ones of ten to twenty marks, eight for ones of thirty to fifty marks, and four for ones of 100 marks. In addition, in the aftermath of the interdict, John was paying a number of large pensions to figures at Rome, and he hoped to convert three of these, of thirty, fifty, and 100 marks, to benefices.[109] The fact that John had to make such anticipatory promises shows that even his wealthy patronage network could not always keep up with demand. Nonetheless, the king could assume that he would be able to regularly grant benefices providing an aristocratic income. Thus, King John sent a message to his favorite, William of Wrotham, ordering him to hand over a church to an even greater favorite, Peter des Roches, bishop of

---

[106] Because some entries are not clear the figures must be approximate. The appointments the king held through vacancies and custodies came in roughly equal portions from bishoprics, monasteries, and secular landholders.

[107] Westminster Abbey Archives, Charter 13155. For similar arrangements, see Hardy, ed., *Rotuli Litterarum Patentium*, 40a, 43a.

[108] Hardy, ed., *Rotuli Litterarum Patentium*, 119b, 121a.

[109] Hardy, ed., *Rotuli Litterarum Clausarum*, 180a. See also Hardy, ed., *Rotuli Chartarum*, 73b.

Winchester, "for by the grace of God we are and will be powerful enough to provide you an equivalent or richer benefice." Indeed, William shortly thereafter received a prebend at the collegiate church of Hastings, one of two such collegiate prebends and seven churches granted to him in the patent rolls.[110]

How did John use the extensive patronage at his command? Much went to reward prominent royal servants like William and Peter. For instance, Walter de Grey, John's chancellor, was one of those who was promised a vacancy of 100 marks, and received the archdeaconry of Totnes, a collegiate prebend, and all or part of at least five churches, in addition to the profits of his office, before he became bishop of Worcester in 1214.[111] The king also used benefices to reward less exalted members of his bureaucracy, such as clerics of his chamber, as well as clerics such as Master Henry of Hereford and Jacob of the Temple who served in the king's chapel.[112] The clerics of important ecclesiastical and secular administrators also received royal largesse. Even a cleric of Bishop Peter des Roches, whose patron dispensed plenty of benefices of his own, could receive a church from the king.[113] Secular administrators, who were less likely than clerical ones to control ecclesiastical patronage, often depended on the king to reward their clerical underlings. At least six different clerics of William Briwerre received a total of eight benefices or promises of benefices from the king.[114] Sometimes, the king rewarded secular followers by giving benefices to their kin: William Briwerre also obtained benefices for two nephews.[115] In addition, John used patronage as a diplomatic tool, rewarding the clerics of figures as diverse as the Emperor Otto, the counts of Flanders and Boulogne, and Llewelyn of Wales, no doubt to gain goodwill.[116] John was particularly intent on gaining favor in Rome, especially after the interdict.[117] He even seems to have used English benefices to try to buy support in Poitou in 1214. In a letter to Peter des Roches, describing his promise of 100 marks in benefices to a Poitevin cleric, Hugh, brother of Geoffrey de Taunay, John wrote that Hugh's friends were very necessary to the king and that he needed their gratitude.[118] Thus, John used his patronage for a variety of purposes, though the chief of them was to support and reward royal administrators and bureaucrats.

Though kinship and lordship were the two major sorts of personal ties that either directly or indirectly determined patronage, friendship also mattered, as King John's promise to Hugh de Taunay indicates. Friendship was a crucial social

---

[110] Hardy, ed., *Rotuli Litterarum Patentium*, 58a, 60a, 68a, 69b, 105b, 106a.

[111] Hardy, ed., *Rotuli Litterarum Patentium*, 58b, 64a, 71b, 75a, 81a, 96b, 102a, 102b. For Walter's successor, Richard Marsh, see Painter, *Reign of King John*, 65.

[112] Hardy, ed., *Rotuli Litterarum Patentium*, 16b, 21b, 58b, 67a, 130a; Hardy, ed., *Rotuli Litterarum Clausarum*, 51b, 62b, 71a, 82a, 183b.

[113] Hardy, ed., *Rotuli Litterarum Patentium*, 89a. For examples of the clerics of prominent royal clerics who were not or not yet bishops receiving benefices, see Hardy, ed., *Rotuli Litterarum Patentium*, 28a, 49a, 69b, 87a.

[114] Hardy, ed., *Rotuli Litterarum Patentium*, 28a, 31b, 75b, 81b, 90b, 111a, 163a.

[115] Hardy, ed., *Rotuli Litterarum Patentium*, 120a.

[116] Hardy, ed., *Rotuli Litterarum Patentium*, 73b, 78b, 89a, 111a, 120b–121a.

[117] Hardy, ed., *Rotuli Litterarum Patentium*, 107a–b, 111a, 117b, 120a, 123b, 126a, 151a, 158b.

[118] John also granted a benefice to a Lusignan cleric; Hardy, ed., *Rotuli Litterarum Patentium*, 113b, 116a, 117a.

institution for the clergy that I will explore more fully in Chapter 8, but here it will be useful to describe its role in patronage. Though William fitz Stephen claimed a kinship tie between Thomas Becket and Archbishop Theobald, he also noted that it was two clerical brothers, frequent guests at the home of Thomas's father, who actually introduced him into Theobald's household. Once there, according to another biographer, Thomas made a pact with two other members of the household, Roger of Neustria and John of Canterbury, to provide mutual support in seeking benefices.[119] It is unclear how big a factor this pact was in the eminently successful careers of the three men (Roger became archbishop of York and John became bishop of Poitou and archbishop of Lyon), especially since Roger soon became an enemy of Thomas, but certainly the three ambitious clerics (or the biographer) thought such a pact would be useful.

Friendship helped clerics seeking benefices in two ways. First, successful clerics who became ecclesiastical magnates might repay friends. Jocelin of Brakelond described how Abbot Samson used his patronage to repay old debts from when he himself had been a secular cleric. He granted the first vacancy during his abbacy to the son of a man who had served him in his youth, granted another benefice to the son of a cleric and master who had admitted him to his school for free out of charity, and granted a third to a chaplain who had helped support his studies at Paris.[120] Second, friendship could be invoked in lobbying powerful people for benefices. For instance, Archbishop Theobald, in a letter written on his behalf by John of Salisbury, which urged Bishop Alfred of Worcester to accede to papal and royal requests to grant churches to one Master Solomon, stressed the latter's claims of friendship upon Alfred.[121] Gilbert Foliot, writing to ask Archbishop Rotrou of Rouen to settle a dispute over a benefice for Ranulf son of Erchemar, emphasized longstanding friendship between them.[122] Friendship worked much like kinship in the quest for benefices, and Jocelin of Brakelond in fact described Abbot Samson as treating his old connections like kin, in contrast to his biological relatives, who had only recognized their kinship once Samson became powerful. In one of Gilbert Foliot's letters to Robert Chesney on behalf of a relative, he deftly combined friendship with kinship, stating floridly that he wrote "in the experience of love, nay rather the favor (*gratia*) of every friendship," asking him to support "our relative and friend."[123] Though friendship was less important than kinship or lordship in the patronage system, the ambitious cleric was still wise to cultivate a strong friendship network.

It is crucial to emphasize just how important it was for clerics to achieve the best possible placement in various networks of influence when seeking to gain and keep patronage. The importance of connections is especially apparent in disputes. When Godfrey de Lucy, early in his career, brought a case against Battle Abbey for a benefice, Abbot Odo only reluctantly opposed him, fearing to offend various powerful men, including Henry II, who had presented Godfrey to the benefice

---

[119] Robertson and Sheppard, eds., *Materials*, 1:4; 3:15.
[120] Jocelin of Brakelond, *Chronicle*, 43–4.   [121] John of Salisbury, *Letters*, 1:151–2.
[122] Gilbert Foliot, *Letters and Charters*, 324.   [123] Gilbert Foliot, *Letters and Charters*, 146.

during a vacancy at the abbey, Archbishop Richard, who had accepted the appointment, and above all Godfrey's father, Richard de Lucy, the justiciar. When the abbot went looking for an advocate, various notable clerics, including Gerard la Pucelle, John of Salisbury, and even Odo's friend Bishop Bartholomew of Exeter, found reasons to turn him down, though Gerard later relented and helped the abbot gain a compromise. Because of his backers, the young Godfrey was a formidable opponent even for the head of a powerful Benedictine house.[124] Similarly, a detailed letter of Gerald of Wales to Hugh of Avalon reveals his struggles to gain an appointment to, and enjoy the profits from, a church in the diocese of Lincoln against the great royal cleric William de Sainte-Mère-Eglise. Gerald fumed that preference for courtiers was wrong, a stance which Bishop Hugh supported, but in the end Gerald, despite having his own networks of connections, was outmatched. According to him, William, as vicar, received twenty marks or more from the church, while he himself received no more than four and a half as rector.[125]

Of course, the importance of networks meant that the influence and power of clerics often depended on the goodwill of others, especially powerful patrons. After Henry II's favorite Ralph of Tamworth bombarded two successive abbots of Abingdon with requests and letters from the king, the pope, and great magnates in order to retain a benefice that the abbey wanted to recover, Abbot Walkelin went to the king, aroused his anger against Ralph by convincing him that Ralph was acting deceitfully, and thereby forced Ralph to give up his claim.[126] Ralph was a powerful figure only so long as the king backed him. Clerics could only gain an independent power base with some important office, such as an archdeaconry or the deanery of a cathedral, and even then remained dependent on the favor of others if they wished to gain a yet higher office. Though the building of networks depended on the efforts of clerics themselves to cultivate whatever ties they could, it was also dependent on others, and of course when it came to the very important ties of kinship, accidents of birth were crucial, though it was up to the clerics to make effective use of the kin ties that fortune had presented them.

Dependent as they were, however, the power and possibilities provided by networks of influence, once one was ensconced in them, could be formidable. Indeed, clerics were often freely offered benefices and pensions by patrons who wanted to tap into their networks. In one such case, Pope Alexander III ruled that the practice smacked of simony, but that did not prevent others from employing it.[127] Thus, St. Albans regained an advowson after a complicated dispute partly by offering appointment to two-thirds of the church to the royal favorite, Richard of Ilchester, and similarly the chronicler of Meaux Abbey claimed that the regular canons of Nostell had offered a church to a married clerical sheriff of Yorkshire in

---

[124] Searle, ed., *The Chronicle of Battle Abbey*, 320–4. For a good discussion of some of the revealing patronage disputes in which Battle Abbey was involved, see Harper-Bill, "Battle Abbey and its Churches," 159–72.

[125] Gerald of Wales, *Opera*, 1:259–68.

[126] Hudson, ed., *Historia Ecclesie Abbendonensis*, 2:244–5.

[127] Duggan, "Decretals of Alexander III," 122.

order to strengthen his support in a dispute with Meaux.[128] In a third case, a cleric complained to the pope that he had been presented to a church and then pushed aside when the patron decided to improve his chances of holding it by presenting it to another cleric who was already "well endowed with prebends and churches."[129]

4. ACQUIRING BENEFICES: MORALS AND EDUCATION

The discussion of patronage so far would seem to support Nigel of Whiteacre's depiction of a patronage system that was thoroughly corrupt and depended purely on the money, practical skills, and personal connections of clerics rather than their religious credentials. There can indeed be no doubt that the system of appointments fell far short of the ideals of reformers, and that men often received benefices for worldly reasons. However, the evidence is also biased towards showing non-religious reasons for patronage. Our sources almost never reveal in detail why patrons selected their nominees for benefices. When the king picked a cleric active in the royal administration for multiple benefices or when nobles appointed relatives to their family churches, one can reasonably infer that lordship or kinship prompted the appointment. Nonetheless, even in these cases, one cannot assume that religious motives and qualifications were entirely absent. A noble father who granted a benefice to a son might be helping him fulfill a genuine vocation. Gilbert of Sempringham, who eventually founded a monastic order and ended up as a saint, started out as priest in two of his father's churches.[130] Royal clerics such as John of Salisbury, Peter of Blois, and Gerald of Wales might also be reformers. Moreover, for the vast majority of appointments, no connections between the patron and the appointee can be found. Were our evidence fuller, no doubt worldly connections would become clear in many cases, but even so the possibility must remain that patrons often chose appointees primarily on religious grounds. Despite pressures from powerful figures, Abbot Odo of Battle ultimately appointed to the local parish church a young deacon noted for his morals and devoted to his studies. According to the abbey chronicler, after the deacon was raised to the priesthood, he taught by "word and example," became a model to his flock, and worked to instill virtue in all. In short, he performed precisely as moralists said a priest should.[131] Even where the motives of patrons may have been partly worldly, religious vocation, learning, and morality could also have been among the factors they considered.

Certainly contemporaries had at least to acknowledge religious considerations, as the many letters recommending individuals for benefices or for other considerations reveal. When Gilbert Foliot wrote to Archbishop Theobald asking the prelate to admit Gilbert's "relative and friend" Richard Belmeis II into a benefice, he wrote of

---

[128] Thomas Walsingham, *Gesta Abbatum Monasterii Sancti Albani*, ed. Henry T. Riley, 2 vols. (London, 1867–9), 1:123–4; Thomas de Burton, *Chronica Monasterii de Melsa*, 1:323–5.

[129] Duggan, "Decretals of Alexander III," 145.

[130] Raymonde Foreville and Gillian Keir, eds., *The Book of St Gilbert* (Oxford, 1987), 16–17.

[131] Admittedly, this was after the abbot tried to appoint a relative, whom the chronicler also described as a worthy appointee: Searle, ed., *The Chronicle of Battle Abbey*, 312–19.

Richard's *scientia* and *mores*. When he wrote subsequently to the pope in support of Richard's elevation to the bishopric of London, he did mention his elevated birth (*stirps generosa*) but also stressed his laudable life and learning. The stress on an individual's learning and character appears again and again not only in Gilbert's letters but in those of Thomas Becket, John of Salisbury, Bartholomew of Exeter, Peter of Blois, and Gerald of Wales.[132] Master David of London, who worked at the papal court on behalf of Gilbert Foliot, the king, and others, obtained a whole sheaf of letters from figures at the papal court attesting to his good character, learning, and eloquence.[133] Even King John, when orchestrating the elections of bishops or deans, would speak of the character and learning of the candidate.[134] Clearly these letters were designed precisely to address the demand, found repeatedly in the writings of reformers, that a priest or cleric should combine learning with a good life or character.

One sees almost a mirror world from different genres. From sermons and moralizing treatises, one could gain the impression that clerics were all badly educated sinners, while the twelfth-century "recommendation letters" would suggest a clergy that was uniformly learned and thoroughly virtuous. Obviously, we must treat the impressions provided by both genres with care. There is a formulaic quality to the praise of character and learning used so often to recommend clerics. A standardized letter in a formulary for bishops' scribes, introducing a cleric entering a new diocese to its bishop, refers to the bearer as "splendidly equipped (*ornatus*) with morals and virtuous in life."[135] Wording very similar to the first half of this appears in a letter of King John concerning the attempted elevation of Hugh Foliot to the bishopric of St. David's.[136] In 1214, the papal legate reported that the chapter at Lichfield had considered an election but accepted the king's nomination of Ralph Neville, "a learned and upright man and of good report," because of his reputation and to keep the king's favor.[137] Was the commendation of the learning and character of Ralph, a prominent royal cleric and member of an important administrative family, simply a deceptive cover for submitting to the king's will? Hugh of Lincoln, when seeking candidates of "proven morals and erudition (*doctrina*)" certainly felt he got many false recommendations due to kinship or friendship.[138] Yet not all recommendations were shams. One of Gilbert Foliot's concerned the chronicler Ralph of Diceto, who was certainly learned and who later

---

[132] Gilbert Foliot, *Letters and Charters*, 38–9, 73–4, 137–8, 157, 316, 341; Duggan, ed., *Correspondence of Thomas Becket*, 1:230–1; John of Salisbury, *Letters*, 1:85; 2:784–5, 800–3; Peter of Blois, *Later Letters*, 68; Gerald of Wales, *Opera*, 1:249.

[133] Liverani, ed., *Spicilegium Liberianum*, 544–5, 671, 735–6, 739–42, 751, 759–60, 767–8.

[134] Hardy, ed., *Rotuli Litterarum Clausarum*, 202b, 203a; Hardy, ed., *Rotuli Litterarum Patentium*, 139b.

[135] Lambeth Palace, MS 105, fo. 271v.

[136] Hardy, ed., *Rotuli Litterarum Clausarum*, 203a. Foliot failed to get this bishopric, but received Hereford a few years later.

[137] H. E. Savage, ed., *The Great Register of Lichfield Cathedral known as Magnum Registrum Album*, William Salt Archaeological Society Collections (Kendal, 1926), 341. For similar comments about Richard Briwerre, nephew of William, when presented by Bishop John of Exeter to the chapter, see Exeter Cathedral Archives, Dean and Chapter Charter 611.

[138] Adam of Eynsham, *Magna Vita Sancti Hugonis*, 2:97–8.

labored hard on behalf of St. Paul's, and a letter of Gerald of Wales was for Robert Grosseteste, who became one of England's greatest intellectuals and reformers.[139] Their recommendations followed standard formulas about character, life, and learning, but in these cases there was nothing hollow about the praise.

One can point, moreover, to instances in which the ideals of the Church influenced appointments. Hugh of Lincoln did largely refuse to appoint royal clerics, as his biographer, Adam of Eynsham, claimed, and this lends credence to Adam's other claims, echoed by Gerald of Wales, about Hugh's careful selection of learned and virtuous clerics.[140] A letter of John of Salisbury to Thomas Becket, then chancellor, over competing candidates to the bishopric of Exeter, shows that John certainly hoped learning would make a difference. John and his patron, Archbishop Theobald, were supporting the learned Bartholomew of Exeter against a candidate whom Theobald had described as "unlearned and useless." However, the other candidate was advanced by Robert fitz Harding to whom Henry II owed a huge debt, since he had helped finance the king's rise to power. This candidate was probably Robert's son, yet Bartholomew became bishop, and it is likely that his learning made a difference in Becket's advice to the king and perhaps in the king's own decision.[141]

More important, clear links between education and advancement show that learning certainly mattered, though whether patrons valued it for religious or practical purposes remains a question. The importance of education to advancement can be detected in a variety of ways. First, the perceptions of contemporaries. As noted in Chapter 3, Walter Map and Ranulf de Glanvill agreed that lower class people were having their sons educated in order to gain riches.[142] A follower of Peter Abelard, whose work survives only in England, contrasted the Jewish practice of educating all the sons in a family with the Christian practice of educating only one son, and that for the purpose of him advancing in the Church and benefiting the family.[143] For Etienne de Fougères, simony was bad partly because it eliminated the incentive for clerics to get an education (and to act well) since churches would simply go to the rich.[144] Strikingly, however, even those who were best placed to receive advancement through personal networks often received an education, and this provides a second sort of evidence for the importance of education to success. Several of Gilbert Foliot's letters show his concern to support or encourage his younger relatives in their studies, including

---

[139] Gilbert Foliot, *Letters and Charters*, 316; Gerald of Wales, *Opera*, 1:249. For Diceto's efforts on behalf of St. Paul's, see Chapter 14, section 3.

[140] Adam of Eynsham, *Magna Vita Sancti Hugonis*, 1:110–13; Gerald of Wales, *Opera*, 7:41, 98.

[141] John of Salisbury, *Letters*, 1:222–3. For Robert, see Hugh M. Thomas, *The English and the Normans: Ethnic Hostility, Assimilation, and Identity, 1066–c.1220* (Oxford, 2003), 196–8; Emilie Amt, *The Accession of Henry II in England: Royal Government Restored, 1149–1159* (Woodbridge, 1993), 37–9; Robert B. Patterson, "Robert Fitz Harding of Bristol: Profile of an Early Angevin Burgess-Baron Patrician and his Family's Urban Involvement," *Haskins Society Journal* 1 (1989), 109–22.

[142] See Chapter 3, section 3; Walter Map, *De Nugis Curialium*, 12–15.

[143] Clanchy, *From Memory to Written Record*, 244.

[144] Etienne de Fougères, *Le livre des manières*, 71.

at Bologna.[145] Philip, son of Earl Patrick, although he had connections such as Henry II's stepbrother, Earl Hamelin, to seek benefices for him, nonetheless studied in the schools.[146] Similarly, Godfrey de Lucy was not able to be present at his case against Battle because he was at the schools.[147] There were various reasons for powerful families to have their clerical members educated or for such individuals to seek out an education, including piety and love of learning. However, it is likely that even those with the best connections believed that education provided a useful edge in the fierce competition for benefices.

The third and most important evidence for links between education and promotion comes from the rise in numbers of *magistri* in important positions, a phenomenon described by various scholars. Clerics with the title *magister* (indicating some level of advanced education) first began appearing commonly in the documents only in the middle third of the twelfth century, and their numbers increased steadily thereafter. John Baldwin has noted the rising numbers of bishops who were *magistri* in England, including ten of thirty-five appointed to certain sees from 1180 to 1223.[148] The rise of the masters was at least as pronounced in the households of bishops. C. R. Cheney found that twenty of the thirty clerics who can be clearly placed in the household of Archbishop Hubert Walter were *magistri*.[149] Marie Lovatt noted that of 180 total witnesses to Geoffrey Plantagenet's charters as Archbishop of York, over fifty were *magistri*.[150] Other editors of episcopal acta have also noted the appearance and rise of *magistri* in the retinues of bishops and my own search for *magistri* in the reigns of Richard and John (to be discussed in Chapter 10) revealed that they were particularly likely to be found in that context.[151] Archdeacons often also had one or more *magistri* in their households by the second half of the twelfth century.[152] In addition, more and more cathedral canons and dignitaries were *magistri*. Julia Barrow has shown that whereas the number of identifiable *magistri* at the cathedrals of Wells, Hereford, London, Lincoln, and Salisbury was negligible in the second quarter of the twelfth century, by the first quarter of the thirteenth century they provided approximately a third of the canons at Wells and half at the other cathedrals.[153] Baldwin indicates that just

---

[145] Gilbert Foliot, *Letters and Charters*, 262–4.

[146] Gervase of Tilbury, *Otia Imperialia: Recreation for an Emperor*, ed. S. E. Banks and J. W. Binns (Oxford, 2002), 578–9.

[147] Searle, ed., *The Chronicle of Battle Abbey*, 326–7.

[148] John W. Baldwin, "Masters at Paris from 1179 to 1215: A Social Perspective," in Robert Louis Benson and Giles Constable, eds., *Renaissance and Renewal in the Twelfth Century* (Cambridge, Mass., 1982), 138–72, at 154; John W. Baldwin, " 'Studium et Regnum': The Penetration of University Personnel into French and English Administration at the Turn of the Twelfth and Thirteenth Centuries," *Revue des Études Islamiques* 44 (1976), 199–215, at 207.

[149] Cheney, *English Bishops' Chanceries*, 11.   [150] Lovatt, ed., *English Episcopal Acta 27*, cvi.

[151] Smith, ed., *English Episcopal Acta 1*, xlv; Burton, ed., *English Episcopal Acta 5*, xxxvi; Harper-Bill, ed., *English Episcopal Acta 6*, xliv; Barrow, ed., *English Episcopal Acta 7*, lvi; Karn, ed., *English Episcopal Acta 31*, cxiii; Karn, ed., *English Episcopal Acta 42*, lxiii–lxiv.

[152] B. R. Kemp, ed., *Twelfth-Century English Archidiaconal and Vice-Archidiaconal Acta*, The Canterbury and York Society, vol. 92 (Woodbridge, 2001), l.

[153] Barrow, "Education and Recruitment," 134, 138. See also Greenway, "Jocelin of Wells and his Cathedral Chapter," 56–7.

under half of the canons at York in the period 1180–1226 were *magistri* and my own perusal of the records of Chichester for the reigns of Richard and John suggest just over a third of the canons there were *magistri*.[154] Clearly the *magistri* had made powerful inroads into important positions in the Church.

Baldwin has noted that *magistri* also entered the English royal administration.[155] Because the position of royal cleric is so ill defined, it would be difficult to determine the percentage of them who were *magistri*. The percentage was certainly smaller than for episcopal clerics and cathedral canons, but *magistri* still played an important role in royal government. Approximately 14 percent of the royal grants of churches and benefices in John's reign specifically gave the title of *magister* to the recipient, though this figure under-represents their number since those who had become archdeacons, like William of Wrotham, received only the latter title. Because secular magnates normally had fairly small clerical trains, they attracted few *magistri* into their households, but they attracted some, and a powerful lord such as Earl William Marshal might have as many as three *magistri* among his followers.[156] Clearly, learned clerics could find many routes to patronage and advancement in England. Indeed, as Barrow and Baldwin have shown, England was unusually open to the advancement of the learned, partly because cathedral appointments were less likely to be controlled by kinship ties and partly because of the strong administrative structures there.[157]

In part education helped advancement because it provided clerics with practical skills that made them attractive to patrons.[158] For instance, Nigel of Whiteacre deplored the practice of studying law or medicine as a route to gaining ecclesiastical benefices, but such studies could in fact be a path to success.[159] The importance of these and other practical skills will be highlighted in the next chapter. Nonetheless, I would argue that the demands of reformers for learning and good character also drove the rise of education in this period. Schools could provide a form of credentialing. Expectations that clerics be learned and lead good lives were sufficiently open ended that it might be hard for a patron to choose between candidates on these criteria. Indeed, it would have been hard to create *any* process that provided credentials for character and morality. However, learning was different, for if a candidate could point to a period of study in the schools, he immediately gained a concrete claim to be learned, and the patron could presumably count on a certain level of competence in religious matters. Even if, or perhaps especially if, the patron had worldly motives for granting a benefice, being able to point to a candidate's studies provided a useful defense against any reformist attacks. Thus, even the most irreligious, well-connected cleric might find it useful to spend time at the schools. However, it is probably unwise to be too cynical here. Given the widely

---

[154] Baldwin, "Masters at Paris," 155; Greenway, *Fasti. 5. Chichester.*

[155] Baldwin, "Studium et Regnum," 204–6.

[156] Green, *Aristocracy*, 210; Crouch, *William Marshal*, 155.

[157] Barrow, "Education and Recruitment," 133–7; Baldwin, "Studium et Regnum," 204–10; Baldwin, "Masters at Paris," 154–7.

[158] Murray, *Reason and Society*, 213–33.

[159] Nigel of Whiteacre, *Tractatus Contra Curiales*, 158–9.

shared belief that appointees to clerical posts should be learned, it is likely that even ambitious clerics might feel that they *ought* to receive an education as well as finding it expedient to do so. In any case, though many factors fueled the rise of education in the long twelfth century, shifts in the patronage structure played an especially important role. With the decline of hereditary benefices, fewer clerics could learn their job from their fathers. At the same time, the fierce competition for benefices made the education and credentialing provided by the growing numbers of schools and by the nascent universities extremely valuable.

5. PATRONAGE, TENSION, AND ANXIETY

The nature of the patronage network was bound to provoke spiritual anxieties among pious clerics. Even allowing for biases in the evidence, the route to success was often bound up with worldly factors. Gerald of Wales reported that at one point he had resigned to the pope all his churches and ecclesiastical benefices, "some gained during boyhood when he was unworthy, some collated to him carnally from his parents and relatives, [or] taken through [their] power from more worthy individuals, or acquired through service at the court, solicitation, and other illicit modes."[160] The pope restored the benefices and churches to Gerald, thus resolving any problems of legality, but clearly Gerald had plenty to feel guilty about if he felt so inclined. Even when they gained benefices licitly, successful clerics could be targets of criticism. For instance, when Stephen Langton sought to recruit Master Adam of Tilney from the household of the abbot of St. Albans, the abbot only reluctantly allowed him to go, and subsequently a house chronicler censured the cleric for being ambitious and desiring rich benefices.[161] Thus the patronage system was almost designed to create spiritual crises, and in subsequent chapters I will discuss more thoroughly the tensions created by service to the powerful and by nepotism.

Patronage could increase other forms of emotional turmoil and anxiety as well, because it paired enormous opportunities with tremendous uncertainties. Most medieval wealth passed from generation to generation through inheritance, and this was particularly true of lay aristocratic wealth, even when one takes into account the possibilities created by royal patronage and marriages to heiresses. For clerics, inheritance of office became a dwindling possibility, especially where the greater prizes were concerned. Thus a great deal of ecclesiastical wealth was up for grabs every generation. Competition for that wealth, and the envy of those who failed in the competition, had the potential for creating social tensions, especially since success was so dependent on the goodwill of others. R. I. Moore has written that "Whether penniless or princely the lot of the clerks (and in this they resembled their

---

[160] Davies, "Giraldus Cambrensis: *De Invectionibus*," 193; Gerald of Wales, *Opera*, 3:326. *Ambitus*, which I have translated as solicitation, could also refer to bribery, so it is possible that Gerald is confessing to simony here.

[161] Thomas Walsingham, *Gesta Abbatum*, 1:243–4; Major, "Familia," 532, 534.

brothers the knights) was at bottom the same—treacherous, precarious, open to constant humiliation."[162] In fact, the comparison holds true mainly for landless knights and secular courtiers, since aristocratic heirs did not face the same uncertainties. That said, Moore has captured the downside of dependence on patronage, a subject I will pursue further in the following chapter. Clerics might opt out of the competition for patronage once they felt that they had received incomes sufficient to their needs, but in general the great opportunities available to clerical elites were accompanied by a deep and potentially humiliating dependency on powerful patrons.

The very possibility of tremendously successful careers in a society of limited expectations could paradoxically create a system rife with jealousy and feelings of failure. Almost every cleric in the country could believe that he might have had a more successful career; even the majority of bishops could point to bishoprics that were wealthier than theirs. Thus, Gerald of Wales and Peter of Blois, for all their successes and wealth, clearly felt that they could have or should have done better. R. W. Southern wrote of losers as well as winners in the competition for success, and though some of his examples of the less successful, such as Peter of Blois, actually did quite well for themselves, there is no doubt their relative failures could have rankled, helping to create, as Southern suggests, the literature of satire and invective that was so widespread in the period.[163] That so many different factors played a role in success or failure, and that the supposed rules of the game differed from those actually in practice, meant that many might feel they had a legitimate grievance. Several scholars have noted that Gerald's complaints about the lack of preferment for the production of learned works smack of disappointment, and so they do.[164] However, Gerald's complaints were also firmly rooted in contemporary beliefs that preferment should be based on learning and character, and though he had done quite well through kinship and lordship, he probably felt that he might have risen higher (and with less sin) in a system that hewed more closely to meritocratic ideals. The negative opinions of Walter Map, Ranulf de Glanvill, and others about the rise of clerics from peasant backgrounds illustrate a different sort of tension. Clearly many believed that the established ecclesiastical and secular elites should maintain their dominance within the Church, and the success of "men raised from the dust" provoked a backlash. Thus, the nature of the patronage system could join social and personal stresses with religious ones to create a psychologically fraught situation for even the most successful careerists.

The shifting patterns of ecclesiastical appointment are fundamental to our understanding of some key developments in the long twelfth century. The decline of heritable churches and benefices opened up ever more wealth to the use of patrons. As a result, the clergy became increasingly incorporated into fluid vertical

---

[162] Moore, *First European Revolution*, 141. See also Stollberg, *Soziale Stellung*, 121.
[163] R. W. Southern, *Scholastic Humanism and the Unification of Europe*, 2 vols. (Oxford, 1995–2001), 1:168–71, 181–5.
[164] Bartlett, *Gerald of Wales*, 17, 58–61; Richter, *Giraldus Cambrensis*, 89–90; Türk, *Nugae curialium*, 100–1.

and horizontal networks of personal influence which allowed patrons to tap into the wealth and power of the Church, but also gave clerics access to the borrowed power of their patrons. The growth of positions available for patronage helped make possible the development of larger royal and ecclesiastical bureaucracies while the fierce competition for benefices encouraged the development of formal education. Though the decline of heritable benefices signally failed to sever clerics from worldly entanglements, it changed the nature of those entanglements and thus posed new challenges to the religious lives of successful clerics. Recruitment through the patronage system helped shape the secular clergy, and the response of clerics to this system deeply influenced their impact on their society.

6

Courtiers, Bureaucrats, and Hell

In his poem, "Quod Amicus Suggerit," Peter of Blois, who was both a courtier cleric and a critic of such clerics, established a dialogue between two figures representing two facets of his career and perhaps of his personality. The courtier makes a compelling case for his choice to serve at court. The court is a place of delights, of alluring cultivation (*cultus delicacior*), and of delicious food. The courtier gains dignity and can make the friendship of magnates. All give way to him and fear him but he fears none. He can also augment the patrimony of his relatives. In short, the courtier can join the elites and be a good kinsman. What of his friend's warnings about the dangers of hell and his urgent demands to repent? From the courtier's perspective, people who voluntarily embrace misery are fools. Why should the courtier be criticized for enjoying the good things God has provided for humanity? Religion is better suited for old age than youth, and the courtier prefers to embrace the desires of the flesh. After all, he argues, Christ's mercy is patient, and penitence should suffice. Besides, can one be sure hell exists? No one has returned thence, and anticipating the afterlife is a little bit like waiting for King Arthur to return; by implication, believing in a fantasy. In short, why worry? To any modern secularist such as myself, the courtier convincingly wins the debate against the moralist who simply reiterates, albeit with passion, typical warnings about hell and ends with a conventional passage about the shortness of life. For a devout medieval believer, of course, the poem would have read quite differently. The courtier was a reckless fool, using dangerous rationalizations to justify yielding to temptation and placing himself in serious danger of suffering the eternal torments of hell. What could make the poem powerful to a contemporary was that Peter was able speak from experience of the allure of the court, could describe the temptations, doubts, and psychological tricks that would cause people like him to take the dangerous spiritual risks the court entailed, and yet hopefully pull the reader back to safety with a forceful and elegant expression of the standard religious truths of the time.[1]

---

[1] Wollin, ed., *Petri Blesensis Carmina*, 265–74. For another edition, a translation, and important discussion of this poem, see Peter Dronke, "Peter of Blois and Poetry at the Court of Henry II," *Mediaeval Studies* 38 (1976), 185–235, at 206–12. For Peter's career in royal and ecclesiastical service, see Cotts, *Clerical Dilemma*, 26–43. Neil Cartlidge, it seems to me, is correct in placing this poem in the context of Peter's sophisticated literary style, his complex self-presentation, and interest in debate and contradiction, but I think the moral point of the poem is nonetheless fairly straightforward: Neil Cartlidge, "An Intruder at the Feast? Anxiety and Debate in the Letters of Peter of Blois," in Ruth Kennedy and Simon Meecham-Jones, eds., *Writers of the Reign of Henry II: Twelve Essays* (New York, 2006), 79–108, at 86.

This chapter explores clerics as courtiers and administrators. Because the long twelfth century was so important to the development of ecclesiastical and secular government, scholars of administration and government have already written extensively on the activities of clerics at court and in bureaucracies. In the first three parts of this chapter I will combine this existing work with my own research in order to isolate the precise clerical contribution to the history of bureaucracy in the period. What made clerics as a group different from the laymen and the occasional regular clerics with whom they worked in households and administrations? To what degree did their areas of expertise overlap with those of others? In particular, what was the role of the secular clergy in Clanchy's shift from memory to written record?[2] Another subject that has received much attention is the tension between religious ideals and the life of the courtier that formed the subject of Peter of Blois's poem. Here again my work will be partly synthetic, but I hope to underscore why moralists were so anxious about service at the court. Overall, an exploration of clerics as courtiers, administrators, and bureaucrats reveals an arena in which they were responsible for fundamental change in the twelfth century, but also shows another crucial area in which conflict between worldly and religious roles created immense moral tension for the clergy.

1. SERVICE TO ECCLESIASTICAL MAGNATES, SECULAR LORDS, AND THE KING

A brief overview of clerical participation in various households, courts, and bureaucratic systems, beginning with ecclesiastical administration, is necessary to lay the groundwork. This period saw dramatic administrative development within the Church in England, as throughout Europe.[3] Great churches of all sorts created increasingly complex administrative structures, and the cathedrals staffed by the secular clergy saw the development of individual prebends and the gradual creation of a chapter administration typically headed by a dean, treasurer, precentor, and chancellor.[4] The example of St. Paul's shows that secular canons were developing sophisticated methods to administer cathedral estates.[5] More important, bishops acquired more and more underlings to assist them in their oversight of the clergy and other duties, and the structures designed to govern dioceses became increasingly complex. The creation of the system of territorial archdeaconries and rural deaneries was crucial.[6] Archdeacons had particularly important tasks, including

---

[2] Clanchy, *From Memory to Written Record.*

[3] Useful overviews of these processes can be found in Barlow, *English Church, 1066–1154,* 104–76; Brett, *English Church,* 34–62, 75–100, 119–215; Cheney, *From Becket to Langton,* 145–9.

[4] Barrow, "Cathedrals, Provosts, and Prebends," 552–63; Blake, "Development of the Chapter of Exeter," 1–11; Crosby, *Bishop and Chapter*; Greenway, "False *Institutio*," 77–101. For secular cathedrals in the later Middle Ages, see Kathleen Edwards, *The English Secular Cathedrals in the Middle Ages* (Manchester, 1967).

[5] See Chapter 4, section 3; Hale, ed., *Domesday of St. Paul's,* 109–17, 140–52.

[6] For archdeacons, see C. N. L. Brooke, "The Archdeacon and the Norman Conquest," in Diana Greenway, Christopher Holdsworth, and Jane Sayers, eds. *Tradition and Change: Essays in Honour of*

holding courts, policing the morals of the population, and overseeing the quality of local churches and clergy.[7] Later in the period began the rise of the bishop's "official."[8] The development of all these offices was closely bound up with the gradual creation of a range of ecclesiastical courts with jurisdiction over many aspects of people's lives.[9] Secular clerics below the level of bishop generally staffed these courts and presided over the lesser ones. In addition, in the second half of the twelfth century, popes began appointing judges delegate to handle individual cases that had been appealed to the papacy, and though at first these judges were normally bishops and abbots, by the end of the period many were secular clerics.[10]

Obviously, the regular as well as secular clergy contributed to the growth of ecclesiastical administration. Because most great religious houses were monastic, the regulars were particularly important in the administration of large churches and their estates. Nonetheless, the ideal and practice of claustration severely restricted the participation of the regular clergy in diocesan governance. Indeed, Peter of Blois argued that monks were less useful than clerics as advisors and in carrying out business.[11] He did so in the divisive context of Archbishop Baldwin's dispute against his cathedral monks, but it is noteworthy that on a couple of occasions Abbot Samson forced the cellarer of his monastery to accept oversight from one of his secular clerics.[12] It is possible that regular clerics *were* on average less prepared by inclination and training to deal with worldly affairs, though one can certainly not ignore the obvious administrative expertise of many monastic officials.[13] In any case, the ideals of claustration mattered, and even at the beginning of the period, when administrative structures were still fairly basic, such thoroughly monastic bishops as Anselm of Canterbury and Wulfstan of Worcester recruited secular clerics to assist them, apparently feeling that some tasks were not the proper province of their monks.[14] The frequent recruitment of secular clerics to the households of abbots and abbesses suggests that their views were widely shared.

Marjorie Chibnall (Cambridge, 1985), 1–19. For rural deans see Thompson, *English Clergy*, 63–9; Brett, *English Church*, 211–15; Karn, ed., *English Episcopal Acta 31*, lx–lxi; B. R. Kemp, "The Acta of English Rural Deans in the Later Twelfth and Early Thirteenth Centuries," in Philippa M. Hoskin, Christopher Brooke, and Barry Dobson, eds., *The Foundations of Medieval English Ecclesiastical History: Studies Presented to David Smith* (Woodbridge, 2005), 139–58.

[7] Brett, *English Church*, 204–8; B. R. Kemp, "Informing the Archdeacon on Ecclesiastical Matters in Twelfth-Century England," in M. J. Franklin and Christopher Harper-Bill, eds., *Medieval Ecclesiastical Studies in Honour of Dorothy M. Owen* (Woodbridge, 1995), 131–49; Kemp, ed., *Archidiaconal Acta*, xlii–xlvii.

[8] David M. Smith, "The 'Officialis' of the Bishop in Twelfth- and Thirteenth-Century England: Problems of Terminology," in M. J. Franklin and Christopher Harper-Bill, eds., *Medieval Ecclesiastical Studies in Honour of Dorothy M. Owen* (Woodbridge, 1995), 201–20.

[9] R. H. Helmholz, *The Canon Law and Ecclesiastical Jurisdiction from 597 to the 1640s* (Oxford, 2004), 106–42.

[10] Jane E. Sayers, *Papal Judges Delegate in the Province of Canterbury, 1198–1254: A Study in Ecclesiastical Jurisdiction and Administration* (Oxford, 1971), 119–20, 125–33.

[11] Gervase of Canterbury, *Historical Works*, 1:368; Peter of Blois, *Later Letters*, 60–1.

[12] Jocelin of Brakelond, *Chronicle*, 79–81, 89–91.

[13] Southern, *Scholastic Humanism*, 1:173–4.

[14] Gribbin and Brett, eds., *English Episcopal Acta 28*, xxxviii–xxxix; Cheney et al., eds., *English Episcopal Acta 33*, lvi.

Outside of the strictly monastic sphere, the secular clergy dominated in the development of ecclesiastical administration.

The administrative importance of household clerics deserves particular attention. I have already noted, in the context of patronage, the dominance of clerics in the households of prelates and their frequent presence in the household of secular magnates.[15] Even lesser figures such as archdeacons might have clerics in their households.[16] Ecclesiastical magnates relied particularly heavily on clerics because of their religious responsibilities. Thus, when Peter of Blois argued for Archbishop Baldwin's plan to found a collegiate church he stressed that many different issues came before the archbishop of Canterbury, who therefore required the advice of prudent men.[17] However, clerics could also play an influential role in the households of secular magnates. Orderic Vitalis described how Richard of Leicester, before becoming a monk, had long served in the court of Robert, count of Meulan, who admitted him to "his most intimate counsels." According to Orderic, Richard had taken a leading part in judging cases and in carrying out the count's business.[18] It is a sign of the trust and authority placed in household clerics (as well as the advantages of their non-combatant status), that they, along with wives, were often entrusted with arranging for the ransoming of lords taken captive during the Magna Carta revolt.[19] As shall become apparent, clerics fulfilled a wide variety of functions in the households and administrations of magnates, and when contemporaries thought about courtier clerics, they were not only thinking about the royal court.

Nonetheless, the most important household/administration was the king's, and the royal government was permeated by the clergy. Space does not allow anything like a full discussion of the role of clerics in the rapidly growing government of England in the long twelfth century, but fortunately previous work makes this unnecessary, for one cannot read modern accounts of royal administration without quickly realizing how crucial the secular clergy were to its functioning.[20] Since such works do not generally single out the role of the clergy from the laity, however, I will focus on a few aspects of clerical participation in royal government to underscore their importance and to highlight three important points: 1) the closeness of some clerics to the rulers of England and their crucial roles in their governments; 2) the manner in which clerics also carried out some of the most mundane and routine tasks of royal government; and 3) the importance of clerics even in such areas as secular justice and warfare that one would expect them to avoid and therefore leave as a lay preserve.

The first point needs little elaboration, since scholars are familiar with figures such as Ranulf Flambard, Roger of Salisbury, and Hubert Walter who could

---

[15] See Chapter 5, section 3.   [16] Kemp, ed., *Archidiaconal Acta*, xlix–lii.

[17] Peter of Blois, *Later Letters*, 60–1; Gervase of Canterbury, *Historical Works*, 1:368.

[18] Orderic Vitalis, *Ecclesiastical History*, 6:488–9.

[19] Hardy, ed., *Rotuli Litterarum Patentium*, 187b, 189b–90a, 190b, 194b, 198b.

[20] Particularly useful are works that provide detail on the personnel of royal government: Green, *Government of England*; Jolliffe, *Angevin Kingship*; Painter, *Reign of King John*; Stollberg, *Soziale Stellung*; Turner, *Men Raised from the Dust*; Turner, *English Judiciary*; Turner, *Judges, Administrators*; Ralph V. Turner, *King John* (London, 1994).

dominate royal government under the king.[21] Nicholas Vincent has studied what the admittedly imperfect evidence of attestations to royal documents can tell us about Henry II's inner circle, and reveals that nearly one third of the king's most frequent witnesses were clerics, overwhelmingly secular clerics.[22] Many of these were bishops or archbishops, but the closest clerical advisors to the king were often royal clerics who had not yet been advanced to the episcopacy. An anecdote from the 1173–4 revolt can serve as one example among many of how influential such clerics could be. When the king's administrators feared the king's position in England was in jeopardy, they sent Richard of Ilchester, then bishop-elect of Winchester, to persuade Henry II that he was most needed there rather than on the continent, because they knew Richard had the king's ear.[23]

Minor players in royal government have received far less attention, and to illustrate the importance of the clergy at the lower levels of royal administration, I will focus on sheriffs' clerics. Sheriffs themselves were the chief local representatives of the king and therefore crucial to royal government, but only a small minority of them were clerics.[24] However, sheriffs increasingly came to rely on clerical subordinates. Individual clerics or priests of sheriffs appear as early as the reign of Henry I, and Thomas Becket himself served in this capacity before entering Archbishop Theobald's household.[25] The duties of sheriffs' clerics were partly financial in nature. The *Dialogue of the Exchequer* envisioned each sheriff having his own cleric at his side during the audit.[26] Sheriffs' clerics can also be found handling monetary matters in the shires themselves, including collecting taxes.[27] In addition, shrieval clerics carried out many of the day-to-day tasks of the county and royal courts, including organizing juries, summoning litigants, delivering writs, taking pledges, and even in one case fetching a poacher who had been caught fishing in an abbot's pond.[28] Collectively, sheriffs' clerics were crucial in helping sheriffs to run royal government in the shires.

The two great duties of kings in the Middle Ages were to provide justice and to win wars. This period was notable for the expansion of royal justice and the development of the common law. Despite the division between ecclesiastical courts

---

[21] Southern, *Medieval Humanism*, 183–205; Kealey, *Roger of Salisbury*; Cheney, *Hubert Walter*; Young, *Hubert Walter*.

[22] Nicholas Vincent, "The Court of Henry II," in Christopher Harper-Bill and Nicholas Vincent, eds., *Henry II: New Interpretations* (Woodbridge, 2007), 278–334, at 293.

[23] Ralph of Diceto, *Opera Historica*, 1:381.

[24] For clerical sheriffs under Henry I, see Judith A. Green, *Henry I: King of England and Duke of Normandy* (Cambridge, 2006), 242. I have noted Wimer the Sheriff under Henry II in Chapter 4. For other clerical sheriffs under Henry II, see *Pipe Roll 7 Henry II*, 8, 41; *Pipe Roll 9 Henry II*, 13; *Pipe Roll 11 Henry II*, 15; *Pipe Roll 17 Henry II*, 55.

[25] A reference to a priest of a sheriff comes from 1100–12 and to a sheriff's cleric from 1127: Cambridge University Library, Add. MS 3021, fo. 414v; Cambridge University Library, Add. MS 3020, fos. 145r–v; Robertson and Sheppard, eds., *Materials*, 3:14–15.

[26] Richard fitzNigel, *Dialogus de Scaccario*, 26–7.

[27] For example, *Pipe Roll 15 Henry II*, 132; *Pipe Roll 27 Henry II*, 26; *Pipe Roll 1 John*, 152–3; Maitland, ed., *Three Rolls*, 78–115.

[28] Palgrave, ed., *Rotuli Curiæ Regis*, 1:76–8, 85, 128–9; 2:32–3; *Curia Regis Rolls*, 1:100, 148, 195; 2:25, 105, 285; 3:100; 4:64; 5:316; 6:45, 62–3; 7:7, 114, 348; Stenton, ed., *Pleas*, 3:61, 83; 4:2.

and secular ones, and the fact that clerics were not supposed to participate in "blood judgments" (cases involving corporal punishment), clerics remained heavily involved with secular justice at the highest levels. Ralph Turner has shown that about *half* the royal justices in the formative period of the common law were clerics.[29] When the office of keeper of the pleas of the crown, or coroner, was established in 1194, three knights and one cleric were chosen from each county, indicating that the creators of this new office thought the participation of clerics was crucial.[30] Thus, secular clerics not only dominated ecclesiastical courts, but they also administered and shaped secular law alongside their lay colleagues.

Clerics only rarely served the king on the battlefield, though there were exceptions. Thomas Becket's military career has been noted and Orderic Vitalis claimed that Robert Curthose was captured at Tinchebray by Henry I's cleric, Waldric, future bishop of Laon.[31] Clerics were far more important in providing logistical support for royal armies.[32] Jolliffe argued that royal clerics did practically all the clerical and financial administration of the war of 1203, and noted that many served John as paymasters of armies and fleets or in other capacities.[33] To give specific examples, Master Richard Marsh, one of John's great favorites, frequently oversaw disbursements to knights in conjunction with various laymen, and during John's Irish expedition of 1210, Henry de Ver, who received several benefices from the king, paid out over £2400 to knights, sergeants, and crossbowmen, often with the help of his own cleric, Nicholas.[34] In the spring and summer of 1212, a royal fleet captured thirteen richly laden Norman merchant ships, and it was the cleric William de Wrotham who disposed of the ships and their contents for the king.[35] This, in fact, was only one of William's actions involving naval affairs, for he oversaw the recruitment, organization, and payment of naval forces throughout the reign.[36] Despite their general avoidance of actual fighting, clerics were essential to the machinery of warfare by the end of the period.

2. LAY AND CLERICAL ADMINISTRATORS

The involvement of clerics in quintessentially non-religious spheres underscores the question of how crucial the contributions of the clergy *as clerics* were to administration, especially outside of the ecclesiastical sphere. Clearly they were often doing the *same* tasks as laypeople. One might, for instance, expect King John's household

[29] Turner, *English Judiciary*, 2, 291.   [30] Roger of Howden, *Chronica*, 3:264.
[31] See Chapter 3, section 1; Orderic Vitalis, *Ecclesiastical History*, 6:90–1.
[32] Michael Prestwich, *Armies and Warfare in the Middle Ages: The English Experience* (New Haven, 1996), 175–7.
[33] Jolliffe, *Angevin Kingship*, 211, 278–81.
[34] Thomas Duffus Hardy, ed., *Rotuli de Liberate ac de Misis et Praestitis, Regnante Johanne* (London, 1844), 172–210.
[35] Beryl E. R. Formoy, "A Maritime Indenture of 1212," *English Historical Review* 41 (1926), 556–9.
[36] F. W. Brooks, "William de Wrotham and the Office of Keeper of the King's Ports and Galleys," *English Historical Review* 40 (1925), 570–9; Powell, "Administration of the Navy," 182–8.

knights and his clerics to have had radically different functions, but apart from fighting on the one hand and chapel duties on the other, there was a remarkable amount of overlap in their roles.[37] I have already discussed the many economic tasks performed by clerics in Chapter 4.[38] Both secular and lay magnates could employ clerics as seneschals, a crucial position of oversight more frequently held by laymen, and Countess Hawise of Aumale had a cleric as her sheriff of Holderness.[39] Magnates also used clerics for a variety of other worldly tasks such as carrying money, serving as messengers, and acting as attorneys in secular courts.[40] In some cases, clerics not only did the same tasks as laypeople but were formally required to act alongside them. Roger of Howden reported that in the forest eyre of 1184, the king divided the country up into circuits and appointed two clerics and two knights as justices in each.[41] Sometimes clerics served their lords in particularly irreligious ways. In a legal case involving a welter of claims and counterclaims, one Baldwin Tirell accused the baron Henry de Pomeray of imprisoning him in his cellar, and claimed that Henry had his cleric John and another cleric arrange for Baldwin to ransom himself![42]

The Angevin royal government is famous for employing all-purpose officials, and many of these were clerics. Two of the best examples come from John's reign: William of Wrotham, and William of Cornhill, archdeacon of Huntingdon and later bishop of Coventry. Jolliffe remarked that these two, along with William of Cornhill's brother Reginald, a layman, had the largest administrative network outside the household.[43] Besides his duties with the tin mines and the royal fleet, William of Wrotham participated in a short-lived but innovative attempt to create a customs tax, worked on initiatives concerning the coinage, handled much of the administrative work involved with royal trade embargoes, oversaw royal forests, and controlled various custodies. As custodian of the ports, he oversaw the construction of a dockyard or mole at Portsmouth. He sometimes had custody of royal castles

---

[37] For the functions of household knights in royal government, see S. D. Church, *The Household Knights of King John* (Cambridge, 1999), 39–73.

[38] See Chapter 4, section 3.

[39] Vincent, ed., *English Episcopal Acta 9*, 177–8, 183–5; Lovatt, ed., *English Episcopal Acta 20*, xliii; Snape, ed., *English Episcopal Acta 24*, xliii, xlvi–xlvii; Mayr-Harting, ed., *Acta of Chichester*, 22; Nicholas Vincent, "Master Elias of Dereham (d. 1245): A Reassessment," in Caroline M. Barron and Jenny Stratford, eds., *The Church and Learning in Later Medieval Society: Essays in Honour of R.B. Dobson* (Donington, 2002), 128–59, at 133–4, 140; Crouch, *William Marshal*, 173; Bearman, ed., *Charters of the Redvers Family*, 41; Thomas de Burton, *Chronica Monasterii de Melsa*, 1:297; C. J. Holdsworth, ed., *Rufford Charters*, 4 vols., Thoroton Society Record Series, vols. 29, 30, 32, 34 (Nottingham, 1972–81), 2:230; Palgrave, ed., *Rotuli Curiae Regis*, 1:381; *Curia Regis Rolls*, 3:237, 4:41–2; Stenton, ed., *Pleas*, 3:25; Farrer and Clay, eds., *Early Yorkshire Charters*, 3:88.

[40] For examples of clerics carrying out these and other tasks for secular magnates, see Robertson and Sheppard, eds., *Materials*, 1:320; Hudson, ed., *Historia Ecclesie Abbendonensis*, 2:146–7, 156–7; Greenway and Watkiss, eds., *Foundation of Walden Monastery*, 78–9, 156–7, 160–1; *Curia Regis Rolls*, 1:152; 5:149. Bishops and heads of religious houses were particularly likely to use clerics as attorneys; Palgrave, ed., *Rotuli Curiae Regis*, 1:30, 123–4, 224, 229, 305, 327, 329, 337, 342, 348, 373; 2:35, 38, 40, 63, 66, 77–8, 179, 187, 199, 260. However, secular magnates also did so: *Curia Regis Rolls*, 1:73, 85, 89, 93, 111, 270, 280, 284, 397, 439.

[41] Roger of Howden, *Chronica*, 2:289–90.   [42] *Curia Regis Rolls*, 7:168–70.

[43] Jolliffe, *Angevin Kingship*, 294.

and at one point had charge of a hostage of Hugh de Lacy for the king. William and those he employed also had surprisingly ordinary tasks such as buying wine for the king, stocking manors, arranging for wine to be transported, and providing eighty fish at the king's command for William Marshal. William of Cornhill, member of a prominent London family with longstanding royal ties, likewise carried out an extraordinary range of tasks: holding custodies; paying or providing necessities for engineers, miners, sappers, and crossbowmen; taking care of a student at Winchester, of sixteen men from Denmark, and of the horses, dogs, and servants of Thomas Bloet; and providing for the purchase, production, or transport of wine, grain, cloth, robes for the king's followers, crossbows, two great pavilions for the king, and, on one occasion, the king's regalia. Eventually he had custody of the Tower of London.[44] The Angevin kings were not the only ones employing all-purpose clerical servants. Nicholas Vincent has shown Master Ralph Basset, Peter des Roches's first steward in the bishopric of Winchester, touring manors, issuing commands by writ, tallaging estates, and even overseeing the installation of glass windows at the bishop's residence at Farnham.[45] It would be hard to distinguish such clerical all-purpose administrators from their lay counterparts on the basis of the tasks they carried out.

On one level, therefore, the secular clergy simply provided large numbers of warm bodies who, as Turner has noted, could largely be employed at the Church's expense.[46] The importance of their numbers can be seen above all in royal government. George Cuttino estimated that 1500 clerics served the government of Edward I.[47] Obviously the number of clerics serving in our period would have been smaller. Nonetheless, when the sergeant of a hundred could have a cleric, and sheriff's clerics might have their own clerics, there were probably a very large number of clerics doing minor tasks, many of whom might not appear in the records.[48] As the previous chapter showed, the patronage system placed large numbers of church positions in the control of kings and others who needed administrators. Though churchmen had served in administrative posts in the Anglo-Saxon period, the long twelfth century saw an increasing percentage of the Church's growing wealth being channeled into secular and ecclesiastical administration. Kings did have resources with which to recruit and reward secular followers, but without control of ecclesiastical revenues would have found it extremely hard to create the bureaucracies they did. As Julia Barrow has written, "It was on the basis

[44] For William's work with fleets and the tin mines, see section 1 within this chapter and Chapter 4, section 3. For some important and some representative entries revealing his other duties and those of William of Cornhill, see Hardy, ed., *Rotuli Litterarum Clausarum*, 3b, 7a, 7b, 13a–b, 17b, 26a–27b, 30b–31b, 33b, 37a–b, 38b, 39a, 41a, 48b, 60a, 64a–b, 70b, 73a, 85b, 102b, 106a, 117a, 121a–b, 122b, 154b; Hardy, ed., *Rotuli Litterarum Patentium*, 42b–43a, 50a, 54b, 57b, 68b, 96a, 154a. See also W. L. Warren, *King John* (Berkeley, 1961), 124–5.

[45] Vincent, ed., *English Episcopal Acta 9*, 183–4.   [46] Turner, *English Judiciary*, 111.

[47] G. P. Cuttino, "King's Clerks and the Community of the Realm," *Speculum* 29 (1954), 395–409, at 403.

[48] Stenton, ed., *Pleas*, 4:236; *Curia Regis Rolls*, 6:230; Farrer and Clay, eds., *Early Yorkshire Charters*, 2:73.

of [a] relatively flexible social system, coupled with the existence of ecclesiastical sinecures, that Angevin bureaucracy could be built."[49]

Sheer numbers mattered, but even outside the Church's administration, clerics also performed duties that were solely or primarily the preserve of the clergy. Chief among these were, of course, religious ones. Religious functions were so routine that they rarely appear in the written records, but occasional glimpses do appear, particularly of unusual religious tasks, as when Bishop Roger of Worcester sent a household cleric, Master Sylvester, to investigate stories of a flying crucifix.[50] There survive some particularly telling glimpses of clerics exercising their religious offices in the households of secular magnates. Orderic Vitalis described how the cleric Gerald of Avranches worked assiduously in the worldly household of Earl Hugh of Chester, devotedly performing his liturgical functions and trying to convert the men of the household to a religious life.[51] A miracle story related how John de Lacy, constable of Chester, called on his chaplain, Anselm, to bring out a relic of St. Gilbert of Sempringham and implore the saint's aid when they were becalmed at sea.[52] Another miracle story spoke of Lambert, chaplain of the countess of Clare, "an honored man of good old age," trying to reconcile his lady to the death of her infant son, James, and advising her (wrongly of course!) that she was being foolishly optimistic in asking the recently martyred Thomas Becket to revive her son.[53] Accounts of household clerics providing religious advice sheds little light, of course, on administrative developments in the period, but they do help explain why clerics could achieve great authority even in secular households. Whatever one thinks of the story of Lambert and the countess of Clare, it does presume a world in which religious authority gave household chaplains the ability to advise their patrons about important and even intensely personal matters.

3. LITERACY, NUMERACY, EDUCATION, AND BUREAUCRACY

The greatest distinctive contribution of the secular clergy to administrative history and to the shift from memory to written record in this period was of course clerical, though in this case in the alternative, record-keeping sense of the word. Monastic houses had been pioneers in making records and using writing in administration, and they remained important exemplars of these practices.[54] However, in this sphere as in others, claustration limited the ability of monastic clergy actively to spread their practices in the wider world. It was therefore the secular clergy who were best able to take the tools of reading and writing, cultivated in the Church for

---

[49] Barrow, "Cathedrals, Provosts, and Prebends," 564.
[50] Gerald of Wales, *Opera*, 7:65–6; Cheney, *Roger, Bishop of Worcester*, 102.
[51] Orderic Vitalis, *Ecclesiastical History*, 3:216–17, 226–7.
[52] Foreville and Keir, eds., *Book of St Gilbert*, 288–91.
[53] Robertson and Sheppard, eds., *Materials*, 2:255–7.
[54] See, for instance, Francesca Tinti, *Sustaining Belief: The Church of Worcester from c.870 to c.1100* (Farnham, 2010), 75–150.

religious purposes, and apply them to administrative tasks in the secular world. Already in the long twelfth century laypeople were acquiring skills in reading and even writing, a point to which I will return, but in this period it was the clergy who were most important to the increased use of the written word in society at large.

As is well known, the royal government was crucial to extending the administrative use of writing in England, and as one might expect, the admittedly limited information on those who actually produced documents indicates that normally they were secular clerics.[55] The chancellor was inevitably a cleric in this period and long thereafter.[56] Systematic records of chancery personnel do not survive, and most scribes were anonymous, but Peter scriptor, a likely royal scribe in the middle of the twelfth century, was a cleric of Archbishop Theobald, and Etienne de Fougères, described both as a scribe and chaplain in documents he prepared, went on to become bishop of Rennes as well as the author of *Le livre de manières*.[57] Incidental evidence reveals men identified as clerics keeping records for justices in eyres, writing out summonses for taxes, or composing summonses for arrears and amercements.[58] Other references reveal shrieval clerics making and keeping various sorts of records, though no such records survive today.[59]

Secular clerics, like monks, nuns, and regular canons, were also expanding the use of writing in ecclesiastical administration, though the surviving evidence indicates that the Church lagged behind the royal government in England.[60] As noted in Chapter 4, large institutional churches, including secular cathedrals, were compiling economic records. They were also compiling collections of charters. More innovative was the increasing use of records in diocesan administration. By the end of the period, the bishops of Winchester had their own pipe rolls, bishops' chanceries were emerging, and some bishops and perhaps archdeacons were apparently keeping at least basic records about parish churches and appointments.[61]

---

[55] Clanchy, *From Memory to Written Record*, 57–80.

[56] For an overview of the debate over the establishment of the chancery, which certainly had antecedents in the Anglo-Saxon period, and for William I's chancellors, see David Bates, ed., *Regesta Regum Anglo-Normannorum: The Acta of William I, 1066–1087* (Oxford, 1998), 96–102. For the chancellors of John's reign, see Painter, *Reign of King John*, 78–80.

[57] T. A. M. Bishop, *Scriptores Regis* (Oxford, 1961), 24–5; Saltman, *Theobald, Archbishop of Canterbury*, 267–8; In addition, Nicholas Karn has identified Bishop's scribe xiii as Robert de Sigillo, future bishop of London: Nicholas Karn, "Robert de Sigillo: An Unruly Head of the Royal Scriptorium in the 1120s and 1130s," *English Historical Review* 123 (2008), 539–53.

[58] Stenton, ed., *Pleas*, 1:131; 2:537; Turner, *English Judiciary*, 211, 297; *Pipe Roll 6 Richard I*, 176; *Pipe Roll 8 Richard I*, xxiv, 290.

[59] Clanchy, *From Memory to Written Record*, 166; *Curia Regis Rolls*, 2:285; 6:208, 230; Stenton, ed., *Pleas*, 1:127; 2:164–5.

[60] Clanchy, *From Memory to Written Record*, 74–6.

[61] For the Winchester pipe rolls, including editions of the first two, see Richard H. Britnell, ed., *The Winchester Pipe Rolls and Medieval English Society* (Woodbridge, 2003); Hubert Hall, ed., *The Pipe Roll of the Bishopric of Winchester for the Fourth Year of the Pontificate of Peter des Roches, 1208–1209* (London, 1903); N. R. Holt, ed., *The Pipe Roll of the Bishopric of Winchester, 1210–1211* (Manchester, 1964). For the gradual coalescence of episcopal chanceries, see Cheney, *English Bishops' Chanceries*, 22–98; Cheney and Jones, eds., *English Episcopal Acta 2*, xliii–xliv; Barrow, ed., *English Episcopal Acta 7*, lxii–lxiii, lxviii–lxix, lxxx–lxxxi; Ramsey, ed., *English Episcopal Acta 10*, xciv–xcix; Barlow, ed., *English Episcopal Acta 11*, lxxviii–lxxx; Neininger, ed., *English Episcopal Acta 15*, lxxvii; Lovatt, ed., *English Episcopal Acta 20*, lxvii; Johnson, ed., *English Episcopal Acta 26*, cviii; Lovatt, ed., *English*

Fragmentary records survive from the highest level of the ecclesiastical courts by the end of the period, though these may only represent ad hoc efforts by Archbishop Hubert Walter.[62] As with the royal government, information about who precisely was responsible for producing and keeping episcopal records is limited, but once again what survives points to the dominance of secular clerics. Chancellors, notaries, and dataries who were clerics occur occasionally in the documents of various bishops: for instance, Peter of Blois was chancellor to Archbishop Richard of Canterbury.[63] In a few cases, the scribes or composers of individual charters issued by bishops identified themselves among the witnesses, and these were often specifically identified as clerics and sometimes were members of the household or cathedral chapter.[64] It is possible that regular clerics also played a role in the expansion of writing in diocesan administration, especially in bishoprics with monastic chapters, but there is no evidence of this.

There are indications that the households of secular lords had a larger role in the shift from memory to written record than scholars have realized. In his courtesy book, Daniel of Beccles urged the cleric of a lord to be a prudent record keeper (*notator*), to make writs and charters, to enroll "receipts, expenses, lawsuits, lands, reliefs, debts, *gersumas*, fines, scutages, and payments," and to enumerate the money and authorize the expenses "which are to the honor of the house."[65] This passage suggests a level of record keeping that surviving records barely hint at, though David Crouch has shown that the poetical biography of William Marshal drew on some quite miscellaneous household records.[66] It is possible that Daniel's advice came from the realm of the ideal rather than reality, but the list of record keeping, with its references to scutages, reliefs, and *gersumas*, clearly emerged out of a specifically English world of landholding. The fact that the earldom of Gloucester had an exchequer by the 1180s makes it more probable that Daniel of Beccles's passing comments reflect reality, and it is likely that by the end of the period, household clerics of powerful lords produced a substantial number of routine records that have since been lost.[67]

Episcopal Acta 27, cxxvii–cxxviii; Mayr-Harting, ed., *Acta of Chichester*, 35–7. For records of churches and appointments, see Cheney, *English Bishops' Chanceries*, 110–19; Kemp, ed., *English Episcopal Acta 18*, cxix, 55; Kemp, "Informing the Archdeacon," 144–8.

[62] Adams and Donahue, eds., *Select Cases*, introduction 3, 6–12, 104–14, text, 1–48.

[63] Cotts, *Clerical Dilemma*, 32; Cheney, *English Bishops' Chanceries*, 28–38; Cheney and Jones, eds., *English Episcopal Acta 2*, xxv–xxvii; Franklin, ed., *English Episcopal Acta 8*, lviii; Harper-Bill, ed., *English Episcopal Acta 6*, xliv; Vincent, ed., *English Episcopal Acta 9*, xliv–xlv; Barlow, ed., *English Episcopal Acta 11*, lxxx; Kemp, ed., *English Episcopal Acta 18*, lxxviii–lxxix; Cheney et al., eds., *English Episcopal Acta 33*, 55–6, 60–1, 91, 129; Cheney et al., eds., *English Episcopal Acta 34*, 53–4.

[64] These include Amicius, a household cleric at Canterbury, elsewhere described as notary, Robert Blund, precentor of Exeter, and Master John of Uffington, a cleric of Bishop Hugh Nunant: Cheney and Jones, eds., *English Episcopal Acta 2*, xxxii n. 25; Barlow, ed., *English Episcopal Acta 11*, 16; Greenway, *Fasti. 10. Exeter*, 10; Franklin, ed., *English Episcopal Acta 17*, lix, 10, 16–17; Johnson, ed., *English Episcopal Acta 26*, cviii–cix, 88; Karn, ed., *English Episcopal Acta 31*, cxl–cxli.

[65] Daniel of Beccles, *Urbanus Magnus*, 40.

[66] Holden, Gregory, and Crouch, eds., *History of William Marshal*, 3:30, 32–5.

[67] Patterson, ed., *Earldom of Gloucester Charters*, 166–7.

What do survive are charters from the households of lords, mostly in cartulary copies but sometimes as originals. Though beneficiaries often produced such documents, particularly early on, the charters of lords were increasingly likely to be produced in their households as time went on, and studies of the charters of various noble families show a gradual movement towards writing offices within their households.[68] Charters issued by secular lords were much more likely than other such documents to identify those who made (*fecit*) or wrote (*scripsit*) them, though the percentage of such charters was still minuscule. Those who can be identified were usually household clerics. Thus, several of the writers or composers of charters of the earls of Chester identified themselves as comital clerics, and some of them may have come from the Barbedavril family associated with the earls over several generations, while another was probably Peter the cleric, who was a prominent figure in Earl Ranulf III's household. Peter was also described as that earl's chancellor, suggesting he had a supervisory role, and the same may have been true of William Barbedavril earlier under Earl Hugh II, for William's counterseal was sometimes used with the earl's seal.[69] Because the earls of Chester were extremely wealthy, their household was more developed than most, but many other nobles had household clerics involved in producing documents. For instance, Anselm, the chaplain whom John de Lacy urged to seek the aid St. Gilbert of Sempringham, also prepared a charter for his lord, and clerics and chaplains who were clearly members of households can be found preparing or writing charters for a number of other noblemen and noblewomen.[70] The title of *notarius* was sometimes applied to household clerics, such as a cleric of the countess of Eu who appears in a miracle story, which provides further evidence of their involvement in

---

[68] Teresa Webber, "The Scribes and Handwriting of the Original Charters," *Journal of the Chester Archaeological Society* 71 (1991), 137–51; Patterson, ed., *Earldom of Gloucester Charters*, 25–30; Greenway, ed., *Charters of the Honour of Mowbray*, lxvii–lxx; Stringer, *Earl David*, 154.

[69] Webber, "Scribes and Handwriting," 140–4; Barraclough, ed., *Charters of the Anglo-Norman Earls of Chester*, 102, 157, 170, 189, 198–200.

[70] Anselm and John de Lacy: Geoffrey Barraclough, ed., *Facsimiles of Early Cheshire Charters* (Blackpool, 1957), 15–16. A countess of Leicester: Stenton, ed., *Documents Illustrative of the Danelaw*, 246. Cecily de Rumilly: Farrer and Clay, eds., *Early Yorkshire Charters*, 7:56 (Hugh the chaplain, who attests half of Cecily's admittedly small number of charters). Matilda II de Senlis: M. J. Franklin, ed., *The Cartulary of Daventry Priory*, Publications of the Northamptonshire Record Society vols. 35, 35 (Northampton, 1988), 3–4. Robert de Brus: Ruth M. Blakely, *The Brus Family in England and Scotland, 1100–1295* (Woodbridge, 2005), 153. Robert Mauduit: Emma Mason, ed., *The Beauchamp Cartulary Charters, 1100–1268*, Publications of the Pipe Roll Society, n.s. vol. 43 (London, 1980), xxxii. Roger de Mowbray: Greenway, ed., *Charters of the Honour of Mowbray*, lxvii–lxix. Simon de Senlis: Stenton, ed., *Documents Illustrative of the Danelaw*, 347 (Julian attested a number of Simon's other charters). Thomas Basset: William T. Reedy, ed., *Basset Charters, c.1120 to 1250*, Publications of the Pipe Roll Society, n.s. vol. 50 (London, 1995), 114–15, 118 (Bartholomew is probably the same figure who attests other Basset charters, in some cases as a chaplain or as rector of Compton Bassett). Earl William of Gloucester: Patterson, ed., *Earldom of Gloucester Charters*, 14, 17, 80–1, 167. Earl William de Mandeville: G. R. Elvey, ed., *Luffield Priory Charters*, 2 vols., Publications of the Northamptonshire Record Society, vols. 22, 26 (Oxford, 1968–75), 1:112–13. Earl William Marshal: Crouch, *William Marshal*, 154. There are a number of other cases where a cleric or chaplain prepares a charter for a noble but cannot be clearly identified as a member of the household due to insufficient evidence.

the production of records.[71] Overall, the evidence would suggest that clerics played a large role in the production of documents on behalf of great magnates.

Trying to apportion the respective role of secular clerics, regular clerics, and professional scribes in the overall production of administrative documents is no easy task. The largest body of evidence about the creation of administrative documents comes from statements of the kind that a particular witness made, wrote, prepared, or composed a charter, that I have already noted in documents of bishops and secular magnates. These statements do not necessarily identify the actual scribe, but do at least show the figure in charge of production.[72] Such statements are very rare; Michael Gervers and Nicole Hamonic were able to identify twenty-five individuals from a database of some 3000 Hospitaller charters and twenty-six from a database of some 10,000 dated charters (both databases extend through the thirteenth century). They found that sixteen of the twenty-five individuals they identified for Hospitaller charters had the title of chaplain, cleric, or *diaconus*.[73] David Postles gathered a larger sample for the twelfth and thirteenth centuries, and reports that of 126 men who subscribed charters, sixty-eight described themselves as clerics, three as deacons, two as priests, and twenty as chaplains, for a total of ninety-three secular clerics.[74] Having, alas, gone far towards reinventing the wheel before encountering these studies, I can report similar findings from an overlapping body of examples for the period up to 1216, with as many as 123 individuals of whom eighty-two identified themselves as some sort of secular cleric, including some who were also *magistri*.[75] Some of the figures discovered by Postles or myself who did not describe themselves as clerics when they took credit for a charter can be identified as such from other documents, so the figures above under-represent the numbers of clerics.[76] Strikingly, Postles only found two who can likely be identified as laymen, and I have found a third.[77] Besides clerics and chaplains in the households of bishops and great secular lords, some composers of charters may have been the chaplains or clerics of lesser landholders granting charters. For instance a charter of Philippa Gulafre was written by Patrick, cleric of Burgate, who also appears as a family attorney as well as rector of Burgate, though unfortunately one cannot be certain if

---

[71] Robertson and Sheppard, eds., *Materials*, 1:320.

[72] Webber, "Scribes and Handwriting," 139 n. 14; Reedy, ed., *Basset Charters*, 115.

[73] Michael Gervers and Nicole Hamonic, "Scribes and Notaries in Twelfth- and Thirteenth-Century Hospitaller Charters from England," in Karl Borchardt, Nikolas Jaspert, and Helen J. Nicholson, eds., *The Hospitallers, the Mediterranean and Europe: Festschrift for Anthony Luttrell* (Aldershot, 2007), 181–92.

[74] David Postles, "County *Clerici* and the Composition of English Twelfth- and Thirteenth-Century Private Charters," in Karl Heidecker, ed., *Charters and the Use of the Written Word in Medieval Society* (Turnhout, 2000), 27–42.

[75] Franklin, ed., *English Episcopal Acta 17*, 10; Barraclough, ed., *Charters of the Anglo-Norman Earls of Chester*, 378; Kemp, ed., *Archidiaconal Acta*, 131–2. See also Patterson, ed., *Earldom of Gloucester Charters*, 17.

[76] For instance, Richard Aaron, who gave himself no title in a charter he wrote for the future king John, but elsewhere appears as a rector: Patterson, ed., *Earldom of Gloucester Charters*, 51; Brown, ed., *Eye Priory Cartulary and Charters*, 1:77–8.

[77] Farrer and Clay, eds., *Early Yorkshire Charters*, 1:413.

ties of lordship or of neighborhood provided the connection.[78] Most scribes or composers of charters, unfortunately, cannot be traced beyond their attestations.

One striking finding is the near absence of monks or nuns. I have found only one example: Luke, monk of Combermere who, strangely enough, prepared a charter from one layman to another far from his monastery.[79] Given the practice of monastic beneficiaries drawing up charters throughout the period, it seems unlikely that no members of the monastic clergy prepared charters. Indeed, Robert Patterson has argued that scribes associated with Margam Abbey in Glamorgan also participated in local administration and the administration of the counts of Gloucester, though the fact that he has to rely overwhelmingly on documents coming from Margam makes it hard to be sure that its scribes normally drafted documents relating to other parties.[80] The absence of monks, nuns, or regular canons claiming credit for charter production may simply reflect distinct monastic scribal practices or ideals of modesty. However, not all scribes associated with monastic houses were necessarily members of the community: for instance, Eye Priory may have relied on a secular cleric for a number of its charters between *c.*1180 and *c.*1210.[81] Though Patterson clearly thinks many of the scribes associated with Margam were monks, which is a reasonable hypothesis, the only three he could identify by name were secular clerics.[82] The secular clergy may therefore have been involved even in monastic document production, which makes it even harder to judge the respective roles of the monastic and regular clergy in producing the growing number of documents in the period.

What of the *scriptores*, the scribes, who appeared occasionally in witness lists, and who very occasionally took credit for writing or making a charter? Were these professional scribes who were laymen and expected pay rather than the hope of a benefice? Possibly, but it would be imprudent to assume so. At least a few of the *scriptores* who explicitly took credit for charters also described themselves as priests or clerics.[83] Both clerics and scribes appeared in the *Dialogue of the Exchequer*, but the cleric of the treasurer was also described as the scribe of his roll and it is hard to see any clear distinction between the two groups in that text.[84] Of course, one could argue that any clerical scribe who made a living from writing was only technically a cleric and would better be described as a clerk. However, as long as they maintained tonsures and wore clerical garb, it is unlikely that contemporaries would have seen such scribes as not "really" being clerics, any more than they

---

[78] Brown, ed., *Eye Priory Cartulary and Charters*, 1:216; 2:39.

[79] Ross and Devine, eds., *Cartulary of Cirencester*, 2:557–8.

[80] Robert B. Patterson, *The Scriptorium of Margam Abbey and the Scribes of Early Angevin Glamorgan: Secretarial Administration in a Welsh Marcher Barony, c.1150–c.1225* (Woodbridge, 2002).

[81] Brown, ed., *Eye Priory Cartulary and Charters*, 2:39.

[82] Two of these, admittedly, were only marginally associated with the abbey, but the third was probably responsible for the only surviving original charter issued by an abbot of the house: Patterson, *Scriptorium of Margam Abbey*, 47, 53, 56, 72–3, 87–8, 93.

[83] Ross and Devine, eds., *Cartulary of Cirencester*, 2:558; Michael Gervers, ed., *The Cartulary of the Knights of St. John of Jerusalem in England: Essex*, 2 vols. (Oxford, 1982), 1:27; Farrer and Clay, eds., *Early Yorkshire Charters*, 7:56.

[84] Richard fitzNigel, *Dialogus de Scaccario*, 26–7.

exempted other kinds of clerical craftsmen or the clerical peasant farmers noted in Chapter 4 from that category.

Indeed, there is clear evidence of clerical scribes who went on to be important churchmen. Richard of Ilchester, the future bishop of Winchester, first appeared in the pipe rolls as Richard scriptor, having previously been a notary in the household of the earl of Gloucester.[85] Thomas Becket worked early on as a scribe for his relative, Osbern Eightpence, recording expenses and rents.[86] One might argue that both figures were "really" administrators rather than clerics but contemporaries were more likely to view them instead as clerics who were too worldly. In addition, there is evidence of clerics combining scribal duties with more purely religious ones. Thomas of Chobham wrote that it was acceptable for clerics and scholars to correct their books, improve their readings, and collect authorities for sermons on holy days as long as they did not accept pay, indicating that secular clerics who were involved in religious duties might also act as paid scribes.[87] Admittedly, the scribal tasks Thomas described were not administrative, but Daniel of Beccles envisioned the same clerics whom he urged to be good record keepers taking care of their lords' chapels as well.[88] Similarly, chaplains who wrote charters presumably also performed masses, heard confessions, and performed other priestly functions. Obviously one cannot rule out the possibility that professional lay scribes were doing much work in the period, given the problems of evidence, but one cannot assume it. Equally obviously, there may have been many clerics who were essentially professional scribes. Nonetheless, much record keeping was clearly the responsibility of clerics who also performed religious duties and might even hold important religious offices.

In discussing the role of the secular clergy in the shift from memory to written record, it is also worth noting that secular clerics produced and preserved records for their own purposes from an early period. In his "Sacerdos ad Altarem," Alexander Neckam advised priests to preserve their privileges, instruments, charters, chirographs, and muniments, either as originals or copies. Alexander wrote, "He who has no inventory is lacking in mature counsel."[89] Some clerics did indeed create small private archives. Bernard the Scribe, one of Henry I's administrators and a cleric, kept a collection of charters that ultimately got preserved because he gave his properties to a religious house. An unusually full series of royal charters for the first two canons of the Lincoln prebend of Asgarby may have resulted from a similar personal collection that was later incorporated into the cathedral archive.[90] Later on, Master David of London asked the unnamed addressee of one of his letters to keep a number of documents with his other charters, yet again suggesting a personal

[85] Duggan, "Richard of Ilchester," 2–3.   [86] Robertson and Sheppard, eds., *Materials*, 2:361.

[87] Thomas of Chobham, *Summa Confessorum*, 269, 309.

[88] Daniel of Beccles, *Urbanus Magnus*, 39–40.

[89] Alexander Neckam, *Alexandri Neckam Sacerdos ad Altare*, ed. Christopher James McDonough (Turnhout, 2010), 19–20.

[90] J. H. Round, "Bernard, the King's Scribe," *English Historical Review* 14 (1899), 417–30; Foster and Major, eds., *Registrum Antiquissimum*, 1:39–41, 71–7.

archive.[91] Gerald of Wales, who had his own *notarius*, also had his own collection of private records and made extensive use of writing in managing his affairs. Gerald was able to detect cheating by a member of his household partly by looking through his *notula* and *scripta*, and one obscure passage might refer to records of expenditures. Gerald relied on letters to keep track of his interests in Wales and apparently arranged to have copies of relevant documents deposited with the prior of Brecon. Sometime after he had technically transferred his archdeaconry and various benefices to his nephew, while continuing to manage them, his nephew demanded he provide an account of their annual revenue.[92] How systematic or well organized Gerald's records were is unclear, but it possible that the household account of the canon of St. Paul's discussed in Chapter 4 is a remnant of a fairly common kind of document for elite clerics from the end of the period. Even fairly minor clerics may have had collections of documents; one rural dean spoke of finding a charter among the records (*scrinia*) of a vicar called Hugh the Chaplain.[93]

The question remains of the extent to which the use of literacy in administration, particularly in the royal government, depended on the clergy. Richardson and Sayles argued for fairly widespread literacy among the upper reaches of lay society, partly on the basis of specific examples, partly on the more problematic argument that administrators *must* have been literate in order to function.[94] Clanchy is sympathetic to their arguments, though more skeptical about the ability of lay administrators to write in than to read Latin since, as he shows, the two abilities were not necessarily joined in the Middle Ages.[95] Turner has argued along similar lines to Richardson and Sayles, though with more examples, and has posed the question, "Must we assume that medieval administrators were always accompanied by clergymen to read to them, write their letters, and figure their accounts?"[96] Most recently and more generally, Aurell has argued that widespread literacy emerged among the lay aristocracy, male and female, over the course of the twelfth and thirteenth centuries.[97]

I have a more skeptical view of the importance of lay literacy in twelfth-century England, including in royal administration, and my answer to Turner's question is that while we should not assume such a state of affairs, it was certainly possible. I will emphasize at the outset that this is not an open and shut case. First, the works noted above have clearly shown that some lay aristocrats were literate or even

---

[91] Z. N. Brooke, "The Register of Master David of London, and the Part he Played in the Becket Crisis," in H. W. C. Davis, ed., *Essays in History Presented to Reginald Lane Poole* (Oxford, 1927), 227–45, at 240.

[92] Gerald of Wales, *Opera*, 1:213; Gerald of Wales, *Speculum Duorum*, 78–83, 118–19.

[93] Kemp, "Acta of English Rural Deans," 153.

[94] H. G. Richardson and G. O. Sayles, *The Governance of Mediaeval England from the Conquest to Magna Carta* (Edinburgh, 1963), 269–82.

[95] Clanchy, *From Memory to Written Record*, 235–6.

[96] Turner, *Judges, Administrators*, 119–36.

[97] Aurell, *Le chevalier lettré*, 15–39, 47–261. See also Nicholas Orme, "Lay Literacy in England, 1100–1300," in Alfred Haverkamp and Hanna Vollrath, eds., *England and Germany in the High Middle Ages* (Oxford, 1996), 35–56.

learned, which is generally what writers meant by *litteratus* in the period.[98] Second, evidence is limited and anecdotal, and there is much we do not know. Nonetheless, the evidence that survives largely points to clerical dominance in the fields of reading and writing. No known author of a text of any size or complexity can be identified with certainty as a lay person in England in this period, which militates against any claim for a particularly strong culture of lay literacy, even with the caveat that it is not possible to establish the status of many individual authors, most obviously the anonymous ones.[99] There was one case of a lay sheriff writing out an acknowledgement of a debt in his own hand.[100] However, I know of no other certain instance of an influential lay administrator writing a document. There is also evidence of a habitual reliance on clerics to read documents out loud. In the *History of William Marshal*, the poet described William having a letter from an ally read out loud, noting in a poetic flourish that the cleric read it exceedingly well.[101] Similar scenes appear in works of romance, which no doubt reflected the expectations of authors and audiences about literate practices in the day.[102] One court case reveals a landholder, who seems by the context to have been a reasonably important figure, receiving a writ and having to send for a cleric to read it; clearly he lacked even basic skills of literacy.[103] Henry I could read, but he too had documents read out loud, perhaps for the benefit of members of his court.[104] Clanchy has emphasized the important of hearing works read aloud, and this clearly held true even for administrative material and correspondence.[105] Those reading aloud were consistently identified as clerics, and given the large numbers of clerics in administrative settings, it would have been perfectly feasible to rely on them for writing and reading most documents. Indeed, one of the striking things is how often a mixed group of clerics and laypeople were appointed to carry out tasks, perhaps because of a desire to ensure that any such group would have access to literate clerics. Though some lay administrators could read and even write, this was probably still a society in which reading and writing was largely associated with the clergy.

Indeed, the well-known linkage writers of the period made between literacy, learning, and clerical status provides circumstantial but powerful evidence for clerical domination of the use of the written word. This almost automatic linkage is particularly apparent in works written in French, where literacy and learning sometimes appear almost to have been defining characteristics of the clergy. Thus,

---

[98] For the meaning of *litteratus*, see Clanchy, *From Memory to Written Record*, 226–31.

[99] For an anonymous text possibly written by a layperson, see Evelyn Mullally, ed., *The Deeds of the Normans in Ireland. La geste des engleis en Yrlande* (Dublin, 2002), 33; Laura Ashe, *Fiction and History in England, 1066–1200* (Cambridge, 2007), 164–5.

[100] Clanchy, *From Memory to Written Record*, 236; Turner, *Judges, Administrators*, 131.

[101] Holden, Gregory, and Crouch, eds., *History of William Marshal*, 1:300–1.

[102] Thomas of Kent, *The Anglo-Norman Alexander (Le roman de toute chevalerie)*, ed. Brian Foster and Ian Short, 2 vols. (London, 1976–77), 1:50; Hue de Rotelande, *Protheslaus*, ed. A. J. Holden, 3 vols. (London, 1991–3), 1:19; 2:29–31, 40, 51–2.

[103] *Curia Regis Rolls*, 7:346–7.

[104] Stuart A. Moore, ed., *Cartularium Monasterii Sancti Johannis Baptiste de Colecestria*, 2 vols., Roxburgh Club (London, 1897), 1:4. Some of the fictional examples noted above also involved literate laymen.

[105] Clanchy, *From Memory to Written Record*, 266–70.

Jordan Fantosme, in his poetic account of the 1173–4 revolt, could write that Earl David of Huntingdon intended no harm "to priest or canon, who knew grammar," and the author of the *Roman de Waldef* could gloss clerics as those "who know how to chant and read."[106] The later use of the reading test for accused criminals claiming clerical status came precisely from this context.[107] As both Clanchy and Turner have discussed, the linkage was so strong that in the context of learning and literacy terms relating to clerical status might be used for laypeople.[108] Once again, vernacular writings provide particularly good examples. For instance, even though Hue de Roteland, in his romance *Ipomedon*, distinguished between laypeople (*leis*) and the learned (*lettrez*), and then almost immediately paired this with a contrast between the clergy and laity (*clerc e lai*), he later described the father of the eponymous hero as being well taught in *clergie* as well as proud of his chivalry. He also used the term *clergie* in commenting on the education of Ipomedon, whom he described as *bien lettrez*.[109] Neither of these imaginary secular aristocrats was actually labeled a cleric, but the semantic slippage here is obvious. Clanchy and Turner noted this occasional tendency to semantic slippage because it clouds the issue of lay literacy by sometimes making it hard to know whether a literate person was in fact a cleric or layperson. Without denying their point, I would stress a different lesson. People in this period imagined literacy and learning to be the province of the religious, and though this was not always true either in reality or in fiction, the close association between learning and clerical status strongly indicates that normally reading, writing, and learning were carried out by the clergy.

Even if my skeptical assessment of the level of lay literacy is correct, there is no denying that lay participation in the literate aspects of administration in the long twelfth century, however limited, was an important harbinger for the future. This point, however, only serves to underline the importance of the secular clergy in spreading the bureaucratic use of literacy outside the monastic sphere. The secular clergy had made possible an administrative world in which powerful laypeople, whether or not they were literate themselves, became deeply involved in processes that relied on the technology of the written word. Even illiterates who had to employ clerics to compose and copy Latin administrative records were involved on some level, because they were giving orders. Even local landholders who had to find a cleric to hear a writ read aloud, or suitors at court who had to rely on the local clergy to orally convey the contents of documents, were operating in an environment in which they needed to deal with the written word. It is no wonder that at least some laypeople were already becoming literate, for a system had been created that inevitably encouraged lay literacy. The process had begun before 1066, of

---

[106] Jordan Fantosme, *Jordan Fantosme's Chronicle*, ed. R. C. Johnston (Oxford, 1981), 84–5 (see also 66–9). A. J. Holden, ed., *Le Roman de Waldef* (Geneva, 1984), 277. Other examples of the association include Paris, "Donnei," 513, 537; Stimming, ed., *Boeve de Haumtone*, 123; A. Ewert, ed., *Gui de Warewic, roman du XIIIe siècle*, 2 vols. (Paris, 1932), 1:28.

[107] Gabel, *Benefit of Clergy*, 65–74.

[108] Clanchy, *From Memory to Written Record*, 226–30; Turner, *Judges, Administrators*, 121–2. See also Aurell, *Le chevalier lettré*, 21–5.

[109] Hue de Rotelande, *Ipomedon*, 63, 69–70.

course, and the use of vernacular documents in the Anglo-Saxon period complicates any assumption about a neat continuous rise of lay involvement in written administration. Nonetheless, the rise of administrative kingship made the long twelfth century crucial in the history of literacy and bureaucracy. Whatever the precise chronology, it was the secular clergy who served as the primary conduit through which the technology of literacy spread into the wider world.

Clerics also played a crucial role in bringing a sophisticated command of numeracy to the government, specifically to the exchequer. Clerics and laypeople worked side by side there, as in other areas of government, and the existence of many merchants in England no doubt precluded any clerical monopoly over the mastery of numbers. Nonetheless, the key figures in the history of the exchequer praised by Richard fitz Nigel, himself a cleric, tended to be other clerics: Bishop Roger of Salisbury; the author's father, Bishop Nigel of Ely; Richard of Ilchester; and Master Thomas Brown, an English expert brought back from service at the royal court of Sicily.[110] Moreover, as Haskins long ago noted, knowledge of the abacus, drawn most immediately from Laon and Lorraine, was crucial to the formation of the exchequer, and that knowledge was preserved and disseminated by clerics.[111] Indeed, there survives, by good fortune, a treatise on the abacus by a scholar named Turchil, which refers to one of Henry I's key officials, Hugh of Buckland, sheriff of eight counties and possibly the married canon of St. Paul's of that name, in setting out a sample problem of how to divide 200 marks among all the hides of Essex, the kind of difficult problem the royal government often faced. Turchil's work shows the complex technical underpinnings that made exchequer calculations possible. Though the exchequer was set up so that people who lacked this technical expertise could participate in the process, the origins of the institution lay in specialized clerical learning.[112]

Given the origins of the exchequer, it is worth exploring the more general influence on government of the higher education that more and more clerics were acquiring, especially since several scholars have emphasized the impact of the schools on administration. John Baldwin stressed the entry of *magistri* into English royal government.[113] Moore contended that governments looked to the schools for solutions to practical problems of governance.[114] Above all, Southern argued for a close symbiosis between the schools and ecclesiastical and secular government, with bureaucracies creating demand for highly trained clerics and clerics in turn furthering the development of administrative structures. Indeed, Southern viewed "the successful application of . . . knowledge, and the skills that had brought it into existence, to the work of government" as one of the three key

[110] Richard fitzNigel, *Dialogus de Scaccario*, 40–1, 52–5, 64–5, 76–7.

[111] Charles Homer Haskins, *Studies in the History of Mediaeval Science* (Cambridge, 1924), 113, 327–35.

[112] Enrico Narducci, "Intorno a due trattati inediti d'abaco," *Bullettino di bibliografica e di storia delle scienze matematiche e fisiche* 15 (1882), 111–62, at 135–54; Green, *Government of England*, 41, 161; Green, *Henry I*, 242.

[113] Baldwin, "Studium et Regnum," 204–10.   [114] Moore, *First European Revolution*, 143.

accomplishments of the schools.[115] Not surprisingly, I concur with these scholars' arguments. Nonetheless, it is not in fact very easy to trace or measure the impact of higher education on the development of government.

One did not, for instance, require an education in Paris or Bologna to write out routine writs or even to help develop the English common law. Of the clerics who served frequently as royal justices, only one, Richard Barre, can be shown to have studied at the famous law schools of Bologna, and of course the Roman or canon law he studied there would have had only indirect application to common law.[116] Once the exchequer was running, hands-on experience was probably more useful than formal training in the quadrivium. The many tasks carried out interchangeably by clerics and laymen manifestly required no training in the schools. One of the standard attacks made on the great clerical administrators, from Ranulf Flambard to Walter de Grey, King John's chancellor, was that they were *illiterati*, in other words unlearned.[117] Peter of Blois described Richard of Ilchester in these terms, and Gerald of Wales attacked Hubert Walter for having been engaged in administrative service at an age when he should have been working on Donatus, whose grammar was a basic textbook, and for coming to the episcopacy from the exchequer rather than the schools.[118] These were all hostile attacks, but they show that the ideal education for a cleric was not necessarily the best training for an administrator. Work in ecclesiastical administration did sometimes require higher training in the schools, which may be why bishops recruited so many masters to their households, but the same was not true of secular government.

Nonetheless, deeply learned men did enter into secular administration. Alexander Neckam lamented that an unnamed friend from the schools, alongside whom he had "fought" in the "castles of philosophy" and who had studied problems of mathematics deep into the night, had entered a morally suspect and intellectually uninspiring career in accounting.[119] Men like Peter of Blois and Gerald of Wales themselves served the king. Both were on the fringes of royal administration but some of the men who devoted their careers to royal administration and gained key positions, like William of Wrotham, were learned *magistri*. Indeed, William was a dedicatee of Geoffrey of Vinsauf's sophisticated rhetorical treatise, *Poetria Nova*, and Richard Barre wrote poetry and made a series of extracts from the Bible for one of his patrons, Bishop William Longchamp.[120] Moreover, whatever Hubert Walter's own educational background, he surrounded himself with deeply learned men in his household, and though it is possible that he retained them primarily to help him fulfill his duties as bishop and archbishop, both he and his household divided

---

[115] Southern, *Scholastic Humanism*, 1:141–5, 180–1; 2:151–218 (quote at 1:180–1). See also Donald Matthew, *Britain and the Continent, 1000–1300* (London, 2005), 109–12.

[116] Turner, *English Judiciary*, 259.

[117] Orderic Vitalis, *Ecclesiastical History*, 5:310–11; Roger of Wendover, *Liber qui Dicitur Flores Historiarum*, ed. Henry G. Hewlett, 3 vols. (London, 1886–9), 2:153.

[118] Peter of Blois, *Later Letters*, 48; Davies, "Giraldus Cambrensis: *De Invectionibus*," 97, 114–15.

[119] Hunt and Gibson, *Schools and the Cloister*, 9.

[120] Geoffrey of Vinsauf, *Poetria Nova*, ed. Margaret F. Nims and Martin Camargo (Toronto, 2010), 95; Richard Sharpe, "Richard Barre's *Compendium Veteris et Novi Testamenti*," *The Journal of Medieval Latin* 14 (2004), 128–46.

their time between secular and ecclesiastical administration.[121] Other bishops serving at court would also have had learned *magistri* in their retinues. Thus, even though a smaller percentage of secular than ecclesiastical administrators would have been trained in the schools, there were enough learned men, particularly in royal government, to have an impact.

Masters and other figures who had studied in the schools were welcomed into administrations and households partly because they brought some important specific skills. Admittedly, not all of these skills mattered in strictly administrative terms. For instance, kings, prelates, and secular lords all sought out clerics trained in medicine, often rewarding them richly.[122] Other skills, however, *were* important for administration. Though only a fairly basic level of Latin was necessary for most administrative tasks, kings and magnates, especially ecclesiastical magnates, needed excellent Latinists in their trains to write elegant letters and serve as emissaries to the papal court and other places where Latin could serve as a common language.[123] Not only communication but also status was involved here: bad Latin could be deeply embarrassing.[124] Even more important in administrative terms was training in canon law. Adam of Eynsham described how Hugh of Avalon, bishop of Lincoln, recruited learned clerics from schools both in England and overseas to assist him in ruling his flock and particularly in running ecclesiastical courts, and also obtained the service of two masters from Archbishop Baldwin.[125] When Abbot Samson of Bury St Edmunds was first appointed as a papal judge delegate, he hired two clerics who were skilled in law to help him out while he gained experience, and Abbot Robert of St. Albans had an Italian cleric and legal expert in his train named Master Ambrose whom he could send to Rome to argue a case before the pope.[126] Most famously, Archbishop Theobald sent Thomas Becket for training in the law schools of Bologna, and summoned Master Vacarius, a specialist in both civil and canon law, to England.[127] Such experts were crucial to the development of ecclesiastical courts, which had a huge influence not only within the Church but also in society as a whole, since they had jurisdiction over many matters of fundamental importance to laypeople, including punishment of moral transgressions and rulings on the legitimacy of marriages and therefore of children.[128]

---

[121] Cheney, *Hubert Walter*, 158–71; Young, *Hubert Walter*, 56–63.

[122] Cheney, *Hubert Walter*, 163; Ramsey, ed., *English Episcopal Acta 10*, lii; Kemp, ed., *English Episcopal Acta 18*, lxxiv; Snape, ed., *English Episcopal Acta 24*, xlii–xliii, xlvii; Franklin, ed., *English Episcopal Acta 17*, 17–18; Crouch, *Beaumont Twins*, 151, 155; Edward J. Kealey, *Medieval Medicus: A Social History of Anglo-Norman Medicine* (Baltimore, 1981), 51–2, 57–81, 135–7, 141–2, 144–6, 151.

[123] Giles Constable, "Dictators and Diplomats in the Eleventh and Twelfth Centuries: Medieval Epistolography and the Birth of Modern Bureaucracy," *Culture and Spirituality in Medieval Europe* (Aldershot, 1996), 37–46.

[124] See Chapter 12, section 3.

[125] Adam of Eynsham, *Magna Vita Sancti Hugonis*, 1:110–13.

[126] Jocelin of Brakelond, *Chronicle*, 33–4; Thomas Walsingham, *Gesta Abbatum*, 1:136–7.

[127] Robertson and Sheppard, eds., *Materials*, 3:17; Gervase of Canterbury, *Historical Works*, 2:384–5.

[128] For early matrimony and bastardy cases, see Adams and Donahue, eds., *Select Cases*, introduction 10, text 1–3, 15–31.

However, scholars like Baldwin, Moore, and Southern have thought not simply in terms of the transfer of specific skills, whether in canon law or the use of the abacus, but of the more general impact of advanced learning. Though tracing such influences is difficult, one suggestive area is in the development of English common law, for although Richard Barre was the only royal justice known to have studied at Bologna, others were *magistri*.[129] As is well known, English common law, unlike much continental law, did not emerge from the revival of the study of Roman civil law but rather from local practices being shaped and standardized by royal government. Yet early writers about the common law and at least some clerical justices were familiar with civil and canon law. As John Hudson has argued most recently, their influence appeared less in the substance of the law than in the structuring of legal argument, the adoption of some of the rhetoric and vocabulary of Roman law, and in the use of Roman legal concepts to clarify such important ideas as the distinction between rights and seisin in land.[130] One might also look at economic administration, as with my argument that figures like Thomas of Hurstbourne and Peter of Waltham, both of whom were *magistri*, were involved in systematic thinking about economic and managerial matters in royal government and beyond.[131]

The teaching of logic, the challenging of received wisdom, and the systematic approach to complex problems in the schools all could have created habits of mind that scholars carried over into administration when they entered the service of monarchs and magnates. There the general lack of specialization would have meant that learned *magistri* would have interacted with equally intelligent laymen and with clerics who might have less formal learning but more experience in the practicalities of estate management or English law. Certainly Peter of Blois described Henry II's practice of discussing difficult questions with a "wedge of clerics," and one could imagine the king and secular administrators and magnates involved in such discussions indirectly absorbing the methods and ideas of the schools.[132] I would suggest that the synergies between formal learning and practical experience, between landholders who knew livestock and *magistri* who knew logic, and between administrators intent on maximizing royal revenues and scholars who sat up late at night struggling with mathematics help explain the administrative creativity and bureaucratic inventiveness of this period. Unfortunately, all of this is necessarily somewhat nebulous, much like arguing for the benefit of a liberal arts education in contemporary society.[133] Nonetheless, even though it is hard to pinpoint many precise contributions of higher education to administrative practices in the long twelfth century, I believe that the habits of mind developed in the schools contributed greatly to the development of successful administrative

---

[129] Turner, *English Judiciary*, 35, 94–5, 259.
[130] John Hudson, *The Formation of the English Common Law: Law and Society in England from the Norman Conquest to Magna Carta* (London, 1996), 150.
[131] See Chapter 4, section 3.   [132] Peter of Blois, *Opera*, 198.
[133] For a more skeptical view, see Rolf Köhn, "Schulbildung und Trivium im lateinischen Hochmittelalter und ihr möglicher praktischer Nutzen," in Johannes Fried, ed., *Schulen und Studium im sozialen Wandel des hohen und späten Mittelalters* (Sigmaringen, 1986), 203–84.

structures and thus represented yet another important contribution of the secular clergy to the medieval origins of modern bureaucracy.

4. THE RELIGIOUS CRITIQUE OF COURTS AND CLERICAL COURTIERS

The immense clerical contribution to administration was accompanied by widespread criticism of clerical courtiers and administrators, but before turning to that subject it is important to more fully describe the allure of service at the royal court and in the households of lay and ecclesiastical magnates. The last chapter showed how service to powerful patrons could provide a route to high position and wealth. The courtier in Peter of Blois's poem claimed that others feared him but he feared none, and though the latter half of this claim is contradicted by the frequent anxieties about patrons that I will discuss shortly, service to great lords was certainly an important route to power. The chronicler of Meaux Abbey explained that despite putting up a struggle the monastery had to be content with a small pension from a rector of one of their churches partly because he was a powerful figure as the seneschal of Baldwin of Bethune, count of Aumale.[134] A writer from Bury St Edmunds described how in 1168, William de Curzon, who wanted to recover family lands that had been taken by others, married the niece of Richard of Ilchester to gain Richard's support. Though Richard was not yet bishop of Winchester, according to the writer he exercised power throughout England by the king's will.[135]

Courts and the households of magnates were also places of luxury, as Peter of Blois's courtier noted. Peter of Cornwall, prior of Holy Trinity, Aldgate, dedicated one part of his *Pantheologus* to Godfrey de Lucy, bishop of Winchester, and in its prologue he described a feast held by the bishop. Peter claimed he was seated fourth from Godfrey's right hand but one thousandth from his left and described tables straining to bear the weight of precious vessels filled with fine wines and food noteworthy as much for its skilled preparation as its cost. "I saw the riches of Croesus, the delights of Sardanopolis [...] the elegance of the Greeks and English abundance [...]." Throughout the prologue, Peter depicted an episcopal household overflowing with luxury, albeit as a prelude to warning about worldly vanities.[136] Similarly, Henry of Huntingdon, in a letter on despising worldly matters, described how in his youth he had been dazzled by the pomp surrounding Bishop Robert Bloet of Lincoln, a royal chancellor. Henry noted the "handsome riders, noble youths, costly horses, gold and gilded vessels, numerous courses [at meals], splendid servers, purple clothing, and satins." Echoing Peter of Blois's courtier, he said that

---

[134] Thomas de Burton, *Chronica Monasterii de Melsa*, 1:297–8.
[135] Thomas Arnold, ed., *Memorials of St. Edmund's Abbey*, 3 vols. (London, 1890–6), 1:148–9.
[136] Peter was also flaunting his command of obscure Latin vocabulary, and his description was not meant to be literally true in every respect: British Library, Royal MS 7 C XIV, fos. 7v–8v.

in his youth he would have considered anyone who suggested rejecting such delights to be "crazier than Orestes."[137]

Service in households and courts brought more than material benefits. As Peter of Blois's courtier noted, it afforded one dignity. Moreover, the friendship of magnates mentioned in his poem brought prestige as well as connections. Though Peter of Cornwall was not in Godfrey's household, his statement about his position in the seating not only gave a (doubtlessly exaggerated) sense of the size of the feast, but also played cleverly with seating and honor. As a humble regular cleric he was a thousand seats from Godfrey, but as an honored guest he was only four places away on the religiously significant right side of the bishop. The occasional gifts of wine by King John to clerical favorites were partly a material reward but mainly a tangible and prestigious sign of royal favor.[138] In a society that valued both vertical and horizontal links, service, particularly in tightknit households, could place one within an emotionally satisfying as well as practically useful network. Anne Duggan, writing on Thomas Becket's household, has spoken of a culture of reciprocity, and of fidelity and honor, parallel to the culture of secular aristocratic retinues.[139] A letter written by the clergy of Exeter about miraculous cures by Becket of the bishop of Exeter and members of his community reveals the episcopal household and cathedral clergy as overlapping communities with strong emotional and religious ties.[140] Certain households could also be intellectually exciting places, as Peter of Blois's passage about Henry II tackling difficult questions with his clerics suggests. John of Salisbury, in a letter to John of Tilbury, recalled how philosophical meditations, discussion of learned works, and pleasant and useful disputations, along with work, kept boredom at bay during their time in Archbishop Theobald's household.[141] Outside of the schools, the royal household and the households of bishops were among the few places where intellectuals were likely to find themselves employed with other intellectuals. Access to wealth, power, and luxury was probably the greatest attraction of courts and households, but there were other attractions of a more subtle sort.

For many moralists and intellectuals, however, the attractions of court life and the robust institutional development in this period were not matters for celebration but for deep anxiety and sharp warnings. Criticism of clerical service of all sorts, but particularly in secular administration, was widespread in the medieval West. The courts of English kings, especially Henry II and his sons, were particularly important targets. Though some of the criticism came from monks like Nigel of Whiteacre, most of the key critics were secular clerics such as John of Salisbury, Peter of Blois, Walter Map, and Gerald of Wales, often themselves courtiers. A number of scholars, among them John Baldwin, Egbert Türk, Stephen Jaeger, John Cotts, and

---

[137] Henry of Huntingdon, *Historia Anglorum*, 586–7. Orestes was driven mad by the Furies after killing his mother, Clytemnestra.

[138] Hardy, ed., *Rotuli Litterarum Clausarum*, 1a, 1b, 48b, 51a, 101a, 162a.

[139] Anne Duggan, "The Price of Loyalty: The Fate of Thomas Becket's Learned Household," in Anne Duggan, ed., *Thomas Becket: Friends, Networks, Texts, and Cult* (Aldershot, 2007), 1–18, at 8–9.

[140] Robertson and Sheppard, eds., *Materials*, 1:407–9.

[141] John of Salisbury, *Letters*, 2:516–19. See also Peter of Blois, *Opera*, 17–18.

Frédérique Lachaud have studied this criticism sensitively and in detail. I will not try, therefore, to do more than summarize the critiques.[142] However, I will summarize them in the context of some of the main arguments of this book and with certain emphases and perspectives that not all scholars would necessarily share or highlight.

Scholars have devoted attention to the critiques in part because it is striking to modern people that governmental institutions, which modern scholars are often predisposed to admire, and ecclesiastical institutions, which one would think religious writers would celebrate, came under so much criticism. It is also striking that so many of the critics themselves had participated in the system which they attacked so fiercely. If one accepts the standard religious premises of the time, however, clerical participation in secular and even in ecclesiastical administration was at best filled with danger and at worst was a short and easy road to perdition. Given these premises, moreover, the administrative systems as they developed in practice were morally flawed, perhaps thoroughly corrupt. Contemporaries recognized in practice nuances that the critics tended to ignore, and some mounted defenses of administrative service. These nuances and defenses help explain why even clerics who attacked courtiers often served at court. The fact remains, however, that in administrative service as in so much else, clerical behavior diverged sharply from the norms clerics were supposed to follow.

A few words are necessary about the nature of critiques of the court, which sometimes borrowed from one another and indeed formed a genre of sorts, before discussing their claims.[143] These critiques must be placed in the broader genre of moral exhortation, not a type of writing given to dispassionate analysis or subtle nuance. Indeed, moral exhortation sometimes slid over into the surprisingly similar genre of slanderous attacks on enemies or general categories of people of whom one disapproved. Peter of Blois (who had himself reacted angrily to a letter attacking him for serving in the households of bishops) protested that the royal clerics who were furious about a letter he wrote attacking them had misinterpreted exhortation as slander.[144] Though such critiques could certainly stem from personal animus, Peter may well have been criticizing clerics at court merely as yet another group of sinners, and the context of moral exhortation helps explain why even those critics who were also courtiers could be so unrelenting. The idea was to shock members of

---

[142] Martin Aurell, *The Plantagenet Empire, 1154–1224*, translated by David Crouch (Harlow, 2007), 60–8; Baldwin, *Masters, Princes, and Merchants*, 1:175–98; Thomas N. Bisson, *The Crisis of the Twelfth Century: Power, Lordship, and the Origins of European Government* (Princeton, 2009), 438–45; Cotts, *Clerical Dilemma*, 131–75; Ferruolo, *Origins of the University*, 131–6, 165–6, 175; Jaeger, *Origins of Courtliness*, 54–100; Rolf Köhn, " 'Militia Curialis'. Die Kritik der Geistlichen Hofdienst bei Peter von Blois in der Lateinischen Literatur des 9–12 Jahrhunderts," in Albert Zimmerman, ed., *Soziale Ordnungen im Selbsverständnis des Mittelalters* (Berlin, 1979), 227–57; Stollberg, *Soziale Stellung*, 123–9; Türk, *Nugae curialium*; Turner, *Judges, Administrators*, 159–79; Turner, *English Judiciary*, 1–11; Lachaud, *L'éthique du pouvoir*, 249–98, 590–8; Frédérique Lachaud, "La figure du clerc curial dans l'oeuvre de Jean de Salisbury," in Murielle Gaude-Ferragu, Bruno Laurioux, and Jacques Paviot, eds., *La cour du prince: cour de France, cours d'Europe XIIe–XVe siècle* (Paris, 2011), 301–20.

[143] For discussion of critiques and borrowing among them, see Cotts, *Clerical Dilemma*, 166–72.

[144] Peter of Blois, *Opera*, 16–19, 440.

the audience into reform, to leave no room for maneuver, no argument by which a clerical courtier could rationalize himself into hell, and also to counteract the allure of households and courts by claims that they were actually quite hellacious places.

Scholars have sometimes attributed harsh critiques partly to the disappointments and consequent bitterness of clerical courtiers such as Gerald of Wales and Peter of Blois who felt they had not been fairly treated or adequately rewarded for their service.[145] This was undoubtedly part of the story, yet more than disappointment was involved in their criticisms. Martin Aurell has pointed out the influence of classical works, particularly Boethius's *Consolation of Philosophy*, in criticism of the court.[146] As Aurell points out, Simund de Freine, a canon of Hereford and friend of Gerald of Wales, rendered this text into French. Strikingly, the narrator of this text, which departed freely from the Latin in places, was called a cleric, and not merely because of his learning, for Simund added a passage attacking clerics who purchased bishoprics.[147] The *Consolation of Philosophy* was widely read because it provided philosophical support for Christian teachings on the vanity of worldly things, and Simund, by making the narrator a formerly rich cleric who had fallen on hard times, was probably trying to make the work resonate more fully with a clerical audience. Other writers used specific examples concerning clerics to drive home lessons about the vanity of the world. Thus, Henry of Huntingdon used stories about the earthly travails of courtiers, including the ill consequences of the loss of royal favor for Bishop Robert Bloet and later for Robert's clerical son, Simon, to show that those who rejected worldly glory were not, in fact, crazier than Orestes.[148] It is likely, therefore, that Gerald of Wales, in using his own experiences in his attacks on the royal court was not only venting spleen, but also using his own history to reinforce widely promulgated arguments about the folly of pursuing worldly success through service at court.[149] Similarly, Peter of Blois stressed that his criticisms of the court came from experience.[150] The relationship between criticism of the court and experience of it was complex. On the one hand, existing models and ideologies might lead clerics to approach courts and households with a far more critical eye than modern scholars are accustomed to using, and certainly led critical writers to provide selective and slanted depictions of courts and courtiers. On the other hand, experiences of the courts, including disappointments but also simple observation of the system in action, might prompt writers to embrace criticisms they once would have rejected. The tendentious nature of the critiques of course means that they exaggerated the moral depravity of the court and the negative aspects of the earthly life of a courtier. Nonetheless, I will argue that the complaints about life at court

---

[145] Bartlett, *Gerald of Wales*, 58–61, 65; Ferruolo, *Origins of the University*, 132–3, 171; Richter, *Giraldus Cambrensis*, 89–90; Türk, *Nugae curialium*, 100–1, 111, 151. See however Cotts, *Clerical Dilemma*, 134–5, 166–7.

[146] Aurell, *Plantagenet Empire*, 66.

[147] Simund de Freine, *Les œuvres de Simund de Freine*, ed. John E. Matzke (Paris, 1909), lxxiv, 2–4, 39–40.

[148] Henry of Huntingdon, *Historia Anglorum*, 586–9, 596–7.

[149] Gerald of Wales, *Opera*, 8:lvii–lix.   [150] Peter of Blois, *Opera*, 43–5.

had at least some basis in fact. As for the moral and religious issues, there were plenty of matters to cause anxiety for any pious cleric.

Critics made a number of claims to argue that even by worldly standards the choice to serve at court was a poor one. They emphasized the hardships involved and the poor lifestyle of courtiers. "Martyrs to the world," Peter of Blois called courtiers, and both he and Walter Map compared them to the ghostly followers of Hellequin, incessantly on the move. Critics complained of vain promises and unfulfilled hopes, of the problems of keeping the favor of the powerful, and of wasting time and money in service but receiving no reward. For instance Alexander Neckam claimed that patrons would put off specific requests, saying that such little rewards were unworthy of such a learned man.[151] According to the critics, one had to lay out money to pay off court officials and gain the favor of other courtiers through gifts and feasts. Flattery and backbiting abounded and the unworthy received great rewards while the worthy were passed over.[152] Walter Map famously made a lengthy metaphorical comparison between the royal court and the hell of classical mythology.[153]

Manifestly, clerics and lay courtiers would not have flocked to the royal court and other households had they been so awful, but even so there was some truth to the criticisms. Though Aurell has shown that the travels of the royal court were better organized and probably less harrowing than some of the critics suggested, nonetheless the logistics of moving large numbers across the medieval countryside were daunting.[154] Service at court may therefore sometimes have entailed poor food and horrible lodgings rather than rich feasts and luxurious settings. Peter of Blois wrote a clever letter to the king on the hardships he encountered tracking him down, and though the letter was designed to underscore his sufferings on behalf of king and archbishop, it is likely that the travails were real.[155] Traveling abroad could be particularly dangerous. Peter, trying to restore one Master Henry to the favor of Reginald, bishop elect of Bath, described how Henry had traveled in the Alps, "strewn with corpses," on Reginald's behalf. The rhetoric was exaggerated, but the Alps were still dangerous.[156] Gerald of Wales at one point wrote that none of the more prominent members of Archbishop Hubert Walter's household would go to Rome for reasons of health, and listed several clerics who had died in missions to the papacy, which was indeed a dangerous proposition due to the susceptibility of travelers to disease.[157]

The objective truth about claims of false promises is impossible to determine, but even the royal patronage system was strained, as promises of future benefices

---

[151] Alexander Neckam, *De Naturis Rerum Libri Duo: With the Poem of the Same Author, De Laudibus Divinæ Sapientiæ*, ed. Thomas Wright (London, 1863), 314–15.

[152] Gerald of Wales, *Opera*, 1:57, 89; 8:lvii–lix; Peter of Blois, *Opera*, 42–51; Walter Map, *De Nugis Curialium*, 370–3; Stubbs, ed., *Epistolæ Cantuarienses*, 335; Nigel of Whiteacre, *Tractatus Contra Curiales*, 159–60.

[153] Walter Map, *De Nugis Curialium*, 2–17, 498–509.

[154] Aurell, *Plantagenet Empire*, 25–7.

[155] Peter of Blois, *Opera*, 121–2; Cotts, *Clerical Dilemma*, 143–4.

[156] Peter of Blois, *Opera*, 175.   [157] Davies, "Giraldus Cambrensis: *De Invectionibus*," 94–5.

show, and it is likely that kings sometimes promised more than they could deliver. It is even more likely that ambitious clerics might delude themselves with overly optimistic hopes of rich bishoprics or collections of benefices which even the king could provide only to a relatively small number of followers. As noted in the previous chapter, this was a system that could easily create jealousy and feelings of failure. Given the fierce competitiveness for benefices, it would hardly be surprising if flattery and backbiting were found in the households of magnates and at the royal court. Certainly several of Becket's biographers believed he had suffered from maneuvers against him in Archbishop Theobald's household, and Peter of Blois frequently claimed that he or others had been the victim of slander in various specific circumstances.[158] Gerald of Wales and Peter of Blois both received rewards for their curial activities, and therefore their claims, echoed in more general critiques, to have labored without recompense might seem odd. However, it is likely that clerics with revenues might be expected to serve for a time without immediate recompense in hopes of future reward. Indeed, among the misuses of ecclesiastical revenues that Thomas of Chobham condemned was serving "in the courts of princes at one's own expense to gain greater benefices."[159] It is probable that such service was something of a gamble, and that clerics might not end up feeling sufficiently recompensed for their labor and expenses, or that they might feel that they deserved new rewards where a patron might think that previous grants of benefices should suffice. With benefices, there could never be a precise correspondence between the amount of work and the amount and timing of the reward, which would lead to inevitable friction and to disappointment for some clerics.

Finally, administrative service in the hope of gain inevitably placed clerics in a situation of dependence on the sometimes unreliable favor of their patrons. Master John of Tynemouth was a leading member of Hubert Walter's household, but Gerald of Wales gleefully recorded John's fears when he failed to decisively end a case Gerald had brought against the archbishop. Gerald described how John anxiously obtained letters from the pope and cardinals stating that the failure was not his fault, how, when both were captured and held in France while returning from Rome during wartime, John fretted that Hubert would not ransom him due to his failure, and how, even after the archbishop had ransomed him, Hubert refused to see John for fifteen days until powerful friends interceded.[160] Worries about patronage appear frequently in the sources, and nowhere more vividly than in the letters of Master David of London. Throughout these letters he can be found seeking reassurances about the favor of his patrons, providing assurances of his own loyalty, attempting to recover favor that he had lost, defending himself against alleged lies, giving copious thanks for benefits, flattering patrons (while condemning flatterers), and, like John of Tynemouth, obtaining letters from the pope assuring his patrons that he was doing his best for them. In one letter he promised

---

[158] Robertson and Sheppard, eds., *Materials*, 2:362; 3:16; 4:9–10; Peter of Blois, *Opera*, 72, 175–8, 221–4, 289–91, 383–6.

[159] Thomas of Chobham, *Summa Confessorum*, 300.

[160] Gerald of Wales, *Opera*, 3:277, 296, 307; Cheney, *Hubert Walter*, 165.

a patron that he had a special link to him, though he held benefices from others, and in another he asked how a patron could think "your boy" (meaning himself) was a traitor. He also received letters of advice about patronage, including one from Arnulf of Lisieux (himself anxious about whether he had Henry II's favor) with suggestions about how to get the king to follow through on promises. David's letter collection provided a guidebook on how to manage patronage networks with the written word, which may be one reason it was preserved, but it also reveals just how hard David felt he needed to work to retain the favor of lords.[161] John Cotts has evocatively described Peter of Blois's letter collection as a micro-history of anxiety; David of London's collection can be described as a micro-history of anxiety about patronage.[162] The court, therefore, was not quite the earthly paradise that Peter of Blois's poetical courtier described it as being.

Nonetheless, the advantages of service at the court and in the households of magnates obviously far outweighed the worldly negatives for many clerics, and the most important attacks by critics were religious in nature. First and foremost, using benefices to reward service distorted the meritocratic system that was supposed to govern the Church. Though administrators might make perfectly adequate church officials, critics were right that clerics were often appointed for secular rather than religious qualifications. Moreover, the granting of benefices in return for service came perilously close to simony. Nigel of Whiteacre wrote that the only distinction between the pay of clerical officials and that of butlers, bakers, and other lay officials was that the latter received a yearly stipend whereas the former received a permanent one once they gained a benefice.[163] More generally, Orderic Vitalis described royal grants to courtiers of bishoprics and abbacies as the pay of hirelings or mercenaries.[164] English moralists in the period usually steered clear of outright claims that such grants constituted simony, but they clearly saw them as deeply problematic.

Service in the secular sphere was particularly problematic, since it involved the kinds of worldly business clerics were supposed to avoid. Nigel of Whiteacre rhetorically asked if it was "divinum negotium," meaning something like proper religious business or God's business, to sit at the king's exchequer, hearing computations and debates from dawn to dusk.[165] Worse, service in the royal judicial system potentially involved clerical administrators in "blood judgments," despite frequent bans in church councils.[166] Clerical service in secular administration also

---

[161] Liverani, ed., *Spicilegium Liberianum*, 544–5, 547, 604–11, 615–28; Arnulf of Lisieux, *The Letters of Arnulf of Lisieux*, ed. Frank Barlow (London, 1939), 125.

[162] Cotts, *Clerical Dilemma*, 56.

[163] Nigel of Whiteacre, *Tractatus Contra Curiales*, 163.

[164] Orderic Vitalis, *Ecclesiastical History*, 2:268–9; 5:202–3.

[165] Nigel of Whiteacre, *Tractatus Contra Curiales*, 189–90.

[166] Turner, *Judges, Administrators*, 171–8; Whitelock, Brett, and Brooke, eds., *Councils and Synods, 1066–1204*, 614, 676, 980, 985; Powicke and Cheney, eds., *Councils and Synods, 1205–1265*, 25. However, fuller evidence from the later thirteenth century indicates that clerical justices might focus on civil rather than crown pleas, thus removing them from blood judgments, and it is possible that this was also the case before 1216: Paul Brand, ed., *The Earliest English Law Reports*, 4 vols., Publications of the Selden Society, vols. 111–12, 122–3 (London, 1996–2007), 3: cv.

meant a huge diversion of ecclesiastical resources, intended to support prayer, pastoral care, and the performance of the liturgy, to secular purposes. The fact that royal clerics often worked to extract money from the Church or supported kings in the great church–state struggles of the period made the diversion of resources to them even more troubling. Ranulf Flambard, that hero of royal administrative history, was hated by church chroniclers partly because of his ability to milk vacant ecclesiastical honors so effectively. For instance, William of Malmesbury noted how he would send a royal cleric to make a thorough inventory, which from a modern perspective was a clear sign of his pioneering administrative acumen, but from William's perspective was an illustration of his ruthless exploitation.[167] Kings were consistently able to retain clerical advisors in disputes with archbishops and popes over ecclesiastical liberties partly no doubt because of genuine royalist sentiment, but also because they were in a position to reward their supporters subsequently with bishoprics, as Henry II did after the Becket dispute and King John did after the interdict.[168] Whatever view one takes of such conflicts, critics of the court surely had a point that there was something amiss in a system of church appointments that favored those who helped kings drain ecclesiastical coffers or who supported monarchs against the champions of the Church.

Attitudes towards clerical service to magnates and particularly to kings were, of course, more complicated than sermonizing attacks would suggest. Even critics saw a place for clerics as religious advisors at court. Notions of public good and of the divine sanction of kingship could provide a more positive view of other forms of service to kings. In a letter responding to criticism of his scathing attack on curial service by clerics, Peter of Blois partially relented and wrote that it could be good and honorable, albeit dangerous, for clerics to serve the king.[169] Richard fitz Nigel, in the *Dialogue of the Exchequer*, strongly defended royal service, using the Pauline idea that the authority of kings and other earthly powers derived from God and emphasizing the utility of royal authority in maintaining peace, supporting the Church, and helping the poor.[170] He would surely have argued that service at the exchequer *was* in some way "divinum negotium." Ralph of Diceto defended the service of certain bishops as royal justices on the grounds that their piety would make them good judges.[171] Nonetheless, defenses of clerical service in the secular sphere were far less common than critiques and were generally hedged with

---

[167] William of Malmesbury, *Gesta Regum Anglorum. The History of the English Kings*, ed. R. A. B. Mynors, Rodney M. Thomson, and Michael Winterbottom, 2 vols. (Oxford, 1998–9), 1:558–9; John of Worcester, *The Chronicle of John of Worcester*, ed. Reginald R. Darlington and P. McGurk, 3 vols. (Oxford, 1995–8), 3:94–5; Blake, ed., *Liber Eliensis*, 224; Orderic Vitalis, *Ecclesiastical History*, 4:170–5; 5:202–3, 310–11.

[168] For expressions of hostility towards clerical courtiers during the Becket controversy, see Robertson and Sheppard, eds., *Materials*, 2:372; 3:42, 243–4, 414. For a comparison between the successful careers of Henry II's supporters and the roadblocks facing Becket's clerics in England, see Duggan, "Price of Loyalty," 1–18. For John's appointments after the interdict, see Painter, *Reign of King John*, 184–6, 197–201; Warren, *King John*, 212; Turner, *King John*, 172–4.

[169] Peter of Blois, *Opera*, 42–51, 439–42. For the latest discussion of this pair of letters, see Cotts, *Clerical Dilemma*, 151–8.

[170] Richard fitzNigel, *Dialogus de Scaccario*, 2–5.

[171] Ralph of Diceto, *Opera Historica*, 1:434–5.

qualifiers. Even Richard fitz Nigel wrote specifically that it was "not absurd" for churchmen to serve kings and other powerful men, particularly in matters that were "not dishonest or dishonorable." This phrasing may have been ironic, but even so it indicates an atmosphere in which Richard's viewpoint was deeply controversial.

More common than active defense was tacit acceptance of secular service. There survives from 1214 a remarkable series of letters from Pope Innocent III on behalf of Richard Marsh, who had helped King John extract large sums of money from the Church during the interdict. The pope noted that some English bishops and churchmen harbored a sense of grievance towards Richard, which could hardly have been surprising. However, the pope issued a specific letter forbidding the recipients to allow anyone to "unjustly trouble" Richard, issued a general letter of protection for him, and also exempted him, on the grounds that he was too busy in royal service, from the requirement that John's major clerical supporters had to travel to Rome to seek absolution. Obviously, these letters represented part of Pope Innocent's effort to conciliate King John, as well as a more specific reward to Richard for his services as royal emissary in the settlement of the dispute. Nonetheless, they also represented an implicit statement by a reforming pope that clerics in royal service served a valuable function and that even those who placed their loyalty to the king above that to the Church deserved a certain leeway. Though an initial attempt to provide Richard with a bishopric in 1214 failed, in 1217 a papal legate promoted him to the rich see of Durham.[172]

Despite ideologies supporting kingship, twelfth-century intellectuals were generally less likely to feel a strong ideological commitment to the nascent government institutions of their period than modern scholars might expect, even if the current generation of scholars is less automatically enthusiastic about "the rise of the state" than previous generations were. One might argue, with Egbert Türk, that an unwillingness by critics to recognize the importance of royal government represented a failure of vision, but the fact remains that their ideals and priorities were different from ours.[173] Moreover, the core of the criticism was directed more at clerical participation in royal government than government itself. Even the most enthusiastic proponents of a well-developed state among modern historians might dislike a system in which a substantial portion of university resources were diverted to non-educational governmental functions, in which every history department had to reserve paid slots for bureaucrats, and in which the best way to become a prominent professor of history was to be a successful auditor for the government's taxation office. It is hardly surprising, therefore, that critics might object to royal reliance on the Church to provide and pay royal servants. One of the great problems of the period, of course, was that secular governments *had* to rely on the Church, and clerics, including figures such as Pope Innocent III, had to cope

---

[172] Cheney and Cheney, eds., *Letters of Pope Innocent III*, 157–8; Painter, *Reign of King John*, 197–8, 201, 205–6; Snape, ed., *English Episcopal Acta 24*, xxxiv.
[173] Türk, *Nugae curialium*, 19, 82–3, 195–8. For a different view, see Aurell, *Plantagenet Empire*, 68.

with this reality. Committed reformers did not, however, have to like it, even when they themselves participated in the system.

As so often, however, reformers focused on personal moral failings and on the individual moral dangers to clerics rather than on any systemic problems resulting from the intertwining of church and state. If the system unduly rewarded secular service, the answer was for clerics to stop being ambitious. Such advice would hardly reform the system but might, reformers could hope, save individual souls. In theory, service within the Church should have been less problematic than secular administrative service, since it would have benefited the Church, and, in fact, one writer, Lucian of Chester, made a forceful distinction by comparing clerics who left episcopal households for the royal palace to the Hellenizing Jews of the Maccabean period who, "imitating gentile rites," built a gymnasium in Jerusalem.[174] Nonetheless, clerics in such households and ecclesiastical officials, particularly archdeacons, also faced fierce criticism on moral grounds. Writers stressed two major, overlapping problems with administrative service and the life of a courtier; the ubiquity of temptation and vice, and the prevalence of corruption.

From the perspective of moralists, most of the characteristics that made life as a courtier attractive involved sin. For them, the search for wealth was simply a form of greed. The ambition of many courtiers and administrators was obviously another sin, and since advancement generally came only with the deaths of incumbents of benefices, critics like John of Salisbury and Nigel of Whiteacre could depict ambitious clerics in a particularly negative light, as hoping for the deaths of others.[175] The dignity that Peter of Blois's fictional courtier spoke of could be reconfigured as pride, his delight in food at court as gluttony. Critics attacked flattery and slander not only because they made the court unpleasant, but also because they were sinful in themselves. The very sophistication of the court was dangerous. In his *Policraticus*, John of Salisbury warned courtiers against all sorts of "frivolities," including hunting, gambling, music, and the performances of actors and entertainers.[176] Even the involvement of clerics in worldly business was a problem largely because it was considered sinful for them as it would not have been for laypeople. Even if one discounts the attacks of critics for exaggeration, one need only acknowledge that their premises were common ones in the period to see why the court was viewed as such a morally dangerous place.

According to the common wisdom of the time, moreover, both secular and ecclesiastical administrations were thoroughly corrupt. John of Salisbury's forceful attack on corruption in secular government in the *Policraticus* included punning references to justices in eyre as errant or erring justices and he claimed that even judges who were clerics rarely refused to take gifts. After an equally forceful attack on ecclesiastical officials, especially rural deans and archdeacons, he noted that if

---

[174] Lucian of Chester, *Extracts from the Liber Luciani De Laude Cestrie*, ed. M. V. Taylor, Lancshire and Cheshire Record Society, vol. 64, part 1 ([London], 1912), 67–8. See also Peter of Blois, *Opera*, 16–17.

[175] John of Salisbury, *Policraticus*, 2:172; Nigel of Whiteacre, *Tractatus Contra Curiales*, 160.

[176] John of Salisbury, *Policraticus*, 1:21–49.

Henry II were asked about them he would say that there was no evil they did not do among the clergy. John ended this section by saying that there were *some* deans, archdeacons, bishops, and papal legates who did God's work, the implication being that most did not.[177] Though the papal curia was a particularly frequent target for criticism, critics saw plenty of corruption within the local Church as well. Church officials were depicted as preying both on the laity, particularly under the guise of punishing immorality, and on the lesser clergy, by making unjust exactions and abusing rights of hospitality. John of Salisbury was clearly right about Henry II's views, for as noted in Chapter 4, the king claimed that rural deans and archdeacons extorted more money each year than he received as income.[178] Gerald of Wales, who attacked the corruption of ecclesiastical officials in several works, told various anecdotes that may have represented popular stories illustrating the ill repute of such officials. In one, an archdeacon cited an innocent man for immoral behavior and refused a ram offered by the man as a bribe, prompting another layman to remark that it was rare for a wolf to refuse a sheep. In another, a cleric who became angry at God after losing most of his money gambling began blaspheming and then offered the rest of his money to anyone who could tell him how to offend God even more. He was advised to become a bishop's official.[179] Etienne of Fougères described rural deans and archdeacons as worse than pagans.[180] Indeed, the corruption and sinfulness of archdeacons was a cliché, and John of Salisbury playfully and ironically congratulated Nicholas de Sigillo, who had formerly claimed that archdeacons were so bad that salvation was impossible for them, for having his eyes opened to their true worth upon being appointed archdeacon of Huntingdon.[181]

Perhaps even more striking than the moralistic and satirical attacks are passages that took corruption for granted. One set of English glosses on canon law simply assumed that secular judges were corrupt and warned ecclesiastical judges against emulating them.[182] Gerald of Wales sent letters to his official representatives and the rural deans in his archdeaconry in Wales warning them against greed, extortion, exactions, simony, and the burdening of local churches by traveling with more than three or four retainers. Though Gerald was trying to make his subordinates practice what he preached, the need for such warnings is telling.[183] One can also find specific accusations of corruption. Gerald claimed that on one occasion papal judges delegate, including a secular cleric, Master Adam of Bromfield, tried to extract bribes from him.[184] King Henry II's anger against rural deans and archdeacons was sparked by a case in which one of the former allegedly extorted the considerable sum of 22s. from a burgess of Scarborough by accusing his wife of

---

[177] John of Salisbury, *Policraticus*, 1:323–34, 344–58.

[178] See Chapter 4, section 1; Robertson and Sheppard, eds., *Materials*, 3:44. See also Robertson and Sheppard, eds., *Materials*, 4:95–6, 201.

[179] Gerald of Wales, *Opera*, 2:322, 325. The first anecdote appears independently in Corpus Christi College, Oxford, MS 32, fo. 95v.

[180] Etienne de Fougères, *Le livre des manières*, 70.   [181] John of Salisbury, *Letters*, 2:24–5.

[182] Kuttner and Rathbone, "Anglo-Norman Canonists," 347.

[183] Gerald of Wales, *Opera*, 1:251–2, 334–5.   [184] Gerald of Wales, *Opera*, 3:212–13.

adultery.[185] In a letter concerning another specific case in which Henry II got involved, John of Salisbury remarked that rural deans and archdeacons seemed to think the spoliation of poor men was a game.[186] Clearly the corruption of secular and ecclesiastical officials was not merely a stereotype.

Of course, moralistic and satirical diatribes about corruption, assumptions about its ubiquity, and anecdotal evidence do not necessarily prove that corruption was endemic. Ralph Turner, in his careful and thoughtful investigation of charges of corruption against royal justices, has rightly emphasized that one must use caution in assessing both the broad claims of moralists and specific accusations of corruption, which might be made by partisan sources. On the whole, Turner is inclined to give royal justices the benefit of the doubt, but he also points to gray areas such as the influence of friendship networks and the practice of giving gifts to important people, which could easily shade over into bribery. He also notes systemic problems, such as the lack of regular pay for justices until well into Henry III's reign, that could encourage corruption.[187] Similar gray areas existed with ecclesiastical justice. A rural dean or archdeacon who *falsely* accused people of immorality was clearly dishonest, but were those who frequently fined laypeople for immorality necessarily corrupt or greedy? Hugh of Avalon, bishop of Lincoln, forbade his archdeacons, their officials, and rural deans from levying monetary fines for fear of corruption. They argued in response that such punishments were highly effective and pointed to Thomas Becket's use of them (Hugh dryly noted that it was not such practices that had made Becket a saint).[188] The arguments of the archdeacons and others may have been self-serving, but were not necessarily false. The systemic problem of pay intruded for church officials as well as justices. The English canonist Honorius referred in his *Summa*, under the heading of simony, to clerics who refused to accept churches unless they were exempted from dues to archdeacons, and to other clerics who refused to accept archdeaconries because the income was insufficient without exactions from clerics. In addressing the first issue, Honorius stated that the key question was whether the dues were licit, but this may not always have been clear in a period when the structure of ecclesiastical governance was undergoing rapid development.[189] Clearly, canonists were coming up against hard practical questions about what constituted acceptable income, and this could create all kinds of problems in differentiating between corruption and acceptable practices. Gray areas aside, I have a more cynical view of royal justice than Turner does, based on past research into cases suggesting remarkably lenient treatment of knights

[185] Robertson and Sheppard, eds., *Materials*, 3:44.

[186] John of Salisbury, *Letters*, 1:193. For other specific accusations, see John of Salisbury, *Letters*, 1:169–71; Saltman, *Theobald, Archbishop of Canterbury*, 393–4; Cheney and Jones, eds., *English Episcopal Acta 2*, 93–5; Spencer Robert Wigram, ed., *The Cartulary of the Monastery of St. Frideswide at Oxford*, 2 vols., Oxford Historical Society Record Series, vols. 28, 31 (Oxford, 1895–6), 1:40–1; Holtzmann, Chodorow, and Duggan, eds., *Decretales Ineditae*, 66; Duggan, "Decretals of Alexander III," 115–17; Cheney and Cheney, eds., *Letters of Pope Innocent III*, 25, 76. See also Thomas of Marlborough, *History of Evesham*, 366–9.

[187] Turner, *English Judiciary*, 3–11, 277–89, 294–8.

[188] Adam of Eynsham, *Magna Vita Sancti Hugonis*, 2:38.

[189] Honorius, *Magistri Honorii Summa*, 324.

and landholders committing acts of violence.[190] As a result, I am more inclined to give credence to claims of widespread corruption by clerical administrators than other scholars might, though obviously one must make allowances for the exaggerations that were expected in the genre of exhortation. The true extent of corruption can never be recovered, but it is clear that there was at least some, that a widespread perception of deep corruption existed, and that even the most idealistic of clerics would have encountered gray areas and moral quandaries in secular and ecclesiastical office holding.

How did clerical administrators and courtiers cope with the chasm between the demanding ideals of moralists and their own conduct, which was viewed as problematic even if they avoided corruption? There was no doubt a widespread acknowledgment, even by moralists, that no one except perhaps a saint could live up to all the ideals expected of clerics. There was a wide gap between the playful nature of John of Salisbury's letter to Nicholas de Sigillo and the strong rhetoric of his *Policraticus*, which suggests that the unyielding stance found in critiques of the court was partly a matter of genre. Probably most audiences approached the genre of exhortation as counseling perfection in an imperfect world and in everyday interactions even moralists probably allowed more nuance than in their fiery treatises. When attacked for his criticisms of clerical courtiers, Peter of Blois not only moderated his criticisms but also wrote that not all could take "the narrow way," in other words that not all could follow the most demanding route to Christian perfection, though even in this concession there was an implicit warning about taking the easy road to hell.[191] As for courtiers, no doubt many of them took the view of Peter's fictional character that repentance could wait and that God would not be so harsh after all. Other clerics surely embraced Richard fitz Nigel's arguments that administrative service was morally acceptable and even laudable. Nonetheless, the chasm between ideal and reality could be troubling for even the most devoted royal servant. Richard Barre was an assiduous royal cleric who was not only an important royal justice but also chancellor for a short time to Henry II's heir, the Young King, and an emissary who traveled as far as Hungary and Constantinople during royal preparations for the Third Crusade. He sided with Henry II against Becket (who called him a prophet of Baal) and was among those sent to try to conciliate the pope immediately after Thomas's murder. When he was transferred from the archdeaconry of Lisieux to that of Ely, his former teacher, Stephen of Tournai, sent him a congratulatory letter, with some warnings about the court but also a quote from a poem that had once been recited to Richard at Bologna: "You will handle the causes of bishops and the business of kings, who prepare you for riches and pleasures." Richard thus appears to have been the model of a loyal courtier. Surprisingly enough, however, Richard wrote a poem, now lost, called "De Molestiis Curie," or "On the Troubles of the Court." This lost poem may partly have reflected the experiences of someone who was caught in the middle

---

[190] Thomas, *Vassals, Heiresses, Crusaders, and Thugs*, 73–8.
[191] Peter of Blois, *Opera*, 440.

of the struggles between Henry II and Becket, between Henry II and the Young
King (who beat and publicly humiliated another clerical follower who stayed loyal
to his father), and between Richard's later patron, William Longchamp, and
Longchamp's many enemies. Most likely, however, the poem also reflected the
internal tensions this loyal courtier and learned cleric faced in reconciling clerical
ideals with the life of the courtier.[192]

Thomas Becket himself was, of course, the figure who most clearly exhibited the
potentially explosive nature of the tensions between service at the court and clerical
ideals. After a miracle that was attributed to him, an unnamed noble who had been
one of his enemies was said to have asked one of Thomas's clerics how someone
who had been so severe on the Church as chancellor could now be among the
saints.[193] Remarkably enough, John of Salisbury dedicated the *Policraticus* to
Thomas as chancellor when he was besieging Toulouse. In doing so, John elided
some of the very tensions he stressed in that work. He described Thomas as "the
light of the clergy" who would cancel unjust royal laws and carry out just ones and
would protect the people and morality. He said Thomas could dress well and
indulge in feasting, because he was so upright. He glossed over the fact that as a
cleric Thomas was carrying out war.[194] John may have been indulging in some of
the obsequious flattery he so deplored in his work, though Cary Nederman and
Karen Bollermann have convincingly argued that the passages making allowances
for Thomas should not be taken at face value and that in fact his attack on clerics
holding office was directed at the chancellor.[195] In either case, he probably already
recognized in Thomas some of the characteristics that would later make him such a
fierce proponent of ecclesiastical rights.[196] However, John himself later compared
the lack of support Thomas received as an exile with how acceptable he was to
everyone when he was "a great trifler (*nugator*) in the court, when he seemed to
despise the law and the clergy," a quotation that shows how tempting it must have
been to act as a comfortably worldly administrator rather than a zealous prelate.[197]
According to Herbert of Bosham, Thomas condemned himself as a former courtier
and disagreed when some of his followers protested that some from the palace and
the world had done well.[198] This is not the place to pursue the complexities of

---

[192] For an overview of Richard's career and the letter from Stephen of Tournai, see Turner, *Judges, Administrators*, 181–98. For Thomas Becket's description of him, see Duggan, ed., *Correspondence of Thomas Becket*, 2:1154–7. For his lost poem, see Teresa Webber and Andrew G. Watson, *The Libraries of the Augustinian Canons* (London, 1998), 208–10, 233. For the Young King's treatment of his clerical vice chancellor, see [Roger of Howden], *Gesta Regis Henrici Secundi*, 1:122–3; Roger of Howden, *Chronica*, 2:94.

[193] Robertson and Sheppard, eds., *Materials*, 2:163–4.

[194] John of Salisbury, *Policraticus*, 1:2, 17; 2:423–4.

[195] Cary J. Nederman and Karen Bollermann, "'The Extravagance of the Senses': Epicureanism, Priestly Tyranny, and the Becket Problem in John of Salisbury's *Policraticus*," *Studies in Medieval and Renaissance History*, 3rd series, 8 (2011), 1–25, at 20–3.

[196] Lachaud, "La figure du clerc curial," 312–19.

[197] *Nugator* was the very term he used for courtiers in *Policraticus*: John of Salisbury, *Letters*, 2:244–5.

[198] Robertson and Sheppard, eds., *Materials*, 3:246–7.

Thomas's remarkable shift from Henry II's courtier to his staunchest foe, which so many able scholars have studied.[199] That said, his history provides clear proof of just how troublesome the tensions between the life of the courtier and the demands of moralists could prove, and the lengths to which at least one prominent royal cleric would go to avoid the condemnation to hell that most contemporaries would have believed was in store for Peter of Blois's blithe and clueless courtier.

---

[199] The bibliography is immense, but the places to start are the biographies of Barlow and Duggan, and Staunton's work on the *vitae*: Barlow, *Thomas Becket*; Duggan, *Thomas Becket*; Staunton, *Thomas Becket and his Biographers*.

7

Clerical Marriage and Clerical Celibacy

A series of related poems, dated by Thomas Wright and A. G. Rigg to the aftermath of the Fourth Lateran Council of 1215, reveal the reaction of a fictional council, in one version made up of 10,000 English clerics, to a decree issued by Pope Innocent ("not innocent, but instead noxious"),[1] demanding that they set aside their women. In these poems a variety of clerics proclaim their dismayed reactions to this decree, of which only a few can be provided here. A scholarly priest says, "To remove the beauties is not a ridiculous thing [. . .] If our lord desires, he can prohibit—but by my soul I cannot abstain." Another priest says, "To violate the wives, daughters, and nieces of neighbors is evil [. . .] you should have your own, and delight in her, and thus await the last day more securely." A husband says that if the pope does prohibit "special marriage," he will soon observe the chorus of holy adulterers to be full. Another priest calls on "Holy Virgin Mary" to be an advocate, since concubines are devoted to her. A fellow devotee of the virgin says, "By the Queen of Glory who is at the North Pole, I will not desert my Malota while I live. What do the pope and legate think? [. . .] Let divine vengeance make me blind unless she sleep with me each night." Another priest, after proudly noting his English birth, says that the nature of virile men is to have sex with wives, not livestock. And finally, in the summation to one version, the last speaker talks of a pope who had excommunicated all who did not procreate, and had had a son by his sister. "What the pope has conceded, who can deny? He commands peasants to work, knights to fight, and, above all, clerics to love. We clerics will have two concubines, monks and canons, the same number or three, deans and bishops, four or five. Thus at last we will fulfill divine law."[2]

---

[1] "Non [. . .] Innocentius, immo nocens vere."

[2] The poems are published in Thomas Wright, ed., *The Latin Poems Commonly Attributed to Walter Mapes*, Camden Society, vol. 16 (London, 1841), 171–82. Longer versions of one of the poems survive in Trinity College, Cambridge, MS O.2.45, pp. 342–4, and Bodleian Library, Bodleian MS 851, fo. 75v. For further discussion of these poems, see Paul Lehmann, *Die Parodie im Mittelalter* (Stuttgart, 1963), 112–16; Brundage, *Law, Sex, and Christian Society*, 402; Rigg, *History of Anglo-Latin Literature*, 233–4, 375; Waters, *Angels and Earthly Creatures*, 161–4. Lehmann suggests a date of *c*.1200. Datings have been based on a supposed link to Innocent III in one version, though for clerical marriage Innocent II, 1130–43, is as likely a candidate, and there does survive a verse attacking an earlier pope, Calixtus II, for ending clerical marriage: Hermann Heimpel, "Reformatio Sigismundi, Priesterehe und Bernhard von Chartres," *Deutsches archiv für Erforschung des Mittelalters* 17 (1961), 526–37, at 529–30. Unfortunately, since the name Innocent is a vehicle for a pun, I am unsure that one should place too much weight on it for dating. Lehmann links the style to the twelfth or thirteenth century, however, and even if the poem is later in the thirteenth century, the dating would not substantively affect my argument. More work needs to be done on these poems and the relationships between them.

Few figures were so likely to provoke comic responses in the Middle Ages as priests (and monks and nuns) who had sex. Yet the drive in the Western Church to thoroughly enforce rules about clerical celibacy was deeply serious. It involved not only a radical change in the behavior expected of individual priests and other clerics, as the doleful clerics in the poem above emphasized, but the elimination of any rights of inheritance in church office, the degradation of the status of the female partners of affected clerics, and the delegitimation of their children. A growing body of scholarship addresses the issue of clerical celibacy, and several scholars, including Christopher Brooke, C. R. Cheney, Mary Cheney, and Julia Barrow, have written on aspects of this campaign in England during our period.[3] Nonetheless, there is still plenty of room for exploration and debate. I have already discussed facets of the issue in Chapter 2 (celibacy as part of the priestly model), Chapter 3 (courtly love), and Chapter 5 (the inheritance of churches). I begin this chapter with a brief discussion of the background and then turn to the drive to enforce celibacy in England in the long twelfth century. A major focus of the chapter, however, is the ideological and practical resistance to this drive. Though satirical, the poems described above give a sense of the furor which the campaign for clerical celibacy met in England, as indeed throughout Western Christendom. Moralists emphasized lust in discussing non-celibate clerics, and sexual desire certainly mattered, but I will explore social and emotional motives for the resistance to clerical celibacy. I will also provide a necessarily tentative assessment of the degree of success or failure of the campaign and of its impact on clerics and their families. Finally, I will touch briefly on the topic of same-sex relationships among clerics.

1. THE CAMPAIGN FOR CLERICAL CELIBACY

From the late Roman period, church councils in the West had legislated against sexual activity by the higher orders of clergy, though early canons allowed them to be married as long as they remained chaste.[4] Although the evidence is scarce, most scholars argue that in the early Middle Ages unchaste clerical marriage remained

---

[3] Brooke, "Gregorian Reform in Action," 69–99; Cheney, *From Becket to Langton*, 126–9, 137–8; Cheney, *Roger, Bishop of Worcester*, 69–78; Barrow, "Hereford Bishops and Married Clergy," 1–8. See also Jennifer Thibodeaux's forthcoming book, *The Manly Priest: Clerical Celibacy, Masculinity, and Reform in England and Normandy, 1066–1300* (Philadelphia, 2015) and, for Normandy, van Houts, "Fate of Priests' Sons."

[4] For a recent overview of the history of clerical celibacy through the Reformation, see Parish, *Clerical Celibacy*. For good overviews of the early history of clerical celibacy, see Barstow, *Married Priests*, 19–104; Frazee, "Origins of Clerical Celibacy," 149–67; Gaudemet, "Le celibate ecclésiastique," 1–31. For the background of early Christian ideas about sex, see Peter Brown, *The Body and Society: Men, Women, and Sexual Renunciation in Early Christianity* (New York, 1988). For a particularly useful set of articles, several of which deal with the neglected period between the initial decrees and the Gregorian Reform, see Frassetto, ed., *Medieval Purity*. For an overview of relationships involving members of the higher clergy after marriage had been eliminated for them, see Ruth Mazo Karras, *Unmarriages: Women, Men, and Sexual Unions in the Middle Ages* (Philadelphia, 2012), 115–64.

common and that priests often had families.[5] Indeed, there are hints from synodal decrees that in some places priests' wives (whether chaste or not is unclear) could even have a special place in religious practice, and of course clerical marriage remained the norm in the Eastern Church.[6] Nonetheless, renewed efforts to eliminate or at least reduce priestly sex came in the Carolingian period and in the tenth century on the continent. In England exhortations to celibacy were common by reformers such as Aelfric and Wulfstan in the years around 1000.[7] The most important effort throughout Western Europe, however, came with the great papal reform movement that began in the middle of the eleventh century. Subsequent popes sustained the drive for celibacy through the long twelfth century and beyond. I have already noted some of the main stated motives behind the drive in Chapter 2, especially cultic purity and concern about church property. Modern scholars have also stressed the role of celibacy in the effort to differentiate clerics from the laity and to raise their status.[8] Reformers of the time would probably have argued instead that they were trying to make sure the clergy lived up to a pre-existing high, even cosmological, status, though no doubt they hoped that by doing so priests, deacons, and subdeacons would raise their social and religious prestige and thus become more effective. Once clerical celibacy became established church policy, widely publicized and backed by the papacy, simple obedience also came into play.

The papal drive for clerical celibacy came to England with the Norman Conquest, through the efforts of archbishops Lanfranc and Anselm. Though some earlier prelates and reformers had demanded celibacy, they had had no clear enforcement mechanism and apparently only limited success. Aelfric championed celibacy but recognized that marriage was widespread and, writing on behalf of Archbishop Wulfstan, said celibacy could not be compelled. Certain law codes of King Æthelred II, which were heavily shaped by Wulfstan, straightforwardly condemned unchastity. They did not, however, specify any penalties for failure to comply, though they did provide an incentive for celibacy by granting chaste priests the rank and wergild of a thegn. One set of regulations of unclear status, called the Northumbrian priests' law, even implicitly recognized priestly marriage

---

[5] For case studies that reinforce this general picture, see Wendy Davies, *Wales in the Early Middle Ages* (Leicester, 1982), 156–7; Valerie Ramseyer, *The Transformation of a Religious Landscape: Medieval Southern Italy, 850–1150* (Ithaca, 2006), 59, 92–6.

[6] Frazee, "Origins of Clerical Celibacy," 157; Jo Ann McNamara, "An Unresolved Syllogism: The Search for a Christian Gender System," in Jacqueline Murray, ed., *Conflicted Identities and Multiple Masculinities: Men in the Medieval West* (New York, 1999), 1–24, at 10–11; Elliott, *Fallen Bodies*, 83–4; Macy, *Hidden History*, 53–80.

[7] Whitelock, Brett, and Brooke, eds., *Councils and Synods, 871–1066*, 198–201, 277–80, 286–7, 289–90; Catherine Cubitt, "Images of St Peter: The Clergy and the Religious Life in Anglo-Saxon England," in Paul Cavill, ed., *The Christian Tradition in Anglo-Saxon England: Approaches to Current Scholarship and Teaching* (Cambridge, 2004), 41–54, at 48–50; Mary Frances Giandrea, *Episcopal Culture in Late Anglo-Saxon England* (Woodbridge, 2007), 120.

[8] From the Frassetto collection alone, see Mayke de Jong, "*Imitatio Morum.* The Cloister and Clerical Purity in the Carolingian World," in Michael Frassetto, ed., *Medieval Purity and Piety: Essays on Medieval Clerical Celibacy and Religious Reform* (New York, 1998), 49–80, at 51; Frassetto, "Heresy, Celibacy, and Reform," 135; R. I. Moore, "Property, Marriage, and the Eleventh-Century Revolution: A Context for Early Medieval Communism," in Michael Frassetto, ed., *Medieval Purity and Piety: Essays on Medieval Clerical Celibacy and Religious Reform* (New York, 1998), 179–208, at 190–1.

by condemning priests who left one woman for another.[9] Clearly, not all agreed with the views of reformers, and in one manuscript a ban on clerical marriage was erased and replaced by the statement that "it is right that a priest love a decent woman as a bedmate."[10] How widespread clerical marriage was remains hard to trace, but there are certainly indications that it was common.[11] As Christopher Brooke noted, the Norman clergy, who took over many of the top positions in the Church after 1066, also came from a society in which clerical marriage was common.[12]

The canons of a 1070 council simply stated that clerics must remain chaste or leave their office, but in 1076 Archbishop Lanfranc and his fellows sensibly (though optimistically) opted for a program that would theoretically have gradually eliminated the marriage of priests, deacons, and canons over the course of a generation. Local priests in castles or villages who were already married did not have to set aside their wives (at this point the marriages of priests were still simply improper marriages—it was only in the aftermath of the first two Lateran Councils that the Church firmly determined that such unions were not marriages at all[13]). However, unmarried priests could not marry and bishops were supposed to extract oaths promising celibacy before ordaining new deacons or priests. Canons of any rank were not to have wives, a ruling that should in theory have affected cathedrals with secular chapters and other collegiate churches immediately, but clearly the overall intention was to ease the English clergy into a regime of clerical celibacy.[14] One of Lanfranc's colleagues may have gone further. According to William of Malmesbury's Latin translation of a lost earlier life of Wulfstan II, bishop of Worcester, this future saint forced priests to choose between their "women" and their churches, and expelled those who chose the former from their positions, causing some to become vagrants and even to starve to death.[15] As Mary Frances Giandrea has suggested, however, William may have invented this episode to present Wulfstan as a saintly and relentless reformer. Wulfstan was the son of a priest, and though he was clearly ambivalent about this (his father's status is known only because of an obit written in cipher in one of Wulfstan's manuscripts), it seems unlikely that he

[9] Whitelock, Brett, and Brooke, eds., *Councils and Synods, 871–1066*, 198–201, 277–80, 336–7, 348–50, 365, 397–8, 459.

[10] Patrick Wormald, *The Making of English Law: King Alfred to the Twelfth Century. Volume 1: Legislation and its Limits* (Oxford, 1999), 203.

[11] Blair, *Church in Anglo-Saxon Society*, 342, 361–2; William M. Aird, *St Cuthbert and the Normans: The Church of Durham, 1071–1153* (Woodbridge, 1998), 116–22; Cubitt, "Clergy in Early Anglo-Saxon England," 284–6; Cubitt, "Images of St Peter," 50–3; Barrow, *Who Served the Altar at Brixworth?*, 5–7.

[12] Brooke, "Gregorian Reform in Action," 83–7. See also Orderic Vitalis, *Ecclesiastical History*, 3:120–3.

[13] Brooke, "Gregorian Reform in Action," 74–5; Barstow, *Married Priests*, 102–4; Gaudemet, "Le celibate ecclésiastique," 16–24.

[14] Whitelock, Brett, and Brooke, eds., *Councils and Synods, 1066–1204*, 576, 619; Barstow, *Married Priests*, 87–8; Cowdrey, *Lanfranc*, 127–8.

[15] William of Malmesbury, *William of Malmesbury, Saints' Lives: Lives of SS. Wulfstan, Dunstan, Patrick, Benignus and Indract*, ed. Michael Winterbottom and Rodney M. Thomson (Oxford, 2002), 124–7.

would have acted so much more harshly than Archbishop Lanfranc.[16] Whatever the truth about Wulfstan of Worcester, as of 1076 the English clergy had been put on notice that clerical celibacy was a requirement for future deacons and priests.

It is not clear that this had much effect, and it was left to Lanfranc's successor, Anselm, to make the next push. Henry of Huntingdon later claimed that Anselm's reform council of 1102 was the first to forbid English clerics to have wives, and though this was clearly untrue, it may have been the first time authorities did more than simply state the rules.[17] Indeed, judging by the surviving evidence, the latter part of Anselm's tenure of office, from 1102 to 1109, may have marked the first and perhaps the last time in the period that a serious and concerted effort was made across England to uniformly enforce clerical celibacy. In 1102, Anselm, having returned from an exile spent partly at the papal court, convened the crucial council that forbade priests, deacons, and canons from having or retaining wives, barred unmarried subdeacons from marrying, and required all those ordained to that rank or above to make a profession of chastity.[18] These measures and the effort to enforce them created a tremendous uproar. Eadmer, followed by William of Malmesbury, recorded that many priests and canons disobeyed the orders, took their women back when Anselm went into a second exile, or even married for the first time.[19] Anselm's own letter collection reveals strong resistance to his efforts. Archbishop Gerard of York complained to him of the difficulties he was having getting his canons to obey the rules, and described the maneuvers they were using to continue seeing their "women." In a letter to Bishop Herbert Losinga, Anselm had to urge the bishop to enforce the rules even if it meant having monks temporarily take the place of deposed clerics who had refused to abandon their wives. An exchange between Anselm and Pope Paschal II indicates that some unchaste priests were essentially going on a strike, refusing to administer last rites and creating more disruptions in pastoral care. A letter from Anselm to the archdeacon of Canterbury reveals him wrestling with the practical difficulties of allowing priests to care for their discarded wives, often necessarily living nearby, while ensuring they remained chaste. The outraged families of the discarded wives may also have been a problem. In this same letter, Anselm gave a certain grace period to priests who feared to give up their women, though they were forbidden to say mass in the meantime. Probably they feared their in-laws, for a subsequent passage in the letter states that those who forbade priests to send away their female relatives must be informed that they would be held accountable for the fornication of the priests and would be excommunicated. This suggests that in 1102 many families considered marriage alliances with priests to be perfectly respectable and

[16] Giandrea, *Episcopal Culture*, 120; Emma Mason, *Saint Wulfstan of Worcester, c.1008–1095* (Oxford, 1990), 30–1.

[17] Henry of Huntingdon, *Historia Anglorum*, 450–1.

[18] Whitelock, Brett, and Brooke, eds., *Councils and Synods, 1066–1204*, 675; Partner, *Serious Entertainments*, 42.

[19] Eadmer, *Eadmeri Historia Novorum in Anglia*, ed. Martin Rule (London, 1884), 175, 193; William of Malmesbury, *Gesta Pontificum Anglorum. The History of the English Bishops*, ed. Michael Winterbottom and Rodney M. Thomson, 2 vols. (Oxford, 2007), 1:184–5.

that the demand that priests discard their wives created explosive tensions by angering important local families. Finally, letters written during Anselm's second exile reveal that many priests did in fact seize the opportunity to return to their wives, as the chroniclers indicated.[20]

In the face of such resistance, Anselm urged Bishop Herbert Losinga to seek help from the laity in expelling disobedient priests from their positions, physically driving such priests and their "women" from their lands, and protecting chaste priests. Seeking help from the laity was common during the Gregorian Reform. However, there was one report (which Anselm downplayed) of laypeople using the absence of priests to try to seize the revenue of churches, so this may have been a dangerous tactic. Certainly, Anselm found his most powerful lay supporter, King Henry I, a problematic ally. Though at one point the king had apparently ruled that priests could keep both wives and churches, he subsequently became an eager backer, though not precisely in the way Anselm wanted. The king undoubtedly hoped to gain credit with Anselm and the papacy by supporting a reform that did not undermine his power, but he also saw an opportunity to raise money by fining clerics who broke the rules. According to Eadmer, this plan spun out of control to the detriment of the parish clergy as a whole, and there survives an awkward exchange of letters between Anselm and the king on the subject.[21]

Nonetheless, Anselm sought and obtained royal and baronial backing for another round of decrees on celibacy in a church council of 1108, forcing the relevant clergy to choose between their women (no longer described as wives) and offices. This council tried to resolve the problem of how to deal with discarded wives by ruling that they must not live in the priest's parish and that the priests could only meet them in the presence of witnesses. More important, these decrees added incentives for bishops to enforce the rules by stating that the movable goods of clerics who lapsed be surrendered to the bishops, along with the goods and persons of their concubines, who by implication would become the property of bishops. This threatened punishment of concubines simply reflected earlier rulings, including one by Pope Leo IX that the women of Roman priests become slaves at the Lateran palace, so it is not certain that anyone seriously intended to enforce it. Nevertheless, the decrees of 1108 were obviously meant to go even further than those of 1102.[22]

During this drive for celibacy, Anselm also took aim at the inheritance of churches by the sons of priests.[23] Many reformers had an even broader goal, to

---

[20] Anselm, *S. Anselmi Cantuariensis Archiepiscopi Opera Omnia*, ed. Franciscus Salesius Schmitt, 6 vols. (London, 1946–61), 4:127, 165–70; 5:266, 318.

[21] Anselm, *Opera Omnia*, 4:166; 5:272–3, 307, 336–9; Eadmer, *Historia Novorum*, 172–3.

[22] Eadmer, *Historia Novorum*, 193–5; Whitelock, Brett, and Brooke, eds., *Councils and Synods, 1066–1204*, 700–3; Barstow, *Married Priests*, 53–4; Bernhard Schimmelpfenning, "*Ex Fornicatione Nati*: Studies on the Position of Priests' Sons from the Twelfth to Fourteenth Century," *Studies in Medieval and Renaissance History*, n.s. 2 (1979), 3–50, at 13, 17.

[23] For the sons of priests and the impact of the campaign for clerical celibacy on the children of clerics, see Schimmelpfenning, "*Ex Fornicatione Nati*," 3–50; Laura Wertheimer, "Children of Disorder: Clerical Parentage, Illegitimacy, and Reform in the Middle Ages," *Journal of the History of Sexuality* 15 (2006), 382–407; van Houts, "Fate of Priests' Sons." Thibodeaux has a good discussion of priests' sons in *The Manly Priest*.

bar the sons of priests from the ranks of the clergy altogether, and this eventually became canon law. However, Pope Paschal gave Anselm a great deal of leeway as regards not deposing and even promoting priests' sons in cases apart from inheritance. Partly this was because they had not committed the sins themselves, a point that Paschal acknowledged and that was generally a source of unease in debates over measures against priests' sons. Partly, according to the pope, it was a concession to the barbarous region in which Anselm found himself. However, the main reason was probably that "the greater and better" part of the clergy were the sons of priests (a testament to the widespread practice of clerical marriage) with the result that any general action against them would have caused even greater disruption in the English Church. In theory, a successful drive for clerical celibacy would have eliminated the problem of priests' sons in the long run, so it is not surprising that Anselm used discretion.[24] Overall, however, Anselm clearly meant business, which did not make him popular among the clergy. According to Eadmer, many priests were elated at his death.[25]

Though at first, Eadmer continued, their hopes were dashed by royal enforcement, the king's rigor was soon relaxed, and priests and canons were able to bribe bishops and archdeacons to take back their former women or, if tired of them, to take new mistresses.[26] Thereafter, with one possible exception, there is no clear evidence of a similar sustained attack on clerical unchastity by the church hierarchy throughout England. Councils of the English Church or of the province of Canterbury did include provisions aimed at enforcing celibacy and ending inheritance of churches on multiple occasions through the twelfth century and beyond.[27] However, the only evidence for a concerted and widespread effort concerns a council of 1129, and this proved abortive. According to the *Anglo-Saxon Chronicle*, this council focused on the wives of archdeacons and priests, but had no effect because the king permitted them to keep their wives. According to Henry of Huntingdon, the bishops entrusted enforcement to the king, who then extracted money from the priests to let them off the hook.[28] If other councils of the English Church produced endeavors to enforce clerical celibacy equal to those of Anselm or even of the 1129 council, it is surprising that no echoes are found in the increasingly informative sources of later periods.

Kings after Henry I, moreover, only rarely got involved. In 1137, according to Ralph of Diceto, King Stephen had the concubines of "certain canons called seculars" arrested and taken to the Tower of London, where they stayed until the canons paid a ransom. Given the size of the Tower of London, this action was clearly limited in scope, and Brooke suggested that the passage referred to

---

[24] Whitelock, Brett, and Brooke, eds., *Councils and Synods, 1066–1204*, 675; Anselm, *Opera Omnia*, 4:127, 199; 5:368.

[25] Eadmer, *Historia Novorum*, 212–13.   [26] Eadmer, *Historia Novorum*, 212–14.

[27] Whitelock, Brett, and Brooke, eds., *Councils and Synods, 1066–1204*, 739–40, 747–8, 752–4, 775–6, 983–4, 1051–2, 1067. For legislation in individual dioceses, see [Roger of Howden], *Gesta Regis Henrici Secundi*, 1:280; Powicke and Cheney, eds., *Councils and Synods, 1205–1265*, 25–6.

[28] Whitelock, Brett, and Brooke, eds., *Councils and Synods, 1066–1204*, 752–4; Henry of Huntingdon, *Historia Anglorum*, 482–5.

concubines of the canons of St. Paul's, some of whom had angered the king by opposing his candidate for bishop the previous year.[29] A couple of generations later, according to Roger of Wendover, King John had the concubines of priests and clerics throughout England seized and put to a heavy ransom during the interdict.[30] Roger was not the most reliable source, but John clearly had precedent and did, earlier in his reign, seize the girlfriend (*amica*), children, and servants of Elias, dean of Nottingham, to force him to come to court, and then made him offer 100 marks for their return.[31] The primary aim in these cases, however, was apparently to raise money and perhaps to put political pressure on the clergy. Given the reliance of kings on worldly clerics with families, from Ranulf Flambard under William II to Godfrey de Lucy late in the period, it is hardly surprising that kings intervened only intermittently. Given their actions and motives when they did intervene, it is hardly surprising that after 1129 the Church was unwilling to call on their support.

Though countrywide efforts disappeared, enforcement devolved to the level of individual bishops and other church authorities who were supported by the increasingly well-established judicial institutions of the Church. A number of papal decretals concerning clerical celibacy and hereditary priests show bishops and others in England taking action. Papal mandates directing bishops to take measures against priests with concubines or priests who tried to inherit churches sometimes came at the bishop's request, suggesting some took an interest in enforcement of the rules.[32] In other cases, however, the initiative came from religious houses. The regular canons of St. Frideswide's sought papal support in replacing priests who had concubines with members of their own house. Abbots of Reading and St. Albans obtained papal mandates demanding that bishops remove unchaste clerics or hereditary priests from churches under their patronage. These suggest that bishops sometimes had to be prompted to enforce the rules.[33] Often, litigants sought papal help in specific cases, and the pope in turn commanded bishops or judges delegate to act.[34] Decretals, then, show efforts to enforce celibacy and prevent priestly inheritance after Anselm, but they also raise the question of whether the church hierarchy was proactive or reactive in tackling violations of canon law. Mary Cheney's discussion of this issue in her book on Roger of Worcester is particularly revealing. Roger, who was certainly a bishop with reform-ist inclinations, may well have sought out a papal letter to help him enforce clerical

---

[29] Ralph of Diceto, *Opera Historica*, 1:249; Brooke, "Composition of St. Paul's," 125.

[30] Roger of Wendover, *Flores Historiarum*, 2:47.   [31] Hardy, ed., *Rotuli de Oblatis*, 144.

[32] Barrow, "Hereford Bishops and Married Clergy," 6; Holtzmann, Chodorow, and Duggan, eds., *Decretales Ineditae*, 104–5; Duggan, "Decretals of Alexander III," 104; Cheney and Semple, eds., *Selected Letters of Innocent III*, 82; Cheney and Cheney, eds., *Letters of Pope Innocent III*, 69, 82; Duggan, ed., *Correspondence of Thomas Becket*, 1:120–1; Philipp Jaffé, ed., *Regesta Pontificum Romanorum*, 2 vols., 2nd edn. (Leipzig, 1885–8), 2:372–3, 383, 387, 407.

[33] Holtzmann, ed., *Papsturkunden*, 3:191, 242, 422, 440–1, 506–7, 577–8.

[34] Cheney, *Roger, Bishop of Worcester*, 326, 331–2, 344, 348, 356–7, 359, 361, 364; Holtzmann, Chodorow, and Duggan, eds., *Decretales Ineditae*, 103; Holtzmann and Kemp, eds., *Papal Decretals Relating to Lincoln*, 10–11; Cheney and Cheney, eds., *Letters of Pope Innocent III*, 82, 125, 183; Ralph of Diceto, *Opera Historica*, 1:xii–xiii; Holtzmann, ed., *Papsturkunden*, 1:430–1, 549–50; 2:382–3.

celibacy, yet he seems to have tackled the issue on a case by case basis and his success was mixed. There is no evidence that he or his officers sought out cases; instead, the impetus for the cases often came from patrons seeking to install their own candidates or rival clerics seeking to win appointment.[35] It is therefore possible that even reformist figures were largely reactive in challenging unchaste priests or those who wished to inherit benefices.

Even a reactive approach could have an impact, since the fierce competition for benefices coupled with the needs of patrons meant that plenty of people had an interest in challenging rival claimants to churches or even in expelling established incumbents. It is not always easy to ascertain motives. Did the canons of St. Frideswide's want to place brothers in local churches because they were disgusted with the flouting of church rules, because they wanted to gain the full income from some of their churches, or for both reasons? Were individual abbots of St. Albans and Reading appalled at the laxness of their predecessors or looking for an excuse to clear out some incumbents to put in their own candidates?[36] There were clearly specific cases where disputants over appointments and patronage rights undermined rivals by accusing them of being the heirs of priests or keeping women themselves.[37] There were also specific cases targeting incumbents. Christ Church, Canterbury, formally complained to Pope Alexander III that a priest in one of their churches was behind on his pension and was a fornicator, and it may have been the first lapse that really prompted them to take action.[38] In 1215, the canons of Dunstable wanted to remove a rector and two vicars from a particularly valuable church and its chapels in order to appropriate half the revenues. There was apparently no dispute about the legitimacy of the long serving rector's appointment. Instead, the canons emphasized that the clerics, among other faults, had concubines and sons. The judges delegate hesitated, saying "it seems hard to us to deprive clerics who have held thirty years or more" and even after they passed sentence a compromise was made whereby the clerics involved got two chapels. Nonetheless, Dunstable got the revenues it wanted.[39] Thus, the interests of patrons and claimants meant that even a reactive system of church courts would often have taken on cases involving clerical concubinage and inheritance.

The cases noted above show how the interests of patrons often worked against clerical inheritance and therefore indirectly against concubinage.[40] Patrons who wanted to provide for relatives and followers through bestowing benefices had practical reasons to oppose clerical inheritance.[41] As Ulrich Rasche has suggested, it also made sense for monasteries to take advantage of the attack on clerical celibacy

---

[35] Cheney, *Roger, Bishop of Worcester*, 69–78. For the involvement of another bishop in individual cases, see Morey, *Bartholomew of Exeter*, 56, 71, 90, 92–3.

[36] For a similar view, see Harper-Bill, "Struggle for Benefices," 127–8.

[37] Holtzmann, ed., *Papsturkunden*, 1:430–1, 549–50.

[38] Holtzmann, ed., *Papsturkunden*, 2:382–3.

[39] Fowler, ed., *Cartulary of Dunstable*, 126–32.

[40] See also Wood, *Proprietary Church*, 910–11.

[41] Southern, *Scholastic Humanism*, 1:136–7; Moore, "Property, Marriage, and the Eleventh-Century Revolution," 193.

to appropriate churches, as Dunstable did.[42] How much of a difference this made overall is unclear. In theory, patrons could simply ignore the claims of hereditary priests by citing church law. In practice, they might be constrained by resistance, local opinion, or the connections of clerics and their families. The chronicle of Battle Abbey reveals how, after the death of an archdeacon to whom it had unwisely granted control of nine of its churches, the abbey fought unsuccessfully for control of one of the churches with the archdeacon's sons, who could call on the aid of Richard of Ilchester and other influential men.[43] Nonetheless, the widespread appointments of bureaucrats, sons of aristocrats, and others who were not the sons of previous incumbents reveal that many patrons did successfully ignore inheritance claims by priests. The interests of powerful lords would not have been opposed to hereditary succession in every case. Clerics from noble families might have sons, and the heads of their families might well decide to let the sons succeed to the benefices of their fathers, as when the Mowbray family arranged for the many rich churches of Samson d'Aubigny, one of its members, to pass to his son Roger.[44] Similarly, lords might sometimes have been willing to help powerful clerical followers arrange for their sons to inherit. Generally, however, the interests of patrons would have militated against clerical succession, which probably gave reformers powerful lay allies in ending hereditary succession of churches as a guaranteed right. It is less clear that such patrons would have appreciated the Church methodically weeding out the sons of priests and priests with concubines, since they might count such figures among their relatives or followers. As Judith Green has noted, even Henry I, who participated in Anselm's systematic drive, clearly turned a blind eye to the families of key clerical administrators such as Roger of Salisbury and Richard Belmeis.[45] The interests of patrons would therefore generally have helped reformers, but would not have created a favorable atmosphere for the *systematic* enforcement of clerical celibacy or even of the ban on inheritance. Instead, a reactive system of church courts that selectively enforced church law would have been most in their interest.

Unfortunately, a major problem in assessing whether church courts were simply reactive, as the surviving evidence suggests, or proactive, is that their records were not systematically preserved. Occasional glimpses appear such as a letter of Gilbert Foliot, bishop of London, to a rural dean, ordering him to suspend some priests and deacons who ignored admonitions and continued to frequent their concubines.[46] However, nothing like the later records of visitations exists. In part this reflects the slow development of church courts and institutions.[47] Nonetheless, the earliest surviving plea rolls from the late twelfth century show the royal courts regularly transferring questions about the validity of marriages to church courts, indicating that by that time such courts were sufficiently robust to handle a large amount of

[42] Rasche, "Early Phase of Appropriation," 229–31.
[43] Searle, ed., *The Chronicle of Battle Abbey*, 236–51.
[44] Greenway, ed., *Charters of the Honour of Mowbray*, lxvi.   [45] Green, *Henry I*, 109–10, 275.
[46] Gilbert Foliot, *Letters and Charters*, 330.
[47] For the development of church courts in England, see Helmholz, *Canon Law*, 106–47.

routine business. They were therefore well enough organized to systematically prosecute unchaste clerics by then as well, though as James Brundage has shown, traditional law, which required eye witnesses, made it difficult to prosecute fornication before certain innovations of Innocent III.[48] Church courts would have been in an even better position to bar clerical inheritance, but without surviving records it must remain unclear how proactive the church hierarchy was.

The records of the royal court do reveal one area in which the reformers gained a clear victory, namely in their use of the ecclesiastical courts to successfully delegitimize clerical marriages and bastardize the offspring of clerics, thereby ending any possibility of formal legal inheritance of churches. Marriage was largely a private matter between families in earlier periods, insulating priestly families from the effects of church law. The growth of church control over marriage, however, made it increasingly difficult for priests, deacons, and subdeacons to claim their unions were marriages, and the cession by secular courts to ecclesiastical courts of cases over the legitimacy of marriages meant that the children of clerics in the major orders were inevitably treated as illegitimate under secular as well as canon law. As early as Henry I's reign, the sons of Osbert, who was sheriff of Yorkshire and Lincolnshire but also a "celebrated" priest, could not therefore automatically inherit his lands but had to make a special arrangement with the king, which fell through.[49] There are a number of cases in the early plea rolls in which litigants sought to defeat their opponents by claiming that they or the person through whom they claimed the land were the children of deacons or priests.[50] The facts were often disputed, but the principle was not. This development may also have indirectly discouraged clerics from forming partnerships and families, since they could not rely on the law to pass on their property and positions to their children but would have to circumvent it. It would also have made clerics in major orders much less attractive to potential partners or their families, who might once have considered unions with such clerics as a good marriage strategy.

2. RESISTANCE TO THE CAMPAIGN FOR CLERICAL CELIBACY

Reformers thus won some signal victories, but they also faced enormous opposition for a variety of reasons. Sexual desire, of course: according to Gerald of Wales, Hugh of Avalon, bishop of Lincoln, once jokingly told a woman complaining of her husband's impotence that if he became a priest, the impotence would

---

[48] James A. Brundage, "Sin, Crime, and the Pleasures of the Flesh: The Medieval Church Judges Sexual Offences," in Peter Linehan and Janet L. Nelson, eds., *The Medieval World* (London, 2001), 294–307.

[49] Thomas de Burton, *Chronica Monasterii de Melsa*, 1:85–6; Green, *Government of England*, 189.

[50] Bartlett, *England under the Norman and Angevin Kings*, 385–6; Stenton, ed., *Earliest Lincolnshire Assize Rolls*, 69–70; Stenton, ed., *Northamptonshire Assize Rolls*, 42–3, 95; Stenton, ed., *Pleas*, 2:187–8; 4:244 *Curia Regis Rolls*, 4:304; 6:143–4.

immediately disappear.[51] Related to lust was infatuation. Thomas of Chobham warned clerical readers against "insane love," and then told humorous anecdotes about bishops who cured priests of this malady, in one case by locking the priest in a room with his lover until, exhausted, he begged to be separated from her.[52] In the humoral framework of medicine, however, sex and sexual desire could be constructed not as sinful or insane, but as natural and healthy. One medical treatise from around the year 1200 even used learned clerics, some of them connected with Hereford Cathedral, to discuss sexual desire and sexual capacity, referring to those "who can do much but desire little," such as Master Hugh de Mapenore, dean and later bishop of Hereford, those "who desire little and can do little," such as Master Reginald de Omine, those "who desire much and are able to do little," such as Master Philip Rufus of Cornwall, and those "who desire much and can do much," such as Master John Burgensis and Master William Chers.[53] One suspects humor here, but doctors sometimes prescribed sex for their clerical patients, and though particularly pious ones might refuse, medical beliefs could provide a motive as well as a pretext for sexual activity.[54] Yet another reason for resistance to demands for celibacy was concern about masculinity. There has been excellent work on clerical masculinity done in the last fifteen years, much of which stresses that clerics developed their own type of masculinity which incorporated celibacy, a point to which I will return.[55] Nonetheless, masculinity was often contested and celibacy was an obvious point of contestation. In one sermon, Bishop Bartholomew of Exeter complained that although people condemned theft and perjury, they did not condemn the visiting of whores, and went on to say that, "If someone lives chastely [. . .] he is

[51] Gerald of Wales, *Opera*, 2:250.

[52] Thomas of Chobham, *Summa Confessorum*, 389–90.

[53] Three of these men can be traced and linked to Hereford; Brian Lawn, ed., *The Prose Salernitan Questions* (London, 1979), xv–xvi, 6.

[54] William of Malmesbury, *Gesta Pontificum*, 1:230–1; Richard of Hexham, "History of the Church of Hexham," 52–3; William of Newburgh, *Historia Rerum Anglicarum*, in *Chronicles of the Reigns of Stephen, Henry II and Richard I*, vols. 1–2, ed. Richard Howlett (London, 1884–5), 1:28–9.

[55] Swanson, "Angels Incarnate," 160–77; P. H. Cullum, "Clergy, Masculinity and Transgression in Late Medieval England," in D. M. Hadley, ed., *Masculinity in Medieval Europe* (London, 1999), 178–96; P. H. Cullum, "Learning to Be a Man, Learning to Be a Priest in Late Medieval England," in Sarah Rees Jones, ed., *Learning and Literacy in Medieval England and Abroad* (Turnhout, 2003), 135–53; Karras, "Thomas Aquinas's Chastity Belt," 52–67; Maureen Miller, "Masculinity, Reform, and Clerical Culture: Narratives of Episcopal Holiness in the Gregorian Era," *Church History* 72 (2003), 25–52; Jacqueline Murray, "Masculinizing Religious Life: Sexual Prowess, the Battle for Chastity and Monastic Identity," in P. H. Cullum and Katherine J. Lewis, eds., *Holiness and Masculinity in the Middle Ages* (Cardiff, 2004), 24–42; Derek G. Neal, *The Masculine Self in Late Medieval England* (Chicago, 2008), 91–122; Jennifer D. Thibodeaux, "Man of the Church, or Man of the Village? Gender and the Parish Clergy in Medieval Normandy," *Gender and History* 18 (2006), 380–99; Jennifer D. Thibodeaux, "The Sexual Lives of Medieval Norman Clerics: A New Perspective on Clerical Sexuality," in Albrecht Classen, ed., *Sexuality in the Middle Ages and Early Modern Times: New Approaches to a Fundamental Cultural-Historical and Literary-Anthropological Theme* (Berlin, 2008), 471–83; Jennifer D. Thibodeaux, ed., *Negotiating Clerical Identities: Priests, Monks and Masculinity in the Middle Ages* (Basingstoke, 2010); Tracy Adams, "'Make me Chaste and Continent, but not yet': A Model for Clerical Masculinity?," in Frederick Kiefer, ed., *Masculinities and Femininities in the Middle Ages and Renaissance* (Turnhout, 2009), 1–29. See also Thibodeaux's forthcoming book, *The Manly Priest*.

embarrassed lest people laugh at him, and say he is not a man."[56] This sermon was directed to the laity, but clerics probably also suffered from such taunts. Moreover, ordinary clerics would surely have valued the domestic skills and work their partners could provide, and it is no accident that *focaria* (hearth-mate) and *coqua* (cook) were common terms for concubines.

A last and crucial reason for resistance to celibacy was a desire for companionship and family life. Like some of the other factors, it is a fairly obvious one, but nonetheless worth discussing at greater length, partly because the English sources for the period provide unusually good evidence for affective ties between clerics, their children, and their wives, and partly because some of this evidence shows that the negative views of the reformers about clerical families were far from universal. The very efforts of reformers such as Gerald of Wales and Thomas Agnellus to attack the attractions of family life show the importance of family ties.[57] Reformers were particularly concerned about the expenditures priests made to provide for their children, and rightly so, for priests did work hard to help their children prosper, which provides indirect but compelling evidence for affective relationships within clerical families. In particular, as we have seen, priests tried to get their sons to succeed them in churches. Priests can also be found providing for sons in other ways, for instance acquiring advowsons of churches to present them to, or obtaining land through purchase or other means.[58] A chaplain named Alured arranged for Oseney Abbey to care for two of his sons until they reached the age of twenty-four and deposited £5 for each of them to receive at that age, also arranging for one son to have the option to join Oseney as an adult if he wished.[59] Priests also provided for their daughters. According to the chronicle of Meaux Abbey, Thomas of Etton, a prominent Yorkshire knight, received 100 marks from a wealthy rector named William after marrying his daughter as a second wife, partly in return for setting aside land for the eldest son of the marriage (Thomas had sons from his first marriage), but perhaps also as a marriage portion.[60] Surviving charters reveal priests and an archdeacon granting property as marriage portions for their daughters.[61]

Occasionally, the sources provide more direct evidence of the love clerics could have for their children. A miracle story from St. Bartholomew's, London, which described how the rural dean Wimund had his daughter educated in letters and moral behavior (providing an extremely rare reference to the education of a girl in this period), stated straightforwardly that Wimund loved his daughter with paternal affection.[62] In a Becket miracle recorded by William of Canterbury, a priest, William of York, blamed the blindness of a son on his own sinfulness in making

[56] Bodleian Library, Bodleian MS 449, fo. 34r.   [57] See Chapter 2, section 2.
[58] Barrow, "Married Clergy," 6; Fowler, ed., *Cartulary of Dunstable*, 85–6, 111; Farrer and Clay, eds., *Early Yorkshire Charters*, 5:149.
[59] Salter, ed., *Cartulary of Oseney Abbey*, 3:52–3.
[60] Thomas de Burton, *Chronica Monasterii de Melsa*, 1:319.
[61] Farrer and Clay, eds., *Early Yorkshire Charters*, 6:245; Ross and Devine, eds., *Cartulary of Cirencester*, 1:205–6; Royce, ed., *Landboc de Winchelcumba*, 2:332.
[62] British Library, Cotton MS Vespasian B IX, fo. 30r; Norman Moore, ed., *The Book of the Foundation of St. Bartholomew's Church in London*, Early English Text Society original series, vol. 163 (London, 1923), 47–8.

an illicit marriage, and then reportedly told the monks of Canterbury, "I sorrowed, for how can a young son be punished without paternal sorrow." According to the story he took steps to cure the boy's blindness by erecting an altar to Becket in his church and by housing and feeding twenty paupers in return for prayers for the child.[63]

Reformers often painted a grim picture of relationships between priests and their women, but the sources sometimes provide revealing glimpses of strong and even loving partnerships. One anonymous monk wrote sarcastically, in reference to clerical concubines, "perhaps you would say not whores but the 'solace' of venerable priests."[64] Perhaps many priests would have said exactly that. Certainly a speaker in one of the poems with which this chapter began protested papal demands by saying, "This is a useless measure, frivolous and vain; he who does not love his companion is not sane!"[65] One of the letters John of Salisbury wrote for Archbishop Theobald reveals the case of a priest who purified the body of his concubine, the mother of his children, who had died without confession or communion, so that she receive Christian burial. The priest was suspended from his office for this transgression, which may have been a simple act of affection or love.[66] More striking still is another miracle story by William of Canterbury. A certain priest had a recently deceased concubine who had done charitable deeds, especially for the poor, in her lifetime. The priest hoped she would be saved because of these deeds, but feared she would go to hell because of her relationship with him. He therefore prayed for Becket's intervention and for a sign of her salvation, which duly appeared at the woman's funeral, though "few or none" other than the priest saw it. The priest, if real, may have imagined or invented a sign, but there is no doubt that this story portrayed a man who cared for his companion, though according to William he also marveled at the mercy shown to his unchastity and reformed his life thereafter.[67]

For all the desire of reformers to vilify priests' women and imagine their families as onerous and dysfunctional, contemporaries could not ignore the fact that the partnerships and families of priests were often like the marriages and families of other men.[68] A writer like William of Canterbury could be quite ambivalent about priests and their families. He expressed concern about encouraging people to abuse the law when recording a miracle about a clerical concubine, and cynically stated

---

[63] Robertson and Sheppard, eds., *Materials*, 1:449–50.
[64] Foreville and Leclercq, "Un débat sur le sacerdoce," 106.
[65] Wright, ed., *Latin Poems*, 177.   [66] John of Salisbury, *Letters*, 1:159–60.
[67] Robertson and Sheppard, eds., *Materials*, 1:294–5. One learned cleric wrote in a letter to Ely about how his *socia*, who was like Sara to his Tobit, had prayed on his behalf, but this cleric may have been in minor orders, and *socia* may mean wife here: Blake, ed., *Liber Eliensis*, 272.
[68] For priests, concubines, and families in later periods, see Daniel Bornstein, "Parish Priests in Late Medieval Cortona: The Urban and Rural Clergy," in Maurizio Zangarini, ed., *Preti nel medioevo* (Verona, 1997), 165–93, at 170–8; Kelleher, "Like Man and Wife," 349–60; Armstrong-Partida, "Priestly Marriage," 221–53; Janelle Werner, "Promiscuous Priests and Vicarage Children: Clerical Sexuality and Masculinity in Late Medieval England," in Jennifer D. Thibodeaux, ed., *Negotiating Clerical Identities: Priests, Monks and Masculinity in the Middle Ages* (Basingstoke, 2010), 159–81, at 168–70.

that the prayers of another concubine for the healing of her clerical companion were motivated by concern about her upkeep. Yet he also recorded some cures of priests' sons without comment and provided a moving picture of affective ties (even while condemning clerical relationships) in the miracles discussed earlier. In one miracle story, in which a priest and his partner mourned their dead son, it was the tears and prayers of the mother that prompted the saint to revive the boy despite the skepticism of the overly rational father.[69] William's main goal was to stress God's mercy as a result of Becket's intervention and he did not always stay "on message" with the condemnation of clerical sexual activity, which perhaps allowed his own ambivalence or the less condemnatory views of those telling him the stories to show through.

Strikingly, many writers of local chronicles and hagiographical works mentioned priests and their concubines or children without any condemnation at all and some even portrayed them in a positive light.[70] Surprisingly enough, given the rivalry between regulars and seculars and the fact that chastity had long been a hallmark of the monastic clergy, such writers tended to be monks. For instance, the monk Thomas of Monmouth, in his notorious "blood libel" account of the supposed boy martyr, William of Norwich, was quite open about the fact that William's mother, Elviva, was the daughter of a priest, Wlward, whom he described as a "presbyter famosus." Even though Thomas finished his work as late as the 1170s, he still described William's aunt as the wife (*uxor*) rather than concubine of a priest and noted that they had a son who was a deacon. He also referred to the wife of a deacon or rural dean in his miracle stories. For Thomas, there seems to have been nothing problematic about priestly marriage or about having his saint come from a clerical lineage.[71] Some monks may have had a relatively tolerant view precisely because they came from clerical families. For instance, Ailred of Rievaulx, a key figure in twelfth-century English monasticism, came from a long line of priests. Perhaps because he himself was a noted monk, because other family members had passed into the regular clergy, and because his family's church of Hexham had become a priory, Ailred felt free to celebrate his ancestors and their relationship to Hexham and its saints. Admittedly, Ailred described his father as a sinner who loved otherwise than was fitting, perhaps a reference to him having a family, and Ailred maintained a discrete silence about his relationship with his ancestors. Nonetheless, he clearly took pride in his family.[72]

The most strikingly positive view of the families of priests comes from John of Ford's *vita* of the hermit Wulfric of Haselbury. Wulfric's confessor, Segar, had four sons who were monks or *conversi* at Ford, which may have influenced John's

---

[69] Robertson and Sheppard, eds., *Materials*, 1:294–5, 341–2, 357–8, 449–50, 504–5, 508, 526.

[70] As also noted in Mayr-Harting, *Religion, Politics and Society*, 118.

[71] Thomas of Monmouth, *The Life and Miracles of St William of Norwich*, ed. Augustus Jessopp and M. R. James (Cambridge, 1896), 10–12, 16, 38, 40, 172, 182.

[72] Ailred of Rievaulx, "On the Saints of the Church of Hexham," in James Raine, ed., *The Priory of Hexham*, Surtees Society, vol. 44 (Durham, 1864), 173–203, at 178–9, 190–2. See also Richard of Hexham, "History of the Church of Hexham," 49–50, 54–6; Aird, *St Cuthbert and the Normans*, 118, 121.

picture. Brictric and Osbern, a father and son who were priests at Haselbury, played an important role in the life, and John devoted extensive praise to Brictic's character and religious practices. John also portrayed Osbern positively and described how, as a boy, he served both his father and Wulfric in ritual functions, perhaps in a form of apprenticeship that was probably common in priestly families. More striking still, John even portrayed clerical concubines in favorable terms. He depicted Osbern's mother making an alb for Wulfric in a scene of domestic piety in one miracle story. Another story concerned the former concubine of a priest who had become an *amica* of Christ and was described as an example of piety and sanctity to the region. Since *amica*, female friend, often meant girlfriend or sexual partner, John of Ford was clearly indulging in word play; the woman had passed from being one kind of *amica* to another, better kind. However, there is no hint of the harsh condemnation often reserved for clerical concubines, no sense that this was a transition similar to that of Mary Magdalen. When one of Segar's sons asked Wulfric how Segar fared in the afterlife, Wulfric said that he had suffered great torments but was now at rest, and though Segar's sins were not specified, there may be the implication that chastity was needed for true holiness. Nonetheless, the gap between the rhetoric of reformers and this work's depiction of pious priests with families involved in the life of the church, or of a holy former concubine, is remarkable.[73]

A final look at affective relations within clerical families comes from John of Salisbury. In a letter to his brother, Robert fitz Gille, a canon at Exeter, celebrating the love between them, John jokingly raised and then dismissed the possibility that Robert's love for his young son had crowded out his brotherly love. The editors of John's letters plausibly suggest that a reference to a sister's as well as a brother's love in another letter may refer to Robert's wife or concubine. Strikingly, this latter letter contains encouragement for Robert in fulfilling his priestly office: apparently John, though generally a staunch moralist, did not see Robert's possession of a family as a contradiction to him having a genuine vocation.[74] Christopher Brooke noted that from one perspective, reformers were simply enforcing the law, but from another they were promoting a devastating social revolution that resulted in broken homes and personal tragedies.[75] The accounts above show that some families simply carried on, but also reinforce Brooke's point about the potential for tragedy and the disruptiveness of the reform program.

Given factors ranging from lust to love, it is no surprise that the efforts of the Gregorian reformers provoked debate and resistance not just in England but throughout Europe. Attempts to enforce celibacy sometimes produced violence. In Normandy, for instance, one archbishop of Rouen had to flee a synod in 1072 when the clergy began stoning him after he launched an effort to bar them from

[73] John of Ford, *Wulfric of Haselbury*, 30–1, 38, 52–4, 102–5, 109.
[74] John of Salisbury, *Letters*, 2:42–7.
[75] Brooke, "Gregorian Reform in Action," 69–70. See also Brundage, *Law, Sex, and Christian Society*, 216–17.

their concubines.[76] Throughout Europe, particularly in the late eleventh century, writers sought to defend the legitimacy of clerical marriage and the ordination of the sons of priests.[77] They drew on scripture, theology, and selected canons to dispute the reforms. Some argued that Paul's admonition that it was better to marry than to burn applied as much to the clergy as to the laity, and that forbidding marriage would only push the clergy into fornication, adultery, sodomy, and bestiality. Others expressed concern that the failure of clerics to live up to the high demands of celibacy would bring the clergy into disrepute. Defenders of clerical marriage sometimes attacked the motives of reformers, arguing, for instance, that they were sodomites. As for the sons of priests, their advocates argued that they should be judged on their merits and not be punished for the sins of their fathers, particularly since baptism cleansed existing sins. Two of the main defenders of clerical marriage or the sons of priests were Normans, the "Norman Anonymous" and Serlo of Bayeux, whose poem "De Filiis Presbyterorum" was copied in an Exeter Cathedral manuscript, presumably by one of the canons there.[78] The influence of writings challenging the reforms should not be exaggerated; they were far outnumbered by the works promoting celibacy and rarely survive in many manuscripts. Nonetheless, they demonstrate that some clerics were willing openly to challenge the reformers, and they probably reflect the views of many more clerics who refused to embrace clerical celibacy or the ban on ordaining the sons of priests.

As the Exeter copy of Serlo of Bayeux's poem indicates, echoes of this debate may be found in England. Indeed, the poems with which I opened the chapter contain, in comic form, arguments made by serious critics of clerical celibacy. One, "De Concubinis Sacerdotum," summarized many of these arguments quite neatly: Old Testament precedents for married priests, the command to be fruitful and multiply, the example of John the Baptist as the son of a priest, lack of clear prohibition in the New Testament, Paul's admonition, and the concern that priests might commit graver sexual sins. The humor in the other versions was broader; one even cited David's lust for Bathsheba as a biblical precedent. Besides many simple statements of defiance (one priest would not give up his concubine for 100 marks!), the clerics in these versions also focused on worldly reasons, including good health, for their opposition. A particularly interesting approach, in view of intellectual developments

[76] Orderic Vitalis, *Ecclesiastical History*, 2:200–1. For examples elsewhere, see Jaeger, *Origins of Courtliness*, 193; Lisa Wolverton, *Hastening toward Prague: Power and Society in the Medieval Czech Lands* (Philadelphia, 2001), 126.

[77] Barstow, *Married Priests*, 105–73; Erwin Frauenknecht, *Die Verteidigung der Priesterehe in der Reformzeit* (Hannover, 1997); Leidulf Melve, "The Public Debate on Clerical Marriage in the Late Eleventh Century," *Journal of Ecclesiastical History* 61 (2010), 688–706; Brigitte Meijns, "Opposition to Clerical Continence and the Gregorian Celibacy Legislation in the Diocese of Thérouanne: *Tractatus pro Clericorum Conubio* (c.1077–1078)," *Sacris Erudiri* 47 (2008), 223–90.

[78] Barstow, *Married Priests*, 133–5, 157–73; Corpus Christi College, Cambridge, MS 190, p. 361. For the identification of this poem as Serlo's, see http://parkerweb.stanford.edu/parker/actions/manuscript_description_long_display.do?ms_no=190 (accessed 23 Nov 2013). For Serlo, see van Houts, "Fate of Priests' Sons." Thibodeaux discusses Norman defenders of clerical marriage in her (forthcoming) book, *The Manly Priest*.

in the twelfth century, was to appeal to nature. One cleric was made to say, "All species of things tend to nature; I pass over how creature bears creature. Therefore if I have intercourse with my wife (*coniux*) I do not surpass the proper bounds (*mensura debita*)." Another said, "When I touch the white thighs of a woman, it is fitting that nature carries out its right." Above all, the poems argued that clerics simply could not live up to the demand for clerical celibacy. "Only angelic life is pure," stated a learned cleric in one version, straightforwardly rejecting the reform ideal that priests strive for angelic purity as simply impossible. These poems may have been satirical, but they undoubtedly included many things that actual clerics thought or said.[79]

Indeed, other writers in England opposed the reformers in a more serious vein. Theobald of Étampes, a Norman who taught at Oxford in the early twelfth century, mounted a strong defense of the ordination of the sons of priests, sometime after 1119, stating, for instance, that the honest son of a priest was more worthy of ordination than the dishonest son of a knight.[80] Godwin, precentor of Salisbury, in his "Meditationes," stoutly attacked those who abandoned their wives, referred to Jesus's prohibition on divorce, quoted Paul's admonition, and argued that because of human imperfection wives were needed to prevent fornication. As with wealth, according to Godwin, it was one's attitude that mattered, for there were two ways to follow the biblical admonition to abandon one's family, in actions and mentally. For Godwin, purity of mind was more important than purity of body, and the proper attitude included having sex for procreation rather than desire, not succumbing to the blandishments of one's wife, and disciplining one's children. As Teresa Webber has noted, Godwin never stated whether he was defending lay or clerical marriage.[81] However, his main discussion of marriage came shortly before a section denying claims about the automatic superiority of monastic life. Such claims, though Godwin did not say so, often involved condemnation of incontinent clerics.[82] Moreover, the strong condemnation of abandoning one's family makes particular sense in a context in which reformers were demanding that priests, deacons, and subdeacons do just that. Such a message would certainly have been welcome to Godwin's bishop, Roger of Salisbury, given that he had a family.[83] Surely, therefore, Godwin was at least implicitly defending clerical marriage, while avoiding any explicit defense in case he was challenged.

Similarly, the attacks of Henry of Huntingdon on the reform movement, which have been discussed by Nancy Partner and Diana Greenway, were veiled and oblique. Henry omitted any clear reference to his status as a family man in his writings, even in the charter in which he passed a rectory to his son (his genealogy

---

[79] Wright, ed., *Latin Poems*, 171–82; Trinity College, Cambridge, MS O.2.45, pp. 342–4; Bodleian Library, Bodleian MS 851, fo. 75v. The passages on nature appear in the unpublished Bodleian and Trinity College versions.

[80] Theobald of Étampes, "Epistola ad Roscelinum," in J.-P. Migne, ed., *Patrologia Latina*, vol. 163 (Paris, 1854), 767–70; Barstow, *Married Priests*, 137–9; Frauenknecht, *Verteidigung der Priesterehe*, 129.

[81] Bodleian Library, Digby MS 96, fos. 12r–15v, 43r–v, 49v; Webber, *Scribes and Scholars*, 125 n. 40, 126–9.

[82] Bodleian Library, Digby MS 96, fos. 18v–29v.

[83] For Bishop Roger's family, see Kealey, *Roger of Salisbury*, 22–4, 272–4.

has been reconstructed from other sources), and he made no direct defense of clerical marriage. However, he subtly undermined the efforts of reformers in a variety of passages, as in his claim that the efforts of 1129 simply resulted in extortion by the king. In the context of Anselm's reforms, he noted that some believed there was a danger that clerics would fall into great uncleanness if they aimed for a purity beyond their capacity. He praised his own father, Archdeacon Nicholas, as the "star of the clergy." In contrast, he told a story of a papal legate who preached the standard line that it was the greatest evil to rise from the side of a whore to go "confect" the body of Christ, and was shortly thereafter found with a whore. A hostile reformer would have found nothing in Henry's writing to definitively mark him as a defiant and rebellious supporter of clerical marriage, but Henry managed to make his views clear.[84]

It is hard to find clear-cut defenses of clerical marriage or the ordination of priests' sons in sources after Theobald of Étampes, but the examples of Godwin and Henry suggest that this reflects the ability of reformers to stifle open dissent rather than an end to debate. Even a later chronicler like Ralph of Diceto could incorporate into his work a passage by Sigebert of Gembloux about the problems caused by Gregory VII's attack on celibacy and draw material from Ivo of Chartres defending the ordination of priests' sons, which suggests a critical stance towards clerical celibacy.[85] There also survive references to oral or informal debate and opposition. Already in 1102 Archbishop Gerard reported to Archbishop Anselm resistance by "sophistic disputers."[86] Much later, Nigel of Whiteacre wrote that unchaste priests pointed to the wives of the apostles to defend their own relations with women, and John of Salisbury noted that clerics were using a biblical passage on bishops having one wife to defend their own practices.[87] Thomas of Chobham's discussion of the issue reveals that there were still objections to enforced clerical celibacy around the time of the Fourth Lateran Council, and Gerald of Wales likewise noted that some argued against it in his time.[88] John Baldwin has placed Gerald himself among a group of thinkers surrounding Peter the Chanter who expressed doubts about clerical celibacy around 1200, and who tried unsuccessfully to reduce its scope.[89] In fact, Gerald's attitude is puzzling. In one passage, he noted that there was no scriptural authority for clerical celibacy, that the Greek Church allowed marriage, and that Peter Comestor had called the Western Church's embrace of celibacy a trick of the devil. He even claimed (implausibly) that Pope Alexander III had intended to reverse the policy.[90] Yet these statements came within a longer passage in which Gerald strongly championed clerical celibacy

---

[84] Henry of Huntingdon, *Historia Anglorum*, xxiii–xxviii, li–lii, 450–1, 458–9, 472–5, 482–5, 830–1; Partner, *Serious Entertainments*, 11–12, 15, 39–47.

[85] Ralph of Diceto, *Opera Historica*, 1:xxi, xxvii–xxviii, 208, 305.

[86] Anselm, *Opera Omnia*, 4:167.

[87] Nigel of Whiteacre, *Tractatus Contra Curiales*, 182; John of Salisbury, *Policraticus*, 2:175.

[88] Thomas of Chobham, *Summa Confessorum*, 377–8; Gerald of Wales, *Opera*, 2:186–8.

[89] John W. Baldwin, "A Campaign to Reduce Clerical Celibacy at the Turn of the 12th and 13th Centuries," in *Études d'histoire du droit canonique dediées à Gabriel le Bras* (Paris, 1965), 2:1041–53.

[90] Gerald of Wales, *Opera*, 2:187–8.

(as he did elsewhere), using the harsh language of cultic purity about touching the bodies of "whores."[91] Perhaps Gerald was acknowledging the arguments of others against celibacy, or perhaps he believed celibacy was an important ideal, but had doubts about the advisability of *enforced* clerical celibacy. In a digression on church wealth immediately following, he depicted that wealth as part of God's plan but nonetheless something that the devil could exploit; perhaps he felt the same about the Western Church's strictures on celibacy.[92] However one explains this passage, it does suggest that the debate was still very much alive in his time. Critics of reform probably never had any real hope of success in overturning church demands for celibacy. The strength of commitment to cultic purity, the long tradition of legislation and exhortation, the moral ascendancy of the reform movement, and the weight of papal authority proved too powerful for counter-arguments to have any institutional chance of success. Nonetheless, ideological opposition to reform continued throughout the long twelfth century.

Practical resistance was even stronger. England saw no riots comparable to those at Rouen and elsewhere, but Peter of Blois's complaints about the canons of Wolverhampton reveal that this resistance could be fierce. Peter claimed the canons, who partnered with each other's female relatives, flaunted their fornication "like Sodom," and ignored his attempts at correction and warnings from the king and archbishop of Canterbury. As noted in Chapter 5, when as dean Peter tried to appoint outsiders when canons died, their heirs claimed heritable rights, fled into the woods, and attacked the newcomers with "fire and iron." In despair, Peter urged turning the church at Wolverhampton into a Cistercian monastery.[93]

Most unchaste clerics and sons of clerics relied on less extreme methods such as bribery. In one of the poems with which I began the chapter, a priest stated, "The pope doesn't scare me with threats and fear, but I will offer coins for the love of God, so that I remain in peace with my dear wife."[94] In 1102, the archbishop of York admitted to Anselm that he had taken money to allow the son of a priest to inherit his father's church, and in 1108, the council of London declared that archdeacons and rural deans must swear an oath not to take bribes to allow priests to keep their women.[95] Etienne de Fougères wrote of archdeacons and rural deans pursuing rumors of women, but only for a payoff. Once that was received, the dean might declare, "That clerk is no *herite* (heretic or perhaps homosexual) who has Horhan and Organite. Good is the home where a woman lives."[96] According to Walter Map, when Reginald de Bohun experienced difficulty being consecrated as bishop of Bath, his father, Jocelin, bishop

---

[91] Gerald of Wales, *Opera*, 2:169–285; 4:313–14, 324–8. For the implausibility of his claim about Alexander III, see James A. Brundage, "Marriage and Sexuality in the Decretals of Pope Alexander III," in Filippo Liotta, ed., *Miscellanea Rolando Bandinelli, Papa Alessandro III* (Siena, 1986), 57–83, at 68.

[92] Gerald of Wales, *Opera*, 2:188–9.   [93] Peter of Blois, *Later Letters*, 25–30.

[94] Wright, ed., *Latin Poems*, 177.

[95] Anselm, *Opera Omnia*, 4:167–8; Whitelock, Brett, and Brooke, eds., *Councils and Synods, 1066–1204*, 702.

[96] Etienne de Fougères, *Le livre des manières*, 70–1.

of Salisbury, told him to give the pope a good smack with a purse full of money.[97]

Priests and their sons could also manipulate the legal system. Bishop William Turbe complained to Alexander III about sons of priests who relied on other sons of priests as witnesses, on forgery, and on frequent appeals to frustrate attempts to dislodge them.[98] Clerics in specific cases were sometimes accused of forging papal letters or acquiring them under false pretenses in order to inherit churches, and in the reign of Innocent III, a father and son defied the attempts of Bury St Edmunds to oust them from their church by alternately claiming to be the rector whenever the other was summoned.[99] A more permanent legal dodge was to remain in lower orders and have a vicar do the work. Indeed, Gerald of Wales noted, apparently with approval, that some argued this was a perfectly reasonable course.[100] Clerics in lower orders supposedly received benefices only with the expectation that they would advance to the necessary rank, but by avoiding advancement they could also avoid violating cultic purity. Since many elite clerics were absentees who had vicars anyway, this may have been a popular gambit.

It is likely that the rejection of reform ideals by many clerics, the existence of bishops and other ecclesiastical officials with families, and the ambivalence even of some pious, celibate clerics, when combined with corruption, reactive tendencies by bishops, and perhaps institutional shortcomings in the ecclesiastical courts, led to patchy enforcement and a widespread practical toleration for clerical sex after Anselm's death. Alexander III, echoing Paschal II, admitted to Bishop Robert Foliot of Hereford the problems of removing offenders from office among a "barbarous" people.[101] During Thomas Becket's dispute with Henry II, the archbishop attacked Gilbert Foliot for corruptly ordaining non-celibate priests and promoting the sons of priests to benefices. Thrown on the defensive, Foliot denied accepting bribes, stated that he had diligently warned all in synods and chapters, and had even corrected some. If the practices had not been eliminated, he continued, it was not his fault, but the fault of many others as well, of the persistence of a "scarcely or never abolished custom," of original sin, and of his archdeacons. Even if Gilbert was not corrupt (and accusations hurled in the heat of the Becket controversy should be treated with caution) he may not have been a zealous enforcer of clerical celibacy. As noted earlier, one letter in his collection did concern proceedings against clerics with concubines; perhaps it was included precisely because of this episode. However, Gilbert, though himself celibate as far as one can tell, had clerical relatives, particularly in the Belmeis family, who were not. In a letter to Bishop Jocelin de Bohun, he joked about the return of the latter's "prodigal" son, Reginald, and in another letter he asked Pope Eugenius III to

[97] Walter Map, *De Nugis Curialium*, 68–9.

[98] Christopher Harper-Bill, "Bishop William Turbe and the Diocese of Norwich, 1146–1174," *Anglo-Norman Studies* 7 (1985), 142–60, at 156–8.

[99] Cheney, *Roger, Bishop of Worcester*, 356–7; Holtzmann and Kemp, eds., *Papal Decretals Relating to Lincoln*, 10–11; Cheney and Cheney, eds., *Letters of Pope Innocent III*, 3.

[100] Gerald of Wales, *Opera*, 2:186.

[101] Barrow, "Hereford Bishops and Married Clergy," 6.

absolve a penitent priest for taking over the church of his father. In his own defense against Becket's charges, moreover, he even revealed that he had promoted to the priesthood a priest's son who had been instituted into a church by a predecessor. He did so, he said, because one of Becket's own clerics extracted such a large pension that the son could no longer afford a vicar and had to minister to the church himself. Gilbert was clearly counterattacking here, blaming his own actions on the greed of Becket's cleric, but it is striking that he apparently saw nothing egregiously wrong with the original situation and felt that his promotion of the son was defensible.[102]

Other ecclesiastical officials clearly shared Gilbert's willingness to overlook or provide exemptions for violations of church law. Thomas of Chobham wrote that bishops nearly everywhere tolerated concubines.[103] A cleric named John who was accused of succeeding his father in a church produced a letter of institution from none other than Henry of Huntingdon, and though there was debate about the authenticity of this document, it seems entirely likely that Henry would institute the son of a priest to a church.[104] Bishop Richard Peche of Coventry was accused of actually forcing the owner of an advowson to accept the son of a priest in his father's church. Since Richard was himself the son of a former bishop and also a father, it seems quite plausible that he might strongly support the son of the priest.[105] More striking is the fact that Hugh of Avalon, subsequently made a saint, appointed so many illegitimate sons to the chapter of Lincoln, based on their merits, that the chapter informed Innocent III that if they elected an internal candidate, they might well end up choosing a bastard.[106]

In this case, the pope replied that such a choice should only be made in compelling circumstances, but in fact the popes themselves clearly felt ambivalent about enforcing rules, particularly when it came to the sons of priests.[107] Innocent himself granted Richard Poore, the son of Richard of Ilchester, bishop of Winchester, leave to hold benefices, citing his learning and good life.[108] In some cases, as with the chronicler Roger of Howden or one Honorius, probably the canonist of that name, learning may indeed have played a role, even prompting popes or their legates to grant dispensations to these sons of priests to succeed their fathers in their churches.[109] One case seems to show Alexander III granting leniency to an alleged son of a priest because of long tenure, and in another, Alexander overruled the local bishop, Bartholomew of Exeter, because he felt compassion for the son of a priest

---

[102] Duggan, ed., *Correspondence of Thomas Becket*, 1:412–13; Robertson and Sheppard, eds., *Materials*, 4:238–40; Gilbert Foliot, *Letters and Charters*, 121, 279, 330.

[103] Thomas of Chobham, *Summa Confessorum*, 385.

[104] Gilbert Foliot, *Letters and Charters*, 319–21.

[105] Duggan, "Decretals of Alexander III," 139–40; Franklin, ed., *English Episcopal Acta 16*, xxiii, xxvii; Franklin, ed., *English Episcopal Acta 17*, xlv n 153; Ralph of Diceto, *Opera Historica*, 1:305.

[106] Though not stated, it is likely that most of these appointments were the sons of clerics, following in the family profession: Cheney and Cheney, eds., *Letters of Pope Innocent III*, 119.

[107] Brundage, *Law, Sex, and Christian Society*, 403.

[108] Cheney and Cheney, eds., *Letters of Pope Innocent III*, 112.

[109] Holtzmann, ed., *Papsturkunden*, 1:510; Lovatt, ed., *English Episcopal Acta 20*, 17–19.

due to his needs and the burdens he had undertaken in the journey to Rome.[110] In light of this last case, the alleged plan of one archdeacon to gain Pope Adrian's indulgence in remaining with his pregnant concubine by naming their child Adriana, if a girl, does not sound as far-fetched as it otherwise might.[111] Popes tried to compromise between enforcement and leniency by regularly granting dispensations, but also restricting the power to grant such dispensations to themselves.[112] This practice would theoretically have limited the scope of the hereditary priesthood, for the sons of priests would have had to go to much trouble to obtain papal dispensation and popes could restrict ordinations only to the most worthy, but it also marked a partial surrender to widespread clerical unchastity. In any case, if the popes were equivocal about consistently enforcing the rules designed to ensure clerical celibacy, it is hardly surprising that other figures might be as well.

A widespread willingness by church authorities to look the other way may explain why clerics sometimes hid either their clerical status or, like Henry of Huntingdon, their families, in public writings and documents. The abbots of Holme patronized at least two dynasties of clerics and were admonished in a papal letter for allowing churches to pass through hereditary succession. Strikingly, two members of the first dynasty, Thomas of Ludham and Thomas of Walton, both of whom were instituted into churches and both of whom had children, were the most frequent witnesses to charters of the abbots in the late twelfth century, but never attested as clerics. As for the second dynasty, two charters granting the church of Fordham and specific parcels of land to Philip, nephew of an earlier abbot, described him as Philip the Chaplain, son of Geoffrey the cleric of Fordham. Yet another charter granted some of the same parcels of land to Philip of Fordham son of Geoffrey, Agnes daughter of Warin de Burgh, and their children. No mention was made in this latter document of Philip as a chaplain, but neither was Agnes described as his wife, and so Philip's status as a priest with a concubine and children was discreetly passed over.[113] At a more prominent level, King John, in a charter confirming to Geoffrey de Lucy a manor his father, Bishop Godfrey, had bequeathed him made no mention of the relationship between them.[114] The status of all these men as priests or bishops with families must have been an open secret. Why bother? In an ecclesiastical culture that loathed open scandal, polite fictions, however transparent, were probably considered proper behavior. However, it is also likely that lenient superiors preferred their subordinates not to call attention to

[110] Cheney, *Roger, Bishop of Worcester*, 361; Duggan, "Decretals of Alexander III," 102–3.

[111] John of Salisbury, *Letters*, 1:25.

[112] Schimmelpfenning, "*Ex Fornicatione Nati*," 3–50; Kathryn Ann Taglia, "'On Account of Scandal...': Priests, their Children, and the Ecclesiastical Demand for Celibacy," *Florilegium* 14 (1995–6), 57–70; Ludwig Schmugge, *Kirche, Kinder, Karrieren: Päpstliche Dispense von der unehelichen Geburt im Spätmittelalter* (Zürich, 1995).

[113] Holtzmann, ed., *Papsturkunden*, 1:486–7; West, ed., *St. Benet of Holme*, 1:52, 56, 66, 96, 102, 131–2, 150; 2:229, 240–1. For the attestations of Thomas of Ludham and Thomas of Walton, see 115, 117–21, 123–5, 127–31, 134–8.

[114] Hardy, ed., *Rotuli Chartarum*, 137a. For an even later example, see Nicholas Vincent, "New Light on Master Alexander of Swerford (d. 1246): The Career and Connections of an Oxfordshire Civil Servant," *Oxoniensia* 61 (1996), 297–309, at 302–3, 308–9.

themselves and to preserve at least some level of plausible deniability, however tenuous.

The most striking witness to a culture of leniency regarding clerical sex was Thomas of Chobham's influential guide for confessors, written around the end of our period. When Thomas noted that some still objected to obligatory clerical celibacy, he said that their objections were frivolous because "it is fitting to obey the Roman Church." He dutifully set out the Church's teachings on clerical celibacy and the official penalties involved. Elsewhere, he even used the language of cultic purity, speaking of priests bringing the odor of the brothel to that of the sacrifice. Yet Thomas also suggested various ameliorations for the penalties against those who broke the rules. Admittedly, some of the penalties he objected to, such as enslaving the concubines or sons of priests, were never seriously enforced, at least in England. However, having said that married acolytes could not licitly hold churches even if they used vicars, Thomas went on to advise confessors that they would not sin too much in advising acolytes who could not remain chaste to secretly marry and even to keep their wives if they were forced to be promoted to keep their churches. He even wrote that priests and clerics should not be forced to abjure concubines, citing a decretal which seems, confusingly, to both permit and forbid concubinage.[115] Whatever Thomas's precise views on clerical celibacy were, he was clearly not an advocate of inflexible enforcement.

The fact that the drive against clerical celibacy faced so much opposition and so many difficulties created a major gap between the rules governing clerical sexuality and the actual behavior of clerics. The willingness of the church hierarchy to tolerate this gap may seem surprising, but it should be placed in the context of similar lapses discussed earlier, such as the embrace of wealth by clerics or their eagerness to serve in the royal court. To modern scholars, conditioned by the greater success of the modern Catholic Church in enforcing celibacy, the ability of clerics to more or less openly have families may jump out more than other clerical breaches of church law. Modern debates about clerical celibacy (as well as modern scandals) also highlight failures to adhere to clerical celibacy in modern eyes. To twelfth-century moralists, clerical sexual activity probably represented one way among many in which clerics failed to live up to angelic standards. Even reformers like Gerald who saw clerical celibacy as desirable probably also saw it as one of several desirable behaviors that were simply impossible to thoroughly enforce. At one point, Gerald, in the middle of a passage using the full arsenal of rhetorical attacks on clerical marriage and fornication, resignedly urged priests at least to be chaste in their old age, and at another point he urged priests to at least remain chaste for three days and nights before performing the Eucharist, so as to minimize the pollution from embracing their "whores."[116]

---

[115] Thomas of Chobham, *Summa Confessorum*, 376–87; Thomas of Chobham, *Summa de Arte Praedicandi*, 126. Brundage, who sees Thomas as essentially opposed to clerical celibacy, provides further discussion: Brundage, *Law, Sex, and Christian Society*, 401–3, 405.

[116] Gerald of Wales, *Opera*, 2:195, 198.

3. EXHORTATION AND THE IMPACT ON PRIESTS' PARTNERS AND CHILDREN

Given the laxity and inconsistency of enforcement, reformers like Gerald continued to use the other key tool of reform, exhortation. I have already discussed in Chapter 2 the core messages of reformers when it came to celibacy. Nonetheless, there are ancillary points to be noted, and it is also important to discuss the impact of the attacks of reformers not only on the clergy but also on their families. The first point is that critics of clerical sexuality not only used sermons and treatises, but also hagiography. Chastity, of course, was considered a common attribute of saintliness, and several biographies of Thomas Becket praised him for remaining chaste even during his most worldly period.[117] Miracle stories sometimes attacked sexual sin by clerics. Gerald of Wales in particular made extensive use of such stories in his section on celibacy in his *Gemma Ecclesiastica*. Some showed divine displeasure, as when an unchaste priest and his son died in a house fire, some showed God issuing warnings before the fact, as when a cleric preparing an assignation with a nun had a vision of hell, and others showed divine aid to those fighting to remain chaste. In a different context, he even recorded a story about a statue of the Virgin Mary coming to life in a Canterbury church and beating up a parish priest who was trying to rape a girl he had failed to seduce.[118] Perhaps the most pointed story about divine displeasure with clerical unchastity comes from the purgatorial vision of a monk of Eynsham. According to this account, the monk saw priests who had repented of sexual activity but not yet performed penance suffering torments in purgatory. Though the visionary saw many such priests there, the number seemed small to him in comparison to the number of guilty, until he was told that most had never repented of their fornication, and therefore gone to hell.[119]

In order to remove the specific fear that celibacy might threaten masculinity, reformers tried to persuade priests that it was in fact *more* manly. Even in the late antique period, renunciation of sex and the struggle against desire could be construed as masculine, and this continued during the Middle Ages.[120] In

---

[117] Robertson and Sheppard, eds., *Materials*, 1:5–6; 2:360, 365; 3:21, 166, 168–72; Hanna Vollrath, "Was Thomas Becket Chaste? Understanding Episodes in the Becket Lives," *Anglo-Norman Studies* 27 (2005), 198–209.

[118] Gerald of Wales, *Opera*, 2:106–7, 212–31, 242–55. For a full and thoughtful analysis of the ways Gerald used stories, supernatural or otherwise, in his discussion of celibacy, see John H. Arnold, "The Labour of Continence: Masculinity and Clerical Virginity," in Anke Bernau, Ruth Evans, and Sarah Salih, eds., *Medieval Virginities* (Toronto, 2003), 102–18. In later periods, such stories often came to be used as *exempla* in sermons: Karras, *Sexuality in Medieval Europe*, 101; Karras, *Unmarriages*, 135–9.

[119] Easting, ed., *Revelation of the Monk of Eynsham*, 116.

[120] Mathew Kuefler, *The Manly Eunuch: Masculinity, Gender Ambiguity, and Christian Ideology in Late Antiquity* (Chicago, 2001), 170–8; Miller, "Masculinity, Reform, and Clerical Culture," 49–50; Karras, "Thomas Aquinas's Chastity Belt," 53–8; Thibodeaux, "Man of the Church," 385–6. Thibodeaux, in her (forthcoming) book, *The Manly Priest*, argues that making priests conform to a monastic model of chaste masculinity was in fact an important motive behind the drive for clerical celibacy.

particular, reformers stressed that to control carnal desires, rather than being controlled by them, was a sign of manliness. The miracle story about Wimund the priest, though describing him as a loving father, stated that he took a lower class temptress (*proletaria succuba*) either for "works of the flesh or night fears (*timores nocturni*)" implicitly linking sex with cowardice and probably by implication with effeminacy.[121] In contrast, Gerald of Wales urged his clerical audience not to be "cowardly" priests but to resist carnal desires manfully (*viriliter*).[122] Likewise, Gervase of Chichester urged priests to "act manfully lest their effeminate flesh subdue them to vice, and rather let moderating reason order one's state of mind and deeds." Gervase used the story of the chaining of Mars and Venus by Vulcan to turn secular ideals of masculinity on their head. According to Gervase, the "effeminate" priest caught by the bishop or his official with his concubine would be chained by episcopal sentence and, just as Mars was humiliated, would be ridiculed and held vile by the whole Church. I have discussed elsewhere how both regular and secular clerics faced challenges to their honor and masculinity in confrontations against armed secular nobles.[123] Here, the effeminate priest was paired with the god of war, and both by implication were unmanly because they could not control their lust.[124] As Ruth Karras has stressed, another way clerics stressed their masculinity, or perhaps their masculine humanity, was to celebrate the use of reason (as Gervase did) and to contrast their behavior with the beastly; Alexander Neckam certainly used this latter approach.[125] Clerical masculinity no doubt remained contested, but reformers probably succeeded in lessening the concerns of clerics that celibacy would undermine their masculinity.

A particularly important characteristic of exhortation was that it was designed to stigmatize priests, deacons, and subdeacons who engaged in sex, along with their children and especially their partners, which had an effect on the social position of those involved, above all the women. Before turning to the children and female partners, however, it is worth emphasizing that reformers could direct extremely harsh rhetoric to the clerics themselves, as when Thomas Agnellus, drawing on the vicious anti-Semitism of the time, compared priests who performed the Eucharist while polluted by sex to the Jews as "Christ killers."[126] The fact that disputants could use marriage and sexual transgressions as a stick with which to beat opponents suggests that the attempts to stigmatize transgressors were effective. Thus, Thomas Becket described Reginald de Bohun as a fornicator and the son of a priest, and one of his biographers, Garnier, scornfully described Geoffrey Ridel, another royal supporter and future bishop, as "the married man."[127]

---

[121] British Library, Cotton MS Vespasian B IX, fo. 30r.   [122] Gerald of Wales, *Opera*, 2:190.

[123] Hugh M. Thomas, "Shame, Masculinity, and the Death of Thomas Becket," *Speculum* 87 (2012), 1050–88.

[124] British Library, Royal MS 3 B X, fos. 42r, 62r.

[125] Ruth Mazo Karras, *From Boys to Men: Formations of Masculinity in Late Medieval Europe* (Philadelphia, 2003), 100–8; Bodleian Library, Wood empt. MS 13, fos. 32r, 33r–v.

[126] Bodleian Library, Laud. Misc. MS 71, fo. 80r.

[127] Duggan, ed., *Correspondence of Thomas Becket*, 2:992–3; Guernes de Pont-Sainte-Maxence, *Vie de Becket*, 147.

Reformers' attacks on the children of the upper clergy tended to be relatively restrained. Their daughters almost never appeared in writing, except in one complaint of priests wasting tithes on adorning daughters as well as wives.[128] As for sons, Nigel of Whiteacre linked the problem of unlearned priests to clerical inheritance, for in that context he told Bishop William Longchamp, to whom his treatise was directed, "If you were a good guard and cultivator of the vines of the Lord of Hosts, you would cut off the hearth-mates of priests with the pruning hook so that so many bastard shoots would not spring forth in your bishopric."[129] Gerald of Wales had a couple of anecdotes about ungrateful sons. In one, the father gave up his prebend at Lincoln Cathedral to his son, and fell into poverty as a result, but the son provided him no help and even kicked him in the face when he prostrated himself to beg aid. These stories, however, appeared not in Gerald's passages on celibacy but in a diatribe against his own supposedly ungrateful nephew.[130] Later sources show that the children of priests were often viewed as scandalous, and this may already have been the case.[131] Laura Wertheimer also makes the intriguing argument that the sons of priests themselves might be seen as polluted, but I do not find direct evidence for this mindset in my sources.[132] All in all, reformers tended to treat the children of priests, deacons, and subdeacons relatively gently, partly because they were seen as innocent of the sin themselves, but perhaps also because so many clerics and monks were themselves the sons of priests. Nonetheless, a certain stigma about being the son of a priest developed, as Thomas Becket's description of Reginald de Bohun indicates. Similarly, Henry II, after a confrontation with Becket's supporter, Herbert of Bosham, said angrily, "What a great provocation, that this son of a priest disturbs my realm and my peace." Herbert responded that he had been born before his father became a priest, but clearly he had been stung.[133] Of course, as the Church gained more control over marriage, the children of priests would increasingly have suffered the stigma of illegitimacy. Indeed, Bernhard Schimmelpfenning has suggested that the drive for clerical celibacy worsened the status for illegitimate children in general.[134] The stigmatization of the children of the upper clergy was largely a by-product of the reform, but it must have been quite painful, especially when combined with the legal consequences of illegitimacy.

Nonetheless, it was the partners of the upper clergy whom reformers targeted most fiercely and who suffered most as a result, experiencing a major degradation of social and legal status during the long twelfth century. The frequent reference to the partners of priests as "whores" (*meretrices*) was both a part of this process and a sign of its success. Even the term *concubina*, though relatively neutral, underscored that

---

[128] Alexander of Ashby, "De Artificioso Modo Predicandi," 65.
[129] Nigel of Whiteacre, *Tractatus Contra Curiales*, 204.
[130] Gerald of Wales, *Speculum Duorum*, 10–15.
[131] Taglia, "On Account of Scandal," 57–70.
[132] Wertheimer, "Children of Disorder," 384, 395. Karras also raises questions about this: Karras, *Unmarriages*, 141.
[133] Robertson and Sheppard, eds., *Materials*, 3:101.
[134] Schimmelpfenning, "*Ex Fornicatione Nati*," 25.

they were not wives. The common term *focaria*, generally translated as hearth-mate, had overtones of domesticity but, as Karras has noted, originally referred to a servant who worked in the kitchen, and thus, like *coqua*, served subtly to downgrade the status of the partners of clerics. As Karras has also noted, there were no equivalent derogatory labels for priests engaged in sexual activities.[135] Though the rulings about the enslavement of the concubines of clerics were probably never enforced, such enactments nonetheless stigmatized priests' wives or women as worthy of being degraded. The complaints about money wasted on the frivolous adornment of the partners of priests utilized negative stereotypes of women, and reformers sometimes used misogynistic anecdotes to try to convince clerics that the pleasures of consorting with women, like the pleasures of the court, were essentially false. Gerald of Wales provided a whole series of these. Playing on stereotypes about women's lust, he told of a priest living near Nottingham who kept his cook as a mistress; she pursued other clerics, and so he became jealous and hanged himself. Playing on negative stereotypes of the demanding, socially ambitious, dominating wife, he described a priest who had to ride behind his servant (*domestica*) or rather lady (*domina*) or mistress (*dominatrix*) as she rode to market to cut an impressive figure. Using both types of stereotype, he told of a priest who had to walk while his concubine rode and therefore received what Gerald considered a just punishment when the concubine connived at her own abduction by two knights and spent the night with them while the priest searched desperately for her. Elsewhere Gerald wrote at length of the dangers of seductive women.[136] The women themselves were not, in some respects, the main focus of such misogynistic attacks. As Maureen Miller has noted, "To understand the crescendo of misogynist discourse in high-medieval Europe, we need to figure how the vilification of women figures in relations between men."[137] However, it was the women involved who suffered most, even if only as collateral damage, in the debates over clerical celibacy.

Ralph of Diceto's account of the arrest of the concubines of canons by King Stephen provides a particularly telling and distressing glimpse into the impact of reform on the honor and status of the partners of the upper clergy.[138] Clearly the women mattered to the canons, since otherwise they would not have been worth holding for ransom, and they were therefore probably long-term partners. If Brooke is correct that they were partners of canons of St. Paul's, the clerics involved were of high status, and the women would have headed well-to-do households. Yet Ralph used the term *focariae*, with its intimations of low status, to describe them.[139] More important, he stated that they had been subject, while in the Tower of London, to

---

[135] Karras, *Unmarriages*, 134–5.

[136] Gerald of Wales, *Opera*, 2:178–84, 235–49, 254–5, 277–8. For such anecdotes in a later period, see Karras, *Sexuality in Medieval Europe*, 101; Karras, *Unmarriages*, 137–8.

[137] Miller, "Masculinity, Reform, and Clerical Culture," 50.

[138] Ralph of Diceto, *Opera Historica*, 1:249; Brooke, "Composition of St. Paul's," 125.

[139] He also used an odd phrase, *raptae sublimes*, to describe them. The term *raptae* might have referred to seduction by the canons, their seizure and treatment by the king's forces, or both. The term *sublimis*, meaning lofty, distinguished, even sublime, seems to give them importance, and though it may only be an ironic reference to their worth as sexual objects or as plunder, it may also allude to a certain social eminence in other circumstances.

ludibrium corporis, at best indicating that they suffered physical mockery and at worst sexual violence. It is unlikely that the king and his followers would have treated the wives of laymen who were the social equivalent of canons of St. Paul's, or even of less eminent canons, in such a humiliating and abusive fashion. The contrast with an earlier generation, when Anselm and fellow reformers apparently had to worry about the attacks on clerics by the relatives of their discarded wives, is striking, and may indicate how much success reformers had achieved in undermining the status of women who formed partnerships with priests, deacons, and subdeacons. Such public humiliation would, of course, only have further degraded their status.

The specific attacks on the female partners of clerics were rooted in existing misogyny, as was the very idea that women's bodies and sexuality were polluting, but one outcome of such attacks was to further entrench misogyny.[140] As noted in Chapter 3, Walter Map's long misogynistic tract attacking marriage, later cited by Chaucer's Wife of Bath, was addressed to a learned and therefore almost certainly clerical friend. Reforming writers such as John of Salisbury and Peter of Blois also authored misogynistic tirades.[141] The extensive debate over celibacy only rooted beliefs about women and pollution more firmly in church thinking and caused them to be publicized more widely, as when Etienne de Fougères wrote, "What a villain is the priest who puts his hand, which ought to anoint and be sacred . . . in a vile place," in a poem composed for a noblewoman![142]

One must be careful about drawing too strong or reductive a link between the drive for clerical celibacy and misogyny. As in so many areas, there could be a major gap between the harsh rhetoric of reform and the more nuanced way people thought and acted in reality. Indeed, this is illustrated by positive or ambivalent views of clerical concubines discussed earlier. Similarly, in a case in which a woman was deserted by her husband, a subdeacon who became a priest, Archbishop Theobald treated her subsequent remarriage as invalid, but sympathized with her and treated her first husband as being most at fault.[143] Nuns were held in esteem, and chaste, saintly women could be favorably contrasted with lecherous clerics, as when the author of the life of Christina of Markyate used the language of cultic purity to describe how she, while still a laywoman, resisted the advances of Ranulf Flambard who, "with the mouth with which he confected the divine mystery, solicited her to commit a wicked deed."[144] Reform attacks on clerical sexuality were not simply about good men and evil women. Nevertheless, the close interaction between misogyny and the drive for clerical celibacy remains clear.

---

[140] Conrad Leyser, however, sees misogyny primarily as a byproduct rather than a cause of concerns about purity: Conrad Leyser, "Custom, Truth, and Gender in Eleventh-Century Reform," in R. N. Swanson, ed., *Gender and Christian Religion* (Woodbridge, 1998), 75–91, at 85–6.

[141] Walter Map, *De Nugis Curialium*, 286–313; John of Salisbury, *Policraticus*, 2:294–306; Peter of Blois, *Opera*, 243–7.

[142] Etienne de Fougères, *Le livre des manières*, 69.   [143] John of Salisbury, *Letters*, 1:153–6.

[144] C. H. Talbot, ed., *The Life of Christina of Markyate: A Twelfth Century Recluse* (Oxford, 1987), 40–5.

4. HOW SUCCESSFUL WAS THE DRIVE FOR CLERICAL CELIBACY?

There is plenty of anecdotal evidence throughout the period for clerics having concubines and families. Indeed, there is probably more evidence for unchaste priests in the later than the earlier decades of the period under study. So dramatic was the growth in written records, however, that this would be possible even if the campaign had dramatic success, which highlights the problems of anecdotal evidence. These problems are increased by the reticence about families in written records discussed earlier, which may have concealed many examples of priests with families. The possibility that the children of the higher clergy were sometimes born before their fathers were required to be celibate, as Herbert of Bosham was probably claiming of himself, also adds problems.[145] At best, one can only venture tentative conclusions, and here earlier scholars have paved the way.

C. N. L. Brooke, in a brief but important article on the subject, argued convincingly that reform had a fairly strong impact in the upper reaches of the ecclesiastical hierarchy over the course of the twelfth century. At St. Paul's, the practice of inheriting prebends virtually disappeared. Bishops and even archdeacons with families became rarer, and ecclesiastical kin groups such as the Belmeis family lost their grip. As Brooke himself recognized, however, this was a slow process.[146] Richard Ruffus, a member of the Belmeis family, was well ensconced at St. Paul's in the late twelfth century and probably had his own family.[147] William of Ely, a member of Bishop Roger of Salisbury's dynasty, lived until 1222 and had a son and probably a daughter.[148] Bishop Herbert Poore of Salisbury, who died in 1217, and his brother Richard, bishop of Chichester, Salisbury, and Durham, who died in 1228, were probably the sons of Richard of Ilchester.[149] Such examples were becoming rarer, however, and Gerald of Wales, even while attacking bishops for their laxity in correcting others, noted that the superior clergy (*clerici majores*) were both firmer in their own chastity and less likely to lapse than their predecessors.[150]

---

[145] Herbert, of course, only denied that his father had been a priest, and it was primarily at the level of priesthood that concerns about celibacy were expressed, which leaves open the possibility that his father was a deacon or subdeacon: Robertson and Sheppard, eds., *Materials*, 3:101. For other cases, real or theoretical, where claims were made that a son had been born while the father had been in minor orders or before he became priest, see Kuttner and Rathbone, "Anglo-Norman Canonists," 345; Ralph of Diceto, *Opera Historica*, 1:391; Cheney, *Roger, Bishop of Worcester*, 326, 348.

[146] Brooke, "Gregorian Reform in Action," 69–99.

[147] Johnson, ed., *English Episcopal Acta 26*, xlvi–xlviii.

[148] Richardson, "William of Ely," 60.

[149] Diana E. Greenway, *Fasti Ecclesiae Anglicanae, 1066–1300. 4. Salisbury* (London, 1991), 3–4. For other examples of powerful churchmen with families, see Franklin, ed., *English Episcopal Acta 8*, liii–liv; Mary G. Cheney, "Master Geoffrey de Lucy, an Early Chancellor of the University of Oxford," *English Historical Review* 82 (1967), 750–63, at 757–61; Barrow, "Hereford Bishops and Married Clergy," 3–4, 7–8; Nicholas Vincent, "Jocelin of Wells: The Making of a Bishop in the Reign of King John," in Robert W. Dunning, ed., *Jocelin of Wells: Bishop, Builder, Courtier* (Woodbridge, 2010), 9–33, at 20–1; Vincent, "New Light on Master Alexander of Swerford," 302–6.

[150] Gerald of Wales, *Opera*, 2:241.

Given Gerald's usual severity, there had clearly been a big enough shift to be undeniable to contemporaries.

However, the general consensus among modern scholars, including Brooke, is that the drive for clerical celibacy was far less successful among the rank and file of the priesthood.[151] If Roger of Wendover's claim that John raised money by ransoming the concubines of priests is true, they obviously existed in sufficient numbers to make it worthwhile. References to the concubines and children of priests or cathedral canons can be found in a variety of sources around 1200, including court records, pipe rolls, and charters.[152] Particularly interesting are documents that show ecclesiastical figures disdaining the discretion noted earlier and openly describing transactions involving the concubines and children of priests. In a charter of 1174 of which the first three witnesses were priests, Peter, rector of Thorner in Yorkshire, granted a carucate of land to his daughter Agace to serve as a marriage portion.[153] Sometime around 1191, the dean and chapter of Chichester helped settle a dispute between their fellow canon, Simon, and his son-in-law.[154] In 1197–8, Peter of Cornwall, prior of Aldgate in London, granted land to William the chaplain, Agnes, the daughter of Richard of Corney, and their sons and daughters.[155] Clearly, the families of priests were a well-established part of the social and ecclesiastical landscape. It is highly unlikely, of course, that the drive for clerical celibacy had no effect on the ordinary clergy. Nonetheless, there clearly remained a sizable number of recalcitrant priests, deacons, and subdeacons who successfully ignored or resisted this drive, took partners, and raised families.[156]

Mayke de Jong, writing about the Carolingian period, has argued that "the long history of clerical celibacy should not be written as a teleological story of failure and success but in terms of a singularly powerful ideal of differentiation which defined the separateness of those who mediated between God and mankind."[157] There is much to be said for this view; reformers were arguing for celibacy as a way to set apart the clergy long before 1066 and long after 1216. Within the Catholic Church the argument continues today. Nonetheless, the Gregorian Reform did set in motion a continuous history of attempted enforcement of clerical celibacy, and

---

[151] Brooke, "Gregorian Reform in Action," 78; Christopher Harper-Bill, "The Anglo-Norman Church," in Christopher Harper-Bill and Elisabeth M. C. van Houts, eds., *A Companion to the Anglo-Norman World* (Woodbridge, 2003), 165–90, at 186; B. R. Kemp, "Hereditary Benefices in the Medieval English Church: A Herefordshire Example," *Bulletin of the Institute of Historical Research* 43 (1970), 1–15, at 1–2.

[152] For instance *Curia Regis Rolls*, 4:304; 5:234, 286; 6:143–4; Stenton, ed., *Northamptonshire Assize Rolls*, 3, 151–2; Stenton, ed., *Pleas*, 4:206; *Pipe Roll 7 Richard I*, 12, 181; Salter, ed., *Cartulary of Oseney Abbey*, 2:195–7; Gervers, ed., *Cartulary of the Knights of St. John*, 1:454–5; Foster and Major, eds., *Registrum Antiquissimum*, 9:239–40; 10:172.

[153] Farrer and Clay, eds., *Early Yorkshire Charters*, 6:245.

[154] Simon was himself son of an earlier dean of the cathedral or of a rural dean: West Sussex Record Office, Chichester Cathedral MS Liber Y, fos. 122v–123r; Greenway, *Fasti. 5. Chichester*, 70.

[155] John Horace Round, ed., *Ancient Charters, Royal and Private, prior to A. D. 1200*, Publications of the Pipe Roll Society, vol. 10 (London, 1888), 104–5.

[156] England was not unique in this respect: G. A. Loud, *The Latin Church in Norman Italy* (Cambridge, 2007), 428–9; Wolverton, *Hastening toward Prague*, 126.

[157] de Jong, "*Imitatio Morum*," 51; de Jong, "Charlemagne's Church," 124.

that history was partly one of success and failure. During the long twelfth century, failure loomed large. Nonetheless the reformers also had important successes. Through a mixture of argument and authority, they won the debate within the Church early on, and thereafter dissent, though widespread, became muted or oblique. The triumph of church law in marriage ensured that the wives of priests would become concubines, and the ongoing degradation of priests' partners made partnerships with priests less desirable. The sons of priests could increasingly become priests only through dispensation, and institutional mechanisms to detect and punish clerical unchastity were also slowly developing within the Church, however underutilized they were. The trend towards celibacy at the top of the ecclesiastical hierarchy was a triumph in itself and ensured that those charged with enforcing celibacy were less likely to oppose the desires of the reformers. Cumulatively, the long twelfth century brought important developments in the history of clerical celibacy.

In England, clerical concubinage and unchastity seem to have remained at least reasonably common well into the thirteenth century, though a number of scholars view that century as the period in which the drive for celibacy began to triumph even among the common clergy. Scholars studying the English clergy in the late medieval period generally argue that clerical infractions of church law on sex were relatively few.[158] However, Janelle Werner has argued against this view, pointing to a visitation of 1397 in the diocese of Hereford in which 14 percent of clerics were charged with sexual infractions. About a quarter of these were involved in long-term relationships with concubines.[159] One's perspective matters here. If one considers clerical celibacy the norm, these figures are an indication of failure, particularly since other sexually active priests surely avoided detection. If, however, clerical marriage was a widespread practice in England before the Gregorian Reform, as I believe, even Werner's figures would indicate a good deal of eventual success by the reformers, though also a continuing pattern of intransigence by a sizable minority. Elsewhere in Europe, regional studies suggest that clerical sexual activity could remain relatively common. At least in some areas, such as Catalonia, many priests seem to have maintained a family life.[160] Taking the Catholic world as a whole, Ludwig Schmugge has found approximately 20,000 children of subdeacons,

---

[158] For clerical concubinage in the thirteenth century, see Lawrence, "English Parish," 659–61; Moorman, *Church Life*, 63–7, 210–13, 234. Lawrence sees a shift in the period, as do Brooke, Cheney, and Cullum: Brooke, "Gregorian Reform in Action," 78; Cheney, *From Becket to Langton*, 129; Cullum, "Learning to Be a Man," 136–7. Laura Wertheimer's study of dispensations in the thirteenth and early fourteenth century reveal surprisingly small numbers of English sons of priests seeking such dispensations, but the question remains how often such men went through any formal process: Laura Wertheimer, "Illegitimate Birth and the English Clergy, 1198–1348," *Journal of Medieval History* 31 (2005), 211–29, at 218–22. For some discussions of celibacy and the English clergy in the later Middle Ages, see Bowker, *Secular Clergy of Lincoln*, 116–20; Heath, *English Parish Clergy*, 104–8, 118–19; Norman P. Tanner, *The Church in Late Medieval Norwich, 1370–1532* (Toronto, 1984), 51–4.

[159] Werner, "Promiscuous Priests," 165–6.

[160] Frazee sees clerical unchastity as widespread in the late Middle Ages: Frazee, "Origins of Clerical Celibacy," 167. For some case studies, see Davis, *Holy Bureaucrat*, 116–20; Vleeschouwers-Van Melkebeek, "Mandatory Celibacy," 681–92. For concubinage and family life, see Kelleher, "Like Man and Wife," 349–60; Armstrong-Partida, "Priestly Marriage," 221–53.

deacons, and priests (overwhelmingly priests) seeking dispensations from 1449 to 1553.[161] The work of Schimmelpfennig suggests that many priests remained the sons of priests in many parts of Europe even in the late Middle Ages.[162] Variations in the willingness of church authorities to prosecute unchaste clergy, in the ability of clerics in different cultures to evade detection, and above all in the kinds of evidence available will inevitably complicate the possibility of mapping out the relative success or failure of the drive for clerical celibacy in the central and late Middle Ages. Nonetheless, as more studies are carried out, the broad outlines will become clearer, which will make it easier to place the findings of studies like this in a broader context.

5. SAME-SEX RELATIONSHIPS AND THE SECULAR CLERGY

In a chapter on clerical sexual activity, it is worth investigating the issue of clerics and same-sex desire, though the evidence for England in the period only allows one to speak of perceptions, attitudes, and constructions rather than practices.[163] In this period, sexual activity between men generally went under the heading of sodomy, a term that could also refer to other sexual activities but was used most frequently for what modern people would call homosexual practices.[164] Though Peter Damian, one of the leaders in the Gregorian reform movement, fulminated at length against sodomy, it was not a priority to English reformers, nor something they saw as particularly common in the priesthood.[165] Ralph Niger, an important English intellectual in the period, did condemn clerics for lusting after other males "against nature," among other sexual sins.[166] Other writers condemned lust for males without specific reference to the clergy. Anselm attacked sodomy at the same time as he attacked clerical marriage.[167] John of Salisbury criticized same-sex relations among a host of other behaviors, and Thomas of Chobham dealt briefly

---

[161] About 11 percent of the total of illegitimate sons seeking dispensation came from England: Schmugge, *Kirche, Kinder, Karrieren*, 33, 166, 183, 193, 195.

[162] Schimmelpfennig, "*Ex Fornicatione Nati*," 38–41. See also Schmugge, *Kirche, Kinder, Karrieren*, 155.

[163] In contrast, see Michael Rocke, *Forbidden Friendships: Homosexuality and Male Culture in Renaissance Florence* (New York, 1996); Guido Ruggiero, *The Boundaries of Eros: Sex Crime and Sexuality in Renaissance Venice* (New York, 1985), 135–45. For discussion of same-sex relations and desire in the period, see John Boswell, *Christianity, Social Tolerance, and Homosexuality: Gay People in Western Europe from the Beginning of the Christian Era to the Fourteenth Century* (Chicago, 1980); Jeffrey Richards, *Sex, Dissidence, and Damnation: Minority Groups in the Middle Ages* (London, 1990), 132–49; Mark D. Jordan, *The Invention of Sodomy in Christian Theology* (Chicago, 1997); Karras, *Sexuality in Medieval Europe*, 132–49.

[164] For sodomy as a category, see Jordan, *Invention of Sodomy*.

[165] For Peter Damian, see Jordan, *Invention of Sodomy*, 45–66. For intolerance and hostility more generally in the period, see Boswell, *Christianity, Social Tolerance, and Homosexuality*, 269–334; Richards, *Sex, Dissidence, and Damnation*, 132–49.

[166] Ralph Niger, *De Re Militari et Triplici Via Peregrinationis Ierosolimitane (1187/88)*, ed. Ludwig Schmugge (Berlin, 1977), 203.

[167] Whitelock, Brett, and Brooke, eds., *Councils and Synods, 1066–1204*, 678–9; Anselm, *Opera Omnia*, 4:169–70.

with them among other forms of non-procreative sex in his guide for confessors.[168] Peter of Blois particularly condemned those who seduced "guileless girls or, worse, boys," because they might cause the damnation of those they had seduced.[169]

Reformers also occasionally condemned sodomitic acts by specific individuals, including clerics. Among many examples of bishops awarding benefices for improper reasons, Gerald of Wales cited an example of an unnamed prelate making boys canons for the "heinous service" of his own body.[170] Most interestingly, the monk of Eynsham claimed that in his vision he saw a place in purgatory reserved for sodomites, male and female, and focused on the case of an anonymous but apparently well-known clerical pluralist and legal scholar he encountered there. According to the account, the cleric had refused to confess his sodomy lest he be despised among those who considered him "glorious and splendid," and instead confessed only lighter sins. As a result of this, of his corruption (presumably as a lawyer or administrator), and of his failure to do good works, he was punished severely in purgatory. Clearly this story was mainly about the importance of confession and penance rather than the particular evils of sodomy, but the writer did go on to make a traditional connection between pride and sodomy and to describe the practice as turning human into beastly or demonic nature. Nonetheless, repentant though unconfessed sodomites might in this vision end up in purgatory rather than hell, unlike unrepentant priests who had sex with women.[171] Clearly one can see in these writings the slow crystallization of sodomy as a category and the increasing tendency to treat it as "unnatural," as well as the general disapproval of non-procreative sex and of any form of clerical sex.[172] Nonetheless, the general silence about clerical sodomy in English sermons and treatises suggests that moralists did not see same-sex relations involving clerics as a major source of anxiety. Alternatively, they may have seen such sexual activities as so self-evidently wrong that they did not need to dwell on them.

Specific claims about sodomitic behavior also appeared in attacks designed to discredit individuals or groups, as when defenders of clerical marriage accused reformers of being sodomites. During the Becket controversy, John of Salisbury claimed that Roger, archbishop of York, while still an archdeacon, "had been accustomed to delight in (lest one speak of nefarious concubinage) one Walter, then a youth with a beautiful face." After Walter's beard grew in and he began to speak of the "disgraceful acts he had suffered, shameful to nature," Roger caused him to be blinded and then, to shut him up, arranged for a corrupt court to have him hanged (Roger claimed that these accusations were lies and that his enemies

---

[168] John of Salisbury, *Policraticus*, 1:220–1; Thomas of Chobham, *Summa Confessorum*, 398–403. For discussion of the passage in the *Policraticus*, see William E. Burgwinkle, *Sodomy, Masculinity, and Law in Medieval Literature: France and England, 1050–1230* (Cambridge, 2004), 65–73.

[169] Peter of Blois, *Opera*, 1083; Peter of Blois, *Later Letters*, 249.

[170] Gerald of Wales, *Opera*, 2:295.

[171] Easting, ed., *Revelation of the Monk of Eynsham*, 78–88, 116.

[172] For intellectual shifts that led to labeling same-sex relations as unnatural, see Boswell, *Christianity, Social Tolerance, and Homosexuality*, 303–34.

were using their "whores" to help spread their lies at the papal curia).[173] Gerald of Wales, in an attack on Richard I's chancellor, William of Longchamp, accused him of being a standard bearer for sodomitic relationships, setting up a household where all reviled those who did not revile *naturalis copula*, and casting out of his bed a girl smuggled into it disguised as a boy once he discovered the subterfuge. According to Gerald's disapproving account, his followers were accustomed to say, in the context of these sexual relations, "If you do not do what is of the court, what do you want with the court?"[174] Gerald also described one of his own rivals, Reginald Foliot, as effeminate to the point of androgyny, and said that he had been "the woman of all men, but is now become the man of all women." Gerald claimed that in his desire for new sexual experiences, Reginald even had sex with a Jewish man, thereby transgressing religious as well as sexual boundaries.[175]

Given the hostility to same-sex relations found in these works, it may seem surprising that clerics would openly display same-sex desire in poetry, but as John Boswell showed in his pioneering work, so they did, even if sometimes in an ambiguous fashion. Some of the most famous of these poets, such as Baudri of Bourgeuil and Marbod of Rheims, were continental, but their works were well known in England, and English manuscripts contain poetry expressing homosexual desire. One poet, Hilary, sometimes called Hilary the Englishman though his origins are unknown, devoted two poems to an English boy, comparing him to Ganymede, and another to William of Anfonia, whom he described as the "splendor of the English world" and from whom he seems to have been seeking patronage. Hilary praised William's looks as well as generosity, and said that if Jupiter had become a bull for a girl, he would have become an eagle for William, thus also placing William in the position of Ganymede. Hilary clearly thought that William, whom unfortunately I have been unable to identify, would consider the comparison flattering. Boswell wrote of a gay subculture, and one of the best Latin poets of English origins, Serlo of Wilton, refers to something like this in a Parisian context. Clearly some English clerics participated in a literary culture of same-sex desire.[176]

Caution must, of course, be employed in developing conclusions from such scattered and problematic material, even if one restricts the discussion to perceptions and constructions of same-sex desire. Each of the anecdotes and references I have recorded could be fruitfully unpacked, but I will limit myself to two general observations. First, the construction of same-sex desire seems to have focused, as commonly in Europe before the eighteenth century, on relationships between older

---

[173] John of Salisbury, *Letters*, 2: 740–1, 746–9.   [174] Gerald of Wales, *Opera*, 4:423.

[175] Davies, "Giraldus Cambrensis: *De Invectionibus*," 106, 121; Gerald of Wales, *Opera*, 3:188. Gerald may also hint at a sexual bond between his nephew and his nephew's tutor: Gerald of Wales, *Speculum Duorum*, 108–9.

[176] Boswell, *Christianity, Social Tolerance, and Homosexuality*, 235, 243–66, 372–4; Thomas Stehling, *Medieval Latin Poems of Male Love and Friendship* (New York, 1984), 68–75, 78–81; Bond, *Loving Subject*, 50–3, 75–6, 95–6; Moser, *Cosmos of Desire*, 197–205. Ruggiero argues that such a subculture existed in Renaissance Venice and that clerics were a part of it: Ruggiero, *Boundaries of Eros*, 135–45.

men and adolescents, though this may have been something of an ideal type since William of Anfonia was apparently old enough to be a potential source of reward.[177] The second point concerns the gap between positive and negative depictions of same-sex desire. On the one hand sex among men was perceived not only as sinful but as a source of shame. On the other, Gerald of Wales could imagine members of Longchamp's household describing sex among males as courtly and poets could advertise their own desires for males. In part, this gap may be explained by what could be called a queer counter-narrative. However, the willingness of some clerics to acknowledge homosexual desire may also provide yet another illustration of a world in which people frequently accepted a wide gap between fiercely expressed norms and the behaviors of individuals.[178]

Angels, presumably, did without sex. Most humans found it harder, and quite likely many of those with a strong personal commitment to celibacy would have chosen the monastic life. Much of this book is about the power, authority, and influence of clerics, their ability to affect and change the world around them. This chapter, insofar as it concerns power, largely involves the ability of those clerics who did not accept clerical celibacy to resist the influence of reformers. In this particular arena of social change, however, it was the clergy who experienced rather than created change. Even taking into account the fact that the ideal of clerical celibacy was present in Anglo-Saxon England and that the movement had only limited success during the long twelfth century, the impact on the clergy and their immediate families in the period was powerful. The families of clerics generally suffered more than the clerics. Despite sympathy for sons of priests, even among reformers, the children of priests, deacons, and subdeacons became illegitimate and thus lost legal rights to inherit land as well as churches. The female partners were degraded from wives to concubines, and rhetorically to whores, and other women suffered from the intensification of misogyny that the drive for celibacy generated. Nonetheless, the drive for celibacy also represented a challenge to those priests, deacons, and subdeacons who did not willingly embrace the reform and therefore faced difficult choices between obedience and sexual desire and between duty and the longing for companionship and family. As a result, sex, sexuality, and procreation created a profound gap between the angelic behavior expected of the upper clergy and the lives many of them led.

---

[177] This pattern is well known for the classical world. For subsequent periods, see Rocke, *Forbidden Friendships*, 87–8, 95; Ruggiero, *Boundaries of Eros*, 116, 124, 145. See, however, Karras, *Sexuality in Medieval Europe*, 141.

[178] A similar gap existed in Renaissance Italy: Guido Ruggiero, *Machiavelli in Love: Sex, Self, and Society in the Italian Renaissance* (Baltimore, 2007), 27–8.

8

Kinship, Household, Hospitality, and Friendship

Sometime in the 1150s, several monks of Selby Abbey were traveling through the countryside on a fundraising tour with their monastery's prized relic, a bone of St. Germanus stolen in an act of *sacra furta* by their founding monk. Finding the church where they wished to stay for the night locked, they sent one of their party to the priest's house where he encountered a sorrowful scene: the priest's sister lying ill, expected to die, surrounded by her weeping and groaning family, including the priest.[1] In the same decade, John of Salisbury, who had been exiled by Henry II, wrote to Thomas Becket, then chancellor and firmly ensconced in the king's favor, seeking his help; in this letter he wrote that none of the afflictions he suffered affected him worse than being deprived of the solace of friends.[2] These two vignettes illustrate two types of relationship crucial to clerics: kinship relationships (beyond the families that they created themselves) and friendship.

This chapter explores both kinship and friendship and also briefly discusses two other important kinds of association, that between clerics and servants or followers and that between guests and hosts. All of these relations created networks of influence and power that reflected and reinforced the standing and influence of secular clerics. However, they also all came fraught with moral and practical problems. Society, it is true, generally viewed these affiliations in a positive light and reformers did not condemn them as they condemned clerical marriage and concubinage. Friendship, indeed, was often seen as having potential spiritual benefits. Yet such relationships brought opportunities for conflicts of interest, corruption, and contentiousness, thus adding to the moral and social tensions highlighted throughout this work. All of these relationships have modern parallels, but all were arguably of greater practical importance for medieval people, including clerics, than for modern individuals. Moreover, all of these relationships had distinctively medieval characteristics that sometimes confound modern expectations.

---

[1] J. T. Fowler, ed., *The Coucher Book of Selby*, 2 vols., The Yorkshire Archaeological Society Record Series, vols. 10 and 13 (Durham, 1891–93), 1:50.
[2] John of Salisbury, *Letters*, 1:45.

1. KINSHIP

Direct glimpses of the affective ties between clerics and their relatives are rare, though another miracle story describes a priest comforting and performing last rites for a beloved kinswoman who appeared to be dying in childbirth.[3] The best evidence of the importance of kin ties to clerics comes from their efforts to provide financial security for younger or dependent kin. Indeed, contemporaries placed a strong emphasis on supporting one's kin, and John of Salisbury, in a letter urging an uncle to subsidize the studies of a nephew, drew on the First Epistle to Timothy to tell him that someone who did not take care of his own was worse than an infidel.[4] Nepotism, the most important way in which clerics sought to provide for their kin, was discussed in Chapter 5. Clerics also found other ways to support relatives, especially laymen and female relatives who could not hold benefices. Bishops, of course, were best placed to do so. Hugh of Avalon, bishop of Lincoln, granted his brother Peter two knights' fees, and William Longchamp, bishop of Ely, provided land worth £30 yearly to help arrange the marriage of his brother's son to the heiress to a barony.[5] Favored royal clerics occasionally acquired custodies partly with the goal of providing good marriages for female relatives. Thus William de Sainte-Mère-Eglise proffered 500 marks to King Richard for custody of the Berkeley family heir and 100 marks for another heir with the stipulation that he be able to marry them to his kinswomen.[6] Few clerics were in a position to establish relatives so prosperously, but many of them, especially cathedral canons, gave land or other property.[7] Generally such grants went to male relatives, but Gervase, archdeacon of Gloucester, provided five virgates of land to arrange a marriage for his niece, Leticia.[8]

Although helping relatives was an important social obligation, moralists feared that it could lead to sin. One treatise, *Moralities on the Gospels*, probably written by Alexander, dean of Wells, stated that devils tempted men to do evil under the guise of good, for instance urging them to serve at court in order to provide for the poor and for their kin.[9] Expending the income of benefices on nephews, nieces, and other kin was no less of a diversion of church resources than spending it on wives, concubines, and children. Above all, nepotism led to unworthy church appointments. Nigel of Whiteacre drew an especially vivid picture of the dangers of nepotism, describing archdeaconries being granted to boys in cradles and nursing

---

[3] Robertson and Sheppard, eds., *Materials*, 2:48–9.

[4] John of Salisbury, *Letters*, 2:274–7. The biblical passage is 1 Timothy 5:8.

[5] Smith, ed., *English Episcopal Acta 4*, 5; Karn, ed., *English Episcopal Acta 31*, 184–5.

[6] For these and similar proffers by clerics, see *Pipe Roll 6 Richard I*, 176, 239; Hardy, ed., *Rotuli de Oblatis*, 180; Hardy, ed., *Rotuli Litterarum Patentium*, 118b.

[7] Foster and Major, eds., *Registrum Antiquissimum*, 3:105–6; 9:81–2, 98, 106–7; 10:172–3; Farrer and Clay, eds., *Early Yorkshire Charters*, 1:344; 5:250 Marion Gibbs, ed., *Early Charters of the Cathedral Church of St. Paul, London*, Camden Society, 3rd ser. 58 (London, 1939), 98–9.

[8] Hollings, ed., *Red Book of Worcester*, 4:431, 440.

[9] E. J. Dobson, *Moralities on the Gospels: A New Source of Ancrene Wisse* (Oxford, 1975), 115. See also Peter of Blois's poem about the courtier: Wollin, ed., *Petri Blesensis Carmina*, 267.

infants receiving churches. He asked how well a child, "who would laugh or cry more readily over an apple than gaining or losing two or three churches," would handle ecclesiastical affairs. Such children would grow up of course, and could be sent to the schools of Paris for a good education, but Nigel suggested that they would probably find study too hard and return home to idle away their time on eating and drinking, falconry and hunting, and spending the tithes and offerings of the faithful on prostitutes.[10] Etienne de Fougères attacked the outcome of nepotism more concisely: churchmen gave benefices "to their nephews who are worth nothing, who still wet their beds [or] live a debauched life through the money they acquire."[11]

Condemnations of nepotism competed with ideals about supporting families and this led to a range and sometimes a muddle of views about nepotism, as can be seen in the works of Peter of Blois. In one of his treatises, Peter condemned the practice, and in a letter to John of Salisbury, then bishop of Chartres, he praised him for preferring a non-relative over a relative. Yet he himself, in a letter asking Bishop Peter of Périgord for preferment, shamelessly exploited the kinship between them, describing himself as the least of the bishop's relations and stating that because his father and mother were dead he had no means of support and relied on the bishop. One might ascribe this merely to hypocrisy, but Peter showed ambivalence in less personal circumstances. In a letter to a friend who was complaining that bishops granted benefices to their relatives rather than to poor, learned scholars, Peter simply treated nepotism as the way of the world: "Friend, this is an old complaint." He claimed that if the friend became a bishop, he too would abruptly forget about merit and worry more about providing for his nephews and marrying his nieces far above their station. In a different letter to John of Salisbury, Peter urged him to promote his nephew, Robert of Salisbury, pulling out all the rhetorical stops. He called upon Aristotle, nature, and the example of animals that cared for their young, cited the same biblical passage that John himself had used, and accused those who advised John against this appointment of being deceitful flatterers. Peter did insist that Robert was honest and learned, but his stress was on urging John to follow his "natural" inclination to favor his nephew. More moderately, Peter defended one of the archbishops of Canterbury whom he served against charges of excessive nepotism, saying that he was affected by concern for family but did not go too far in this matter, and that he favored other figures over close relatives. Finally, in a letter to a bishop who had been dispossessed and was lamenting the harm to his relatives among other things, Peter mixed a warning about the seductive dangers of affection for relatives with an admission that concern for them was natural and even good.[12]

Peter's ambivalence about nepotism and his desire to find a compromise between the ideals of meritocracy and the responsibilities of kinship were not unique.

---

[10] Nigel of Whiteacre, *Tractatus Contra Curiales*, 157–8.
[11] Etienne de Fougères, *Le livre des manières*, 71.
[12] Peter of Blois, *Opera*, 110–13, 118–19, 178–81, 217–19, 341–3, 1015–16; Peter of Blois, *Later Letters*, 61, 85–7.

Thomas of Chobham attacked the promotion of bad relatives over good outsiders but raised the question of whether one could legitimately favor good candidates who were relatives or friends over others who were even better. He recorded the differing opinions on this issue of other thinkers but refused to express his own.[13] Gervase of Chichester said that merit should matter more than kinship and that Aaron had become high priest on the basis of merit, not because he was Moses's brother. However, this allowed Gervase to suggest that promoting kinsmen because of merit was acceptable, and to urge a middle way between favoring kin too much and excluding them altogether from benefices.[14]

Kinship not only created moral dilemmas but sometimes presented individual clerics with extremely difficult relationships; judging by the surviving evidence, clerical uncles and nephews often had particularly tense relations. The best example concerns Gerald of Wales, who composed an entire work attacking his nephew, also named Gerald.[15] Gerald wrote in a separate work that his brother Philip, lord of Manorbier, had asked him to aid Philip's youngest son and to help him gain benefices, particularly Gerald's archdeaconry of Brecon and his prebend at St. David's.[16] As noted in Chapter 5, Gerald arranged for his succession to the archdeaconry, the prebend, and a church, by resigning them but appointing himself as his nephew's administrator.[17] However, the younger Gerald was not content with the pensions his uncle paid him or with waiting for Gerald's death to take full control of the benefices. After several years, according to Gerald's account, he seized control, costing his uncle more than fifty marks annual revenue and, still worse, humiliating him.[18] Moreover, he and his chief supporter, William, whom the senior Gerald had originally appointed as his tutor, conducted their attack ably and ruthlessly. The younger Gerald stole or seized charters concerning the prebend and a church. He also copied provocative passages his uncle had written in both private and public writings, and he and the tutor wrote down and (according to Gerald) exaggerated provocative statements Gerald made in private, using them to stir up prominent figures, particularly the bishop of St. David's, against him.[19]

Gerald reacted strongly in his account of the conflict, not only recording his version of the dispute, but also providing a broader picture of their relationship in which he depicted himself as the benevolent, deeply concerned uncle victimized by an ungrateful and good-for-nothing nephew. Gerald described his own efforts not just to provide for the younger Gerald, but also to educate him and to use reproofs to improve his morals.[20] If anything, Gerald implied, he was too lenient and too eager to please. Defending himself against his nephew's complaints of bad temper and harshness, he wrote that he had not punished his nephew at all as a child when

---

[13] Thomas of Chobham, *Summa de Arte Praedicandi*, 191.
[14] British Library, Royal MS 3 B X, fos. 79r–v.
[15] Gerald of Wales, *Speculum Duorum*.   [16] Gerald of Wales, *Opera*, 3:326.
[17] See Chapter 5, section 2; Gerald of Wales, *Speculum Duorum*, xxvi–xxvii.
[18] Gerald of Wales, *Speculum Duorum*, xxx–xxxv, 26–31, 72–3, 116–19, 194–7, 219–21, 242–53.
[19] Gerald of Wales, *Speculum Duorum*, 36–7, 142–5, 216–17.
[20] Gerald of Wales, *Speculum Duorum*, 4–5, 44–5, 50–1, 72–3.

teaching him, and had corrected him verbally, rather than with blows, as a youth.[21] He also claimed that the tutor, William, had often stated that the younger Gerald only had to polish his own boots to get anything he wanted from his uncle.[22] Whatever their relationship might once have been, Gerald attacked his nephew's character relentlessly after their dispute. He described him as depraved, corrupt, deaf to correction, insolent, and a disappointment from an early period. He criticized him as a poor student, unable to learn French or Latin properly, who devoted himself to frivolous pastimes such as hunting hares or playing the Welsh lute. He mocked him for his stutter; for playing with cats, dogs, and children; and for preferring the company of actors and pages to that of good men. He savagely attacked the reputations and characters of his nephew's maternal kin, constantly imputing all his nephew's shortcomings to their blood. For page after page, Gerald denigrated the nephew who had outmaneuvered him.[23]

Individual personalities obviously mattered greatly in the clash between this particular uncle and nephew, and one must treat Gerald's over-the-top attack on his nephew with skepticism. Some of his contemporaries clearly did so, for he had to write a letter to Hugh de Mapenore, dean of Hereford, and other prominent Hereford clerics to defend himself after an angry letter to his nephew backfired.[24] Nonetheless, the younger Gerald may well have been an indifferent scholar, and there is independent evidence that he was a less than zealous churchman, for Julia Barrow has uncovered a later charter in which he deposited over £200 on behalf of his sons at Dore Abbey.[25] On the flip side, the nephew's complaints about his uncle's temper and harshness receive corroboration from Gerald's own writings, not least his attack on his nephew. Reading between the lines of that text, the older Gerald, for all he did to assure his nephew's future, and perhaps despite an early affection for him, must have been a nightmare as a guardian, mentor, and patron, especially for someone of the nephew's apparent interests and inclinations. This relationship cannot therefore be considered a model with which to study all relationships between clerical uncles and nephews. Even so, there are plenty of other indications that such relationships could be prone to difficulties.

Peter of Blois, like Gerald, considered himself a benevolent uncle plagued by ungrateful nephews. During a dispute over the family patrimony on the continent, and after one of his nephews organized a letter-writing campaign in which influential figures, including the pope, urged Peter to turn over various continental benefices to him, Peter lashed out. He complained to his nephews of their ingratitude, threatening to fill France with letters attacking them. He wrote that he had adopted them like sons, educated them, and spent far more than he could

---

[21] Elsewhere, however, Gerald claimed that had he been able to oversee his nephew at a crucial time, he would have taught him letters and manners through fear of the rod: Gerald of Wales, *Speculum Duorum*, 20–1, 42–3.

[22] Gerald of Wales, *Speculum Duorum*, 94–5.

[23] Gerald of Wales, *Speculum Duorum*, 20–77, 124–53.

[24] Gerald of Wales, *Speculum Duorum*, 160–7.

[25] Julia Barrow, "Gerald of Wales's Great-nephews," *Cambridge Medieval Celtic Studies* 8 (1984), 101–6.

afford on them, and condemned them for repaying him badly. He claimed they had usurped the lands he had inherited from his father, and accused both of them of usury, and one of them of tricking him through forgery.[26] Likewise, Bishop Arnulf of Lisieux complained strongly about his nephews, including Hugh Nunant, future bishop of Coventry, saying they had turned against him when he fell into Henry II's disfavor despite having received many benefices from him.[27] John of Salisbury had to intervene with Thomas Becket on behalf of one of Thomas's nephews, whom the archbishop had cut off without money during his studies.[28] Gerald of Wales told an admittedly improbable story of an uncle who ceded a church to a nephew, only to have the nephew try to murder him, and Walter Map humorously depicted his own nephews lording it over him in making use of his property, "soldiering" against him by treating every expenditure on them as their due, and returning not a word of thanks.[29]

Why is the limited evidence that narrative sources provide about relations with nephews so negative? Given the small number of relationships discussed here, coincidence may partly be involved. Moreover, relationships gone wrong were more likely to generate comment than ones that ran smoothly, and in some cases writers may have wished to give warnings that nepotism, like attending court or having a family, did not always turn out well, though they showed little remorse about their own participation in the practice. One also suspects that a stereotype of the disappointing, ungrateful nephew had arisen in the period. Thus, the unremittingly negative portrayal of relations between clerics and their nephews is partly an artifact of the sources. Nonetheless, relations between clerical uncles and nephews may well have been particularly prone to problems. Clerical uncles in some ways filled the roles of fathers, and though relations between fathers and sons can be wonderful, they have also been potentially explosive throughout history. There were also specific aspects of medieval family life that probably increased tensions across generations. Families were very patriarchal, with younger members firmly subordinated to the family patriarch. One of Gerald's complaints about his nephew was that he remained seated when others stood in Gerald's honor, showing how a member of the younger generation might resent his subordination.[30] Once uncles had provided benefices for their nephews, as Arnulf of Lisieux did with his nephews, the latter had a practical independence that allowed them, if they wished, to act independently and even contrary to the interests of their uncles, naturally provoking charges of ingratitude. Moreover, there might easily have been room for disagreements over whether uncles had exerted themselves sufficiently persistently or skillfully in the search for patronage for their nephews, with the potential for disappointed expectations on the one side and anger over insufficient gratitude on the other. Moral qualms about nepotism may sometimes have increased stresses.

---

[26] Peter of Blois, *Later Letters*, 37–41, 121–2, 124–6.
[27] Arnulf of Lisieux, *Letters*, 201–3, 211–13.
[28] Duggan, ed., *Correspondence of Thomas Becket*, 1:76–7.
[29] Gerald of Wales, *Speculum Duorum*, 16–17; Walter Map, *De Nugis Curialium*, 22–3.
[30] Gerald of Wales, *Speculum Duorum*, 126–7.

Often enough, moreover, it was an uncle's own benefices that might be earmarked for the nephew, and this brought problems similar to those facing aristocratic and royal families, in which family patriarchs and their adult sons could not easily share wealth and authority. The problems Henry II faced with his rebellious sons formed a good example of what might ensue, and according to Gerald of Wales, Walter Map used this very example in criticizing Gerald's decision to resign in favor of his nephew while attempting to maintain actual authority.[31] The potential divisiveness of dealings between uncles and nephews and the similarities with relations between fathers and sons show just how important such relationships could be, and they clearly deserve further study, especially within the context of scholarship on the medieval family.

2. HOUSEHOLD AND HOSPITALITY

Successful clerics not only had relatives but also servants and followers.[32] Households may sometimes have been quite large, as indicated by the account of the archdeacon of Richmond traveling with a retinue of ninety-three.[33] Even the injunctions at church councils that rural deans should travel with no more than five horses and archdeacons with no more than seven presupposes a reasonably large household if one factors in followers remaining at the dean's or archdeacon's home base.[34] Some of these followers would have been servants or clerics in minor orders, but others could be priests or learned men in their own right. Thus, clerics prominent in the household of the bishop of Durham had their own chaplains and, as noted in Chapter 5, archdeacons could have *magistri* in their followings.[35] Geoffrey Ridel, as archdeacon, even had a doctor in his service.[36] Ordinary parish priests would have had smaller households, particularly if celibate, but Gerald of Wales's admonition that such priests should have a modest *familia*, with no more than a cleric and a key-bearer (*claviger*—perhaps someone who managed the house), suggests that in fact many had more followers.[37] Of course, many ordinary clerics could not have afforded a household or might live in someone else's, but there were still thousands of priests and other clerics who served as the head of a household, whether it included a family or not.

Servants and followers provided many benefits to prosperous or wealthy secular clerics. Above all, they provided practical assistance, from carrying out the ordinary chores to skilled work such as Geoffrey Ridel's doctor would have provided. Parish

---

[31] Gerald of Wales, *Speculum Duorum*, 10–11. See also 16–17, 124–5.

[32] For the households of cathedral canons in the later Middle Ages, see Lepine, *A Brotherhood of Canons*, 114, 123–31.

[33] See Chapter 3, section 1; Farrer and Clay, eds., *Early Yorkshire Charters*, 5:347.

[34] For limitations in English councils, see Whitelock, Brett, and Brooke, eds., *Councils and Synods, 1066–1204*, 1062–3; Powicke and Cheney, eds., *Councils and Synods, 1205–1265*, 36.

[35] See Chapter 5, section 4; Snape, ed., *English Episcopal Acta 24*, xliii; Kemp, ed., *Archidiaconal Acta*, l.

[36] Robertson and Sheppard, eds., *Materials*, 1:187.   [37] Gerald of Wales, *Opera*, 2:275.

priests who embraced celibacy would have needed at least one servant or follower to take over responsibilities normally handled by wives. Clerics with prebends, glebes, or administrative functions would often have needed assistance managing their properties or carrying out their duties. Heading a household generally also provided prestige. Derek Neal, in stressing that one should consider factors other than sex in considering clerical masculinity, has argued that heading households gave even celibate priests social standing and made them more like other respectable men.[38] Gerald of Wales's nephew may not have stood to show him deference, but others in his household at Lincoln did.[39] The collection of clerical anecdotes at Corpus Christi, Oxford, contains one attributed to Walter Map with the condescending moral that the lord of a household was more perceptive than its members.[40] Thus, being head of a household could clearly bolster feelings of self-worth. For the most powerful, large retinues could bring even more prestige. Peter of Blois warned courtier clerics that the retinues they sought to attract were vanities, and that followers were drawn by their money, not loyalty, but his diatribe clearly acknowledged that powerful clerics, like other great men, gloried in having large followings.[41]

The relationship between clerics and their followers could combine elements of public lordship with the intimacy of the domestic sphere. One letter of John of Salisbury described a man who was "a familiar cleric from the table of Master John of Oxford," the latter being described as a cleric of the king.[42] Here the chain of lordship, familiarity, and patronage extended from Henry II to his favorite, John of Oxford, and from John to his cleric, who was placed, metaphorically at least, within John's household. In diatribes against servants who aided or were connected with his nephew, Gerald of Wales emphasized that some of them, like his nephew, had eaten his bread. He even described one, William the tutor, as boasting of being able to share Gerald's table and actual dish, a clear mark of favor.[43] The sharing of food provided by Gerald created the expectation both of a close bond and of gratitude. The relationship between well-to-do clerics and their followers or servants was supposed to be closer than that between modern employers and their employees, more akin to ties of family or lordship. Indeed, clerics could support their followers much as they did their kin, sometimes acting as patrons similar to great magnates, though on a smaller scale, as when courtier clerics obtained benefices from the king for their own clerics.[44] Walter Map can be found trying to help the "reeve" (perhaps steward) of his household get promoted to the subdiaconate.[45] Occasionally, clerics can be found giving their followers land.[46] Clearly, relations between clerics and members of their households were meant to be close.

---

[38] Neal, *Masculine Self*, 7–8, 105–7.   [39] Gerald of Wales, *Speculum Duorum*, 126–7.
[40] Walter Map, *De Nugis Curialium*, 515–16.   [41] Peter of Blois, *Opera*, 44.
[42] John of Salisbury, *Letters*, 2:124–5.
[43] Gerald of Wales, *Speculum Duorum*, 2–5, 96–7, 110–11.
[44] See Chapter 5, section 3.   [45] Adam of Eynsham, *Magna Vita Sancti Hugonis*, 2:130–1.
[46] Karn, ed., *English Episcopal Acta 31*, 39–41, 103; Snape, ed., *English Episcopal Acta 24*, 2–3; *Ninth Report of the Royal Commission of Historical Manuscripts, Appendix* (London, 1883), 35.

Heading a household, however, brought its own moral difficulties and possible tensions. As Peter of Blois's comments indicate, overly large households could be linked with vainglory or excessive expenditure. Directing ecclesiastical patronage towards household members no doubt contributed to the general concerns about abuse of patronage and unjust appointments. Relations with members of the household, like those with relatives, could also be quite problematic. Walter Map's complaints about his nephews came in the context of an admittedly humorous account of how difficult his household was in general. According to Walter, even though he tried to be a good and generous head of his *familia*, his household was dominated by greedy, lying, stubborn individuals who constantly took advantage of him and made life impossible for anyone who tried to serve him well. They circumvented any attempt he made to improve matters, and when he tried to economize they went out and invited guests so that he was forced to keep the food and drink flowing.[47] Gerald of Wales's rage at his nephew spilled over to various servants, followers, and former followers, above all his nephew's tutor, Master William de Capella, whom he blamed for leading the younger Gerald astray. Gerald insisted that he had treated William well, paying him five marks a year for teaching his nephew, granting him various forms of authority, and even protecting him from some angry men armed with swords. Nonetheless, he claimed that William had defrauded him in many ways, including peculation and lying about the productivity of one of Gerald's estates to divert its revenues. Gerald also accused him of other moral failings, including having a concubine, misusing Gerald's seal and that of a knight to forge documents in order to succeed his father in a church, and obtaining a church through simony. Gerald even wrote a poem accusing William of having sex with his sister, described as a whore and the daughter of a priest.[48] It seems safe to say that relations in Gerald's household were not entirely happy. Obviously, one should not take these accounts as representative or necessarily trustworthy. Nonetheless, as with any relationship involving power and dependency, relations between heads of households and their servants or followers were susceptible to resentment and hostility. Walter's account, even if exaggerated for satirical affect, probably reflected stereotypes about "servant problems" that in turn reflected inevitable tensions in a highly unequal and status conscious society.

The relationship between guest and host was less close than the other affiliations discussed in this chapter, but hospitality was a cherished ideal. It formed an important kind of social glue and helped make travel easier in a period when inns were few. It was also an important religious value. Monasteries were particularly important in providing hospitality, and Julie Kerr has explored both monastic and lay hospitality in England.[49] However, secular clerics also provided hospitality, and

---

[47] Walter Map, *De Nugis Curialium*, 16–23.
[48] Gerald of Wales, *Speculum Duorum*, 2–9, 74–5, 78–123, 154–5.
[49] Julie Kerr, *Monastic Hospitality: The Benedictines in England, c.1070–c.1250* (Woodbridge, 2007); Julie Kerr, "Food, Drink and Lodging: Hospitality in Twelfth-Century England," *Haskins Society Journal* 18 (2006), 72–92; Julie Kerr "'Welcome the Coming and Speed the Parting Guest.' Hospitality in Twelfth-Century England," *Journal of Medieval History* 33 (2007), 130–46.

were anxious to have a reputation for being good hosts.[50] Nigel of Whiteacre described the rich rector of one of his cautionary anecdotes as having a great name because he showed hospitality to rich and poor along a great public road.[51] A miracle story from the *vita* of Wulfstan of Worcester reveals an archdeacon anxious about his inability to provide sufficient hospitality for the bishop's retinue (fortunately, a miracle of unending mead ensued).[52] A surviving fragment of a letter reveals John, rector of Kirkby Lonsdale, requesting that the abbot of Furness have his fishermen provide John with fish which he needed because the vice-archdeacon of Richmond was coming and he did not wish to lose his reputation for hospitality (*honorem hospicii*).[53] It was, of course, just such attitudes about hospitality that allowed Walter Map's household to outmaneuver him.

Often enough hospitality was an obligation and as such could be subject to abuse, as when the archdeacon of Richmond showed up at a local church with his huge retinue. He was apparently not unique: the abbey of St. Frideswide obtained from Pope Celestine III a letter allowing it to bar archdeacons and rural deans from visiting churches if they showed up with more horses and men than allowed in canon law or if they appeared with hunting dogs and birds of prey.[54] Gerald of Wales condemned a bishop who extorted money from churches on the pretext of hospitality.[55] Peter of Blois, in a letter urging an official of the bishop of Chartres to leave office for the sake of his soul, noted the harm such officials did to hosts with their excessive retinues.[56] Clearly, powerful churchmen often used their rights of hospitality in local churches as a way to help support large retinues and even to pay for hunting excursions. The very limitations placed on the retinues of visiting officials, as well as the limits placed in a Canterbury council of 1213–14 on the number of visits archdeacons and officials could make to individual churches, indicates the prevalence of such abuses.[57] As with kinship, medieval writers viewed the relationship between host and guest positively, but there was clearly always the potential for abuse and corruption.

3. FRIENDSHIP

One of the most important types of relationship for clerics, nearly as important as kinship, was friendship. In recent years there has emerged a growing body of work on medieval friendship, including its expression in the letters and other writings of

---

[50] For a later period, see Lepine, *A Brotherhood of Canons*, 131–4.

[51] Nigel of Whiteacre, *Tractatus Contra Curiales*, 164.

[52] William of Malmesbury, *Saints' Lives*, 128–31.

[53] Nicholas Vincent, "William Marshal, King Henry II and the Honour of Châteauroux," *Archives* 25 (2000), 1–15, at 2–3, 15.

[54] Farrer and Clay, eds., *Early Yorkshire Charters*, 5:347; Wigram, ed., *The Cartulary of the Monastery of St. Frideswide at Oxford*, 1:40–1.

[55] Gerald of Wales, *Opera*, 2:294.   [56] Peter of Blois, *Opera*, 90.

[57] Whitelock, Brett, and Brooke, eds., *Councils and Synods, 1066–1204*, 1062–3; Powicke and Cheney, eds., *Councils and Synods, 1205–1265*, 36.

John of Salisbury and Peter of Blois.[58] This scholarship reveals that although there is much overlap between medieval and modern notions of friendship there are also important differences. Educated medieval clerics (though probably not other medieval people) may have been more attuned than most modern people to theoretical and philosophical approaches to friendship due to the widespread knowledge of Cicero's treatise, *Laelius de Amicitia*. This work was so influential that the English Cistercian Ailred of Rievaulx described himself as christianizing Cicero in his own treatise on spiritual friendship, from which Peter of Blois drew heavily in writing *his* work on the subject, *De Amicitia Christiana*.[59] Cicero's influence led to an idealizing of friendship and much pondering on it; letter writers often discoursed on friendship, sometimes at length.[60] Partly, perhaps, as a result, friendship often had a formal, abstract quality to it. For instance, whereas modern people would generally expect friendship to emerge spontaneously among acquaintances, medieval clerics might write to people they had never met, formally requesting friendship. Moreover, as Constant Mews and Neville Chiavaroli have argued, letter-writing manuals used two different sets of concepts for describing friendship: one as a bond or tie, but the other as an agreement or pact, conceptualizing friendship as a deliberate arrangement rather than an affective link.[61] To the extent that one can distinguish between a public and a private sphere in the medieval period, friendship was more likely to be part of the public arena than in the modern period, with friendships being stressed in letter collections meant to be read widely and with ideals of friendship playing a role in thinking about lordship and politics.[62] Extrapolating from this secondary work and from my

---

[58] John McLoughlin, "*Amicitia* in Practice: John of Salisbury (*c.*1120–1180) and his Circle," in Daniel Williams, ed., *England in the Twelfth Century: Proceedings of the 1988 Harlaxton Symposium* (Woodbridge, 1990), 165–81; Laurence Moulinier-Brogi, "Jean de Salisbury: un réseau d'amitiés continentales," in Martin Aurell, ed., *Culture politique des Plantagenêt, 1154–1224* (Poitiers, 2003), 341–61; Cary J. Nederman, "Friendship in Public Life during the Twelfth Century: Theory and Practice in the Writings of John of Salisbury," *Viator* 38 (2007), 385–97; Cotts, *Clerical Dilemma*, 66–7, 82–94, 241–7; Cary J. Nederman, "Textual Communities of Learning and Friendship Circles in the Twelfth Century: An Examination of John of Salisbury's Correspondence," in Constant J. Mews and John N. Crossley, eds., *Communities of Learning: Networks and the Shaping of Intellectual Identity in Europe, 1100–1500* (Turnhout, 2011), 73–83. For more general works on friendship in the period, see Reginald Hyatte, *The Arts of Friendship: The Idealization of Friendship in Medieval and Early Renaissance Literature* (Leiden, 1994); Julian Haseldine, "Understanding the Language of *Amicitia*. The Friendship Circle of Peter of Celle (*c.*1115–1183)," *Journal of Medieval History* 20 (1994), 237–60; Julian Haseldine, "Love, Separation and Male Friendship: Words and Actions in Saint Anselm's Letters to his Friends," in D. M. Hadley, ed., *Masculinity in Medieval Europe* (London, 1999), 238–55; Julian Haseldine, ed., *Friendship in Medieval Europe* (Stroud, 1999); Walter Ysebaert, "Medieval Letter-Collections as a Mirror of Circles of Friendship? The Example of Stephen of Tournai, 1128–1203," *Revue Belge* 83 (2005), 285–300; Constant J. Mews and Neville Chiavaroli, "The Latin West," in Barbara Caine, ed., *Friendship: A History* (London, 2009), 73–110; Lachaud, *L'éthique du pouvoir*, 151–7; Burger, *Bishops, Clerks, and Diocesan Governance*, 210–38.

[59] Peter of Blois, *Opera*, 871–96; Cotts, *Clerical Dilemma*, 14, 241–5; Ailred of Rievaulx, "Liber de Spirituali Amicitia," in J.-P. Migne, ed., *Patrologia Latina*, vol. 195 (Paris, 1855), 659–702.

[60] For example, Gerald of Wales, *Opera*, 1:229–34, 238–41.

[61] Mews and Chiavaroli, "Latin West," 95–6.

[62] Gerd Althoff has been particularly important in stressing friendship in politics. For an overview of his views in English, see Gerd Althoff, "Friendship and Political Order," in Julian Haseldine, ed., *Friendship in Medieval Europe* (Stroud, 1999), 91–105.

own observations, I would argue in addition that medieval ideas of friendship could encompass a more formalized version of the modern phenomenon of networking: making contacts for mutually beneficial relationships. Julian Haseldine, a leading researcher on medieval friendship, has also suggested that the language of friendship could be used to mark writers as members of a "spiritual aristocracy" through their learned and religious exchanges.[63] Thus one must approach medieval friendship with its many distinctive elements firmly in mind.

Friendship in the long twelfth century served spiritual, emotional, and utilitarian purposes. The spiritual aspect may have been more pronounced among monastic writers like Ailred of Rievaulx, but, as Cotts has argued, a secular cleric like Peter of Blois could tap into monastic ideas of spiritual friendship.[64] Besides his treatise, Peter of Blois wrote many letters of spiritual advice and rebuke, often addressed to people he described as friends. Even in his letter denouncing clerics at court, he addressed the courtiers as his friends (and lords), and in a letter reacting to the angry response he received, he again greeted them as friends and spoke of his love for them. Protestations of friendship may have been tactical here, but probably also represented a belief, mirroring friendship theory of the time, that one duty towards friends was to help improve their morals. Indeed, when he sent a copy of his treatise on spiritual friendship to the great courtier cleric, William de Sainte-Mère-Eglise, by this time bishop of London, Peter spoke of the mutual love between them but included a gentle warning about worldly entanglements.[65] Other clerics also embraced ideals of spiritual friendship. For instance, Joseph of Exeter, nephew of Archbishop Baldwin, wrote letters expressing his strong friendship for Guibert, abbot of Fleury, and sought spiritual guidance from Guibert because he was disturbed by sinful thoughts and inclinations.[66] Friendship for secular clerics, as for monks and nuns, could clearly have a strong religious component.

This religious component, naturally enough, was closely intertwined with the emotional aspect of friendship. Friends, then as now, provided emotional support, whether through the sharing of troubles, expressions of esteem, or encouragement in times of trouble. Joseph of Exeter, like John of Salisbury, spoke of the solace of friendship, and in one letter to Guibert expressed anxieties about his approaching participation in the Third Crusade, asking for Guibert's prayers. In the sole surviving letter from Guibert to Joseph, the abbot provided spiritual council, but also gratifyingly fulsome praise.[67] Gerald of Wales exchanged poems with two other writers of the time, Walter Map and Simon de Freine, in which these intellectuals praised each other in witty and sophisticated ways. Simon de Freine, described as a friend in the rubric, also wrote a poetic defense of Gerald against the attacks of a monk. Gerald, who frequently felt underappreciated, also clearly drew emotional sustenance from the praise of his work by Walter and another intellectual, Robert

---

[63] Haseldine, "Language of *Amicitia*," 260.   [64] Cotts, *Clerical Dilemma*, 241–5.

[65] For examples, see Peter of Blois, *Opera*, 24–7, 42–51, 171–2, 190–5, 243–9, 439–42; Peter of Blois, *Later Letters*, 212–17, 329–32.

[66] Joseph Iscanus, *Werke und Briefe*, ed. Ludwig Gompf (Leiden, 1970), 220–2.

[67] Joseph Iscanus, *Werke und Briefe*, 220–8.

de Bello Fago.[68] When Walter of Coutances, a prominent English cleric who became archbishop of Rouen, got into a major confrontation with Richard I, he initiated an exchange of letters with Ralph of Diceto in which the latter expressed his support and praised Walter. Ralph was not in a position to help Walter materially; indeed he wrote to him anonymously for fear of the king, though Walter reported that he recognized the "style of the lover." Nonetheless, Walter thanked Ralph for his sympathy and clearly appreciated his emotional support.[69] Because of the formality of friendship and because friendship was so often expressed in conventionalized if very strong terms in letters, historians have rightly expressed skepticism about what such language can tell about the affective nature of specific relationships.[70] Nonetheless, just as the entirely conventionalized phrases of modern greeting cards can be used equally to express heartfelt emotions and those conveyed merely as a matter of form, so too could conventional affective expressions found in letter writing manuals express genuine as well as more formalized or artificial sentiments. Though not every use of the language of friendship reveals affective, emotional ties, such bonds were an important part of medieval as well as modern friendship.

Nonetheless, medieval friendship also had a very strong instrumental aspect, as much of the recent scholarship has stressed, and friends were expected to provide favors to each other. In a letter to Robert of Inglesham, archdeacon of Surrey, in which he was seeking help for the exiled Thomas Becket, John of Salisbury drew on Cicero to write that although friends could refuse dishonorable requests, they should fulfill honorable ones without hesitation.[71] In 1163, Richard de Almaria, precentor of Lincoln Cathedral, received a letter from Bishop Arnulf of Lisieux in which the bishop described at length how friendship obliged the precentor to grant an unspecified request made by the letter's bearer and seconded by the bishop.[72] As these letters suggest, friendship language was often used to pressure others, and at times claims of friendship seem almost to have functioned as a form of emotional blackmail, though it is likely that powerful people developed an ability to ignore such rhetoric if needed.

Friendship served a wide range of instrumental purposes. I have already discussed the most important one for clerics, the search for patronage.[73] In addition, clerics could use friendship to rally support in political disputes, as John of Salisbury was trying to do for Thomas Becket, and both Julian Haseldine and Anne Duggan have discussed how friendship networks helped the archbishop in his dispute with

---

[68] Gerald of Wales, *Opera*, 1:362–3, 382–7, 412–14; 3:335–6; Davies, "Giraldus Cambrensis: *De Invectionibus*," 178–9. A. K. Bate suggests that Gerald and Walter were not close friends, that Walter was slyly mocking Gerald in his supposed praise, and that Gerald was too vain to notice. I am not convinced, and in any case Gerald certainly saw Walter's praise as genuine: A. K. Bate, "Walter Map and Giraldus Cambrensis," *Latomus* 31 (1972), 860–75.

[69] Ralph of Diceto, *Opera Historica*, 2:135–43.

[70] See particularly Ysebaert, "Medieval Letter-Collections," 285–300.

[71] John of Salisbury, *Letters*, 2:528–9.

[72] Arnulf of Lisieux, *Letters*, 64–5.   [73] See Chapter 5, section 3.

Henry II.[74] Similarly, when the monks of Christ Church, Canterbury, were battling with Archbishop Baldwin, they asked Ralph of Sarre, a Kentish follower of Becket who had become dean of Rheims Cathedral, to intercede with Pope Gregory VIII, to whom he was very close.[75] One could also use the intercession of friends to help recover the favor of powerful people, as John of Salisbury was trying to persuade Thomas Becket to do with Henry II in the letter noted at the beginning of this chapter.[76] Later on, John, while trying unsuccessfully to arrange for his own peace with Henry during the Becket controversy, did successfully intervene on behalf of the son of a friend, Master Geoffrey of St. Edmund, through the intercession of other friends, particularly a royal cleric, Walter de Insula. One can incidentally see John working to keep the friendship network functioning smoothly in this episode, for he urged Geoffrey to thank Walter, and have *his* friends, including Earl Geoffrey de Mandeville, do likewise. John subsequently asked Master Geoffrey to reciprocate by interceding for him with the bishop of Norwich.[77] Gilbert Foliot and Peter of Blois can also be found writing letters of intercession for secular clerics, using the language of friendship.[78] Friends could also serve as intermediaries in disputes, as some of Gerald of Wales's friends tried to do in his feud with his nephew and the nephew's tutor.[79] When reconciliation proved fruitless, disputants might call on friends for legal help. In the dispute between Battle Abbey and Godfrey de Lucy discussed in Chapter 5, Abbot Odo sought support from Gerard la Pucelle on the basis of established friendship (*familiaritas*), and though at first Gerard refused, he eventually agreed.[80] Friendship could also prompt all sorts of miscellaneous favors. Gerald of Wales stated that he was fulfilling the obligations of friendship when he recorded recent miracles of Hugh of Avalon at the request of Roger of Rolleston, dean of Lincoln, and though this statement clearly fits into the modesty topos of authors, it is likely that Gerald saw writing as one way to provide favors within his friendship network.[81] John of Salisbury even lamented to a friend his loss of other friends during the Becket controversy by way of introducing a request that the recipient help persuade the bishop of Norwich to pay three marks he owed John to John's brother.[82] It is important not to take too cynical a view of medieval friendship, but clearly the hope for practical advantages played a very large role in the creation of friendship networks among twelfth-century clerics.

Such networks of friendship and influence could be very large and complex. Analysis of the correspondence of John of Salisbury and Peter of Blois by John McLoughlin and John Cotts reveals what an extensive circle of contacts these two

---

[74] Julian Haseldine, "Thomas Becket: Martyr, Saint—and Friend?," in Richard Gameson and Henrietta Leyser, eds., *Belief and Culture in the Middle Ages: Studies Presented to Henry Mayr-Harting* (Oxford, 2001), 305–17; Anne Duggan, "Thomas Becket's Italian Network," in Anne Duggan, ed., *Thomas Becket: Friends, Networks, Texts, and Cult* (Aldershot, 2007), 1–21.
[75] Stubbs, ed., *Epistolæ Cantuarienses*, 113, 124–5.   [76] John of Salisbury, *Letters*, 1:45–6.
[77] John of Salisbury, *Letters*, 2:76–83.
[78] Gilbert Foliot, *Letters and Charters*, 118; Peter of Blois, *Opera*, 175–8.
[79] Gerald of Wales, *Speculum Duorum*, 112–13.
[80] Searle, ed., *The Chronicle of Battle Abbey*, 322–3, 328–31.
[81] Gerald of Wales, *Opera*, 7:137.   [82] John of Salisbury, *Letters*, 2:72–5.

men had, and though they did not use friendship language with all of their correspondents, they did so frequently enough to show the importance of friendship in their networking.[83] The schools and nascent universities provided ample opportunities for building up friendship networks. Though the fact that Gerald of Wales and Adam, bishop of St. Asaph, had formerly been close associates in Paris did not prevent them from engaging in a fierce dispute in Wales, both referred to their times together in the schools in trying to soften the other's antagonism and make peace.[84] When Peter of Blois wrote to Conrad, archbishop of Mainz, about the captivity of Richard I in Germany after the Third Crusade, he reminded him of their friendship in the schools, when they studied under the same master and lived in the same lodgings.[85] Thomas of Marlborough, a former secular cleric who became a monk at Evesham, was imprisoned on one occasion during an epic struggle between the convent and the abbot. Fortunately for Thomas, three of his former teachers, John of Tynemouth, Simon of Sywell, and Honorius of Richmond, were important canonists and favorites of Archbishop Hubert Walter. Their friendship helped win Thomas the archbishop's support, which gained Thomas his freedom.[86] The schools not only provided learning and credentialing but also the possibility of making contacts and forming friendships with clerics who might someday be highly influential.

Friendship formed a particularly useful way for contemporaries to envision and build social ties in the socially fluid world of the clergy, because it allowed for bonds between both those of equal and those of unequal status and could accommodate changes in the relative standing of friends. Even friends of equal or inferior status could be quite useful to clerics, partly because they might themselves be in a position to provide favors but also because they could bring their own networks to bear, particularly in interceding with powerful figures they knew. Nonetheless, having friends who were powerful figures such as bishops and archbishops was even better. Mews and Chiavaroli have contrasted the explicit "pacts of protection and obedience," in feudal relationships (drawing on Marc Bloch) with the "tacit pacts of mutual service and legitimate expectation" in friendship.[87] Though not all relationships of lordship were particularly formal in the period, friendship nonetheless provided a more socially flexible type of social bond. Even when there was an existing vertical relationship between clerics, as between bishops and their officials or followers, friendship could strengthen such a relationship and be used to lessen the social distance between the parties if they desired.[88] Friendship could also be used to build and conceptualize informal bonds of loose patronage between clerics and figures with whom they had no official relation. Ambitious clerics who developed many friendships at a young age might hope to end up with friends who were bishops or great royal clerics and who could therefore help advance their

---

[83] McLoughlin, "Amicitia in Practice," 168–74; Cotts, *Clerical Dilemma*, 63–7.
[84] Gerald of Wales, *Opera*, 1:36–8.   [85] Peter of Blois, *Opera*, 428–32.
[86] Thomas of Marlborough, *History of Evesham*, 232–7.
[87] Mews and Chiavaroli, "Latin West," 97, 99.
[88] Burger, *Bishops, Clerks, and Diocesan Governance*, 210–38.

careers. In a world in which two young clerics might start out as rough equals but end up with radically different statuses because one had had a far more successful career than the other, friendship worked better than lordship as a way of conceptualizing and sustaining relationships. Peter of Blois announced to Archbishop Conrad of Mainz that he was sure that the latter's promotion would not affect their friendship, and though this may have been a tactical effort by Peter to try to ensure just that, friendship could provide a way of accommodating the sharp changes in status that would have been more common among elite clerics than in other social groups.[89]

Though friendship clearly had many practical, emotional, and even spiritual advantages, it too created moral dilemmas. Peter of Blois, in his treatise on friendship, argued that although friends should help each other, friendship based on self-interest was not true friendship, an idea he drew from Ailred of Rievaulx and ultimately from Cicero.[90] Cotts, however, has noted that Peter's own friendships, as seen in his letters, arguably did not follow this ideal of disinterested friendship.[91] In practice it must have been hard to distinguish between improper friendships based solely on mutual self-interest and proper ones that were based on mutual disinterest but nonetheless fostered exchanges of favors. Even so, it is likely that friendship was yet another arena in which reality often fell short of contemporary ideals. Moreover, Bishop Hugh of Lincoln complained and Thomas of Chobham implied that friendship as well as nepotism might lead to the recommendation or promotion of unworthy candidates, and Gerald of Wales classed benefices he had gained through the help of friends, along with those he had gained through nepotism or service at court, as morally problematic.[92] An anonymous story tells how a cleric asked Gerard la Pucelle to make a request of Archbishop Richard of Canterbury on his behalf. Gerard, who did not really support the request, made it anyway, but when the archbishop said that he would grant it if Gerard advised him to, Gerard replied there was a great distance between petition and advice.[93] The point of the story seems to be the cleverness with which Gerard navigated between his obligation to the petitioner and his duty to provide the archbishop with wise advice, but is shows how the responsibilities of friendship could easily clash with other obligations.

Friendships could also go wrong. Peter of Blois complained bitterly to a former friend in Rouen, saying he had treated Peter with pride and abuse. Peter also accused him of never having been useful but always asking for help, in other words of failing to fulfill the obligations of *mutual* help entailed in friendship.[94] Cotts has written sensitively and in detail about the stresses in the friendship between Peter and Reginald of Salisbury, bishop of Bath, whose patronage Peter relied on, but

---

[89] Peter of Blois, *Opera*, 428.   [90] Peter of Blois, *Opera*, 877–8.
[91] Cotts, *Clerical Dilemma*, 242. Nederman argues that John of Salisbury *did* put Ciceronian ideals into practice in his own friendships, as revealed in his letters: Nederman, "Friendship in Public Life," 385–97; Nederman, "Textual Communities of Learning and Friendship Circles," 73–83.
[92] Adam of Eynsham, *Magna Vita Sancti Hugonis*, 2:97–8; Thomas of Chobham, *Summa de Arte Praedicandi*, 191; Gerald of Wales, *Opera*, 3:326.
[93] Corpus Christi College, Oxford, MS 32, fo. 99v.   [94] Peter of Blois, *Opera*, 75–7.

whom he also reprimanded in moral terms, and with whom he had practical differences as well.[95] Yoko Hirata has written similarly about the breakdown of friendship between John of Salisbury and Gerard la Pucelle, partly over Gerard's decision, without consulting his friends, to teach in Germany (then on the other side of a papal schism), partly over Gerard's decision to desert Becket's party for the king, and perhaps partly over intellectual jealousies and differences.[96] One of the most spectacular breakdowns of a friendship was that between Gilbert Foliot and Master David of London. David had served both Gilbert and Henry II during the Becket controversy, and been rewarded for his service. The relationship may always have been rocky, given that David sought and obtained Gilbert's reassurance about their friendship on at least one occasion, though David was chronically anxious about such matters. In this case the anxiety was ultimately warranted, because when David sought the deanship of St. Paul's, London, where Gilbert was bishop, and then went over Gilbert's head to the pope to try to achieve his aim, the bishop grew furious. In a letter to Bishop Roger of Worcester, Gilbert expressed his anger over David's ingratitude for past favors, attacked him for betraying their friendship, and used his own friendship with Bishop Roger to try to persuade him not to support David. Toward the end of the letter Gilbert expressed his intractable opposition to David: "For I prefer to exhaust whatever I command in body, spirit, emotion, or property, rather than to succumb to so great an enemy."[97]

As the case of Gilbert Foliot and David of London illustrates, the breakdown of friendship could easily lead to the creation of a new relationship of open enmity. Similarly, when the monks of Great Malvern denied Gilbert Foliot's request to grant a benefice to a relative, he wrote at length about their betrayal of friendship and implied that they might suffer from his displeasure if they did not change their minds.[98] Gilbert was not alone in threatening to hold grudges. The letter that John of Salisbury wrote on Archbishop Theobald's behalf to Bishop Alfred, urging him to grant a benefice to Master Solomon, also hinted at enmity if Alfred did not accept his request.[99] Peter of Blois threatened his former friend at Rouen by saying that he had become a canon through the help of his friends and that he could lose his position through the same means if they informed the pope of his moral shortcomings.[100] Writers moved remarkably quickly from the language of friendship to the language of enmity in these cases.

Paul Hyams, focusing on feuds and violence among the laity, has shown how closely friendship and enmity could be linked in the thinking of the period. Indeed, many twelfth-century people seem to have conceptualized enmity as the flip side of

---

[95] Cotts also discusses how Peter edited his letters to manipulate his image within this relationship: Cotts, *Clerical Dilemma*, 82–94.

[96] Yoko Hirata, "John of Salisbury, Gerard Pucelle and *Amicitia*," in Julian Haseldine, ed., *Friendship in Medieval Europe* (Stroud, 1999), 153–65.

[97] Gilbert Foliot, *Letters and Charters*, 262, 274–5, 280–2, 288, 312–13; Liverani, ed., *Spicilegium Liberianum*, 610–11; Brooke, "Register of Master David," 237–45.

[98] Gilbert Foliot, *Letters and Charters*, 68–9.

[99] See Chapter 5, section 3; John of Salisbury, *Letters*, 1:151–2.

[100] Peter of Blois, *Opera*, 76.

friendship, pairing the terms *freond* and *feond* (enemy) in Old English and *amicitia* and *inimicitia* in Latin.[101] Just as medieval friendship had its oddly formal side, so too did enmity. Ever since Jolliffe wrote on the subject, scholars have been aware of how the Angevin kings used their "ira et malevolentia" as a political tool, and how people would pay to have the king set wrath aside, which seems a strangely commercial way to settle what modern people would see as a purely emotional conflict.[102] Stephen White and Richard Barton have argued that secular magnates could stage almost ritualized displays of anger as a way of sending signals, bringing others into negotiation, and achieving a settlement on their terms.[103] Regular and secular clerics may have used the contrast between friendship and enmity in similar ways. When Master Jordan de Ros confronted Abbot Samson with strong claims, backed by charters, to hold a benefice during an advowson dispute, Samson deliberately and publicly withheld his friendship from Jordan until Jordan backed down and resigned. In the end, a compromise was reached, but Samson had made his point.[104] It is possible that medieval views of friendship as an important abstract category with strong instrumental as well as affective and emotional elements may have helped strengthen a parallel category of enmity.

As Hyams has also shown, English society in the central Middle Ages cherished enmity as well as friendship and reconciliation, and clerics did not entirely avoid this tendency.[105] It is striking how quick clerics were to assume that rivals and enemies were working to do them down and how eagerly they attributed tensions with superiors or failures to win benefices to the machinations of others. Master David of London claimed in one letter that false rumors about why he sent a messenger to the bishop of Worcester were the work of enemies. In another, asking the recipient to help him reconcile with a patron, he spoke of plotting by antagonists.[106] Peter of Blois wrote of rivals and enemies harming his prospects through sheer envy or even spreading rumors about his father to undermine him. In a case in which he was interceding for a third party with Bishop Reginald of Bath, he claimed that a flatterer was using slander to harm his friend's standing with the bishop.[107] John of Salisbury had to defend Thomas Becket against Gerard la Pucelle's suspicions that Thomas had forwarded a letter of his to the pope in hope of causing him harm, and that Thomas's followers were speaking against him before the French king. On another occasion, John himself claimed that an enemy had forged an insulting letter in his name to get him in trouble with a bishop and a prominent cleric.[108]

---

[101] Paul R. Hyams, *Rancor and Reconciliation in Medieval England* (Ithaca, 2003), 3–4, 21–32.

[102] Jolliffe, *Angevin Kingship*, 87–109.

[103] Stephen D. White, "The Politics of Anger," in Barbara H. Rosenwein, ed., *Anger's Past: The Social Uses of an Emotion in the Middle Ages* (Ithaca, 1998), 127–52; Richard E. Barton, "'Zealous Anger' and the Renegotiation of Aristocratic Relationships in Eleventh- and Twelfth-Century France," in Barbara H. Rosenwein, ed., *Anger's Past: The Social Uses of an Emotion in the Middle Ages* (Ithaca, 1998), 153–70.

[104] Jocelin of Brakelond, *Chronicle*, 61–2.

[105] Hyams, *Rancor and Reconciliation*, 111–276.

[106] Liverani, ed., *Spicilegium Liberianum*, 620–1, 624–6.

[107] Peter of Blois, *Opera*, 146, 175–8, 221–3.   [108] John of Salisbury, *Letters*, 2:80–3, 590–7.

Such accusations might at first simply suggest that twelfth-century England had its own "paranoid style" of clerical politics.[109] Yet in a society in which enmity was valued and was a recognizable model of behavior, one should not automatically dismiss fears about the activities of enemies as paranoid. A particularly important case in point involves Gerald of Wales. During his conflict with Archbishop Hubert Walter over the status of the see of St. David's, Gerald clashed frequently at the papal court with Hubert's representative and favorite, John of Tynemouth. On their way back from Rome, as noted in Chapter 6, both fell foul of the warfare between England and France early in John's reign. According to Gerald, John was taken prisoner in France first and maliciously described Gerald so that he would be taken prisoner as well. In retaliation, Gerald told their captors that John was a favorite of Hubert Walter and had benefices worth more than 100 marks, thus ensuring that John would be held for ransom although he himself was freed. Though one might reasonably question Gerald's claim's about John's malice, Gerald can presumably be taken as an authoritative source for his own motives, and there is no doubt that he took great pleasure in boasting about what he saw as a skillful act of revenge.[110] It is likely that the frequent claim of writers that royal courts and great households were filled with slanderers and backbiters was more than merely a cliché. Clerics, of course, were supposed to remain aloof from the embrace of enmity and feuding by the laity, but obviously they did not always do so, and though all the actions described above were non-violent, clerical involvement in the "enmity culture" of the period helps explain the violence to be discussed in the next chapter. The enemies of clerics were not always former friends. Nonetheless, clerics and others in this society clearly saw a closer relationship between friendship and enmity than most modern people do. Ironically, the culture of friendship, which churchmen idealized, may have fed obliquely into a culture of enmity that they criticized.

Secular clerics were invariably involved in a web of worldly connections. Though the relationships discussed here have their modern parallels, they also had their distinctive aspects: for instance the sometimes crucial practical importance of kinship ties beyond the nuclear family; the patriarchal nature of medieval households; the close link between hospitality and reputation; and the sometimes formal nature of friendship and enmity. Most of these relationships enhanced the power and influence of individual secular clerics and of the secular clergy as a whole. As with so many aspects of their lives, however, such ties also enmeshed them in moral dilemmas and added to the personal and social tensions inevitable for religious figures living in the world.

---

[109] The phrase is from a famous 1964 article in Harper's Magazine by Richard Hofstadter, "The Paranoid Style in American Politics."

[110] Gerald of Wales, *Opera*, 3:265–6, 274–81, 292–7, 307.

9

Violence, Clerical Status, and the Issue of Criminous Clerks

Right around the time of Thomas Becket's consecration as archbishop, Philip de Broi, a secular canon of St. Paul's, Bedford, was accused of killing a knight. He cleared himself of the charge in the ecclesiastical court of the bishop of Lincoln, but not all were satisfied of his innocence. When he was tried again in a royal court, he resisted on the grounds that he was being tried twice for the same crime and roundly abused a royal justice, thus provoking the anger of King Henry II.[1] This murder case, one of thousands from the period, is notorious because it was one of the sparks that ignited the dispute between Henry and Thomas Becket over the problem of how to deal with "criminous clerks."[2] The precise issues at dispute between king and archbishop had to do with procedure and jurisdiction, but the underlying problem, clerical violence, was a particularly important example of the fissure between the ideals and reality of clerical behavior, one that had wider social and political consequences than most.

The first part of the chapter investigates rules and customs relating to the use of violence both against and by clerics. I explore exceptions to the rules, both in theory and in practice, but argue that the ideal of separating the clergy from any taint of violence, whether as perpetrators or victims, remained a powerful one. After summarizing the place of the debate over criminous clerks in the Becket controversy, I turn to evidence for the criminal activities and the use of violence by the secular clergy. A study of the plea rolls from the reigns of Richard I and John suggests that secular clerics were no less likely than adolescent and adult laymen to commit acts of violent crime. Though Henry II may have exaggerated the problem of criminous clerks, it is clear that secular clerics did participate in criminal activity in the period. It is therefore not surprising that contemporaries saw the problem of violent, lawless clerics as a serious one. The final section of the chapter briefly explores the motives of secular clerics in employing violence and notes the surprisingly common use of force in disputes among churchmen.

---

[1] Robertson and Sheppard, eds., *Materials*, 1:12–13; 2:374–5; 3:45, 265; 4:24–5.
[2] The phrase has become so hallowed by time that I will use it despite the fact that it substitutes clerk for cleric, a practice I otherwise avoid, and that criminous is an obsolete word in every other context.

1. CLERICS, VIOLENCE, AND TABOOS

The view that the clergy, both secular and regular, should receive special protection from violence was longstanding and widely accepted by laypeople as well as the religious. For instance, the *Leges Henrici Primi*, which purported to describe royal law in the early twelfth century and treated Anglo-Saxon practices of wergild as still being in practice, contained various passages mandating additional payments of compensation to the church as well as to the victim or his kin for those who struck, injured, mistreated, or killed clerics.[3] Church authorities and intellectuals were, of course, even more concerned than royal officials about protecting clergy. Thomas of Chobham wrote that killing a cleric was equivalent to patricide.[4] The Second Lateran Council in 1138 issued a decree, occasionally noted by English writers, that anyone who merely "laid violent hands" on a cleric or monk was automatically excommunicated and had to travel to Rome to be absolved by the pope.[5] How often this decree was followed, particularly in cases of minor violence, is unknown, but a papal mandate in 1213 discussed a man who, as an adolescent, had beaten students his master had placed in his charge to extort money from them, though the fact that the man was himself a cleric complicates matters.[6] In any case, the principle that the bodies of the clergy should remain inviolate was clearly established.

This principle was mirrored by the belief that clerics should refrain from using violence; indeed, in Bishop Bartholomew's penitential a section on those who killed clerics was immediately followed by one on clerics who killed others, illustrating the close connection of the two principles.[7] Several English church councils or synods repeated standard decrees against clerics fighting or bearing arms.[8] More striking was how broadly Thomas of Chobham's *Summa Confessorum* interpreted the ban on clerical violence. Thomas wrote that even those who killed by accident were degraded from the clergy if they had not tried sufficiently hard to avoid the accident or if they were doing something forbidden, such as shooting arrows. Strikingly, another mandate of Innocent III concerned a priest who had not performed mass since he had lost control of his horse and it had crushed a child.[9] Thomas also wrote that even those who killed pagans in defense of the faith would be demoted. Thomas not only included the typical ban on clerical participation in blood judgments, but wrote that clerics could not *attend* such judgments except to speak in defense of an accused. For Thomas, it was even problematic for a priest

---

[3] L. J. Downer, ed., *Leges Henrici Primi* (Oxford, 1972), 112–13, 208–11, 216–17.
[4] Thomas of Chobham, *Summa Confessorum*, 455.
[5] Anne Duggan, "Conciliar Law, 1123–1215: The Legislation of the Four Lateran Councils," in Wilfried Hartmann and Kenneth Pennington, eds., *The History of Medieval Canon Law in the Classical Period, 1140–1234: From Gratian to the Decretals of Pope Gregory IX* (Washington, D.C., 2008), 318–66, at 331; Morey, *Bartholomew of Exeter*, 285; Thomas of Chobham, *Summa Confessorum*, 113.
[6] Cheney and Cheney, eds., *Letters of Pope Innocent III*, 151, 265.
[7] Morey, *Bartholomew of Exeter*, 212–15.
[8] Whitelock, Brett, and Brooke, eds., *Councils and Synods, 1066–1204*, 581, 777, 988.
[9] Cheney and Semple, eds., *Selected Letters of Innocent III*, 23.

to say he was robbed, since that could lead to the robber being hanged, though he considered it permissible as long as the priest sought justice rather than vengeance. Thomas was not opposed to a harshly violent judicial system in principle; he wrote that priests could preach to judges that they should hang evildoers as long as they did not refer to specific cases. What was problematic was the involvement of clerics themselves, however indirectly, in judicial violence.[10] In theory, what might be called a taboo against clerical involvement in violence was as strong as the taboo against subjecting clerics to violence.

These taboos stemmed partly from Christian ideals of pacifism. Though the commitment to pacifism had been eroded by the theory of just war, by a long-standing acceptance of the use of violence in justice, and by the embrace of the crusades after 1095, it remained a force in Christian thinking, as the Peace of God movement reveals. Amy Remensnyder has shown that prohibiting clerics from the use of arms, as well as protecting them from violence, formed an important aspect of this movement.[11] Though it never spread to England, the Peace of God was adopted in Normandy by the dukes themselves and its influence must have been felt across the channel. More generally, Paul Hyams, in his work on feuding in England, has stressed that church writers continued to express negative views on vengeance, hatred, and anger.[12] Though religious writers accepted that lay people could sometimes licitly exercise violence and even encouraged them to do so in crusades, still they refused to endorse the exercise of arms by clerics. Clerics were supposed to serve as exemplars of Christian pacifism to others, and since the ban on them carrying arms undermined their security, they warranted the extra protection that bans on harming them could provide.

These taboos, however, had even more to do with the continuing effort, redoubled after the Gregorian Reform, to set the clergy apart as a "chosen people," a "genus electum," to use the phrase from the vulgate so often applied by medieval writers to priests or clerics. The decrees of a church council at Westminster in 1138, quoting an earlier pope, stated that it was as ridiculous for a cleric to go to battle as it was disgraceful for a lay person to perform mass.[13] Laypeople could think the same. When an armed cleric named Hugh de la Mare urged Richard I to get away from some fighting in Sicily during the king's journey to the Holy Land, Richard supposedly responded "Sir cleric, concentrate on your scriptures and get away from the press. Leave chivalry to us, by God and Saint Mary."[14] The king's comment was dismissive, but for clerics themselves, the taboos against clerical involvement with violence derived from the special, exalted status of the clergy. As part of their special status, clerics, particularly priests, were not supposed to suffer from physical deformity, which of course could result from a serious wound. However, the separation from violence was itself a crucial marker of clerical distinctiveness.

---

[10] Thomas of Chobham, *Summa Confessorum*, 64–5, 70, 78, 304–8, 423–6, 436–7, 445–7.

[11] Remensnyder, "Pollution, Purity, and Peace," 280–307.

[12] Hyams, *Rancor and Reconciliation*, 44–54.

[13] Whitelock, Brett, and Brooke, eds., *Councils and Synods, 1066–1204*, 777.

[14] Ambroise, *The History of the Holy War: Ambroise's* Estoire de la guerre sainte, ed. Marianne Ailes and Malcolm Barber, 2 vols. (Woodbridge, 2003), 1:26.

A passage by the monk Lucian of Chester, which exalted their status in typical fashion, for instance by describing the secular cleric as "an angel of God and the light of the world," stressed that among their privileges they were spared in times of warfare and violence by "solemn custom."[15] Like celibacy, the barriers between the clergy and violence also separated them from the laity. Indeed, similar pollution concerns were involved, for Remensnyder has argued that pollution fears about money, clerical sexuality, and clerical violence were all tied together in the Peace movement.[16] Blood carried a multivalent symbolism in the Middle Ages, and because of Eucharistic theology was often viewed positively.[17] However, blood that was shed in an act of violence could represent or could *be* a form of pollution, as when the spilling of blood in a church forced its reconsecration. This is why writers like Thomas of Chobham used the term "blood judgment" to emphasize that clerics should avoid participation in judicial violence. Thus, taboos about violence were crucial to the very identity of the clergy as a distinct group.

In practice, social norms about the clergy and violence were somewhat flexible. I have written elsewhere that powerful people in the reigns of Henry II and his sons, including prelates, had little hesitation about using limited and carefully calibrated violence against secular clerics and monks. However, I also showed that they tried to limit their transgressions and that they often employed proxy violence (for instance, attacks on servants) to apply pressure without committing sacrilege.[18] I have also written that clerics, like laypeople, could be kidnapped for ransom in Stephen's reign, but norms commonly broke down under the intense pressures of war.[19] Even so, the use of clerics to gather ransoms for their lords during the Magna Carta rebellion suggests that in wartime clerics had a better chance of safely carrying large sums of money about the countryside than laymen would have had.[20] Though the norms, rules, and taboos protecting the clergy from violence were not inviolable, they still had a potent influence.

More important, in the present context, was the flexibility of laws and norms with regard to the use of violence *by* clerics.[21] Canon law itself gave a certain amount of leeway. Clerics could licitly use limited forms of violence to discipline servants or students, even though the latter were generally clerics; the adolescent

[15] Bodleian Library, Bodleian MS 672, fo. 120v. Monks, of course, had the same privileges, but Lucian was here speaking of clerics.

[16] Remensnyder, "Pollution, Purity, and Peace," 280–307.

[17] Nicholas Vincent, *The Holy Blood: King Henry III and the Westminster Blood Relic* (Cambridge, 2001); Caroline Walker Bynum, *Wonderful Blood: Theology and Practice in Late Medieval Northern Germany and Beyond* (Philadelphia, 2007).

[18] Thomas, "Shame, Masculinity, and Becket," 1053–6.

[19] Hugh M. Thomas, "Violent Disorder in King Stephen's England: A Maximum Argument," in Paul Dalton and Graeme J. White, eds., *King Stephen's Reign (1135–1154)* (Woodbridge, 2008), 139–70, at 152–3.

[20] See Chapter 6, section 1; Hardy, ed., *Rotuli Litterarum Patentium*, 187b, 189b–90a, 190b, 194b, 198b.

[21] See also Kirsten Fenton's discussion of the use of violence by saints in the works of William of Malmesbury: Kirsten A. Fenton, *Gender, Nation and Conquest in the Works of William of Malmesbury* (Woodbridge, 2008), 30–2, 47–50, 75–7.

student teacher noted above got into trouble because he used violence for an improper purpose. Violence in self-defense by clerics was also licit, and Thomas of Chobham noted that it was the custom in many areas to allow clerics to dress as laymen and carry arms when fearing ambushes by enemies or when traveling on pilgrimage or to the schools.[22] This may be why Gerald of Wales owned a good quality Lombard sword which he accused his nephew's tutor of stealing, though the aristocratic prestige of owning such a weapon probably also formed a major incentive.[23] Norms about clerical use of violence were even more flexible than church law. The fact that about half of the most active early justices were clerics, as noted in Chapter 6, may indicate that bans against participating in blood judgments were widely ignored.[24] I have also noted a couple of examples of clerics, one of them Thomas Becket, actively serving the king on the battlefield; ideals of just war or of service to the king may have partially offset strictures against clerical violence.[25] Celebration of crusading provided an even stronger motive for clerics to ignore prohibitions against violence. Ralph de Hauterive, archdeacon of Colchester, received favorable notice from several chroniclers for his rescue of beleaguered survivors of a rout during the Third Crusade. One writer praised Ralph for his abilities in both kinds of "military service," meaning actual fighting and the metaphorical struggles of churchmen, and described Ralph as famous for his learning and distinguished for his use of arms.[26] This was, of course, a period in which Archbishop Turpin could be viewed as a heroic military figure in such works as *The Song of Roland*.

Even so, the core belief that clerics should avoid the use of arms remained largely intact. Presumably the fact that clerical judges would not themselves have hanged or mutilated those convicted meant that the breach was not felt to be so serious. Though Thomas Becket engaged in combat himself, bishops and other clerics who led military contingents may, like judges, have felt that they were sufficiently removed from the actual spilling of blood to remain unstained by the violence. The same was no doubt even truer for the many clerics who served royal armies in logistical capacities.[27] Indeed, that so few clerics actually served in combat reveals the essential effectiveness of the ban on clerics bearing arms. Even on crusades, the theory that clerics should not fight remained dominant. Ralph Niger, admittedly one of the few clerics at all critical of the crusades, censured the archetypal fighting crusader bishop, Turpin, "about whose excesses performers

---

[22] Thomas of Chobham, *Summa Confessorum*, 70–1, 84, 228, 426–7, 442; Baldwin, *Masters, Princes, and Merchants*, 1:141–2.

[23] Gerald of Wales, *Speculum Duorum*, 96–7.

[24] See Chapter 6, sections 1 and 4; Turner, *English Judiciary*, 2, 291.

[25] See Chapter 3, section 1 and Chapter 6, section 1.

[26] The writer of the *Itinerarium* also recorded Archbishop Baldwin participating in the fighting and described Hubert Walter, the bishop of Salisbury, as a knight in battle: William Stubbs, ed., *Itinerarium Peregrinorum et Gesta Regis Ricardi* (London, 1864), 91, 115–16; Roger of Howden, *Chronica*, 3:70; Ralph of Diceto, *Opera Historica*, 2:84.

[27] Though figures in Peter the Chanter's circle expressed concern about prelates providing fighters for war and the church providing financial support, administrative logistical support received surprisingly little criticism: Baldwin, *Masters, Princes, and Merchants*, 1:206–20.

(*histriones*) make up stories."[28] Peter of Blois was far more favorable to the crusades and urged clerics to participate, but in doing so he posed a question he thought clerics might ask: "What should I do as a cleric among knights, an unarmed and unwarlike man among the armed and warlike?" Peter's response was that prayer and exhortation were also important, and the whole imagined interchange worked on the assumption that clerics would not fight.[29] Innocent III, in a mandate to England, said that clerics who had taken crusade vows as a form of imposed penance should normally redeem them because they were noncombatants.[30] Thus, even deeply committed supporters of the crusades believed that clerics should avoid the actual fighting.

2. CLERICAL VIOLENCE AND THE BECKET DISPUTE

Clearly there were gray areas when it came to clerics and violence, but it was the question of what to do about "criminous clerks" who clearly transgressed the ban on clerical violence without an acceptable excuse that divided Henry II and Thomas Becket so deeply.[31] As Michael Staunton has shown, almost all contemporaries agreed that this was one of the major issues in the controversy.[32] Everybody could agree that clerics should not commit crimes, particularly violent ones; the problem was what to do with those who broke the rules. To employ the punishments of mutilation and execution commonly used against convicted lay criminals would break the taboo against violating the bodies of clerics with violence. However, many people, including some clerics, thought that treating the clergy differently and more leniently was unfair and would make it harder to suppress violent crime. The dilemma created by the corporal punishment of clerics was not the only issue at stake in the dispute over criminous clerks, for there were important jurisdictional issues that affected the Church as an institution, but it is the debate over violent forms of punishment that matters most in this context, since that was what most involved clerics as individuals.

The dispute over criminous clerks must be set squarely in the context of a drive by Henry II to reduce crime and maintain peace, and Hyams has recently stressed how much effort the king and his government put into various initiatives for this purpose.[33] "I am thinking thoughts of peace," said Henry in 1163, according to a summary of the dispute, "and I am much moved for the good of the peace, which is badly disturbed in my kingdom by the evils of clerics, who

---

[28] Ralph Niger, *De Re Militari*, 79–80.

[29] Peter of Blois, *Petri Blesensis Tractatus Duo: "Passio Raginaldi, Principis Antiochie," "Conquestio de Dilatione Vie Ierusolimitane,"* ed. R. B. C. Huygens (Turnhout, 2002), 67–8.

[30] Cheney and Cheney, eds., *Letters of Pope Innocent III*, 57–8.

[31] For accounts of this controversy, see Barlow, *Thomas Becket*, 91–3, 102–4; Duggan, *Thomas Becket*, 38–40, 48–58; Gabel, *Benefit of Clergy*, 25–8; David Knowles, *Thomas Becket* (Stanford, 1971), 79–86; Smalley, *Becket Conflict*, 123–32, 161–2; W. L. Warren, *Henry II* (Berkeley, 1973), 459–69, 481, 540–2; Hanna Vollrath, *Thomas Becket: Höfling und Heiliger* (Göttingen, 2004), 70–83.

[32] Staunton, *Thomas Becket and his Biographers*, 99.

[33] Hyams, *Rancor and Reconciliation*, 155–74. See also Warren, *Henry II*, 460–1.

perpetrate many robberies, thefts, and homicides."[34] For Henry and his supporters, the exalted status of the clergy only made their crimes worse.[35] Implicit in their argument was a sense that clerics who had broken taboos by committing violence had morally forfeited the protection from violence that clerical status provided them, and that their clerical status should therefore not work to their benefit but rather to their detriment. Herbert of Bosham also reported the royalist argument that the sort of men who committed serious crimes would worry little about losing their clerical status, which was the worst punishment an ecclesiastical court could inflict on clerics.[36]

The response of Becket and his supporters was not by and large to dispute the king's premises, motives, or arguments, but to argue that clerical privileges and ecclesiastical liberty had to trump royal concerns, however justified. The punishments meted out in Henry's judicial system may seem harsh and barbaric to a modern audience, but clerics of the time expressed no objection on those grounds.[37] The concern of Becket's supporters was to remove the clergy from involvement in blood judgment in any capacity, including as criminals, rather than to soften the system as a whole. Indeed, Herbert of Bosham, one of Becket's most loyal supporters and the writer who presented the archbishop's case at greatest length, went out of his way to praise the king's zeal for preserving peace for his people.[38] Nor did Becket's followers argue that clerical crime was not a problem. The anonymous author of one passage defending clerical privilege wrote of clerics that "some of these or many are evil, and commit robberies or are thieves, arsonists, or murderers."[39] At most, there was some hedging here with the "some." Herbert of Bosham recorded Becket himself as acknowledging royalist concerns about the lack of deterrence in ecclesiastical penalties and arguing that strict imprisonment of criminous clerks could answer this problem.[40] Later sources reveal that even after Becket's martyrdom, churchmen had doubts about Becket's position and about the efficacy of ecclesiastical penalties against criminals. Cotts has argued convincingly that a letter Peter of Blois wrote on behalf of Archbishop Richard of Canterbury, about the ineffectiveness of ecclesiastical punishment against laypeople who attacked clerics, represented an indirect criticism of the systematic reliance on ecclesiastical sanctions against clerical criminals that came about in England as a result of Becket's death.[41] The regular canon William of Newburgh, though he thought the king had pursued his case too zealously, believed that the king's

---

[34] A similar passage also appears in Edward Grim's *vita* of Becket: Robertson and Sheppard, eds., *Materials*, 2:386–7; 4:202.

[35] Robertson and Sheppard, eds., *Materials*, 3:266; 4:202.

[36] Robertson and Sheppard, eds., *Materials*, 3:266.   [37] Knowles, *Thomas Becket*, 80.

[38] Robertson and Sheppard, eds., *Materials*, 3:272–3.

[39] Robertson and Sheppard, eds., *Materials*, 4:148.

[40] Robertson and Sheppard, eds., *Materials*, 3:271.

[41] Cotts, *Clerical Dilemma*, 190–3. See also Vollrath, *Thomas Becket*, 82. Cotts's argument about the true purpose of this letter is bolstered by the fact that the royal government was perfectly willing to pursue those who killed clerics despite the ostensible concerns of the letter. See, for instance, G. Herbert Fowler, "Rolls of the Justices in Eyre at Bedford, 1202," *Publications of the Bedfordshire Historical Record Society* 1 (1913), 133–247, at 228–9; Stenton, ed., *Pleas*, 3:78; 4:101, 115.

concern about widespread criminal activity by clerics had been valid, and he also complained that bishops were too lax even in using what disciplinary powers they had.[42] In short, most clerics, including even Henry's adversaries, conceded most of his arguments. Nonetheless, his opponents argued that the king's effort to subject clerical bodies to corporal punishments was unacceptable.

The fullest statement of this view appears in Becket's own arguments at a council at Westminster in 1163, as reconstructed by Herbert of Bosham, who was present and wrote that he was providing the gist of these arguments even if not the precise words. In this reconstructed speech, Becket emphasized that clerics were a race set apart and chosen for the service of God, and as a result their bodies, which could in some sense be described as spiritual, were to be without mutilation of limbs or deformation. To use ordinary punishments on them would be to deform the image of God in men. Becket went on to construct a complicated word picture, saying that it would be indecent and disgraceful to tie hands consecrated to God behind the back of an offending cleric, since only a little before they had made the image of the cross at the altar, but now would provide the image of a public thief. It would be no better for an anointed head, at whose feet royal majesty had sought grace and mercy shortly before, to hang on an ignominious gibbet. Nor was it fitting that hands from which the king himself might seek blessing be mutilated. Over the course of this long speech, Becket used various arguments, including standard Gregorian ideas about the relation of church and state, but the core had to do with the special status of the clergy.[43] The idea of physical contact with God through the Eucharist that moralists used so often could not be employed to the same extent here, because the debate concerned the clergy as a whole, not just priests. Nonetheless, ideas about the sacral nature of clerics and their bodies that preachers and writers so often used to try to shame clerics into behaving better were employed here to protect their privileges. Thus the belief that clerics should have special privileges, though potentially self-serving when it came to punishment, was rooted in widespread and longstanding ideas about the distinctive and exalted position of the clergy that were by no means invoked only in self-interested ways.

Henry and his legal advisors tried to find a way to circumvent the dilemma they too perceived between trying to repress clerical crime and the imperative to preserve clerical bodies from violence. They also sought to compromise on another key issue in the dispute, namely the longstanding claim of the Church to jurisdiction over its members, by backing away from any attempt to try clerics in secular courts. The wording of the relevant passage in the Constitutions of Clarendon is not very clear, but Maitland long ago convincingly argued that the intention was for clerics to be tried in a church court and then, after being stripped of clerical status if found guilty, turned over to the secular courts for punishment.[44] Since clerical exemption adhered to the status, not the person (indeed, even Becket and his supporters

---

[42] William of Newburgh, *Historia Rerum Anglicarum*, 1:140–1.

[43] Robertson and Sheppard, eds., *Materials*, 3:268–72.

[44] Frederic William Maitland, "Henry II and the Criminous Clerks," in H. A. L. Fisher, ed., *The Collected Papers of Frederic William Maitland* (Cambridge, 1911), 232–50.

agreed that deposed clerics could be tried for *subsequent* crimes and punished as laymen), the solution was an ingenious one. Becket, however, rejected the process on the grounds that it was contrary to canon law and constituted a kind of double jeopardy, for even if it involved only one trial, it created a double punishment for a single crime. He may also have felt, as Anne Duggan has suggested, that the process put forward at Clarendon was designed to fulfill the letter rather than the spirit of canon law and thereby to circumvent its intent.[45] Unfortunately for all involved, canon law as yet provided no clear guidance on this subject. Maitland famously argued that Becket's stance was in fact more innovatory than the king's, though other scholars, notably Charles and Anne Duggan, have disagreed.[46] Whatever one thinks of Becket's precise interpretation of canon law or of his rejection of the royal attempt at compromise, however, it must be emphasized that a strong and widely shared belief in the special, exalted status of the clergy lay behind his stance on this issue and behind his eventual willingness to embrace martyrdom partly because of it.

How serious was the problem of clerical criminality?[47] Most contemporary accounts of the dispute provided only broad generalizations, such as Henry's claims about widespread criminal activity by clerics or the concession that "some or many" committed crimes. William fitz Stephen, however, did note a couple of specific and notorious crimes besides the *cause célèbre* of Philip de Broi. More important, William of Newburgh wrote that Henry's advisors spoke to the king in 1163 of clerics having committed more than a hundred murders, as well as many other crimes, during his reign, which at that point was less than a decade old.[48] William, however, was writing some decades later, so there is no way of knowing if his figure of a hundred murders actually represented claims made during the debate, let alone whether the figure had any validity. Fortunately, enough early plea rolls containing accusations of criminal activity survive to give at least a rough idea of the extent of clerical criminality and violence.

Tables 1 through 3 represent the results of a study of accusations of criminal activity from the surviving eyre rolls of the reigns of Richard and John that record serious criminal activity. These consist of eighteen sets of pleas of the crown from fourteen counties and eight different years between 1194 and 1208.[49] Table 1

[45] Duggan, *Thomas Becket*, 56–7.

[46] Maitland, "Henry II and the Criminous Clerks," 241–50; Duggan, "Becket Dispute and the Criminous Clerks," 1–28; R. M. Fraher, "The Becket Dispute and Two Decretist Traditions: The Bolognese Masters Revisited and Some New Anglo-Norman Texts," *Journal of Medieval History* 4 (1978), 347–68; Duggan, *Thomas Becket*, 48–58.

[47] For accounts of criminous clerks and how they were treated in the later Middle Ages, see Gabel, *Benefit of Clergy*, 30–115; Heath, *English Parish Clergy*, 119–33; Swanson, *Church and Society*, 149–53.

[48] Robertson and Sheppard, eds., *Materials*, 3:45–6; William of Newburgh, *Historia Rerum Anglicarum*, 1:140.

[49] Wiltshire, 1194; Buckinghamshire and Bedfordshire, 1195; Hertfordshire, Middlesex, Essex, and Staffordshire, 1199; Cornwall and Somerset, 1201; Lincolnshire, Bedfordshire, Northamptonshire, and Rutland, 1202; Northamptonshire, Staffordshire, and Shropshire, 1203; Lincolnshire, 1206; Yorkshire, 1208. Maitland, ed., *Three Rolls*, 77–115, 141–8; Palgrave, ed., *Rotuli Curiæ Regis*, 1:159–65, 202–11, 214–18; George Wrottesley, "Staffordshire Suits, Extracted from the Plea Rolls temp. Richard I and King John," *William Salt Archaeological Society Collections for a History of Staffordshire* 3 (1882), 1–163, at 38–45, 91–8; Stenton, ed., *Earliest Lincolnshire Assize Rolls*, 93–168, 266–71; Fowler, "Bedford Eyre, 1202," 214–47; Stenton, ed., *Northamptonshire Assize Rolls*, 1–21, 112–21; Stenton, ed., *Pleas*, 2:1–15, 48–96, 176–8, 211–25; 3:69–87; 4:94–117.

Table 1. Accused Clerics as a Percentage of Total Accused

Crimes	Total Number of those Accused	Number of Accused Clerics	Percentage of Accused who are Clerics
Murder	523	22	4.2%
Assault	261	10	3.8%
Robbery	221	5	2.3%
Violating the King's Peace	229	9	3.9%
Rape	90	8	8.9%
All Crimes[50]	1646	65	3.9%

Table 2. The Ranks of the Sixty-five Accused Clerics

Rank	Number	Percent
Unspecified (cleric)	45	69%
Acolyte	2	3%
Subdeacon	6	9%
Deacon	2	3%
Priest	10	15%

Table 3. Procedural Outcomes for the Sixty-five Accused Clerics

Outcome	Number	Percent
Transfer to Church Court	32	49%
Plaintiff does not follow up	17	26%
Cleric fails to appear	3	5%
Cleric flees	2	3%
Cleric settles the case	2	3%
Cleric outlawed	1	2%
Cleric cleared	1	2%
Case transferred to the Exchequer	1	2%
Outcome unclear or unknown	6	9%

shows the total numbers of those accused of crimes with the numbers of clerics as a subset. The second table breaks down the accused clerics by rank. The great majority were simply described as clerics and were therefore probably only in minor orders, but a significant minority were in major orders.[51] Table 3 shows that the system created in the aftermath of the Becket controversy was used in the vast majority of cases. Where secular courts were not relieved of responsibility by

[50] This last category includes not only the crimes listed in the Table, but also other kinds of serious, mostly violent crimes such as arson, as well as harboring fugitives, that could make their way into records of the royal courts, but are insufficient in number to make a breakdown by category useful.

[51] Gabel believed that before Henry III's reign, only clerics in major orders were protected by clerical immunity, but this was clearly not the case: Gabel, *Benefit of Clergy*, 29, 62–3.

the flight of clerics or the failure of the plaintiffs to follow up, they almost always turned the accused over to ecclesiastical courts.[52]

Caution is needed in using the figures from the Tables, for the records used present various problems. The investigation necessarily concerns those who were accused rather than found guilty since the outcomes of most cases cannot be known: survival of royal records is patchy, and surviving records from the relevant church courts are practically nonexistent. Given the methods of proof in the period, a study of those found guilty of crimes would only provide a somewhat more useful picture, but the fact remains that we have here only a picture of those initially thought to be responsible for crimes. However, there is no reason to think that clerics were more likely to be falsely accused of crimes than laypeople, and there would have been many crimes where the identity of the perpetrators would have been manifest, so the percentage of accused criminals who were clerics probably conforms broadly to the percentage of actual perpetrators who had that status. Unfortunately, the surviving plea rolls are only a fraction of those even from just the years 1194–1208, and there are none from the early years of Henry II's reign, which were most relevant to the Becket controversy. Though the total number of cases is reasonably large, for individual types of crime the number is often very small. The much higher percentage of accused rapists than accused robbers who were clerics *might* say something about the impacts of clerical celibacy and wealth, but given that there were five accused clerical robbers and eight accused clerical rapists (six of them from one eyre visitation in one county), the likelihood of a sampling error is high. Despite their shortcomings, however, these figures can cast at least some light on the debate over criminous clerks.

To properly assess the figures in the first Table, it is necessary to estimate what percentage of the population consisted of clerics. Unfortunately, there are no sources providing good evidence about the total number of clerics or of the general population around 1200. However, one can extrapolate from various estimates to make very rough guesses. Based on poll tax evidence, Swanson argued for a figure of 24,000–25,000 secular clerics after the Black Death in England.[53] Moorman, based on ordination figures, estimated that there were approximately 40,000 clerics in the thirteenth century, and there is no reason to think there were substantially more clerics in the late twelfth century.[54] As for the general population, one must rely on finding a plausible figure between estimates for the late eleventh century based on *Domesday Book* and ones for the late fourteenth century based on the poll taxes. J. L. Bolton suggests a figure of between 3.5 and 4 million as a "valid guess" for 1200.[55] If one takes, for the sake of argument, Moorman's figures and a more conservative (and convenient) figure of 3.2 million for the population around 1200, this would make the secular clergy roughly 1.25 percent at the time of the

---

[52] William *clericus* of Harrowden was presumably outlawed because he had fled and was not able to invoke clerical privilege: Fowler, "Bedford Eyre, 1202," 240–3. I would like to thank Paul Brand for help with this point.

[53] Swanson, *Church and Society*, 31.   [54] Moorman, *Church Life*, 52–3.

[55] J. L. Bolton, "The English Economy in the Early Thirteenth Century," in S. D. Church, ed., *King John: New Interpretations* (Woodbridge, 1999), 27–40, at 31–32 n 22.

eyre records I have analyzed, whereas a figure of 4 million for the population would make the clergy 1 percent of the population.

If one looks at the percentage of crimes attributed to clerics, Henry II chose to pursue a costly and not very productive fight in the battle over criminous clerks, though of course he could not have predicted that the dispute would end in Becket's death. Even had his position won, and even if one allowed the dubious proposition that harsher penalties would have had sufficient deterrent value to spark a massive drop in clerical crime, the drop in the overall percentage of crime would have been quite limited. Nor did the lighter punishments afforded clerics allow large numbers of hardened criminals to save their lives by claiming to be clerics. In later periods, because of the introduction of the reading test to determine clerical status and because of the spread of lay literacy, this came to be perceived as a problem, but that point was far in the future.[56] I did note in the Introduction a couple of dubious claims of clerical status, one of them from a criminal case, but one case from over 1600 accused laypeople (only a minority of them women who were automatically barred from clerical status) suggests that the problem was insignificant. The victory of Thomas Becket's policy on the treatment of clerical criminals clearly did not unleash a massive crime wave.

However, the study of the plea rolls also suggests why there was a perception of widespread criminal activity by clerics. Given the taboo against violence by clerics, violent clerical crimes would have been particularly memorable, and though they were only a small percentage of total crimes, cumulative numbers across England might well have seemed serious. If only a small percentage of county visits by eyres between 1194 and 1208 produced accusations of murder against twenty-two clerics, William of Newburgh's figure of over one hundred suspected murders by clerics across England between 1154 and 1163, whatever its source, was quite reasonable. When other crimes were added in, criminal activities by clerics were sufficiently common for the royal government not to be able to ignore them or treat them as inconsequential. Moreover, clerics were sometimes accused, both in the plea rolls and in other sources, of crimes that would no doubt have been particularly shocking or noteworthy to contemporaries. The Wiltshire eyre of 1194 included the case of a cleric who was suspected, along with a widow, of murdering a man because he had sued the widow for breach of faith after she had spurned him for the cleric.[57] The Cornish eyre of 1201 reveals that two clerics were among those suspected of killing two Hospitallers on subsequent days, and an early town and gown crisis occurred at Oxford in 1209 after a student killed his mistress and fled.[58] Ironically enough, a subdeacon named Hugh, with the byname of Malus Clericus, or evil cleric, was among the attackers of Thomas Becket. After the knights had struck Thomas down, Hugh splattered the archbishop's brains on the pavement of the cathedral to ensure that he was dead.[59] This was not a society in which people dispassionately

---

[56] Gabel, *Benefit of Clergy*, 69–70. [57] Maitland, ed., *Three Rolls*, 83.
[58] Stenton, ed., *Pleas*, 2:70–1; J. I. Catto, *The History of the University of Oxford. Vol. 1. The Early Oxford Schools* (Oxford, 1984), 26.
[59] Robertson and Sheppard, eds., *Materials*, 2:435, 438; 3:142.

analyzed crime statistics. Between the notoriety of individual crimes by clerics, the cumulative number of criminal clerics that the systematic operations of the royal courts would have uncovered, and the taboo against violence by clerics, it is not surprising that a perception arose that criminous clerks posed a serious problem.

It is also worth noting that the evidence suggests that clerics were committing violent crimes at least as frequently as other adult and adolescent males. In evaluating the finding that clerics represented 1 percent or 1.25 percent of the population but roughly 4 percent of those accused of serious crimes, one must factor in the fact that women were far less likely than men to commit serious crimes and that young children were not likely to do so at all. Even so, the figures in Table 1 indicate that clerics were *more* likely than other adolescent and adult males to commit crimes. Given the problems of all the figures discussed in this calculation, one would not want to put too much weight on this apparent finding. Nonetheless, it is hard to argue from the available data that the taboos against clerics employing violence made them significantly less likely to participate in violent crime.

Here one must note a contrast with the regular clergy. Moorman suggested a figure of 17,000 for the regular clergy (including friars, who only arrived in England in the 1220s) yet the regulars basically do not appear in the plea rolls as accused criminals. Monks and nuns did not completely eschew violence, as illustrated by the occasional employment of armed bands by religious houses to enforce their will, or the famous incident in which the nuns of Watton forced one of their number to castrate a brother of the house with whom she had had sex.[60] To some extent, the apparent difference may mark the fact that any monastic violence would normally have been contained by the cloister walls and that monastic authorities could therefore have handled it themselves or taken it directly to church courts (such practices would also have made fewer instances of monastic violence visible to the lay community). Nonetheless, there may have been a real difference in behavior. Nuns, as women, were less likely to employ violence than male religious were in this period. The greater likelihood of a strong religious vocation may have made monks less likely to practice violence. More important, claustration removed regular clerics from many of the kinds of worldly situation that led to violence and made it less likely that they would be armed or have access to arms. As a result, Henry II and his successors had to worry about criminous clerks disrupting the peace, but not, apparently, about criminous monks or nuns. Given this contrast the activities of violent clerics would only have stood out more. Henry II and his supporters may have overestimated the negative impact of criminous clerks on law and order in the period, but one can understand why they felt outrage about them.

[60] Moorman, *Church Life*, 52, 410–12; Elkins, *Holy Women*, 106–11; Giles Constable, "Aelred of Rievaulx and the Nun of Watton: An Episode in the Early History of the Gilbertine Order," in Derek Baker, ed., *Medieval Women* (Oxford, 1978), 205–26; Palgrave, ed., *Rotuli Curiæ Regis*, 1:11; C. R. Cheney, "Harrold Priory: A Twelfth-Century Dispute," *Bedfordshire Historical Record Society* 32 (1952), 1–26, at 7–8, 19.

3. CAUSES AND MOTIVES OF CLERICAL VIOLENCE

The surprising level of clerical participation in crime raises the only partially answerable question of why clerics committed acts of violence. Poverty could have been a motive for some members of the clerical underclass, as suggested by Thomas of Chobham's warning that badly trained students would not be able to gain a post and might therefore become thieves, robbers, or sorcerers.[61] As Hanna Vollrath has noted, the empress Matilda herself saw a connection between clerical poverty and clerical crime.[62] In some cases ties of family, service, and patronage led secular clerics into violence. One father allegedly had his three sons, one of them a subdeacon, murder two men who had come to collect a debt from him.[63] Samson, a cleric of William de Redvers, earl of Devon, allegedly authorized some of the earl's men to lay hands on the bishop of Exeter and other clerics on the porch of the church of Plympton.[64] In one complicated case, Wimer the chaplain was accused of coming with an armed band, breaking into buildings of Master Thomas, cleric of Earl Hugh Bigod and rector of Bungay, and carrying off ecclesiastical goods worth forty marks. Wimer and Thomas were disputing over the church of Bungay, but Wimer was also sheriff of Norfolk and Suffolk, and it is likely that he carried out that raid in the context of Earl Hugh's rebellion against the king during the 1173–4 revolt, for raiding was a common military practice in the period, including in that particular conflict.[65] More generally, clerics, despite all the efforts to make them act differently from lay people and to avoid worldly concerns and entanglements, had the same passions and got involved in violence for many of the same reasons as laypeople did. Indeed, clerics were frequently accused of collaborating with lay-people in individual crimes.

Some scholars have suggested an additional motive particular to the clergy, arguing that the prohibition against clerical violence itself encouraged such violence by casting doubt on the masculinity of clerics.[66] I have already noted the threat that clerical celibacy posed to claims of clerical masculinity, and in a society that often linked masculinity to the use of violence, the prohibition on the bearing of arms by the clergy only added to this threat. Clerics may therefore have participated in brawls and other forms of violence precisely to demonstrate their masculine status. I have discussed the issue of violence and clerical masculinity in an article on the Becket dispute.[67] There, I argued that the main response to questions about clerical

---

[61] Thomas of Chobham, *Summa Confessorum*, 298.

[62] Vollrath, *Thomas Becket*, 76–7; Duggan, ed., *Correspondence of Thomas Becket*, 1:166–7.

[63] Stenton, ed., *Pleas*, 2:211–12.

[64] Cheney and John, eds., *English Episcopal Acta 3*, 116–17. For Samson's connections with the earl, see Bearman, ed., *Charters of the Redvers Family*, 41.

[65] Holtzmann, Chodorow, and Duggan, eds., *Decretales Ineditae*, 81–5, 92–5, 112; Cheney, *Roger, Bishop of Worcester*, 318, 328, 347–8, 362. For raiding during that revolt, see Thomas, "Violent Disorder," 141–2, 161.

[66] Cullum, "Clergy, Masculinity and Transgression," 186; Thibodeaux, "Man of the Church," 391–4.

[67] Thomas, "Shame, Masculinity, and Becket," 1050–88.

masculinity was for the clergy (both regular and secular) to create a model of a peaceful yet honorable, spiritual, and manly warrior who could stand up to lay aggression using tools available to the clergy such as excommunication. Nonetheless, this was a somewhat defensive model, and the writings of the day offer much indirect evidence of anxiety about clerical masculinity. Though it is hard to prove, I therefore concur with the argument that concerns about masculinity likely fueled violence, which helps explain why secular clerics were no less likely than other adolescent and adult males to commit violent crime.

Finally, one type of clerical misdeed, the use of violence against other clerics, both secular and regular, deserves more attention, for it broke the rules and taboos about violence both *by* and *against* the clergy. Given that violence among churchmen seems largely to have been left to church courts, which left few records, a surprising number of examples survive. The actions of Wimer the chaplain and Samson, cleric of the earl of Devon, fell into this category. A decretal of Pope Celestine from 1196 records the accusation of a vicar that a new rector, an important royal cleric named Geoffrey of Buckland, forced him to resign under fear of death. Another rector was accused of having one of his men "lay violent hands" on a vicar to pressure him to resign.[68] Yet another rector was accused of using an armed band to resist eviction after papal judges delegate issued a sentence against him for failing to pay a pension to Bury St Edmunds.[69]

Judging by the surviving sources, the most frequent use of violence by secular clerics against other religious came in arguments with Cistercian monasteries over exemptions from tithes, and these were particularly important because they were unusually spectacular manifestations of the rivalry between the secular and regular clergy that forms the subject of Chapter 15. One detailed account of such an incident comes from the cartulary of Pipewell Abbey, which records a dispute in or around the year 1213 between the monks and Alexander, rector in the nearby village of Braybrooke. According to this account, Alexander was a proud man who hated and envied the monks because of their growing wealth and because they paid no tithes on land they cultivated with their own labor. After a time his "sorrow and fury" proved too much. Accompanied by an armed band of servants and hirelings, he took wagons to the fields of the monks, seized their grain, and carried it off. When the monks heard this, they ran with their lay brothers to stop Alexander and his followers, only to receive severe beatings. The monks appealed to the papacy and won a favorable judgment from papal judges delegate, but ended up having to make peace with Alexander, dropping claims to any damages in return for a promise that he would not harm them in the future.[70] Though fuller than most, this account was not unique: the chronicle of Meaux Abbey records similar raids by clerics; papal and archiepiscopal documents reveal accusations of rectors leading armed bands to seize and harvest the grain of the monks of Fountains and Bordesley; and Pope Alexander III, in a mandate on behalf of the Cistercian houses

[68] Holtzmann and Kemp, eds., *Papal Decretals Relating to Lincoln*, 36–9, 58–9.
[69] Holtzmann, ed., *Papsturkunden*, 3:372–4.
[70] British Library, Cotton MS Caligula A XII, fos. 79r–80r.

of Rufford and Roche, wrote that he had heard of "insolent" clerics in the dioceses of York, Lincoln, and Chester who violently seized property of monks in tithe disputes.[71] One should not exaggerate the violence in most of these cases. All of the descriptions come directly or indirectly from Cistercians, who had an interest in playing up the violent and illicit nature of the acts of their opponents. The clerics may simply have considered themselves to be forcefully asserting their rights in a society in which "self-help" was a common legal practice. Generally, only the seizure of property was involved and in the Pipewell case it may have been the monks who initiated the actual fighting. Nonetheless, the apparent willingness of clerics to resort to force in disputes against other religious is striking.

The tensions created by clerical violence differed from those produced by most other forms of transgression. As noted in Chapter 2, criminal violence by clerics was so obviously wrong that moralists did not need to fulminate against it.[72] Instead, the question of how to deal with those who broke the rules divided the clergy and the laity. Clerical violence probably formed the most blatant way in which clerics failed to live up to the ideals demanded of their high status in the eyes of laypeople. We have little evidence of what English laypeople thought about clerical marriage, but it is clear that the perception that clerics might get away with murder drove at least one prominent layperson, Henry II, to fury, and he seems to have had much support on this issue. There were many reasons why the Becket controversy ended as it did. Nonetheless, the intensity of emotions surrounding clerical violence and the difficulties involved in reconciling twelfth century beliefs about proper punishment of evildoers with the rules and taboos against violating clerical bodies helped make Thomas Becket a martyr. Ironically, Thomas's deep concern with protecting the sacred clerical body from violation led to his murder, one of the most famous examples of a violation of a clerical body in the Middle Ages.

---

[71] Thomas de Burton, *Chronica Monasterii de Melsa*, 1:297, 311–13; Holtzmann, ed., *Papsturkunden*, 3:293–4, 399–400; Cheney and John, eds., *English Episcopal Acta 3*, 12–13.

[72] See Chapter 2, section 2. See also Smalley, *Becket Conflict*, 219–20, 224; William of Newburgh, *Historia Rerum Anglicarum*, 1:141.

PART III

THE CULTURAL AND INTELLECTUAL IMPACT OF THE CLERGY

10

English Secular Clerics and the Growth of European Intellectual Life in the Twelfth-Century Renaissance

In the late 1160s, Bishop Gilbert Foliot wrote to his nephew Robert Banastre, archdeacon of Essex, urging him to persevere in his studies in Bologna. He proclaimed that Bologna was worthy to be called a city of letters, and that it sharpened the dull world with the subtlety of high genius, opened the treasures of the law, and shed bright light on the secrets of great wisdom. He praised what the city had to offer the student with its abundant goods for sale, large number of masters, and pleasing company of fellow students. He then urged Robert not to return without sufficient learning lest his period of study in Bologna, which brought glory to most, bring shame to him.[1] Foliot was clearly employing all of his rhetorical powers to persuade his apparently unmotivated nephew to embrace his studies, but this letter provides some idea of the great potential appeal of a relatively recent but nonetheless already influential continental center of learning to English students and scholars.

This chapter explores the participation of the English secular clergy in various continental centers of learning, briefly discusses the intellectual activities of some noteworthy learned clerics and of some more average ones, and describes the emergence of a large group of highly educated *magistri* in England. More generally, it introduces the subject of the rapid expansion of intellectual life among the secular clergy of England. The emergence of places such as Paris, Bologna, Salerno, and Toledo as magnets for scholars and students from throughout Catholic Europe was a fundamentally important historical development. Several of these centers emerged as universities, creating a model that would soon be replicated at Oxford and Cambridge and over time throughout Western Europe and eventually the world.[2] These centers, and above all Paris, also fostered many of the most important intellectual changes in Europe in the long twelfth century. Collectively they emerged from but simultaneously encouraged a vibrant transnational intellectual culture noteworthy for an accelerating international exchange of knowledge, including both interchange within Catholic Europe and the absorption of much learning

---

[1] Gilbert Foliot, *Letters and Charters*, 263–4.
[2] For an overview of the development and history of medieval universities, see Hilde de Ridder-Symoens, ed., *Universities in the Middle Ages* (Cambridge, 1992).

from the Arabic world. England participated fully in the explosion of intellectual life in the period, and many English secular clerics became intellectuals. Admittedly, the vast majority of them did not make major individual contributions to the scholarly life of the period, but, as I will argue, ordinary intellectuals collectively mattered as much as the towering intellects upon whom we tend to focus.

Though the main goal of this chapter is to begin to show the crucial importance of the secular clergy, in England as elsewhere, to the intellectual and cultural developments of the Twelfth-Century Renaissance, the developments studied here can also serve as a platform to rethink England's place in that renaissance. R. W. Southern, one of the great scholars of intellectual life in the High Middle Ages, did not think highly of England's cultural and intellectual contributions in the period. "Culturally the most obvious thing about England in the twelfth century is its dependence on France. It was a colony of the French intellectual empire, important in its way and quite productive, but still subordinate. Scholars, poets, architects and religious reformers in England did the same thing as their contemporaries in France, rather less well, and in a provincial and derivative way. England made no great, distinctive contribution in any of the fields which are the special glory of the twelfth century."[3] Yet a fuller look at the involvement of English secular clerics in the intellectual world of the twelfth century can suggest an alternative to the colonial model for England's place in the Twelfth-Century Renaissance, and provide the basis for a more positive assessment of the English contribution.

1. ENGLISH CLERICS AND CONTINENTAL CENTERS OF LEARNING

When contemporaries thought about the best place for people to train in specific fields, they generally thought of places outside England. For instance, late in our period, Geoffrey of Vinsauf, a typical English scholar who worked mostly in France, described Paris as the place to study the trivium; Toledo, the quadrivium; Bologna, law; and Salerno, medicine.[4] There is no doubt that English intellectual life depended heavily on centers of learning outside of England, particularly Paris, and that for most of the period secular clerics seeking the best higher education had to go abroad. Yet dependence did not flow only in one direction. The creation of these centers of advanced learning required both a critical mass of scholars and the economic support that large numbers of students could bring, and at first this depended on recruiting students and teachers from many areas across Europe. The symbiotic relationship between the emerging intellectual centers and the lands from

---

[3] Southern, *Medieval Humanism*, 140–7, 158–80. See also Cheney, *Hubert Walter*, 12. For a more positive depiction of England's role in the renaissance, see Rodney M. Thomson, "England and the Twelfth-Century Renaissance," *Past and Present* 101 (1983), 3–21; Rodney M. Thomson, *Books and Learning in Twelfth-Century England: The Ending of "Alter Orbis"* (Walkern, 2006), 94–100; Moser, *Cosmos of Desire*, 102; Swanson, *Twelfth-Century Renaissance*, 211.

[4] Edmond Faral, *Les arts poétiques du XIIe et XIIIe siècle* (Paris, 1962), 283–4.

which they recruited was fundamentally important, with personnel, ideas, talent, and resources flowing in, and personnel, refined ideas, and polished talent flowing back out to culturally enrich other areas. The participation of large numbers of English secular clerics in this symbiotic relationship was important in its own right, because England was a particularly important source of scholars and students in these schools, and also because their participation is representative of a wider European phenomenon.

Three crucial factors lay behind the ability of English clerics to foster the development of European intellectual centers during the long twelfth century: the demand for education; wealth and the capacity to move money; and above all personal mobility. In earlier chapters I discussed the reasons why there was a high demand for education among English secular clerics, including not only the pragmatic skills education could provide but also the credentialing that gave clerics an advantage in a highly competitive patronage system. At the same time, there was probably less ability to meet that demand in England, at least beyond the most basic levels, than elsewhere.[5] As Barrow and Southern have argued, France and Germany had a stronger tradition of cathedral schools than England, and of course many English cathedrals were staffed by monks, who were probably not very interested in educating secular clerics.[6] This lack, combined with ties to the continent due to the Norman Conquest, prompted many clerics to go or send younger relatives to various French schools in the generations following 1066.[7] Within England, it is true, schools began to emerge outside of monasteries at various places during the long twelfth century, increasing the ability of clerics to get more than a basic education nearer home. Already, in the 1120s or 1130s, the anonymous monk involved in a debate with Theobald of Étampes wrote of the latter having sixty or one hundred students at Oxford and of schoolmasters being scattered everywhere in England and other countries.[8] Later in our period, Alexander of Ashby wrote of the increase in number of learned masters teaching in England since his youth.[9] However, on the continent, large groups of teachers were already gathering at specific places like Paris and Bologna in the middle third of the twelfth century. Only towards the end of the period could Oxford and Cambridge even begin to compete with such centers.

As for wealth, I have also underscored the remarkable amount of money that flowed collectively and sometimes individually to the English secular clergy. Such income could provide for further education for incumbents. For instance, Gilbert Foliot wrote two letters asking the chapter of Hereford Cathedral to allow his nephews, in one case possibly Robert Banastre, to continue receiving income

---

[5] For overviews of education in England in this period, see Barlow, *English Church, 1066–1154*, 220–47; Bartlett, *England under the Norman and Angevin Kings*, 506–25; Nicholas Orme, *Medieval Schools: From Roman Britain to Renaissance England* (New Haven, 2006), 46–50, 189–217.

[6] Southern, *Medieval Humanism*, 162–4; Barrow, "Education and Recruitment," 120–6, 130–2. See also Matthew, *Britain and the Continent*, 60–3.

[7] Southern, *Medieval Humanism*, 164; Barlow, *English Church, 1066–1154*, 248–54.

[8] Foreville and Leclercq, "Un débat sur le sacerdoce," 65.

[9] Alexander of Ashby, "De Artificioso Modo Predicandi," 52–3.

from prebends while they were at the schools. As early as 1158, statutes of St. Martin-le-Grand treated time at the schools as an allowable reason for absenteeism, a practice that eventually became standard for just about any kind of benefice, including parish churches.[10] As universities coalesced, benefices were often provided to teachers to support them, and when Pope Lucius III urged St. Augustine's Canterbury to grant Honorius, possibly the specialist in canon law of that name, his father's church to sustain himself in the schools, he may have had such an arrangement in mind.[11] It is not clear where Honorius taught, but earlier on, in the early 1140s, the theologian Robert Pullen had become embroiled in a dispute with the bishop of Rochester for teaching at Paris while holding the post of archdeacon of Rochester and other English benefices, thus showing that English money could support teaching as well as study in continental centers.[12] The importance of education for those seeking lucrative benefices would also have encouraged both clerical and lay families to invest in education for their younger members.

As Barrow and R. N. Swanson have stressed, the mobility of money as well as people was crucial for the success of Paris, and the same could be said of other key centers of learning.[13] In Chapter 4 I emphasized the involvement of clerics in the commercial economy, and anecdotal evidence reveals that this extended to the credit market for scholars and students working abroad. For instance, Gerald of Wales borrowed money in Paris in anticipation of messengers bringing him income from his benefices, Master David of London complained several times of his debts in Bologna, and Gilbert Foliot referred in passing to the debts one of his nephews had acquired there as well.[14] During his great embassy to Paris in 1158, Thomas Becket not only entertained the masters and scholars at Paris but also the local creditors of the English students (*cives scholarium Angligenarum creditores*), suggesting that there was a fairly established practice of lending to foreign students there.[15] As Gerald's difficulties indicate, getting money from England was not always easy, but Southern noted various means of coping with these problems such as sending several younger scholars with an older one so that the group as a whole could survive on the remittances to each as they arrived.[16] Despite the difficulties, English secular clerics were clearly in a position to provide a substantial proportion of the wealth necessary to support the great centers of learning on the continent.

As for mobility, the ability of clerics to cross borders not just in their studies but even their careers in this period was remarkable. Of course, circulation between England and Normandy would have been particularly strong. For instance, the chapter of Bayeux had a number of canons named for specific villages, towns, or

---

[10] Gilbert Foliot, *Letters and Charters*, 260–2; Franklin, ed., *English Episcopal Acta 8*, 52–3.
[11] Holtzmann, ed., *Papsturkunden*, 1:510.   [12] Courtney, *Cardinal Robert Pullen*, 9–14.
[13] Barrow, "Education and Recruitment," 136; Swanson, *Twelfth-Century Renaissance*, 27.
[14] Gerald of Wales, *Opera*, 1:49; Liverani, ed., *Spicilegium Liberianum*, 603–4, 622–4, 626–8; Gilbert Foliot, *Letters and Charters*, 263.
[15] Robertson and Sheppard, eds., *Materials*, 3:32.
[16] Southern, *Scholastic Humanism*, 1:164–6.

counties in England.[17] However, many careers went beyond the Anglo-Norman sphere. Gerard la Pucelle taught at Paris and Cologne before returning to England to eventually become bishop of Coventry.[18] Gervase of Tilbury taught at Bologna, served in the courts of Henry II and the Young King, was a cleric of an archbishop of Rheims, entered the service of King William II of Sicily, and finally settled in Arles in the entourages of the archbishop of that city and of the emperor Otto, rising to a position of prominence.[19] The remarkable capacity of churchmen not only to function but to flourish throughout Catholic Europe is suggested by a list of some of the places where Englishmen (not all of them secular clerics, admittedly) became bishops or archbishops during the long twelfth century: Rouen and Poitou in the French dominions of the English kings; Lyons and Chartres in other parts of France; Lisbon in Iberia; Messina, Syracuse, and Compsa in the Norman kingdom of Sicily; perhaps Olomouc (Olmütz) in what is now the Czech Republic; Ribe and Bergen in Scandinavia; Tyre in the Holy Land; and Rome, where Pope Adrian IV was pope in the middle of the twelfth century.[20] The expansion of Catholic Europe seems to have created something analogous to the "aristocratic diaspora" described by Robert Bartlett, with clerics moving outward from core areas of Europe to its peripheries, but clearly English clerics could also achieve success within Europe's core areas.[21] If clerical careers could be so international, it is hardly surprising that clerics could also be quite mobile in seeking out places to study.

Together, these factors allowed English clerics to play a significant role in the formation of key continental intellectual centers, and above all at Paris, a center both for the liberal arts, as Geoffrey of Vinsauf wrote, and for theology.[22] Paris could become a dominant intellectual center precisely because it did not depend only on its immediate region but drew scholars like Abelard from the provinces and intellectuals like Peter Lombard from other parts of Europe. Just how important a role English scholars played can be seen from John Baldwin's findings that of the known masters teaching at Paris from 1179 to 1215, just over one third were English, including nine, or exactly one third, of the twenty-seven such masters who

[17] David Spear, *The Personnel of the Norman Cathedrals during the Ducal Period, 911–1204* (London, 2006), 61, 64, 72, 74, 77, 86.

[18] Kuttner and Rathbone, "Anglo-Norman Canonists," 296–303.

[19] Gervase, who married and became marshal of the imperial court, may not have ended his career as a cleric, but he certainly started as such: Gervase of Tilbury, *Otia Imperialia*, xxv–xxxiii.

[20] Cary J. Nederman, *John of Salisbury* (Tempe, 2005), 37–9; Charles Wendell David, ed., *De Expugnatione Lyxbonensi. The Conquest of Lisbon* (New York, 1936), 178–81; Haskins, *Mediaeval Science*, 187; Pixton, *German Episcopacy*, 205; Matthew, *Britain and the Continent*, 98; Jean Dunbabin, "Canterbury, John of (c.1120–1204?)," *Oxford Dictionary of National Biography*, Oxford University Press, 2004 [http://www.oxforddnb.com/view/article/2062, accessed 23 Nov 2013, subscription required]; Ralph V. Turner, "Coutances, Walter de (d. 1207)," *Oxford Dictionary of National Biography*, Oxford University Press, 2004 [http://www.oxforddnb.com/view/article/6467, accessed 23 Nov 2013; subscription required]; Orderic Vitalis, *Ecclesiastical History*, 6:128–9; Brenda Bolton and Anne Duggan, eds., *Adrian IV, the English Pope, 1154–1159: Studies and Texts* (Aldershot, 2003).

[21] Robert Bartlett, *The Making of Europe: Conquest, Colonization and Cultural Change 950–1350* (Princeton, 1993), 24–59.

[22] For the rise of Paris, see Southern, *Scholastic Humanism*, 1:198–233; Ferruolo, *Origins of the University*, 11–26.

left writings. English masters in that period outnumbered those from the French royal demesne and fell not far short of the total number from France as a whole.[23] Strikingly, the important university statutes of 1215 were promulgated by Robert de Courson, an English cardinal and former Parisian master.[24] Individual English students were less likely to appear in the records than masters, but chance references survive in various sources. For instance, one English student in Paris wrote partisan notes in English in the margins of one of his texts about events in Philip Augustus's war on Richard I.[25] Jordan Fantasma or Fantosme, later a cleric of the bishop of Winchester, even appears in an illuminated manuscript as a pupil of Gilbert de la Porrée (see Plate 1).[26] Numbers or percentages are hard to come by, but the anecdote about Thomas Becket hosting the creditors of English students suggests such students were already fairly numerous by 1158. When Nigel of Whiteacre wrote his *Speculum Stultorum* in the late twelfth century, English scholars formed a distinct group at the university, and they became numerous enough that when the nation system was founded at the university over the course of the first half of the thirteenth century, the English nation, which included Germans and Scandinavians, became one of four nations there.[27]

Although England produced no scholars at Paris as important as Peter Abelard or Peter Lombard, some English masters were quite influential. Adam of Balsham, also known as Adam of Petit Pont from the location where he taught in Paris, wrote a new textbook on logic in 1132. Though the long-term influence of this textbook was limited, Adam was important enough in the short term to found a school which lasted several generations, and Southern called him the central Parisian logician of his time.[28] Indeed, he was almost certainly the Magister Adam who was depicted along with Socrates, Plato, and Aristotle surrounding "Lady Dialectic" in a manuscript made in Paris in the 1140s, now in Germany (see Plate 2), which indicates a remarkably high standing among contemporaries.[29] Marcia Colish describes the

[23] Baldwin, "Masters at Paris," 149–50.

[24] For discussion of these statutes, see Stephen C. Ferruolo, "The Paris Statutes of 1215 Reconsidered," *History of Universities* 5 (1985), 1–14.

[25] N. R. Ker, *Catalogue of Manuscripts Containing Anglo-Saxon* (Oxford, 1957), 331; British Library, Royal MS 10 C V, fos. 18r, 74v.

[26] For a discussion of English students as well as masters at Paris, see Astrik L. Gabriel, *Garlandia. Studies in the History of the Mediaeval University* (Frankfurt, 1969), 1–37. For Jordan Fantosme, who may have studied with Gilbert at Poitiers rather than Paris, see Jordan Fantosme, *Chronicle*, xi–xiii; Iain MacDonald, "The Chronicle of Jordan Fantosme," *Studies in Medieval French Presented to Alfred Ewert* (Oxford, 1961), 242–58, at 247–54. For German students and scholars at Paris, to serve as a comparison, see Joachim Ehlers, "Deutsche Scholaren in Frankreich wärend des 12. Jarhhunderts," in Johannes Fried, ed., *Schulen und Studium im sozialen Wandel des hohen und späten Mittelalters* (Sigmaringen, 1986), 97–120.

[27] Nigel of Whiteacre, *Speculum Stultorum*, 64–5; Gabriel, *Garlandia*, 1, 25–6; Pearl Kibre, *The Nations in the Mediaeval Universities* (Cambridge, Mass., 1948), 16–18.

[28] Southern, *Scholastic Humanism*, 1:216.

[29] L. Minio-Paluello, "The *Ars Disserendi* of Adam of Balsham 'Parvipontanus'," *Mediaeval and Renaissance Studies* 3 (1954), 116–69; L. Minio-Paluello, ed., *Twelfth Century Logic; Texts and Studies. Vol. 1. Adam Balsamiensis Parvipontani Ars Disserendi* (Rome, 1956); Matthew, *Britain and the Continent*, 62–3; Erich Zimmermann and Kurt H. Staub, *Buchkunst des Mittelalters: Zimelien der Hessischen Landes- und Hochschulbibliothek Darmstadt* (Wiesbaden, 1980), 30–1.

English theologians Robert Pullen and Robert of Melun as two of Peter Lombard's chief competitors in systematizing theology. Their long-term significance could hardly compare to his, but they too were influential in the period.[30] John Baldwin has shown the impact in moral theology of the circle of the Parisian master Peter the Chanter. Among the important members of this group were Stephen Langton, Thomas of Chobham, Gerald of Wales, and Robert de Courson, all of whom were from England or were closely associated with that country.[31] Langton was, of course, a particularly important theologian in his own right.[32] The schools of Paris would not only have been much smaller but also far less productive without the participation of secular clerics from England.

English clerics were also an important presence at Bologna, the key European center for the study of law. Though there were probably fewer English students in Bologna than in Paris, there is plenty of anecdotal evidence for English clerics studying there, including very influential ones such as Thomas Becket. Not long after he was made a saint, an altar was dedicated to him in a church in Bologna, and though this may be a sign of his international fame, it probably also resulted from the number of English scholars in that city, for it attracted many donations from English figures, including Master William of London, who left a number of books at his death in 1187, and William Anglicus, who left money when he died in 1211.[33] Teaching by English masters at Bologna began later than in Paris, but in the 1190s Richard de Morins, also known as Richard Anglicus, moved from Paris to Bologna, where he became a prominent master before returning to England for a second career as a regular canon at Dunstable. Richard composed a number of works on canon law, including commentaries on Gratian and on more recent papal decretals. In 1203, Gilbert Anglicus made an intermediate collection of decretals, albeit in Pisa rather than Bologna, and Alan Anglicus made another soon thereafter, as well as composing various works of commentary. The collections of Gilbert and Alan were two of the important intermediate collections of decretals that lay behind the official compilation of 1234.[34]

---

[30] Marcia L. Colish, *Peter Lombard*, 2 vols. (Leiden, 1994), 1:65, 68–77. See also Courtney, *Cardinal Robert Pullen*, 55–280; Smalley, *Becket Conflict*, 39–58; D. E. Luscombe, *The School of Peter Abelard: The Influence of Abelard's Thought in the Early Scholastic Period* (Cambridge, 1969), 281–98.

[31] Baldwin, *Masters, Princes, and Merchants*, 1:19–31, 34–6, 41–3.

[32] Beryl Smalley, *The Study of the Bible in the Middle Ages* (Oxford, 1952), 196–200, 205–28, 233–8, 241–2, 249–63; F. M. Powicke, *Stephen Langton* (Oxford, 1928), 34–8, 62–74; Louis J. Bataillon et al., eds., *Étienne Langton: prédicateur, bibliste, théologien* (Turnhout, 2010).

[33] Robertson and Sheppard, eds., *Materials*, 3:17; A. Allaria, "English Scholars at Bologna during the Middle Ages," *Dublin Review* 112 (1893), 66–83.

[34] Kenneth Pennington, "The Decretalists 1190–1234," in Wilfried Hartmann and Kenneth Pennington, eds., *The History of Medieval Canon Law in the Classical Period, 1140–1234: From Gratian to the Decretals of Pope Gregory IX* (Washington, D.C., 2008), 211–45, at 215–16, 219–21; Kenneth Pennington, "Decretal Collections 1190–1234," in Wilfried Hartmann and Kenneth Pennington, eds., *The History of Medieval Canon Law in the Classical Period, 1140–1234: From Gratian to the Decretals of Pope Gregory IX* (Washington, D.C., 2008), 293–317 at 304–6; Robert C. Figueira, "Ricardus de Mores and his *Casus Decretalium*: The Birth of a Canonistic Genre," in Stanley Chodorow, ed., *Proceedings of the Eighth International Congress of Medieval Canon Law* (Vatican City, 1992), 169–87, at 169–71.

What is striking about Bologna, however, is that England was not just providing people (and money) for the schools there, but also what one might call intellectual raw material. A disproportionate percentage of the papal decretals that ended up in canon law came from England, and Charles Duggan has shown that this was because several of the important primitive decretal collections were made in England, whence they traveled to Bologna where they were incorporated into the intermediate collections and ultimately into canon law.[35] Equally strikingly, Jane Sayers has shown that formularies on canon law procedure, perhaps originally created in England for the use of judges delegate, can be found copied in Italy.[36] Here we see intellectual material flowing out from England as well as into it, and this underscores the strong symbiotic relationship between the intellectual centers and the areas from which they recruited. England and other regions depended on Bologna for the development of canon law, but Bologna depended on input from these regions as well, and could not have achieved anything like the same level of importance drawing only on its own region or even Italy as a whole.

For Salerno, the evidence of English clerical participation is generally more circumstantial. Salerno was one of the places (along with Montpellier) where John of Salisbury and Alexander of Neckam imagined people going to study medicine, and there is plenty of evidence of travel between England and the Norman kingdom of Sicily.[37] However, few English secular clerics can be placed in Salerno itself and fewer still can be shown teaching or studying there. Gervase of Tilbury mentions being in Salerno at one point, though there is no evidence he studied there.[38] Peter of Blois spent time convalescing in the household of the archbishop of Salerno, where perhaps he picked up some medical learning, since he later wrote about treating his own ague.[39] Sometime before 1183, a secular cleric named Master Matthew, who was from Cambridge but who had studied medicine at Salerno, vowed to join St. Albans along with two learned relatives and two "associates and students." One of the latter was named Robert of Salerno, and it is possible that the entire group had studied there.[40] Though the direct evidence for English scholars at Salerno is limited, the indirect evidence of ties between England and Salerno is strong. Monica Green has shown how important England was, along with Normandy and other parts of northern France, in the twelfth-century reception of Salernitan medical writing. Indeed, one treatise associated with the celebrated Salernitan woman physician, Trota, has English vernacular words in it, suggesting that an English speaker was involved in the composition of the

---

[35] Charles Duggan, *Twelfth-Century Decretal Collections and their Importance in English History* (London, 1963), 66–117; Charles Duggan, "Decretal Collections from Gratian's *Decretum* to the *Compilationes Antiquae*: The Making of the New Case Law," in Wilfried Hartmann and Kenneth Pennington, eds., *The History of Medieval Canon Law in the Classical Period, 1140–1234: From Gratian to the Decretals of Pope Gregory IX* (Washington, D.C., 2008), 246–92.

[36] Sayers, *Papal Judges Delegate*, 47–54.

[37] John of Salisbury, *Ioannis Saresberiensis Metalogicon*, ed. J. B. Hall and K. S. B. Keats-Rohan (Turnhout, 1991), 18; Alexander Neckam, *De Naturis Rerum*, 311.

[38] Gervase of Tilbury, *Otia Imperialia*, 578–9.   [39] Cotts, *Clerical Dilemma*, 28.

[40] Thomas Walsingham, *Gesta Abbatum*, 1:194–6.

text or intervened at a very early stage in its transmission.[41] The English compilation of *c.*1200 that discussed the sexual desires and capacities of Hugh de Mapenor and other English clerics, and that probably had some connection with Hereford Cathedral, drew heavily on Salernitan material.[42] Overall, it seems clear that England had the same sort of symbiotic relationship with Salerno as it did with Paris and Bologna.

With Toledo (and its region), the direct evidence for the participation of English clerics is stronger. Toledo was important primarily as the chief center for the translation of Arabic material into Latin. As Haskins first made clear, English clerics played an important and indeed disproportionate role in that transmission from the time of Adelard of Bath, early in the twelfth century, though admittedly not always at Toledo itself.[43] More recently, Charles Burnett and others have shed extensive light on this subject.[44] Much of this work was scientific, proto-scientific, or magical in nature, and Southern himself viewed science as one of England's few strengths.[45] England does seem to have been unusually receptive to such material, but the role of English clerics in the transmission of science and magic shows important similarities to the general participation of English clerics in the transnational intellectual life of the time. English scholars often went abroad to international centers of learning and cooperated with scholars from all around Europe. Of course, for translation from Arabic, cooperation had to extend beyond the normal cultural boundaries of Catholic Europe to include Jews, Jewish converts to Christianity, Mozarabic Christians, and perhaps Muslims, all steeped in Arabic culture. This cooperation across religious boundaries has deservedly received much attention, but it is nonetheless also worth stressing the cooperation of English clerics with clerics from other parts of Europe. Gerard of Cremona, an Italian translator in Toledo, started systematically translating Aristotelian or pseudo-Aristotelian texts that had been identified by the Muslim scholar al-Farabi as key works. Where Gerard left off, presumably at his death, Alfred of Shareshill took up, suggesting a link between them.[46] Two Englishmen, one of whom was possibly William of Stafford, archdeacon of Madrid, commissioned an account of differences among astronomical tables from Master John Hispanus.[47] One of the most

---

[41] Monica Green, "Rethinking the Manuscript Basis of Salvatore de Renzi's *Collectio Salernitana*. The Corpus of Medical Writings in the 'Long' Twelfth Century," in Danielle Jacquart and Agostino Paravicini Bagliani, eds., *La* Collectio Salernitana *di Salvatore de Renzi* (Florence, 2008), 15–60; Monica H. Green, ed., *The Trotula: A Medieval Compendium of Women's Medicine* (Philadelphia, 2001), 50.

[42] Lawn, ed., *Prose Salernitan Questions*, xv–xvii.

[43] Haskins, *Mediaeval Science*, 20–42, 45–9, 113–29.

[44] See particularly Charles Burnett, *The Introduction of Arabic Learning into England* (London, 1997). For ways in which Toledo differed from other European schools, see Charles Burnett, "The Institutional Context of Arabic–Latin Translations of the Middle Ages: A Reassessment of the 'School of Toledo'," in Olga Weijers, ed., *Vocabulary of Teaching and Research Between Middle Ages and Renaissance* (Turnhout, 1995), 214–35.

[45] Southern, *Medieval Humanism*, 164–71.

[46] Burnett, *Introduction of Arabic Learning*, 71–2; James K. Otte, "The Life and Writings of Alfredus Anglicus," *Viator* 3 (1972), 275–91, at 283–5.

[47] Charles Burnett, "Communities of Learning in Twelfth-Century Toledo," in Constant J. Mews and John N. Crossley, eds., *Communities of Learning: Networks and the Shaping of Intellectual Identity in Europe, 1100–1500* (Turnhout, 2011), 9–18, at 15.

important English translators, Robert of Ketton, worked intimately with Hermann of Carinthia, also known as Hermann of Dalmatia or Hermann the Slav, who came from the other end of Catholic Europe. At one point they worked with the Leonese translator, Hugh de Santalla, to bring parts of the Arabic hermetic tradition into Latin. They were also part of a team assembled by Peter the Venerable to translate Muslim religious texts for the purposes of refutation.[48] As in Paris, Bologna, and Salerno, English clerics played an important role at a center of learning where scholars from all over Europe come together to create a critical mass in the investigation of one or more subjects, thereby revolutionizing European learning.

How did the frequent travel of English clerics to study and work in European intellectual centers affect scholarly life in England? It is arguable that England suffered something of a "brain drain" during the period. For instance, Adam of Balsham ended up a canon at Notre-Dame de Paris, Robert Pullen was made papal chancellor and a cardinal, and Robert of Ketton became archdeacon of Pamplona. Nonetheless, many more scholars returned to England. Often enough, they returned with books of newly developed or translated learning: for instance, Daniel of Morley, who traveled to Toledo in search of Arabic learning, emphasized the books he had brought back in the preface to his treatise on the natural world.[49] Moreover, the permanent departure of some English scholars was offset by the immigration of continental scholars educated in these and other centers to England. Peter of Blois, who was born in the region of Blois to a Breton father, studied at Chartres, Tours, Bologna, and Paris, and worked in the Norman kingdom of Sicily and Normandy before coming to England, is a noteworthy example.[50] Similarly, the Lombard scholar Master Vacarius, who bridged the study of Roman and canon law and also wrote on theological matters, was recruited into the household of Archbishop Theobald. He settled in England, became a canon at the collegiate church of Southwell, and founded a school of legal scholars called the *pauperistas* after his most important legal text, the *Liber Pauperum*.[51] Despite the permanent loss of some important thinkers, intellectual life in England benefited enormously from interaction with the continental schools.

For most of the period, scholars coming or returning from abroad would have dispersed into the households of the powerful or ended up with prebends in cathedral churches or collegiate churches rather than creating centers of learning comparable to the ones on the continent, though it must be noted that those centers did not develop until well into the twelfth century. This pattern created or

---

[48] Thomas E. Burman, *Reading the Qur'ān in Latin Christendom, 1140–1560* (Philadelphia, 2007), 15–16; Charles Burnett, "The Establishment of Medieval Hermeticism," in Peter Linehan and Janet L. Nelson, eds., *The Medieval World* (London, 2001), 111–30, at 114–24.

[49] Gregor Maurach, "Daniel von Morley 'Philosophia'," *Mittellateinisches Jahrbuch* 14 (1979), 204–55, at 212; Burnett, *Introduction of Arabic Learning*, 61–9.

[50] Cotts, *Clerical Dilemma*, 17–48.

[51] Southern, *Scholastic Humanism*, 2:155–66; Leonard Boyle, "The Beginnings of Legal Studies at Oxford," *Viator* 14 (1983), 107–31, at 114–30; Taliadoros, *Law and Theology*, 25–53; Vacarius, *The Liber Pauperum of Vacarius*, ed. Francis de Zulueta, Publications of the Selden Society, vol. 44 (London, 1927); Francis de Zulueta and Peter Stein, eds., *The Teaching of Roman Law in England around 1200*, Selden Society supplementary series, 8 (London, 1990).

strengthened many small, informal centers of learning. The royal court famously attracted some of the greatest scholars in England, including John of Salisbury, Peter of Blois, and Gerald of Wales. Herbert of Bosham emphasized the number of *eruditi* in Thomas Becket's retinue and other prelates, such as Hubert Walter or Richard fitz Nigel, attracted a number of educated churchmen in their trains.[52] Such cathedrals as Salisbury, Lincoln, and Hereford could also become moderately important centers of learning.[53] Such local centers certainly had their importance. For one thing, the scattering of scholars and the rise of many small intellectual circles would have fostered the dissemination of knowledge throughout England. Moreover, the presence of scholars in influential households was essential to the kind of interaction between learned clerics and laypeople discussed in Chapters 4 and 6. Nonetheless, small and, in the case of households, peripatetic centers of learning could not achieve the scholarly critical mass that made places like Paris, Bologna, Salerno, and Toledo so intellectually important.

Towards the end of the period, however, English clerics took the university model that was evolving in Paris and Bologna and replicated it in their own land, at Oxford and Cambridge. The early history of these institutions has been extensively studied, so only a brief review of their origins is needed here.[54] The early history of the schools at Oxford is obscure, but by the 1190s, and probably before, it had emerged as the pre-eminent center for learning in England. Like the universities at Bologna and Paris it was not founded, but rather coalesced. Nonetheless the influence on its development of the continental centers, particularly Paris, is clear. Cambridge then spun off from Oxford in the early thirteenth century. Though neither university approached the size of Paris or Bologna, they neverthe-less acquired the necessary critical mass of scholars to attract students, sustain themselves over the long term, and slowly transform into stable, established

---

[52] Robertson and Sheppard, eds., *Materials*, 3:206–7, 237, 523–31; Barlow, *Thomas Becket*, 77–9; Cheney, *English Bishops' Chanceries*, 12–19; Smith, ed., *English Episcopal Acta 1*, xlv; Cheney and Jones, eds., *English Episcopal Acta 2*, xxvii–xxviii; Johnson, ed., *English Episcopal Acta 26*, liv–lv; Lovatt, ed., *English Episcopal Acta 27*, cvii–cviii.

[53] Webber, *Scribes and Scholars*, 82–112; Thomson, *Books and Learning*, 44; Xenia Muratova, "Bestiaries: An Aspect of Medieval Patronage," in Sarah Macready and F. H. Thompson, eds., *Art and Patronage in the English Romanesque* (London, 1986), 118–44; Frans van Liere, "The Study of Canon Law and the Eclipse of the Lincoln Schools, 1172–1225," *History of Universities* 18 (2003), 1–13; Charles Burnett, "Mathematics and Astronomy in Hereford and its Region in the Twelfth Century," in David Whitehead, ed., *Medieval Art, Architecture, and Archaeology at Hereford* ([London], 1995), 50–9. For contemporary praise of learning at Hereford, see Gerald of Wales, *Opera*, 1:382–4; R. W. Hunt, "English Learning in the Late Twelfth Century," *Transactions of the Royal Historical Society* 4th ser., 19 (1936), 19–42, at 36–7.

[54] For the early development of Oxford University, see R. W. Southern, "From Schools to University," in J. I. Catto, ed., *The History of the University of Oxford. Vol. 1. The Early Oxford Schools* (Oxford, 1984), 1–36; M. B. Hackett, "The University as a Corporate Body," in J. I. Catto, ed., *The History of the University of Oxford. Vol. 1. The Early Oxford Schools* (Oxford, 1984), 37–95. For recent arguments (in a long debate) that would push Oxford's rise back to an earlier date, see Rodney M. Thomson, "Serlo of Wilton and the Schools of Oxford," *Medium Aevum* 68 (1999), 1–12. For the early history of Cambridge University, see Damian Riehl Leader, *A History of the University of Cambridge: Volume 1, The University to 1546*, ed. C. N. L. Brooke (Cambridge, 1988), 16–44. Quite recently, Nicholas Karn has questioned the traditional accounts of the founding of Cambridge: Karn, ed., *English Episcopal Acta 42*, lx–lxxi.

institutions. Though it would be a long time before Oxford and Cambridge had anything like the influence of Paris or Bologna, they emerged long before universities in many parts of Europe, suggesting the relative strength of intellectual life in England. Even if their beginnings were modest, the long-term importance of these two institutions, both created by secular clerics, goes without saying.

2. ENGLAND AND THE TWELFTH-CENTURY RENAISSANCE

Having discussed English clerics and European intellectual centers, it is worth returning to Southern's unflattering characterization of England's place in the Twelfth-Century Renaissance. Southern did see some bright spots (historical writing, intellectual contributions to government, interest in wonders, and, as noted earlier, science), and at the end of his major piece on the subject backed off slightly from his initial claims. Nonetheless, he was firm in stressing England's dependence on France and the derivative nature of its culture, a view most neatly stated in his description of it as a colony of the French intellectual empire. Southern's picture, though exaggerated, has merit, particularly for the late eleventh and early twelfth centuries. Intellectual and cultural influence did tend to flow more from France to England than the reverse, partly as a result of the Norman Conquest. During the post-Conquest period, an elite drawn from northern France transformed England in various ways, introducing its own culture and taking northern French models to guide it in confronting changes that were affecting all of Europe. The tendency of powerful secular clerics, many from Norman families, to study on the continent only reinforced this pattern, and at first glance the importance of Paris to English intellectual life simply seems to provide more evidence of English cultural and intellectual dependence on France.

 Yet the parallels between English clerical participation in the schools of Paris and English involvement in centers of learning outside of France suggest that, at least from the middle of the twelfth century, England must be seen in a European context rather than simply as a cultural appendage of France. Indeed, even when attending the Parisian schools, English clerics were involved as much in an international endeavor as in a French one. Walter Map studied there under the Englishman, Gerard la Pucelle, with a cleric named Lucas who later became archbishop of Esztergom in Hungary.[55] When William of Tyre, a student from the Kingdom of Jerusalem, studied in Paris, his teachers included the English masters Robert of Melun and Adam of Balsham, and also Robert Amiclas, a noted master who later retired to an English monastery and was therefore probably English too.[56] Southern argued that John of Salisbury should be viewed primarily as a product of the French intellectual scene, and therefore as an example of French

---

[55] Walter Map, *De Nugis Curialium*, 142–5.
[56] Southern, *Scholastic Humanism*, 1:213; Rodney M. Thomson, "Robert Amiclas: A Twelfth-Century Parisian Master and his Books." In *England and the Twelfth-Century Renaissance* (Aldershot, 1998), 238–43.

rather than English intellectual prowess. John did study at Paris with many French masters, but three of his formal or informal teachers, Robert Pullen, Robert of Melun, and Adam of Balsham, were from England, and another was German.[57] Did John receive a French education or a cosmopolitan and international Parisian one? In any case it was obviously not the allure of French culture that drew English clerics to Bologna, Salerno, and Toledo.

In discussing the participation of the English secular clergy in European intellectual life, particularly from the middle decades of the twelfth century on, a different model might be useful. For Southern's anachronistic political model of English colony and French metropole I would substitute an equally anachronistic economic model of Catholic Europe as an intellectual free trade zone with personnel and resources flowing from place to place and with certain centers of particularly intensive activity emerging as a result. Instead of being envisioned as a colony in this model, England could be imagined as an important hinterland that provided resources to several continental centers of intellectual and cultural development. This was a relationship less like that of colonial India or Jamaica to imperial Britain and more like that of various contemporary countries and regions to Silicon Valley. England, however, was probably a particularly important hinterland for the continental centers of learning because of the wealth and number of its clerics, and it was one of the first hinterlands to duplicate the existing models through the formation of its own universities. This model would suggest that England and particularly its clergy had a more important role in the Twelfth-Century Renaissance than indicated by Southern's depiction of the country as a backward colony. However, this model is useful not just for evaluating England's place in the Twelfth-Century Renaissance, but also for looking at the role of clerics from regions throughout Europe in the rise of important intellectual centers and therefore in the scholarly transformations of the period. Admittedly, the role of clerics from different regions varied. For instance, Barrow has shown some specific reasons why German secular clerics were less likely to participate in the international schools than were their counterparts in France and England.[58] Nonetheless, the mobility and wealth of secular clerics made these centers of learning possible, and clerics from throughout Europe participated.

3. THE PROLIFERATION OF INTELLECTUALS AMONG THE SECULAR CLERGY

Before leaving Southern's discussion of England's place in the Twelfth-Century Renaissance, it is worth noting one of his other arguments. To demonstrate

---

[57] John of Salisbury, *Metalogicon*, 70–3.
[58] Barrow, "Education and Recruitment," 126–9, 131–7. Thomson builds on this, to show a variety of ways in which the Twelfth-Century Renaissance was somewhat different in Germany: Rodney M. Thomson, "The Place of Germany in the Twelfth-Century Renaissance," in Alison I. Beach, ed., *Manuscripts and Monastic Culture: Reform and Renewal in Twelfth-Century Germany* (Turnhout, 2007), 19–42.

England's provincial and derivative culture, he compiled a list of what one might call the intellectual giants of Europe in the twelfth century, among whom the only English figure was the French-educated John of Salisbury.[59] Southern must be allowed his point about the absence of such figures from England. Different scholars would come up with different lists of the leading fifteen or twenty intellectuals of the twelfth century, but it is hard to imagine one in which scholars from England would play a substantial role. Yet to focus simply on the intellectual giants in a discussion of broad intellectual shifts, let alone cultural ones, is dangerously close to a romantic vision of progress through the work of lone, towering geniuses, and therefore seems to me too limited. Jean Leclercq, writing of monks, stated: "Monastic culture is the culture of a milieu; it is not merely the privilege of a few great minds. The life of a milieu depends on its elite; but without it, an elite could not exist."[60] The same view could be extended to intellectual and cultural life more broadly. There can be no question that a figure like Abelard mattered tremendously through sheer intellect, or that the work of an individual like Peter Lombard could have a huge influence over a society, but neither of these figures should be seen in isolation. At the very least they needed to have students and readers who could understand and disseminate their ideas; otherwise, their influence would have been negligible. Moreover, quantitative difference can lead to qualitative difference, and many of the greatest intellectual achievements of the day were helped along by the more mundane activities of ordinary intellectuals.

A brief discussion of some of the work of clerical intellectuals of middling or minor importance can illustrate this point and also begin the process of showing the increasing intellectual dynamism of the secular clergy. One subject of great interest to scholars in recent decades is the fraught but sometimes fruitful interchange between religions and cultures in the Middle Ages, and a discussion of three "second-tier" scholars can show English involvement in this cultural arena. Robert of Ketton is hardly a household name, even to medievalists, but among his works was the earliest translation of the Qur'an into Latin, which has recently been investigated by Thomas Burman. Robert's translation has often been criticized, with some justification, but the pioneering nature of his effort needs to be stressed, and it is hardly surprising that his work had flaws. Moreover, Burman has revealed some surprising strengths of Robert's work. For instance, Robert's departures from literal translation, which have attracted some of the criticism, often derived from his incorporation of Arabic exegetical tradition, indicating his deep immersion in Arabic learning.[61] Herbert of Bosham, subject of the previously cited monograph by Deborah Goodwin, was another writer who tackled linguistic and religious barriers, in his case with Hebrew and Judaism, in the search for useful learning. Herbert was the author of an important *vita* of his patron Thomas Becket and a student of Peter

---

[59] Southern, *Medieval Humanism*, 158–9. For a recent overview of John and his work, see Nederman, *John of Salisbury*.

[60] Jean Leclercq, *The Love of Learning and the Desire for God: A Study of Monastic Culture* (New York, 1961), 309.

[61] Burman, *Reading the Qur'ān*, 7, 9, 13–17, 26–40, 43–4, 46–7, 49–52, 57–87.

Lombard who sought to produce an improved version of his master's glosses, but he was also a pioneer in reviving the use of Hebrew among Christians as a tool of Bible study. Working with Jewish scholars, he even drew on Jewish exegesis by commentators such as Rashi, though of course he reacted strongly against the thinking of such figures when it was directed against Christian teachings.[62] Gerald of Wales was a versatile intellectual who worked in a variety of genres, including autobiography, moral theology, hagiography, satire, invective, letter writing, poetry, history, cosmography, and advice to princes. His most innovative work, however, was his study of Welsh and Irish culture and geography, what Robert Bartlett has described as his "ethnographic achievement." Gerald's ethnographic studies had roots in the work of classical geographers and historians, and had some rough parallels in his own time, but was nonetheless quite unusual for the period.[63] None of these individuals were among the leading European intellectuals of their time, but their work was innovative and important, and crossed cultural boundaries in fascinating ways.

Peter of Waltham was a far less important intellectual. His only surviving work is a series of moral extracts from Gregory the Great, not the kind of original composition modern scholars admire. Yet seventeen manuscripts survive. One of the more important, if mundane, efforts of the Twelfth-Century Renaissance was to reorganize existing knowledge in ways that made it more accessible and useful to contemporary intellectuals, and Peter's work obviously filled a perceived need.[64] As noted in Chapter 4, Peter was also the owner of a copy of the late Roman agricultural treatise of Palladius, and in the same manuscript he had Cetius Faventinus's *De Diversis Architectonicae Fabricis*, a world chronicle, a fragment of the *Gesta Normannorum Ducum*, and Vigilius of Thapsus's *Contra Arrianos*.[65] From a modern perspective, Peter's reading was more interesting than his writing: he provides a good example of twelfth-century engagement with classical works, in his case some unusual ones. As I suggested in Chapter 4, Peter may also have been involved in the systematic thinking about estate management characteristic of the period. Many more intellectuals left no surviving writings and probably most never wrote anything more than ephemera; their intellectual work might have consisted of such activities as teaching, administration, or the practice of medicine and law. The *Liber Eliensis* contains a letter, composed in ornate Latin and containing learned references to cosmology, various religious texts, and a Greek term for God, written by a Master Ralph about a miracle. This chance survival suggests a

---

[62] Goodwin, *Take Hold of the Robe of a Jew*; Smalley, *Study of the Bible*, 186–95; Staunton, *Thomas Becket and his Biographers*, 63–74.

[63] Gerald of Wales, *Opera*. Gerald's works on Ireland and Wales are in volumes 5 and 6. See also Gerald of Wales, *Expugnatio Hibernica*. For recent work on Gerald as an intellectual, and particularly for his work on Ireland and Wales, see Bartlett, *Gerald of Wales*, 103–210; Richter, *Giraldus Cambrensis*, 66–86.

[64] Peter of Waltham, *Remediarium Conversorum: A Synthesis in Latin of Moralia in Job by Gregory the Great*, ed. Joseph Gildea (Villanova, 1984).

[65] Bodleian Library, Rawlinson MS G 62; Elisabeth M. C. van Houts, ed., *The Gesta Normannorum Ducum of William of Jumièges, Orderic Vitalis, and Robert of Torigni*, 2 vols. (Oxford, 1992–5), 1:xcviii–xcix.

deeply learned man about whom we would know nothing otherwise.[66] The individual contributions to the great intellectual developments of the day by figures such as Peter of Waltham and Master Ralph were minor. Cumulatively, however, the work of such figures to these intellectual developments was crucial. Indeed, even a figure like Robert Banastre played his role; if nothing else, the money expended on his studies helped fund the schools of Bologna.

The growing impact of ordinary intellectuals among the secular clergy depended heavily on their increasing numbers, and though the number of clerical intellectuals is hard to measure, one can get a rough idea of the number of *magistri* by the last decades of the period. Unfortunately, it is not certain what entitled individuals to take the title of *magister* before a defined system of taking degrees emerged, but it obviously involved some claim to distinction in learning that could be measured, even if only informally, since many important clerics chose not to assume the title. In other words, it was not merely a courtesy title such as *dominus* later became for important clerics. By the end of the period, it may already have signaled recognition of the completion of a course of higher studies.[67] The term *magister* was also beginning to be used for craft masters, which can lead to confusion, but scribes generally seem to have been reluctant to use the term for figures other than clerics in our period. Urban charters abound with important figures in various trades who almost never receive the title. Indeed, in one charter of a grant by a mason to Oseney Abbey, though the donor had had himself described as a *magister* on his seal, the scribe gave him no such title.[68] Overall, I have found fewer than a dozen craft masters with the title outside of royal records. The compilers of royal records in John's reign seem to have been somewhat more willing to give the title to laypeople, particularly military specialists, but even here the number of lay *magistri* is fairly limited.

In the course of my research, I have accumulated the names of as many distinctly identifiable *magistri* as I can find who appear in the reigns of Richard and John (1189–1216) in narrative sources, charters, and the royal records. Practical problems abound in this endeavor. Even for the best of editors, the dating of undated charters is often not very precise, and generally one can only supply ranges of dates. I have drawn only on documents whose dates are described as falling fully within the two reigns, thus discarding some *magistri* who probably flourished during the period, though perhaps also including some from misdated documents. *Magistri* sometimes appear with just a forename, and it is impossible to tell, for instance, how many different individuals various references to "Magister William" involve, and how many were men who were identified more fully elsewhere. I have therefore

---

[66] Blake, ed., *Liber Eliensis*, 270–4.

[67] For some brief discussions of the term, see Cheney, *Roger, Bishop of Worcester*, 102–3; Barrow, "Education and Recruitment," 118; Clanchy, *Abelard*, 65–7; Lovatt, ed., *English Episcopal Acta 27*, cvii. For the quite different use of the Anglo-Norman *mestre* for secular mentors of heroes in romances, see Judith Weiss, "*Mestre* and Son: The Role of Sabaoth and Terri in *Boeve de Haumtone*," in Jennifer Fellows and Ivana Djordjević, eds., *Sir Bevis of Hampton in Literary Tradition* (Woodbridge, 2008), 25–36.

[68] Salter, ed., *Cartulary of Oseney Abbey*, 2:276.

not counted such figures unless they had unusually distinctive forenames. Individuals sometimes used more than one byname in the period, which may sometimes have resulted in counting a single individual as two. Though by 1189 scribes had become more consistent than earlier in identifying *magistri* by their titles, they were never entirely consistent, which may lead to missing out some individuals. Some *magistri* were regular clerics, and though I have avoided including them when their monastic status is known, I have undoubtedly included some because their status is not clear from the sources. However, monastic *magistri* usually appeared only in the relatively rare surviving documents issued by, rather than for, religious houses, and their numbers seem to have been surprisingly low.[69] Though I have searched broadly in the published records and in some unpublished cartularies, I have by no means made a complete search, and given the number of *magistri* who appear in only one or two sources, it is likely that many others appear in texts and documents that I did not search or that have not survived. Overall, despite some likely instances of over-counting, my figures are likely to fall well short of the actual number of *magistri* that existed, though certainly not by orders of magnitude.

I have found approximately 550 *magistri* in the period who can clearly be identified as clerics because of titles, the holding of benefices, or other relevant information. In addition, I have found over 400 who cannot be certainly identified as clerics, regulars, or laypeople. The vast majority of these probably *were* clerics, given the reluctance to use the title for the laity and the contexts in which many of their names are found, such as the witness lists to episcopal acta.[70] Even though at least some would have been laypeople or monks, the reasons to believe that the overall count is an underestimate indicate that there were almost certainly over a thousand clerical *magistri* (and probably some hundreds more) established in England during the reigns of Richard and John.

The rise of a large number of *magistri* around 1200 was simply one aspect of the massive expansion of intellectual activity by the secular clergy in England in the long twelfth century. Intellectual life in Anglo-Saxon England had been dominated by the regular clergy, even more so than was the case in other lands, where cathedrals staffed by secular clerics could be important centers of learning. Some evidence does survive of intellectual activity by non-monastic clergy in the late Anglo-Saxon period, such as historical writings from the clerics of Durham (who were only replaced by monks after the Conquest), a section of an anonymous chronicle at York almost certainly copied from contemporary or near contemporary accounts of the last Anglo-Saxon archbishops there, and the work of gathering manuscripts at Exeter under Bishop Leofric.[71] No doubt if lost texts had survived and if more anonymous works could be confidently attributed to authors, the amount of intellectual activity by secular clerics in the Anglo-Saxon period would

[69] Gransden, *History of Bury St Edmunds*, 136 n 253.

[70] Only a small percentage of these 400 come from the royal records.

[71] H. H. E. Craster, "The Red Book of Durham," *English Historical Review* 40 (1925), 504–32, at 519–32; Ted Johnson South, *Historia de Sancto Cuthberto: A History of Saint Cuthbert and a Record of his Patrimony* (Cambridge, 2002), 1, 25–36; Raine, ed., *Historians of the Church of York*, 2:342–54; Giandrea, *Episcopal Culture*, 89–91; Frank Barlow et al., eds., *Leofric of Exeter* (Exeter, 1972).

appear greater, and there were no doubt deeply learned secular clerics before 1066 as after who never composed anything but ephemeral writings. Nonetheless, the expansion of writing and other forms of intellectual activity among the secular clergy during the long twelfth century is remarkable, as the following chapters will further demonstrate.

The secular clergy, of course, had no monopoly on intellectual activities during the long twelfth century. Because lay literacy in Latin was limited in England, the laity played a relatively small part in intellectual life there, but even so their roles as patrons, participants in discussions, and occasionally as literates should not be ignored. The regular clergy may have lost the overwhelming dominance of intellectual activity it had had in the Anglo-Saxon period, but between the continuing intellectual vitality of the old Benedictine houses and the growing contributions of the many new houses of various orders founded after the Norman Conquest, the regulars remained very important to intellectual life in the period. Moreover, the intellectual worlds of the regular and secular clergy were deeply intertwined. Learned secular clerics like Alexander Neckam sometimes entered religious houses.[72] Ideas flowed freely between the regular and secular clergy and it would be hard to find a major field of study or a major intellectual debate in the period in which both regulars and seculars did not play a large role. Nonetheless, it was among the secular clergy that intellectual activity expanded most rapidly, and although one certainly cannot speak of any absolute decline in the intellectual activities of the regular clergy, one can speak of a *relative* decline in their importance in the intellectual life of twelfth-century England and Europe.[73]

Moreover, it was the secular clergy who were crucial to the development of the great centers of learning discussed earlier and therefore to the increasing internationalization of learning and to the formation of universities. It is true that the regular clergy contributed to the internationalization of learning in other ways, partly through transnational monastic networks and partly through the ability of any thinker, even if cloistered, to communicate through writings. It is also true that the regular clergy did make at least some contribution to the international centers of learning. For instance, the regular canons of St. Victor, including ones from England and Scotland, played an important role in Paris. However, the participation of the regular clergy in the schools and nascent universities was initially limited. Not only did claustration inhibit monks and regular canons from attending non-monastic schools, but monks might even be forbidden to attend the schools in this period, and of course nuns could not attend schools outside their cloisters until the modern period.[74] Only later did friars become important in universities, and other regular orders establish mechanisms to allow their members to study at such

---

[72] Hunt and Gibson, *Schools and the Cloister*. For the influence of those schoolmen who entered monasteries, see Knowles, *Monastic Order in England*, 502–5.

[73] The shift in balance between the intellectual contributions of the secular and regular clergy may have been even greater in England than elsewhere because of the greater earlier predominance there of the monasteries.

[74] Ferruolo, *Origins of the University*, 6–7.

institutions. The later participation of the regular clergy in universities should not obscure the dominance of the secular clergy at the beginning.[75] English secular clerics contributed greatly to the creation of these institutions and to intellectual life in general, and partly because of this, England did in fact play a crucial role in the Twelfth-Century Renaissance.

[75] One cannot forget the laity in the Mediterranean centers of Bologna and Salerno, but even there, the English scholars were likely to have been clerics.

11

Secular Clerics as Collectors and Donors of Books

Gerald of Wales was a man who loved books. He loved best the books that he himself wrote; indeed, he even composed a poem on the *cupboard* containing those books. However, he also loved the books he had collected. On one occasion when he was pursuing the bishopric of St. David's he deposited the "treasury" of books he had acquired since boyhood at the Welsh Cistercian abbey of Strata Florida, and sought to borrow money from that house to pursue his case at Rome with his books of theology as pledge. On the eve of his departure the monks claimed that the rules of their order prevented them from taking pledges and he was forced to sell them the books. In a later diatribe against the Cistercians he lamented that he had had to exchange priceless treasure for vile money and wrote that the loss felt like having his guts ripped out.[1] Gerald was trying to score points in this passage, but clearly he hoped that the description of his visceral reaction would gain sympathy from other bibliophiles. For Gerald was a representative of a phenomenon that first became common in England in the second third of the twelfth century, the private collector of books, the vast majority of whom were secular clerics.[2]

Research on medieval book collections, particularly those of the early and central Middle Ages, tends to focus on institutional libraries both for intellectual and for practical reasons. Such libraries were fundamentally important to the intellectual history of the period. Until the late twelfth century, moreover, books were usually copied in the great churches that also housed libraries, thus linking book production closely to the creation of libraries. Indeed the twelfth century itself was a great age of English monastic scriptoria.[3] On the practical side, there is simply a lot

---

[1] Gerald of Wales, *Opera*, 1:369; 4:154–5.

[2] Rosamond McKitterick has shown that there were private lay libraries in the Carolingian world, and so it cannot be ruled out that such libraries existed in the Anglo-Saxon period, but if so, little evidence survives: Rosamond McKitterick, *The Carolingians and the Written Word* (Cambridge, 1989), 157–9, 245–52. For kings, nobles, and books in England in our period, see Thomson, *Books and Learning*, 62–5. For the private collections of later cathedral canons and of the late medieval parish clergy, see Lepine, *A Brotherhood of Canons*, 161–6; Heath, *English Parish Clergy*, 87–9.

[3] Christopher de Hamel, *A History of Illuminated Manuscripts* (London, 1994), 74–107; Rodney M. Thomson, "Monastic and Cathedral Book Production," in Nigel J. Morgan and Rodney M. Thomson, eds., *The Cambridge History of the Book in Britain. Vol. 2, 1100–1400* (Cambridge, 2008), 136–67; Teresa Webber, "Monastic and Cathedral Book Collections in the Late Eleventh and Twelfth Centuries," in E. S. Leedham-Green and Teresa Webber, eds., *The Cambridge History of Libraries in Britain and Ireland. Volume 1, To 1640* (Cambridge, 2006), 109–25.

more surviving evidence for the libraries of religious houses. The loss of medieval manuscripts over the centuries has been staggering, and almost all books that survived did so *because* they were housed in institutional libraries.[4] Indeed, this was true even of books that were initially in private hands, and the majority of information about private book ownership comes, one way or another, from the libraries of religious houses. Though many such libraries were decimated, some have left catalogues, large blocks of manuscripts for paleographers to study, or both. Thus, our knowledge of medieval institutional libraries is much greater than that of private ownership of books. That said, there is sufficient if scattered evidence for private ownership of books by secular clerics to make an overview of that evidence worthwhile. Rodney Thomson has already provided a brief discussion of private ownership by clerics and others in his *Books and Learning in England in the Twelfth Century*.[5] He and other paleographers and historians have also discussed collections of various individual clerics. Drawing on their work and my own investigations, I wish to explore what the surviving evidence about their books can tell us about the intellectual life of the secular clergy in England in the long twelfth century.

This chapter has several arguments. The first is that by the end of the period, clerics collectively owned large numbers of books. The second is that the various interests of book owners reveal a lively intellectual culture among the secular clergy. Third, while there was much overlap in the sorts of books found in institutional and private libraries, there were also differences in emphasis, which has important implications for our understanding of the availability of various kinds of books to scholars in the period. Fourth, the evidence suggests that secular clerics played an important role in helping institutional libraries catch up to new intellectual trends from the mid-twelfth century on. Fifth, secular clerics were important in bringing books out of churches and into the world where the laity could more easily observe their use. Sixth, secular clerics fostered one of the key developments in the history of the book in the West: the rise of a professional book trade. This last argument fits in with a larger argument, which I will pursue in Chapter 13, about the importance of secular clerics as cultural patrons (I will reserve discussion of manuscript illumination to that chapter). Overall, a study of private book ownership reveals the growing importance of secular clerics to the book culture of the period.

---

[4] For a discussion of reasons for such losses, with a focus on the manuscripts of the friars, see David L. d'Avray, *Medieval Marriage: Symbolism and Society* (Oxford, 2005), 40–53; D. L. d'Avray, "Printing, Mass Communication, and Religious Reformation: The Middle Ages and After," in Jane Annette Roberts and Pamela Robinson, eds., *The History of the Book in the West: Volume I, 400 AD–1455* (Farnham, 2010), 301–21, at 303–12. Many of d'Avray's arguments about the books of friars hold even truer for secular clerics. For the particular vulnerability of books in private hands, see also Carla Bozzolo and Ezio Ornato, *Pour une histoire du livre manuscrit au Moyen Âge: trois essais de codicologie quantitative* (Paris, 1983), 73–4, 82–3.

[5] Thomson, *Books and Learning*, 62–6.

1. NUMBERS OF BOOKS OWNED BY SECULAR CLERICS

The sources revealing private book ownership are various. Sometimes secular clerics recorded their donations in the manuscripts themselves when they gave them to institutional libraries. For instance, the inscription of Ralph Foliot, a late twelfth-century archdeacon of Hereford, is found in nine Hereford Cathedral volumes and reveals that he gave twenty volumes.[6] However, surviving inscriptions are fairly rare, and normally appear only in one or two manuscripts. Occasionally, paleographic work can link inscribed manuscripts to others, as with Foliot and a few other manuscripts at Hereford lacking his inscription. Most impressively, Jennifer Sheppard and Rodney Thomson have used paleographical study of annotations to link up to twenty manuscripts from Buildwas Abbey to one inscribed with the name of Robert Amiclas, the former master at Paris who presumably retired to that monastery.[7] Many more books connected to secular clerics can be located in the book catalogues or records of donations of religious houses, and can sometimes be identified as surviving manuscripts from the houses in question. Though some of these works may have been commissioned by secular clerics for monasteries, most were probably first acquired for the personal use of the donors, and only subsequently ended up in religious houses, often when the owner joined the institution or died. In most cases records survive of only one, two, or a handful of manuscripts being given by a single individual, but occasionally clerics can be found giving more, as with donations of a number of works by Herbert Medicus to Durham, Master Hamo to Rochester, and Thomas of Marlborough to Evesham.[8] These larger donations provide particularly helpful insights into the interests of individual clerics. Perhaps the most useful sources, however, are three which record private collections: a list of books deposited by Master Robert of Edington at St. Victor's in Paris; a list of books in one of the Amiclas manuscripts, which probably describes books he owned but did not pass on to Buildwas; and a will from 1223–5 distributing the books of Bartholomew of St. David's, a canon of Crediton.[9] In addition, a twelfth-century copy of Amalarius of Metz's *Liber Officialis*, given to Ely by William, priest of Stradsett, contains a list of nine works, including the Amalarius, which may have belonged to William and originally been bound

[6] R. A. B. Mynors and Rodney M. Thomson, *Catalogue of the Manuscripts of Hereford Cathedral Library* (Cambridge, 1993), xviii–xix.

[7] Jennifer M. Sheppard, *The Buildwas Books: Book Production, Acquisition and Use at an English Cistercian Monastery, 1165–c.1400* (Oxford, 1997), lvi–lviii, 171–261; Thomson, "Robert Amiclas," 238–43.

[8] R. A. B. Mynors, *Durham Cathedral Manuscripts to the End of the Twelfth Century* (Durham, 1939), 62; R. Sharpe et al., *English Benedictine Libraries: The Shorter Catalogues* (London, 1996), 136–8, 505, 521–2; Mary P. Richards, *Texts and their Traditions in the Medieval Library of Rochester Cathedral Priory* (Philadelphia, 1988), 16, 18, 39–40; Thomas of Marlborough, *History of Evesham*, 490–1. Master Hamo remains a somewhat shadowy figure, but is probably the same Master Hamo who gave property to Rochester in return for a corrody, and was thus not a monk: British Library, Cotton MS Domitian A X, fos. 162v–163r.

[9] Mynors, *Durham Cathedral Manuscripts*, 78–82; Thomson, "Robert Amiclas," 241–2; Thomson, *Books and Learning*, 65–6.

together in the same manuscript.[10] These sources are particularly useful because they provide a check on the institutional bias of sources: donors and religious houses both may have thought that certain types of books made more suitable donations than others, which may skew our picture of the kinds of books clerics tended to have. In addition to these sources, there are various of miscellaneous references to specific books in private hands.[11]

The discussion in this chapter will be based on a corpus in the neighborhood of 350 manuscripts, including those from Bartholomew of St. David's somewhat later will. Of these, more than ninety survive. Some of these manuscripts include or included multiple texts. Establishing an exact count of either manuscripts or of individual works clearly related to secular clerics in the period is difficult. Catalogues and lists were not always clear about whether individual works were bound together or not. Identifications of the status of book owners are sometimes uncertain. For instance, Master Alured, whose inscription has been found in three manuscripts, has been identified as a royal cleric who was later bishop of Worcester, as a regular canon of Cirencester, as an abbot of Haughmond, or as some combination thereof. Unfortunately, Alured or Alfred was such a common name that these identifications must remain speculative. Though I have included Alured's works, because I think he was probably a secular cleric, generally I have been cautious about including manuscripts of individuals with an uncertain status.[12] Another problem concerns secular clerics who became monks or regular canons. I have included the books of such individuals when they had a long career outside the monastery, but the example of Thomas of Marlborough, who both brought books to Evesham and acquired books for the monastery after he joined, reveals potential problems. In his case, there is little ambiguity, because he described the circumstances of his donations in detail, but in other cases I may inadvertently have included some manuscripts acquired by secular clerics only after they became monks or regular canons.[13] Conversely, I have probably excluded books linked with monks whose previous status as secular clerics is not clear from the sources. I have not included any manuscripts donated by bishops, since such figures were in a position to collect books on a scale other clerics could not, but at least some books owned by bishops would have been acquired before their elevation. Because

---

[10] Corpus Christi College, Cambridge, MS 416, fo. 1. It is possible that William should be identified with the William of Stradsett who attested a charter of Bishop William Turbe to Ely in 1158–73 along with his son Master Daniel. William is not described as a priest in the charter (as other witnesses are), but this may be another case of an omission of clerical title because a priest was not celibate: Harper-Bill, ed., *English Episcopal Acta 6*, 75–6.

[11] One also finds references to clerics as owners of book collections without the titles being specified: Robertson and Sheppard, eds., *Materials*, 2:193–5; Thomas Walsingham, *Gesta Abbatum*, 1:73.

[12] All Souls College, Oxford, MS 82; Bodleian Library, Jesus College, Oxford MS 26; Mynors and Thomson, *Catalogue of Hereford Cathedral Library*, 13; Christopher Baswell, *Virgil in Medieval England: Figuring the Aeneid from the Twelfth Century to Chaucer* (Cambridge, 1995), 44–5. Alured's books ended up at Cirencester, where manuscripts were often linked to specific canons of the house. The fact that Alured's inscriptions did *not* identify him as a canon suggests he was not one: N. R. Ker, *Medieval Libraries of Great Britain: A List of Surviving Books* (London, 1964), 248–9.

[13] Thomas of Marlborough, *History of Evesham*, 490–3.

of the uncertainties, the survey of manuscripts belonging to secular clerics must be somewhat impressionistic.

Before turning to these manuscripts, however, some discussion of the institutional libraries of secular clerics and their limitations is necessary. All the cathedrals staffed by secular clerics would have had libraries, and reasonably large numbers of books survive from four of them: Salisbury, Exeter, Lincoln, and Hereford. Most likely the large collegiate churches in England also had libraries, though little evidence survives. Waltham did have a good library in the early thirteenth century, but how much this was owed to the original secular clerics and how much to the regular canons with whom Henry II replaced them is unclear.[14] About smaller collegiate churches it is also generally hard to speak, but in the 1220s the very small one at Heytesbury, which was connected to Salisbury cathedral, had Gregory the Great's *Pastoral Care*, a book of sermons, and a collection of papal decretals in addition to sixteen service books.[15] However, there were far more houses of the regular than of the secular clergy that would have had libraries, including the cathedral priories and the great Benedictine monasteries, but also many of the houses of the newer orders, some of which assembled impressive collections. On this basis alone, the contribution of regulars would have overshadowed that of the seculars in building up libraries in England.

Moreover, the libraries of those secular cathedrals for which information survives prove surprisingly disappointing. Salisbury, it is true, was quite dynamic in the fifty years after the Norman Conquest. Teresa Webber has shown the effort put into creating an up-to-date library there, with an emphasis on building up patristic works and a strong interest in the classics. She has also shown how this was linked to an active intellectual life there. However, even at Salisbury, the growth of the library tapered off at mid-century, though there was an upsurge in the late twelfth century with the acquisition of glossed Bibles and recent theological works from Paris.[16] As for the libraries at Hereford and Lincoln, Thomson has described them as disappointingly small compared to monastic libraries, and not very scholarly. They were adequate but unimpressive reference libraries, and because a twelfth-century catalogue survives for Lincoln, it is clear that the evidence there is not distorted by accidents of survival. Thus, when it came to institutional libraries, the secular clergy apparently compared poorly to the regular clergy in quality as well as quantity. Yet this conclusion raises a puzzle. As Thomson has pointed out, it is hard to square the quality of the libraries with the reputations of Lincoln and Hereford as centers of learning. On a more specific note, Diana Greenway has shown that Henry of Huntingdon's knowledge was not restricted to books in the cathedral library. Both Thomson and Greenway suggest that the apparent discrepancy between a relatively weak cathedral library and the strength of learning in a

---

[14] Watkiss and Chibnall, eds., *Waltham Chronicle*, xxix–xxx.

[15] Jones, ed., *Register of S. Osmund*, 1:294. A rare surviving manuscript from a collegiate church is a twelfth-century martyrology from the collegiate church of St. Chad, Shrewsbury: Bodleian Library, Rawlinson MS D 1225.

[16] Webber, *Scribes and Scholars*.

cathedral community might be explained partly by the personal books owned by the canons.[17]

To assess the importance of private ownership by clerics, one must first ask how many manuscripts were in clerical hands, though unfortunately the answers will necessarily be speculative. The figures I have given above of manuscripts connected to clerics could easily be matched or bettered by a single large institutional library with a decent survival rate of manuscripts.[18] One should not make too much of this fact, however. Given the inconsistency in the writing and survival of inscriptions and the absence of catalogues for many houses for which manuscripts do survive, it is possible that many more surviving manuscripts were owned by individuals before passing into the hands of religious houses. Certainly the many twelfth-century manuscripts given to religious houses later in the Middle Ages must have been in private hands between their creation and donation. More important, however, are the overwhelming odds against the survival of manuscripts outside of an institutional setting. Nigel Morgan has estimated that some 40,000 missals existed in England in the Middle Ages, the majority of them in local churches. Around ninety relatively complete ones survive, of which only nineteen can clearly be linked to parish churches, none of them to my knowledge from the period discussed in this book.[19] The Reformation made such manuscripts particularly vulnerable to loss, but so too did the fact that most were not in libraries, as the large percentage of surviving ones that come from institutional libraries indicates. The proportion of surviving records and manuscripts provides a poor basis for judging the relative proportion of manuscripts inside and outside of libraries in the twelfth century.

The size of certain private collections suggests the possibility that the cumulative number of manuscripts owned by secular clerics was quite large. The biggest one associated with a secular cleric with English connections is the 140-volume collection of Philip de Harcourt, who was dean of Lincoln in the 1130s. However, Philip spent over two decades of his life as bishop of Bayeux, and he may have accumulated much of his library then.[20] Other figures had much smaller but still reasonably large collections: Ralph of Sarre, an English cleric who became dean of Rheims Cathedral, gave thirty-eight volumes to Canterbury Cathedral, Robert of Edington had perhaps the same number, Bartholomew of St. David's thirty to thirty five, and Robert Amiclas close to thirty, if one counts the works listed in one of his manuscripts. Of this group, only Amiclas, who appears in two lists of masters at

---

[17] Thomson, "Where were the Latin Classics?," 28–9; Thomson, *Books and Learning*, 43–60; Mynors and Thomson, *Catalogue of Hereford Cathedral Library*, xvii–xviii; Rodney M. Thomson, *Catalogue of the Manuscripts of Lincoln Cathedral Chapter Library* (Woodbridge, 1989), xv–xvi; Henry of Huntingdon, *Historia Anglorum*, xxxii–xxxix.

[18] Knowles, *Monastic Order in England*, 525; Rodney M. Thomson, *Manuscripts from St. Albans Abbey, 1066–1235*, 2 vols. (Woodbridge, 1982), 1:4–5.

[19] Nigel J. Morgan, "Books for the Liturgy and Private Prayer," in Nigel J. Morgan and Rodney M. Thomson, eds., *The Cambridge History of the Book in Britain. Vol. 2, 1100–1400* (Cambridge, 2008), 291–316, at 291.

[20] Richard H. Rouse and Mary A. Rouse, "'Potens in Opere et Sermone': Philip, Bishop of Bayeux, and his Books," in Aldo S. Bernardo and Saul Levin, eds., *The Classics in the Middle Ages* (Binghamton, 1990), 315–41. His books are not included in my tally.

Paris, can be described as a noted intellectual. Ralph of Sarre was obviously an important churchman and Robert of Edington was a leading cleric in the bishopric of Durham, but Bartholomew of St. David's seems to have been a modest figure. Even more striking is the record, from a case in the royal courts, of two cartloads of books belonging to Richard, rural dean of Worcester in 1221, just outside our period.[21] Apparently even relatively minor figures could own many books. By later standards, admittedly, collections of two or three dozen manuscripts may not seem large. However, if one multiplies such figures by the number of potential collectors the cumulative number of works in private hands starts to appear impressive.

The great question, of course, is what sort of multipliers to use. It is useful first to distinguish between service books necessary to conduct the ordinary rituals of Christian worship, which any priest or cleric might have owned, and those types of works such as school books, glossed Bibles, theological works, and law books that were more likely to be in the hands of intellectuals. I will start with the latter category. Thomson has written that "The impression one gets is that churchmen generally owned something between a handful and a few dozen books."[22] This seems correct to me, at least for the elite clergy, and particularly for masters. If one takes from the previous chapter a minimum figure of 550 clerical *magistri* from around 1200 and a conservative estimate of an average of five manuscripts per master excluding basic service books, this would lead to a total of 2750 manuscripts. If one takes the more likely figure of at least 1000 masters and an average of ten manuscripts per master it would lead to a total of over 10,000 manuscripts. These figures exclude masters of earlier periods (though one must also allow for the passage of books from one generation to the next) and the hundreds of cathedral canons, archdeacons, wealthy rectors, and other elite clerics who were not masters, at least some of whom would have owned manuscripts. Approaching the problem from another angle, there is no reason to think that the libraries of figures such as Robert of Edington and Bartholomew of St. David's were particularly unusual among the elite clergy. One hundred such libraries would produce 3000 to 4000 manuscripts. Five hundred such libraries, which is not beyond the realm of possibility, would produce between 15,000 and 20,000 volumes. If one includes the whole period, I would venture that a figure of 20,000 or more manuscripts, beyond service books, is at least possible.[23] On the conservative end, a figure of less

---

[21] Thomson, *Books and Learning*, 66, 90; Thomson, "Robert Amiclas," 238, 241.

[22] Thomson, *Books and Learning*, 65. Eltjo Buringh provides some figures for the size of inventories or donations for twelfth-century France and for all of Europe in the period of the Avignon popes. Unfortunately, his categories of book owners do not closely match mine, and for the Avignon period one has to take into account the greater book production for later periods. However, his figures suggest that the calculations here are not unreasonable. He gives an average of thirty-eight for twelfth-century French donations. Many of these involve archbishops, but some may involve donations of a few books which may not represent the entire collections of individuals. For the Avignon period he gives an average of thirty manuscripts for monks, priests, and clerics: Eltjo Buringh, *Medieval Manuscript Production in the Latin West: Explorations with a Global Database* (Leiden, 2011), 354–5, 416.

[23] This might seem a large though not impossible number in light of Buringh's estimated output of 810 manuscripts a year in Britain (p. 349), even if one takes into account importation of books from Paris. However, I wonder if Buringh sufficiently takes into account the rise of secular clerics as book

than 5000 manuscripts seems to me unlikely. These figures should obviously be taken with caution, as they are extrapolated from very limited data. However, even the more conservative estimate would indicate that book ownership by secular clerics needs to be considered seriously in thinking about book culture in England beginning in the second third of the twelfth century, when private book collection first seems to have become common.

The secular clergy probably also played a significant role in providing service books to parish churches and chapels. In later periods, the responsibility for these and other items necessary for worship was transferred to the churchwardens and the parishioners.[24] In the long twelfth century, they remained the responsibility of the priests. Charters from before 1216 sometimes required specific vicars to provide books for their churches, and critiques of priests for misusing tithes indicate that this was a general expectation for the parish clergy.[25] For instance, Gervase of Chichester attacked greedy priests for providing "old and corrupt" books and Alexander of Ashby complained of priests who had old, damaged, unornamented books or none at all, though their concubines and daughters were adorned "like the Temple."[26] Not all priests neglected their duties in this respect. A visitation of churches held by the dean and canons of Salisbury in the early 1220s reveals that four priests had given a total of fourteen service books in nine volumes to their churches.[27] Priests also sometimes held service books as their own property: Gerald of Wales urged priests to bequeath books to their churches rather than to sons, daughters, or nephews.[28] That priests did sometimes leave books to their relatives is indicated by a charter of around 1200 in which John, son of a priest named Gervase, bought land in return for one mark and a psalter worth two shillings.[29] More generally, exemptions on taxation of the property of clerics included books along with other items that in later periods would have belonged to parish churches.[30]

The demand for service books by priests was therefore probably high. Each church was expected to have several basic works such as missals, psalters, and antiphonals. Inventories of eleven churches connected with Salisbury Cathedral in the early 1220s show an average of just over eight works each, sometimes

collectors in his figures. I also suspect that his discussion of loss rates, as impressive and useful as it is, may suffer from relying too heavily on institutional libraries, and does not take into account the greater wastage rates of manuscripts in parish churches and private hands: Buringh, *Medieval Manuscript Production*, 54–7, 179–251, 272, 288–9, 291–2, 353–4, 357, 403–14.

[24] Moorman, *Church Life*, 140–1; Cheney, *From Becket to Langton*, 160.

[25] Johnson, ed., *English Episcopal Acta 26*, 25–6, 156; Christopher Harper-Bill and Richard Mortimer, eds., *Stoke-by-Clare Cartulary: BL Cotton Appx. xxi*, 3 vols., Suffolk Charters, 4–6 (Woodbridge, 1982–84), 1:68–9.

[26] British Library, Royal MS 3 B X, fo. 17r; Alexander of Ashby, "De Artificisoo Modo Predicandi," 65. See also British Library, Cotton MS Vespasian E X, fo. 182v; Gerald of Wales, *Opera*, 4:335–6.

[27] Jones, ed., *Register of S. Osmund*, 1:276, 279, 291, 295–6.

[28] Gerald of Wales, *Opera*, 2:37–8; 4:335.

[29] Gervase's father is only identified as a priest in a separate charter: Ransford, ed., *Early Charters of Waltham Abbey*, 85–7.

[30] Sydney Knox Mitchell, *Taxation in Medieval England* (New Haven, 1951), 118–19; William E. Lunt, "The Text of the Ordinance of 1184 Concerning an Aid for the Holy Land," *English Historical Review* 37 (1922), 235–42, at 242; Roger of Howden, *Chronica*, 2:335.

unbound or bound together in a smaller number of manuscripts.[31] Early twelfth-century leases and inventories of three London churches list a smaller number of works, between four and seven each.[32] Even if one assumes that many churches were inadequately endowed with books or had none at all, the fact that England had over 10,000 local churches, including chapels, meant that there were still probably thousands and perhaps tens of thousands of service books throughout England. Some books may have dated back to the Anglo-Saxon period: one of the churches in the Salisbury visitation had an "old missal" with *littera Anglica* and another had "a very old book" on which oaths were sworn.[33] However, unusually old books clearly stood out, and even where books already existed, there would have been a demand for new ones to replace others that had worn out or gone out of fashion. Lay donors may well have provided some such books, though I have found no evidence for this. What evidence does survive suggests that over the course of the long twelfth century, the secular clergy, including quite ordinary priests, were collectively responsible for procuring large numbers of manuscripts for everyday worship.

2. TYPES OF BOOKS OWNED BY SECULAR CLERICS

What sorts of books did secular clerics own? Though service books would un-doubtedly have been the most common, they form only about a seventh of the manuscripts for which I have collected information. Religious houses probably did not want ordinary service books as donations and such texts may not normally have been worth recording in other circumstances. Lavishly produced service books were a different matter, and of particular note are more than thirty luxury manuscripts given by ten secular clerics to Saint Paul's Cathedral before 1216 and recorded in thirteenth-century inventories.[34] These donations include approximately a quarter of the manuscripts recorded in the inventories, and compare favorably in number to the ten given by bishops in the period. Indeed, twenty-two were given just by the dean and historian Ralph of Diceto and two other canons.

By far the most common type of book associated with the secular clergy in the surviving record were glossed Bibles. I have found records of over 130 manuscripts associated with at least twenty-seven members of the secular clergy containing various books of the Bible with glosses. Such manuscripts can be found not only in monastic and cathedral catalogues and records of donations but also in lists of the books owned by individual clerics, showing that their prominence was not simply a matter of the acquisition policies of libraries. Indeed, roughly half of Robert of

---

[31] Jones, ed., *Register of S. Osmund*, 276, 279–83, 290–1, 295–6, 311–12, 314. See n. 15 for Heytesbury, which also had pastoral responsibilities.
[32] *Ninth Report*, 63–4.   [33] Jones, ed., *Register of S. Osmund*, 1:280, 291.
[34] N. R. Ker, "Books at St Paul's Cathedral before 1313," in Andrew G. Watson, ed., *Books, Collectors, and Libraries: Studies in the Medieval Heritage* (London, 1985), 209–42, at 215–35.

Edington's manuscripts consisted of glossed books of the Bible.[35] These figures illustrate the centrality of such Bibles to the intellectual life of the secular clergy, at least from the time of their development in the middle of the twelfth century, and it seems likely that glossed Bibles formed a far higher percentage of the manuscripts in private than in institutional libraries in the late twelfth and early thirteenth centuries.

In striking contrast stands the paucity of patristic works in surviving records of private ownership, at least outside of the large and perhaps atypical collection of Philip of Harcourt.[36] Master Alfred of Hemel Hempstead, who held property in Oxford and therefore probably taught there, gave Missenden Abbey a copy of the homilies of Augustine that Ker dated to about 1200.[37] Thomas of Marlborough brought two works of Isidore of Seville with him when he became a monk at Evesham.[38] Ralph of Sarre gave a copy of Boethius's *De Trinitate* and works by Hilary of Poitiers and Leontius Byzantinus to Canterbury Cathedral; he and Bartholomew of St. David's both owned copies of Pseudo-Dionysius; and William of Stradsett's collection contained a work attributed in the period to Jerome.[39] Given the importance of patristic texts in the Middle Ages, and the efforts to acquire such texts for English libraries after the Norman Conquest, this is not an impressive result, so small that it is unlikely to be simply an aberration of the evidence. One important way in which private collections may therefore have radically differed from institutional libraries was the relative lack of such texts. Quite likely clerics expected to gain patristic learning mainly through the glossed Bibles, though the absorption of patristic material in such a manner would have been a markedly different experience from learning it through whole texts.

The paucity of patristic texts is underscored by the fact that secular clerics possessed just as many works of earlier medieval theology, including Bede's commentaries on Luke and Mark and his *De Tabernaculo*, and such Carolingian works as Amalarius's *Liber Officialis*, Defensor's *Liber Scintillarum*, Alcuin's treatise on virtues and vices, and Hrabanus Maurus's commentary on John. They also possessed writings from the early part of the Twelfth-Century Renaissance such as Anselm's *Meditations*, Odo of Tournai's treatise on the mass, and Ivo of Chartres's sermons.[40] Not surprisingly, the collections and donations of secular clerics were

[35] Mynors, *Durham Cathedral Manuscripts*, 79.

[36] Rouse and Rouse, "Philip, Bishop of Bayeux and his Books," 324.

[37] Bodleian Library, Auct. MS D.1.10; Ker, *Medieval Libraries*, 282; Salter, ed., *Cartulary of Oseney Abbey*, 1:243.

[38] Thomas of Marlborough, *History of Evesham*, 490–1.

[39] Montague Rhodes James, *The Ancient Libraries of Canterbury and Dover* (Cambridge, 1903), 87; Trinity College, Cambridge, MS B.2.31; Ker, *Medieval Libraries*, 31, 242; Thomson, *Books and Learning*, 65; Corpus Christi College, Cambridge, MS 416, fo. 1.

[40] Bodleian Library, Bodleian MS 729 (Alard of Burnham, dean of St. Paul's: Bede and Hrabanus); Kealey, *Medieval Medicus*, 62 (Clarembald, a royal physician: *De Tabernaculo*); Corpus Christi College, Cambridge, MS 416, fo. 1 (William of Stradsett: Amalarius and Alcuin); Reginald Maxwell Woolley, *Catalogue of the Manuscripts of Lincoln Cathedral Chapter Library* (London, 1927), viii (Roger of Almaria, precentor of Lincoln: Defensor); Webber and Watson, *Libraries of the Augustinian Canons*, 445–6 (Philip Apostolorum, canon of Lincoln; Anselm); Thomson, "Robert Amiclas," 241 (Robert Amiclas: Ivo's sermons and Defensor); James, *Libraries of Canterbury and Dover*, 87–8 (Ralph of Sarre:

still stronger when it came to the theology of the schools from the later twelfth century. A number of clerics gave Peter Lombard's *Sentences* to libraries, and a couple also made donations of Peter Comestor's *Historia Scholastica*.[41] Master Robert of Edington owned both of these books along with Peter of Poitiers's commentary on Psalms and four Parisian sermon collections.[42] In addition to Peter Lombard's *Sentences*, Bartholomew of St. David's owned works of Richard and Hugh of St. Victor.[43] Master Hamo gave to Rochester a work of John of Cornwall.[44] Indeed, recent works of the schools, like glossed Bibles, were probably more important, in proportional terms, in private collections than in institutional ones. In addition, secular clerics had a smattering of other miscellaneous religious writings. Master Robert of Edington owned a copy of the life and miracles of St. Cuthbert (as was fitting for a Durham cleric), Bartholomew of St. David's owned works on the virtues and vices, and William of Stradsett had works on the antichrist, St. Eustace, and St. Augustine of Canterbury.[45] Hamo, chancellor of Lincoln, gave his cathedral library a collection of sermons for the whole year and one of the Lincoln canons gave a penitential.[46]

Clerics also owned books on law and medicine. Master Peter of Paxton, who served Earl Simon de Senlis III and Earl David of Huntingdon, at one point pledged the *Codex*, *Digest*, and *Institutiones* of Justinian's *Corpus Iuris Civilis*, along with a Bible, to Holyrood Abbey.[47] When Thomas of Marlborough entered Evesham, he brought works of both canon and civil law with him.[48] A number of other clerics bequeathed legal works, including Justinian's *Codex*, Ivo of Chartres's *Panormia*, Gratian's *Decreta*, and perhaps Huguccio's *Summa Decretorum*, to various institutional libraries.[49] Fewer secular clerics can be connected to medical

---

Odo of Tournai, a sermon or sermons of Ivo, and also works attributed to Remigius of Auxerre and Hildebert of Lavardin).

[41] Master Hamo, Ralph Foliot, Richard Barre, Ralph of Sarre, Richard, chaplain of Thomas Becket, Master Gilbert, and Walter Gross, probably a canon of Lincoln, made donations of Peter Lombard's work: Sharpe et al., *English Benedictine Libraries*, 424, 521; Mynors and Thomson, *Catalogue of Hereford Cathedral Library*, 57–8; Webber and Watson, *Libraries of the Augustinian Canons*, 217; James, *Libraries of Canterbury and Dover*, 87; Alan Coates, *English Medieval Books: The Reading Abbey Collections from Foundation to Dispersal* (Oxford, 1999), 26, 114; Woolley, *Catalogue of Lincoln Cathedral Library*, ix. Robert Bellofago and Samson, canon of Lincoln, gave copies of Peter Comestor's work: Edward Maunde Thompson and S. M. Lakin, *A Catalogue of the Library of the Cathedral Church of Salisbury* (London, 1880), 10; Woolley, *Catalogue of Lincoln Cathedral Library*, vii. A Master David of London gave a miscellany, including works of Stephen of Tournai and various quodlibets and tracts, from around 1200, to Merton, but this manuscript seems late for the letter writer of that name and may have belonged to a later figure: British Library, Royal MS 9 E XII, fo. 1r; Ker, *Medieval Libraries*, 282.

[42] Mynors, *Durham Cathedral Manuscripts*, 78–9.

[43] Thomson, *Books and Learning*, 65–6.

[44] Sharpe et al., *English Benedictine Libraries*, 521–2.

[45] Mynors, *Durham Cathedral Manuscripts*, 78; Thomson, *Books and Learning*, 66; Corpus Christi College, Cambridge, MS 416, fo. 1.

[46] Woolley, *Catalogue of Lincoln Cathedral Library*, viii.

[47] Foster and Major, eds., *Registrum Antiquissimum*, 3:164; Stringer, *Earl David*, 152–3.

[48] Thomas of Marlborough, *History of Evesham*, 490–1.

[49] Bodleian Library, Jesus College, Oxford MS 26 (Alfred: Ivo of Chartres's *Panormia*); Woolley, *Catalogue of Lincoln Cathedral Library*, viii (Hugh, Archdeacon of Leicester: Gratian); Coates, *English*

books, but Thomas of Marlborough brought three such works to Evesham and Peter of Blois referred in a letter to a collection of books on medicine that were stolen from him.[50] Moreover, Herbert Medicus gave to Durham at least five manuscripts containing a total of twenty-five works, almost all of them medical in nature. They included translations from Arabic texts and works by contemporary writers such as Master Roger of Salerno and Master Reginald of Montpellier.[51] The overall number of legal and medical texts is not huge, but such books may not have been a high priority for institutional libraries seeking donations, so it is possible that this kind of book is under-represented in our sample. Since the limited evidence does suggest that specialists in medicine and the law often owned such texts it is likely that a good number of them existed outside of institutional libraries.

Another type of professional text consisted of books associated with the trivium. Among the volumes Master Hamo granted to Rochester were a pair devoted to glosses and *summae* on rhetoric, dialectic, and grammar, as well as a work of the prominent twelfth-century grammarian Ralph of Beauvais. Robert Amiclas had the *Eclogae* of Theodolus, a common work for teaching grammar and rhetoric (Bartholomew of St. David's also had a copy), a work on poetry, and the treatise of another twelfth-century scholar, Peter Helias, on the Roman grammarian Priscian. Thomas of Marlborough entered Evesham with "many" works on grammar and even Herbert Medicus had a work of Priscian.[52] One might expect to see more copies of basic works on grammar, given their importance in teaching, but such basic works were probably not of interest to institutional libraries and perhaps not even always worth including in the lists of books owned by masters. The appearance of contemporary works on grammar, rhetoric, and dialectic, however, is worth noting.

The secular clergy were also very interested in classical and late antique works. As Thomson has noted, Bartholomew of St. David's distributed a remarkable number of classical works in his will, including texts by Lucan, Virgil, Juvenal, Ovid, Cato, Avianus, Maximianus, Statius, Claudian, Aristotle, and Horace. Ralph, the priest of Whitchurch, gave to Reading Abbey the *Eclogues* and *Georgics* of Virgil, the *Odes*, *Epistles*, *Ars Poetica*, and *Epodes* of Horace, and Juvenal's *Satires*. Master Hamo gave works of Aristotle, Cicero, Ovid, Claudian, and Suetonius to Rochester, and

---

Medieval Books, 25, 114 (copy of "decreta" given by Master Gilbert who may have held a living from the monastery); Sharpe et al., *English Benedictine Libraries*, 422, 505, 521 (Master Hamo: Gratian and commentaries on the *Decreta*); Webber and Watson, *Libraries of the Augustinian Canons*, 340, 343, 406 (Richard Barre: Gratian and Justinian's *Codex*; Robert fitz Gille, Archdeacon of Totnes: Gratian); B. C. Barker-Benfield, *St Augustine's Abbey, Canterbury*, 3 vols. (London, 2008), 3:1621 (Master Stephen: probably Huguccio, *Summa Decretorum*); James, *Libraries of Canterbury and Dover*, 87–8 (Ralph of Sarre: a work on civil law and glosses on the *Decreta*).

[50] Thomas of Marlborough, *History of Evesham*, 490–1; Peter of Blois, *Later Letters*, 41. For some other possibilities, see Kealey, *Medieval Medicus*, 127, 132, 135.

[51] James Raine, *Catalogi Veteres Librorum Ecclesiae Cathedralis Dunelmensis*, Surtees Society, vol. 7 (London, 1838), 7–8; Mynors, *Durham Cathedral Manuscripts*, 62; Bartlett, *England under the Norman and Angevin Kings*, 589–90; Kealey, *Medieval Medicus*, 44–7.

[52] Sharpe et al., *English Benedictine Libraries*, 522; Thomson, "Robert Amiclas," 241; Thomson, *Books and Learning*, 66; Thomas of Marlborough, *History of Evesham*, 490–1.

Thomas of Marlborough brought Lucan, Juvenal, various works of Cicero, and "many other *auctores*" to Evesham.[53] The classics played an important role in teaching the trivium at more advanced levels, and it is noteworthy that one of the manuscripts associated with Master Alured was a copy of Virgil's *Aeneid* with annotations, some perhaps by Alured himself, designed for teaching the poem at both a basic and a more advanced level.[54] Nonetheless, the range of works owned by secular clerics suggests interests beyond the standard classroom texts. According to a later inventory, William of Chichester, a canon of Exeter, gave to his cathedral library not only works of Statius and Persius, but also works by several late antique Christian writers, including Prudentius, Arator, Prosper of Aquitaine, Sedulius, and Boethius.[55] When Master Gerard, canon of Lincoln, lost one of the cathedral's books, he gave as a substitute a copy of Vegetius's *De Re Militari* with the *Roman History* of Eutropius. From Archdeacon Hugh of Leicester, Lincoln received a copy of Josephus.[56] Robert of Edington owned the *Letters* of Sidonius Apollinaris, and William of Stradsett the *Antonine Itinerary* and *Apollonius of Tyre*.[57] A certain Gerard pledged a twelfth-century copy of Calcidius's translation of part of Plato's *Timaeus* to St. Mary's, York.[58] Finally, there was Peter of Waltham's donation to Waltham Abbey of Palladius's treatise on agriculture and Cetius Faventinus's *De Diversis Architectonicae Fabricis*, a work on architecture based on Vitruvius.[59] Taken together, this evidence suggests that the classics, including comparatively rare or obscure works, played a very important role in private libraries, perhaps even more important proportionally than in institutional ones. The evidence also suggests that there was widespread use of and access to classical material through whole works, not just through basic grammar texts and florilegia. Clearly, in assessing the place of the classics in the latter part of the Twelfth-Century Renaissance, scholars need to keep private collections in mind.

Some clerics had an interest in more contemporary literary and historical works. Herbert Medicus gave a copy of Petrus Alphonsus's *Parables* to Durham, as well as a

---

[53] Thomson, *Books and Learning*, 65–6; Coates, *English Medieval Books*, 43; Sharpe et al., *English Benedictine Libraries*, 447, 521–2; Thomas of Marlborough, *History of Evesham*, 490–1.

[54] The early glosses could have been added at Cirencester after Master Alured gave the work, but they make sense as a tool for a master teaching in a school: All Souls College, Oxford, MS 82; Baswell, *Virgil in Medieval England*, 41–62.

[55] George Oliver, *Lives of the Bishops of Exeter and a History of the Cathedral* (Exeter, 1861), 307. It must be noted, however, that this gift bears a close resemblance to some of the works given by Bishop Leofric, as Joyce Hill pointed out to me after a conference presentation, so it is possible that this is a later misattribution.

[56] Woolley, *Catalogue of Lincoln Cathedral Library*, vi, viii.

[57] Mynors, *Durham Cathedral Manuscripts*, 78; Corpus Christi College, Cambridge, MS 416, fo. 1.

[58] Cambridge University Library, MS Ee.6.40, fo. 44v. Gerard's identity is unknown, but a possible candidate is Gerard son of Lewin, who held the church of Stokesley and land in York from St. Mary's. Gerard came from a very wealthy family which had to pay huge sums to the crown. Thus Gerard was someone who could easily have afforded books but might have needed to pledge one in return for money and been unable to redeem it. In his handwritten notes in Cambridge University library, M. R. James dated the inscription to the twelfth or thirteenth century, in other words, broadly around 1200, which would fit Gerard son of Lewin's dates: Farrer and Clay, eds., *Early Yorkshire Charters*, 1:231–2, 443; Thomas, *English and the Normans*, 185.

[59] Van Houts, ed., *Gesta Normannorum Ducum*, 1:xcix; Bodleian Library, Rawlinson MS G 62.

Liber Aurelii Ambrosii, which must surely refer to Geoffrey of Monmouth's *Historia Regum Britanniae* or some offshoot thereof.[60] Thomson has identified three of Bartholomew of St. David's books as Walter of Châtillon's *Alexandreis*, Matthew of Vendôme's *Tobias*, and Peter Riga's *Aurora*.[61] As for history, besides Peter of Waltham's ownership of a world chronicle and fragments of the *Gesta Normannorum Ducum*, Master Robert of Edington owned some "rolls" of history, and Alfred of Chard, a canon of Exeter, gave part of a chronicle of England to his cathedral library.[62] Several writers, including Ralph of Diceto, Richard Barre, Gerald of Wales, and Ralph Niger, granted their own works to a cathedral or monastery.[63] Authors are, of course, a special case, since they would have desired to propagate their own work, but the other donations show a more disinterested appreciation for the literary culture and historical interests of the Twelfth-Century Renaissance.

A final category of works shows the interest of some secular clerics in the natural world. Daniel of Morley, unfortunately, did not specify the books he brought back from Spain, but clearly they included works in this category.[64] Herbert Medicus had a professional interest in such works, and his books included Dioscorides's treatise on medicinal plants and a *Liber de Natura Lapidum*, probably a treatise on the medicinal or magical properties of stones of the sort common in the period.[65] Bartholomew of St. David's, William of Stradsett, and Philip Apostolorum, canon of Lincoln, owned bestiaries, and Philip also possessed a mappa mundi.[66] Master Hamo of Rochester and Master Robert of Edington had works on algorismus, the form of calculation with Hindu-Arabic numerals that was slowly penetrating Western Europe at this time. The latter also had material on astrology and on *phisica*, which could have referred either to medicine or other aspects of the natural world.[67] Ralph of Sarre and Robert fitz Gille both had books on *phisica* as well.[68] Master Robert Amiclas had a work entitled *De Scientia Lune* and a table on rhythmomachy, a mathematically oriented game of the period.[69] Aside from these pieces that can be associated with specific individuals, many surviving manuscripts containing works on the natural world seem originally to have been

---

[60] Raine, *Catalogi Veteres*, 8.   [61] Thomson, *Books and Learning*, 65.

[62] Bodleian Library, Rawlinson MS G 62; van Houts, ed., *Gesta Normannorum Ducum*, 1:xcix; Mynors, *Durham Cathedral Manuscripts*, 78; Oliver, *Lives of the Bishops*, 305.

[63] Ker, "Books at St Paul's Cathedral before 1313," 234; Woolley, *Catalogue of Lincoln Cathedral Library*, vii–viii; Thomson, *Lincoln Cathedral Library*, 13–14, 18–20; Webber and Watson, *Libraries of the Augustinian Canons*, 140, 208. A Lincoln catalogue lists several works by Gerald as Gerald's own gift. It does not so list the seven volumes of Ralph Niger's work, but since he was a canon there it seems likely.

[64] For some of the books he likely acquired, based on his own writings, see Burnett, *Introduction of Arabic Learning*, 63–7.

[65] Raine, *Catalogi Veteres*, 7–8.

[66] Thomson, *Books and Learning*, 66; Corpus Christi College, Cambridge, MS 416, fo. 1; Webber and Watson, *Libraries of the Augustinian Canons*, 445–6.

[67] Sharpe et al., *English Benedictine Libraries*, 521; Mynors, *Durham Cathedral Manuscripts*, 78.

[68] Webber and Watson, *Libraries of the Augustinian Canons*, 405–6; James, *Libraries of Canterbury and Dover*, 88.

[69] Thomson, "Robert Amiclas," 241–2.

made for personal rather than institutional use, and so may have been made for secular clerics.[70]

3. THE IMPACT OF BOOK OWNERSHIP
BY SECULAR CLERICS

Any overall assessment of the importance of the private collections of secular clerics for the intellectual life of England in the period must take into account the fragmentary nature of the evidence, since the 350 manuscripts discussed here represent only a fraction of what once existed. Extrapolation from this sample would suggest a very large number of manuscripts of glossed Bibles and significant numbers of manuscripts of standard texts such as Peter Lombard's *Sentences*. Given the variety of texts secular clerics possessed, some of them fairly rare, it is also likely that the surviving evidence provides only a very partial glimpse of the range of titles owned by secular clerics. It is therefore difficult to fully assess the collective nature and influence of such collections. That said, book collecting and patronage by secular clerics clearly reflected the major intellectual trends of the period: the influence of the schools; the rise of the professions of law and medicine; a growing interest in the classics; the importance of contemporary works of theology, litera-ture, and history; and a desire to understand the natural world. The evidence of private collections also mirrors the international nature of English intellectual life. Northern French influence is most obvious, but one can also point to works of Roger of Salerno or Petrus Alphonsus. In addition, this evidence reveals the diverse interests of the secular clergy, both collectively and as individuals. Even Herbert Medicus's professionally specialized collection included literary works. The variety of interests of clerics such as Master Hamo of Rochester, Master Robert of Edington, and Bartholomew of St. David's will be apparent from the discussion above.

Private libraries were obviously not adequate substitutes for institutional ones. Outside of Philip de Harcourt's library, those private libraries for which we have evidence were fairly limited. This is not surprising, since scholarly books could be expensive. A note in one of Ralph of Sarre's books reveals him spending over £28 for copies of the Pentateuch, Job, the twelve prophets, Matthew, and Luke, as well as parchment for a psalter and for a volume of the Epistles. Even if this sum was in a less valuable currency than sterling, the outlay was considerable.[71] Similarly, in 1295, two glossed manuscripts of the epistles of Paul, given by a twelfth-century canon to Exeter, were valued at £3 and fifty shillings respectively, and a twelfth-century inventory valued a lectionary at a London church at thirty shillings.[72] These may have been unusually expensive books, but even cheap books were

[70] Thomson, *Books and Learning*, 98.
[71] Christopher de Hamel, *Glossed Books of the Bible and the Origins of the Paris Booktrade* (Woodbridge, 1984), 54.
[72] Oliver, *Lives of the Bishops*, 307; *Ninth Report*, 64.

expensive by modern standards. Another reason for small libraries was that elite clerics often had a peripatetic career and books were not easy to cart about. For instance, John of Salisbury worried whether it was worth bringing his books back to England when trying to repair his relations with Henry II in 1165.[73] Costs and logistics may help explain why glossed Bibles were so popular among secular clerics. Such Bibles not only arranged biblical commentary in a convenient manner, but they also packed a great deal of useful material into a relatively small number of books. A set of glossed books of the Bible could run to many volumes, but even so was cheaper and more easily transportable than a library of patristic texts.[74]

Yet glossed Bibles were ultimately no substitute for larger libraries of theological works and, judging by the surviving evidence, few if any secular clerics owned anything like an adequate library for serious scholarship. A hint of the resulting difficulties comes from Peter of Blois's *Compendium in Job*, in which he excused his supposed rudeness of style by writing that he had been spending much time in castles and courts in service of the archbishop of Canterbury, where, among other problems, there was a deficiency of books.[75] He was no doubt employing the modesty topos, but his complaints about his working conditions were surely genuine. If any secular cleric was likely to have a large private collection, it was Peter, but he obviously found lack of access to an adequate institutional library problematic.

The borrowing of books, however, could help overcome the deficiencies of individual libraries. Letters of John of Salisbury, Peter of Blois, Gerald of Wales, and Master David of London show all of them borrowing and lending books and seeking new texts, often for the purposes of copying. For instance, when Gerard la Pucelle was in Cologne in 1166, John of Salisbury asked him to inform him of anything new he found in the book cupboards he was "plundering" and to send him works of Hildegard of Bingen.[76] These chance references in letters suggest that the flow of books among secular clerics and between secular clerics and institutions was quite active, and though the peripatetic lives of many clerics hindered the accumulation of large personal libraries, they also allowed clerics to come into contact with many other book collections, facilitating the circulation of texts.

There is also good evidence of borrowing from the Lincoln Cathedral library.[77] Lincoln and Hereford probably became centers of learning partly because they provided access to libraries that were in the hands of secular clerics and could make up for many of the deficiencies in private collections. However, it was the *combination* of cathedral library, private collections, and the circulation of books that was

---

[73] John of Salisbury, *Letters*, 2:48–9. John bequeathed only twenty-four manuscripts to Chartres when he died as bishop there, but he may well have bequeathed additional books to other institutions and to individuals: Clement C. J. Webb, *John of Salisbury* (London, 1932), 165–9.

[74] Lesley Smith, *The* Glossa Ordinaria: *The Making of a Medieval Bible Commentary* (Leiden, 2009), 231.

[75] Peter of Blois, *Opera*, 797.

[76] John of Salisbury, *Letters*, 1:55–8; 62–3; 2:224–5, 294–5, 424–5, 534–5; Peter of Blois, *Opera*, 116; Peter of Blois, *Later Letters*, 116–17; Gerald of Wales, *Opera*, 1:237–8; Liverani, ed., *Spicilegium Liberianum*, 620.

[77] Thomson, *Lincoln Cathedral Library*, xvi.

crucial. For instance, the Hereford Cathedral library shows little sign of the scientific interests for which Hereford was noted, but clearly the books necessary for that kind of research existed in private collections.[78] Of course, secular clerics may also have been able to borrow from monastic libraries; Janet Martin has suggested that John of Salisbury relied on the library at Christ Church, Canterbury.[79] Nonetheless, the learned communities surrounding some secular cathedrals indicate the potential importance of private as well as institutional collections to centers of learning. The rise of Oxford and then Cambridge only underscores this point. One cannot rule out the use of local monastic collections, particularly by masters at Oxford. However, when Master William of Tonbridge entered Oseney Abbey, he brought his theological texts with him, suggesting that local monasteries may have relied as much on scholars for books as the reverse.[80] It is hard to imagine that even the nascent universities could easily have depended fully on monastic collections for all their needs and they must have relied heavily on the books of their masters and students.

The evidence discussed above suggests that secular clerics had a major role in the dissemination of texts, particularly in certain genres. Richard and Mary Rouse have noted Philip de Harcourt's role in the transmission of ancient Latin texts, including rare ones, but he was clearly not alone.[81] Likewise, secular clerics probably had an enormous impact in spreading the work of the schools, and may also have had a disproportionate influence in the transmission of other writings of the Twelfth-Century Renaissance. Part of their impact came through donations to the libraries of cathedrals and monasteries. Thomson and Lesley Smith have described masters as an important conduit through which glossed Bibles entered England and its libraries, and a donation of a set of volumes containing an entire Bible could substantially update an institutional library's holdings.[82] However, donations of other sorts of books also reshaped libraries: Durham would have been unlikely to have acquired such an up-to-date medical library without the donation of Herbert Medicus. How big a role did donors play in reshaping and increasing the size of libraries? Christopher de Hamel has noted that over a quarter of the approximately 200 surviving manuscripts of glossed Bibles in England were associated with donors, including bishops as well as lesser clerics, which is a sizable percentage given the inconsistent recording and survival of inscriptions by donors.[83] Precisely how important a role the secular clergy played in reshaping libraries will probably never be entirely clear, and certainly monasteries were still capable of copying books themselves or of acquiring them through purchase. De Hamel has suggested that bishops and abbots may have sent clerics to Paris to make copies of glossed Bibles,

---

[78] Thomson, *Books and Learning*, 44, 48.

[79] Janet Martin, "John of Salisbury as Classical Scholar," in Michael Wilks, ed., *The World of John of Salisbury* (Oxford, 1984), 179–201, at 180–90.

[80] Salter, ed., *Cartulary of Oseney Abbey*, 3:78.

[81] Rouse and Rouse, "Philip, Bishop of Bayeux and his Books," 316.

[82] Thomson, *Books and Learning*, 90–2; Smith, *Glossa Ordinaria*, 163–7, 171–2, 174, 180, 192. Smith suggests this was true in other countries as well.

[83] de Hamel, *Glossed Books*, 11.

which were then illuminated by Parisian artists, and gives an example of a manuscript inscribed by Robert de Neville, cleric of an abbot of Peterborough, that ended up in Peterborough's library.[84] However, it is just as likely that Robert copied the manuscript for himself during studies in Paris, and ended up giving it to Peterborough because of his connections there.[85]

Secular clerics also brought book ownership out of churches into the broader world and helped familiarize laypeople with the use of books. Master Peter of Paxton's patrons, the earls of Huntingdon, would obviously have seen him use his books when working on legal questions.[86] Ralph, priest of Whitchurch, who gave a psalter and classical texts to Reading Abbey, was the incumbent of a church in the patronage of the fitz Gerald family, and his probable attestations to some of their charters makes it reasonably likely that he served in their household. William de Briane, Ralph's successor as rector of Whitchurch-on-Thames and chaplain to Warin fitz Gerald, translated the *Pseudo-Turpin Chronicle* into Anglo-Norman at the behest of Warin and his wife, Alice de Courcy.[87] Ralph of Whitchurch may have conveyed his interest in and familiarity with Latin works to his patron's family and thus paved the way for the next generation to seek a book containing a translation of a Latin text. Peter of Paxton and Ralph of Whitchurch thus show one important avenue through which nobles in particular became exposed to the culture of the book. Indeed, Ralph of Whitchurch's connection to the fitz Geralds suggests the kind of setting in which a work like the *Roman d'Eneas*, a French version of Virgil's *Aeneid*, might have been produced.

Finally, the role of secular clerics in the production of manuscripts deserves attention, given their large and increasing demand for books. To some degree they met this demand by copying books themselves or by employing scribes. John of Ford's *vita* of Wulfric of Haselbury records that as a hermit the former parish priest devoted time to writing books for himself and for the church in which he resided, though he employed Richard, son of the priest Segar, as a scribe, and the latter may have done most of the copying.[88] Philip of St. Edward, a canon of Salisbury who corrected scribal mistakes in cathedral manuscripts, was presumably capable of writing or overseeing the production of a missal he presented to the altar of St. Stephen at the cathedral.[89] Secular clerics could even provide scribes for regulars who wished to have books copied. In 1192–3 a student and scribe of Master Robert Bonn or Boun of Bedford (possibly the Master Robert of Bedford who was precentor of Lincoln) made a copy of Peter Comestor's *Historia Scholastica* for

---

[84] de Hamel, *Glossed Books*, 58–61.   [85] See Smith, *Glossa Ordinaria*, 180.

[86] Stringer, *Earl David*, 152–3.

[87] A Ralph *clericus* attested two family charters and Ralph cleric of Digeneswella another. Ralph may possibly also be the Master Ralph who attested a family charter: Sharpe et al., *English Benedictine Libraries*, 444, 447; Coates, *English Medieval Books*, 32, 43, 114; Nicholas Vincent, "Warin and Henry fitz Gerald, the King's Chamberlains: The Origins of the FitzGeralds Revisited," *Anglo-Norman Studies* 21 (1999), 233–60, at 254–6, 260; William de Briane, *The Anglo-Norman* Pseudo-Turpin Chronicle *of William de Briane*, ed. Ian Short (Oxford, 1973), 2–4.

[88] John of Ford, *Wulfric of Haselbury*, 45, 105.

[89] Kemp, ed., *English Episcopal Acta 18*, 100; Jones, ed., *Register of S. Osmund*, 2:140.

the abbess of Elstow.[90] One must be cautious about generalizing from a handful of examples, but secular clerics may have played an important role in the production of their own books.

However, secular clerics clearly also helped bring about the great shift, in the decades surrounding 1200, from the production of books in the scriptoria of large churches to a commercial system of book manufacture.[91] Given strong clerical participation in the commercializing trends of the period, it is no surprise that they bought and sold books. Besides Gerald of Wales's forced sale and Ralph of Sarre's expenditure on books, one can point to Peter of Blois's complaints about a bookseller in Paris who had agreed to sell him some legal texts but then sold them to another.[92] Thomas of Monmouth, the monk who promoted the blood libel cult of William of Norwich, reported that a psalter stolen from him was sold (for a mere three pence) to a Norwich priest.[93] De Hamel has made a very convincing case for the production of glossed Bibles in Paris leading gradually to the creation of a book trade there involving scribes, illuminators, book binders, and others; strikingly, many of the examples he used concerned the acquisition of books by English secular clerics.[94] Circumstantial evidence links secular clerics to professionals in the book trade in England as well. A charter of *c.*1195–1215 to the dean and chapter of St. Paul's, London, is attested by Michael "who sells books" and John "who binds books."[95] These figures could have provided books for the cathedral, but also for the cathedral clergy. Similarly, Thomson notes various scribes and painters in Hereford from the late twelfth century and early thirteenth and suggests that the cathedral relied on such professionals to make its books.[96] There is no reason that individual clerics could not have done the same. More telling still, a handful of Oxford charters from the 1190s on reveal a number of illuminators and parchment makers there along with at least one binder.[97] Such professionals may well have received commissions from monasteries, but clearly they were settled in Oxford because of business from the masters and students at

---

[90] British Library, Royal MS 7 F III; De Hamel, *Glossed Books*, 56. See also Hunt, "English Learning," 33 n. 3.

[91] For this shift, see M. A. Michael, "Urban Production of Manuscript Books and the Role of the University Towns," in Nigel J. Morgan and Rodney M. Thomson, eds., *The Cambridge History of the Book in Britain. Vol. 2, 1100–1400* (Cambridge, 2008), 168–94; Richard H. Rouse and Mary A. Rouse, *Illiterati et Uxorati: Manuscripts and their Makers: Commercial Book Producers in Medieval Paris, 1200–1500*, 2 vols. (Turnhout, 2000), 1:17, 23–49; De Hamel, *Illuminated Manuscripts*, 108–40.

[92] Peter of Blois, *Opera*, 219–21.   [93] Thomas of Monmouth, *William of Norwich*, 201–2.

[94] De Hamel, *Glossed Books*, 12–13, 39–40, 49–52, 60–1, 76.

[95] Gibbs, ed., *Early Charters*, 166–7. See also M. B. Parkes, *Their Hands before our Eyes: A Closer Look at Scribes* (Aldershot, 2008), 39–40, 134–6.

[96] Mynors and Thomson, *Catalogue of Hereford Cathedral Library*, xix.

[97] T. E. Holland, "The University of Oxford in the Twelfth Century," in Montague Burrows, ed., *Collectanea II* (Oxford, 1890), 137–92, at 178–9; H. E. Salter, ed., *A Cartulary of the Hospital of St John the Baptist*, 3 vols., Oxford Historical Society Record Series, 66, 68–9 (Oxford, 1914–17), 1:419, 446–7. See also M. A. Michael, "English Illuminators *c.*1190–1450: A Survey from Documentary Sources," *English Manuscript Studies 1100–1700* 4 (1993), 62–113, at 63–5, 79–80; Michael, "Urban Production," 169–70.

the emerging university. Though many secular clerics may have been able to copy out their own books, they would not have had all the skills, from making parchment to binding, needed to produce a book. Nor did individuals generally have the resources to bring together a variety of skilled artisans in the way that a monastery could, and therefore it would have made sense for them to rely on commercial producers. There were doubtless many factors in the rise of the book trade, but the increasing practice of private book collection by the secular clergy was clearly an important one.

The collective evidence of books associated with individual secular clerics provides an important window into the scholarly lives of clerics, especially in the later stages of the Twelfth-Century Renaissance. This evidence exposes some possible weaknesses, particularly a likely tendency to absorb patristic texts indirectly through glossed Bibles. In general, however, it underscores the strength and liveliness of intellectual life among the secular clergy and their broad range of interests. It also underscores the importance of ordinary intellectuals to that renaissance in various ways, including transmitting texts and thereby disseminating knowledge, helping modernize institutional libraries, familiarizing the laity with book culture, and providing a crucial market for the emerging book trade. Judging by the English evidence, one of the key results of the Twelfth-Century Renaissance was the emergence of a book culture outside of institutional libraries, and in this process the secular clergy played a crucial role.[98]

---

[98] This was certainly not unique to England, for clerics in France (and no doubt elsewhere) also owned and donated books: A. M. Genevois, J.-F. Genest, and A. Chalandon, *Bibliothèques de manuscrits médiévaux en France: relevé des inventaires du VIIIe au XVIIIe siècle* (Paris, 1987), 173, 195, 203, 205–6, 242–4.

12

Secular Clerics as Authors and Intellectuals

In his *Otia Imperialia*, Gervase of Tilbury told the story of an English master, a man named Richard according to one annotator, who went to King Roger II of Sicily and asked for the bones of Virgil, thought to be buried in Naples. Was this master an early humanist, eager to establish some monument to the great classical author? In fact, the English scholar, who was described as being "strong and acute in the trivium and quadrivium, efficacious in medicine, and an unrivalled astronomer," sought the bones for magical purposes. Virgil had a reputation as a skilled wizard and Richard believed he could use Virgil's bones to recover his magic, though because of opposition from the citizens of Naples he came away only with a book of magic that was entombed with the bones. This story is improbable and does not focus on the mainstream of intellectual endeavor of the time, which was religious scholarship. Nonetheless, it does illustrate some important aspects of twelfth-century intellectual life: the international search for learning, which I have already stressed, the interest in the classical past, the frequent strangeness of intellectual endeavors from a modern perspective, the desire of intellectuals to gain knowledge that had practical application (for what could be more useful than magic, if it worked?), and the frequent willingness of clerics to seek controversial knowledge for worldly purposes.[1]

This chapter focuses on the intellectual work of the secular clergy, chiefly on their writings, but also on professional practices such as law, medicine, and preaching that had a strong learned component.[2] The primary aims of the chapter are to provide some sense of just how intellectually productive the secular clergy had become, to further illustrate their broad range of interests, to explore the contributions not just of the most famous scholars but also of more ordinary intellectuals, and to provide more evidence of their collective importance to the intellectual life of the period. I will pursue these aims through a survey of the activities and writings of clerics in a variety of fields and genres, though discussion of one genre, training guides for pastoral care, will be reserved for Chapter 14. As will become clear, secular clerics were deeply involved with many well-known aspects of the Twelfth-Century Renaissance: the abiding interest in theology and religion, the efflorescence of

---

[1] Gervase of Tilbury, *Otia Imperialia*, 802–5. For discussion of this story, see Peters, *Magician, Witch, and Law*, 54–6; Jean-Patrice Boudet, *Entre science et nigromance: astrologie, divination et magie dans l'occident médiéval, XIIe–XVe siècle* (Paris, 2006), 274–5.

[2] Overviews of English learning in the period which do not restrict themselves to the secular clergy may be found in Bartlett, *England under the Norman and Angevin Kings*, 492–525; Hunt, "English Learning," 19–42.

literature, the fascination with antiquity, and the translation of works from Arabic. Within their wide array of interests, however, I wish to stress efforts by some scholars to master and manipulate the material world. Generally, these scholars had no more success than Gervase's astronomer/magician, but had their dreams been realized, they would have transformed scholarship and society every bit as much as the scientific revolution later did. As it was, English secular clerics helped engineer developments in learning that had profound religious and social implications. With all this intellectual activity, however, came severe moral tensions. Moralists often stressed that a good cleric was a learned cleric, but the expansion of learning in the long twelfth century fostered fierce debates about what kinds of learning were useful and moral.

1. THE VARIETIES OF INTELLECTUAL WORK BY SECULAR CLERICS

Theology and the study of the Bible lay at the heart of intellectual life in the period, and it is hard for most modern people to comprehend just how riveting these subjects must have been to scholars in the twelfth century. The employment of a range of skills, including literary criticism and the emergent tool of dialectic, in a rapidly developing and extremely prestigious field designed to lay bare the fundamental truths of the universe, must have been heady indeed. Paris became the center of such scholarship during the course of the twelfth century, and I have already discussed the importance there of English scholars such as Robert of Melun, Robert Pullen, and Stephen Langton. Other lesser but still important English theologians such as John of Cornwall, who was very much engaged in some of the major debates of the day, also operated there.[3] English clerics were unusually important to a couple of aspects of bible study. An admittedly fairly mechanical but nonetheless noteworthy project was the division of the books of the Bible into the chapters still used. Medieval sources ascribed this development to Stephen Langton, and though recent work has revealed earlier instances of these chapter divisions, he probably helped popularize them. Herbert of Bosham and Alexander Neckam were also pioneers in this process.[4] For reasons that are not entirely clear, scholars from England, including not only Herbert of Bosham but also Ralph Niger and Stephen Langton, were also influential in the more exciting effort to gain some mastery of Hebrew and apply it to Christian biblical studies.[5]

---

[3] Eleanor Rathbone, "John of Cornwall: A Brief Biography," *Recherches de théologie ancienne et médiévale* 17 (1950), 46–60; Taliadoros, *Law and Theology*, 149–50, 152.

[4] Powicke, *Stephen Langton*, 34–7; Smalley, *Study of the Bible*, 221–4; Paul Saenger, "The British Isles and the Origin of the Modern Mode of Biblical Citation," *Syntagma: Revista de Historia del Libro y de la Lectura* 1 (2005), 77–123, at 82–3, 94–5; Paul Saenger and Laura Bruck, "The Anglo-Hebraic Origins of the Modern Chapter Division of the Latin Bible," in Javier San José Lera, Francisco Javier Burguillo López, and Laura Mier Pérez, eds., *La fractura historiográfica: las investigaciones de Edad Media y Renacimiento desde el tercer milenio* (Salamanca, 2008), 177–202.

[5] Smalley, *Study of the Bible*, 190–1, 235–6; Goodwin, *Take Hold of the Robe of a Jew*, 9–10, 48–50; Ralph Niger, *De Re Militari*, 80–2.

Of course, most theologians were not working at the cutting edges of European scholarship, and precisely because theology and bible study were such popular fields they provide a good opportunity to stress the work of ordinary intellectuals. A particularly telling example of an intellectual who was not at the center of European intellectual life, but nonetheless created an accomplished, substantial, and sometimes inventive body of work, was William de Montibus, who returned to Lincoln from Paris in the 1180s and served as chancellor there from 1194 at the latest until his death in 1213. His works included an introduction to theology called the *Numerale*, guides to penance and the seven sacraments, and collections of similes and images, proverbs and quotations, and mnemonic and didactic verses. Joseph Goering, who has studied his mostly unpublished writings, emphasizes his use of new pedagogical techniques, of innovative forms of organization, such as alphabetization, and of other popularizing practices.[6] Throughout this work, I have had frequent occasion to mention other theologians and biblical commentators who were not giants in the field, but did interesting, solid work, including Godwin of Salisbury, Gervase of Chichester, Master Vacarius, and Peter of Blois; the writing of treatises on theology and the Bible by secular clerics in England was surprisingly common.

Moving beyond treatises, one can point to clerics who left behind densely annotated manuscripts, such as Robert Amiclas and Peter de Melida, a canon of Lincoln Cathedral about whom little is known today but who was described as a famous figure in a Becket miracle.[7] Glosses were a very important medium of biblical and theological study in this period, but at this point most of the relatively limited work on them has understandably focused on the emergence of the standard *Glossa Ordinaria*.[8] Though many glosses were simply copied, others reveal original thought. For instance, Webber has used annotations in Salisbury Cathedral manuscripts to help reconstruct the lively intellectual life there in the twelfth century.[9] It is likely that future work will reveal much more about the scholarship of the period, and may even reveal unexpected riches in the margins of manuscripts. Theology and biblical explication can also be found in letters. Julie Barrau has shown how John of Salisbury, who in earlier letters had tended to cite classical sources, used an array of biblical citations to justify radical positions during the Becket controversy. John was, of course, no ordinary intellectual, but his techniques were not unusual, and show how other clerics who wrote no treatises on theology or the Bible could nonetheless have put to use the knowledge they had gained in their studies. Though few individuals could ever be pathbreakers in the fields of theology and bible study, large numbers of secular clerics, in England as elsewhere, were actively engaged in these fields.

---

[6] Goering, *William de Montibus*.

[7] For Amiclas's glosses, see Sheppard, *Buildwas Books*, lvii. For Peter de Melida and his manuscripts, see Smith, ed., *English Episcopal Acta 1*, xliv; Robertson and Sheppard, eds., *Materials*, 2:103; Thomson, *Lincoln Cathedral Library*, xv, 57, 138, 142, 150.

[8] Smith, *Glossa Ordinaria*.   [9] Webber, *Scribes and Scholars*, 132–9.

Further evidence of this may be found in sermons, a genre designed partly to transmit theology and biblical learning. I will be discussing preaching more fully in Chapter 14, but here I wish to discuss the writing of sermons as an intellectual activity. A number of secular clerics were the authors of sermon collections in Latin.[10] Though I have used these collections mainly for sermons about clerical behavior, most Latin sermons were devoted to commenting on biblical passages. They have received relatively little scholarly attention, but represented a substantial portion of the intellectual production of the period, and some were quite sophisticated. When it came to sermons, however, the vast majority of secular clerics would have worked as practitioners. Preaching was supposed to be one of the crucial activities of the clergy and even allowing for doubts about how common preaching was at the parish level (see Chapter 14), clearly there would have been large numbers of clerics spreading theology and biblical teachings at various levels of sophistication through the spoken word. Reformers were particularly attuned to the importance of sermons, and it was in this context that Thomas of Chobham wrote an early guide to preaching a few years after 1216.[11]

English secular clerics also made important contributions to the liberal arts. I noted Adam of Balsham's influential treatise in the field of logic in Chapter 10, for instance, and he also wrote a work, *De Utensilibus*, that was designed to help students master obscure Latin vocabulary.[12] While teaching in Paris, Dunstable, or Oxford, Alexander Neckam wrote a similar work and also some other pedagogical pieces, including fables and a commentary on Martianus Capella.[13] Robert Blund, probably the canon of Lincoln of that name, wrote a *summa* on Priscian and grammar.[14] Late in the period, Geoffrey of Vinsauf, an English cleric who studied at Paris but taught at least for a time at Northampton, wrote various treatises on rhetoric, one of which, the *Poetria Nova*, became one of the most influential works on rhetoric in Europe in the later Middle Ages, with over 220 manuscripts surviving, making it the equivalent of a medieval "bestseller."[15] Even more important for fostering the liberal arts were the many secular clerics who served as masters at the growing number of schools and eventually at Oxford and Cambridge, many of whom would have been deeply learned even if they left no

---

[10] Lambeth Palace, MS 458 part 2; Bodleian Library, Wood empt. MS 13; Trinity College, Cambridge, MS B.14.8, fos. 1r–102v; Bodleian Library, Laud. Misc. MS 71; Peter of Blois, *Opera*, 559–776; Goering, *William de Montibus*, 515–66; Thomas of Chobham, *Sermones*, ed. Franco Morenzoni (Turnhout, 1993); Roberts, *Sermons of Stephen Langton*.

[11] Thomas of Chobham, *Summa de Arte Praedicandi*. For a discussion of his guide, see Morenzoni, *Des écoles aux paroisses*.

[12] "Adam of Petit Pont's *De Utensilibus*," in Tony Hunt, ed., *Teaching and Learning Latin in Thirteenth-Century England* (Woodbridge, 1991), 1:165–76.

[13] Hunt and Gibson, *Schools and the Cloister*, 19–20, 32–3, 41–2.

[14] Barker-Benfield, *St Augustine's Abbey*, 3:1856–8. Barker-Benfield suggests that Robert, who died a monk at St. Augustine's, Canterbury, was a monk who served on detached duty as a canon, but I think his alternative scenario, that Robert became a monk only after being a canon, makes more sense.

[15] Geoffrey's works are edited in Faral, *Les arts poétiques*, 194–327. For his impact, see Marjorie Curry Woods, *Classroom Commentaries: Teaching the Poetria Nova across Medieval and Renaissance Europe* (Columbus, 2010).

surviving writings. The *Liber Eliensis* described one such teacher, the rhetorician Julian, who entered Ely after a career of teaching on the continent and in London, as "a man admirable for his knowledge, second to none in grammar, to be preferred to any in the Latin world."[16]

Fascination and engagement with the Latin classics, long considered a hallmark of the Twelfth-Century Renaissance, was closely linked to the liberal arts and was common among the secular clergy, as indicated by their frequent ownership of classical texts.[17] John of Salisbury is acknowledged as one of the most accomplished classicists in the period.[18] Less famous secular clerics could also write works intimately connected to the classics. For instance, Alberic, a canon at St. Paul's, almost certainly wrote or revised an important compilation of mythological material from the classical world which was informed by Stoic, Neo-platonic, and Aristotelian thinking. Jane Chance has described this work as "the most influential mythography in the Middle Ages," and it had a direct or indirect influence on such writers as Boccaccio, Petrarch, Salutati, and Chaucer.[19] More generally, the widespread interest in the Latin classics among the learned clergy is indicated by the pervasive use of classical quotations and allusions.[20] Neither the historian Henry of Huntingdon nor William fitz Stephen, the biographer of Becket, have the reputation of someone like John of Salisbury for classical learning, yet the former could use incidents from classical history to shape his own work and the latter could use classical allusions to compare London favorably to Rome and to describe Becket's worldly greatness before he became archbishop.[21] Indeed, the use of

---

[16] Blake, ed., *Liber Eliensis*, 341–2.

[17] For classical learning and influence in the Twelfth-Century Renaissance, see Haskins, *Renaissance of the Twelfth Century*, 93–152; Janet Martin, "Classicism and Style in Latin Literature," in Robert Louis Benson and Giles Constable, eds., *Renaissance and Renewal in the Twelfth Century* (Cambridge, Mass., 1982), 537–68; Swanson, *Twelfth-Century Renaissance*, 40–50.

[18] John and others may often have relied on florilegia and epitomes rather than complete texts, but that did not make the classical influence any less important: Martin, "John of Salisbury as Classical Scholar," 184–5; Rodney M. Thomson, *William of Malmesbury* (Woodbridge, 2003), 9–10; Anne Duggan, "Classical Quotations and Allusions in the Correspondence of Thomas Becket: An Investigation of their Sources," *Viator* 32 (2001), 1–22, at 7–11.

[19] Georg Heinrich Bode, ed., *Scriptores Rerum Mythicarum Latini Tres Romae Nuper Reperti*, 2 vols. (Zell, 1834), 1:152–256; Jane Chance, *Medieval Mythography: From Roman North Africa to the School of Chartres, A.D. 433–1177*, 2 vols. (Gainesville, 1994), 2:138–84. Burnett has raised doubts about whether Alberic was the "Third Vatican Mythographer," but Alberic was named in many manuscripts and most scholars still accept that attribution. His association with liturgical development and with books at St. Paul's makes it seem likely that he was at least the reviser: Eleanor Rathbone, "Master Alberic of London, 'Mythographus Tertius Vaticanus'," *Mediaeval and Renaissance Studies* 1 (1941–43), 35–8; Charles Burnett, "A Note on the Origins of the Third Vatican Mythographer," *Journal of the Warburg and Courtauld Institutes* 44 (1981), 160–6; Baswell, *Virgil in Medieval England*, 134; Richard W. Pfaff, *The Liturgy in Medieval England: A History* (Cambridge, 2009), 483; Adgar, *Le gracial*, 13, 327. Added complications arise from the appearance of a second Alberic of London (judging by the dates) as the witness to an Oxford charter in the 1180s: Salter, ed., *Cartulary of Oseney Abbey*, 1:217. Alexander Neckam is another potential candidate for authorship of this work.

[20] See, for example, Duggan, "Classical Quotations," 1–22.

[21] Henry of Huntingdon, *Historia Anglorum*, xxxiv–xxxviii, 853–5; Diana E. Greenway, "Authority, Convention and Observation in Henry of Huntingdon's *Historia Anglorum*," *Anglo-Norman Studies* 18 (1996), 105–21, at 105, 112–14; Staunton, *Thomas Becket and his Biographers*, 59; John Scattergood, "Misrepresenting the City: Genre, Intertextuality and William Fitz-Stephen's

classical allusions and quotations was so widespread that the proper question might be what learned writings did not display classical influence?

The occasional appearance of classical references in sermons is particularly striking, because it showed the willingness to use pagan works in a thoroughly Christian setting (albeit often to provide negative examples) and because in some cases it presupposed a shared familiarity with the classical world between preacher and audience. Peter Maude, in a sermon to priests, could contrast the school of Christ with the school of Epicurus.[22] Thomas Agnellus quoted a skeptical satire of Horace about the powers of a wooden carving of Priapus in a passage contrasting pagan gods with the Christian deity.[23] Alexander Neckam made particular use of the classics in preaching, drawing explicitly on Ovid and Virgil and referring to pagan gods, individuals from the Trojan wars, and figures such as Narcissus and Perseus. Some of these references even appeared in sermons he addressed to laypeople. Perhaps Alexander was aiming beyond his audience's reach, but it is possible that classical knowledge so permeated the clergy that many stories reached the laity in oral form.[24]

Naturally enough, classical influence was particularly apparent in the contributions of secular clerics to the rich tradition of contemporary Latin literature. Our genre boundaries differ from theirs, sometimes making it hard to delineate what should count as twelfth-century literature, but plays written in imitation of classical comedies certainly fit the bill. About twenty Latin comedies survive from the long twelfth century, and one, *De Tribus Sociis*, was probably composed by Geoffrey of Vinsauf. Judging by the manuscript tradition, two others, *De Clericis et Rustico* and *Babio*, came from England, with the former possibly also being by Geoffrey. These two plays have clerics as characters, and because they provide interesting glimpses into clerical self-mockery, in one case ridiculing intellectual pretension, it is worth pausing to describe them briefly. *Babio* concerned a married priest of that name who lusted after his own step-daughter, Viola, and suffered comic retribution not only by seeing the lord of the village win Viola's favor but also by being cuckolded by his wife, Petula. The play is filled with slapstick, sexual humor, and trickery, but also punning, alliteration, and, fittingly enough, classical allusions. *De Clericis et Rustico*, drawn from an anecdote of Petrus Alfonsus, concerned two clerics and a peasant who were traveling together but found themselves with insufficient food, whereupon the clerics tried to trick the peasant out of his share by making a deal that whoever saw the most marvels in his sleep would get the food. One cleric used his knowledge of astronomy to invent a dream of being drawn into the heavens, describing spheres and poles, cycles and epicycles, and the signs of the zodiac. The other called on his command of classical mythology to describe Tantalus, Sisyphus,

Description of London (c.1173)," *Reading the Past: Essays on Medieval and Renaissance Literature* (Dublin, 1996), 15–36.

[22] Trinity College, Cambridge, MS B.14.8, fo. 25r.

[23] Bodleian Library, Laud. Misc. MS 71, fo. 34v. The passage quoted is from book 1, satire 8 of Horace's *Satires*.

[24] Bodleian Library, Wood empt. MS 13, fos. 17r, 23r, 26r, 35r, 81r–v, 88v–89r, 120r; Hunt and Gibson, *Schools and the Cloister*, 91.

the Furies, and other aspects of the pagan afterlife. The peasant, however, had already outwitted them by getting up in the middle of the night and eating the food.[25]

A number of English clerics composed Latin poetry. Admittedly, a sizable poetic corpus survives for only a few, including Henry of Huntingdon, Gerald of Wales, and Peter of Blois.[26] However, scraps of poetry can be found from other figures, including Gerald's friend Robert de Bello Fago; Hugh Sottovagina, precentor and house historian of York Cathedral; Geoffrey Trocope, archdeacon of Nottingham; and John of Leicester, a canon of Bridgnorth.[27] When the prayer roll of Abbess Matilda of Caen, daughter of William the Conqueror, was circulated in England to solicit prayers for her, two schools and the cathedrals of Exeter, York, and Lincoln contributed poems in her honor.[28] Such scattered evidence suggests that the composition of poetry was a widespread skill among the secular clergy, which would hardly be surprising since composing poetry could be a part of their education. Secular clerics may therefore also have been responsible for a fair proportion of the many anonymous poems that survive from the period. The greatest Latin poets of the twelfth century, such as the secular clerics Marbod of Rennes, Hildebert of Lavardin, and the Archpoet, tended to be continental, but Serlo of Wilton, who was active on both sides of the Channel, was one of the more accomplished poets of the twelfth century, as noted in Chapter 3.[29] Likewise, Joseph of Exeter, nephew of Archbishop Baldwin of Canterbury, composed a poetic retelling of the Trojan War that enjoyed popularity in England and on the continent and that A. G. Rigg has described as a high point in medieval Latin verse.[30]

[25] The plays discussed here are edited by Andrea Dessì Fulgheri and Enzo Cadoni in the second volume of *Commedie latine del XII e XIII secolo*, 5 vols. (Genoa, 1976–86), 2:129–377. See also Rigg, *History of Anglo-Latin Literature*, 113–14, 152. Babio is specifically described as a priest in a manuscript from the late twelfth century or early thirteenth. It is possible that the anonymous plays come from a monastic background, but the themes seem more in keeping with a context involving the secular clergy.

[26] Henry of Huntingdon, *Historia Anglorum*, 778–825; A. G. Rigg, "Henry of Huntingdon's Herbal," *Mediaeval Studies* 65 (2003), 213–92; Winston Black, "Henry of Huntingdon's Lapidary Rediscovered and his *Anglicanus Ortus* Reassembled," *Mediaeval Studies* 68 (2006), 43–87; Henry of Huntingdon, *Anglicanus Ortus: A Verse Herbal of the Twelfth Century*, ed. Winston Black (Toronto, 2012); Gerald of Wales, *Opera*, 1:341–87; Wollin, ed., *Petri Blesensis Carmina*. The extent of Peter of Blois's corpus is highly debated and Wollin's edition contains many poems of disputed attribution.

[27] Wollin, ed., *Petri Blesensis Carmina*, 281; Thomas Wright, ed., *The Anglo-Latin Satirical Poets and Epigrammatists of the Twelfth Century*, 2 vols. (London, 1872), 2:219–29; Raine, ed., *Historians of the Church of York*, 2:267–9; Adam of Eynsham, *Magna Vita Sancti Hugonis*, 2:231–2; Bodleian Library, Bodleian MS 656, fos. 149v–150r; Rigg, *History of Anglo-Latin Literature*, 52–3, 86. For John of Leicester as a canon of Bridgnorth, see Hardy, ed., *Rotuli Litterarum Patentium*, 38a.

[28] Léopold Delisle, ed., *Rouleaux des morts du IXe au XVe siècle* (Paris, 1866), 189, 191–2, 199–200.

[29] See Chapter 3, section 2. For Serlo's poetry, see Jan Öberg, ed., *Serlon de Wilton: Poèmes Latins* (Stockholm, 1965). Godman nicely situates the Archpoet in the world of the clerical elite of Germany, similar in many ways to the milieu discussed in this book: Peter Godman, *The Silent Masters: Latin Literature and its Censors in the High Middle Ages* (Princeton, 2000), 202–27.

[30] Joseph also composed religious poetry: Rigg, *History of Anglo-Latin Literature*, 67–8, 99–102; Joseph Iscanus, *Werke und Briefe*, 75–211; A. K. Bate, "Joseph of Exeter, Religious Poet," *Medium Aevum* 40 (1971), 222–9.

Modern scholars do not generally assign as much aesthetic value to letter collections as to plays or poems, but for medieval scholars letter writing was the equivalent of an art form as well as being an important practical task.[31] Gerald of Wales preserved a number of his letters, partly to illustrate his various travails but clearly also to enhance his literary status, since he included them in the same work as his poetry, speeches, and prologues.[32] Master David of London and John of Salisbury also left collections.[33] However, Peter of Blois was the greatest master of letter writing in the period and his letter collection, designed to provide models for other practitioners, had enormous influence in subsequent years. Versions of his collection survive in over 300 manuscripts, making it another medieval "bestseller," and there were even a number of editions published between 1480 and 1667.[34] Letter writing, moreover, may have been the written medium though which the largest numbers of clerics demonstrated their learning and literary skills, for though only a small minority of clerics would have compiled letter collections, hundreds would have written formal letters in the course of their careers.

Beyond these works in relatively well-defined literary genres, secular clerics associated with England also produced miscellaneous works in Latin that had strong literary elements. The anonymous cleric, probably English, who was noted in Chapter 3 for his adherence to the peasantry, produced an undeservedly neglected collection of anecdotes, stories, and commentary, with subjects ranging from the death of Nero to the wife of a Spanish warrior who had sex with Muslims.[35] Better known today is Walter Map's rich collection of anecdotes, historical snippets, marvels, and stories.[36] More influential during the Middle Ages was the *Otia Imperialia* of Gervase of Tilbury, a vast miscellany that was particularly noteworthy for its collection of what might now be considered folk tales, including one of a demon hound near Carlisle that burned down a house of a priest with his "less than legitimately born" family inside.[37] It was, however, Geoffrey of Monmouth who had the greatest long-term literary impact, even though his works purported to be history, prophecy, and biography. Though Geoffrey was presumably from Wales and identified with the Britons rather than the English, he spent much of his career in Oxford, where he was probably associated with the collegiate church of St. George.[38] Julia Crick has catalogued over two hundred manuscripts of his most important work, the *Historia Regum Britanniae*. Many of these were of continental

[31] For the epistolary genre, including its literary aspects, see Giles Constable, *Letters and Letter-Collections* (Turnhout, 1976).

[32] Gerald of Wales, *Opera*, 1:199–335.

[33] Brooke, "Register of Master David," 227–45; John of Salisbury, *Letters*.

[34] Southern, *Scholastic Humanism*, 2:194–5, 216–18; Cotts, *Clerical Dilemma*, 4–5, 49–95.

[35] Colker, ed., *Analecta Dublinensia*, 181–257.   [36] Walter Map, *De Nugis Curialium*.

[37] Gervase of Tilbury, *Otia Imperialia*.

[38] Geoffrey of Monmouth, *The History of the Kings of Britain: An Edition and Translation of* De Gestis Britonum (Historia Regum Britanniae), ed. Michael D. Reeve and Neil Wright (Woodbridge, 2007); Geoffrey of Monmouth, *The Vita Merlini*, ed. John Jay Parry (Urbana, 1925); Michael J. Curley, *Geoffrey of Monmouth* (New York, 1994); John Gillingham, "The Context and Purpose of Geoffrey of Monmouth's *History of the Kings of Britain*," in *The English in the Twelfth Century: Imperialism, National Identity, and Political Values* (Woodbridge, 2000), 19–39.

provenance, showing a widespread geographical dissemination of the text that reached even to Germany and Italy.[39] The literary impact of Geoffrey's work, which not only reshaped the Arthurian cycle but also planted the seed for such works as Shakespeare's *King Lear*, hardly requires further discussion.

England had a particularly strong tradition of historical writing to which both the regular and the secular clergy contributed.[40] Clerics such as Henry of Huntingdon, Roger of Howden, and Ralph of Diceto were among the best historians of the twelfth century and their works are still fundamentally important for reconstructing the history of the period.[41] Gerald of Wales wrote one of the key sources for the English invasion of Ireland and various other secular clerics also wrote chronicles and histories.[42] Hagiography was one of the most culturally and religiously significant genres of the period, and a number of secular clerics, including Gerald of Wales, Peter of Blois, and John of Salisbury, produced collections of miracles stories and *vitae* of saints old and new, including some of the most important lives of Thomas Becket.[43]

Another noteworthy aspect of the Twelfth-Century Renaissance was the rise of vernacular writing, particularly in French. As a result of the Norman Conquest, French became an important written language in England and England in turn became a surprisingly important center for the development of written French.[44] Though laypeople would have participated far more in the development of vernacular than Latin literature, the contributions of the religious remained crucial, and Michael Clanchy has noted that it was often the very learned who experimented with using the vernacular in writing.[45] Many vernacular texts, of course, were written by monks, and this was an area in which nuns were especially important.[46] That said, secular clerics played an influential role in the development of the French vernacular tradition in England. Indeed, the combination of their learning and

[39] Julia C. Crick, *The* Historia Regum Britanniae *of Geoffrey of Monmouth: III. A Summary Catalogue of the Manuscripts* (Cambridge, 1989); Julia C. Crick, *The* Historia Regum Britanniae *of Geoffrey of Monmouth: IV. Dissemination and Reception in the Later Middle Ages* (Cambridge, 1991), 206–17.

[40] For secular clerics who were historians in the period, see Antonia Gransden, *Historical Writing in England c.550–c.1307* (London, 1996), 1:123–5, 186, 193–212, 219–46, 271.

[41] Henry of Huntingdon, *Historia Anglorum*; [Roger of Howden], *Gesta Regis Henrici Secundi*; Roger of Howden, *Chronica*; Ralph of Diceto, *Opera Historica*.

[42] Gerald of Wales, *Expugnatio Hibernica*; John of Salisbury, *Historia Pontificalis*; Alfred of Beverley, *Annales, sive Historia de Gestis Regum Britanniæ*, ed. Thomas Hearne (Oxford, 1716); Hugh the Chanter, *History of the Church of York*; Watkiss and Chibnall, eds., *Waltham Chronicle*.

[43] Gerald of Wales, *Opera*, 3:377–404; 4:357–431; 7:1–147; Cotts, *Clerical Dilemma*, 260; Nederman, *John of Salisbury*, 80; Whatley, ed., *Saint of London*; Robertson and Sheppard, eds., *Materials*, 2:299–322, 353–450; 3:1–534; Raine, ed., *Historians of the Church of York*, 1:261–347; 2:259–91, 531–43. I have included some anonymous saints' lives and collections of miracle stories related to Beverley and York that were probably composed by clerics at those churches.

[44] For overviews of Anglo-Norman writing, see Legge, *Anglo-Norman Literature*; Susan Crane, "Anglo-Norman Cultures in England, 1066–1460," in David Wallace, ed., *The Cambridge History of Medieval English Literature* (Cambridge, 1999), 35–60; Ian Short, "Patrons and Polyglots: French Literature in Twelfth-Century England," *Anglo-Norman Studies* 14 (1992), 229–49.

[45] Clanchy, *From Memory to Written Record*, 215–20.

[46] M. Dominica Legge, *Anglo-Norman in the Cloisters: The Influence of the Orders upon Anglo-Norman Literature* (Edinburgh, 1950).

their interactions with the secular elites put them in a particularly good position to foster vernacular written culture.

One important contribution by secular clerics was the translation of material from Latin. Various clerics translated a number of Latin works from a variety of genres, including hagiographical works, the bestiary, and the book of Proverbs from the Bible.[47] Understandably enough, most modern readers are more interested in chivalric romance than translations of Latin texts, but the importance of such translations for the development of vernacular written culture, including chivalric romance, should not be underestimated. For instance, Master Thomas of Kent, possibly a monk but most likely a cleric, used a Latin version of Pseudo-Callisthenes to create his own version of Alexander the Great's highly fictionalized adventures. Like more famous works such as the anonymous *Eneas* and *Le Roman de Troie* of Benoît de Sainte-Maure, this work contributed to the creation of the subgenre of the Romance of Antiquity, reimagining the ancient world in a medieval framework in which, for instance, Athens could be a center of chivalry and "courtoisie" as well as of scholarship in the seven liberal arts. With all manner of marvels and wonders, such as Alexander exploring the ocean in an underwater vessel or hippopotamuses attacking and devouring 200 knights, translations of the Alexander romance helped contribute to the development of the marvelous in medieval vernacular literature.[48] Though the vernacular literature of romance and poetry that arose in the twelfth century depended heavily on aristocratic and popular oral traditions, it also drew deeply from translated Latin texts, which is precisely why the work of someone like Geoffrey of Monmouth, who was translated into French by the Norman cleric Wace, and whose stories provided the inspiration for so many Arthurian romances, could be so influential.[49]

Secular clerics also produced original works in French. One important original composition for modern historians was the chronicle of Jordan Fantosme, a key source for English events in the 1173–4 rebellion against Henry II.[50] Hue de

[47] For works by men who were certainly or almost certainly secular clerics, see William de Briane, *The Anglo-Norman* Pseudo-Turpin Chronicle *of William de Briane*, ed. Ian Short (Oxford, 1973); Simund de Freine, *Œuvres*; Philippe de Thaon, *Comput (MS BL Cotton Nero A. V)*; Philippe de Thaon, *Le livre de Sibile*, ed. Hugh Shields (London, 1979); Philippe de Thaon, *Le Bestiaire de Philippe de Thaün*, ed. Emmanuel Walberg (Lund, 1900); Paul Studer and Joan Evans, eds., *Anglo-Norman Lapidaries* (Paris, 1924), 200–76; Adgar, *Le gracial*. For some works by men who were likely secular clerics, see Sanson de Nantuil, *Les proverbes de Salemon by Sanson de Nantuil*, ed. Claire Isoz, 3 vols. (London, 1988–94); Chardri, *La vie des set dormanz*, ed. Brian S. Merrilees (London, 1977). Chardri probably also composed an original collection of moral reflections called the *Petit plet*: Chardri, *Le petit plet*, ed. Brian S. Merrilees (Oxford, 1970).

[48] Thomas of Kent, *Anglo-Norman Alexander*, 1:74–5, 154–5, 198–201. A later illuminator believed Thomas to have been a monk of St. Albans, but the editors of his work argue against this: Legge, *Anglo-Norman Literature*, 106; Thomas of Kent, *Anglo-Norman Alexander*, 2:70–1.

[49] Wace, *Wace's* Roman de Brut: *A History of the British, Text and Translation*, ed. Judith Weiss (Exeter, 2002).

[50] Besides being a historian, Jordan was a student of Gilbert de la Porrée, a schoolmaster in Winchester, and the author of a learned Latin poem on the incarnation. Disconcertingly he was also accused of causing the death of a cleric named Herbert: Jordan Fantosme, *Chronicle*, xi–xiv; MacDonald, "Chronicle of Jordan Fantosme," 247–54. Another historian who was working in the vernacular and was likely a secular cleric was Gaimar, who translated large parts of the *Anglo-Saxon*

Roteland's romances, *Ipomedon* and *Protheslaus*, are important works which were unduly neglected in the past but have been receiving increased attention in recent decades. *Ipomedon* in particular has a rich vein of comedy.[51] Master Thomas, who wrote *The Romance of Horn*, had a son, but his reference to himself chanting in Latin at the end of the poem, his self-ascribed title as master, and the Latin and clerical influence on his vocabulary indicate he was an educated man of clerical status. Dominica Legge has described his work as perhaps the finest surviving Anglo-Norman romance.[52] The status of other writers, such as Thomas of Britain, author of the now fragmentary version of the Tristan legend used by Gottfried von Strasbourg, or the anonymous authors of the influential Anglo-Norman romances of Guy of Warwick and Boeve of Hampton, must remain unknown, but it is certainly possible that they were clerics. Even if one sets such uncertain examples aside, the surviving evidence clearly shows the importance of secular clerics in the flowering of writing in French in England during the long twelfth century.

The secular clergy also aided the preservation of French as a spoken language in England. Though the Norman Conquest established French as the language of the elite, it is likely that over the course of the twelfth century it gradually became an second language even for aristocrats, at least for those without holdings on both sides of the Channel.[53] The prestige of the French language, the appeal of French culture in general, and the continuing political ties of England with parts of France helped French remain an important language for the lay elites. However, French was also useful to the clerical elites. For learned clerics as for the laity, command of French could be a marker of elite status: Walter Map recorded how he embarrassed his enemy, Geoffrey Plantagenet, illegitimate son of Henry II, by wittily mocking his poor French.[54] Many clerics, like many secular aristocrats, had careers that spanned the Channel, making knowledge of French a necessity. A command of French would also have made life easier when studying in French schools, and sojourns in Paris or elsewhere would have given clerics who were not already bilingual a good mastery of the language. Gerald of Wales once asked a young cleric, Master John Blund, who spoke French like a native, how long he had spent in France. As it turned out, John had not been there at all, but had learned to speak it well by carefully imitating two clerical uncles who had spent much time studying across the Channel.[55] It was clearly in the interest of many clerics to use and promote the use of French, and their role in the survival of spoken French in England should not be underestimated.

Chronicle into French; Geffrei Gaimar, *Estoire des Engleis. History of the English*, ed. Ian Short (Oxford, 2009).

[51] Hue de Rotelande, *Ipomedon*; Hue de Rotelande, *Protheslaus*. For discussion of Hue's works, see Legge, *Anglo-Norman Literature*, 85–96; Crane, *Insular Romance*, 134–74. It is possible but unlikely that Hue was not a cleric: see Chapter 3, n. 41.

[52] Master Thomas, *The Romance of Horn*, ed. Mildred K. Pope and T. B. W. Reid, 2 vols. (Oxford, 1955–64), 1:173–4; 2:1–2; Legge, *Anglo-Norman Literature*, 96.

[53] W. Rothwell, "The Role of French in Thirteenth-Century England," *Bulletin of the John Rylands Society* 58 (1976), 445–66; R. M. Wilson, "English and French in England, 1100–1300," *History* 28 (1943), 37–60; Ian Short, "On Bilingualism in Anglo-Norman England," *Romance Philology* 33 (1980), 467–79; Short, "Patrons and Polyglots," 246–8.

[54] Walter Map, *De Nugis Curialium*, 496–7.   [55] Gerald of Wales, *Speculum Duorum*, 56–7.

What of the secular clergy and English? As a result of the Norman Conquest written English declined in relative importance to writing in Latin and subsequently to French. However, recent work has shown that the decline was not as sharp as once thought: Old English works continued to be copied and various new works appeared.[56] Some English writing can be traced to the regular clergy and much is anonymous, but here too secular clerics played a role. Bruce O'Brien, editor of the post-Conquest *Laws of Edward the Confessor*, suggests that they might have emerged out of the household of a bishop, which would make authorship by a secular cleric likely.[57] Far more important was Laȝamon, author of the largest and most ambitious work in Early Middle English, a poetic translation of Wace's French translation of Geoffrey of Monmouth's *Historia Regum Britanniae*. This work was most likely composed before 1216, and the author explicitly described himself as the parish priest of Areley Kings in Worcestershire.[58]

2. SECULAR CLERICS AND "PRACTICAL" KNOWLEDGE

Secular clerics were also involved in intellectual endeavors designed to have practical or worldly utility. It would, of course, be unwise to make too sharp a distinction between utilitarian and non-utilitarian subjects. The same basic learning in the liberal arts that prepared one to grapple with theology could have practical applications as well, and the advantages a reputation for learning gave in gaining benefices has been discussed in Chapter 5.[59] Moreover, there was a specific expectation, or at least hope, that the writing of learned works of literature, history, or religion might bring patronage from rulers and prelates who were supportive of learning and desirous of the immortal fame that their beneficence would theoretically bring. Gerald of Wales frequently sought to gain rewards for his many works (despite occasionally protesting otherwise) by flattering dedicatees and by lamenting at length that princes were no longer as generous as they had once been, thus hinting that prospective patrons should reverse the trend.[60] Across

---

[56] Mary Swan and Elaine M. Treharne, eds., *Rewriting Old English in the Twelfth Century* (Cambridge, 2000); Mary Swan, "Old English Textual Activity in the Reign of Henry II," in Ruth Kennedy and Simon Meecham-Jones, eds., *Writers of the Reign of Henry II: Twelve Essays* (New York, 2006), 151–68; Elaine Treharne, "The Life of English in the Mid-Twelfth Century: Ralph D'Escure's Homily on the Virgin Mary," in Ruth Kennedy and Simon Meecham-Jones, eds., *Writers of the Reign of Henry II: Twelve Essays* (New York, 2006), 169–86; Elizabeth Solopova, "English Poetry of the Reign of Henry II," in Ruth Kennedy and Simon Meecham-Jones, eds., *Writers of the Reign of Henry II: Twelve Essays* (New York, 2006), 187–204; Thomson, *Books and Learning*, 10–18; Elaine M. Treharne, *Living through Conquest: The Politics of Early English, 1020–1220* (Oxford, 2012).

[57] Bruce R. O'Brien, *God's Peace and King's Peace: The Laws of Edward the Confessor* (Philadelphia, 1999), 49–61.

[58] Laȝamon, *Laȝamon: Brut*, ed. G. L. Brook and R. F. Leslie, 2 vols. (London, 1963–78), 1:2–3. For the date, see Françoise H. M. Le Saux, *Layamon's Brut: The Poem and its Sources* (Cambridge, 1989), 1–10.

[59] Cotts, *Clerical Dilemma*, 114–15; Stollberg, *Soziale Stellung*, 132–5.

[60] Gerald of Wales, *Opera*, 5:3–5; 6:3–8, 161–2; 7:136; Gerald of Wales, *Expugnatio Hibernica*, 8–12, 22–5, 264–5.

the Channel, the Norman cleric Wace made the connection between writing and patronage quite straightforwardly: "I speak to rich men, who have money and a good income, for through them books are composed and good deeds written down and properly recounted." Wace criticized those who provided him with no more than praise and encouragement, highlighted his poverty, and echoed Gerald in lamenting the lost generosity of past rulers, but he also revealed that Henry II had provided him a prebend at Bayeux.[61] Thus, writers could have thoroughly pragmatic motives for studies and writings that were not designed for worldly utility.

That said, government, law, and medicine were three noteworthy areas of clearly pragmatic intellectual activity. I have already stressed the importance of the contributions of secular clerics as intellectuals and as bureaucrats to the development of English government in Chapter 6. However, it is worth underscoring here the achievement of Richard fitz Nigel in writing about and explaining government accounting in the *Dialogue of the Exchequer*.[62] In the context of government one must also note John of Salisbury's *Policraticus*, generally considered the first major work on political philosophy from the Middle Ages and one of the most important medieval treatises in that field, which emerged at least in part from John's experience in ecclesiastical and royal government in England.[63]

Secular clerics were particularly active in writing about, teaching, and practicing law. Canon law was of course a particularly important field for the clergy. I noted the activities of English scholars in Bologna in Chapter 10 and Stephan Kuttner and Eleanor Rathbone have described the many activities elsewhere of English canonists, who can overwhelmingly be identified as secular clerics.[64] A number of English clerics (including Gerald of Wales and Gerard la Pucelle) taught at various centers in England and on the continent. Later in the period, though precisely when is debated, Oxford became an important center for the study of canon law in England.[65] Glosses reveal the teaching activities of a number of English clerics, many of them prominent administrators and intellectuals, such as John of Tynemouth, Simon of Sywell, and the theologian John of Cornwall. Master Odo of Dover wrote a treatise of which only fragments survive, and Master Honorius composed a *summa* of canon law.[66] Most clerics who studied canon law, of course,

---

[61] Wace, *Roman de Rou*, 2–3, 110–11, 214–15. I have quoted Burgess's translation.

[62] Richard fitzNigel, *Dialogus de Scaccario*.

[63] John of Salisbury, *Policraticus*. For an overview of this work and its importance, see Nederman, *John of Salisbury*, 51–62.

[64] Kuttner and Rathbone, "Anglo-Norman Canonists," 279–358. See also Charles Duggan, "The Reception of Canon Law in England in the Later-Twelfth Century," in *Canon Law in Medieval England: The Becket Dispute and Decretal Collections* (London, 1982), 359–90; Rudolf Weigand, "The Transmontane Decretists," in Wilfried Hartmann and Kenneth Pennington, eds., *The History of Medieval Canon Law in the Classical Period, 1140–1234: From Gratian to the Decretals of Pope Gregory IX* (Washington, D.C., 2008), 174–210, at 182–4, 193–202.

[65] Southern, *Scholastic Humanism*, 2:155; Boyle, "Beginnings of Legal Studies," 107–31; Taliadoros, *Law and Theology*, 35–42; Henry Mayr-Harting, "The Role of Benedictine Abbeys in the Development of Oxford as a Centre of Legal Learning," in Henry Wansbrough and Anthony Marett-Crosby, eds., *Benedictines in Oxford* (London, 1997), 11–19.

[66] Honorius, *Magistri Honorii Summa*.

displayed their knowledge as practitioners, whether as papal judges delegate, church administrators, or representatives of patrons in lawsuits.

Roman civil law never gained the importance in England that it had elsewhere, but even so, Master Vacarius, the Italian specialist in that field, and his followers, the *pauperistae*, gained prominence there.[67] Comments by Ralph Niger and Daniel of Morley suggest that study of Roman law was popular in England in the late twelfth century.[68] As for the early development of the common law, it was clearly an effort in which clerics worked alongside laypeople, as the number of royal justices who were royal clerics suggests.[69] It is likely that clerics were particularly important in compiling or composing legal treatises. Patrick Wormald has suggested that the *Quadripartitus*, a Latin compilation of Anglo-Saxon laws, and the *Leges Henrici Primi* emanated from the circle of Archbishop Gerard of York, which would place them, like the *Laws of Edward the Confessor*, in the context of the secular clergy.[70] There has been much debate about who wrote the key treatise on the early common law later attributed to the layman Ranulf de Glanville, an attribution no longer generally accepted. Given the involvement of so many secular clerics in royal government and their dominance in the field of writing, the likelihood is that this work too came from the hand of a secular cleric, and Ralph Turner has suggested Godfrey de Lucy as a possible author.[71]

In the field of medicine, there is less evidence of writing by clerics, partly because so much material is anonymous.[72] The reference to masters associated with Hereford Cathedral in the *Prose Salernitan Questions* suggests the likelihood that the author was a cleric there.[73] Edward Kealey has proposed a couple of possible links between clerics and lost works in library catalogues.[74] There is, however, much more evidence of learned secular clerics *practicing* medicine, albeit alongside other types of practitioners ranging from monks to village healers. Kealey, whose work focused on the Anglo-Norman period to the middle of the twelfth century, noted that about 25 percent of recorded practitioners were secular clerics, though given that another 22 percent could not be classified, this figure is low.[75] No similar study has been done for the second half of our period, but certainly a number of *magistri* from the reigns of Richard and John were also described as *medici, fisici,* or with some similar title, and some had benefices and churches, showing they were

---

[67] See Chapter 10, section 1.   [68] Turner, *Judges, Administrators*, 51–2.

[69] See Chapter 6, section 1; Turner, *English Judiciary*, 2, 291.

[70] Wormald, *Making of English Law*, 473.

[71] Hall, ed., *Glanvill*, xxx–xxxiii; Turner, *Judges, Administrators*, 71–101.

[72] The influential medical writer Gilbert Anglicus was once identified with a physician working during John's reign, but Michael McVaugh has convincingly argued that he is a later figure: Faye Getz, *Medicine in the English Middle Ages* (Princeton, 1998), 3–4, 39–42; Michael McVaugh, "Who Was Gilbert the Englishman?," in George Hardin Brown and Linda E. Voigts, eds., *The Study of Medieval Manuscripts of England: Festschrift in Honor of Richard W. Pfaff* (Tempe, 2010), 295–324.

[73] Lawn, ed., *Prose Salernitan Questions*, xv–xvi, 6.   [74] Kealey, *Medieval Medicus*, 127, 135.

[75] Kealey also provides brief biographies of or notes on a number of clerical healers: Kealey, *Medieval Medicus*, 39, 49, 51–2, 58–64, 74–5, 126–8, 130, 132, 135–9, 141–2, 144–6, 151. See also Getz, *Medicine*, 4–7.

clerical rather than lay *magistri*.[76] Occasionally, narrative sources show clerical doctors practicing in their dual capacity as healers of bodies and of souls. For instance, a miracle story described a dean of Wells (almost certainly Dean Alexander Medicus) giving up hope of saving the life of a nobleman after inspecting his urine, and promising to say masses and prayers for him.[77] Learned physicians were probably outnumbered by local healers, who are less likely to appear in the sources, and since the chief centers for medical education were in the south of Europe, where laypeople were more likely to attend the schools, it is possible that some learned doctors were laymen. Nonetheless, it is clear that secular clerics played an important role in spreading learned medicine in England.

English clerics were involved in a number of fields such as medicine designed to understand and manipulate the physical world, including mathematics, magic, the study of the stars, and the revival of the broad Aristotelian corpus of natural philosophy. As various scholars have noted, boundaries between science, magic, and even religion were fluid in this period, and though contemporaries did make distinctions, they often disagreed.[78] Modern distinctions between science and pseudo-science also create difficulties. I will therefore treat works grappling with the physical world as a unity. England's importance in science or proto-science in this period is well known.[79] Hereford, site of a cathedral staffed by secular canons, may have been a particularly important center.[80] Though a few members of the English regular clergy were important students of the physical universe, like Walcher, prior of Malvern, the majority of intellectuals working in this area were secular clerics.[81]

The most important English scientist in the period was Adelard of Bath, who traveled as far as Salerno and Antioch in pursuit of learning.[82] He was most

[76] Examples include Adam Fisicus, succentor of Wells, Master Nicholas Fisicus (Geoffrey fitz Peter's doctor), who received a prebend at Hastings, and Master Matthew Fisicus or Medicus, who received a prebend at Bridgnorth and churches in Lancashire: Greenway, *Fasti. 7. Bath and Wells*, 23; Hardy, ed., *Rotuli Litterarum Patentium*, 51a, 59a–b, 89a; *Curia Regis Rolls*, 2:250. For more on Master Matthew and for some other examples from later in the period, see C. H. Talbot and E. A. Hammond, *The Medical Practitioners in Medieval England: A Biographical Register* (London, 1965), 10–11, 91, 125–6, 197–8, 212–13, 207, 329.

[77] Reginald R. Darlington, ed., *The Vita Wulfstani of William of Malmesbury*, Camden Society, 3rd ser., vol. 40 (London, 1928), 144

[78] Charles Burnett, "The Translating Activity in Medieval Spain," *Magic and Divination in the Middle Ages: Texts and Techniques in the Islamic and Christian Worlds* (Aldershot, 1996), 1036–58, at 1038; Clanchy, *Abelard*, 26; Richard Kieckhefer, *Magic in the Middle Ages* (Cambridge, 1989), 8–17. C. S. Watkins deals at length with many ambiguities concerning the supernatural in England in the twelfth century: C. S. Watkins, *History and the Supernatural in Medieval England* (Cambridge, 2007).

[79] Southern, *Medieval Humanism*, 164–71; Burnett, *Introduction of Arabic Learning*; Haskins, *Mediaeval Science*, 113–29. For other overviews of the study of the natural world and related subjects in England, see Barlow, *English Church, 1066–1154*, 257–65; Bartlett, *England under the Norman and Angevin Kings*, 645–92; Southern, *Robert Grosseteste*, 83–107.

[80] Hunt, "English Learning," 36–7; Southern, *Robert Grosseteste*, 104; Burnett, "Mathematics and Astronomy in Hereford," 50–9.

[81] Haskins, *Mediaeval Science*, 113–17; Burnett, *Introduction of Arabic Learning*, 39–40.

[82] Louise Cochrane, *Adelard of Bath: The First English Scientist* (London, 1994); Charles Burnett, ed., *Adelard of Bath: An English Scientist and Arabist of the Early Twelfth Century* (London, 1987).

influential as a translator from Arabic of Euclid's *Elements*.[83] He also translated or wrote works on astronomy or astrology; composed a broad-ranging treatise of his own on *Quaestiones Naturales*; wrote works dealing with the seven liberal arts, the care of falcons, and the abacus; and had his teachings on music quoted in glosses.[84] Adelard was yet another English scholar whose work had an impact on Catholic Europe as a whole, and the *Quaestiones Naturales* were even translated into Hebrew.[85] Robert of Ketton's most notable work was his translation of the Qur'an, but he stated that he was more interested in studying the heavens and geometry. He may have been responsible for another version of Euclid, and translated astronomical and astrological works by the Arab scholars al-Battani and al-Kindi.[86] Other clerics interested in the natural world included Robert of Chester, who helped introduce alchemy into the Latin West, translated Al-Khwarizm's work on algebra, composed a treatise on the astrolabe, and compiled astronomical tables for London;[87] the influential geometer John of Tynemouth (perhaps identical to the canon lawyer of that name);[88] and Roger of Hereford who wrote a work on the computus aimed at calendar reform, adapted astronomical tables to Hereford, and had various astrological works attributed to him.[89] Robert Grosseteste, one of the great

---

[83] There is uncertainty about just which of the versions of the translation attributed to Adelard he was in fact responsible for, but later versions or redactions may also have been done by English secular clerics, for which see notes 86 and 88; H. L. L. Busard, ed., *The First Latin Translation of Euclid's* Elements *Commonly Ascribed to Adelard of Bath* (Toronto, 1983), 5–7, 16–18.

[84] Abū Ma'šar, *The Abbreviation of the Introduction to Astrology together with the Medieval Latin Translation of Adelard of Bath*, ed. Charles Burnett, Keiji Yamamoto, and Michio Yano (Leiden, 1994), 91–143; Paolo Lucentini and V. Perrone Compagni, *I testi e i codici di Ermete nel Medioevo* (Firenze, 2001), 66–7; Adelard of Bath, *Adelard of Bath, Conversations with his Nephew: On the Same and the Different, Questions on Natural Science, and On Birds*, ed. Charles Burnett (Cambridge, 1998); Emmanuel Poulle, "Le traité de l'astrolabe d'Adélard de Bath," in Charles Burnett, ed., *Adelard of Bath: An English Scientist and Arabist of the Early Twelfth Century* (London, 1987), 119–32; Charles Burnett, "Adelard, Music and the Quadrivium," in Charles Burnett, ed., *Adelard of Bath: An English Scientist and Arabist of the Early Twelfth Century* (London, 1987), 69–86.

[85] Thomson, *Books and Learning*, 100; Burnett, *Introduction of Arabic Learning*, 59.

[86] H. L. L. Busard and Menso Folkerts, eds., *Robert of Chester's (?) Redaction of Euclid's* Elements, *the So-called Adelard II Version*, 2 vols. (Basel, 1992), 11–31. Robert of Ketton has often been treated as identical to Robert of Chester, but for the distinction, and brief biographies of both men, see Charles Burnett, "Ketton, Robert of (*fl*. 1141–1157)," *Oxford Dictionary of National Biography*, Oxford University Press, 2004 [http://www.oxforddnb.com/view/article/23723, accessed 23 Nov 2013; subscription required].

[87] R. Lemay, "L'authenticité de la préface de Robert de Chester à sa traduction du Morienus (1144)," *Chrysopœia* 4 (1991), 3–32, at 6–7; Louis Charles Karpinski, ed., *Robert of Chester's Latin Translation of the Algebra of al-Khwarizmi* (New York, 1915); Lucentini and Compagni, *I testi e i codici di Ermete*, 66–7.

[88] Wilbur Knorr, who has done most work on this geometer, doubts that he can be identified with the canonist, but given the range of intellectual interests of other secular clerics I am less skeptical than Knorr about such an identification: Wilbur R. Knorr, "John of Tynemouth alias John of London: Emerging Portrait of a Singular Medieval Mathematician," *British Journal for the History of Science* 23 (1990), 290–323; H. L. L. Busard, ed., *Johannes de Tinemue's Redaction of Euclid's* Elements, *the so-called Adelard III Version*, 2 vols. (Stuttgart, 2001), 1:12–13. Wilbur R. Knorr, "Tynemouth, John of (*fl*. early 13th cent.)," *Oxford Dictionary of National Biography*, Oxford University Press, 2004 [http://www.oxforddnb.com/view/article/52685, accessed 23 Nov 2013; subscription required].

[89] Haskins, *Mediaeval Science*, 124–6; Lynn Thorndike, *A History of Magic and Experimental Science, Vol. 2* (New York, 1923), 2:181–6; Jennifer Moreton, "Before Grosseteste: Roger of Hereford and Calendar Reform in Eleventh- and Twelfth-Century England," *Isis* 86 (1995),

scientific minds of the thirteenth century, probably composed his treatise *De Sphera*, which provided an overview of the structure of the heavens, as early as *c*.1215.[90]

One crucial development in which English clerics played an important role, both before 1216 and after, was the reception into the Latin West of Aristotle's natural philosophy, along with pseudonymous Aristotelian tracts and Arabic commentaries on his work. Daniel of Morley, in his treatise describing various aspects of the natural world, drew on Arabic works in the Aristotelian tradition and often referred to Aristotle as an authority.[91] Later sources indicate that several masters were teaching Aristotle at Oxford in the first decade of the thirteenth century, including Edmund Rich, future archbishop of Canterbury, and John Blund.[92] The poet Henry of Avranches described Blund as, "the first man to investigate deeply the books of Aristotle, when the Arabs had recently handed them over to the Latins, and the man who had lectured on Aristotle first and with the most renown in both Oxford and Paris."[93] John's career lasted well past 1216, but he wrote a treatise, *De Anima*, which drew heavily on Aristotle and Avicenna, early in his career.[94] However, the most important English Aristotelian scholar of the period was Alfred of Shareshill, who spent time in Iberia but ended up as a canon of Lichfield. In Chapter 10, I noted how he took up Gerard of Cremona's program of translating Aristotelian texts. His Aristotelian, or rather pseudo-Aristotelian translations, *De Mineralibus* and *De Plantis*, were both very influential, and 170 manuscripts of the latter survive, making it yet another "bestseller" in medieval terms. Alfred also wrote commentaries on these and other Aristotelian works, and composed his own treatise, *De Motu Cordis*, which drew on a wide range of Aristotelian and Arabic sources. A contemporary continental scholar, David of Dinant, described him as *dux naturae*, revealing the high esteem in which he was held.[95]

Various factors drove this learned interest in the natural world. Pure thirst for knowledge was no doubt as important in this period as any other. Learning about the natural world could also be applied to religious purposes, as was common in

---

562–86; Roger French, "Foretelling the Future: Arabic Astrology and English Medicine in the Late Twelfth Century," *Isis* 87 (1996), 453–80.

[90] Southern, *Robert Grosseteste*, 142–6.

[91] Thorndike, *History of Magic*, 2:171–81; Theodore Silverstein, "Daniel Morley, English Cosmogonist and Student of Arabic Science," *Mediaeval Studies* 10 (1948), 179–96; Southern, *Robert Grosseteste*, 88–90; Burnett, *Introduction of Arabic Learning*, 61–8; Maurach, "Daniel von Morley 'Philosophia'," 204–55.

[92] Daniel A. Callus, "The Introduction of Aristotelian Learning to Oxford," *Proceedings of the British Academy* 29 (1943), 229–81, at 238–52.

[93] J. A. Weisheipl, "Science in the Thirteenth Century," in J. I. Catto, ed., *The History of the University of Oxford. Vol. 1. The Early Oxford Schools* (Oxford, 1984), 435–69, at 437; Burnett, *Introduction of Arabic Learning*, 69.

[94] Iohannes Blund, *Tractatus de Anima*, ed. D. A. Callus, R. W. Hunt, and Michael W. Dunne (London, 2013).

[95] Otte, "Alfredus Anglicus," 275–91; Alfred of Shareshill, *Alfred of Sareshel's Commentary on the Meteora of Aristotle*, ed. James K. Otte (Leiden, 1988); R. James Long, "Alfred of Sareshel's Commentary on the Pseudo-Aristotelian *De Plantis*: A Critical Edition," *Mediaeval Studies* 47 (1985), 125–67; Southern, *Robert Grosseteste*, 90–2; Burnett, *Introduction of Arabic Learning*, 70–2.

bestiaries. Daniel of Morley argued that study of the natural world could improve understanding of the Bible and Robert of Chester claimed that the alchemical work he was translating drew from a hermetic tradition that proved the truth of the Old and New Testaments.[96] However, one major goal was utility, despite the seemingly esoteric nature of much of this work. About 40 percent of the total number of translations from Arabic in the central Middle Ages had to do with astronomy, astrology, magic, and divination.[97] Adelard's *Liber Prestigiorum*, his translation of a work by Thābit b. Qurra, described the making and use of astrologically based talismans that could have performed extremely useful functions, had they worked, including winning the love of an equal or a king, regaining the love of one's spouse, recovering stolen money, winning a law suit, or destroying a city. As Burnett noted in this context, "Talismans are *useful*."[98]

Scholars saw knowledge about mathematics and the natural world as having various practical uses. Adelard argued that geometry had originally been designed to measure land and had helped people to avoid disputes and even wars over boundaries.[99] Roger of Hereford viewed astrology as essential to medicine.[100] The most widespread aim, however, was to gain a means of accurately foretelling the future. Various writers on astrology, including Roger of Hereford and Daniel of Morley, emphasized the utility of seeing into the future.[101] For instance, Daniel wrote to his patron, John of Oxford, bishop of Norwich, the following: "Since the astronomer knows about future events, he can repel or avoid disasters such as civil wars or famine, earthquakes, conflagrations, floods, and general pestilences of men and beasts. Even if he cannot altogether escape them, he can prepare for them in advance, which will make them more tolerable than they are to those who are overtaken unawares. I interject this to refute the errors of those who malign the studies of astronomers."[102] As Haskins noted, "astrology is only applied astronomy, wrongly applied as we now believe, but a thoroughly practical subject in the eyes of the later Middle Ages."[103]

Scattered evidence for the practice of astrology suggests that clerical astrologers often tried to put theory into practice and that astrology had quickly gained a fair

[96] Southern, *Robert Grosseteste*, 89; Maurach, "Daniel von Morley 'Philosophia'," 212–13; Lemay, "L'authenticité de la préface de Robert de Chester," 6.

[97] Boudet, *Entre science et nigromance*, 35. See also Murray, *Reason and Society*, 110–16.

[98] Burnett, "Establishment of Medieval Hermeticism," 113–14; Charles Burnett, "Talismans: Magic as Science? Necromancy among the Seven Liberal Arts," in *Magic and Divination in the Middle Ages: Texts and Techniques in the Islamic and Christian Worlds* (Aldershot, 1996), 1–15; Boudet, *Entre science et nigromance*, 138–44, 161–2.

[99] Adelard of Bath, *Conversations with his Nephew*, 56–61.

[100] French, "Foretelling the Future," 454–9, 468–75, 486.

[101] In stressing the utility of astrology, English clerics were only echoing the claims of their guides, such as Petrus Alfonsus and Abū Ma'šar, and of their contemporaries, such as Raymond of Marseilles, who dedicated a treatise on astrology to the earl of Leicester: Burnett, *Introduction of Arabic Learning*, 39; French, "Foretelling the Future," 454–6, 467; Southern, *Robert Grosseteste*, 104; Maurach, "Daniel von Morley 'Philosophia'," 239.

[102] Southern's translation: Southern, *Robert Grosseteste*, 105.

[103] Haskins, *Mediaeval Science*, 259. See also Watkins, *History and the Supernatural*, 232.

amount of credence.[104] Though horoscopes are an inherently ephemeral kind of document, a number survive from Stephen's reign, possibly cast by Adelard of Bath or Robert of Chester, and a couple of them dealt with crucial political questions in 1151. One stated that no army would come from Normandy and the other that King Stephen would be able to compel his barons to do homage to his son Eustace, but only with the help of an astrologer. These horoscopes used the coordinates of Cordoba, making them invalid even in astrological terms, but there is no doubt that they aimed to provide useful information.[105] A horoscope attributed to Roger of Hereford seems to have been designed for Eleanor of Aquitaine, indicating that he had either won her patronage or hoped to do so.[106] John of Salisbury, in a letter of 1167 to Peter scriptor, reported the pronouncements of astrologers that there would be widespread political disturbances that year. John claimed not to place any faith in the predictions, but promptly admitted that events in Germany and France had proved them partly correct.[107] Several chroniclers reveal that predictions of disasters based on an unusual conjunction of planets in 1186 were widely discussed and even prompted Archbishop Baldwin of Canterbury to ordain a three-day fast throughout his province. Among the astrologers who issued predictions in that year was William, a cleric of the English magnate John, constable of Chester.[108] Hilary Carey suggests that astrology was much less commonly practiced than later, noting the dearth of surviving horoscopes and arguing that the technical deficiencies in the horoscopes about Stephen's reign argue for a lack of competence in the period.[109] Perhaps so, but there was clearly great excitement about the possible utility of astrology, and secular clerics were at the forefront in trying to use astrological predictions to better cope with the future.

Clerics also used other means to try to predict the future. Simund de Fresne, in a poem praising learning in Hereford, not only mentioned an *astrologus* there (possibly Roger of Hereford), but also described a geomancer using his art to predict whether a man or woman would get their way. Simund's description of the geomancer's methods was specific enough for Burnett to conclude that they were derived from a work by Gerard of Cremona, thus showing the applied use of a translation from Arabic.[110] John of Salisbury described how when he was a boy the priest to whom he had been entrusted for his basic education had used him and another boy in divination ceremonies involving reflective surfaces and the summoning of spirits. John failed in this magic and was barred from further

[104] Chroniclers also occasionally mention bishops practicing astrology: William of Malmesbury, *Gesta Pontificum*, 1:392–3, 458–9, 474–5; Orderic Vitalis, *Ecclesiastical History*, 5:8–11.

[105] Burnett, *Introduction of Arabic Learning*, 46; John North, "Some Norman Horoscopes," in Charles Burnett, ed., *Adelard of Bath: An English Scientist and Arabist of the Early Twelfth Century* (London, 1987), 147–61.

[106] French, "Foretelling the Future," 463.   [107] John of Salisbury, *Letters*, 2:392–3.

[108] Gervase of Canterbury, *Historical Works*, 1:335; Roger of Howden, *Chronica*, 2:290–6; Southern, *Robert Grosseteste*, 106; Boudet, *Entre science et nigromance*, 76–81. Boudet provides a careful technical analysis of William's forecast, as reported by Howden.

[109] Hilary M. Carey, *Courting Disaster: Astrology at the English Court and University in the Later Middle Ages* (London, 1992), 30–1; North, "Some Norman Horoscopes," 151.

[110] Hunt, "English Learning," 36–7; Burnett, "Mathematics and Astronomy in Hereford," 57.

attempts, to his later relief, but stated that he knew many who practiced the art. John also chastised Thomas Becket for employing divination, specifically palm reading, as chancellor during Henry II's expedition to Wales in 1157, and again criticized him as archbishop for studying auguries in a letter of 1170.[111]

Elite clerics attempted to manipulate the physical world through magic or natural powers in other ways as well. Many may have sought to do so through the possession of gemstones, particularly ones with carvings.[112] One important genre in the period was the lapidary, which sometimes treated stones allegorically, but often described the useful properties of specific types of gems or of gems carved with particular symbols. The most influential lapidary of the period was that of the continental bishop Marbod of Rennes, but Henry of Huntingdon, Gervase of Tilbury, and Alberic of London all included passages on lapidary lore in their writings.[113] There also survive anonymous treatises in Latin and Anglo-Norman in twelfth- and thirteenth-century English manuscripts, and some of the vernacular ones have been attributed to the cleric and translator Philippe de Thaon.[114] These works claimed that gemstones, particularly carved ones, had many useful powers, including aiding success in various arenas, among them battle and robbery; helping to win the love and favor of other humans or even God; promoting health; improving virtue; and even breaking free from chains or gaining invisibility.[115] The ownership of gemstones in general and of classical intaglios in particular was popular among wealthy clerics as among the lay elites in the long twelfth century, as I shall discuss more fully in the next chapter.[116] There were various reasons for the popularity of such objects, but it is likely that some owners hoped to utilize the natural or magical powers of their gemstones.

The overall fascination with magical or natural powers, and the hopes, aspirations, fantasies, and fears that esoteric forms of learning could engender, are best illustrated by contemporary images of the learned man of enormous magical or technical power. In the story by Gervase of Tilbury with which I began this chapter, Virgil was clearly such a figure, and the English master who wanted his bones was trying to step into his shoes. One of the characters that surely made the Alexander romance exciting to Thomas of Kent and his audience was Nectanabus, a magician and astronomer who taught Alexander's mother about the stars and then seduced her, disguised as the god Ammon, thus becoming Alexander's father. Later in the work, the Athenians were described as fearing Alexander partly because of the knowledge he gained from Aristotle, particularly concerning astronomy.[117]

[111] John of Salisbury, *Policraticus*, 1:144, 164; John of Salisbury, *Letters*, 2:708–11.

[112] Boudet, *Entre science et nigromance*, 167.

[113] Black, "Henry of Huntingdon's Lapidary," 43–87; Gervase of Tilbury, *Otia Imperialia*, 610–19; Bode, ed., *Scriptores Rerum Mythicarum*, 203–5.

[114] For other works by Phillipe, see n 47 in this chapter.

[115] Joan Evans, *Magical Jewels of the Middle Ages and the Renaissance, Particularly in England* (Oxford, 1922), 33–7, 53–139, 220–3; Studer and Evans, eds., *Anglo-Norman Lapidaries*; Thomas Wright, "On Antiquarian Excavations and Researches in the Middle Ages," *Archaeologia* 30 (1844), 438–57; Boudet, *Entre science et nigromance*, 122–4.

[116] See Chapter 13, section 2.   [117] Thomas of Kent, *Anglo-Norman Alexander*, 1:8–21, 75.

William of Malmesbury, a contemporary of Adelard of Bath, recorded a wildly inventive short biography of Gerbert of Aurillac, who became Pope Sylvester II, involving him acquiring knowledge of the abacus, the astrolabe, astrology, and divination from Muslims in Spain; making a pact with a demon; inventing a mechanical clock, a water powered organ, and a magical talking head; and using his magical arts to uncover treasures buried by pagans in antiquity.[118]

The most influential inventor of such figures was Geoffrey of Monmouth, and the most famous of his creations was Merlin.[119] In Geoffrey's *Vita Merlini*, Merlin was a deeply learned magician. He studied astrology and requested a house with seventy windows to view the stars and seventy scribes to record his prophecies. Geoffrey had Merlin and Taliesen discuss the cosmos, drawing heavily on Isidore of Seville but also making a reference to Arab sayings on Venus.[120] This vision of Merlin as scholar was less pronounced in the *Historia Regum Britanniae*, but the prophecies recorded there included astrological elements. Merlin and other learned magicians in the *Historia* often proved to be very powerful and useful. Merlin transported Stonehenge from Ireland to England and disguised Uther Pendragon so that he could seduce Arthur's mother, Ygerna. King Edwin had a magician from Spain, Pellitus, who could predict future events through the stars and through flights of birds; his warning allowed Edwin to defeat an invading army. Arthur himself had in Caerleon a school of no less than 200 philosophers, skilled in astronomy and other arts, who studied the course of the stars and predicted future events for the king.[121]

It is hard for modern scholars to take the real or imagined magical and quasi-magical endeavors of twelfth-century scholars seriously. Few modern historians would think that any astrologer could have done King Stephen much good even if he had used the correct coordinates. And why did those 200 astrologers fail to warn Arthur about Mordred? Such skepticism is not entirely anachronistic, for medieval thinkers had been primed by writers like Augustine to be skeptical about astrology.[122] Gervase of Canterbury, for instance, mocked Archbishop Baldwin for ordering the three-day fast, saying that the predictions of astrologers were belied by the plenty of crops and the calmness of the atmosphere; the only serious "storm" was Baldwin's oppression of the monks at his cathedral.[123] The appearance of magic in literary sources may often have been designed for entertainment or moral edification.

---

[118] William of Malmesbury, *Gesta Regum*, 1:278–95. For discussion of this story, see Watkins, *History and the Supernatural*, 164–8; Boudet, *Entre science et nigromance*, 269–71. For its context in William's work, see Peters, *Magician, Witch, and Law*, 28–32. Gerbert was interested in the abacus, but was not unique in his time: Burnett, *Introduction of Arabic Learning*, 10–11. For a more accurate view of his role in this sort of learning, see S. J. Tester, *A History of Western Astrology* (Woodbridge, 1987), 131–2.

[119] J. S. P. Tatlock placed Merlin and other characters of Geoffrey of Monmouth in a similar context: John S. P. Tatlock, *The Legendary History of Britain: Geoffrey of Monmouth's* Historia Regum Britanniae *and its Early Vernacular Versions* (Berkeley, 1950), 360–70.

[120] Geoffrey of Monmouth, *Vita Merlini*, 54–7, 62–85, 96–111, 122–4.

[121] Geoffrey of Monmouth, *History of the Kings of Britain*, 36–7, 136–61, 170–5, 178–81, 186–9, 210–11, 264–73.

[122] For Augustine's views, see Tester, *Western Astrology*, 108–12.

[123] Gervase of Canterbury, *Historical Works*, 1:335.

Nonetheless, various scholars (including John of Salisbury) took Merlin seriously, and the theologian John of Cornwall even wrote or compiled his own version of Merlin's prophecies.[124] It is therefore worth suspending both medieval and modern disbelief for a moment to give due consideration to the aim of learned clerics to learn accurate methods of forecasting the future and to develop other esoteric powers.

After all, if there were good twelfth-century reasons for skepticism about astrology and magic there were also ones for confidence. Astrology and many of the other magical and quasi-magical practices had their roots in classical and Muslim learning, and twelfth-century Christian scholars had a profound if deeply ambivalent respect for those traditions. Much of the astronomy and mathematics that was being absorbed during the twelfth century from the Arab world was sound. The abacus, which William of Malmesbury claimed Gerbert had brought to the Latin West from the Muslims, helped revolutionize English government in the period. One has only to read Turchil's treatise on the abacus to realize how esoteric that knowledge would have seemed in a society in which numeracy was not widespread. Yet it obviously had tremendously useful applications.[125] In a pre-Copernican universe, two of the heavenly bodies, the sun and the moon, clearly had a profound influence on the earthly environment, and a writer such as the influential Arab astrologer, Abū Ma'šar, could point to phenomena such as the seasons and tides to make the case for astrology.[126] Moreover, because learned clerics were trying to introduce methods of forecasting the future and exercising power in esoteric ways that were new to their society, they did not initially face the widespread experience of repeated failure. All in all, the clerics studied in this section had reason to hope that their exploration of astrology and similar practices could yield powerful results for themselves, for their patrons, and by extension for society as a whole. Their hopes did not materialize, but this should not detract from the audaciousness of their endeavor to use learning for ambitious worldly ends.

I will round out the discussion of the intellectual activity of clerics by reviewing three works (or in one case, a compilation of works) illustrating the surprisingly wide range of clerical interests and the varied aspects of life to which they could apply their learning. First, Daniel, cleric of Beccles, who was perhaps a married cleric in minor orders, wrote a fascinating early courtesy book.[127] This work was a guide to civilized life (*vita urbana*), providing advice on table manners, household management, proper conduct in various professions, relations with women (from a misogynistic standpoint), and a host of other topics, emphasizing the virtues of moderation and restraint and the importance of hierarchy throughout. It had a fair

---

[124] Kieckhefer, *Magic*, 105–15; Clanchy, *Abelard*, 25; Watkins, *History and the Supernatural*, 145–6; Michael J. Curley, "A New Edition of John of Cornwall's *Prophetia Merlini*," *Speculum* 57 (1982), 217–49.

[125] Narducci, "Intorno a due trattati inediti d'abaco," 135–54.

[126] French, "Foretelling the Future," 455–6.

[127] Daniel granted land with the consent of his son and heir, which indicates he was claiming the son as legitimate. However, he quitclaimed rights in an advowson, which suggests the possibility of membership in a hereditary family of rectors, though other explanations could be made for this quitclaim: *Curia Regis Rolls*, 4:20; Christopher Harper-Bill, ed., *Blythburgh Priory Cartulary*, 2 vols., Suffolk Charters, 2–3 (Woodbridge, 1980–81), 1:98.

amount of influence on the subsequent development of the genre of courtesy books in England.[128] Second, John of Tilbury, who was among the *eruditi* of Thomas Becket, was probably also the author of a treatise in which he described how he had developed a new form of shorthand that would allow students to copy out the lectures of a master in full.[129] Third, Patrick Gautier Dalché convincingly ascribes to the historian Roger of Howden, who traveled to the Holy Land on the Third Crusade, three closely related treatises on geography and sailing from the years immediately following 1191. The first seems to be a verbal description of a mappa mundi. The second, the *Liber Nautarum*, updated Isidore of Seville's discussion of maritime affairs, for instance by including the names of some modern types of ship. The third is a description of sea routes from Roger's home region of Yorkshire to the Indies. It discusses distances, landmarks, ports, anchorages, and towns, with the occasional reference to trade, such as the suggestion that one could buy tin in the region of Dartmouth and sell it for double the price in the Mediterranean. Taken together, the texts attributed to Howden show a fascinating intersection between the intellectual world of the schools and the nautical realm of mariners and merchants.[130]

It was not only the clergy as a whole that had diverse interests, but sometimes individual clerics as well. Even if one cannot be certain that Roger of Howden was a specialist in maritime matters as well as history, other figures for whom we have substantial writings and evidence, such as Gerald of Wales, John of Salisbury, and Peter of Blois, were clearly polymaths. Peter of Blois, for instance, was not only a writer in many genres, but also a teacher and active courtier, who also had legal and perhaps medical training.[131] He even had some knowledge of astrology, having read in his youth the work of Abū Ma'šar (in John of Seville's translation) at the behest of an uncle who had studied in Toledo.[132] A less well-known figure, Ralph Niger, not only composed many biblical commentaries and his unusually critical discussion of the crusades, but also a revision of Jerome's work on Hebrew names,

---

[128] Daniel of Beccles, *Urbanus Magnus*. For discussion of this work, see Bartlett, *England under the Norman and Angevin Kings*, 582–8; John Gillingham, "From *Civilitas* to Civility: Codes of Manners in Medieval and Early Modern England," *Transactions of the Royal Historical Society* 6th ser. 12 (2002), 267–89, at 272–8; Frédérique Lachaud, "L'enseignement des bonnes manières en milieu de cour en Angleterre d'après l'*Urbanus magnus* attribué à Daniel de Beccles," in Werner Paravicini and Jörg Wettlaufer, eds., *Erziehung und Bildung bei Hofe* (Stuttgart, 2002), 43–53; Frédérique Lachaud, "Littérature de civilité et 'processus de civilisation' à la fin de XIIe siècle: le cas anglais d'après l'*Urbanus magnus*," *Les Échanges culturels au Moyen Âge: XXXIIe congrès de la SHMES* (Paris, 2002), 227–39. For its later influence, see Jonathan Nicholls, *The Matter of Courtesy: Medieval Courtesy Books and the Gawain-Poet* (Woodbridge, 1985), 162–6.

[129] Valentin Rose, "Ars Notaria: tironische Noten und Stenographie im 12. Jahrhundert," *Hermes* 8 (1874), 303–26; Charles Burnett, "Give Him the White Cow: Notes and Note-Taking in the Universities in the Twelfth and Thirteenth Centuries," *History of Universities* 14 (1995–6), 1–30, at 3–5, 21–2; Robertson and Sheppard, eds., *Materials*, 3:527.

[130] Patrick Gautier Dalché, *Du Yorkshire à l'Inde: une "géographie" urbaine et maritime de la fin du XIIe siècle (Roger de Howden?)* (Geneva, 2005); Paul Hughes, "Roger of Howden's Sailing Directions for the English Coast," *Historical Research* 85 (2012), 576–96.

[131] Cotts, *Clerical Dilemma*, 23–4, 28, 104–9.   [132] Peter of Blois, *Later Letters*, 236.

two chronicles, and devotional texts for the Virgin Mary.[133] This was not generally an age of specialization, but even so the range of interests and talents possessed by some clerics was remarkable.

3. CONTROVERSIES OVER LEARNING

Serlo of Wilton once experienced an admonitory visit from hell. At least, so says a story that apparently originated with him, though he later equivocated about it; perhaps he had made it up as an *exemplum* and subsequently regretted having it taken as literally true. In this story, Serlo depicted himself as a master at Oxford with many students, one of whom, Richard, made the mistake of challenging him in a weekly public disputation, hoping to gain glory by besting his master. After Serlo crushed Richard's argument, the latter returned to his lodgings and fell sick, apparently out of pure chagrin. A priest was summoned and, seeing the boy close to death, called on him to confess, but Richard responded by asking the priest if he knew anything about dialectic. Richard then died and went to hell. Three times on the following three evenings he returned to Serlo, warning his master of his approaching death and of the dangers to his soul. Serlo eventually got the message and became a monk. However his first reaction, despite the horrific appearance of Richard, which displayed the punishments that he was suffering, was to plan how he could use his dead student to convey his latest thinking to Plato, Aristotle, and other thinkers residing in hell. For contemporaries, Serlo's reaction would have seemed ludicrous not because of his plan to use Richard as an infernal courier to classical philosophers but because Serlo could think primarily about his latest scholarship even when presented with clear and vivid evidence of the punishments of hell. The monastic recorder of the anecdote noted one moral of the story: that even a learned master needed to abandon the world to find true religion. However, there was clearly another moral. By becoming too absorbed in their learning, Richard and Serlo had lost sight of the religious ends of education, to the damnation of one and the severe peril of the other.[134]

Learning was one of the main accomplishments expected of an ideal cleric, but nonetheless the lively intellectual life of the period was, for a variety of reasons, a source of social tension and moral stress for many clerics. One reason was the prestige learning brought, which could lead to arrogance for the learned.[135] Scholars certainly hungered after this prestige. Peter of Blois, in a letter to a namesake poet, wrote in congratulatory tones of how they had both achieved enduring fame through their writings, and Gerald of Wales relentlessly promoted

---

[133] Ralph Niger, *De Re Militari*; G. B. Flahiff, "Ralph Niger—An Introduction to His Life and Works," *Mediaeval Studies* 2 (1940), 104–26; Goodwin, *Take Hold of the Robe of a Jew*, 48–50.

[134] This story was uncovered through some ingenious detective work by Rodney Thomson: Thomson, "Serlo of Wilton," 2–4, 10–12. For a somewhat similar anecdote, see Baswell, *Virgil in Medieval England*, 2–3.

[135] For the prestige afforded by learning, see Murray, *Reason and Society*, 227–33; Moser, *Cosmos of Desire*, 107–16.

himself to assure he gained glory for his erudition.[136] However, pride was no virtue, and Nigel of Whiteacre could mock the pretensions of scholars by describing how the donkey, Brunellus, the protagonist of his *Speculum Stultorum*, decided to become a learned master and daydreamed about the "senate and people" rushing out to greet him and the plebeians shouting "Behold, the master is here." Unfortunately, after years of study the donkey could still only bray.[137] On the flip side, a lack of learning was simply embarrassing. Gerald of Wales delighted in pointing out mistakes in Latin and other failures of learning. Sometimes, such passages were directed at enemies like Archbishop Hubert Walter, as when Gerald passed on another cleric's joke about the archbishop's poor Latin grammar or described how Hubert had misunderstood a theological point in a sermon by Peter of Blois.[138] In other cases, Gerald's efforts had a didactic purpose. For instance, he told the story of a student who asked John of Cornwall about the identity of Busillis in the Bible. No doubt puzzled, John, upon checking the passage, discovered that because of a break in a word from one column to the next, the student had misread the phrase "in diebus illis" ("in those days") as "in die busillis," construing it as "in the day of Busillis," a nonexistent individual. John suggested that the student ask in front of other students, since the phrase appeared near the beginning of one of the gospels (it is in the first chapter of both Mark and Luke). When the unfortunate student's question provoked laughter, John used it to illustrate "the shame and scandal of ignorance and poor learning in a cleric."[139]

Most tensions over learning had to do with content, however. Heresy (or perceived heresy) was of course the greatest potential spark for controversy, and both Adam of Balsham and Robert of Melun were involved in the accusations of heresy against the influential theologian Gilbert de la Porrée.[140] However, heresy accusations within the learned environment were rare, and no English scholars were accused. Even aside from heresy, however, learning provoked all kinds of controversies, and clerics associated with England, like Peter of Blois, Gerald of Wales, and above all John of Salisbury joined an international debate over the purposes and proper methods of education. Indeed, John of Salisbury's *Metalogicon* was probably the most important treatise in the period on the subject of education.[141] Much has been written on John's views and the debates in the period more generally, so little discussion is needed here.[142] Suffice it to say that critics were

---

[136] Peter of Blois, *Opera*, 237–9; Gerald of Wales, *Opera*, 1:45–8, 72–3, 79–80, 409–23; 3:333–6; 5:3–5; 6:3–7; Cotts, *Clerical Dilemma*, 123–4.

[137] Nigel of Whiteacre, *Speculum Stultorum*, 58, 65.

[138] Davies, "Giraldus Cambrensis: *De Invectionibus*," 100–1.

[139] Gerald of Wales, *Opera*, 2:343.

[140] For this conflict and their involvement, see Minio-Paluello, "Adam of Balsham," 117; Southern, *Scholastic Humanism*, 2:123–32; Godman, *Silent Masters*, 123–34. Godman's whole book provides a good overview of the worries about the potential of learning to produce heterodoxy and the sharp conflicts that these worries produced in the long twelfth century.

[141] John of Salisbury, *Metalogicon*. See also John of Salisbury, *Policraticus*, 2:122–9, 136–45. For other writers, see Peter of Blois, *Opera*, 311–14; Cotts, *Clerical Dilemma*, 110–12; Gerald of Wales, *Opera*, 2:348–57.

[142] Ferruolo, *Origins of the University*, 131–83; Baldwin, *Masters, Princes, and Merchants*, 1:77–83, 96–101; Jaeger, *Envy of Angels*, 278–91; K. S. B. Keats-Rohan, "John of Salisbury and Education in

concerned about various matters, including superficiality of learning, excessive subtlety, and an undue concentration on logic and dialectic at the expense of grammar and rhetoric. One set of critiques I do wish to emphasize, however, concerned careerism and excessive worldliness in intellectual endeavors.

I have already discussed criticism of government service by clerics, and of the study of medicine and law for purposes of advancement.[143] For Peter of Blois law itself was potentially dangerous as a subject because it encouraged avarice and pride, was often misused for socially destructive purposes, and in general was simply too worldly for clerics.[144] However, in an educational system that emphasized religious subjects, any non-religious subject could be viewed as problematic. Gerald of Wales's works on Ireland were among his most successful books in his own time. However, William de Montibus, despite initial praise, later objected strongly to them (particularly because of depictions of sex with animals) and suggested that Gerald really ought to be writing theology. Gerald defended himself vigorously, but nonetheless at some point he himself composed a similar letter to Walter Map, urging him to abandon the composition of secular writing and take up the writing of theological works.[145] Certain subjects, of course, were especially problematic. Peter of Blois, in his letter to his relative and namesake, criticized him for wasting time on frivolous verse, condemning its scurrility, use of classical pagan stories, and emphasis on worldly love.[146] Anxiety about and condemnation of the use of pagan classical works, whether in the arena of literature or philosophy, were particularly well-established traditions, and it was no accident that Serlo placed his interest in

Twelfth Century Paris from the Account of his *Metalogicon*," *History of Universities* 6 (1986–87), 1–45; Nederman, *John of Salisbury*, 46–7, 62–75; M. T. Clanchy, "*Moderni* in Education and Government in England," *Speculum* 50 (1975), 671–88; Morenzoni, *Des écoles aux paroisses*, 73–80; Godman, *Silent Masters*, 149–90.

[143] See Chapter 5, section 4, and Chapter 6, section 4.

[144] Peter of Blois, *Opera*, 91–2, 416–22, 1120; Cotts, *Clerical Dilemma*, 106–7, 121–2. See also Nigel of Whiteacre, *Tractatus Contra Curiales*, 158–9; Ralph Niger, *De Re Militari*, 214–17; Turner, *Judges, Administrators*, 51–2; Zulueta and Stein, eds., *Teaching of Roman Law*, xxxiv–xxxv. Taliadoros, it should be noted, has shown that Peter's attitude towards law, even in his later years, was more ambivalent than some of his statement might suggest: Jason Taliadoros, "Communities of Learning in Law and Theology: The Later Letters of Peter of Blois (1125/30–1212)," in Constant J. Mews and John N. Crossley, eds., *Communities of Learning: Networks and the Shaping of Intellectual Identity in Europe, 1100–1500* (Turnhout, 2011), 85–107. For further discussion of disputes over clerics, law, and also medicine, see Baldwin, *Masters, Princes, and Merchants*, 1:83–7, 192–8; Stollberg, *Soziale Stellung*, 129–33, 139; Ferruolo, *Origins of the University*, 101–3, 126, 163–5, 181–2.

[145] Gerald of Wales, *Speculum Duorum*, 168–75; Gerald of Wales, *Opera*, 1:271–89; Bartlett, *Gerald of Wales*, 146–8. See also Gerald of Wales, *Expugnatio Hibernica*, 4–9.

[146] The suggestion of some scholars that Peter was writing to himself is probably mistaken, but he did refer to himself having written trifles and love poetry as a youth, and there is clearly a certain amount of introspection in the letter: Peter of Blois, *Opera*, 231–37; Reto R. Bezzola, *Les origines et la formation de la littérature courtoise en Occident (500–1200)*, 3 vols. (Paris, 1968), 3:41–2; Dronke, "Peter of Blois and Poetry," 196–8; R. W. Southern, "The Necessity of Two Peters of Blois," in Lesley M. Smith and Benedicta Ward, eds., *Intellectual Life in the Middle Ages: Essays Presented to Margaret Gibson* (London, 1992), 103–18; Southern, *Scholastic Humanism*, 2:180–4, 204–7; Cotts, *Clerical Dilemma*, 124–9.

Plato and Aristotle at the center of his story [147] In a sermon to scholars at Oxford, Alexander Neckam chastised them at length for being more interested in pagan than Christian subjects, for instance wanting to hear about how Minerva was born from the head of Jove, not the Son from the Father, or favoring Plato's *Timaeus* over Genesis.[148] He, Thomas of Chobham, and the English canonist Honorius all issued cautions about and guidelines for the use of secular and particularly classical literature.[149] Study of non-religious subjects was, of course, widely justified because they were seen as preparing scholars for religious learning. Like Serlo of Wilton, however, Robert Pullen and Gerald of Wales expressed worries about scholars getting so involved in the excitement over what were supposed to be preparatory fields, such as logic and dialectic, that they lost sight of the true purpose of learning, the study of divine truth.[150]

Nowhere, however, did English clerics venture into more controversial intellectual territory than in the pursuit of astrology, divination, and magic.[151] John of Salisbury devoted approximately 13 percent of his large work, the *Policraticus*, to condemning magic and divination.[152] Thomas of Chobham also discussed magic at length in his treatise for confessors and in his treatise on preaching he urged priests to strongly attack divination and magic.[153] Even the stories revealing fascination with learned magicians could be hostile or cautionary. Nectanabus was a villain and William of Malmesbury's Gerbert was an immoral figure who was ultimately deceived by the demon with whom he made a pact.[154] Though this hostility extended to all practitioners, there was particular concern about learned clerical magic because so much of it was being introduced in the period.[155] For instance, though Adelard of Bath was widely admired, his work on astrological talismans was considered highly suspect. Albertus Magnus later warned against this work, and another later scholar described it as abominable.[156] An example of one of the

---

[147] The literature on this is extensive. See, for example, Baldwin, *Masters, Princes, and Merchants*, 1:78–80, 102–7; Bartlett, *England under the Norman and Angevin Kings*, 517–18; Leclercq, *Love of Learning*, 139–48; Haskins, *Renaissance of the Twelfth Century*, 94–8.

[148] Bodleian Library, Wood empt. MS 13, fos. 88v–89r.

[149] Haskins, *Mediaeval Science*, 372–3; Alexander Neckam, *Sacerdos ad Altare*, 174–5; Thomas of Chobham, *Summa de Arte Praedicandi*, 15; Honorius, *Magistri Honorii Summa*, 125.

[150] Lambeth Palace, MS 458 part 2, fos. 148r–151r; Gerald of Wales, *Opera*, 350–1.

[151] For some works that explore the controversies surrounding learned magic and astrology in depth, see Peters, *Magician, Witch, and Law*, 63–84; Kieckhefer, *Magic*, 116–75; Boudet, *Entre science et nigromance*; Watkins, *History and the Supernatural*, 129–69.

[152] John of Salisbury, *Policraticus*, 1:49–169. For the percentage, see Carey, *Courting Disaster*, 29. For a good discussion of how John adapted Isidore and for John's attack in general, see Boudet, *Entre science et nigromance*, 89–108. See also Thorndike, *History of Magic*, 2:155–70.

[153] Thomas of Chobham, *Summa Confessorum*, 420–1, 466–87; Thomas of Chobham, *Summa de Arte Praedicandi*, 167.

[154] Thomas of Kent, *Anglo-Norman Alexander*, 1:8–21; William of Malmesbury, *Gesta Regum*, 1:278–95. As Watkins notes, William of Malmesbury was somewhat more ambivalent about new forms of learning such as astrology than his cautionary tales about Gerbert and other figures would indicate: Watkins, *History and the Supernatural*, 164–8.

[155] For ecclesiastical sanctions and the gradual hardening of hostility, see Peters, *Magician, Witch, and Law*, 85–109; Kieckhefer, *Magic*, 176–201; Boudet, *Entre science et nigromance*, 205–78. For particular worries about clerical magic, see Watkins, *History and the Supernatural*, 129–30.

[156] Burnett, "Talismans," 6; Boudet, *Entre science et nigromance*, 142–3.

incantations, designed to be read while fumigating the talisman with incense, may show why:

> O shining spirits of the planets, you who descend from al-'alām [i.e. the macrocosm], effectors of good and evil! Bind the spirit of Socrates, son of Sophroniscus, to the heart of Plato. Let their will and desire be one; let loathing and rejection be absent; but let the imagination and memory [of the other] be always present. Be present, too, spirits of the hours of the planets, not only by day, but also in the night and in their dreams. Bring the picture of Socrates' image before Plato's eyes to such an extent that, all other feelings excluded, he gives himself totally to him, by the power of God.[157]

This charm encapsulates many aspects of intellectual life in the period, such as the interest in Arabic learning, the fascination with classical pagan figures (even if their names are used only as placeholders for the intended subjects of the incantation), and the interest in manipulating the natural world; but it was clearly not likely to please conservative religious figures, despite the final invocation of God.

It is noteworthy how many clerics were open to such religiously suspect subjects as magic, astrology, and divination. This could occur partly because of the difficulty of separating the magical and demonic from the natural. Even a harsh critic like John of Salisbury had to wrestle with the existence of everyday forms of prognostication such as sailors searching for signs of a shift in the weather. These were clearly based on natural phenomena and therefore not sinful, but where did one draw the line?[158] He and most other scholars grudgingly accepted that astrology had at least some scientific basis, and acceptance of the natural properties of stones was also widespread.[159] Even the use of astrological talismans such as Adelard's could be presented as the manipulation of natural phenomena using hermetic knowledge. The idea of natural magic had not yet emerged, but scholars in the period were struggling to unravel which kinds of esoteric forces were natural and therefore acceptable and which were not, giving proponents of such practices a certain amount of wiggle room.[160] Another factor providing latitude to clerics working on the borderlands between nature and magic was that attitudes towards magic had not hardened as they would later in the Middle Ages. Though concerns about demonic involvement were already present, they were not nearly as pervasive as in subsequent centuries.[161] It was only later that the intellectual basis for the great witch hunts of the early modern period was established. Though condemnation appeared in many types of sources, including ecclesiastical law, in this period the sanction was still generally only excommunication, along with loss or

---

[157] Burnett, "Establishment of Medieval Hermeticism," 113–14. Translation by Burnett.

[158] John of Salisbury, *Policraticus*, 1:69. See also Baldwin of Ford, *Opera*, 433; Thomas of Chobham, *Summa Confessorum*, 479.

[159] John of Salisbury, *Policraticus*, 1:107–15, 133–43; Thomas of Chobham, *Summa Confessorum*, 476, 478; Tester, *Western Astrology*, 147, 175–83.

[160] Kieckhefer, *Magic*, 12–14; Boudet, *Entre science et nigromance*, 125–33; Watkins, *History and the Supernatural*, 133–40.

[161] Ralph Niger, *De Re Militari*, 219; John of Salisbury, *Policraticus*, 1:164; Kieckhefer, *Magic*, 151–3.

suspension of office for clerics, rather than death.[162] Adelard of Bath even described how he and his nephew visited an old sorceress to learn about incantations, and as Jean-Patrice Boudet has remarked, this would have been unimaginable in later centuries.[163] Moreover, though clerical magic appears particularly incongruous to modern people, the religious dangers may have seemed less distinctive for people living in a time when moralists argued that the clerics who put ordinary learning to use in government service also placed their salvation at risk. Even so, it is startling how willing clerics were to venture into spiritually dangerous territory when it came to astrology and magic.

The interest of clerics in magic and astrology or in other worldly forms of learning such as law or love poetry may simply represent one more way in which many failed to live up to the demanding ideals expected of them, but one wonders if some aspects of learning also represented escape from or even resistance to the prevailing Christian ideology. There were clearly escapist elements to some of the literature written or translated by clerics. This was particularly true of chivalric romance, and though the escapism of such works was designed primarily for a lay audience, one should not rule out its attractions for clerics as well. The pagan classics may sometimes have provided a more serious form of escapism. Modern scholars generally pay little attention to the anxiety about pagan learning in the period, since this ambivalence was an old story extending back to the early church and since pagan classical works had seemingly long since been domesticated, so that even justifications of their use had become conventional.[164] However, we may be too quick to dismiss the unsettling yet potentially liberating effects for clerics of reading such works. In a religiously homogeneous place like England, where the only non-Christians were small communities of Jews, pagan Roman writers provided the main exposure most clerics would have had to worldviews that strongly contradicted their own. As accustomed as Christians were to using pagan works for their own purposes, young clerics must nonetheless often have found it profoundly shocking, sometimes delightfully so, to encounter frank discussions of paganism, sex, or magic, and to study ethical systems that overlapped with but did not depend on Christian morality. As Alexander Neckam's warning to the scholars of Oxford indicates, many found the exotic, intellectually captivating world of pagan Rome intoxicating. Indeed, there seems to have been a widespread fascination among clerics with the ancient world, as suggested by their collecting of antique intaglios, noted earlier. Similarly, an English cleric named Gregory who wrote a description of Rome, probably around 1200, included many pagan classical buildings and objects as well as Christian ones, clearly expecting that his audience would be

---

[162] For English synodal condemnations, see Whitelock, Brett, and Brooke, eds., *Councils and Synods, 1066–1204*, 614, 741; Powicke and Cheney, eds., *Councils and Synods, 1205–1265*, 24–5, 33. See also Morey, *Bartholomew of Exeter*, 271–3.

[163] Adelard of Bath, *Conversations with his Nephew*, 192–5, 233 n 72; Boudet, *Entre science et nigromance*, 158–9.

[164] See, for instance, Baldwin, *Masters, Princes, and Merchants*, 1:78; Hunt and Gibson, *Schools and the Cloister*, 43.

interested in them.[165] There were many reasons for interest in pagan antiquity, but given the profound moral and religious stresses to which secular clerics were exposed, the opportunity to immerse themselves in a literary and intellectual world in which Christianity was absent and writers dealt freely with and often celebrated politics, wealth, power, and sex must have proven tempting to many clerics. Students unfamiliar with the Middle Ages are often startled by the importance of pagan classics in the period, but as scholars we may have become so familiar with their importance that we overlook how disruptive they may have been even within a Christian worldview that had long incorporated and theoretically tamed them.

There was also a strong element of the carnivalesque in some literary works written by the secular clergy and also in works about them. The concept of the carnivalesque was developed by the Russian scholar Mikhail Bakhtin, and he and many of the scholars who followed in his footsteps have associated it primarily with popular culture.[166] However, though positing popular origins for the phenomenon, Bakhtin rightly noted that many of its important medieval manifestations were linked to the clergy, including both clerical writings and festivities such as the feast of fools.[167] We have only limited evidence for such festivals in England in the long twelfth century, but certainly there were props for the feast of fools and a feast of boys at Salisbury Cathedral when a new treasurer made an inventory there in 1214.[168] That such clerical phenomena had a primarily popular basis is no more than an assumption, and trying to apply modern distinctions between popular and elite culture to the Middle Ages may be a problematic enterprise. Nonetheless, one can reasonably apply the idea of the carnivalesque to certain kinds of transgressive writings and behaviors both by clerics and by ordinary people. Though clerical authors were generally well off or rich, they were constrained by demanding codes of behavior and formed part of a strongly hierarchical structure in which they always had to deal with powerful superiors. It is hardly surprising that some might have wanted to disrupt things by their writings and by satirical festivals. Admittedly, many of the most raucous works of the period had a moralizing purpose, but even those could attack the status quo by mocking powerful people, including popes and bishops. Many scholars have argued that the carnivalesque sometimes acted as a social safety valve, and it is perhaps not accidental that a certain leeway seems to have been given to youthful writings about love and other problematic

---

[165] M. R. James, "Magister Gregorius de Mirabilibus Urbis Romae," *English Historical Review* 32 (1917), 531–54; Herbert Bloch, "The New Fascination with Ancient Rome," in Robert Louis Benson and Giles Constable, eds., *Renaissance and Renewal in the Twelfth Century* (Cambridge, Mass., 1982), 615–36, at 630–1.

[166] M. M. Bakhtin, *Rabelais and his World* (Cambridge, Mass., 1968). For discussion of the concept with particular reference to medieval England, see Chris Humphrey, *The Politics of Carnival: Festive Misrule in Medieval England* (Manchester, 2001).

[167] Bakhtin, *Rabelais and his World*, 74–6, 82–3, 85, 293–5. Here the clergy would include the regular clergy, such as Nigel of Whiteacre, whose *Speculum Stultorum* Bakhtin mentions. In a recent book, Max Harris argues that the unruly (and therefore carnivalesque) aspects of the feast of fools have been greatly exaggerated. He is clearly right up to a point, but in my view goes too far in dismissing evidence contrary to his view: Max Harris, *Sacred Folly: A New History of the Feast of Fools* (Ithaca, 2011).

[168] Jones, ed., *Register of S. Osmund*, 2:128, 135.

subjects, since young clerics may have felt the constraints of their profession most strongly. Bakhtin himself described the feast of fools as providing a "vent for laughter" in a setting weighed down by the seriousness of church morality.[169] Whether as protest or safety valve, however, works of disruptive literature may well have served as a response to the social and religious pressures that secular clerics felt.

Even though learning could add to the moral and social stresses facing the secular clergy, it could also be a source of pleasure and contentment for them. Gerald of Wales extolled the delight of dwelling among books and wrote that he preferred living in his small residence in Wales, suitable to study and work, to having the riches of Croesus. Upon occasion, he claimed he would prefer a life of study to being a bishop, at least of any place but St. David's.[170] Given his dogged efforts to gain wealth and his pursuit of the bishopric of St. David's, such statements clearly oversimplified Gerald's complex character. Given the vicissitudes and frustrations of his career, however, it is likely that scholarship did sometimes provide a refuge, and the massive amount of scholarship he produced surely indicates that he took joy in learning. Perhaps the most evocative account of the pleasures of quiet religious scholarship, however, comes from a story in the collection of clerical anecdotes at Corpus Christi College, Oxford. In this account, which is fictional or highly garbled at best, Master Anselm, a theologian, was elected bishop of London with the consent of the "elder" King Henry. A delegation went to Paris to fetch him, but on their first approach got no response. The next day, they returned to his house, asking that he not delay. Anselm took them out to the garden in the courtyard of his house in which, the account says, he was accustomed to meditate and read about God. Describing the good work he had done there, he asked how he could leave it for a bishopric. The end of the story is lost, but it seems safe to surmise that Master Anselm preferred the schools to the power, wealth, and authority of being a bishop.[171] Some clerics clearly envisioned the scholarly life as the good life.

Though England was not the epicenter of the Twelfth-Century Renaissance, secular clerics associated with that land were clearly important to intellectual life in the period. Often their intellectual paths led into controversial areas, and it is a sign of the dynamism of the period that severe disapproval by moralists did little to quell the adventurousness of clerical scholars. Most of England's learned secular clerics can best be described as practicing intellectuals, putting their training to use through preaching sermons, composing letters, practicing canon law, examining patients, casting horoscopes, or teaching subjects ranging from grammar to theology in local schools and eventually at Oxford and Cambridge. Many, however, produced written works in a remarkable range of fields. Not all of their works were

---

[169] Bakhtin, *Rabelais and his World*, 75.

[170] Gerald of Wales, *Opera*, 1:87, 93, 98–9; 6:47; Davies, "Giraldus Cambrensis: *De Invectionibus*," 122–3.

[171] There was an Anselm who briefly became bishop of London in Stephen's reign before his election was quashed by the pope, but he had been an abbot of Bury: Corpus Christi College, Oxford, MS 32, fo. 99v; Diana E. Greenway, *Fasti Ecclesiae Anglicanae, 1066–1300. 1. St Paul's, London* (London, 1968), 1.

particularly innovative, but many were, and a large number both reflected and promoted important intellectual and cultural trends of the day, such as the growing interest in the natural world or the development of vernacular literature. Some clerics, including John of Salisbury, Peter of Blois, Geoffrey Vinsauf, Alfred of Shareshill, and Geoffrey of Monmouth produced texts that had enormous influence in the later Middle Ages and in some cases beyond. Monks, nuns, regular canons, and even laypeople all contributed to the intellectual life of the long twelfth century, but this chapter shows once more just how important were the secular clergy, in England and elsewhere, to the Twelfth-Century Renaissance.

13

Secular Clerics as Cultural Patrons and Performers

One of the most generous donors to the treasury of St. Paul's, as revealed by an inventory of 1245, was a late twelfth-century canon of the cathedral, Master Henry of Northampton. Henry's most impressive gift was a cross ornamented with gilded images, two engraved gems, and a variety of other precious stones. Another precious gift was a heavy silver chalice accompanied by a paten engraved with an image of the Trinity. In addition, he gave two complete sets of vestments, three chasubles, and a cope, all made of valuable textiles and richly embroidered with a variety of images, such as lions, flying serpents, eagles, the angels Uriel and Barathiel, and saints and bishops of London. Lastly, he gave eight service books, some bound with covers of gilded silver or decorated with rich illumination, including a combined breviary and antiphonal with musical notation and an illuminated initial depicting a bearded man holding a scroll.[1]

This chapter explores secular clerics as cultural patrons and performers. Though Haskins focused primarily on intellectual matters, the cultural and artistic achievements of the period are crucial to the widespread acceptance of the existence of a Twelfth-Century Renaissance. Above all there was the flourishing of Romanesque architecture and the origins of the Gothic. In addition, the flowering of manuscript illumination, achievements in metalwork, textiles, and other art forms, and developments in music and drama have contributed to modern appreciation of the twelfth century. This chapter shows that the secular clergy made an important and underappreciated contribution to many of the key cultural and artistic movements of the day. The chapter begins by exploring secular clerics as patrons of *histriones*, *joculatores*, and other sorts of entertainers. It then turns to clerics as performers of the liturgy, and particularly as producers of sacred music and drama, before discussing the activity of some courtier clerics as entertainers, particularly through their witty conversation. There follows a section showing that secular clerics were important patrons of work in precious metals and stones, textiles and embroidery, and manuscript illumination, and another describing their involvement with architecture, architectural sculpture, and wall painting. The chapter ends with a discussion, somewhat speculative, of the influence of secular clergy as intellectuals on art.

---

[1] W. Sparrow Simpson, "Two Inventories of the Cathedral Church of St. Paul, London," *Archaeologia* 50 (1887), 439–524, at 465, 471, 476, 483, 487, 496, 499; Ker, "Books at St Paul's Cathedral before 1313," 215–16, 218–21, 230–1.

I must stress that the category of "culture" used here is anachronistic and perhaps idiosyncratic. I am drawing in this instance not on inclusive anthropological definitions of culture, but on modern concepts of high culture which would have seemed odd, perhaps even morally offensive, to twelfth-century thinkers. Medieval people, including secular clerics, clearly valued artistic creations highly, given the investments they made in them in a poor society. Occasionally, they expressed their appreciation in writing. Gerald of Wales, for instance, praised the artistry of the initials in an early medieval Irish manuscript, and Master Gregory, in his description of Rome, extolled the naturalism of a late Roman bronze and a statue of Venus, stressing how he had visited the latter three times even though it required a long walk from his lodgings.[2] Nonetheless, the concept of art for art's sake would no doubt have seemed idolatrous at a time when even art for religion's sake could be problematic and when many cultural artifacts we now value would have been judged irreligious.[3] For example many modern people view the literary and musical products of minstrels as among the glories of the Middle Ages, but most medieval moralists viewed such works as sinful, and their creators as beyond the pale of Christianity. Moreover, the prestige and value medieval people assigned to various cultural activities, and the reasons they assigned such values, could sharply differ from ours. For instance, some of the treasures commissioned by Henry of Northampton may well have been valued more for the precious materials employed than for the artistry, as suggested by the description of his chalice as being fifty shillings by weight. By setting the art of conversation alongside drama and by giving as much weight to textiles as to manuscript illumination, I am to some degree shaking up modern conventions, though in a time when scholars and artists delight in challenging canons, even this is a fairly conventional approach. Nonetheless, modern values that place a high premium on art, architecture, music, and drama fundamentally shape our approach to our past, and so in arguing for the importance of the secular clergy to historical change in the period, it is worth stressing their contributions even to aspects of culture that twelfth-century people valued less than we do.

1. SECULAR CLERICS AND THE "PERFORMING ARTS"

Medieval clerics inherited from Roman Christianity their extreme hostility towards actors and other entertainers, which was inspired in the ancient period by the close association of these figures with paganism. As John Baldwin and Christopher Page have shown, figures from late in our period, such as Peter the Chanter and Thomas of Chobham, revealed a certain amelioration in attitudes with regard to some entertainers. In Thomas's case, those *histriones* who sang about saints or the deeds of rulers were

[2] Gerald of Wales, *Opera*, 5:123–4; James, "Magister Gregorius de Mirabilibus Urbis Romae," 546, 548.

[3] T. A. Heslop argues that even these responses reflect their authors' association of the objects with sanctity or with the magic of ancient Rome as much as with their own beauty: T. A. Heslop, "Late Twelfth-Century Writing about Art, and Aesthetic Relativity," in Gale R. Owen-Crocker and Timothy Graham, eds., *Medieval Art: Recent Perspectives* (Manchester, 1998), 129–41, at 138.

distinguished from other entertainers.[4] Nonetheless, the general hostility, even on the part of Peter and Thomas, remained strong, with writers often pairing entertainers with prostitutes and expressing the assumption that they were destined for damnation. Indeed, as Carla Casagrande and Silvana Vecchio have pointed out, moralists generally considered entertainers so far beyond redemption that they focused on trying to dissuade their patrons from supporting them rather than reforming the entertainers themselves.[5] Naturally enough, moralists were particularly concerned about clerics providing money to entertainers. Alexander Neckam attacked those who rewarded *histriones* in a couple of his sermons, and in one of these he addressed Oxford scholars directly, urging them to give to young scholars instead.[6] Thomas Agnellus, dwelling on the misuse of tithes by clerics, complained of *histriones* carrying off property sanctified to the Lord, and Thomas of Chobham attacked clerics who gave to *histriones* and prostitutes for similar reasons.[7]

What these criticisms of misplaced clerical generosity indicate, of course, is that clerics, including parish clergy, were in fact sponsoring entertainers. Nor do we have to rely solely on moral invectives to know this. One Becket miracle reveals that Henry, precentor of Chichester, kept a fool not out of charity but for the sake of humor from his "strange words and actions."[8] Becket himself admitted that he was a patron of *joculatores* and *histriones* as chancellor, though not as archbishop.[9] The earliest surviving private accounts of an English secular cleric include a payment to Waggestaf *istrio*, whose very stage name suggests the scurrility that moralists condemned in entertainers.[10] As so often, secular clerics did precisely what they were told not to do, though Adam of Eynsham reveals that even the saintly monastic bishop of Lincoln, Hugh of Avalon, had *histriones* and musicians at feasts in his household for the sake of his followers and guests (what made Hugh saintly was that he paid no attention to them).[11] How important the collective patronage of secular clerics was for entertainers is hard to say, but if Hugh of Avalon sponsored entertainers, it is a safe bet that many other bishops and elite clerics did as well, and the attacks of moralists give the impression that even local priests were a widespread source of support.

[4] Thomas of Chobham, *Summa Confessorum*, 291–2.

[5] Baldwin, *Masters, Princes, and Merchants*, 1:198–204; John W. Baldwin, "The Image of the Jongleur in Northern France around 1200," *Speculum* 72 (1997), 635–63, at 639–42; Christopher Page, *The Owl and the Nightingale: Musical Life and Ideas in France, 1100–1300* (London, 1989), 8–41; Carla Casagrande and Silvana Vecchio, "Clercs et jongleurs dans la société médiévale (XIIe–XIIIe siècles)," *Annales* 34 (1979), 913–28, at 913–15. For condemnations of entertainers by John of Salisbury and Bishop Bartholomew of Exeter, see John of Salisbury, *Policraticus*, 1:46–9; Morey, *Bartholomew of Exeter*, 274.

[6] Bodleian Library, Wood empt. MS 13, fos. 30r, 112r–v; Hunt and Gibson, *Schools and the Cloister*, 91.

[7] Bodleian Library, Laud. Misc. MS 71, fos. 3r, 12r; Thomas of Chobham, *Summa Confessorum*, 300. See also Foreville and Leclercq, "Un débat sur le sacerdoce," 103.

[8] Robertson and Sheppard, eds., *Materials*, 1:207–8.

[9] Robertson and Sheppard, eds., *Materials*, 3:289–90; 4:156.

[10] Woolgar, ed., *Household Accounts*, 1:124.

[11] Adam of Eynsham, *Magna Vita Sancti Hugonis*, 1:125.

In the religious sphere, clerics were performers themselves. Indeed, as some scholars have argued, this made them in certain respects rivals to entertainers. Casagrande and Vecchio suggested that moralists, in stressing what they viewed as the immodest distortions of bodies and the misuse of language by entertainers, were implicitly comparing them negatively to the ways clerics were supposed to use their bodies and voices.[12] Carol Symes, drawing on modern theories of performance, has urged scholars to widen their view of medieval theater, and has discussed commentaries on the ways clerics carried out duties and even on clerical behavior in terms of performance. She and Claire Waters have also discussed preaching as a form of performance. Both utilize the work of medieval authors, such as Ailred of Rievaulx, Peter the Chanter, and Alain of Lille, who contrasted clerics with entertainers in ways that also pointed to awkward similarities.[13] Secular clerics connected with England could do the same. For instance, Gerald of Wales, drawing on a passage from Peter the Chanter, compared priests who adapted masses to suit their audiences to minstrels who, seeing the audience did not like the song of Wacher, switched to one about Landeric.[14] Strikingly, the angry laborer who condemned clerics in the collection of Erkenwald miracles was made to say that the their occupations were less like business than *ludicra*, which in classical Latin referred to games or to plays, a potentially embarrassing claim that presumably helped provoke the saint's wrath.[15] Clerics would have emphasized that their methods of performance and, more important, their goals and motives, were very different from those of entertainers, but the comparison was apparently inescapable to contemporary minds.

No clerical duty involved performance more than the conduct of the liturgy, which was deeply enmeshed in the history of European music and drama. The list of Henry of Northampton's gifts provides a glimpse of the "props" and "costumes" that could be used. The consuetudinary of Salisbury Cathedral, first composed between 1173 and 1220, provides what may be called the stage directions for the performance of the liturgy there throughout the year. This work provides guidelines on everything from specific movements in specific services to the organization of processions (approximately 120 a year) to what vestments should be worn on what occasions.[16] Liturgy itself has a history, but unfortunately, the loss of relevant manuscripts for churches of secular clerics in England in this period makes a straightforward exploration of their contributions to this history impossible. A few works associated with Exeter and Wells from right around the Norman Conquest survive, but almost everything else in the period is monastic in nature.[17]

---

[12] Casagrande and Vecchio, "Clercs et jongleurs," 916–17.
[13] Carol Symes, *A Common Stage: Theater and Public Life in Medieval Arras* (Ithaca, 2007), 2, 150–68; Waters, *Angels and Earthly Creatures*, 44–8.
[14] Gerald of Wales, *Opera*, 2:290; Baldwin, *Masters, Princes, and Merchants*, 1:203–4.
[15] Whatley, ed., *Saint of London*, 112–13. For this incident, see Chapter 3, section 3.
[16] This is published as the first volume of Walter Howard Frere, *The Use of Sarum*, 2 vols. (Cambridge, 1898–1901). For the date, see Pfaff, *Liturgy in Medieval England*, 368–9. For the number of processions, see William Peter Mahrt, "The Role of Old Sarum in the Processions of Salisbury Cathedral," in George Hardin Brown and Linda E. Voigts, eds., *The Study of Medieval Manuscripts of England: Festschrift in Honor of Richard W. Pfaff* (Tempe, 2010), 129–41, at 133.
[17] Pfaff, *Liturgy in Medieval England*, 124–6, 129–38.

Fortunately, Richard Pfaff, the leading authority on the medieval English liturgy, has indirectly but ingeniously traced the development of the Sarum use, the most important liturgical set of customs in England in the later Middle Ages, back into the twelfth century. He does so not only by extending backwards the dating of the consuetudinary but also by linking prayers for specific saints to the likely adoption of their cults at Salisbury in the early and mid-twelfth century. Pfaff also shows that thirteenth-century figures at St. Paul's, London, associated an earlier stage of liturgical development there with a mid-twelfth-century canon named Alberic, presumably Alberic of London.[18]

Whatever the role of the secular clergy in liturgical innovation, they were certainly liturgical performers in settings ranging from the parish church to great cathedrals. Indeed, laypeople were much more likely to experience liturgical performances by secular than by regular clerics. Of course, such performances had primarily religious rather than artistic functions, but their very religious importance meant that they also had broader cultural or artistic significance, and medieval people could clearly value artistry in the performance of the liturgy, particularly in singing. One Marian miracle concerned a canon at Salisbury named Arez who was dismissed from his prebend for having a concubine and children despite the fact that he had a beautiful singing voice. Talent may have mattered less than morality in this case, but it clearly mattered.[19] A monastic writer, Lucian of Chester, stated that the psalms of monks reached God's ears alone whereas those of bishops and the secular clergy delighted the ears of the people. Lucian's aim was to contrast the functions of monks and clerics, but his assumption was that the laity took pleasure in the performances of the clergy.[20] Certainly some members of the royal house did. William of Malmesbury noted Queen Edith-Matilda's love of hearing divine service, and even suggested that she was too generous to clerics with good voices and to scholars with new songs and poems.[21] Ralph of Coggeshall wrote that Richard I also delighted in the divine office, encouraging the clerics singing in his chapel with gifts and requests, even walking among the choir and urging them on with voice and gesture.[22] The clerics of the royal chapel who sang "Christus Vincit" at major festivals routinely received generous gifts of 25s or even 50s in John's reign, a practice that seems to have gone back at least to Henry II's reign.[23] Others could appreciate the artistry of the royal chaplains as well: the author of the poetic

---

[18] Pfaff, *Liturgy in Medieval England*, 350–69, 384–5, 482–8. See also Mahrt, "Role of Old Sarum," 129–41.

[19] Corpus Christi College, Oxford, MS 32, fos. 92b–93r. The name Arez is not close to that of any known canon at Salisbury, but there was a canon named Robert Araz at Exeter who died in 1123: Greenway, *Fasti. 10. Exeter,* 67. For a similar story, see William of Malmesbury, *Gesta Regum,* 1:342–3.

[20] Bodleian Library, Bodleian MS 672, fo. 189r.

[21] William of Malmesbury, *Gesta Regum,* 1:756–7.

[22] Ralph of Coggeshall, *Chronicon Anglicanum,* 97.

[23] *Pipe Roll 34 Henry II,* 19; Hardy, ed., *Rotuli Litterarum Clausarum,* 4a, 26b, 34b, 51b, 62b, 71a, 82a, 85b, 183b; Hardy, ed., *Rotuli Litterarum Patentium,* 58b, 130a; Ian Bent, "The English Royal Chapel before 1300," *Proceedings of the Royal Musical Association* 90 (1963–4), 77–95, at 86–93.

history of William Marshal referred in passing to the beautiful singing of a mass at the court of Richard I.[24]

Page, in exploring how the gap in the ancient world between aristocratic theoreticians and servile performers of music was bridged and how the performance of music therefore became respectable during the Middle Ages, has emphasized that many powerful and educated clerics had experience as members of choirs.[25] Thus, William of Malmesbury could praise Thurstan, a canon of Bayeux who became archbishop of York, not only for his learning, but also for being first among his contemporaries in his command of music.[26] Similarly, Adelard of Bath, noted for his command of musical theory among other subjects, wrote of being asked by a master of learned music and a queen to play the *cithara* before them.[27] The deeply learned scholar Ralph Niger was also a composer: the set of four offices he composed in honor of the Virgin Mary included dozens of pieces with musical notation (see Plate 3).[28] Admittedly, in the late twelfth century, in England as elsewhere, liturgical and therefore musical duties at cathedrals were increasingly transferred to vicars choral.[29] This shift may itself have reflected an appreciation for good performance; Barrow suggests that an increasingly complex liturgy and the resulting desire for a trained auxiliary played a role, and a desire for increased musical quality may also have contributed.[30] However, the shift also indicates that many powerful clerics felt they had more important things to do. Even so, Page's point that powerful and learned clerics had at least performed musically at some point remains valid, and indeed the emphasis in this book on the elite social status of many secular clerics strengthens his argument. They could scorn secular entertainers, but could hardly view the performance of music as inevitably lower class.

How much did English clerics participate in the musical developments of the period, particularly in the arena of polyphony? Unfortunately, the evidence for this issue is problematic. There is little doubt that the secular clergy in Paris were very important. A late thirteenth-century treatise by an anonymous English scholar attributed key developments in polyphony to figures in the cathedral of Notre-Dame de Paris, and most scholars have seen Paris late in our period as central to developments in sacred music as in theology, with Parisian influence then radiating outwards to places like England though the influence of scholars who studied at

---

[24] Holden, Gregory, and Crouch, eds., *History of William Marshal*, 2:86–7.

[25] Christopher Page, "Music and the Origins of Courtliness," in Keith Busby and Christopher Kleinhenz, eds., *Courtly Arts and the Art of Courtliness* (Cambridge, 2006), 29–48, at 30, 33–6.

[26] William of Malmesbury, *Saints' Lives*, 60–1.

[27] Adelard of Bath, *Conversations with his Nephew*, 52–3; Burnett, "Adelard, Music and the Quadrivium," 69–86.

[28] Lincoln Cathedral Library, MS 15, fos. 33r–43r; K. D. Hartzell, *Catalogue of Manuscripts Written or Owned in England up to 1200 Containing Music* (Woodbridge, 2006), 212–13. For a brief discussion of his music, see Andrew Hughes, "British Rhymed Offices: A Catalogue and Commentary," in Susan Rankin and David Hiley, eds., *Music in the Medieval English Liturgy* (Oxford, 1993), 239–84, at 250–1. Scraps of music can be found in manuscripts associated with Salisbury Cathedral early in our period, and music can also be found in manuscripts of Bishop Leofric of Exeter: Hartzell, *Catalogue* 18–22, 212–13, 280–5, 293–303, 389–93, 400–27, 559–61, 564.

[29] Barrow, "Vicars Choral and Chaplains," 87–97; Edwards, *English Secular Cathedrals*, 252–73.

[30] Barrow, "Vicars Choral and Chaplains," 90–1.

Paris.[31] This would fit in with the model of interchange between Paris and England that I discussed in Chapter 10. However, the earliest surviving evidence of a cleric bringing Parisian polyphony to England dates from the late 1220s, when William de Fauconberg, treasurer of St. Paul's, gave that cathedral a manuscript that probably included a piece by the key Parisian composer, Perotin.[32] Some scholars argue that polyphony, which was already employed at Winchester in the Anglo-Saxon period, underwent development in England as well as France, in which case English secular clerics were likely to have been involved, but other scholars have raised questions. Unfortunately, the evidence for the early history of polyphony is so limited that assigning pieces or developments to specific places, even generally to Paris, is tricky.[33] There is, however, one set of polyphonic songs, though not from the liturgy, that can almost certainly be assigned at least to the Angevin Empire. This is a group of conductus whose Latin lyrics concerned political and royal affairs such as the Becket controversy, the revolt of 1173–4, the death of Henry II, the coronation of Richard I, and the regency of Bishop William Longchamp while Richard was on crusade. There is no way of knowing with certainty where these pieces originated, but the households of the kings or of great figures such as Longchamp seem obvious possibilities. If this supposition is correct, the compositions were probably by educated secular clerics in these households, given the use of Latin and the lack of regular clerics in such contexts. Of course, even if these suggestions are accepted, there is no guarantee that the clerics involved were English, since the subjects of the songs were all of interest throughout the Angevin empire. Some of the songs do, however, seem to evince a particular interest in England. Thus, there is a strong possibility that English secular clerics were involved in developments in polyphony in the period, though beyond that it would be rash to go.

With sacred drama, which evolved partly out of the liturgy, we are on firmer ground, for two famous and early references to specific performances involve secular clerics in England in our period or just after.[34] A St. Albans source tells how in the early twelfth century a learned cleric, Geoffrey, brought from the continent by the abbot in the early twelfth century to serve as the local schoolmaster, borrowed copes from the monastery to stage a play of St. Katherine. When these burned in his house, along with his books, he entered the monastery as a form of recompense.[35] A miracle story from around 1219 describes as customary the

---

[31] Page, *Owl and the Nightingale*, 134–54; Craig M. Wright, *Music and Ceremony at Notre Dame of Paris, 500–1550* (Cambridge, 1989), 235–99.

[32] Nicky Losseff, *The Best Concords: Polyphonic Music in Thirteenth-Century Britain* (New York, 1994), 14.

[33] Andrew Hughes and Randall Rosenfeld, "John of Salisbury," *Grove Music Online*, accessed November 20, 2013; Losseff, *Best Concords*, 3–24, 181–93; Robert Falck, *The Notre Dame Conductus: A Study of the Repertory* (Henryville, 1981), 89–96; Olga Elizabeth Malyshko, "The English Conductus Repertory: A Study of Style" (PhD, New York University, 1989), 21–35; Mark Everist, "Anglo-French Interaction in Music, *c.*1170–*c.*1300," *Revue Belge de Musicologie* 46 (1992), 5–22.

[34] For the partially liturgical roots of medieval drama, see William Tydeman, *The Theatre in the Middle Ages: Western European Stage Conditions, c.800–1576* (Cambridge, 1978), 30–45.

[35] Thomas Walsingham, *Gesta Abbatum*, 1:72–3.

staging of plays about the resurrection at the great collegiate church of Beverley.[36] One must be hesitant about extrapolating too much from two examples, but it does seem likely that secular clerics would have been more important than monks or nuns at helping move religious drama from its roots in the liturgy into the lay community, where it eventually ended up with the guild cycles of the later medieval period.

With the profane Latin comedies discussed in Chapter 12, we are back in the realm of uncertainty, not only in terms of authorship, but even in terms of performance. Many scholars have expressed doubts about whether these plays were meant to be staged, but Symes has argued persuasively that they were designed with some kind of performance in mind. The existence of Latin *conductus* concerning politics, clearly meant to be performed outside a narrowly religious context, provides additional weight to her argument that Latin works could be performed as well as read. Symes even suggests that *Babio* might have been destined for an audience of professional clerks such as gathered at the court of Henry II. One cannot rule out monastic authorship or audience for these plays; one of the most sexually explicit, *Alda*, was written by Peter of Blois's brother, William, at one time an abbot in the Norman kingdom of Sicily. Nonetheless, the secular clergy provide the most likely context for the creation and performance of profane Latin plays. In addition to the royal court, bishops' households, schools, cathedrals, and even collegiate churches could have been possible venues.[37]

Another kind of entertainment was conversational, and apparently nobody was better at it than Walter Map.[38] Though Walter left behind a substantial written work in his *De Nugis Curialium*, it was for his talk that he was best known in his own time. According to Gerald of Wales, Walter had contrasted Gerald's writings with his own conversational gifts, saying that the former were more praiseworthy and durable than the latter but had brought fewer tangible rewards because Walter's words were in the vernacular and because the age of discerning patrons had passed.[39] Gerald himself cherished Walter's ability to make witty insults, since he recorded several Walter had scored against their mutual enemies, the Cistercians. For instance, when a Cistercian abbot boasted to King Henry II of the discipline in his abbey by saying that it was a place that was hateful to the devil because of the many beatings there, the king glanced at Walter who said that it was no surprise

---

[36] Raine, ed., *Historians of the Church of York*, 1:328. For the dating and a translation, see Susan E. Wilson, *The Life and After-life of St. John of Beverley: The Evolution of the Cult of an Anglo-Saxon Saint* (Aldershot, 2006), 12–13, 204–5.

[37] Carol Symes, "The Performance and Preservation of Medieval Latin Comedy," *European Medieval Drama* 7 (2003), 29–50. See also Martin W. Walsh, "*Babio*: Toward a Performance Reconstruction of Secular Farce in Twelfth-Century England," in Daniel Williams, ed., *England in the Twelfth Century: Proceedings of the 1988 Harlaxton Symposium* (Woodbridge, 1990), 219–40; Moser, *Cosmos of Desire*, 102–4, 216.

[38] Robert Levine objects to M. R. James's description of Walter as a "great after-dinner speaker," but what he really shows is that Walter was not a great *modern* after-dinner speaker. I accept his arguments that Walter should be taken seriously, but I do not believe that that is incompatible with a reputation as a renowned and amusing conversationalist: Robert Levine, "How to read Walter Map," *Mittellateinisches Jahrbuch* 23 (1991), 91–105.

[39] Gerald of Wales, *Expugnatio Hibernica*, 264–5.

that the devil hated a place where his friends were whipped.[40] Gerald was not the only one who copied Walter's jokes, for the anonymous compiler of the collection of anecdotes in Corpus Christi College, Oxford, MS 32 also did so.[41] An even clearer indication of Walter's fame as an amusing raconteur comes from a humorous passage in Hue de Roteland's *Ipomedon*: "Now understand this clearly lords: Hue says that he never tells a lie in it; well hardly ever, and then not much. No one can keep himself entirely from it . . . .Don't lay it all on me! I'm not the only person who knows the art of lying. Walter Map is very good at it too."[42] Walter himself, in *De Nugis Curialium*, implicitly contrasted his own written work with the vernacular rhymes of the *scola mimorum*, but he also described it as a form of entertainment, placing it, at least metaphorically, in the realm of the theater and applying to it terms such as *ludicrum* and *ludus*, referring to plays, sports, or games. Walter wrote that his audience could either read or hear it, and the work probably gives an idea of the kinds of oral entertainment which he provided at court.[43] Indeed, this rambling account may represent his attempt to put onto the page various jokes, anecdotes, and stories he had heard or invented over the years.

Courtier clerics like Walter Map, then, could serve as a species of entertainer at court, as did Adelard of Bath when he played before a queen.[44] Similarly, clerical authors of vernacular histories and romances may have expected their works to be read aloud, performed as it were, in courtly settings. Nigel of Whiteacre, in his diatribe about improper ways in which clerics sought advancement, attacked clerical courtiers who passed their time with trifles (*nugae*—the very term used for Walter Map's writings), compiling genealogies of kings and princes and inserting the house of their lords into them. Nigel criticized them for flattering their lords, but they were also clearly entertaining them. What separated clerical performers in the secular sphere from the entertainers whom moralists despised? Adelard and Walter Map would probably have pointed to their learning, but social status and wealth may have been the chief distinction, for Nigel also criticized clerics who entered the service of lords and then demanded benefices lest they be forced to consort with *histriones* through poverty.[45] Walter Map was a distinguished courtier; Roland the Farter, to cite another entertainer at the royal court, was likely not.[46]

Clerics, then, acted as performers in a variety of contexts, and also composed various kinds of works, including songs, poems, and plays, for others to perform. Some types of performance, such as the liturgy, were central to the very existence of the clerical order. Other types were considered irreligious. Whatever the moral or

---

[40] Gerald of Wales, *Opera*, 4:220.
[41] Corpus Christi College, Oxford, MS 32, fos. 93r–99r. An edition of the passages relating to Walter may be found in Walter Map, *De Nugis Curialium*, 515–16.
[42] Hue de Rotelande, *Ipomedon*, 379–80. The translation is taken, with minor changes, from Legge, *Anglo-Norman Literature*, 94–5.
[43] Walter Map, *De Nugis Curialium*, 210–11, 404–5.
[44] Adelard of Bath, *Conversations with his Nephew*, 52–3.
[45] Nigel of Whiteacre, *Tractatus Contra Curiales*, 162–3.
[46] Bartlett, *England under the Norman and Angevin Kings*, 236.

social standing of various types of performance, however, secular clerics, both as patrons and participants, were central to twelfth-century developments in what would later be called the performing arts.

2. SECULAR CLERICS AS PATRONS OF ART

As patrons, the secular clergy were also crucial to the development of artisanship and artistry in a variety of materials. Often clerics purchased well-crafted items for personal or familial use, as indicated by the complaints of moralists about priests buying luxurious clothing or jewelry, particularly for their concubines.[47] As the same complaints make clear, however, they were supposed to be buying treasures for their churches, and the lamentations about the lack or poor quality of altar cloths and vestments, the neglect of reliquaries and images of saints, and the use of tin rather than silver or gold for chalices give some idea of the many precious objects and works of art clerics were supposed to acquire.[48] In the course of the thirteenth century, parishioners would take over responsibility for such items, but in the long twelfth century the onus was still on the rectors or vicars, as several agreements about vicarages makes clear.[49] Indeed, exemptions for clerics from a proposed tax in 1184 and from the Saladin tithe included books, vestments, church treasures and decorations, and other articles necessary for church ritual, indicating that items that would later belong to churches were often the private property of the priests in the long twelfth century.[50] Admittedly, a visitation of churches and chapels belonging to the dean and canons of Salisbury not long after the period suggests a more complex picture, with both individual clerics and individual laypeople granting vestments, banners, altar cloths, and reliquaries, or in one case a parishioner and priest working together to provide a chasuble.[51] Nonetheless, priests were clearly buying many decorations and ritual objects for their churches. Between the luxury items they purchased for themselves and their families, the objects such as chalices they purchased to carry out their duties, and the ornaments they bought for their churches, secular clerics must collectively have played a major role in patronizing artists and artisans.

One example is their patronage of jewelry and of gold and silver plate. The claims that priests bedecked their women with jewelry were tendentious, but no doubt some clerics did purchase jewelry for their concubines or themselves. When Master

---

[47] Bodleian Library, Laud. Misc. MS 71, fos. 3r–3v; British Library, Cotton MS Vespasian E X, fos. 182v–183r; Morris, ed., *Old English Homilies*, 162–3.

[48] Gerald of Wales, *Opera*, 2:34–6; Bodleian Library, Laud. Misc. MS 71, fos. 3r–v, 68v, 88r; British Library, Royal MS 3 B X, fo. 17r; Morris, ed., *Old English Homilies*, 162–3; John of Salisbury, *Letters*, 1:159.

[49] Johnson, ed., *English Episcopal Acta 26*, 25–6, 51–4, 56–7, 156; Harper-Bill and Mortimer, eds., *Stoke-by-Clare Cartulary*, 1:68–9. For the shift in the thirteenth century, see Moorman, *Church Life*, 140–2.

[50] Mitchell, *Taxation*, 118–19; Lunt, "Text of the Ordinance of 1184," 242; Roger of Howden, *Chronica*, 2:335.

[51] Jones, ed., *Register of S. Osmund*, 1:275, 281, 292, 296, 313.

Osbert de Camera granted property in London to St. Paul's, he also gave a gold ring with a ruby, which was to hang from the charter with the seal.[52] Wealthy clerics also invested heavily in elaborate clasps or brooches for their liturgical copes. These were generally made of gold and silver and often had sapphires, amethysts, pearls, and other precious and semi-precious stones on them. One archdeacon gave to Salisbury a brooch with a total of fifty-four stones, many of them pearls, and a couple of other clerics there gave ones with thirty-eight stones.[53] As for church plate, the inventory of St. Paul's treasury included several chalices, engraved patens, and engraved or gilded silver vials given by clerics from our period. One canon, Richard of Stortford, gave two heavy silver candelabra worked with men riding lions.[54] Similarly, Henry of Warwick, canon and later chancellor of Exeter, gave his cathedral two silver basins adorned with images of the early bishops of the see.[55] Judging by the descriptions and by comparison with surviving medieval metalwork, some of these pieces may have been true works of art; for instance, one wonders if Richard of Stortford's candelabra bore any resemblance to the Gloucester candlestick at the Victoria and Albert Museum, with its many fantastic figures.

One particularly interesting type of art collected in the long twelfth century consisted of carved gemstones and cameos, noted in the last chapter for their alleged natural or magical powers.[56] Most were of classical origin, though Hugh Nunant, bishop of Coventry, had one with "Allah" inscribed on it in Arabic.[57] Bishops and members of the secular elites collected these enthusiastically, but so too did secular clerics below the level of bishop. Henry of Northampton, Peter of Blois, and three other canons of St. Paul's or Salisbury had cameos as parts of the brooches of their copes, and a dean and a canon of St. Paul's had carved carnelians on theirs.[58] Such intaglios could also be incorporated into seal matrices, and often knowledge of them survives only from their impressions in wax seals. For instance, Thomas Becket, before becoming archbishop, used one with an image of Mercury as a counterseal.[59] The counterseal William Barbedavril used during his oversight of the earl of Chester's writing office had one with the faces of Silenus and Mercury.[60] Like much of the art discussed in the section, intaglios were valued for being rare and precious as well as for their artistry, and their alleged powers no doubt added to

---

[52] Gibbs, ed., *Early Charters*, 56–7.

[53] Simpson, "Two Inventories," 475–7, 481; Jones, ed., *Register of S. Osmund*, 2:129–30.

[54] Simpson, "Two Inventories," 464–8.   [55] Oliver, *Lives of the Bishops*, 300, 310.

[56] See Chapter 12, section 2. An excellent discussion of the phenomenon can be found in Martin Henig, "The Re-use and Copying of Ancient Intaglios set in Medieval Personal Seals, Mainly Found in England: An Aspect of the Renaissance of the 12th Century," in Noël Adams, John Cherry, and James Robinson, eds., *Good Impressions: Image and Authority in Medieval Seals* (London, 2008), 25–34.

[57] Franklin, ed., *English Episcopal Acta 17*, lxxviii–lxxix.

[58] Simpson, "Two Inventories," 476–7, 481; Jones, ed., *Register of S. Osmund*, 2:129.

[59] Ursula Nilgen, "Intellectuality and Splendour: Thomas Becket as a Patron of the Arts," in Sarah Macready and F. H. Thompson, eds., *Art and Patronage in the English Romanesque* (London, 1986), 144–58, at 146–7.

[60] Barraclough, ed., *Charters of the Anglo-Norman Earls of Chester*, 153. For other examples, see Mason, ed., *Westminster Abbey Charters*, 253; Stenton, ed., *Documents Illustrative of the Danelaw*, 257–8; Kemp, ed., *Archidiaconal Acta*, xli.

their allure. Nonetheless, Martin Henig has commented on the connoisseurship sometimes employed in collecting these seals, which suggests that artistic appreciation also played a role.[61]

Written sources reveal the ownership of other miscellaneous pieces of craft or art. Gerald of Wales sent a belt adorned with gold and silver to the papal chancellor, and after it went astray, sent another, along with a knife decorated with silver and ivory.[62] Godwin of Salisbury criticized clerics who imitated laypeople in splendidly decorating the trappings of their horses.[63] That such trappings could indeed be elaborate is indicated by Gerald's story of the priest's concubine who had a saddle decorated with pictures and carvings and engraved in gold, and by Adam of Eynsham's contrast between the simple style of Hugh of Avalon, when traveling, and the ostentatiousness of his clerics, whose horses had saddles adorned with gold.[64] One of the parish churches of Salisbury Cathedral had a processional cross and another had a pyx described as being of Limoges work. Two churches each had an *iconia* of Mary, which in the latter case was described as in need of being painted and compared to a *statua* of John. Probably these were statues.[65] Miracle stories written by Gerald of Wales also record statues in parish churches, one of which was described as being made of wood but decorated with gold and silver, and remnants of a wooden crucifix, including the head of Christ, survive from a parish church in Gloucestershire, where they were hidden at the Reformation.[66] None of these statues or pieces of Limoges work can be linked to specific clerics, but the fact that they were in parish churches means that they were likely commissioned by a rector or vicar.

Some of the best evidence for clerical patronage of crafts and artistic endeavors concerns textiles and textile art. Clerics were supposed to wear simple clothes, but the complaints of moralists suggested that some spent lavishly on clothing. Herbert of Bosham once showed up before Henry II, during the Becket controversy, wearing a tunic made of green cloth of Auxerre and a cloak cut in German style, which perhaps helped prompt the king's remark, "Behold, here comes a proud one."[67] More impressive still, Peter of Blois, in one of his letters, thanked the archbishop of Palermo for sending him a gold belt, a silk garment, and samite cloth (a heavy silk fabric).[68] However, Peter's items were probably intended for liturgical garments rather than personal clothing, for wealthy clerics invested astonishing amounts of income in extraordinarily lavish sets of vestments. Documents from Exeter and Salisbury reveal many donations by clerics of rich vestments, and the inventories of St. Paul's included thirty-three copes, nine chasubles, and fourteen complete sets of vestments given by clerics before 1216. Ralph of Diceto alone gave nine copes, a chasuble, and six sets of vestments, some of them for the use of the

---

[61] Henig, "Re-use and Copying of Ancient Intaglios," 27–8.
[62] Gerald of Wales, *Opera*, 1:308–9.   [63] Bodleian Library, Digby MS 96, fo. 23r.
[64] Gerald of Wales, *Opera*, 2:277; Adam of Eynsham, *Magna Vita Sancti Hugonis*, 1:102–3.
[65] Jones, ed., *Register of S. Osmund*, 1:280–1, 312–13.
[66] Gerald of Wales, *Opera*, 2:105–7; George Zarnecki, Janet Holt, and Tristram Holland, eds., *English Romanesque Art, 1066–1200* (London, 1984), 160.
[67] Robertson and Sheppard, eds., *Materials*, 3:99–100.   [68] Peter of Blois, *Opera*, 196.

lesser clergy, including boys.[69] Fortunately for us, the St. Paul's inventories described the donated vestments in particularly rich detail. Most of them were made of samite, though cloth of gold and brocade were noted in some cases and a few were made of "the silk cloth which is called imperial." Various colors were used, including black, white, red, green, saffron, purple, and a "black purple like marble." Gold thread abounded. Yet it is the range of embroidered designs that was truly remarkable. There were designs in the form of stars, moons, gold coins, roses and other flowers, vines, trees, peacocks, eagles, stags, leopards, lions, griffons, and flying dragons. There were archers; individual saints and angels identified by name; angels with thuribles, crowns, or silver bells; and God in majesty. The canon Richard, chaplain of Windsor, had Windsor Castle embroidered on his vestments along with a depiction of himself reading the gospels before the bishop. It is true that vestments used in lesser churches, such as those recorded as gifts by cathedral personnel and local clerics to a couple of Salisbury Cathedral's parish churches, would generally have been plainer, but even so some were made of silk.[70] When elite clerics performed the liturgy, however, they dressed themselves in works of art.

Clerics also bought or commissioned textile art in other forms. A chaplain at one parish church gave three linen altar cloths with some sort of depictions on them.[71] At Salisbury, a canon gave an altar cloth of silk and one of the deans of the cathedral gave one of red samite, embroidered in gold.[72] At St. Paul's, Ralph of Diceto was the donor of a *tapetium*, a tapestry or carpet of some sort. Among the hangings in the choir were a saffron-colored one given by the wealthy royal cleric, William of Wrotham, and a particularly large purple one donated by Diceto. Given that other donors of hangings included bishops and King John, these pieces were likely to have been magnificent.[73] Textile art is undervalued in the modern world but was clearly treasured in the Middle Ages, and clerics were obviously important patrons of this art.

With the textiles and metalwork discussed so far we must mainly rely on written descriptions, but with manuscript illumination we are fortunate in having surviving works associated with specific clerics from our period.[74] Even so, it is worth starting with the descriptions in the thirteenth-century inventories of books given to St. Paul's, for these provide an idea of near-contemporary reactions. Clearly the makers of these inventories had a deep appreciation for many books given by their predecessors before 1216, since the compilers of the inventories could speak, for instance, of a "large and beautiful" gradual or a "very beautiful" troper, both given by Ralph of Diceto. In part the later canons appreciated the quality of the lettering, which was often described as large, excellent, or even "thoroughly wonderful."

---

[69] Oliver, *Lives of the Bishops*, 299–301; Jones, ed., *Register of S. Osmund*, 2:129–33; Simpson, "Two Inventories," 475–80, 483, 487–90.

[70] Jones, ed., *Register of S. Osmund*, 1:275, 292.   [71] Jones, ed., *Register of S. Osmund*, 1:292.

[72] Jones, ed., *Register of S. Osmund*, 2:134.   [73] Simpson, "Two Inventories," 495.

[74] Vestments and metal objects buried with Archbishop Hubert Walter do survive: Neil Stratford, Pamela Tudor-Craig, and Anna Marie Muthesius, "Archbishop Hubert Walter's Tomb and the Furnishings," in Nicola Coldstream and Peter Draper, eds., *Medieval Art and Architecture at Canterbury before 1220* (London, 1982), 71–93.

Utility must have been a factor in this appreciation, particularly for books meant to be used during services, but there may also have been admiration for the quality of handwriting—a valuing of calligraphy that is rare in modern Western cultures.[75] There was, however, also an appreciation for illumination, which admittedly overlapped with calligraphy in illuminated initials. William of Potterne, a canon and important royal bureaucrat, had given a "beautiful epistolary with excellent letters," that began with "a thoroughly beautiful golden letter," clearly an initial with gold leaf. However, the compilers also appreciated art that was separate from lettering, for they described a missal given by the canon Robert of Clifford as having a calendar with the "months depicted and beautiful symbols (*signis pulcherrimis*)."[76] None of these particular manuscripts survives, but the manuscripts connected with clerics in the long twelfth century that do survive can give us a sense of why later canons valued these lost manuscripts so much.

I have looked at over thirty of the more than ninety surviving manuscripts associated with secular clerics, along with detailed modern catalogue descriptions of many of the remainder.[77] The vast majority of surviving manuscripts had some form of decoration, though mostly the decoration consisted of initials in ink of various colors, employing scrollwork, foliage, and other designs. Such initials would have been fairly inexpensive, but many are quite beautiful, and some manuscripts contain a large number. A smaller percentage of manuscripts have what might be termed a touch of luxury, marked by more exuberant ink initials and one or two initials with gold leaf and illumination. For instance, Lawrence, archdeacon of Bedford, gave to St. Mary's, Huntingdon, a manuscript containing the prophetic books of the Bible with glosses, which contains an elaborate ink initial for each book and each accompanying gloss, with the use of gold leaf for the first prophetic book.[78] Some surviving manuscripts, however, include a good number of high quality illuminations. The highest concentration of these comes from Lincoln Cathedral. For instance, Hamo the Chancellor gave a glossed psalter with at least ten splendid initials (some now excised), including one with an image of David playing the harp (see Plate 4). Other examples include a large two-volume Bible given by Henry of Huntingdon's father, Nicholas, around 1100 (see Plate 5); and manuscripts given by David, archdeacon of Buckingham; Jordan, treasurer in the mid-twelfth century (see Plate 6); and Ralph Medicus, a canon and royal physician who died in 1170.[79] Manuscripts with high quality illumination also survive from other centers. For example, Bodley MS 725, probably given by the canon Robert de

[75] Parkes, *Their Hands before our Eyes*, 103; Clanchy, *From Memory to Written Record*, 278–83.

[76] Ker, "Books at St Paul's Cathedral before 1313," 215–30.

[77] Catalogue entries may be found below for some of the ninety; of these, I have looked at a fair sampling of the Lincoln and Hereford manuscripts: Sheppard, *Buildwas Books*, 176–261; Mynors, *Durham Cathedral Manuscripts*, nos. 135–45; Mynors and Thomson, *Catalogue of Hereford Cathedral Library*, 7, 12–13, 20, 26–30, 32, 38–40, 57–60, 79, 101–2; Thomson, *Lincoln Cathedral Library*, nos. 1, 15, 18, 23–7, 79, 170–1, 174, 176, 178, 187.

[78] Cambridge University Library, MS Kk.4.21. For a similar example associated with Roger, vice dean of Hereford, see Bodleian Library, Jesus College, Oxford, MS 66.

[79] Lincoln Cathedral Library MSS 1 (Nicholas, archdeacon of Huntingdon), 18 (David, archdeacon of Huntingdon), 171 (Jordan the Treasurer), 174 (Hamo the Chancellor), 176 (Ralph

Hanc to Exeter, is a glossed copy of the Epistles of Paul with a skillfully painted initial with gold leaf at the beginning of the text and accompanying gloss of each letter. Subjects include animals playing musical instruments, a man hacking at a lion with an ax, and a fiddler on the back of a bird (see Plate 7).[80]

Perhaps the most impressive single manuscript associated with a secular cleric other than a bishop is the bestiary given to Worksop Priory by Philip Apostolorum, a canon of Lincoln cathedral. This famous manuscript, now at the Morgan Library, contains 106 illuminations and is one of the most important surviving bestiaries from the period.[81] Even more impressive, however, is the collective program of illumination that appears in the four large surviving manuscripts which Herbert of Bosham gave to Christ Church, Canterbury, containing his revisions of Peter Lombard's glosses on the psalter and the Epistles of Paul. The sheer amount of illumination in these works is astonishing. In the psalter, for instance, every verse of every psalm starts with three small initials and every psalm begins with a large one. Marginal figures abound in all the volumes, often commenting on the text (see Plate 8). Whimsical figures appear such as a lion with the head of a monk or a naked blue man lying on his stomach and staring out at the reader. Altogether, there are scores of large and medium sized initials and hundreds of small ones.[82] Whatever one thinks of the quality of the individual illuminations (de Hamel judged them as less than professional in quality) the overall effect of this program is quite striking, and Herbert himself clearly supervised the illumination as well as the text.[83]

Thus, the survival of a number of illuminated manuscripts connected with clerics can give us some idea of their importance as patrons of illumination. Admittedly, none of the surviving manuscripts reaches the heights of such works as the St. Alban's Psalter or the Winchester Bible. In particular, none of them have the great cycles of illustration of some of the greatest English illuminated manuscripts of the period. Individual clerics simply did not have sufficient resources to finance such works. Nonetheless, clerics could be patrons of beautiful works of illumination, and the lesser but still luxurious and noteworthy manuscripts they commissioned must have greatly stimulated artistic production and created demand for many skilled illuminators.

Medicus). Half of Nicholas's Bible is Trinity College, Cambridge, MS B.5.2. See Thomson, *Lincoln Cathedral Library*, xiv–xv, 3, 15, 137–8, 140–1, 212.

[80] Bodleian Library, Bodleian MS 725. For Robert de Hanc or de Auco's possible link with this manuscript, see de Hamel, *Glossed Books*, 61. Another impressively illuminated manuscript, given by Master Hamo to Rochester, is British Library, Royal MS 4 C X.

[81] Morgan Library, MS 81. All the images from this manuscript may be found on the Morgan Library website. For further discussion, see Muratova, "Bestiaries," 118–44.

[82] The surviving manuscripts are Trinity College, Cambridge, MSS B.5.4, B.5.6, B.5.7; Bodleian Library, Auct. MS E.inf.6.

[83] de Hamel suggested Herbert might have been the illuminator, but subsequent research indicates that this was not the case: de Hamel, *Glossed Books*, 60; Stella Panayotova, "Tutorial in Images for Thomas Becket," in Stella Panayotova, ed., *The Cambridge Illuminations: The Conference Papers* (London, 2007), 76–86, at 78–9.

3. SECULAR CLERICS, ARCHITECTURE, ARCHITECTURAL SCULPTURE, AND WALL PAINTING

Apart from manuscript illumination, the bulk of remaining art from this period survives in the form of buildings, mainly churches, along with architectural sculpture and a limited amount of wall painting. Though most of the great churches from the period were monastic, some cathedrals, a diminishing number of collegiate churches, and the vast majority of parish churches were staffed by secular clerics. Unfortunately, the question of who was responsible for the building, rebuilding, and decoration of such churches remains a highly vexed question about which written sources reveal little. To address the role of the clergy in patronizing architecture and related arts, I will therefore begin with some fairly straightforward evidence of their involvement and then move to more indirect or suggestive evidence.

The clearest evidence of clerical patronage of architecture concerns domestic architecture rather than churches, albeit sometimes dwellings associated with cathedrals or collegiate churches. A letter concerning the attempt of the archbishop of Canterbury to build a collegiate church at Hackington against the will of his monks notes that the canons were building their houses, "nay, rather palaces," at great speed.[84] Similarly, during the temporary expulsion of monks from Coventry the monk Richard of Devizes wrote that the newly installed canons were building ample and splendid lodgings for themselves.[85] Elsewhere, clerics were building or purchasing dwellings around great churches in a more piecemeal fashion. In the late 1180s, Richard fitz Nigel, royal treasurer and at that point dean of Lincoln Cathedral, expressed astonishment that hitherto the dean of Lincoln had had no fixed abode in Lincoln, but had had to stay in lodgings, "like a pilgrim." He remedied the situation by buying the ruined houses of a recently deceased canon and rebuilding them as a residence for future deans.[86] Similarly, late in the twelfth century, Ralph of Diceto, two other cathedral dignitaries, and Master Henry of Northampton gave houses they had built to St. Paul's for the use of their successors.[87] Julia Barrow has found a similar pattern at Hereford and elsewhere of cathedrals acquiring stocks of well-built houses near the cathedral from the late twelfth century on.[88] It is not clear in these cases that there was yet a systematic plan to create a cathedral close or precinct, but several grants refer to the cathedral's "courtyard." In King Richard's reign the bishop and canons of Salisbury were already contemplating the later removal of their cathedral, and in this case there seems definitely to have been a plan to allot spaces for each canon to build a

---

[84] Stubbs, ed., *Epistolæ Cantuarienses*, 80.   [85] Richard of Devizes, *Chronicle*, 70.

[86] Foster and Major, eds., *Registrum Antiquissimum*, 3:322–3.

[87] Holtzmann, ed., *Papsturkunden*, 1:480; Gilbert Foliot, *Letters and Charters*, 445–6; Gibbs, ed., *Early Charters*, 76–9, 97–8; Johnson, ed., *English Episcopal Acta 26*, lxxxi–lxxxiii.

[88] Barrow, "Canons and Citizens of Hereford," 7–8. See also Derrick Sherwin Bailey, *The Canonical Houses of Wells* (Gloucester, 1982), 42–3, 45, 48, 53, 62, 123. For the substantial houses of later canons, see Lepine, *A Brotherhood of Canons*, 114–21.

dwelling.[89] Cathedral precincts, whether planned or haphazard, were slowly coming into existence in this period, and it seems to have been the clerics themselves who funded the process.

That the townhouses of clerics could be quite impressive is indicated by several pieces of evidence beyond the hostile monastic comments noted above. Some of these houses were made of stone, an expensive material only slowly coming into use in domestic architecture.[90] Gerald of Wales revealed in passing that his house in Lincoln had a solar: a private room that was a mark of an elite dwelling.[91] Thomas of Hurstbourne had a townhouse that was large enough to contain its own chapel and was apparently worthy of purchase by the abbot of Peterborough, presumably for his own use, after Thomas's death.[92] Master Alard, when dean of St. Paul's, and one of the canons there bought two houses each from Herbert of Antioch, for eighty marks (£53 6s 8d) and eighty-one marks (£54) respectively.[93] These may have been investment properties, but their purchases give some idea of how expensive a London townhouse could be, and how much a rich cleric could afford to invest in housing.

Clear evidence for architectural patronage by secular clerics also comes from their funding of monastic buildings. I noted in Chapter 4 that William de Rule, rector of Cottingham, built a refectory for the monks of Meaux Abbey from his own funds.[94] Other clerics also financed major building works for religious houses: Peter of Waltham constructed buildings for a house of nuns and a guesthouse or almshouse for Waltham Abbey; Richard, dean of Wells, built a hall for the abbots of Evesham; and Robert fitz Gille, archdeacon of Totness, built a refectory and infirmary for Plympton Priory.[95] After Waverley Abbey was almost destroyed by floods early in John's reign, William, rector of Broadwater, sponsored the building of the abbey church itself, which he was still financing during the interdict.[96] Thus some wealthy clerics were obviously in a position to finance surprisingly large buildings.

This evidence suggests the possibility that secular clerics had an important role in the building and rebuilding of parish churches in the long twelfth century, though it must be emphasized just how little we know about the patronage of parish architecture. Various parties might have been responsible: the owners of the church advowsons, the parishioners (whether as a group or as individuals), or the clerics of the church. Generally, scholars have assumed that the owners of church advowsons,

---

[89] Jones, ed., *Register of S. Osmund*, 2:3.

[90] Gibbs, ed., *Early Charters*, 76–9, 168, 189–90; Charles T. Clay, ed., *York Minster Fasti*, 2 vols., Yorkshire Archaeological Society Record Series, 123–4 (Wakefield, 1958–9), 2:143.

[91] Gerald of Wales, *Speculum Duorum*, 30–1.   [92] *Ninth Report*, 26.

[93] Gibbs, ed., *Early Charters*, 189–90; *Ninth Report*, 18.

[94] Thomas de Burton, *Chronica Monasterii de Melsa*, 1:217.

[95] Peter eventually became a canon at Waltham; Peter of Waltham, *Remediarium Conversorum*, 491–2. For more on Peter's career, see Karn, ed., *English Episcopal Acta 31*, 136. For Richard, see Thomas of Marlborough, *History of Evesham*, 188–9. For Plympton, see Webber and Watson, *Libraries of the Augustinian Canons*, 406.

[96] Henry Richards Luard, ed., *Annales Monastici*, 5 vols. (London, 1864–9), 2:253, 255, 296; Hardy, ed., *Rotuli Litterarum Clausarum*, 110a.

mainly lay landowners and religious houses, had most responsibility, and there is certainly evidence to suggest widespread involvement on their part, particularly in the original foundation of churches, which would often have occurred before 1066.[97] In contrast, scholars have largely ignored the possible involvement of the clergy, probably on the assumption that the parish clergy, who were most intimately linked to parish churches, were too poor to make any significant contribution.[98] Such assumptions may not always be correct. Broadwater church in Worthing, Sussex, has some very impressive twelfth-century remains and if one of its rectors could finance the rebuilding of an abbey church it is perfectly possible that its rectors also rebuilt parts of their own church.[99]

As Carol Cragoe has shown, clerics in our period were still theoretically responsible for the fabric of their entire churches, though starting in the 1220s synodal decrees show a gradual shift of responsibility for the naves to the parishioners.[100] Maintenance of the fabric is not, of course, construction, but rebuilding could be very extensive under certain circumstances. For instance, after the church of North Deighton in Yorkshire burned down, Alexander of Dorset, a pluralist and prominent royal cleric, apparently took charge of rebuilding, since he received a grant of timber from a prominent landowner for that purpose.[101] Moreover, it is worth noting that starting in 1200 there was a frequent tendency to increase the size of chancels, which remained the responsibility of the rectors, and it is possible that such partial renovations of churches often came at their initiative.[102] Even if one downplays the implications for architectural patronage of clerical responsibility for the fabric, it is at least suggestive for patronage of wall paintings. William de Montibus complained about clerics who left their chancel walls bare while adorning their concubines and whitewashing their dovecotes ("even if men are silent, the walls shout").[103] If priests were responsible for maintenance and whitewashing of walls, they probably commissioned wall paintings, particularly given their responsibility for ornaments like wall hangings.[104] One must be cautious about drawing too many implications from the responsibility of priests for the fabric of chancels and whole churches, but one should not too easily dismiss such implications either.

[97] Much of the evidence is anecdotal, but John Blair's observation that many churches in Surrey were placed next to manor houses rather than in villages is noteworthy: Blair, *Early Medieval Surrey*, 134–5.

[98] See, for instance, Peter Draper, *The Formation of English Gothic: Architecture and Identity* (New Haven, 2006), 40.

[99] Nikolaus Pevsner and Ian Nairn, *Sussex* (Harmondsworth, 1965), 390–1.

[100] Carol Davidson Cragoe, "The Custom of the English Church: Parish Church Maintenance in England before 1300," *Journal of Medieval History* 36 (2010), 20–38.

[101] *Curia Regis Rolls*, 6:337.

[102] Paul Binski, *Becket's Crown: Art and Imagination in Gothic England, 1170–1300* (New Haven, 2004), 176; Draper, *Formation of English Gothic*, 179, 200. In the fourteenth century individual rectors sometimes rebuilt chancels on a splendid scale: Thompson, *English Clergy*, 128–9.

[103] British Library, Cotton MS Vespasian E X, fos. 182v–183r. This quotation suggests that an informal division of responsibility for nave and chancel may have begun before that division first appears in a set of synodal decrees of 1224.

[104] For the surviving corpus of wall painting in the period, much of it in parish churches, see Ernest William Tristram, *English Medieval Wall Painting: The Twelfth Century* (London, 1944).

Moreover, there is at least some concrete evidence of parish clergy being responsible for the building of new churches. In 1147, Bishop Simon of Worcester consecrated a church belonging to Great Malvern Priory, which the rector, Athelard, and the vicar, Edwin, had built "de novo" in Pershore at their own expense.[105] Hugh of Wells, another pluralist and great royal cleric, received twelve acres from one Geoffrey de Bosco for building a church at Aldefrith near Little Yarmouth.[106] It is admittedly hard to imagine that most parish clergy would be able to fund the building of a whole church, and it is likely that patrons did play an important role, as scholars have generally assumed. Often enough, there may have been cooperation between clerics and wealthy laypeople, as in a couple of cases noted above. Insufficient evidence survives to reconstruct the relative importance of different groups in the building and remodeling of parish churches, but clearly the secular clergy played at least some role and it is possible that their role was very important indeed.

In one subset of parish churches, those belonging to collegiate churches or cathedral chapters and clergy, secular clerics must normally have been the key patrons, since both the owners of the advowsons and the rectors or vicars were drawn from their ranks. One cannot, it is true, rule out contributions to building by wealthy parishioners, and it is not always clear precisely when such churches came into the possession of colleges or cathedrals. Even so, study of such churches suggests that the secular clergy could be enthusiastic patrons of rebuilding, sculpture, and painting, whether as incumbents or as owners of advowsons. For instance, Lawrence Butler and Richard Morris have linked some parish churches with impressive architecture and sculpture to patronage by the personnel of York Minster. In particular, North Newbald, which was held by the canons in *Domesday Book* and later became a prebend, has an impressive cruciform church built around 1140 with a sculpted doorway. Similarly, a doorway from the cathedral treasurer's church at Alne has carved scenes with fashionable subjects such as the labors of the month, zodiac signs, and figures from a version of the bestiary that only became available in the middle of the twelfth century.[107] A study of churches linked to dignities and prebends, using the *Buildings of England* series, reveals that the churches connected to York Minster were not unique. For instance, the deans of Lincoln held many churches and chapels first granted to the cathedral by William II or Henry I, and many of these still include architectural and sculptural elements from the period.[108] At Wedmore in Somerset, in a church that financed several prebends of Wells, there survives a doorway so much in the style of Wells Cathedral

[105] Cheney et al., eds., *English Episcopal Acta 33*, 42–3.

[106] Admittedly, since Hugh was described as rector, this might be another instance of rebuilding: Hardy, ed., *Rotuli Litterarum Clausarum*, 159b.

[107] Carvings at Riccall and on the font at Thorpe Salvin, both connected with prebends, also depict the labors of the month: L. A. S. Butler, "'The Haunted Tanglewood': Aspects of Late Twelfth-Century Sculpture in Yorkshire," *Proceedings of the Leeds Philosophical and Literary Society* 18 (1982), 79–95; Morris, *Churches in the Landscape*, 279, 282–3.

[108] The dean is not recorded specifically as holding most of these churches until the late twelfth or thirteenth century, but a number were described as prebendal from the time of donation and most of the rest from 1146 at the latest: Greenway, *Fasti. 3. Lincoln*, 5–7; Nikolaus Pevsner and Elizabeth

that Pevsner, who praised it, suggested that workmen from the cathedral also worked there.[109] Many more examples could be cited and most churches linked to cathedrals which were not completely rebuilt at a later date include architectural and sculptural elements from this period. As for painting, one of the most important surviving wall paintings from the long twelfth century, a depiction of the psychomachia or battle between the vices and virtues from around 1200, survives from a church belonging to the collegiate church of Bridgnorth.[110]

When it comes to collegiate churches themselves, their deans and chapters might well have played a dominant role in building. Early in Stephen's reign, the canons of St. Martin-le-Grand in London issued a charter authorizing a chaplain to collect money to continue work that had been started on their church. They emphasized their fear of the impending ruin of the old church but also extolled the beauty of the new one. It cannot be ruled out that Henry of Blois, who was dean of the church as well as bishop of Winchester, and who granted an indulgence for those who donated money, was the driving force behind this project. Judging by this document, however, the canons were either in charge or had embraced the program enthusiastically.[111] Very little architectural material survives from the long twelfth century from collegiate churches that were not episcopal foundations dominated by bishops, making any assessment of the quality of their contributions to the developments of the period difficult, but Pevsner did describe the small collegiate church of Gnosall as including "Some of the most exciting Norman work in the country."[112]

Contemporary sources generally attributed to bishops the great building projects at cathedrals and at collegiate churches attached to bishoprics. Peter Draper argues, however, that there may be a certain bias in the sources, and suggests that deans, priors, and cathedral chapters played a larger role in the process than written records indicate. He points to the development of chapter houses as a sign of cathedral clergy expressing their increasing power and independence, and convincingly suggests that the rebuilding of Wells, begun late in the twelfth century, reflected the desire of the canons there to regain cathedral status in competition with the monks of Bath.[113] Given the efforts of individual clerics to build housing for themselves and their successors around cathedrals, it does seem likely that they would also have been interested in building projects in the cathedrals themselves. When Bishop Richard Poore of Salisbury made plans late in our period to build a

---

Williamson, *Derbyshire* (Harmondsworth, 1978), 57, 106, 245, 261, 296–7, 340, 348, 358; Nikolaus Pevsner and Elizabeth Williamson, *Nottinghamshire* (Harmondsworth, 1979), 168, 315–16.

[109] Greenway, *Fasti. 7. Bath and Wells*, 72; Nikolaus Pevsner, *South and West Somerset* (Harmondsworth, 1958), 332. After 1220, the canon Elias of Dereham (for whom see the end of this section) rebuilt the church of Potterne, a prebend of Salisbury cathedral, in the cathedral style: Binski, *Becket's Crown*, 72–3.

[110] Tristram, *English Medieval Wall Painting*, 48–9, 111–13. Images of this painting may be found at http://www.paintedchurch.org/jousclav.htm.

[111] Westminster Abbey, Muniments MS 13167, no. 109.

[112] Nikolaus Pevsner, *Staffordshire* (Harmondsworth, 1974), 135–6.

[113] Draper, *Formation of English Gothic*, 40–3, 128, 228. See also Binski, *Becket's Crown*, 53, 68, 103–6.

new cathedral at a new site, which was begun not long after King John's death, he certainly consulted the canons of his cathedral, and the canons themselves pledged income, which was a common practice, as Draper notes.[114] Since bishops were generally quite busy, individual canons may also have had managerial roles. Certainly kings often used clerics (frequently in the company of laymen) to oversee building projects at castles, palaces, and other buildings, and bishops could easily have tapped cathedral clergy to do the same.[115] Indeed, Elias of Dereham, a familiar of various bishops whose career stretched from the late twelfth century to his death in 1245, was connected with various artistic and architectural projects, including a new shrine for Thomas Becket and, most notably, the rebuilding of Salisbury Cathedral, where he was a canon. Matthew Paris described him as an *artifex incomparabilis* and scholars have debated over the years whether he could be considered an architect as well as a manager. Recently, the view of him as something like an architect has regained strength and at the very least he was clearly, in Paul Binski's words, "a favoured guru of good building."[116] Bishops were probably the only figures with the power, authority, and wealth to take the lead in any extensive rebuilding of a cathedral, but it is likely that cathedral chapters and individual clerics played a larger role than the sources reveal, which would have made them important figures in the development of architecture in the period.

4. INTELLECTUALS AND ART

As the debate over Elias of Dereham indicates, we have almost no knowledge of the divisions of responsibility between patrons of art and the artists themselves over issues of design, whether in architecture, painting, sculpture, or other kinds of art. Could secular clerics, whether as patrons or in other capacities, have sometimes had a say in the design of works of art and architecture even when they were not artists? It is worth noting that Peter of Waltham owned a treatise on architecture, though we have no way of knowing whether this work had any influence on Peter's thinking about the buildings he sponsored.[117] Clerical translations of works on geometry may indirectly have played an important role in the architectural history of the period, though clear evidence is hard to find.[118] Another important area in which secular clerics may have had an important role was iconography, as when Herbert of Bosham oversaw the images produced in his glossed books of the

---

[114] Jones, ed., *Register of S. Osmund*, 2:7–9, 11–12; Draper, *Formation of English Gothic*, 47. See also Bird, *Manuscripts of Wells*, 490.

[115] For examples just from Henry II's second decade, see *Pipe Roll 12 Henry II*, 17, 35; *Pipe Roll 15 Henry II*, 107–8, 136; *Pipe Roll 16 Henry II*, 67, 70, 72, 74; *Pipe Roll 17 Henry II*, 118–19; *Pipe Roll 18 Henry II*, 124, 130, 135; *Pipe Roll 19 Henry II*, 113, 132; *Pipe Roll 20 Henry II*, 3, 121, 137.

[116] Vincent, "Elias of Dereham," 128–59; Adrian Hastings, *Elias of Dereham: Architect of Salisbury Cathedral* (Much Wenlock, 1997), 18–23; Draper, *Formation of English Gothic*, 45–6; Binski, *Becket's Crown*, 73–4.

[117] The work of Palladius, which was in the same manuscript, also contains a section on buildings: Bodleian Library, Rawlinson MS G 62.

[118] Cochrane, *Adelard of Bath*, 63–70.

Bible.[119] Religious iconography must normally have come ultimately from the clergy, secular as well as regular. Of course artists, even when laypeople, would have learned much iconography through training and experience, and lay patrons would also have acquired knowledge through viewing religious art. However, it seems likely that clerical patrons would have had iconographic preferences when they commissioned works and it also seems probable that lay patrons would have consulted their chaplains, as well as other religious, in making choices. More generally, Binski, in placing art and architecture from 1170 to 1300 in its religious and cultural context, has emphasized the intellectual background to artistic choices, sometimes in very specific cases such as the color of stones in the Trinity Chapel at Canterbury Cathedral, designed to house Becket's shrine. Binski relates these to the allegorical use of colors by intellectuals, including in accounts of Becket's murder by such secular clerics as William fitz Stephen and Edward Grim. The thinking and writing of the regular as well as the secular clergy were often intertwined in the kinds of choices Binski describes, but Binski places particular emphasis on the masters who trained at Paris.[120] Thus, secular clerics may have had a crucial artistic influence not only as patrons but also as intellectuals.

People from every social group, ranging from wealthy lay patrons and ecclesiastical prelates to artisans and embroiderers from humble backgrounds, played crucial roles in the cultural and artistic developments of the period. That said, secular clerics had a greater importance in these developments than most scholars have realized. Obviously, the contributions of secular clerics often took place in cooperation with others such as lay artists or episcopal patrons, which means that these contributions should be viewed as individual strands woven into a much larger tapestry. Equally obviously, some of the arguments I have advanced in this chapter are speculative, inevitably so given the gaps in our knowledge of cultural and artistic production in the period. Nonetheless, I hope that the cumulative evidence presented here will convince readers of the profound cultural influence of the secular clergy. As performers and composers of liturgy, music, and drama; as patrons of entertainers, metalwork, textiles, painting, sculpture, and architecture; as intellectuals; and even possibly as architects, secular clerics in England and elsewhere played a crucial role in the cultural efflorescence of the Twelfth-Century Renaissance.

---

[119] Panayotova, "Tutorial Images," 178–83.
[120] Binski, *Becket's Crown*, 8–14, 29–51, 61–77, 179–86.

PART IV

THE RELIGIOUS LIFE OF THE CLERGY

14

Clerics and Religious Life

In 1196, an anonymous monk of Eynsham Abbey claimed to have had a vision in which he saw, among many other things, a venerable priest who had entered paradise. "Joining righteous zeal and an exemplary life with the grace of preaching," this priest, according to the account of the vision, had freed multitudes from the devil, not only in his own parishes but also in other churches, by recalling them from mortal sins and showing them how they could profit from virtue and persevere in justice and sanctity. The account did not describe the priest as a saint, since it indicated that he was a pluralist and claimed that he had spent some time in purgatory. Nonetheless, this imperfect priest was described as succeeding in the most important task of pastoral care: saving his parishioners and others from eternal torment, and helping them win everlasting salvation.[1]

Reformers, as we have seen, usually focused on the perceived shortcomings of the clergy, and though their diatribes often exaggerated these faults there was certainly a large gap between the rigorous demands of moralists and the actual behavior of the clergy. As we have also seen, there were, nonetheless, also priests who were praised by contemporaries for their zeal and diligence, such as the priest in the vision, the worthy candidate appointed by Abbot Odo of Battle Abbey to the parish church in Battle, and the father and son priests Osbern and Brictric at Haselbury.[2] Earlier chapters have shown evidence of strong religious commitment by many clerics, including the efforts of the reformers themselves to chastise and improve the clergy, the religious writings of the clergy, and even the struggles moralists faced in coping with their own sinful behavior. This chapter explores the religiosity of the secular clergy further by examining several topics. The first section discusses efforts by a number of influential clerics, particularly in the later decades of the long twelfth century, to train and reform the clergy and thereby improve pastoral care, particularly in the areas of preaching and teaching. The second section examines clerical performance of the sacraments and of worship more generally, emphasizing how clerics, by their routine conduct of their duties, constantly reinforced Christianity in English society. It also notes the growing role of the secular clergy in intercession for souls due to the development of the chantry at the end of the period. The third section explores evidence for a variety of activities indicating personal piety on the

---

[1] The author may have been Adam of Eynsham, and the visionary may have been his brother Edmund: Easting, ed., *Revelation of the Monk of Eynsham*, xxxiii–xliii, 156.

[2] See Chapter 5, section 4 and Chapter 7, section 2; Searle, ed., *The Chronicle of Battle Abbey*, 312–19; John of Ford, *Wulfric of Haselbury*, 30–1, 52–4.

part of clerics, arguing that many clerics encouraged practices of lay piety by example as well as by exhortation. A fourth section discusses two contrasting aspects of clerical religiosity: skepticism and intolerance. Overall, the chapter explores what the admittedly limited and problematic sources tell us about clerical piety, zeal, and commitment to duty, and assesses their religious impact on society as a whole.

1. EFFORTS TO IMPROVE PASTORAL CARE

The most striking efforts to improve the performance of pastoral care came late in the period with the writing of manuals designed for that purpose.[3] Though such manuals were novel, they did have earlier roots in the teachings in the schools. For instance, though William de Montibus normally wrote for a fairly small elite among the clergy, as Goering has argued, he composed a brief poem on penance, "Peniteas Cito Peccator," that "became one of the most popular vehicles for conveying the essentials of penance to medieval European confessors." Over 150 manuscript copies survive and it was printed at least fifty-one times between 1485 and 1520.[4] Even a work like Robert Pullen's *Sentences*, designed for a sophisticated intellectual audience in the schools, contained information on clerical behavior or on such priestly duties as confession that could help its readers serve in the parish or, more likely, oversee those who did.[5] However, it was only at the very end of the twelfth century and in the early thirteenth century that intellectuals began writing larger works designed specifically to aid the parish clergy. An early example was Gerald of Wales's *Gemma Ecclesiastica*, written before 1199, which was written for the guidance of the clergy of his Welsh archdeaconry but could have been used by clerics anywhere.[6] Several others were written around the time of the Fourth Lateran Council. Most important were *Qui Bene Presunt* by Richard of Wetheringsett, a student of William de Montibus, and Thomas of Chobham's *Summa Confessorum*. Goering has described these two works as establishing a new type of didactic religious literature, and both had enormous influence in subsequent centuries.[7] Such manuals appeared too late to have influence in our period, but they do reveal the desire among intellectuals to improve pastoral care.

---

[3] Leonard Boyle, "The Inter-Conciliar Period 1179–1215 and the Beginnings of Pastoral Manuals," in Filippo Liotta, ed., *Miscellanea Rolando Bandinelli, Papa Alessandro III* (Siena, 1986), 43–56.

[4] Goering, *William de Montibus*, 59–67, 107–38.

[5] Robert Pullen, "Sententiarum," 901–19, 922–36.   [6] Gerald of Wales, *Opera*, 2:5–7.

[7] Joseph Goering, "The Summa *Qui Bene Presunt* and its Author," in Richard Newhauser and John A. Alford, eds., *Literature and Religion in the Later Middle Ages: Philological Studies in Honor of Siegfried Wenzel* (Binghamton, 1995), 143–59; Goering, *William de Montibus*, 83–91; Morenzoni, *Des écoles aux paroisses*, 178–82; Thomas of Chobham, *Summa Confessorum*. For another work, see Joseph Goering, "The Summa *de Penitentia* of John of Kent," *Bulletin of Medieval Canon Law* new series, 18 (1988), 13–31. Riccardo Quinto has also placed some of Langton's works in the context of the literature of pastoral care: Riccardo Quinto, "Stephen Langton: Theology and Literature of the Pastoral Care," in B.-M. Tock, ed., *In principio erat verbum: mélanges offerts en hommage à Paul Tombeur* (Turnhout, 2005), 301–55.

For the long twelfth century itself, the most important vehicles for improving and training the clergy were sermons, particularly those addressed to synods, priests, or the clergy. Even early in the period, *ordines* for the conduct of synods often contained the text of a standard sermon, with roots going back to the tenth century, which covered the most basic ritual, pastoral, and moral responsibilities of the priest.[8] As time went on, sermons for the clergy multiplied, became more varied, and in some cases more sophisticated. One important subset of these sermons, which I used extensively in Chapter 2, focused on exhorting priests and other clerics to lead better lives, since one way of improving pastoral care, as reformers stressed, was for the clergy to set better examples to their flocks. Many other sermons explicitly addressed to synods or the clergy, along with the vast majority of sermons written by Thomas Agnellus, Alexander Neckam, and the other English authors of Latin sermon collections, consisted of examination of biblical passages, often accompanied by explication of various religious concepts. Ferruolo has suggested that although some of the sermons produced by Parisian masters in the period were directed towards the laity, many were directed toward students, in hopes of training an elite clergy who could train other clerics.[9] I suspect that many sermons written by English secular clerics served as the second step in this "trickle down" process of teaching ordinary clerics. Unfortunately, the audience of most sermons cannot be determined, and so this must remain a surmise until more work is done on these collections. However, the discussions in many sermons seem more complex than one would expect for the laity, and may instead have been designed to provide parish clergy with the religious learning that reformers stressed was so important to pastoral care. Occasionally, sermons also provided practical guidance on pastoral duties such as preaching, correcting parishioners, or conducting the mass, though less often than one would think.[10] Sermons to the clergy seem primarily designed to convey moral exhortation, knowledge of the Bible, and theology.

How effective a method preaching was for training the clergy must have depended partly on how commonly clerics attended synods. This was particularly true of attempts to provide even a relatively simple training in theology and the Bible, which would have required multiple sermons. Unfortunately, we do not know how frequent even diocesan synods were, let alone the regional meetings of clerics called by archdeacons or rural deans, but certainly in the later decades of the period clerics must have met fairly often to deal with the increasing amount of routine business within the Church.[11] We also do not know how well attended

[8] Herbert Schneider, ed., *Die Konzilsordines des Früh- und Hochmittelalters*, Monumenta Germaniae Historica (Hannover, 1996), 87–90, 489–96, 498–500.

[9] Ferruolo, *Origins of the University*, 198–9.

[10] Bodleian Library, Wood empt. MS 13, fos. 45r, 109v; Bodleian Library, Laud. Misc. MS 71, fos. 91v–92r; Trinity College, Cambridge, MS B.14.8, fos. 73r–v. Morenzoni suggested that there was a relative lack of specific advice on preaching in Langton's sermons because he was preaching to an educated audience in the schools, but practical guidance in sermons was rare in other collections as well: Morenzoni, "Pastorale et ecclésiologie dans la prédication d'Étienne Langton," 455, 459, 462–3.

[11] For a good overview of diocesan synods and their responsibilities, see J. Avril, "L'Évolution du synode diocésain principalement dans la France du nord du Xe au XIIIe siècles," in Peter Linehan, ed., *Proceedings of the Seventh International Congress of Medieval Canon Law* (Vatican City, 1988), 302–35.

such meetings were likely to be. Bishop Herbert of Salisbury wrote in 1203 that not even a tenth of the rectors and perpetual vicars showed up to one of his synods, but apparently "annual vicars," who would have done much of the actual work in the parishes, attended in larger numbers. Moreover, the *vita* of William of Norwich noted in passing a priest who attended a synod because it was compulsory, and one of the few surviving documents from the ecclesiastical courts referred to a rector being suspended for not coming to a synod.[12] Thus, attendance may have been fairly common for the parish clergy and as a result synodal sermons, along with other sermons addressed to priests and clerics, were potentially an important avenue by which the learned clerical elite could spread knowledge of the ideals, teachings, and rules of the Church to the parish clergy before much of the literature of pastoral care was developed.[13] In addition, when bishops issued synodal statutes, they could have used them in combination with sermons and perhaps informal discussions as a teaching as well as a legislative tool.[14]

Another way learned reformers could aid pastoral care was by providing model sermons. Thus William de Montibus, after lamenting the lack of preaching by many priests, devised two sets of brief Latin sermons which he said learned but lazy preachers could use for their flocks, presumably in translation.[15] Given the lack of any clear indication about the intended audience in most Latin sermons it is hard to know how many other surviving ones were designed for a lay audience. Unfortunately, moreover, very little evidence survives for the authorship of vernacular sermons, which may best represent preaching in the parishes, and it is therefore difficult to know whether any were the work of secular clerics.[16] That said, at least some other Latin sermons written by elite clerics represented versions of ones delivered to the laity. Peter of Blois explicitly described one of his sermons as having been translated into Latin at the request of an acquaintance after being offered to the "crude" laity.[17] Similarly, Alexander Neckam sometimes directly addressed laypeople in his sermons. For instance, in one sermon he compared their weeping over lost money unfavorably to Jesus's weeping for Jerusalem (Alexander

[12] Kemp, ed., *English Episcopal Acta 18*, 210; Thomas of Monmouth, *William of Norwich*, 71; Adams and Donahue, eds., *Select Cases*, 33. For a witness list almost certainly from a local synod that includes three priests, two masters, three clerics, and seven chaplains, see Kemp, "Acta of English Rural Deans," 145–6.

[13] See also Brett, *English Church*, 155–60; Cheney, *From Becket to Langton*, 141–6; Lawrence, "English Parish," 664.

[14] C. R. Cheney, *Medieval Texts and Studies* (Oxford, 1973), 185–202; Roy Martin Haines, *Ecclesia Anglicana: Studies in the English Church of the Later Middle Ages* (Toronto, 1989), 129–37; Morenzoni, *Des écoles aux paroisses*, 163–71.

[15] Goering, *William de Montibus*, 516–17, 544–57. For the complex question of the language of preaching, see Giles Constable, "The Language of Preaching in the Twelfth Century," *Viator* 25 (1994), 131–52; David L. d'Avray, *The Preaching of the Friars: Sermons Diffused from Paris before 1300* (Oxford, 1985), 6–7, 90–5; Hunt and Gibson, *Schools and the Cloister*, 93–4.

[16] The general tendency has been to associate anonymous vernacular texts from the period with monastic houses, partly on the basis of manuscript affiliation. There is no doubt the regular clergy were involved, but the higher survival rate of manuscripts in institutional libraries may distort the picture. For recent work on sermons and other religious texts in the vernacular, see Swan and Treharne, eds., *Rewriting Old English*.

[17] Peter of Blois, *Opera*, 750.

was trying to overcome their reluctance to pay tithes).[18] Presumably clerical readers of the sermon collections could have used such sermons themselves or mined them for ideas. Thus, at least some of the sermon writing by learned clerics could have been used to improve preaching to the laity.

Most sermons written by learned English clerics were very traditional in style, but a few writers were involved in the important transformations in preaching that took place during the twelfth and thirteenth centuries.[19] Many of these changes were associated with the friars, but as various scholars have shown, the masters in the schools were also closely involved.[20] For instance, some of the teaching techniques William de Montibus helped develop, such as distinctions, short discussions of specific biblical or religious terms that could summarize theological learning in an accessible format, could also be used in sermons.[21] Hints of the practices that made sermons more interesting to ordinary audiences can also be found in some sermons. For example, Neckam took care to speak to the laity in ways that addressed their own interests and experiences, in one case admonishing them for refusing to embrace a new religious life when otherwise they desired nothing but novelty, whether in clothes or in the music which minstrels used to accompany love songs. He also made an early and explicit use of *exempla* in sermons, if only sparingly.[22] A sense of how another cleric might inject humor through an *exemplum* comes from a story recorded in the collection of clerical anecdotes at Corpus Christi College, Oxford, as one which Master Walter of London used in a sermon to the laity. In this *exemplum*, Walter, when staying at the house of a knight, drank too much after being toasted in turn by his host and the host's wife and daughter. The next morning, after his horse had drunk its fill of water, Walter told it to drink again for his love, for love of his host, and for love of his host's wife and daughter. The horse did not do so, showing, Walter told the congregation, more wisdom than he himself had.[23] Though most sermons from the period were quite dry, change was clearly coming. Moreover, some aspects of the transformations in preaching may have had their roots in sermons directed to

---

[18] Bodleian Library, Wood empt. MS 13, fos. 74r–v; Hunt and Gibson, *Schools and the Cloister*, 24, 84.

[19] John W. O'Malley, "Introduction: Medieval Preaching," in Thomas L. Amos, Eugene Green, and Beverly Mayne Kienzle, eds., *De Ore Domini: Preacher and Word in the Middle Ages* (Kalamazoo, 1989), 1–11; d'Avray, *Preaching of the Friars*, 13–28; Phyllis Roberts, "The *Ars Praedicandi* and the Medieval Sermon," in Carolyn Muessig, ed., *Preaching, Sermon, and Audience in the Middle Ages* (Leiden, 2002), 41–62, at 44–9; Nicole Bériou, "Les sermons latins après 1200," in Beverly Mayne Kienzle, ed., *The Sermon* (Turnhout, 2000), 363–447.

[20] Ferruolo, *Origins of the University*, 198–206; Bériou, "Les sermons latins," 367, 400; Mark A. Zier, "Sermons of the Twelfth Century Schoolmasters and Canons," in Beverly Mayne Kienzle, ed., *The Sermon* (Turnhout, 2000), 325–62.

[21] Goering, *William de Montibus*, 69–72; Roberts, "*Ars Praedicandi*," 57–9.

[22] Bodleian Library, Wood empt. MS 13, fos. 88r, 89v–90r; Ferruolo, *Origins of the University*, 201–2; Hunt and Gibson, *Schools and the Cloister*, 84. For the use of *exempla*, which had a long history but came into prominence in the thirteenth century, see Claude Bremond, Jacques Le Goff, and Jean Claude Schmitt, *L'"Exemplum"* (Turnhout, 1996). For Langton's interest in preaching to the laity, and his use of *exempla*, see Smalley, *Study of the Bible*, 253–7; Roberts, *Sermons of Stephen Langton*, 84–9.

[23] Corpus Christi College, Oxford, MS 32, fos. 95r–v. This assemblage of stories may be a forerunner of later collections of *exempla*.

priests and other clerics, for as shown in Chapter 2 these often addressed clerical behaviors and circumstances in very concrete ways, anticipating the way in which later preachers would tackle the sins and behaviors of the laity.

Many of the elite clerics who sought to improve the clergy and pastoral care through their writings also held offices that allowed them to pursue these goals through other means. For instance, some of the letters of Peter of Blois to other archdeacons show him providing advice on difficult pastoral problems they faced, and serve as a reminder that he and other reformers often handled real problems and oversaw actual clerics.[24] Similarly, as chancellor of Lincoln Cathedral, William de Montibus would presumably have used his teaching and oversight of teaching to advance reform ideals, and Thomas of Chobham, as an official of the bishop of Salisbury, could have helped put into practice the standards set forth in his writings.[25] As the many diatribes about the shortcomings of archdeacons and other officials show, the holders of these offices were often *not* zealous reformers, but at least some were.

Reform-minded clerics can also be found urging the advancement of reform to others, especially to bishops, who were expected to play the central role in overseeing and improving pastoral care through investigating the qualifications of ordinands, conducting visitations, organizing synods, and issuing synodal decrees. According to the *vita* of Bishop Hugh of Lincoln, a local cleric was commanded by a vision to go to Hugh and urge him to call on Archbishop Hubert Walter to reform the sinful clergy.[26] Herbert of Bosham used his *vita* of Thomas Becket as a platform to urge bishops and archbishops to take greater care in ordinations, and Gerald of Wales criticized bishops for not taking sufficient care in vetting ordinands and overseeing the clergy.[27]

How widespread the impetus to reform was is uncertain. There is plentiful evidence for the failure of reform efforts in this book, and there were obviously many clerics at various levels of the hierarchy who were profoundly unconcerned with improving themselves or the clergy as a whole and many others whose attitudes were lukewarm. Only a small number of reformers, mainly from the elite clergy, can be identified because of their writings, though of course many more zealous clerics may have existed who did not express their commitment to reform in writing, or whose writings have not come down to us. Ultimately, there is no way of knowing how widespread was the commitment to reform, but there was at least a vocal and influential minority who strongly championed the improvement of the clergy and of pastoral care.

It is unfortunately also hard to measure the impact of the reform impetus among the ordinary clergy, or even to have a good sense of the general quality of pastoral care. Two major factors impinged on how well the clergy performed their duties:

---

[24] Some of the problems were fairly obscure, and he clearly included the relevant letters in the collection to reveal his erudition and ability to solve knotty problems, but it seems likely that the incidents were real: Peter of Blois, *Later Letters*, 239–43, 249–51, 273–6.

[25] Goering, *William de Montibus*, 42–57; Kemp, ed., *English Episcopal Acta 18*, lxxvii.

[26] Adam of Eynsham, *Magna Vita Sancti Hugonis*, 2:87–91.

[27] Robertson and Sheppard, eds., *Materials*, 3:238–47; Gerald of Wales, *Opera*, 2:334–7.

commitment and training. The critiques by moralists of the clergy must raise questions about the religious zeal of many clerics, but one must also take into account the rhetorical exaggerations in such diatribes and the likelihood that some priests may have been committed pastors without conforming to all of the ideals of reformers. Brictric had a good reputation as priest of Haselbury despite having a family, and clerical participation in church ales, which Gerald of Wales saw as a sign of personal laxity, may just as easily have stemmed from a strong involvement in parish life and a desire to improve the finances of the church.[28] However, the evidence simply does not exist to measure how assiduously the clergy in general carried out their tasks. Only very occasionally, usually in miracle stories, do we even get glimpses of priests or other clerics carrying out pastoral duties.[29] There has been a fair amount of work done on preaching, but in fact little evidence survives about how common it was, especially at the parish level, and opinions vary among scholars. Thus Giandrea is optimistic about the late Anglo-Saxon period, but Watkins more pessimistic about the twelfth century.[30] Certainly reformers stressed the importance of preaching, but some scholars argue that not until the age of the friars did preaching to ordinary laypeople become common.[31] We simply do not know.

The question of training and education has been of concern to medieval moralists and modern scholars alike. As reformers frequently emphasized, it was crucial for parish priests to acquire the knowledge they needed to be effective moral and religious guides, and moralists therefore harshly attacked deficiencies in learning.[32] Nigel of Whiteacre had a particularly vivid image of badly educated priests who, when a book was opened before them, marveled "as if suddenly within theatrical games, knowing nothing except that these are tools of clerics, as a blacksmith knows nets to be tools of the fisherman and the fisherman knows the hammer and forge to be tools of the blacksmith."[33] Modern scholars have taken complaints about ignorance among the clergy seriously for the obvious reason that even with the increase of schools in the twelfth century it is not clear that many ordinary parish clergy had much formal schooling. Modern opinions vary about the education of parish priests, even when discussing the thirteenth century, for which we have more evidence. Moorman was pessimistic, while others, such as

---

[28] John of Ford, *Wulfric of Haselbury*, 30–1, 52–4, 109.

[29] Robertson and Sheppard, eds., *Materials*, 1:245; 2:48–9, 111–12; Scammell, *Hugh du Puiset*, 99–100; James Raine, "Vita Oswini Regis," *Miscellanea Biographica*, Surtees Society, vol. 8 (London, 1838), 1–59, at 32.

[30] Giandrea, *Episcopal Culture*, 110–12; Watkins, *History and the Supernatural*, 106.

[31] For arguments about the strength of preaching in earlier periods, see Thomas L Amos, "Preaching and the Sermon in the Carolingian World," in Thomas L. Amos, Eugene Green, and Beverly Mayne Kienzle, eds., *De Ore Domini: Preacher and Word in the Middle Ages* (Kalamazoo, 1989), 41–60; McKitterick, *Frankish Church*, 80–114. For arguments that the thirteenth century was a crucial turning point, see d'Avray, *Preaching of the Friars*, 6, 13–28. For preaching and sermons in the thirteenth century and the later Middle Ages, see Moorman, *Church Life*, 78–81; Owst, *Preaching in Medieval England*; H. Leith Spencer, *English Preaching in the Late Middle Ages* (Oxford, 1993); Wenzel, *Latin Sermon Collections*, 229–52, 333–53.

[32] See Chapter 2, section 1.   [33] Nigel of Whiteacre, *Tractatus Contra Curiales*, 203–4.

Clanchy and Denton, have been somewhat more optimistic, though all acknowledge the difficulties of the evidence.[34]

There are certainly indications that the parish clergy were poorly educated. Some of the earliest and most famous concrete evidence comes from the visitation of the the network of chapels connected to Sonning and held of Salisbury Cathedral in 1222. This revealed a painful, albeit sometimes comic ignorance on the part of most of the chaplains. When one chaplain was probed on the Latin phrase "Te igitur, clementissime Pater," he could not translate what *clemens* meant or describe the case of *clementissime* or how it was declined. Likewise, he could not describe the case of *te*, and when asked by what word it was ruled, he pointed to the word *Pater* on the grounds that God ruled everything.[35] These chaplains were in fact relatively well supplied with books in their churches, but one could imagine them being as boggled by those books as the priests in Nigel of Whiteacre's diatribe. There is no guarantee that the chaplains examined here were typical and, as Clanchy pointed out, action was taken against them.[36] Nonetheless, the evidence from this visitation gives pause when it comes to the educational attainments of the parish clergy.

On the other hand, one can also point to local priests and clerics who were at least reasonably learned. Orderic Vitalis and John of Salisbury both received their initial education from local priests, and though John's teacher may have engaged in dubious magical practices, his teaching was sufficiently good to enable John to go on to become one of the great scholars of the twelfth century. Indeed, given the amount of intellectual excitement about magic in the period, the priest's interest in divination may have been a sign of deeper learning. Sigar, priest of Newbald in Yorkshire, recorded the account of a vision by a boy named Orm.[37] A handful of Becket miracles came to the attention of the monks of Canterbury through letters sent by local priests or clerics.[38] In Chapter 11 I noted that the hermit and former parish priest Wulfric of Haselbury worked on books for his own use and that of the local parish church.[39] One must, however, be as careful about extrapolating from this handful of positive examples as from the negative ones.

Assessments of the overall quality of learning among the parish clergy in the long twelfth century will inevitably remain tentative, and will depend in turn on judgments about how much impact the growth of schooling had on ordinary clerics, how common the kind of tutoring Orderic Vitalis and John of Salisbury

---

[34] Moorman, *Church Life*, 90–5; Clanchy, *From Memory to Written Record*, 241–2; Jeffrey H. Denton, "The Competence of the Parish Clergy in Thirteenth-Century England," in Caroline Barron and Jenny Stratford, eds., *The Church and Learning in Later Medieval Society: Essays in Honour of R. B. Dobson* (Donington, 2002), 273–85, at 273–8. See also Lawrence, "English Parish," 655, 662–4; Townley, "Unbeneficed Clergy," 62–4; Morenzoni, *Des écoles aux paroisses*, 144–63; Joseph Goering, "The Changing Face of the Village Parish II: The Thirteenth Century," in J. A. Raftis, ed., *Pathways to Medieval Peasants* (Toronto, 1981), 323–33.

[35] Jones, ed., *Register of S. Osmund*, 1:304–7.

[36] Clanchy, *From Memory to Written Record*, 241.

[37] Orderic Vitalis, *Ecclesiastical History*, 3:6–9; 6:552–3; John of Salisbury, *Policraticus*, 1:164; Hugh Farmer, "The Vision of Orm," *Analecta Bollandiana* 75 (1957), 72–82. These three examples are also noted in Watkins, *History and the Supernatural*, 74–5.

[38] Robertson and Sheppard, eds., *Materials*, 1:238–9; 2:184–5, 239

[39] John of Ford, *Wulfric of Haselbury*, 45, 105.

received was, and even how much the rise of celibacy decreased the passage of learning through priestly families.[40] Nonetheless, the positive examples show that at least some parish priests took the demands of the Church seriously enough to acquire a fair amount of learning. It is also worth pointing out that the increasing investment in education in the period, though it had much to do with professional advancement, was no doubt also a response to the need for an educated clergy and thus to some degree a measure of the influence of the reform impetus.

2. SACRAMENTS, WORSHIP, INTERCESSION, AND THE CHRISTIAN HABITUS

The discussion so far has focused mostly on preaching and teaching, but the clergy had other important tasks, above all performing the sacraments, which was argually their central function, at least in the case of priests. As Cotts has written, "The male clergy, through its learning and ordination, had a monopoly on the keys to salvation, that is, the sacraments of baptism, communion, confirmation, ordination, penance, extreme unction (last rites), and marriage." There were exceptions to this monopoly, as Cotts acknowledges, but the clergy dominated a series of rites that shaped the religious lives of people and were designed to hopefully save their souls. The sacraments had a long history, of course, but the long twelfth century, with the lead up to the Fourth Lateran Council, was vital to their theological development and saw a growing emphasis on their importance. To quote Cotts once more, "Over the course of the twelfth century, canon lawyers worked out unanswered questions, until by 1215 they had established a reasonably coherent sacramental theology that exalted the role of the clergy."[41] It is no surprise, therefore, that large parts of Gerald of Wales's pioneering treatise for parish priests, the *Gemma Ecclesiastica*, was devoted to instruction in the purposes, handling, and administration of the sacraments.[42]

Just as it is hard to detect the actual practice of preaching in the sources, so it is difficult to judge how the sacraments actually functioned in society, how ordinary Christians perceived them, and how they affected religious life on an everyday basis. What really excited comment were the miracles of saints. Though the sacraments were supposed to convey vast religious power and to bring about fundamentally important religious transformations, the fact that they were routine meant that the day-to-day impact or experience of the sacraments was rarely recorded, whereas accounts of unusual and dramatic religious incidents survive by the thousands. This makes it hard to judge precisely how important clerical exercise of sacramental functions was. Interestingly, though lay interest in the mass increased in the later Middle Ages, it did not apparently translate into increased respect for the clergy: the angelic, godlike stature attributed to priests on account of the Eucharist by moralists

---

[40] For the last point, see Barlow, *English Church, 1066–1154*, 147.
[41] Cotts, *Europe's Long Twelfth Century*, 111.
[42] Gerald of Wales, *Opera*, 2: 12–38, 43–5, 110–61.

certainly did not pass into the popular imagination. Because of the inevitable sinning of clerics, and because theologians had insisted, at least from the time of the Donatist heresy, that sacramental power stemmed from ordination rather than personal piety, the clergy were often viewed merely as a conduit for the powers of the sacraments, thus diminishing the religious importance these rites might have given them. Yet, as the medieval prescriptive literature demonstrates, the sacraments were crucially important to Christian life, which in turn made the clergy crucial, even if only as a conduit for sacramental power.

Priests and clerics were also fundamentally important to the conduct of worship, most notably in the sacramental performance of the mass, but also in the saying of prayers, the chanting of psalms, and various other forms of worship. Modern scholars often focus on how clerics served their parishioners directly, through hearing confession, visiting the sick, or preaching, but medieval people also considered acts of worship directed towards God to be crucial. Such practices had various purposes: to honor God, to acknowledge obedience to Christian teachings, and to please God and thereby to avert his wrath or gain his blessing on earth. More important still, Christians hoped that prayers and other forms of worship could help people achieve salvation and, as the idea of purgatory became more prominent, help move souls to heaven more speedily.

Secular clerics were not, of course, alone in conducting Christian worship. All Christians could actively participate in some forms of worship, such as prayer, and could at least witness other forms such as the saying of the mass. Monks, nuns, and regular canons had a particularly important role in the performance of worship. Partly this was because medieval people, particularly rich donors, valued continuous, large-scale worship in larger churches by groups of specialists: in some senses, religious houses were like factories, organized to produce worship and intercession on an industrial scale. Because their rules required them to live communally, the regular clergy were particularly well placed to provide such worship. Laypeople also favored the intercession of monks, nuns, and regular canons because they believed that their piety and their way of life would make their worship more pleasing to God and thus more effective than that of others, including the secular clergy. In many ways, indeed, the primary function of the regular clergy was to intercede with God, and monastic writers sometimes suggested that it was a job largely and rightly reserved to them. The anonymous monk who debated with Theobald of Étampes stated that just as people resorted to castles in times of rebellion and invasion, so they relied on monasteries to intercede with God in the face of plagues or famines.[43] Lucian of Chester wrote of the importance of the prayers and tears of monks when war, famine, or pestilence afflicted Christian people, "because God can deny nothing to them when they ask."[44] Despite such claims and the undoubted importance of the regular clergy as worshippers, the significance of the secular clergy in conducting Christian worship should not be underestimated.

---

[43] Foreville and Leclercq, "Un débat sur le sacerdoce," 97.
[44] Bodleian Library, Bodleian MS 672, fos. 189r–v.

Though the parish clergy may not have been "elite" worshippers they were certainly performing the mass and other forms of worship on a regular basis. Thus the *vita* of Wulfric of Haselbury could praise the parish priest Brictric for his performance of prayers, psalms, and vigils.[45] Though most people surely knew something about worship in monastic churches and perhaps witnessed it occasionally, possibly on pilgrimage, they would have had far more exposure to the ritual activities of their local clergy. Moreover, secular clerics in collegiate churches and secular cathedrals did contribute to organized worship on a large scale. The emphasis that secular clerics, like regulars, could place on such worship is revealed in the Waltham chronicler's account of his training there as a boy in the early twelfth century, when it was still a collegiate church. After referring briefly to education in the reading and composition of Latin, he described at greater length the disciplined and dignified manner in which the boys were taught to participate in the choir during divine worship.[46] The residency statute of 1192 for St. Paul's, drawn up under Dean Ralph of Diceto, stressed that performing the hours by chanting, reading, and praying, was an important part of serving the church well.[47] The discussion in Chapter 13 provides a hint of how wealthy secular clerics could create particularly spectacular kinds of liturgical performance, dressed in their ornate vestments embellished with embroidery and fastened with brooches loaded down with precious stones.[48] Some observers undoubtably preferred the plainer habits of regular clergy, but others surely reveled in the magnificence of the seculars. Processions, which were held for many purposes, from greeting kings to seeking miracles, were a particularly important kind of occasion for elite secular clerics to impress the laity with their magnificence, and by extension to reveal the glory of the Church and of the Christian God. Roger of Howden described how at Richard I's coronation, the priors, abbots, and bishops were led by a group of secular clerics dressed in silk copes and carrying processional crosses, candles, and thuribles.[49] If their vestments and other accoutrements were anything like those described in cathedral inventories, the visual impact must have been powerful.

One particularly important purpose of worship was intercession for souls, and the development of the chantry in the late twelfth century introduced a major shift of such intercession from the regular to the secular clergy.[50] Of course, the secular clergy had been involved all along, despite the early dominance of the regular clergy in this arena. As David Crouch has pointed out, the founders of collegiate churches must have expected the secular canons of the foundations to pray for their souls.[51] In *Domesday Book*, priests held land in return for saying masses for the king

---

[45] John of Ford, *Wulfric of Haselbury*, 30–1.
[46] Watkiss and Chibnall, eds., *Waltham Chronicle*, 66–7.
[47] Ralph of Diceto, *Opera Historica*, 2:lxxi.   [48] See Chapter 13, sections 1–2.
[49] Roger of Howden, *Chronica*, 3:9.
[50] For the background and early development of the chantry, see K. L. Wood-Legh, *Perpetual Chantries in Britain* (Cambridge, 1965), 1–5; Howard Colvin, "The Origin of Chantries," *Journal of Medieval History* 26 (2000), 163–73; Crouch, "Origin of Chantries," 159–80.
[51] Crouch, "Origin of Chantries," 160, 173–4.

and queen.[52] Gerald of Wales, in letters to the officials in his archdeaconry, ordered them to organize widespread prayers and masses for Gerald's soul, for the souls of two recently deceased archdeacons, and for the faithful.[53] The vision of the Eynsham monk tells of a knight in purgatory who commanded a cleric in a dream to tell the knight's wife to request intercession from five "continent and honest priests" named by the knight.[54] As noted in Chapter 2, Gerald and Thomas of Chobham criticized priests who performed intercessory masses for pay.[55] Thus, even in the heyday of monastic intercessory prayer, the secular clergy also had an important role.

Nonetheless, the real institutionalization of widespread intercessory worship by the secular clergy came with the development of the chantry, which eventually created employment for large numbers of secular clerics and channeled to them resources that in earlier periods might have gone to monastic houses. Chantries became popular partly because monasteries were overwhelmed with the intercessory duties they had accumulated, but also because they were relatively cheap to found and because the founders had a great deal of control over the kinds of services that would be performed for them. The vast majority of chantries were founded after 1216, but the model for this type of institution came into being in the long twelfth century. To what degree the impetus for the creation of chantries came from clerics offering their services and to what degree it came from donors seeking intercession is unclear, but it is worth noting that secular clerics played an important early role as *patrons* of chantries. Of the seven chantries founded at St. Paul's before 1216, three were founded by bishops, one by an archdeacon, and three by cathedral canons. Of the seventeen in total founded there by 1250, all but one were founded by bishops or other clerics associated with the cathedral.[56] Secular clerics can also be found endowing early chantries at York and at Lincoln.[57] Lay donors, including members of the royal house, also founded many early chantries, but secular clerics were often pioneers not only as employees of this novel kind of religious institution but also as founders.

Innovations such as chantries are obviously noteworthy, but it is important to emphasize just how crucial the secular clergy's performance of their ordinary duties, however uneven, was to the continual maintenance of Christianity in society. Pastoral care and the constant performance of Christian rituals by clerics created what might be called a Christian habitus, and the Christian marking of crucial rites of passage such as birth and death through baptism and burial consistently

---

[52] Julia Barrow, "The Clergy in English Dioceses *c*.900–*c*.1066," in Francesca Tinti, ed., *Pastoral Care in Late Anglo-Saxon England* (Woodbridge, 2005), 17–26, at 21–2; Lennard, *Rural England*, 325.

[53] Gerald of Wales, *Opera*, 1:251–2, 270, 334–5.

[54] Easting, ed., *Revelation of the Monk of Eynsham*, 138–40.

[55] See Chapter 2, section 2; Gerald of Wales, *Opera*, 2:126–38, 281–93; Thomas of Chobham, *Summa Confessorum*, 12, 322–3.

[56] Marie-Hélène Rousseau, *Saving the Souls of Medieval London: Perpetual Chantries at St. Paul's Cathedral, c.1200–1548* (Farnham, 2011), 12, 173–5.

[57] Clay, ed., *York Minster Fasti*, 2:139–43; Foster and Major, eds., *Registrum Antiquissimum*, 10:274–5; Dorothy M. Owen, "Historical Survey, 1091–1450," *A History of Lincoln Minster* (Cambridge, 1994), 112–63, at 150.

reinforced the Christian identity of individuals and communities. Even badly performed rites mattered. Most parishioners would have been unaware of garbled Latin by poorly trained priests. Though they might have noticed glaring errors through long observation or been scandalized by a visibly intoxicated priest performing the Eucharist, the rituals themselves would still have held significance. Preaching may often have failed to conform to the ideals of reformers or perhaps to later standards, but it is likely that most of the parish clergy felt some obligation to provide moral and religious teachings, and cumulatively this would have influenced beliefs and social mores. The impact of so many clerics throughout society carrying out even the basics of Christian worship, even if many of them were lukewarm or not very effective, would still have had the effect of maintaining and strengthening the powerful hold Christianity had on this society.[58]

In his recent work, *Medieval Religious Rationalities*, David d'Avray has stressed how medieval Christianity, through various institutions, practices, and beliefs, created an interlocking set of beliefs that powerfully reinforced each other. As he notes, however, such beliefs had to be constantly reproduced.[59] D'Avray describes various channels of reproduction, including godparents, but obviously the activities of the secular clergy were crucial. England, of course, had long been thoroughly Christian, but it is easy to underestimate how much effort is required to maintain the strength of even a well-established religion. A religious faith is not like a physical object that once set in motion remains in motion due to inertia. Any religion has to be constantly renewed through teaching, practice, and the development of a habitus to remain strong. John Arnold, after describing Christianity as a dominant culture, emphasized that, "Dominant cultures are not passive, inert things. They produce and reproduce themselves, to ensure continued communication and [...] maintain hegemony."[60] In twelfth-century England as throughout the Middle Ages, this depended heavily on the secular clergy. They may have failed to live up to the hopes of idealists in performing this task, and one cannot point to any pastoral revolution in the period, but that should not obscure their importance in sustaining and intensifying the already thorough Christianization of English society through their daily fulfillment of their religious duties.

3. THE PIOUS ACTIVITIES OF SECULAR CLERICS

Given how hard it is to find evidence about clerics performing their routine duties, it is surprising how much one can find about their acts of personal piety.[61] It is worth emphasizing the widespread evidence for such acts because it can offset the excessive focus of twelfth-century moralists on the religious failings of the clergy.

[58] For a similar point, see Loyn, *English Church*, 118.
[59] D. L. d'Avray, *Medieval Religious Rationalities: A Weberian Analysis* (Cambridge, 2010), 31–62, 94–106.
[60] John Arnold, *Belief and Unbelief in Medieval Europe* (London, 2005), 28.
[61] For a later period, see Lepine, *A Brotherhood of Canons*, 139–55.

I have just noted the role of secular clerics as early patrons of chantries. More important, secular clerics were often generous to traditional religious institutions. In previous chapters I have noted gifts of books, ornaments, vestments, and even buildings to cathedrals and monasteries. Clerics also gave land, whether inherited or purchased, and such gifts can be found scattered throughout cartularies and other sources. Most such donations were small, but occasionally they were more substantial, as when Isaac of Skeftlynge, gave twelve bovates to Meaux Abbey.[62] Clerics were collectively far less important than laypeople as donors of land to religious houses, but there were far fewer of them and their wealth tended to come in other forms. In earlier periods, when churches were more like private property, clerics can be found giving churches, particularly in urban settings.[63] Records of gifts of money rarely survive, because there was no need to keep permanent records as with land, but it is likely that clerics, who could have rich incomes even when they had little private property, often made gifts in this form. For instance, The chronicler Orderic Vitalis recorded that his father Ordelarius, a wealthy priest, initially gave the new monastery of Shrewsbury £15, and later gave it £200.[64]

Gifts by clerics can sometimes provide indirect glimpses into the piety of the clergy. Thus, the founding of chantries clearly represented a strong belief in the efficacy of prayers and masses for the dead. Clerical endowments for annual distributions of food or money to other clerics and to the poor, in return for intercession for their souls, provide further evidence of this belief.[65] Gifts might suggest a personal preference or fondness for certain festivals or ceremonies. For instance, Dean William of Lichfield gave rent from land he had bought to finance the purchase of candles for processions at the feast of the Invention of the Holy Cross.[66] The generosity of a number of cathedral clerics to their own cathedrals suggests that although many canons may have been absentee time-servers, some had a strong devotion to the church in which they served. This is particularly apparent at St. Paul's, where Ralph of Diceto was at the center of a circle of dedicated cathedral clergy, including Henry of Northampton, Robert of Clifford, Richard of Stortford, Hugh of Reculver, Osbert de Camera, and Master Alard (the future dean), all of whom were present at the promulgation of the statute on residency of 1192, and some of whom oversaw a survey of the cathedral's property in 1181. This group carried out what seems to have been a concerted effort to support the cathedral by gifts of houses, property, vestments, books, and ornaments.[67] However, secular clerics could also be generous to houses of the regular

---

[62] He later tried to give four of them to his mistress: Thomas de Burton, *Chronica Monasterii de Melsa*, 1:161–2.

[63] For instance, Smith, ed., *English Episcopal Acta 4*, 132; Harper-Bill, ed., *English Episcopal Acta 6*, 95–6.

[64] Orderic Vitalis, *Ecclesiastical History*, 3:146–9.

[65] West Sussex Record Office, Chichester Cathedral MS Liber Y, fos. 142r, 148r, 180r; Gibbs, ed., *Early Charters*, 78–9, 94; Barrow, ed., *English Episcopal Acta 7*, 141–2; Johnson, ed., *English Episcopal Acta 26*, 31–2.

[66] Franklin, ed., *English Episcopal Acta 16*, 56–7.

[67] Ker, "Books at St Paul's Cathedral before 1313," 215–30; Simpson, "Two Inventories," 464–500; Gibbs, ed., *Early Charters*, 56–7, 76–9, 93–4, 96–8, 204–5, 246–7; Johnson, ed., *English*

clergy, showing that despite the rivalry between the groups, many secular clerics placed a high value on the religious contributions of monks, nuns, and clerics.

In giving gifts to religious houses, clerics were giving to the patron saints of those institutions, and clerics were active participants in the cult of saints in other ways as well. Thus priests and other clerics appear frequently among supplicants to saints and as participants in miracle stories, as shown by a number of such stories noted throughout this work. Clerics might also show interest in relics. For instance, Godfrey de Lucy, while dean of St. Martin-le-Grand, obtained from Durham a piece of the cloth in which St. Cuthbert had long been wrapped.[68] In addition, clerics might show special devotion to the feast of a particular saint. Among the many services that Roger the Chaplain, canon of London, specified in return for a gift of two valuable houses to St. Paul's was a special distribution of money on the feast day of St. Radegund.[69] As supplicants and devotees of cults, secular clerics often differed little from laypeople, but their skills and positions could sometimes give clerics an important role in promoting cults. This is most obvious in the production of hagiographical works. In some cases, it might be noted, such works were connected with corporate attempts by the clerics of cathedrals and other collegiate churches to sanctify a bishop or raise awareness of an existing saint. Secular clerics can be found promoting cults in other ways as well, for instance by holding feasts for a saint or by encouraging parishioners to seek help from a particular cult. This is particularly apparent in Reginald of Durham's account of the miracles of St. Cuthbert. Cuthbert was the greatest saint of northern England, and his cult was controlled and promoted by the Benedictine monks of Durham. However, priests can be found encouraging and supporting Cuthbert's cult locally in villages ranging from Nottinghamshire to Cumberland and to Teviotdale in Scotland.[70]

Clerics can also be found extending charity to the poor and sick, often in ad hoc and informal ways. For instance, one paralyzed man in Salisbury received alms from none other than Thomas of Chobham, and the canon Philip of St. Edward had a rough shelter built for the same unfortunate.[71] Miracle stories in Gerald of Wales' *vita* of Hugh of Avalon show the dean and precentor of Lincoln respectively supporting a blind boy and a paralyzed one.[72] Sometimes charity to the poor could be connected with ritual veneration of saints. A Marian miracle records that a priest in Thomas Becket's time not only chanted the psalter before an image of Mary on each of her feast days but also fed 100 poor people.[73] Clerics may also have

---

Episcopal Acta 26, lxxxi–lxxxiii; Hale, ed., *Domesday of St. Paul's*, 109; Ralph of Diceto, *Opera Historica*, 2:lxxii. For corporate loyalty in a later period, see Lepine, *A Brotherhood of Canons*, 180–90.

[68] Snape, ed., *English Episcopal Acta 24*, 82–3.

[69] Gibbs, ed., *Early Charters*, 189–90. The chantry he founded was attached to Radegund's altar: Rousseau, *Saving the Souls*, 173.

[70] Reginald of Durham, *Libellus de Cuthberti Virtutibus*, 32–7, 127–34, 138–48, 242–5, 284–90.

[71] A. R. Malden, *The Canonization of Saint Osmund* (Salisbury, 1901), 37–9; Bartlett, *England under the Norman and Angevin Kings*, 590–1.

[72] Gerald of Wales, *Opera*, 7:127, 143–5.

[73] Sidney Sussex College, Cambridge, MS 95, fos. 40r–v. This was a much later collection but one that copied miracles from earlier sources. For another example, see Reginald of Durham, *Libellus de Cuthberti Virtutibus*, 127.

served as informal intermediaries in helping others get aid. For instance, a miracle story of the hermit Godric of Finchale tells how the mother of a leprous girl went to the parish priest for help, and he found a place for the girl in a hospital.[74] Some secular clerics participated in the founding and growth of hospitals, which first began to appear in England after the Norman Conquest.[75] A few wealthy clerics were even able to found hospitals themselves: Henry of Northampton founded one with the aid of Ralph of Diceto and placed it under the auspices of St. Paul's.[76] Other powerful clerics used their influence to help support existing hospitals, as when John of Brancaster, archdeacon of Worcester and a prominent royal cleric, obtained from King John a license for a fair, the proceeds of which would go to support a hospital in Fakenham, Norfolk.[77]

In an article published in 2007 I argued that lay piety was already very strong in the long twelfth century, even though the evidence for it is more scattered than for later periods and though some specific practices had not yet developed.[78] Clerics in the long twelfth century as in later periods no doubt supported the development of lay piety by exhortation. As moralists emphasized, however, priests were supposed to preach by example as well as by word, and when it came to acts of piety, many clerics clearly did serve as models to the laity. The laity were not, of course, merely passive recipients of clerical indoctrination. In particular, the willingness of priests to cater to suggestions from laypeople in their practice of the liturgy indicates that lay piety developed through a discourse between the laity and clergy.[79] Nonetheless, the secular clergy were in a powerful position to shape lay piety, and in part they did so by their actions.

4. SKEPTICISM AND INTOLERANCE

Though personal acts of piety suggest that many secular clerics held a deep commitment to their faith, the religiosity of clerics obviously varied widely, and it is worth noting some striking evidence for clerical doubts and skepticism, generally about specific but often crucial aspects of Christian belief.[80] The courtier of Peter of Blois's poem, who treated hell as a fantasy on a par with King Arthur's return, may have been a figment of Peter's imagination, but could just as easily have represented a noteworthy strand of skepticism among worldly clerics.[81] Gerald of

---

[74] Reginald of Durham, *Vita Sancti Godrici*, 456.

[75] For the history of medieval hospitals, see Nicholas Orme and Margaret Webster, *The English Hospital, 1070–1570* (New Haven, 1995).

[76] Gibbs, ed., *Early Charters*, 246–7. For another example, see Barrow, "Canons and Citizens of Hereford," 13–14.

[77] Hardy, ed., *Rotuli de Oblatis*, 96.   [78] Thomas, "Lay Piety," 179–82.

[79] See Chapter 2, section 2 and Chapter 13, section 1.

[80] For recent discussions of skepticism and doubt in the period, see Susan Reynolds, "Social Mentalities and the Cases of Medieval Scepticism," *Transactions of the Royal Historical Society* 6th ser., 1 (1991), 21–41; Sabina Flanagan, *Doubt in an Age of Faith: Uncertainty in the Long Twelfth Century* (Turnhout, 2008), 67–89; Arnold, *Belief and Unbelief*, 216–30.

[81] See beginning of Chapter 6.

Wales told the story of a priest who, when criticized for the sloppiness of his liturgical performance, expressed doubts about transubstantiation, the incarnation, and the resurrection, saying that priests told fables invented by the ancients to restrain behavior through fear. How many similar to that priest, Gerald went on to ask, "are hidden among us today?" Gerald also told of another cleric, an English master named Richard Albericanus whom he had known in Paris, who had lectured on Peter Lombard's *Sentences*, fasted, performed vigils, abstained from sex, given alms, and prayed often. Though Richard had seemed a mirror of religion and morals, at the end of his life he could not bring himself to receive the Eucharist because, as Gerald put it, he had never managed to have faith in it. The Eucharist was a particular source of doubt for many educated figures, and Gerald himself was happy to have his faith strengthened by a eucharistic miracle, though he said he had always believed firmly.[82] Individual stories of unbelief must be treated as skeptically as those about belief, piety, and sanctity, since they were generally designed with a moral in mind. Nevertheless, the fact that the point was often to attack or to allay doubt suggests that skepticism among clerics did exist.

As always with inner beliefs, a large area of uncertainty must remain, particularly when dealing with a society so different from our own. Because it was the job of priests and other clerics to act in religiously prescribed ways, the question of inner motivation is particularly acute with them. In the highly competitive ecclesiastical patronage networks of the day, cultivating an appearance of piety was a good career move. Socially ambitious clerics, denied some aspects of prestige available to secular aristocrats, might have been particularly eager for the social capital that could be acquired through performance and patronage of religious activities. Of course, the scenario of large numbers of unbelieving clerics supporting reform initiatives or performing pious actions for purely cynical motives seems unlikely. Probably more common, in a period when many had economic motives for joining the secular clergy, was a tepid, fluctuating spirituality, which created, as we have seen, its own struggles and stresses. Nonetheless, some clerics at least seem to have had profound doubts about basic tenets of Christianity.

However, the evidence suggests that other secular clerics were strongly devoted to the religious ideals and practices of the day. From a modern perspective, including that of most modern Christians, this devoutness did not always have positive results. In recent decades scholars have increasingly depicted the long twelfth century as a period of growing intolerance for a number of groups, including lepers and people who did not follow sexual norms, but particularly for heretics and non-Christians. Moore has tied the rise of intolerance firmly to governments and to the clerical, literate elites who staffed them.[83] It must be noted that clerical attitudes were neither simple nor uniform. Not surprisingly, the outlook of someone like Herbert of Bosham who worked with Jewish scholars

---

[82] Gerald of Wales, *Opera*, 2:33, 40–1, 285. For eucharistic doubts by Herbert of Bosham, see Flanagan, *Doubt in an Age of Faith*, 6, 81–5.

[83] Moore, *First European Revolution*, 146–59; Moore, *Formation of a Persecuting Society*, 94–147, 165–70.

could be quite complex, as Goodwin has shown, containing some positive attitudes as well as strong elements of hostility towards Judaism.[84] Alfred of Shareshill could describe his Jewish master, Solomon Avenraza, as "a celebrated Israelite, and the chief of modern philosophers," and Burnett has even suggested that a passage by Adelard of Bath in praise of a fictional land of philosophers near the equator contained a message of religious toleration.[85] Nonetheless, there is no doubt that secular clerics could be deeply intolerant and that collectively they played an important role in the rising religious intolerance that characterized the period.

Both the extent and the impact of clerical intolerance can most clearly be seen in the case of the Jews. The development of the cult of William of Norwich was a key moment in the rise of the blood libel against Jews and therefore of European anti-Semitism. Though the monk Thomas of Monmouth probably played the largest role in this bizarre episode, priestly members of William's family were also important. Indeed, John McCulloch has argued that William's uncle, a priest, was crucial in initially setting out the accusation against the Jews.[86] Less important incidents reveal the pervasiveness of anti-Semitism. The sacral status of the clergy was sometimes highlighted by the perceived provocation of non-Christians, and Walter Map told approvingly a story of how King Louis VII had burned the richest Jew in France for dragging a cleric from a procession and throwing him in a cesspool because the cleric had hurt his son.[87] No such dramatic event (assuming it was true) occurred in England, but some admittedly brief and therefore difficult to interpret passages in the pipe rolls may indicate Jews being punished for confrontations with clerics. Late in Henry II's reign, Beleasez of Oxford was amerced £100 for speech with a cleric of the Earl Ferrers, and not long thereafter Jacob of Lincoln paid forty marks partly for the cope of a cleric "abstrata."[88] Heresy was relatively unimportant in England in this period, but English clerics were certainly aware of and strongly disapproved of continental movements. For instance, Thomas Agnellus, in passages extolling the unity of the church, spoke of those involved in heresy and contention being ejected from the womb of the church "like abortions."[89] Peter of Blois zealously expressed his intolerance against various groups. His hostile views of heretics appear in sermons and the preface to his *Tractatus de Fide*. Among his many writings were a treatise against the Jews and works supporting the crusades, including a *vita* of the

---

[84] Goodwin, *Take Hold of the Robe of a Jew*, 175, 178–9, 196–201, 215–26, 230–1, 233.

[85] Otte, "Alfredus Anglicus," 281; Alfred of Shareshill, *Commentary on the* Metheora, 51; Burnett, *Introduction of Arabic Learning*, 44–5.

[86] Thomas of Monmouth, *William of Norwich*, 38–45; Gavin I. Langmuir, "Thomas of Monmouth: Detector of Ritual Murder," *Speculum* 59 (1984), 820–46; John W. McCulloch, "Jewish Ritual Murder: William of Norwich, Thomas of Monmouth, and the Early Dissemination of the Myth," *Speculum* 72 (1997), 698–740; Jeffrey J. Cohen, "The Flow of Blood in Medieval Norwich," *Speculum* 79 (2004), 26–65. Langmuir argued that Thomas of Monmouth was the main instigator.

[87] Walter Map, *De Nugis Curialium*, 452–5.

[88] *Pipe Roll 27 Henry II*, 113; *Pipe Roll 30 Henry II*, 71; *Pipe Roll 32 Henry II*, 78.

[89] Bodleian Library, Laud. Misc. MS 71, fos. 36r–v, 41v–44r For other strong reactions to heresy, see Ralph Niger, *De Re Militari*, 187–93; Walter Map, *De Nugis Curialium*, 118–29.

infamous Reginald of Antioch.[90] Clearly the secular clergy were doing their part to foster religious intolerance in the long twelfth century.

Moore's arguments about clerics and intolerance focus on politics and power. For him, the rise of governments was crucial, and he describes Henry II as a pioneer in using oppression against heretics. *Clerici*, as key props and beneficiaries of government, would naturally have been involved. In particular, Moore notes the participation of two of Henry's clerical advisors, Reginald de Bohun and John of Canterbury, in a papal mission to Toulouse in 1178 after Count Raymond called for help against the heretics, and suggests that this might illustrate the manner in which oppressive tactics could be conveyed from one government to another. Moore also argued that rivalry between the *clerici* and highly literate Jews for posts in government might have prompted them to promote intolerance, though more recently he has suggested instead that envy of Jewish prosperity, fueled by clerical insecurity and anxiety, may have been the most important factor. As for heresy, he suggests that clerical pride in literacy and opposition to the *rustici*, whom they associated with heresy, similarly prompted intolerance.[91] Assessing Moore's arguments about clerics and intolerance is not easy, especially based on English evidence, since England was not one of the centers of the efforts to suppress heresy, for all of Henry II's precocity. Moreover, motives such as status envy are by their nature hard to uncover. Certainly the manifold anxieties and pressures affecting the clergy that I have discussed throughout the book might have prompted them to lash out at convenient scapegoats. Nonetheless, I suspect that the core motives for clerical intolerance were straightforwardly religious. Intolerance both for internal dissidents and for other religions had a long history within Christianity, and the success of the First Crusade and the subsequent devotion by Catholic Europe of massive resources to religious warfare only strengthened the existing strands of intolerance within the Western Church. As a church that had chosen to embrace intolerance became more institutionally effective, it is hardly surprising that intolerance grew. As more and more clerics, both secular and regular, wrote more and more material, it was inevitable that expressions of intolerance would grow. English clerics in the long twelfth century may not uniformly have been intolerant zealots, but they were supposed to be, according to mainstream Christian thinking at the time, and rising intolerance may partly have been a product of reformers demanding greater zeal from the clergy. Obviously many factors were involved in intolerance: for instance, Peter of Blois's complaints about being "crucified" by Jewish money lenders indicate that piety was not the only motive for his attacks on Jewish religion.[92] Nonetheless, the clerical piety discussed in this chapter was probably the most important reason for the support secular clerics gave to rising religious intolerance.

---

[90] Peter of Blois, *Opera*, 738, 740, 825–70; Peter of Blois, *Later Letters*, 326; Peter of Blois, *Tractatus duo*.

[91] Moore, *First European Revolution*, 146–59; Moore, *Formation of a Persecuting Society*, 94–147, 165–70.

[92] Peter of Blois, *Opera*, 450.

Whether for good or for ill, there is plentiful evidence of the secular clergy acting in ways that indicated pious zeal, which can be put alongside the evidence for indifference, incompetence, and irreligion among them. It is, perhaps, inevitable to measure the clergy of the period against reformist standards and therefore to underestimate their general level of religious commitment. Whatever their level of commitment, however, the secular clergy, through providing the bulk of pastoral care and through performing the acts of worship that would have been most visible to the majority of the laity, were crucial to maintaining the religious dominance of Christianity in this society. Because England already had a deeply Christianized culture in 1066, Christianity's continuing power to shape society can seem static, timeless, and effortless, but in fact the Christian religion retained such a strong grip only because of a continuous effort to maintain and increase its influence. Popes, bishops, the regular clergy, and the laity all played important roles in this process, and many of the most zealous were hermits, recluses, monks, regular canons, and nuns. Indeed, to a large degree the new orders, such as the Cistercians, the Augustinians, and, in the early thirteenth century, the friars, provided the standard bearers for reform and religious enthusiasm in the Christian West. Nonetheless, many clerics were deeply pious. More important still, because of their role out in the world ministering to the laity, the secular clergy were arguably more important than any other group in maintaining and deepening the influence of Christianity on society as a whole.

15

The War against the Monks

Bernard of Clairvaux was one of the most revered religious figures of the twelfth century, and like so many who became saints in the Middle Ages was a member of the regular clergy. Not all secular clerics, however, held him in high esteem, as illustrated by two of Walter Map's stories. In one, John Planeta, a cleric of Thomas Becket, provoked by two Cistercian abbots who celebrated Bernard's attack on Peter Abelard while they were guests at the archbishop's table, recounted a failed attempt by Bernard to exorcise a demon from a madman. When Bernard ordered the man to be released, in this story, the man began throwing rocks at him and chasing him through the streets. According to Walter's account, a displeased Becket asked John what kind of miracle this was, whereupon John replied that the madman had always been gentle to everyone but hypocrites and that the miracle represented a judgment on Bernard's presumptuousness. In the other story, two Cistercian abbots who were guests of Gilbert Foliot recounted various miracles of Bernard, but also noted a case in which he tried unsuccessfully to resurrect a dead boy, lying down on the corpse and praying. At this point, Walter himself intervened, saying, "What an extremely unlucky monk. For I never heard of any monk lying down on a boy without the boy getting up right after him." According to Walter, the abbot who had told the story turned red, and others left the room in order to laugh.[1]

These satirical attacks on Bernard and supposed monastic sexual practices took place in the context of a strong rivalry between the regular and secular clergy that sometimes erupted into virulent animosity. Walter's invective against various monastic orders, particularly the Cistercians, and similar attacks by Gerald of Wales are well known, and David Knowles discussed their criticisms at length.[2] However, the broader rivalry between secular clerics and monks has received only cursory attention, particularly compared to other disputes such as the later competition between the secular clergy and the friars.[3] There were many aspects to this rivalry, including disputes over resources, conflicts over authority, and struggles over claims to moral superiority. To speak of war between the two orders is

---

[1] Walter Map, *De Nugis Curialium*, 78–81.

[2] Knowles, *Monastic Order in England*, 662–78. See also Brian Golding, "Gerald of Wales and the Monks," *Thirteenth-Century England* 5 (1995), 53–64.

[3] For brief references to the rivalry, see Bartlett, *England under the Norman and Angevin Kings*, 477; Partner, *Serious Entertainments*, 88–90, 162–4; Rigg, *History of Anglo-Latin Literature*, 69–70; Harper-Bill, "The Anglo-Norman Church," 180; Stollberg, *Soziale Stellung*, 152–4; van Houts, "Fate of Priests' Sons."

admittedly hyperbolic, but the animosity between the two groups was sometimes remarkably vitriolic. Various writers criticized the rivalry, and of course there was much interaction and cooperation between the two groups, who were theoretically united in service to the Church and its ideals, but the level of hostility between the two groups remained high. The long twelfth century was noted for many rivalries between religious groups, such as the Cistercians and the Cluniacs or monks and regular canons, and in some ways this rivalry was simply one more. It was, however, a particularly important one because of the size and influence of both groups, even though regular canons, who held an ambiguous position between monks and secular clerics, came into the conflict rarely, and nuns do not appear at all. Ultimately monks and secular clerics undermined each other with their attacks, but on the whole, the monks had the upper hand in this dispute.

1. THE RIVALRY AND ITS CAUSES

Though the invective of Walter Map and Gerald of Wales has received most attention, it was so broad and exaggerated that it serves to obscure the main issues in the rivalry between the regular and secular clergy as much as to reveal them, and their animus was also unusual in being focused so heavily on a single monastic order, the Cistercians. Walter, criticizing the alleged rapacity of the Cistercians (particularly in depopulating land to set up granges), compared them to a royal army ravaging the lands of rebels or to the Israelites plundering the Egyptians. He accused them of trickery, forgery, and even the murder of a knight and his household in their efforts to increase their holdings.[4] Gerald later claimed that when Walter heard that two Cistercians had converted to Judaism, he remarked that it was strange that although they had rightly left behind a perverse monastic order they had not gone further and actually become Christians, a witty insult, but also a powerful one given the religious bigotry of the day.[5] Gerald himself attacked Cistercians and other monks even more broadly than Walter, adding more stories of greed, trickery, and depopulation, and also including tales of armed raids by monks against other houses, of the poaching of corpses to obtain gifts associated with burial, and of untrained monks fraudulently practicing medicine, in the process killing the heir of the earl of Winchester. In addition, Gerald included many anecdotes of sexual misbehavior and drunkenness, and of monks breaking their own particular rules, for example by eating meat.[6] In the context of an attack on an individual monk, Gerald claimed that he regularly included among his litanies, "From the malice of monks, Lord, deliver us."[7]

Walter's and Gerald's attacks on monks are so over the top that they are hard to take seriously, and certainly many of their individual stories must be treated with extreme skepticism if not dismissed outright. As Knowles and Brian Golding have pointed out, some of their animus was rooted in their own specific disputes with

---

[4] Walter Map, *De Nugis Curialium*, 84–113.
[5] Gerald of Wales, *Opera*, 4:140.
[6] Gerald of Wales, *Opera*, 4:26–244.
[7] Gerald of Wales, *Opera*, 1:213.

monks. Indeed, Gerald says as much about Walter.[8] Nevertheless, for all of the personal elements in their attacks, and despite their colorful and vindictive exaggerations, Walter and Gerald directly or indirectly addressed many of the issues dividing the regular and secular clergy, as shall become apparent. Moreover, their works are far from being the only evidence of rivalry and hostility between the two groups. For instance, early in the twelfth century, an abbot wrote to Herbert Losinga complaining of vituperative criticism of monks by secular canons and urging Herbert to take Archbishop Anselm's place as defender of the monastic order by writing a treatise defending monasticism.[9] Late in the period, Lucian of Chester lamented the tendency of clerics and monks to attack one another, with clerics criticizing monks for gluttony, sloth, and deceitfulness, and monks attacking clerics for lasciviousness, doing nothing but playing, and being the "darlings" of women. Drawing on two passages from Horace, he imagined the cleric saying of the monk, "He alone consumes what would satisfy three bears, on which account you can ridicule him as a pig from the herd of Epicurus," at the same time drawing on Claudian to envision monks describing the clergy as useless eunuchs.[10] Towards the middle of the century John of Salisbury provided some of the same criticisms of the regular clergy as Walter and Gerald later did, and though he himself wrote in a moderate tone, he stated that anyone who criticized the monastic orders was called an enemy of religion, showing how high tempers could run.[11] Indeed, the regular clergy were no slouches when it came to vitriol. The anonymous monk who clashed with Theobald of Étampes compared bad clerics (whom he saw as the rule) to locusts; described them as having "beaked beards, curled hair, effeminate clothes, and distorted feet like hooves;" likened priests to water in an outhouse which in cleaning away filth also merged with it; and urged that they should be rewarded with a place in hell like "wanton Ganymede."[12]

So strong was the rivalry between the regular and secular clergy that it often emerged in disputes that had independent causes. For instance, tension between clerics and monks appears in Hugh the Chanter's discussion of the dispute between Canterbury and York, even though the clash was basically about Canterbury's claims to primacy and had nothing to do with divisions between religious orders, except for the fact that York was staffed by canons and Canterbury by monks.[13] Similarly, late in the century, when Abbot Samson of Bury ordered his cleric, Master Ranulf, to supervise the monks' incompetent cellarer, many monks reacted vigorously, saying, among other things, "the abbot scorns his monks and holds them suspect, he consults and loves clerics [. . .]. We are made a reproach to our

---

[8] Knowles, *Monastic Order in England*, 665–7, 675; Golding, "Gerald of Wales and the Monks," 61–4; Gerald of Wales, *Opera*, 4:140, 219.

[9] Robert Anstruther, ed., *Epistolae Herberti de Losinga, Primi Episcopi Norwicensis, Osberti de Clara et Elmeri, Prioris Cantuariensis*, Publications of the Caxton society, 5 (London, 1846), 102–5.

[10] Bodleian Library, Bodleian MS 672, fos. 125v–126r. The passages from Horace are from his *Epistles*, 1.4.16 and 1.15.35. For Claudian, Lucian quotes *In Eutropium*.

[11] John of Salisbury, *Policraticus*, 2:190–201.

[12] Foreville and Leclercq, "Un débat sur le sacerdoce," 57, 103, 108.

[13] Hugh the Chanter, *History of the Church of York*, 72–3, 116–17.

neighbors. All we monks are considered faithless or improvident; he believes the cleric, not the monk."[14] Moreover, when an election dispute broke out after Samson's death, and Archbishop Stephen Langton proposed to send two clerics to investigate, the convent objected to scrutiny of monks by "clerics, who are always assiduous in plots against them."[15] The rivalry was strong enough even to create periodic debates over whether the archbishop of Canterbury should be a monk or a secular cleric.[16] These debates stemmed partly from Canterbury's status as the premier monastic cathedral in England and from the desire of the cathedral monks to be ruled by a fellow monk, but they also derived from the power and symbolism of the archbishop as head of the English Church. Reactions were often fierce. When the regular canon William of Corbeil became archbishop in 1123, apparently as a compromise between the monastic party and many of the bishops, who wanted a secular cleric, Orderic Vitalis lamented that in the past the English, including clerics, had honored monks, but that now, "customs and laws are changed and clerics raise clerics to humble and crush the monks."[17] When Abbot Lawrence of Westminster objected to Thomas Becket's candidature on the grounds that he was not a monk, Bishop Hilary of Chichester asked if he thought there were no good men but monks.[18]

There were various reasons for this hostility between groups that should have been united by their religious commitments. As Stephen Ferruolo in particular has shown, tensions arose between monks and the masters of the emerging schools.[19] The tendency of monastic intellectuals to be conservative and of schoolmen to be innovative could lead to clashes such as that between Bernard of Clairvaux and Peter Abelard, though intellectual disputes did not generally break down neatly along monastic versus secular lines. To some degree, the rise of the schools undermined the religious pre-eminence of monasteries, particularly in the intellectual sphere. Monasteries competed with the schools for some of the most promising religious scholars and there was debate about whether the monasteries or the schools provided the better environment for scholarship and were more useful generally in religious terms. Because of the dominance of French schools, particularly Paris, much of this debate took place in France, but English figures like Robert Pullen, Alexander Neckam, and Stephen Langton were all involved.[20]

More important was competition for resources. Most obvious in this respect was the shift of control of cathedrals and collegiate churches from the secular to the regular clergy. Some of the most important cathedrals, such as Canterbury and Winchester, had become monastic in the tenth century, but others, such as Durham and Norwich, had made the transition only after the Norman Conquest.

---

[14] Jocelin of Brakelond, *Chronicle*, 79–80, 89–91.
[15] Rodney M. Thomson, ed., *Chronicle of the Election of Hugh, Abbot of Bury St. Edmunds and Later Bishop of Ely* (Oxford, 1974), 18–19.
[16] Eadmer, *Historia Novorum*, 222.
[17] Cecily Clark, ed., *The Peterborough Chronicle, 1070–1154* (Oxford, 1958), 43; Orderic Vitalis, *Ecclesiastical History*, 6:318–21; William of Malmesbury, *Gesta Pontificum*, 1:232–3.
[18] Barlow, *Thomas Becket*, 65.   [19] Ferruolo, *Origins of the University*, 47–92.
[20] Ferruolo, *Origins of the University*, 208–12; Smalley, *Becket Conflict*, 44.

Given the rarity of monastic cathedrals elsewhere in Christendom, it must have been frustrating to many clerics to see so many wealthy cathedral churches in the hands of monks, and the continuing transformation of collegiate churches into houses of monks or regular canons must also have been maddening. That such transformations generally occurred because of the perceived superiority of the regular clergy only added insult to injury, even in the case of transfers that had taken place long before. For instance, any secular cleric upset about such monastic appropriations would hardly have been calmed by reading comments like those of the monastic chronicler William of Malmesbury on secular clerics making way for "better" men in the tenth-century takeover of cathedrals, especially when compared to William's description of his own abbey of Malmesbury being turned into a "stable" of secular clerics during an early interruption of monastic life there.[21] It must have been even harder for secular clerics to encounter similar sentiments in contemporary papal documents such as one proclaiming that Durham Cathedral had been turned over to monks because of the incorrigible and depraved life of the clergy there.[22]

With the conversion of Waltham into an Augustinian house, one can in fact see the reactions of two secular clerics to claims that regular clergy were replacing corrupt secular clerics. Henry II, who championed this conversion partly to fulfill a vow to found two religious houses in atonement for Becket's death, stated in his charter that he was motivated by the irreligious and worldly life of the secular canons there; and Alexander III referred to reforming Waltham into a better state.[23] Not surprisingly, the fiercely monastic chronicler Gervase of Canterbury echoed their sentiments.[24] In contrast, Ralph of Diceto did accept that there were scandals associated with the dean and the canons of Waltham, but lamented that the innocence of many was tainted by the crimes of a few; clearly he felt unhappy and defensive about how the episode would affect the reputation of the secular clergy as a whole.[25] Gerald of Wales reacted more aggressively, saying that the canons had long served in a particularly holy manner and claiming that the king was simply attempting to fulfill his vow cheaply.[26] In fact, at least one of the displaced canons had children, and it is hardly a stretch to believe the accusation that the canons of Waltham were worldly individuals, given the findings of this book.[27] If anything, however, the widespread worldliness of secular canons would only have made them more sensitive about such accusations and more concerned about their potential use in depriving them of yet more resources. Moreover, there may well have been an element of propaganda in some instances, as William Aird has suggested in the case of monastic accounts of the early clerics at Durham.[28]

[21] William of Malmesbury, *Gesta Pontificum*, 1:34–5, 602–3.
[22] Holtzmann, ed., *Papsturkunden*, 2:132–6, 138–40, 220–1.
[23] Ransford, ed., *Early Charters of Waltham Abbey*, 14–15; Dugdale, *Monasticon Anglicanum*, 6:63–4; Holtzmann, ed., *Papsturkunden*, 1:445–6.
[24] Gervase of Canterbury, *Historical Works*, 1:260.
[25] Ralph of Diceto, *Opera Historica*, 1:420.   [26] Gerald of Wales, *Opera*, 8:170.
[27] *Pipe Roll 24 Henry II*, 33; Ransford, ed., *Early Charters of Waltham Abbey*, 177–8.
[28] Aird, *St Cuthbert and the Normans*, 104–8.

The diversion of parish resources to monastic houses through appropriation, pensions, and the holding and withholding of tithes was also a major source of contention. According to Gerald of Wales, it was Newnham Abbey's large holdings in Walter Map's parish of Westbury that excited Walter's hostility to the Cistercians.[29] Walter himself emphasized that secular clerics drew their livelihoods from service at the altar since they did not inherit patrimonies and could not licitly engage in business. He stated that God had granted this livelihood to the clergy, but went on to lament that the regulars held almost all the altars (i.e. churches) and that the clergy had to pay part of their income to hold from them.[30] As Giles Constable has shown, debate over monastic possession of tithes that would otherwise have gone to local churches was widespread.[31] One particularly illuminating document in this controversy was the debate between Theobald of Étampes and the anonymous monk. Theobald's argument was simple. Drawing from a distant past when most monks had been laymen, he wrote that because monks were not clerics and did not exercise pastoral care, they should not receive income from tithes. He admitted that the regular clergy sometimes performed pastoral care, but viewed this as an exceptional measure, when clerics were lacking, and argued that making monks clerics was a problematic way to allow them to gain financial resources meant for the clergy.[32] The anonymous monk, as already noted, made a bitter response.[33] His attacks on priests were not simply abuse, however, for his intent was to argue that monks were *more* worthy than priests to receive tithes. He therefore drew sharp contrasts, stating, for instance, that monks stayed awake praying for their benefactors while priests stayed awake having sex with their wives, and that the prayers of monks flowed forth while the homes of priests resounded with the crying of babies.[34]

Despite Theobald's sweeping attack on monastic receipt of tithes, diversion of parish incomes to monasteries was so well established that secular clerics were fighting a rearguard action to limit the damage. Walter Map's argument about clerics living by the altar came in the context of a debate over the privileges of *one* crusading order, the Hospitallers, not of monastic possession of advowsons more generally. Similarly, John of Salisbury argued against the ability of another crusading order, the Templars, to hold advowsons, and otherwise limited himself to criticizing monastic houses for acquiring churches without consulting bishops. A particularly hot issue, despite its limited scope, was the refusal by the Cistercians and some other orders to pay tithes on lands they held. John of Salisbury, William de Montibus, and Peter of Blois (in a letter written for the archbishop of Canterbury) all criticized this practice, and Walter Map, Gerald of Wales, and John of Salisbury emphasized depopulation by Cistercians for granges partly because of the resulting impact on tithes and the churches they

---

[29] Gerald of Wales, *Opera*, 4:219.   [30] Walter Map, *De Nugis Curialium*, 70–1.
[31] Constable, *Monastic Tithes*, 136–85.
[32] Foreville and Leclercq, "Un débat sur le sacerdoce," 53–4.
[33] Foreville and Leclercq, "Un débat sur le sacerdoce," 55–111.
[34] Foreville and Leclercq, "Un débat sur le sacerdoce," 78.

supported.[35] At times, as described in Chapter 9, disputes over this issue erupted into violence, and the willingness of priests to raid Cistercian properties reveals the anger they felt.[36] Appropriation of churches, which surely diverted more resources, provoked less fury, which is somewhat puzzling but may stem from the fact that the loss of tithes affected existing incomes held by rectors, whereas appropriation, which normally took place in vacancies, merely affected the prospective incomes of clerics. As I argued in Chapter 4, one should not exaggerate the extent to which monasteries successfully absorbed parish revenues. Nonetheless, religious houses sought to increase their revenues from parish sources throughout the long twelfth century, and one gets the sense that the secular clergy felt beleaguered, wondering when and if the process would ever end. Thus, when describing the acquisition of benefices by the Hospitallers, Walter Map lamented that the regulars always increased and the seculars always decreased.[37]

Another source of friction may have been competition for gifts from the laity, as well as jealousy by secular clerics of the fundraising ability of monks. Though the number of large corporate churches held by secular clerics was declining, canons of the ones that remained might well have hoped for donations, and there is scattered evidence for gifts to parish churches, which were common later in the Middle Ages.[38] Monastic success at acquiring donations, however, would have limited the scope for secular clerics to win donations. The evidence for the resulting friction is indirect but suggestive. Specifically, John of Salisbury, Walter Map, and Gerald of Wales all criticized some of the practices monasteries used to encourage donations. John spoke of religious houses attracting potential donors into fraternities, hearing their confessions (which infringed on the rights of secular clerics), and exercising too much leniency in hopes of encouraging generosity.[39] Walter, when describing the methods monks used to attract generosity from knights, compared them to hawks hunting their prey.[40] Gerald also described various unscrupulous methods of monastic fundraising by the Cistercians, including in one case getting a patron drunk and then affixing his seal to a charter.[41] None of these writers described the monks as succeeding at the expense of secular clerics, and quite likely they felt genuine distaste for some fundraising practices, but it also seems likely that envy and frustration at seeing so much wealth flowing into monastic hands, especially when monks were sucking other resources away from the secular clergy, sharpened their distaste.

Conflicts between abbots and their monks or between bishops and cathedral priories could also exacerbate tensions between the regulars and the seculars, as in the disagreement between Abbot Samson and his monks. Indeed, since secular clerics generally dominated the households of abbots and bishops, such conflicts

[35] John of Salisbury, *Policraticus*, 2:194, 196–8; Goering, *William de Montibus*, 198; Peter of Blois, *Opera*, 252–5; Walter Map, *De Nugis Curialium*, 92–3, 96–7; Gerald of Wales, *Opera*, 4:135–7, 177. For this practice and debate over it more generally, see Constable, *Monastic Tithes*, 198–306.

[36] See Chapter 9, section 3.   [37] Walter Map, *De Nugis Curialium*, 70–1.

[38] For generosity to parish churches, see Thomas, "Lay Piety," 182–3.

[39] John of Salisbury, *Policraticus*, 2:195–6.   [40] Walter Map, *De Nugis Curialium*, 84–5.

[41] Gerald of Wales, *Opera*, 4:178, 198–203.

almost inevitably pitted monks against clerics. In some cases, household clerics may even have instigated strife. The *Liber Eliensis* not only recorded that Bishop Nigel of Ely received support from his clerics in his many disputes with his cathedral monks, as one would expect, but in several instances also accused Nigel's entourage or individual clerics within it of encouraging Bishop Nigel to act against the monks.[42] The *Liber Eliensis* was a highly partisan work, and the tendency to blame the actions of powerful men on evil counselors was common in the period. Nevertheless, conflicts between monastic churches and their abbots or bishops were often at least partly about revenues, and it would have been in the interests of household clerics to encourage their patrons. Thomas of Marlborough depicted one cleric, Master William of Verdun, urging his patron, the bishop of Worcester, to take over Evesham in order to increase his revenues; had the bishop done so, it would have provided him with far more resources with which to reward followers like Master William.[43]

Monastic cathedral priories were particularly obvious targets for ambitious household clerics, as can be seen from two major disputes in the late twelfth century. The first stemmed from the failed attempts of Archbishops Baldwin and Hubert to found a college of secular canons to house their household clerics at Hackington near Canterbury or later at Lambeth. The second arose from Bishop Hugh of Coventry's temporarily successful replacement of monks with secular clerics at Coventry. The latter dispute, for which only scattered sources survive, represented a straightforward clash of interests between the cathedral monks and the canons who replaced them.[44] The former dispute, for which far more evidence survives, including the convent's letters on the subject and large sections of the chronicles of the monk Gervase of Canterbury, was more complicated.[45] Ostensibly, the collegiate churches at Hackington and Lambeth were designed simply to create a church in honor of Thomas Becket that would also serve as a convenient place to house the archbishop's clerical advisors, and thus represented no threat to the cathedral priory. However, the monks were worried that the college would create a powerful and organized body of rivals who could draw resources and influence away from them. They even feared that the foundation might be the first step in an attempt to replace them.[46] Though their concerns were sometimes

[42] Blake, ed., *Liber Eliensis*, 286–7, 294–6, 322, 325, 334–5, 338–40. See also Karn, ed., *English Episcopal Acta 31*, cvii–cxii.

[43] Thomas of Marlborough, *History of Evesham*, 260–1. William used the ultimately unsuccessful takeover of Glastonbury by Savaric, bishop of Bath and Wells, as a model. For this takeover and the resulting dispute, see Knowles, *Monastic Order in England*, 327–30.

[44] For overviews of this dispute, see Palgrave, ed., *Rotuli Curiæ Regis*, 1:xviii–xxii; Knowles, *Monastic Order in England*, 322–4; D. E. Desborough, "Politics and Prelacy in the Late Twelfth Century: The Career of Hugh de Nonant, Bishop of Coventry, 1188–98," *Historical Research* 64 (1991), 1–14, at 6–8; Franklin, ed., *English Episcopal Acta 17*, xxx–xxxvii; Crosby, *Bishop and Chapter*, 126–30.

[45] Stubbs, ed., *Epistolæ Cantuarienses*; Gervase of Canterbury, *Historical Works*, 1:29–68, 337–69, 375–432, 436–84, 498–502, 534–93. Stubbs, in the introduction to the letters, gives a good overview of the dispute. See also Knowles, *Monastic Order in England*, 318–22, 325–6; Cheney, *Hubert Walter*, 135–57.

[46] For some statements of their concerns, see Gervase of Canterbury, *Historical Works*, 1:36–7, 337–8, 473; Stubbs, ed., *Epistolæ Cantuarienses*, 62–4, 378–80, 449–51, 532–8.

expressed in exaggerated fashion, they were certainly understandable, given the acquisitiveness and power of so many secular clerics. From the beginning, more-over, the dispute was intertwined with the ultimately successful attempts of the archbishops to recover the advowsons of four very wealthy churches which they wanted to use to support their clerics.[47] One cannot know what the actual intentions of the archbishops were, and the monks may have over-reacted, but it is not surprising that they resisted the new foundation so fiercely.

Both disputes were fought bitterly over a span of years and both escalated to violence. At Coventry, Bishop Hugh expelled the monks with the help of an armed band, though only after some of them had taken a cross from the cathedral and struck him on the head with it, bloodying him, while he was at a synod.[48] At Canterbury, Archbishop Baldwin had the monks besieged three times, once for eighty-four weeks. Baldwin made sure his men, who numbered nearly 500 at one point, did not go too far, beating servants but not the monks, and invading the monastic precincts but not the cathedral in which Thomas Becket had been martyred. Nonetheless, the extent of his willingness to use force and intimidation was remarkable.[49] The monks there remained intransigent despite the pressure applied on them, and eventually carried the day on their major goals, as did their fellows at Coventry, who won a papal ruling on their behalf in 1197.

Some bishops and clerics may have seen the Canterbury and Coventry disputes as test cases for a general clerical takeover of cathedral priories, for the prior of Canterbury at one point wrote to the priory's representatives in Rome claiming that the conflict had escalated into a plan to eject monks from every cathedral.[50] This seemingly unlikely claim gets support from a source hostile to the monks, Gerald of Wales, who wrote that Hugh Nunant, after emphasizing the unusual nature of English monastic cathedrals, urged the bishops of those cathedrals to contribute to a fund to lobby to have the monks removed, volunteering to contribute a large sum himself and to lead the effort. According to Gerald, the bishops generally approved this except for Archbishop Baldwin, who was himself a monk, though of the Cistercian rather than the Benedictine order.[51] More modestly, one of the Canter-bury letters refers to a plan rejected by the bishop of Ely to create prebends in his diocese which would be financed by churches belonging to the priory, with the priory being compensated by newly developed agricultural land. This proposal would seem to suggest a supplementary collegiate church along the lines of what Baldwin and Hubert were proposing, but the Canterbury writers placed it in the context of broader fears of monks, including themselves, being replaced by canons.[52] Clearly, plans to replace or supplement monks with canons through-out England never amounted to anything more than talk, particularly after the

---

[47] Stubbs, ed., *Epistolæ Cantuarienses*, xxxviii.

[48] Palgrave, ed., *Rotuli Curiæ Regis*, 1:3, 66–7; William of Newburgh, *Historia Rerum Anglicarum*, 1:394–5; Roger of Howden, *Chronica*, 4:35; Richard of Devizes, *Chronicle*, 8; Gerald of Wales, *Opera*, 4:64–5.

[49] Thomas, "Shame, Masculinity, and Becket," 1053–6.

[50] Stubbs, ed., *Epistolæ Cantuarienses*, 450.

[51] Gerald of Wales, *Opera*, 4:65–7.   [52] Stubbs, ed., *Epistolæ Cantuarienses*, 534–5, 538.

ultimately decisive victory of the monks at Canterbury and Coventry. Nonetheless, it would not be surprising if many bishops and clerics dreamed about how many lucrative benefices could have been created from cathedral priories.

The sources on these struggles naturally focused on the leadership of Archbishops Baldwin and Hubert and of Bishop Hugh, but the household clerics and the canons of the foundations they were trying to establish naturally supported the prelates strongly. Peter of Blois was a lynchpin in Archbishop Baldwin's efforts, representing him in Rome and writing letters to garner support.[53] Other clerics and canons expressed vociferous support and served the archbishops in various tasks, including the seizure of manors, incursions into monastic precincts, and the occupation of monastic buildings during the Canterbury dispute.[54] One of these clerics, William de Sancta Fide (William of St. Faith), whom the monks called William Sine Fide (William the Faithless), was also active in the Coventry dispute, where he was the chancellor of Hugh's secularized church and served as one of the attorneys for the canons after the monks brought a suit of novel disseisin against them.[55] Gervase of Canterbury claimed that the real architects of Baldwin's plans were in fact household clerics, singling out Peter of Blois in particular. Though this represents another example of the evil counselor topos, and though Peter later disavowed responsibility, the accusation is at least plausible.[56] The Canterbury priory sources certainly depicted the archbishop's clerics as committed partisans who threatened, taunted, and insulted the monks at various points.[57] In the process, they composed certain damning if amusing vignettes: Master Henry Pigun saying jokingly, in the context of appeals to the pope about the seizure of monastic lands, "we appeal and plunder"; Roger of Tanton, a canon of Hackington, saying in the same context, "I would not cease any more for the lord pope, even if he were here, than for the vilest servant (*garcio*) of the whole house"; and Master Sylvester exclaiming "Ptrut" in mocking response to papal documents.[58] Obviously these vignettes were recorded to sway opinion, particularly at the papal court, but they are sufficiently concrete that they may well have recorded real reactions. In any case, these were clearly not just disputes between prelates and their convents but also between clerics and monks.

Not surprisingly, these rancorous conflicts provoked bitter and sharply divided responses. The Canterbury monks considered some of their representatives who had fallen ill and died at Rome to be martyrs, and the canons of Hackington,

[53] Stubbs, ed., *Epistolæ Cantuarienses*, 81, 107–8; Gervase of Canterbury, *Historical Works*, 1:354, 356; Peter of Blois, *Later Letters*, 52–62; Peter of Blois, *Opera*, 534–5; Cotts, *Clerical Dilemma*, 36–7, 150.

[54] Stubbs, ed., *Epistolæ Cantuarienses*, 76–7, 131–2, 141, 152, 170–1, 312, 315–16; Gervase of Canterbury, *Historical Works*, 1:349, 359, 361, 425, 467, 473.

[55] Palgrave, ed., *Rotuli Curiæ Regis*, 1:3; Franklin, ed., *English Episcopal Acta 17*, 7–8; Stubbs, ed., *Epistolæ Cantuarienses*, 107–8, 290, 312, 315–16.

[56] Gervase of Canterbury, *Historical Works*, 1:332, 349, 354, 361; Peter of Blois, *Opera*, 534–5.

[57] Gervase of Canterbury, *Historical Works*, 1:419, 470, 473; Stubbs, ed., *Epistolæ Cantuarienses*, 25–6, 127–8, 141, 290, 486.

[58] Stubbs, ed., *Epistolæ Cantuarienses*, 77, 185.

according to Gervase, boasted of dubious miracles on behalf of the archbishop.[59] Gerald of Wales gave the following heading for a lost chapter on the conflict: "On the chapel of Lambeth by the envy and pride of the monks alone destroyed to the grave injury of the clergy."[60] As for Coventry, Nigel of Whiteacre attacked the canons fiercely, describing them as pimps who brought "public whores" into the cathedral complex.[61] Another monastic writer, Richard of Devizes, sarcastically extolled the replacement at Coventry of charitable monks living a simple life by canons who built splendid residences but were always absent, leaving their tasks to their less wealthy vicars who would have to turn the poor away from their doors.[62] In contrast, Gerald of Wales, who had visited Coventry during its brief secular phase, proclaimed that the canons had been a vast improvement upon the monks, including in their exercise of charity and hospitality, and claimed that upon enquiry the locals had agreed with him, even though many were kin to the monks.[63] In some cases the bitter commentary linked the specific disputes to the general rivalry between the secular and regular clergy. Gerald's heading on the Canterbury dispute can certainly be interpreted that way, and Richard of Devizes labeled the allegedly bad behavior of the Coventry canons as the *religio* of clerics. William of Newburgh, a regular canon, marveled that Archbishop Baldwin would propagate secular canons when he was a Cistercian monk himself and Gervase placed the dispute with Baldwin in the context of broader anti-monastic sentiment. Gervase also included a vignette in which Bishop Hugh, hoping to intervene in Archbishop Baldwin's dispute, said that if King Richard agreed, there would not be a monk left in England.[64] Most strikingly, in a statement prepared for Pope Celestine III, the monks of Canterbury wrote that there was an old saying that between groups with distinct customs (*mores*) there could be no certain friendship or firm concord, and that to intrude men of another order or "sect" would be like a lance in the side and a nail in the eye to the prior and convent. Elsewhere, the monks stated simply that seculars hated monastic simplicity.[65]

2. COMPETITION OVER AUTHORITY AND MORALITY

Deeply intertwined with the contests over wealth and control of churches were fierce disagreements over more abstract issues of authority. Particularly controversial was the claim that because secular clerics had the duty of pastoral care, they had superiority and authority over monks. As Theobald of Étampes put it, "The pastor is truly said to be the cleric, the monk, moreover, the sheep. Whence Jerome,

[59] Stubbs, ed., *Epistolæ Cantuarienses*, 269–70; Gervase of Canterbury, *Historical Works*, 1:529–31.
[60] Gerald of Wales, *Opera*, 4:63. See also Ralph of Diceto, *Opera Historica*, 2:165.
[61] Nigel of Whiteacre, *Tractatus Contra Curiales*, 196–7.
[62] Richard of Devizes, *Chronicle*, 70–1.   [63] Gerald of Wales, *Opera*, 4:67–8.
[64] William of Newburgh, *Historia Rerum Anglicarum*, 1:393; Gervase of Canterbury, *Historical Works*, 1:34, 470.
[65] Stubbs, ed., *Epistolæ Cantuarienses*, 379, 413.

although a monk, says, 'the cleric shepherds and I am shepherded.' Because the monk is herded and ruled by the cleric, it is obvious that the cleric is superior to the monk."[66] Gerald, also drawing on Jerome, likewise claimed that clerics should be the rulers, and monks the ruled.[67] Like Theobald's claim about tithes, such assertions ignored the entry of many monks into clerical orders, and it also ignored longstanding changes in church organization and the practical power of the monastic orders. Not surprisingly, therefore, such claims incensed monks. The abbot who urged Herbert Losinga to take up the monastic cause was reacting to this sort of claim when he wrote that secular canons asserted "with an inane profusion of words that they are of higher grade than monks and that adopting the monastic habit provides little or no help to the health of souls."[68] Not surprisingly, Theobald of Étampes's respondent opened his work with a long rebuttal of Theobald's claims on this score. He also developed a lengthy exegesis of the story of Jacob and Esau to argue that monks were in fact superior in authority to clerics, who had frittered away their birthright through sin.[69]

This monk's exegesis of Jacob and Esau shows the degree to which the rivalry between monks and clerics turned on claims of moral superiority, and how such claims were used to justify arguments about authority and about which group should control churches and other resources. As a result, attacks on the morality of the other group were potentially powerful weapons, and as the discussion so far demonstrates, such attacks were often used in specific disputes. Indeed, Nigel of Whiteacre's entire treatise against courtier clerics should clearly be read in the context of the disputes at Canterbury and Coventry. Nigel himself was a Canterbury monk. More important, he dedicated his treatise against courtly clerics to Bishop William Longchamp, who as papal legate had overseen the removal of the monks from Coventry, and he appealed to William to investigate his conscience on the subject. Quite probably the treatise was designed to undermine the moral standing of the kinds of powerful clerics who threatened the monks as well as to urge them to change their ways.[70] Unfortunately, analysis of the use of such rhetorical assaults is complicated by the belief that religious writers should fiercely correct their audiences and the fact that reformers and moralists did sometimes launch harsh attacks on their own groups. Thus, critics of other groups could claim that their motive was simply to do their duty, and such claims should not be altogether dismissed. Gerald of Wales was as willing to tell scandalous tales about secular clerics as about monastic groups, and his scathing critique of the regular clergy appeared in a work that criticized every branch of the Church. Nigel of Whiteacre's criticisms of secular canons in another work, the *Speculum Stultorum*, were accompanied by attacks on various monastic groups as well.[71] Clearly the monk who responded to Theobald of Étampes was more interested in undermining

[66] Foreville and Leclercq, "Un débat sur le sacerdoce," 52.
[67] Gerald of Wales, *Opera*, 4:66, 83.
[68] Anstruther, ed., *Epistolae Herberti de Losinga*, 103.
[69] Foreville and Leclercq, "Un débat sur le sacerdoce," 55–67, 79–89, 108–10.
[70] Nigel of Whiteacre, *Tractatus Contra Curiales*, 195–7. See also Cotts, *Clerical Dilemma*, 170–2.
[71] Nigel of Whiteacre, *Speculum Stultorum*, 76–86.

priests than reforming them, but his arguments overlapped heavily with those of reformers who were intent on improving the clergy. It can be difficult to distinguish between hostile and friendly critics, and often enough the writers themselves may have had complex motives. The fact remains, however, that the same kinds of attacks used to reform fellow Christians were also sometimes used to weaken rivals.

Partly because of this, secular clerics had to struggle against a widespread belief in the superiority of monastic morals and the monastic life, which put them constantly on the defensive. Gervase of Canterbury recounted a conversation between a Canterbury monk and Archbishop Hubert, in which the latter argued that a collegiate church would keep the clergy living correctly through mutual fear of detection. Gervase easily turned this statement to the advantage of the monks by stating that the archbishop remained silent about what specifically the clerics were accustomed to do in their scattered homes, "day and night," lest he inadvertently give support to the monks' cause by providing an *exemplum* of clerics living badly.[72] In Chapter 4 I discussed the defense of clerics owning property by Godwin, precentor of Salisbury in the early twelfth century. Besides his positive arguments he made several counter jabs concerning collective monastic wealth. Monks, he stated, may argue that they gave up goods in this life for benefits in the next, but the many who left humble abodes for the large habitations and properties they inhabited with their brothers were benefiting in this life. Nor, he continued, did one read of the apostles receiving estates, infinite numbers of animals, and fields for cultivation after abandoning the world.[73] Godwin's points were telling, but he was clearly struggling against a presumption that private ownership of property made secular clerics inferior to the regular clergy, and more generally, as Webber has pointed out, against an idea that there was a hierarchy of religious orders.[74] An anecdote of Gervase of Canterbury, in which Henry II compared monks and clerics, reveals particularly well how reform rhetoric undermined the secular clergy by increasing the perception of their moral inferiority compared to monks. In this story the king noted monastic wealth, but then trotted out all the standard attacks of reformers on priests: their misuse of ecclesiastical revenues, their greater concern for decorating their concubines than their churches, their drunken feasts, and so forth.[75] Concerns about such use of reforming critiques may in fact explain an odd passage in one of Thomas Agnellus's sermons. Right in the midst of rebuking priests for having material rather than spiritual concerns, he suddenly shifted to monks, criticizing them in an elaborate series of word-plays for being concerned more with the table (*mensa*) than with mass (*missa*), with salmon than with Solomon, with potation than with oration.[76] Thomas was probably trying to launch a pre-emptive strike, but clearly it was hard for clerics not to argue from a largely defensive position.

---

[72] Gervase of Canterbury, *Historical Works*, 1:537.
[73] Bodleian Library, Digby MS 96, fos. 26v–27r.
[74] Webber, *Scribes and Scholars*, 123–9.
[75] Gervase of Canterbury, *Historical Works*, 1:540.
[76] Bodleian Library, Laud. Misc. MS 71, fo. 101v.

The superiority ascribed to monks and the resulting defensiveness felt by secular clerics help explain the aggressive, scorching attacks of Walter Map and Gerald of Wales. First, there was probably an emotional response to claims about the inferiority of their own order. Gerald complained of monastic arrogance, which he averred was based on wealth and ignored the inferior status and lesser erudition of monks. In doing so he wrote that it was remarkable "how they do not cease to insult clerics." Shortly thereafter, he attacked the belief that monks were so superior that even a failed monk could still make a good cleric.[77] Walter Map's comparison of the Cistercians to the Israelites plundering the Egyptians, referring to a biblical account of divinely sanctioned looting during the departure from Egypt, and his reference to "we Egyptians" at first seems strange, for it compares the Cistercians to the chosen people and their victims, including Walter, to the enemies of the Israelites. Walter, however, used the comparison ironically to highlight Cistercian arrogance, for in Walter's account, the Cistercians claimed to have the only true path to heaven and justified unscrupulous trickery on the grounds of their holy status.[78] There was probably also a tactical element involved in the attacks, designed purposely to undermine perceptions of monastic moral superiority. This is suggested by the similarity between Gerald's attacks on monks in general and his attacks on the many alleged moral failings of a specific monk whom he considered an enemy and therefore wished to discredit.[79] For Gerald, writing after the Canterbury dispute, monastic intransigence may also have justified the strength of his attacks. After describing Archbishop Baldwin's rejection of Bishop Hugh's attempt to make a concerted attack on cathedral priories, Gerald wrote that the archbishop tried but failed to "conquer" his monks by patience and generosity.[80] Gerald clearly felt that a harsher approach was needed.

Walter's criticisms largely focused on the avarice of the Cistercians and other orders and should be placed in the context of the debate over wealth and private ownership of property. If their eschewal of private wealth theoretically made monks better, an exposé of their greed could undermine their claims to superiority. In addition, however, Walter's complaints of monastic arrogance and hints at sexual impropriety could affect perceptions of monastic moral pre-eminence more broadly. Gerald was more systematic in trying to dismantle the reputations of the regular clergy, expanding on Walter's critique of monastic greed and discussing other areas of sin more explicitly. Though Gerald could hardly deny that sexual activity was widespread among clerics, by including lurid anecdotes about the sexual activities of monks he could counteract monastic propaganda about the inferiority of the secular clergy. By pointing to instances of monks lusting after boys, and thereby playing on stereotypes about monks, he could even hope to turn the tables on them.[81] Similarly, stories about excessive eating and drinking by monks could counter claims that the regular clergy lived more austere lives than the secular

---

[77] Gerald of Wales, *Opera*, 4:82–4.
[78] Walter Map, *De Nugis Curialium*, 86–9, 98–9, 102–13.
[79] Gerald of Wales, *Opera*, 1:203–18.   [80] Gerald of Wales, *Opera*, 4:66–7.
[81] Gerald of Wales, *Opera*, 4:33–4, 44–5, 51–3, 86–90, 100–2, 168–9, 172–3, 233–5.

clergy. Of particular note was one in which a parish priest who had been generous to a Cistercian house abruptly halted his donations after seeing the monks feast, for by depicting a clerical admirer of monks who has his illusions shattered it implied that belief in monastic superiority, particularly by clerics, was naive.[82] It is hard to know how effective the harsh diatribes of Walter and Gerald were in changing perceptions about the exalted moral status of monks, but their works certainly would have given ammunition to other secular clerics who were engaged in disputes with the regular clergy or simply frustrated with claims of monastic superiority.

3. PEACEMAKING, COOPERATION, AND AMBIVALENCE

Naturally enough, the strife between the secular and regular clergy provoked dismay. Constable has drawn attention to writers who condemned strife and urged toleration between different monastic orders, as well as among Christian groups more generally.[83] English authors made similar condemnations of fighting between clerics and monks. When Robert Pullen sharply distinguished between the functions of clerics and monks in a sermon, he also stated that they were of one baptism and one faith, that they should love each other fraternally, and that they should sorrow rather than laugh that they often did otherwise. In his *Sentences* he emphasized that both those who led the active and those who embraced the contemplative life served useful functions.[84] When John of Salisbury criticized various monastic orders, he made sure to balance his criticism with praise, wrote that there were faithful as well as reprobate men in religious orders, and humbly stated that the secular clergy could not compare with the regulars for rigor of religious life.[85] Even the most vigorous polemicists generally felt the need to avoid being uniformly negative: Walter Map interlarded his criticisms with grudging praise, and Nigel of Whiteacre allowed that there were some praiseworthy secular clerics. Indeed, Nigel actually lamented the discord between monks and clerics, admitting that some monks could be proud and that even clerics accustomed to vestments decorated with gold might be humble.[86]

Some writers stated their disapproval of strife more forcefully. When Herbert Losinga was asked to take up the cause of the monks, he replied that he would not attack clerics, "who are sacred ministers of altars and [. . .] the producers (*conficientes*) of the body and blood of God, by whose vigils the sheepfold of God is guarded and the sheep of Christ are pastured with the delights of doctrine." Herbert could not in

---

[82] Gerald of Wales, *Opera*, 4:38–42, 55, 57, 98–100, 208–19, 244.

[83] Giles Constable, "The Diversity of Religious Life and Acceptance of Social Pluralism in the Twelfth Century," in *Culture and Spirituality in Medieval Europe* (Aldershot, 1996), 29–47.

[84] Lambeth Palace, MS 458 part 2, fo. 137r; Robert Pullen, "Sententiarum," 936–40.

[85] John of Salisbury, *Policraticus*, 2:190–210.

[86] Walter Map, *De Nugis Curialium*, 50–9, 62–3, 68–9, 112–17; Nigel of Whiteacre, *Speculum Stultorum*, 83; Nigel of Whiteacre, *Tractatus Contra Curiales*, 195–6.

fact wholly restrain himself from suggesting monastic superiority, but he clearly disapproved of strife between the two groups.[87] However, it was Lucian of Chester, writing in the diocese of Coventry either during or in the aftermath of Bishop Hugh's conflict with the cathedral monks, who most fully condemned strife between monks and clerics, as well as between monks and bishops, though he never referred directly to the Coventry conflict. His condemnation of wrangling between monks and clerics, noted above, was only part of his conciliatory approach. Before addressing relations between clerics and monks, Lucian praised the secular clergy at length, and stressed their status, privileges, and importance. Like many reformers, he compared them to angels, and he emphasized their superiority to laypeople. His echoing of reformers was deliberate: part of his intent was to remind clerics of their exalted (and very comfortable) status in order to urge them to live up to their responsibilities. However, Lucian also intended to get his clerical readers in a mood receptive to his arguments about the proper relations between the two groups. After praising clerics, Lucian called for unity, with justice to the cleric who lived rightly, peace to the monk who was not proud, and companionship between the two. A skilled practitioner of the humility topos, Lucian stated that if the cleric could not accept the monk as a brother, he should accept him as a son, for the cleric was the greater and the monk, the lesser. In his view, however, the superiority of clerics gave them, along with bishops, the duty to support and protect monks. Like many others, he believed that clerics and monks should complement each other with their separate functions rather than be rivals, saying that "the cleric shines through learning, the monk through discipline," and "the cleric is potent in scripture, the monk noteworthy through merits." Lucian clearly hoped he had the blueprint for harmony between monks, clerics, and bishops.[88]

Good relations between clerics and monks existed in reality as well as in the hopes of peacemakers like Lucian of Chester. I have noted the great generosity from many clerics to monastic houses.[89] There was obviously at least as much intellectual cooperation between monks and clerics as rivalry. Bernard of Clairvaux may have opposed Peter Abelard, but he supported the careers of Robert Pullen and John of Salisbury.[90] Alexander Neckam addressed various monastic audiences with flattering humility in sermons he wrote while still a secular cleric.[91] One could object that he was atypical, since he subsequently became a regular canon, but that simply suggests that he, like many other secular canons who entered religious houses, admired the life of the regular clergy. Individual instances of friendships and cooperation between clerics, monks, and monasteries can be found throughout the sources, as when the chronicler of Walden Abbey described how a cleric

[87] Anstruther, ed., *Epistolae Herberti de Losinga*, 106–7.

[88] Most of his discussion is in the unpublished sections of his work: Lucian of Chester, *Liber Luciani*, 69; Bodleian Library, Bodleian MS 672, fos. 117r–132r, 188v–190r.

[89] See Chapter 14, section 3.

[90] C. N. L. Brooke, "John of Salisbury and his World," in Michael Wilks, ed., *The World of John of Salisbury* (Oxford, 1984), 1–20, at 8.

[91] Bodleian Library, Wood empt. MS 13, fos. 53r, 60r, 86r; Hunt and Gibson, *Schools and the Cloister*, 87.

named Henry, who was on terms of close familiarity with the monks, resigned from a church he held and persuaded his nephew, the patron, to grant it to Walden.[92] Even during the Canterbury conflict, the monks were able to call on a prominent English cleric, Ralph of Sarre, dean of Rheims, to help them. More surprisingly, the monks representing the cathedral priory at Rome reported that they received crucial financial support as a legacy from one of the archbishop's clerics.[93]

Because of the contradictory factors encouraging hostility and closeness, ambivalence was a common reaction of secular clerics towards the regular clergy. Peter of Blois provides the best example of this, and Cotts has done an excellent job of elucidating his ambivalence, though perhaps one can fully appreciate just how fraught Peter's situation was only in the context of the polemics and disputes discussed in this chapter.[94] Peter's actions and attitudes towards monks ranged from hostility through a prickly defensiveness to a warm embrace. As noted above, Peter was a key player in the Canterbury dispute. On another occasion, when a regular canon criticized him for advocating simplicity but being a wealthy courtier, Peter framed his response partly in terms of the broader conflict of orders, and described his critic as attacking clerics generally. In that response, Peter argued that a diversity of religious orders was useful and defended private clerical wealth in similar terms to Godwin of Salisbury, but also counter-attacked by referring to the arrogance of those in religious orders and the accumulation of churches and property by the critic's own house.[95] More broadly, as Cotts has argued, Peter defined his own place in the church and in society, and by extension that of other secular clerics, partly in contrast to that of monks. Yet Peter was closely attuned to monastic thought, wrote hagiography in praise of monastic saints, and sought the prayers of members of religious orders, particularly in his old age. He frequently urged monastic correspondents to live up to their vows. In his response to his critic, he counterbalanced criticism of the regular clergy with extensive praise. More important, he apologized abjectly to the Canterbury monks, shifting the blame elsewhere, and stressed that God had punished him for his actions.[96] Most strikingly, as discussed in Chapter 7, when he became fed up with the secular canons at Wolverhampton, where he was dean, he urged its conversion to a Cistercian house.[97] In a letter lamenting his own sinful worldliness and requesting prayers from the monks of Meaux Abbey, Peter remarked that, "It may perhaps seem absurd to some [monks] to pray for a secular cleric," encapsulating both the rift between the two orders and the desire to overcome that rift.[98]

---

[92] Greenway and Watkiss, eds., *Foundation of Walden Monastery*, 62–3.
[93] Stubbs, ed., *Epistolæ Cantuarienses*, 13–14, 113, 124–5, 220–1, 230, 282, 287.
[94] Cotts, *Clerical Dilemma*, 215–17, 247–62.
[95] Peter of Blois, *Opera*, 1113–26; Cotts, *Clerical Dilemma*, 251–5.
[96] Peter of Blois, *Opera*, 534–5.   [97] Peter of Blois, *Later Letters*, 25–30.
[98] Peter of Blois, *Later Letters*, 168–71.

4. THE SECULAR CLERGY AS SECOND BEST

Nonetheless, the complexity and ambiguity of relationships between the secular and regular clergy should not obscure the importance of their rivalry, one in which the regular orders had much greater success in the long twelfth century, as indicated by their acquisition of so many resources at the expense of the secular clerics. A takeover of monastic cathedrals by secular clerics would have reversed this trend, but that effort failed at Coventry and did not get off the ground elsewhere. It is likely that even at Coventry, Hugh Nunant accomplished as much as he did only because of being struck by the monks. In terms of the competition for gifts, the surviving evidence indicates that the regular clergy won hands down. Some nobles did found collegiate churches staffed by secular clerics early on, but their numbers were dwarfed by the scores of new monasteries founded in the period, sometimes with the very endowments of those earlier colleges. Cathedral churches and collegiate churches did continue to receive gifts. For instance, Lincoln Cathedral received major donations from various monarchs up through Henry II and also received scores of gifts, large and small, from other donors through the period.[99] Even so, the number of gifts to secular cathedrals and collegiate churches pales in comparison to the thousands upon thousands of gifts recorded in surviving monastic cartularies.

Some reasons for the greater success of the regular clergy were practical in nature. Until the popularization of chantries, monastic houses were the organizations best designed to offer systematic intercession for souls and society, creating a demand for their services. Collectively the monastic orders commanded tremendous wealth and therefore power. Individually, large monastic churches had the structures and resources to court donors, win lawsuits, or lobby the papacy. As monks and regular canons took over cathedrals and collegiate churches, there were fewer and fewer churches of secular clerics that could compete on the same level, though of course this raises the question of why secular clerics were not able to defend against such takeovers more successfully. Monks were more likely than secular canons to focus their energies and efforts on the well-being of the great churches they staffed. As the previous chapter has shown, some secular canons had a strong commitment to their

---

[99] Foster and Major, eds., *Registrum Antiquissimum*, 1:25–31, 39–41, 49, 51–5, 62–3, 71–7; 2:241; 3:1–5, 11–14, 16, 29–33, 35–6, 40–3, 48, 122, 128–9, 136–7, 155–6, 158–60, 165–6, 169–72, 189–200, 202–12, 215–17, 220–3, 226, 234–8, 250–6, 259–66, 278–9, 295–6; 4:6–18, 23–4, 26–7, 33–4, 36–7, 44, 49, 50–2, 55–6, 63–6, 72–4, 76–7, 79–80, 82–91, 96–100, 102–13, 116–18, 122–9, 132–5, 142–60, 163, 167–9, 172–85, 192–3; 6:1–2, 7–13, 16–20, 22–3, 30, 34–6, 46–7, 49, 51, 63–9, 72–3, 77–8, 85–93, 100–3, 108–11, 121–2, 124–5, 128–9, 132–3, 135–9, 141–7, 151–7; 7:1, 3–15, 17, 19–23, 26, 28, 31, 35–6, 41, 44–8, 58, 92–3, 95–6, 99–101, 103–8, 111–12, 121–32, 197–8; 8:1, 3–6, 69, 77–8, 83–6, 113–14, 125–6, 150–1, 188–9; 9:1–3, 48–9, 63–6, 69–70, 75–6, 199–200, 207–8, 214, 226, 235–7, 239–40; 10:8–9, 58, 62, 232, 288–90, 315–16. For an overview of aristocratic involvement with and generosity to secular cathedrals, see Stephen Marritt, "Secular Cathedrals and the Anglo-Norman Aristocracy," in Paul Dalton, Charles Insley, and Louise J. Wilkinson, eds., *Cathedrals, Communities and Conflict in the Anglo-Norman World* (Woodbridge, 2011), 151–67.

churches. Given the frequent absenteeism and pluralism of secular canons, however, most were unlikely to show the same level of fierce devotion as monks and regular canons, who were normally bound to a single institution for the remainder of their lives. Yet the practical advantages of the monks should not be exaggerated. Secular clerics too had enormous collective influence, power, and wealth. Because of their service in secular and ecclesiastical bureaucracies and households, they had the ears of the powerful. The increasing dominance of secular clerics in the ranks of the bishops as the twelfth century went on also gave them an advantage. In practical terms, therefore, the success of the regular clergy was by no means guaranteed.

Ultimately, the regular clergy had the upper hand because their reputation for moral superiority remained largely intact, despite the efforts of their clerical critics. Bartlett has compiled a list of twenty-one English saints living in the period 1075–1225, and the great majority were regular clerics or hermits. Thomas Becket had been a secular cleric, but had secretly taken on a monastic habit, and would have been an unlikely candidate for canonization but for the extraordinary circumstances of his death. The cults of Archbishop William of York, Bishop Remigius of Lincoln, and Bishop Osmund of Salisbury emerged from the milieu of the secular clergy, for all were promoted by the canons of their cathedrals, but their cults had only limited success.[100] The deathbed conversion to the monastic life of many laypeople and some clerics was a sign that most believed it to be the surest route to heaven. Indeed, the abbot who wrote to Herbert Losinga pointedly noted that when priests, laypeople, and even kings feared the approach of death, they became monks, not priests or canons.[101] Strikingly, even Hugh Nunant joined a monastery before he died, a traditionally commendable end that Gerald of Wales described in detail.[102] The massive generosity of laypeople to religious houses surely also represented a widespread vote of confidence in the special efficacy of their prayers resulting from a belief in their superior morality. Critics of the monks probably damaged their reputations to some degree, but could not overcome a widespread view that they remained better than the secular clergy.

There were many reasons why it was difficult for secular clerics to counteract beliefs about monastic moral superiority, even though monks too were far from flawless. First, the idea of monastic superiority was too well entrenched to overturn easily. Second, the demands on monks in terms of giving up private property and adopting certain ascetic practices *were* higher. When they succeeded in following their ascetic practices, it gave them extra prestige. Even when they failed, criticism by clerics unwilling to adopt such practices in the first place may not have been particularly effective. Monks in wealthy monasteries no doubt had a higher standard of living than the poorest parish clergy, but because of the ostentatious lifestyles of the wealthier secular clergy, that fact probably had little impact. Moreover, the discipline and oversight that claustration was designed to provide probably did make sexual activity and the employment of violence far less common among the

---

[100] Bartlett, *England under the Norman and Angevin Kings*, 462.
[101] Anstruther, ed., *Epistolae Herberti de Losinga*, 103.
[102] Gerald of Wales, *Opera*, 4:68–74.

regular than the secular clergy. It is likely that most monks were as prone as secular clerics to indulge in vices such as anger or gluttony, but sexual sins and the employment of violence were far more likely to affect reputations. Furthermore, as I have also argued, monastic behavior was more easily hidden from view, and this included not just sex and violence but also minor sins such as feasting or quarreling. Indeed, some of Gerald of Wales's stories concerned the secret feasting by monks, and were designed precisely to counteract this monastic advantage, though probably with only limited success.[103] Moreover, those males who were most fervent probably did tend to enter monasteries, especially when caught up in the excitement generated by new, rigorous movements. While fervor was not guaranteed to last, self-selection may have resulted in a certain overall difference in behavior between the regular and secular clergy and the initial fervor itself probably influenced perceptions. The evidence does not exist to systematically judge whether or not monks and regular canons generally came closer than secular clerics to living up to the high standards of religious writers, but I strongly suspect that the perception of their moral superiority stemmed partly from actual differences in behavior as well as from the greater visibility of the shortcomings of the secular clergy.

As an alternative to claiming moral superiority or even equality with monks, secular clerics sometimes emphasized the importance of the tasks entrusted to them, above all pastoral care. As already noted, Theobald of Étampes stressed pastoral care in the debate over tithes and he and others focused on it when asserting the authority of the secular over the regular clergy. Godwin of Salisbury, in defending private clerical wealth, emphasized its use to support preaching, ministering to the flock, and caring for the poor.[104] Gerald of Wales stressed the productivity of pastoral work by comparing the monk to a single grain of wheat and the cleric to the farmer who planted wheat and brought in much grain to the barn of the Lord.[105] Where appropriate, secular clerics stressed the utility of administrative work within the Church, as Peter of Blois did in advocating Baldwin's plan for a collegiate church and in defending his and other clerics' participation in ecclesiastical administration.[106] As Ferruolo has pointed out, Stephen Langton and other scholars also emphasized the importance of the teaching and learning that went on in the schools. As Ferruolo and Smalley both argued, various figures connected to the schools, including Langton, Pullen, and Gerald of Wales, argued more generally for the worth of the active life in comparison to the contemplative life of the regular clergy.[107]

Even in emphasizing the importance of their functions, however, secular clerics were fighting an uphill battle, for the view that the contemplative life was superior, though contested, was widespread. Frequent reference to the story of Martha and

---

[103] Gerald of Wales, *Opera*, 4:98–100, 208–13.

[104] Bodleian Library, Digby MS 96, fo. 21r. The relevant passage is edited in Webber, *Scribes and Scholars*, 128 n 54.

[105] Gerald of Wales, *Opera*, 4:83.

[106] Peter of Blois, *Opera*, 17–18; Peter of Blois, *Later Letters*, 60–1.

[107] Ferruolo, *Origins of the University*, 211–12; Smalley, *Study of the Bible*, 249–51; Smalley, *Becket Conflict*, 43–8. See also Morenzoni, *Des écoles aux paroisses*, 90–3.

Mary in Luke gave the regular orders a strong rhetorical boost, given Jesus's praise for Mary, who listened to him and was often considered a symbol of the regular clergy, over Martha, who was busy taking care of things. Peter of Blois, in answering the criticisms of the anonymous regular canon, argued that even though Jesus commended Mary, he was not displeased with Martha's busy activities. An argument that the active life was worthy but second best was hardly a strong one, and it was difficult for clerics to work their way around this problem in pursuing their rivalry against the regular clergy.[108] For scholars, one possible route was to argue that learning was a form of contemplation, a reasonable argument, but one that had to overcome the strong traditional association of contemplation with the monastic rather than scholastic life. Another was to argue that one could incorporate contemplation into an active life. In the end, even the Parisian masters often had to resort to a convoluted argument that the contemplative life was better "in essence," but that some sort of mixed life was best.[109]

Even granted the difficulties of overcoming established views about the superior value of the monastic life, however, one cannot help but feel that secular clerics missed an important opportunity. Reformers established a powerful model of the exalted status and importance of priests due to their ritual functions (admittedly shared by priests among the regular clergy), and to their pastoral duties. Because those same works aimed at improvement and correction, they emphasized the moral shortcomings of many priests, thus undermining the secular clergy. However, one wonders why, in their rivalry with the monastic clergy, secular clerics did not combine arguments about the profound importance of pastoral care with more positive portrayals of clerics, rather than resorting to counterattacks against monks. Various possibilities may explain this failure. The combative nature of so many debates in the period may have made counterattack the automatic response. The humility topos made self-congratulatory rhetoric problematic, though that did not stop monastic writers from building up a largely positive picture of monks and monastic life. The fact that so few learned clerics, the ones who were composing arguments, were active in the parishes may have made such an approach less useful to their own situations. Perhaps defenders of the secular clergy felt that emphasizing the importance of pastoral care would only allow their monastic rivals to quote back to them the criticisms made by clerical reformers about the deficiencies of those entrusted with guiding the laity. It is even possible that the image of the morally corrupt secular clergy was sufficiently entrenched in their own minds for defenders to feel that any approach involving the praise of clerics would not be credible. Whatever the reasons, secular clerics in England failed to effectively exploit existing

---

[108] Peter of Blois, *Opera*, 1121. Interpretations of the story of Martha and Mary were complex, as Constable has shown, and many writers praised Martha or urged a combination of the virtues of both: Giles Constable, "The Interpretation of Mary and Martha," in *Three Studies in Medieval Religious and Social Thought* (Cambridge, 1995), 1–141. Nonetheless, one strong strand of interpretation used the story to favor the contemplative life.

[109] Ferruolo, *Origins of the University*, 208–9, 211–12; Smalley, *Study of the Bible*, 249–50; Smalley, *Becket Conflict*, 44; Morenzoni, "Pastorale et ecclésiologie dans la prédication d'Étienne Langton," 455.

views about the importance of pastoral care and the exalted status of its practitioners in their rivalry with the regular clergy.

In the end, the failure of the secular clergy to successfully defend their order, combined with the emphasis of many reformers on the importance of pastoral care, opened the door for a new set of rivals, the friars, who entered England in the 1220s and soon achieved enormous success in that country, as throughout Catholic Europe. No doubt the reputations of both the secular clergy and the existing monastic orders suffered from the aggressive bickering between the two groups. The superiority of monastic life was challenged, but with only partial success. Secular clerics and reformers established the importance of many functions of the secular clergy which cloistered monks and even regular canons could not or would not fulfill on any large scale basis. Yet reformers also emphasized the widespread inadequacy of the clerics who were assigned those tasks, and even those defending the clergy against the attacks of monks did not systematically challenge this view. In this overall setting, the mendicant orders could appear to offer an ideal solution by combining the active life, including aspects of pastoral care such as preaching, with the supposedly superior moral life of the regular clergy. In the long term, of course, medieval people became as disillusioned with the friars as with other groups of religious. In the short term, however, their success illustrates just how little success the secular clergy had in reconciling the tensions created by the high expectations placed on them and the worldly duties, entanglements, and temptations they faced in the course of their lives.

Conclusion

Given the importance of secular clerics below the episcopal level to English society in the long twelfth century, and indeed to Christian Europe throughout the Middle Ages, it is stunning how little they figure in the historiography of the medieval period. It is not, of course, that they are entirely absent, but rather that they generally appear intermittently and only in specific roles, mainly as scholars, bureaucrats, or parish priests, rather than as a group. Historians need to place secular clerics nearer to the heart of the story of historical change in the Middle Ages, and our understanding of medieval society will be deeply flawed until we research this powerful and influential group more fully. In this book I have made a start on the process with a large case study concerning the secular clergy of England during the long twelfth century. In this conclusion I have two aims. The first is to review my findings on how great an impact this important group had on their society. The second is to suggest some ways in which a focus on the secular clergy can help us rethink some of our views of medieval society.

The impact of the secular clergy was particularly strong in the intellectual and educational spheres. Two key developments of the long twelfth century were the transmission of Arabic and Greek learning into Catholic Europe and the rise of the schools and universities. This study has emphasized just how crucial the secular clergy were to both. The personal mobility of the secular clergy made them ideal transmitters of knowledge both within and beyond the religious and cultural boundaries of the Catholic world, and their worldliness made them more likely than the regular clergy to seek out non-Christian learning. Despite the later importance of the regular clergy, particularly friars, in the universities, and despite the contributions even in the twelfth century of some regular clerics, secular clerics were essentially the founders of the university system, particularly in northern Europe. Secular clerics had the mobility, the resources, and the motives to create the critical mass of masters and students at places like Paris, Oxford, and Cambridge, where early universities would emerge. Thus they played a crucial role in one of the most important developments in the history of medieval education.

In England, at least, the secular clergy had an outsized role in the expansion of intellectual life more generally. Monastic learning grew too, but the intellectual productivity of the secular clergy simply exploded. Because of the monastic dominance of intellectual life in England before 1066, the *rate* of expansion of clerical intellectual activity may have been greater there than in some areas on the continent where cathedral schools had a much larger presence in the eleventh century. Nonetheless, the expansion of intellectual activity by secular clerics occurred throughout much of Catholic Europe in the central Middle Ages, and contributed greatly to the intellectual efflorescence of the period. As the long twelfth century proceeded, the English secular clergy produced increasing numbers of works in a remarkable array of fields, from theology to law and from vernacular romance to geography. Some works produced by secular clerics associated with England, such as Peter of Blois's letters or Geoffrey Vinsauf's *Poetria Nova*, achieved great influence in the Middle Ages and a few, such as John of Salisbury's *Policraticus*, had an impact that stretched well beyond the end of the medieval period. Moreover, this intellectual expansion was not limited to authorship, for increasing numbers of clerical teachers, doctors, lawyers, and even astrologers applied their learning to what might be somewhat anachronistically described as professional practice. Obviously, there was a wide overlap between the intellectual activities of secular clerics and those of monks, nuns, and regular canons, but the greater involvement of the secular clergy in the world meant that clerical learning was more often directed towards such practical subjects as law and government and also to some theoretically utilitarian subjects like astrology and magic which, had they worked, would have changed the world. Learned secular clerics were also both distinctive and influential because they helped bring learning out of the cloisters, as is clearly illustrated in their fundamental but previously ignored role as book collectors, thus helping to create the professional book trade and exposing the laity to the culture of the book. Moving beyond the intellectual sphere, clerics were also surprisingly important in the cultural life of the period, both as participants in music, drama, and entertainment, and as patrons of art and architecture.

The wealth and leisure available to many secular clerics, and the expectations that they be educated, that they perform the liturgy, and that they ornament their churches and rituals, meant that they provided one broad base on which the intellectual and cultural achievements of the period could be built. As a result, when one studies the clergy as a group, the collective intellectual and cultural importance of ordinary intellectuals, performers, and patrons becomes clear, and this shows one way in which expanding the focus to the entire secular clergy can influence our understanding of historical change in the period. We are accustomed to focusing upon intellectual and cultural geniuses, such as Anselm or Marie de France, and certainly the secular clergy provided their fair share of these, especially when one looks at Europe as a whole, but this study has shown that a mass of generally far less impressive figures could also play a huge role in intellectual and cultural development, at least when they had the kind of advantages afforded to the secular clergy.

The focus on the secular clergy has also allowed me to suggest a new model of England's place in the Twelfth-Century Renaissance. England was, in some senses, on the periphery of this renaissance, but its clergy were not. This was a thoroughly international renaissance; indeed, in a society that was miserably poor by modern standards, only a pooling of resources from throughout Catholic Europe made it possible. Partly because of the mobility of secular clerics, resources and knowledge flowed to and from such centers of learning as Paris, Bologna, Salerno, and Toledo, and developments in parts of Europe could influence all of Europe. England was less an intellectual colony of France, though French influence remained strong there, than an unusually wealthy and productive European region that participated in intellectual and cultural developments involving Catholic Europe as a whole.

Another important aspect of twelfth-century history is the rise of administration, and though scholars have long understood the importance of the secular clergy in this process, few have looked at their distinctive contributions. In part, this is because many of their functions and duties *did* overlap with those of their lay counterparts. Even when they were not functioning in distinctive ways, however, the ability of secular clerics to operate freely in the world while drawing on the tremendous wealth of the church was crucial to the growth of secular as well as ecclesiastical administration. Moreover, the clergy were also profoundly important to the growth of administrative institutions because of their learning, above all because of their literacy. One of the key developments of the period was that the lay elites were beginning to participate in the culture of literacy, but the clergy were still dominant in the use of reading and particularly writing, and it was only through their examples and guidance that literacy among lay administrators started developing. The rise of ecclesiastical and above all secular bureaucracy was crucial to European history, and though it was a slow and gradual process, the long twelfth century was a critically important period, especially in the history of English royal administration. Without the secular clergy, the administrative developments of the period are unimaginable.

Administrative service was one of several factors that gave some clerics great power, and this study suggests that medievalists need to seriously rethink their conception of the social elites by acknowledging the importance of influential secular clerics among them. Modern discussions of elite groups almost never include the secular clergy except for bishops; instead, scholars think primarily of the secular aristocracy or perhaps of courtiers, generally undifferentiated between clerics and laypeople. In contrast, medieval writers who paired elite clerics with knights as equally important although distinctive social groups clearly did treat the upper clergy as a branch of the elites. Secular clerics were thoroughly ensconced in powerful aristocratic patronage networks of lordship and friendship, and worked alongside secular aristocrats in the households of magnates and at the royal court. Despite religious strictures, clerics participated in aristocratic culture, including hunting, courtly love, courtly entertainment, and the production of vernacular romances and poetry, and though some scholars, particularly Jaeger, have investigated their importance in these arenas, most historians continue to focus on the secular aristocracy in this context. Because secular clerics, other than bishops, did not tend to be important landholders, they do not fit our preconceptions about membership in the economic elites, yet the wealthiest clerics could wield extensive economic power, live aristocratic lifestyles, and act as influential cultural patrons. Some influential clerics were aristocratic by birth, but even those who were not could gain high status and influence. It is true that the majority of clerics were not members of the English elite, but that should not blind us to the fact that many were, and indeed that a significant portion of that elite was made up of secular clerics.

Despite their status and power, the secular clergy had less influence in shaping social and economic developments than intellectual, cultural, and political ones. Admittedly, their influence on the economy, as managers, administrators, and above all consumers, was greater than has commonly been acknowledged. Generally, however, the clergy experienced rather than generated social change. Nonetheless, a study of the secular clergy can provide fascinating perspectives on the social history of the period. Along with service to the king, the church provided one of the few potential paths for upward social mobility, and reactions to successful clerics of low birth show how much this could be resented. An even more remarkable aspect of clerical history in the period was the denial of marriage to a group among whom it had once been widespread. One can see kinship networks adjusting to cope with the end of normal inheritance by sons; nuclear families became much more problematic, but broader clerical kin groups could survive, albeit with difficulty, through nepotism and ensconcing themselves in powerful networks of influence. The rise of clerical celibacy obviously makes clerics and their partners key loci for the study of gender and sexuality. Clerics had to establish their own models of masculinity and the attacks on the wives and concubines of priests increased the already powerful misogyny of the period. It is also fascinating to see an influential group eschewing violence or, in many cases, failing to do so, and the dispute between Becket and Henry II reveals just how central the clergy were to thinking about violence and privilege in the period. Precisely because the secular clergy were both an important and a distinctive group, their social history can powerfully illuminate many of the social dynamics of the time. More importantly, one can no more understand the social history of the Middle Ages without including the secular clergy than one could without including a group like the secular nobility.

Because clerics were theoretically set apart, by their ordination, as a group devoted entirely to religion, one reason for their neglect in the scholarship may be their apparent lack of involvement in exciting new religious developments in the period. Among the regular clergy, one can find the rise of new orders with new practices, including the regular canons, Cistercians, England's own order of Sempringham, and, slightly later, the friars. Among the secular clergy one can at most speak of administrative change, for instance with the spread of such officials as territorial archdeacons and rural deans, developments which were far less captivating to contemporaries or to most modern historians. For the most part, the secular clergy were more the objects of reform than the instigators, as moralists and church authorities sought to enforce clerical celibacy, eliminate clerical violence, prevent clerics from conducting secular business, bar them from service at the royal court, and reshape their lives in many other ways. Indeed, the secular clergy became a locus of thinking about masculinity, sexuality, purity, worldliness, piety, and religiosity largely because they were objects of so much exhortation and controversy, not because they were pioneers of religious renewal. Religious writers may have stressed the cosmic importance of priests, due to their performance of the Eucharist and their pastoral duties, but contemporaries were more interested in other more zealous religious groups, and modern scholars have followed suit.

Yet for all the worldliness and resistance to reform of the secular clergy, they were profoundly important to religious life and religious change in the period. Even when reforms were imposed on them, as with the demand for celibacy, their responses, both positive and negative, helped shape religious change. Moreover, many of the writers trying to reform the secular clergy were themselves secular clerics. Though the growth of church bureaucracy did not arouse the same excitement as the development of new religious orders, and indeed created much ambivalence, it was crucially important in giving the church a greater potential to make its influence and authority felt in society. As part of the overall explosion of clerical intellectual activity, secular clerics were fundamentally important to the development of scholasticism and the flowering of religious learning more gener-ally, which were among the greatest religious developments in the period. Most important of all, the secular clergy had a huge impact simply by fulfilling their duties, however imperfectly they did so. By providing many of the Church's officials, by offering the most accessible performances of Christian rituals, and above all by carrying out the vast majority of pastoral care, the secular clergy guaranteed the continuing inculcation of Christian beliefs and values into society. They even fostered the growth of lay piety by their own private acts of piety. Overall, the secular clergy were indispensable to the functioning and success of the Church in the secular world.

A focus on the secular clergy can also add useful perspectives on religious history, as on social history, and perhaps even help us rethink aspects of it. First, the accomplishments of the secular clergy reveal the limitations that claustration placed on the influence of the regular clergy. Monasteries and nunneries had been crucial to the survival and spread of Christianity in the early Middle Ages, often serving as the chief centers of learning or acting as catalysts for the revitalization of the religion in local areas, and they continued to be important religious institutions throughout the Middle Ages. However, though claustration served to intensify the religious experience, it also reduced the impact of monks, nuns, and regular canons on the world beyond. They performed only limited pastoral care, rarely served even in diocesan administration, and generally had less interaction with the laity than secular clerics did. Of course, claustration never cut the religious off from the world completely, but the regular clergy, for all their prestige, had far less direct impact on the laity than the secular clergy did.

Second, the pattern of constant if not particularly effective exhortation discussed in Chapter 2 and elsewhere can prompt us to rethink the concept of reform in fruitful ways. Scholars often envision reform in terms of specific movements bringing specific changes within a limited time frame. One cannot, however, speak of a specific reform movement in England, except insofar as writers and preachers were trying to implement the Gregorian Reform over the long term. Efforts at bringing specific change did have some results, as the slow decline of clerical marriage and concubinage indicates, but generally the gap between the expectations placed on clerics and their actual behavior remained huge. Indeed, reformers themselves, such as Peter of Blois and Gerald of Wales, could be selective about the rules and norms they chose to accept, for instance when it came to pluralism. A certain amount of hypocrisy may have come into play and, more important, contemporaries recognized that there would be an inevitable gap between ideal and reality and between preaching and practice. Yet there can be no doubt that there was a sustained and powerful effort throughout the period to change the behavior of the clergy, in other words, to reform them. In a situation in which the expectations for clerical morality were so high, and in which there were so many temptations and competing social and political expectations, the effort to improve the clergy or indeed to prevent them from falling away from reform ideals was inevitably going to be a perpetual slog rather than a swift historical change. Perhaps one should think of reform not only in terms of specific movements, but also in the context of long-term, even perpetual efforts that were designed as much to prevent decline as to promote what the reformers viewed as positive change.

Third, it is important not to think of Christianity's hold on medieval society, however well established, as a given, but rather to treat it as an ongoing process that constantly had to be renewed. Admittedly, there was nothing likely to challenge Christian dominance in England in the long twelfth century, and in retrospect the fears of some English preachers about heresy seem exaggerated. Already in 1066, the Christian church had structures, institutions, and practices in place to constantly renew Christian beliefs and practices among the populace. Even so, any religion needs the constant repetition of rituals, teachings, and practices to survive and flourish. Like efforts to reform the clergy, this too was an ongoing slog and therefore unlikely to capture the historical imagination. Nonetheless, the process, however unexciting, was a crucial one. Who was chiefly responsible for the ongoing maintenance of religion in medieval society? In most times and places it was the secular clergy.

A final important point to take away from the study of the secular clergy was just how explosive and yet also how creative the nexus between the sacred and the secular could be in the Middle Ages. Modern people unfamiliar with the terminology often find the term "secular cleric" puzzling, sometimes taking it for an oxymoron. The term does indeed suggest an awkward hybridity, which makes it fitting for a group that was caught between the religious and the worldly. On the one hand, the secular clergy were defined and set apart by their ecclesiastical office and religious functions, and of course most secular clerics *were* deeply involved in religious activities. Yet most clerics also failed, as their critics charged and as this study has amply demonstrated, to consistently follow the guidelines designed to set them apart as a distinctive, unworldly, quasi-angelic group. Throughout this work I have stressed the various moral, social, and psychological tensions that this group faced, and many of these stemmed from the very ambiguity encompassed in the term "secular clergy." All humans face a struggle to live up to the ideals and behaviors expected of them, but the secular clergy, faced with unusually demanding moral expectations combined with circumstances that often discouraged conformity to those expectations, experienced more challenges than most. To be a secular cleric was to be torn between the demands of religion and the world.

Yet the very fact that secular clerics had to straddle the sacred and the worldly was a large part of what made them so influential and so much a part of the creativity and ferment associated with the Twelfth-Century Renaissance. They could bring the skills of reading, writing, and logic, long cultivated almost solely for religious purposes, into the secular world in the spheres of government, economy, and even secular aristocratic culture. If Jaeger and Aurell are correct, it was partly the clerical presence among the social and political elites that made a number of profound changes in aristocratic culture possible.[1] Secular clerics had a huge part in the creation of the universities and the book trade, the accumulation of knowledge about the natural world, and the gradual rise of the legal and medical professions, all developments that had tremendous secular as well as religious impact over the long term. Even in religious terms, the worldly presence of the secular clergy was crucial, for it was what allowed them to do their primary job, to influence and Christianize the laity. Reformers focused heavily on the intersection of the sacred and the secular because of their fear of the impact of worldly entanglements on the secular clergy and, for that matter, on Christians in general. We too should focus on this intersection, though for historical rather than religious reasons. Historians are well aware of the constant entanglement between religious and secular life throughout the Middle Ages, but there is still a tendency for religiously minded scholars to focus on religious topics and secularly minded scholars to focus on secular ones, partly for practical reasons, but also out of a modern desire to divide the religious and the secular into distinct spheres. Medieval studies, however, could benefit from greater attention to the contentious, stressful, and yet creative zone in which the sacred and the profane met, intermingled, and clashed.

More particularly, medieval studies could benefit from more work on the secular clergy. This surprisingly neglected group can provide extremely fertile ground for future research. Any of the major topics discussed in this book could be pursued further, particularly if one moves beyond the temporal and geographical boundaries of this study. For instance, we are beginning to get individual studies concerning clerical marriage, concubinage, and celibacy, but only after many more of these have been carried out will our understanding of the history of clerical celibacy be fully satisfactory. For some topics, study of the secular clergy has hardly begun. At the same time, broad-ranging studies of the clergy like this one need to be carried out for different periods and places. To what degree did the social, economic, cultural, and religious position of the clergy vary from society to society? How did such specific developments as the rise of the friars influence the position of the clergy over time? Conversely, to what degree did the role of the clergy operate similarly across cultures, allowing the clergy to help bind together the cultures of Catholic Europe and to distinguish Western Europe from other cultures? Indeed, to what degree did the clergy help facilitate what Bartlett has described as the "The Making of Europe" in the central Middle Ages?[2] Much more research on the secular clergy is needed for an adequate understanding of medieval history, and unless we incorporate the secular clergy more fully into our picture of medieval society, that picture will be woefully incomplete.

---

[1] See Chapter 3, section 2. [2] Bartlett, *Making of Europe*.

In the introduction, I made the argument that the secular clergy contributed more to the Twelfth-Century Renaissance, broadly defined, than any other group. Readers can judge for themselves whether I have made good on the claim, and judgments may differ. Nonetheless, there can be no doubt that this understudied group was very significant. Indeed, the sheer number of areas of life in which the secular clergy had great influence and brought about significant historical development is a mark of their importance within medieval society. It is worth ending, however, by noting that the influence of many of the changes the secular clergy wrought in the long twelfth century, or in the longer sweep of the Middle Ages, are still felt today. Anyone reading a book or watching a movie on King Arthur and his knights, or studying Arthurian literature, is dealing with a literary and cultural phenomenon that had earlier medieval roots but was first widely popularized by Geoffrey of Monmouth, a secular cleric working in Oxford in the twelfth century. Max Weber and others have considered bureaucratization as one of the hallmarks of modern society, and secular clerics had a huge role in the early stages of the slow development of modern European bureaucracies, both in the long twelfth century and in later periods.[3] Finally, anyone studying or teaching in a university is working within a kind of institution which was largely invented by secular clerics. The secular clergy were therefore a group that had a profound influence not only on medieval history but also on the history of the modern world.

---

[3] Weber himself recognized the importance of England's bureaucracy in the period after the Norman Conquest, though in a feudal and patrimonial context, and noted the reliance of English kings on clerical benefices: Max Weber, *Economy and Society: An Outline of Interpretive Sociology*, 3 vols. (New York, 1968), 3:970, 1036, 1089. For an interesting discussion of medieval papal bureaucracy and law in Weberian terms, see d'Avray, *Medieval Religious Rationalities: A Weberian analysis*, 122–49.

Bibliography

MANUSCRIPT SOURCES

Cambridge: Cambridge University Library

MS Ee.6.40.	Manuscript belonging to Gerard (son of Lewin?)
MS Kk.4.21.	Manuscript donated by Lawrence, archdeacon of Bedford
Peterborough D & C MS 1.	Peterborough Cartulary
Add. MS 3020 and 3021.	Thorney Cartulary

Cambridge: Corpus Christi College Library

MS 190, p. 361	Copy of Serlo of Bayeux's poem on priests' sons
MS 416.	Manuscript belonging to William, priest of Stradsett

Cambridge: Sidney Sussex College Library

MS 95.	Compilation of Marian Miracles

Cambridge: Trinity College Library

MS B.2.31.	Manuscript belonging to Ralph of Sarre
MS B.5.2.	Bible of Archdeacon Nicholas
MSS B.5.4, B.5.6, B.5.7	Manuscripts of Herbert of Bosham
MS B.14.8.	Sermons of Peter Maude
MS O.2.45, pp. 342–4	Copy of the poem "Convocacio Sacerdotum"

Chichester: West Sussex Record Office

Chichester Cathedral MS Liber Y.	Chichester Cathedral Cartulary

Exeter: Exeter Cathedral Archive

Dean & Chapter	Charter 289
Dean & Chapter	Charter 611

Lincoln: Lincoln Cathedral Library

MS 1.	Bible of Archdeacon Nicholas
MS 15.	Manuscript of Ralph Niger
MS 18.	Manuscript donated by David, archdeacon of Huntingdon
MS 171.	Manuscript donated by Jordan the Treasurer
MS 174.	Manuscript donated by Hamo the Chancellor
MS 176.	Manuscript donated by Ralph Medicus

London: British Library

Add. MS 35296.	Spalding Cartulary
Cotton MS Caligula A XII.	Pipewell Cartulary
Cotton MS Claudius D XIII.	Binham Cartulary
Cotton MS Domitian A X.	Rochester Cartulary
Cotton MS Vespasian B IX.	Account of the Foundation of St. Bartholomew's Hospital

Cotton MS Vespasian E X.   William de Montibus, "Numerale"
Harley MS 3650.   Kenilworth Cartulary
Royal MS 3 B X.   Gervase of Chichester, "Commentary on Malachi"
Royal MS 4 C X.   Manuscript belonging to Hamo of Rochester
Royal MS 7 C XIV.   Peter of Cornwall, "Pantheologus"
Royal MS 7 F III.   Manuscript produced by scribe of Robert Bonn
Royal MS 8 G II.   William de Montibus, "Distinctions"
Royal MS 9 E XII.   Manuscript belonging to Master David of London
Royal MS 10 C V.   Manuscript annotated by an English student in Paris

London: Lambeth Palace
MS 105.   Clerical Formulary
MS 458 part 2.   Sermons of Robert Pullen

London: Westminster Abbey Archives
Charter 13155.
Muniments MS 13167.   Charter Roll

New York City: Morgan Library
MS 81.   Worksop Bestiary (accessed online)

Oxford: All Souls College Library
MS 82.   Manuscript belonging to Master Alured

Oxford: Bodleian Library
Auct. MS D.1.10.   Manuscript belonging to Alfred of Hemel Hempstead
Auct. MS E.inf.6.   Manuscript of Herbert of Bosham
Bodleian MS 449.   Sermons of Bartholomew of Exeter
Bodleian MS 656, fols.   John of Leicester's poem on Godfrey de Lucy
  149v–150r.
Bodleian MS 672.   Manuscript version of Lucian's *De Laude Cestrie*
Bodleian MS 725.   Manuscript belonging to Master Robert de Hanc
Bodleian MS 729.   Manuscript belonging to Master Alard
Bodleian MS 851, fol. 75v. Copy of the poem "Convocacio Sacerdotum"
Digby MS 96.   Godwin of Salisbury, "Meditationes"
Jesus College, Oxford MS 26. Manuscript belonging to Master Alured
Jesus College, Oxford MS 66. Manuscript belonging to Roger, vice-dean of Hereford
Laud Lat. MS 17.   Clerical Formulary
Laud. Misc. MS 71.   Sermons of Thomas Agnellus
Rawlinson MS D 1225.   Manuscript formerly at St. Chad's, Shrewsbury
Rawlinson MS G 62.   Manuscript belonging to Peter of Waltham
Wood empt. MS 13.   Sermons of Alexander Neckam

Oxford: Corpus Christi College Library
MS 32.   Collection of Clerical Anecdotes

PUBLISHED PRIMARY SOURCES

Abū Ma'šar. *The Abbreviation of the Introduction to Astrology together with the Medieval Latin Translation of Adelard of Bath*, edited by Charles Burnett, Keiji Yamamoto, and Michio Yano. Leiden, 1994.

Adam of Eynsham. *Magna Vita Sancti Hugonis: The Life of St. Hugh of Lincoln*, edited by Decima L. Douie and David Hugh Farmer. Repr. with corrections. 2 vols. Oxford, 1985.

Adam of Petit Pont. "Adam of Petit Pont's *De Utensilibus*." In *Teaching and Learning Latin in Thirteenth-Century England*, edited by Tony Hunt, 1:165–76. Woodbridge, 1991.

Adams, Norma, and Charles Donahue, eds. *Select Cases from the Ecclesiastical Courts of the Province of Canterbury, c.1200–1301*. Publications of the Selden Society, vol. 95. London, 1981.

Adelard of Bath. *Adelard of Bath, Conversations with his Nephew: On the Same and the Different, Questions on Natural Science, and On Birds*, edited by Charles Burnett. Cambridge, 1998.

Adgar. *Le gracial*, edited by Pierre Kunstmann. Ottawa, 1982.

Ailred of Rievaulx. "Liber de Spirituali Amicitia." In *Patrologia Latina*, edited by J.-P. Migne, vol. 195, 659–702. Paris, 1855.

Ailred of Rievaulx . "On the Saints of the Church of Hexham." In *The Priory of Hexham*, edited by James Raine, 173–203. Surtees Society, vol. 44. Durham, 1864.

Alexander Neckam. *De Naturis Rerum Libri Duo: With the Poem of the Same Author, De Laudibus Divinæ Sapientiæ*, edited by Thomas Wright. Rolls Series. London, 1863.

Alexander Neckam. *Alexandri Neckam Sacerdos ad Altare*, edited by Christopher James McDonough. Corpus Christianorum, Continuatio Mediaevalis, vol. 227. Turnhout, 2010.

Alexander of Ashby. "De Artificioso Modo Predicandi." In *Alexandri Essebiensis Opera Omnia*, edited by Franco Morenzoni. 2 vols. 1:1–104. Turnhout, 2004.

Alfred of Beverley. *Annales, sive Historia de Gestis Regum Britanniæ*, edited by Thomas Hearne. Oxford, 1716.

Alfred of Shareshill. *Alfred of Sareshel's Commentary on the* Metheora *of Aristotle*, edited by James K. Otte. Leiden, 1988.

Ambroise. *The History of the Holy War: Ambroise's* Estoire de la guerre sainte, edited by Marianne Ailes and Malcolm Barber. 2 vols. Woodbridge, 2003.

Anselm. *S. Anselmi Cantuariensis Archiepiscopi Opera Omnia*, edited by Franciscus Salesius Schmitt. 6 vols. London, 1946–61.

Anstruther, Robert, ed. *Epistolae Herberti de Losinga, Primi Episcopi Norwicensis, Osberti de Clara et Elmeri, Prioris Cantuariensis*, Publications of the Caxton society, vol. 5. London, 1846.

Arnold, Thomas, ed. *Memorials of St. Edmund's Abbey*. 3 vols. Rolls Series. London, 1890–6.

Arnulf of Lisieux. *The Letters of Arnulf of Lisieux*, edited by Frank Barlow. Camden Society, 3rd series, vol. 61. London, 1939.

"Babio," edited by Andrea Dessì Fulgheri. In *Commedie latine del XII e XIII secolo*. Vol. 2. 129–301. Genoa, 1980.

Baldwin of Ford. *Opera*, edited by David N. Bell. Corpus Christianorum, Continuatio Mediaevalis 99. Turnhout, 1991.

Barlow, Frank, ed. *English Episcopal Acta. 11, Exeter, 1046–1184*. Oxford, 1996.

Barlow, Frank, ed. *English Episcopal Acta. 12, Exeter, 1186–1257*. Oxford, 1996.

Barraclough, Geoffrey, ed. *Facsimiles of Early Cheshire Charters*. Blackpool, 1957.

Barraclough, Geoffrey, ed. *The Charters of the Anglo-Norman Earls of Chester, c.1071–1237*. Record Society of Lancashire and Cheshire, vol. 126. Chester, 1988.

Barrow, Julia, ed. *English Episcopal Acta. 7, Hereford, 1079–1234*. Oxford, 1993.

Bates, David, ed. *Regesta Regum Anglo-Normannorum: The Acta of William I, 1066–1087*. Oxford, 1998.

Bearman, Robert, ed. *Charters of the Redvers Family and the Earldom of Devon, 1090–1217*, Devon and Cornwall Record Society, n.s. vol. 37. Exeter, 1994.

Biddle, Martin, Frank Barlow, Olof von Feilitzen, and D. J. Keene. *Winchester in the Early Middle Ages: An Edition and Discussion of the Winton Domesday*. Oxford, 1976.

Bird, William Henry Benbow. *Calendar of the Manuscripts of the Dean and Chapter of Wells. Vol. 1. Register Books*. London, 1907.

Black, Winston. "Henry of Huntingdon's Lapidary Rediscovered and his *Anglicanus Ortus* Reassembled." *Mediaeval Studies* 68 (2006), 43–87.

Blake, E. O., ed. *Liber Eliensis*. Camden Society, 3rd series, vol. 92. London, 1962.

Bode, Georg Heinrich, ed. *Scriptores Rerum Mythicarum Latini Tres Romae Nuper Reperti*. 2 vols. Zell, 1834.

Brand, Paul, ed. *The Earliest English Law Reports*. 4 vols. Publications of the Selden Society, vols. 111–12, 122–3. London, 1996–2007.

Brown, R. Allen, ed. *The Memoranda Roll for the Tenth Year of the Reign of King John, 1207–8*, Publications of the Pipe Roll Society, n.s. vol. 31. London, 1957.

Brown, Vivien, ed. *Eye Priory Cartulary and Charters*. 2 vols., Suffolk Charters, vols. 12–13. Woodbridge, 1992–4.

Burton, Janet E., ed. *English Episcopal Acta. 5, York, 1070–1154*. Oxford, 1988.

Busard, H. L. L., ed. *The First Latin Translation of Euclid's Elements Commonly Ascribed to Adelard of Bath*. Toronto, 1983.

Busard, H. L. L., ed. *Johannes de Tinemue's Redaction of Euclid's* Element, *the So-called Adelard III Version*. 2 vols. Stuttgart, 2001.

Busard, H. L. L., and Menso Folkerts, eds. *Robert of Chester's (?) Redaction of Euclid's* Elements *the So-called Adelard II Version*. 2 vols. Basel, 1992.

Camargo, Martin, ed. *Medieval Rhetorics of Prose Composition: Five English* Artes Dictandi *and their Tradition*. Binghamton, 1995.

Chardri. *Le petit plet*, edited by Brian S. Merrilees. Anglo-Norman Texts, vol. 20. Oxford, 1970.

Chardri. *La vie des set dormanz*, edited by Brian S. Merrilees. Anglo-Norman Texts, vol. 35 London, 1977.

Cheney, C. R., and Mary G. Cheney, eds. *The Letters of Pope Innocent III (1198–1216) Concerning England and Wales*. Oxford, 1967.

Cheney, C. R., and E. John, eds. *English Episcopal Acta. 3, Canterbury, 1193–1205*. Oxford, 1986.

Cheney, C. R., and Bridgett E. A. Jones, eds. *English Episcopal Acta. 2, Canterbury, 1162–1190*. Oxford, 1986.

Cheney, C. R., and W. H. Semple, eds. *Selected Letters of Pope Innocent III Concerning England (1198–1216)*. London, 1953.

Cheney, Mary, David Smith, Christopher Brooke, and Philippa M. Hoskin, eds. *English Episcopal Acta. 33, Worcester, 1062–1185*. Oxford, 2007.

Cheney, Mary, David Smith, Christopher Brooke, and Philippa M. Hoskin, eds. *English Episcopal Acta. 34, Worcester, 1186–1218*. Oxford, 2008.

Clark, Cecily, ed. *The Peterborough Chronicle, 1070–1154*. Oxford, 1958.

Clay, Charles T., ed. *York Minster Fasti*. 2 vols. Yorkshire Archaeological Society Record Series, vols. 123–4. Wakefield, 1958–9.

Colker, Marvin L., ed. *Analecta Dublinensia: Three Medieval Latin Texts in the Library of Trinity College, Dublin*. Cambridge, MA, 1975.

Constable, Giles, and Bernard Smith, eds. *Libellus de Diversis Ordinibus et Professionibus qui sunt in Aecclesia*. Oxford, 1972.

"Constitutio Domus Regis." In *Dialogus de Scaccario and Constitutio Domus Regis*, edited by Emilie Amt and S. D. Church, 195–215. Oxford, 2007.

Craster, H. H. E. "The Red Book of Durham." *English Historical Review* 40 (1925), 504–32.

Curia Regis Rolls. Vols. 1–7. London, 1922–35.

Curley, Michael J. "A New Edition of John of Cornwall's *Prophetia Merlini*." *Speculum* 57 (1982), 217–49.

Daniel of Beccles. *Urbanus Magnus Danielis Becclesiensis*, edited by J. Gilbart Smyly. Dublin, 1939.

Darlington, Reginald R., ed. *The Vita Wulfstani of William of Malmesbury*, Camden Society, 3rd series, vol. 40. London, 1928.

David, Charles Wendell, ed. *De Expugnatione Lyxbonensi. The Conquest of Lisbon*. New York, 1936.

Davies, W. S. "Giraldus Cambrensis: *De Invectionibus*." *Y Cymmrodor* 30 (1920), 1–248.

Davis, H. W., Charles Johnson, H. A. Cronne, and R. H. C. Davis, eds. *Regesta Regum Anglo-Normannorum, 1066–1154*. Oxford, 1913–69.

Davis, R. H. C., ed. *The Kalendar of Abbot Samson of Bury St. Edmunds and Related Documents*. Camden Society, 3rd series, vol. 84. London, 1954.

"De Clericis et Rustico," edited by Enzo Cadoni. In *Commedie latine del XII e XIII secolo*. Vol. 2. 351–77. Genoa, 1980.

Delisle, Léopold, ed. *Rouleaux des morts du IXe au XVe siècle*. Paris, 1866.

Dickinson, J. C., and P. T. Ricketts. "The Anglo-Norman Chronicle of Wigmore Abbey." *Transactions of the Woolhope Naturalists' Field Club* 39 (1969), 413–46.

Dobson, E. J. *Moralities on the Gospels: A New Source of Ancrene Wisse*. Oxford, 1975.

Douglas, D. C., ed. *Feudal Documents from the Abbey of Bury St. Edmunds*. London, 1932.

Downer, L. J., ed. *Leges Henrici Primi*. Oxford, 1972.

Dugdale, William. *Monasticon Anglicanum*. 6 vols. in 8. London, 1846.

Duggan, Anne, ed. *The Correspondence of Thomas Becket, Archbishop of Canterbury, 1162–1170*. 2 vols. Oxford, 2000.

Duggan, Charles. "Decretals of Alexander III to England." In *Miscellanea Rolando Bandinelli, Papa Alessandro III*, edited by Filippo Liotta, 85–151. Siena, 1986.

Eadmer. *Eadmeri Historia Novorum in Anglia*, edited by Martin Rule. Rolls Series. London, 1884.

Easting, Robert, ed. *The Revelation of the Monk of Eynsham*. Early English Text Society, vol. 318. Oxford, 2002.

Elvey, G. R., ed. *Luffield Priory Charters*. 2 vols. Publications of the Northamptonshire Record Society, vols. 22, 26. Oxford, 1968–75.

Etienne de Fougères. *Le livre des manières*, edited by R. Anthony Lodge. Geneva, 1979.

Ewert, A., ed. *Gui de Warewic, roman du XIIIe siècle*. 2 vols. Paris, 1932.

Faral, Edmond. *Les arts poétiques du XIIe et XIIIe siècle*. Paris, 1962.

Farmer, Hugh. "The Vision of Orm." *Analecta Bollandiana* 75 (1957), 72–82.

Farrer, William, and Charles T. Clay, eds. *Early Yorkshire Charters*. 13 vols. Yorkshire Archaeological Society Record Series, Extra Series. Edinburgh and Wakefield, 1914–65.

Fonge, Charles, ed. *The Cartulary of St Mary's Collegiate Church, Warwick*. Woodbridge, 2004.

Foreville, R., and J. Leclercq. "Un débat sur le sacerdoce des moines au XIIe siècle." In *Analecta Monastica*, edited by Raymonde Foreville, J. Leclercq, J. Morson, and H. Farmer, 8–118. Studia Anselmiana, vol. 41. Rome, 1957.

Foreville, Raymonde, and Gillian Keir, eds. *The Book of St Gilbert*. Oxford, 1987.

Formoy, Beryl E. R. "A Maritime Indenture of 1212." *English Historical Review* 41 (1926), 556–9.

Foster, C. W., and Kathleen Major, eds. *The Registrum Antiquissimum of the Cathedral Church of Lincoln*. 10 vols. Publications of the Lincoln Record Society, vols. 27–9, 32, 34, 41, 46, 51, 62, 67. Hereford, 1931–73.

Fowler, G. Herbert. "Rolls of the Justices in Eyre at Bedford, 1202." *Publications of the Bedfordshire Historical Record Society* 1 (1913), 133–247.

Fowler, G. Herbert, ed. *A Digest of the Charters Preserved in the Cartulary of the Priory of Dunstable*, Bedfordshire Historical Record Society Publications, vol. 10. Aspley Guise, 1926.

Fowler, J. T., ed. *The Coucher Book of Selby*. 2 vols. The Yorkshire Archaeological and Topographical Association Record Series, vols. 10 and 13. Durham, 1891–3.

Franklin, M. J., ed. *The Cartulary of Daventry Priory*. Publications of the Northamptonshire Record Society, vol. 35. Northampton, 1988.

Franklin, M. J., ed. *English Episcopal Acta. 8, Winchester, 1070–1204*. Oxford, 1993.

Franklin, M. J., ed. *English Episcopal Acta. 14, Coventry and Lichfield, 1072–1159*. Oxford, 1997.

Franklin, M. J., ed. *English Episcopal Acta. 16, Coventry and Lichfield, 1160–1182*. Oxford, 1998.

Franklin, M. J., ed. *English Episcopal Acta. 17, Coventry and Lichfield, 1183–1208*. Oxford, 1998.

Frere, Walter Howard. *The Use of Sarum*. 2 vols. Cambridge, 1898–1901.

Gautier Dalché, Patrick. *Du Yorkshire à l'Inde: une "géographie" urbaine et maritime de la fin du XIIe siècle (Roger de Howden?)*. Geneva, 2005.

Geffrei Gaimar. *Estoire des Engleis. History of the English*, edited by Ian Short. Oxford, 2009.

Geoffrey of Monmouth. *The Vita Merlini*, edited by John Jay Parry. University of Illinois Studies in Language and Literature, vol. 10, no 3. Urbana, 1925.

Geoffrey of Monmouth. *The History of the Kings of Britain: An Edition and Translation of De Gestis Britonum (Historia Regum Britanniae)*, edited by Michael D. Reeve and Neil Wright. Woodbridge, 2007.

Geoffrey of Vinsauf. "De Tribus Sociis," edited by Enzo Cadoni. In *Commedie latine del XII e XIII secolo*. Vol. 2. 303–49. Genoa, 1980.

Geoffrey of Vinsauf. *Poetria Nova*, edited by Margaret F. Nims and Martin Camargo. Rev. ed. Toronto, 2010.

Gerald of Wales. *Giraldi Cambrensis Opera*, edited by J. S. Brewer, James F. Dimock, and George F. Warner. 8 vols. Rolls Series. London, 1861–91.

Gerald of Wales. *Speculum Duorum, or A Mirror of Two Men*, edited by Brian Dawson, Robert Burchard Constantijn Huygens, Yves Lefevre, and Michael Richter. Cardiff, 1974.

Gerald of Wales. *Expugnatio Hibernica: The Conquest of Ireland*, edited by A. B. Scott and F. X. Martin. Dublin, 1978.

Gervase of Canterbury. *The Historical Works of Gervase of Canterbury*, edited by William Stubbs. 2 vols. Rolls Series. London, 1879–80.

Gervase of Tilbury. *Otia Imperialia: Recreation for an Emperor*, edited by S. E. Banks and J. W. Binns. Oxford, 2002.

Gervers, Michael, ed. *The Cartulary of the Knights of St. John of Jerusalem in England: Essex*. 2 vols. Oxford, 1982.

Gibbons, A., ed. *Liber Antiquus de Ordinationibus Vicariarum Tempore Hugonis Wells, Lincolniensis Episcopi, 1209–1235*. Lincoln, 1888.

Gibbs, Marion, ed. *Early Charters of the Cathedral Church of St. Paul, London*. Camden Society Society, 3rd series, vol. 58. London, 1939.

Gilbert Foliot. *The Letters and Charters of Gilbert Foliot, Abbot of Gloucester (1139–48), Bishop of Hereford (1148–63), and London (1163–87)*, edited by Z. N. Brooke, Adrian Morey, and C. N. L. Brooke. Cambridge, 1967.

Godber, Joyce, ed. *The Cartulary of Newnham Priory*. 2 vols. Bedford Historical Record Society Publications, vol. 43. Bedford, 1963–4.

Green, Monica H., ed. *The Trotula: A Medieval Compendium of Women's Medicine*. Philadelphia, 2001.

Greenway, Diana E., ed. *Charters of the Honour of Mowbray, 1107–1191*. London, 1972.

Greenway, Diana E., and Leslie Watkiss, eds. *The Book of the Foundation of Walden Monastery*. Oxford, 1999.

Gribbin, Joseph A., and Martin Brett, eds. *English Episcopal Acta. 28, Canterbury, 1070–1136*. Oxford, 2004.

Guernes de Pont-Sainte-Maxence. *La vie de saint Thomas Becket*, edited by Emmanuel Walberg. Paris, 1936.

Hale, William, ed. *The Domesday of St. Paul's*. Camden Society, vol. 69. London, 1858.

Hall, G. D. G., ed. *The Treatise on the Laws and Customs of the Realm of England, Commonly called Glanvill*. Oxford, 1993.

Hall, Hubert, ed. *The Red Book of the Exchequer*. 3 vols. Rolls Series London, 1896.

Hall, Hubert, ed. *The Pipe Roll of the Bishopric of Winchester for the Fourth Year of the Pontificate of Peter des Roches, 1208–1209*. London, 1903.

Hardy, Thomas Duffus, ed. *Rotuli Litterarum Clausarum in Turri Londinensi Asservati*. London, 1833.

Hardy, Thomas Duffus, ed. *Rotuli de Oblatis et Finibus in Turri Londinensi Asservati, Tempore Regis Johannis*. London, 1835.

Hardy, Thomas Duffus, ed. *Rotuli Litterarum Patentium in Turri Londinensi Asservati*. London, 1835.

Hardy, Thomas Duffus, ed. *Rotuli Chartarum in Turri Londinensi Asservati*. London, 1837.

Hardy, Thomas Duffus, ed. *Rotuli de Liberate ac de Misis et Praestitis, Regnante Johanne*. London, 1844.

Harper-Bill, Christopher, ed. *Blythburgh Priory Cartulary*. 2 vols. Suffolk Charters, vols. 2–3. Woodbridge, 1980–81.

Harper-Bill, Christopher, ed. *English Episcopal Acta. 6, Norwich, 1070–1214*. Oxford, 1990.

Harper-Bill, Christopher, and Richard Mortimer, eds. *Stoke-by-Clare Cartulary: BL Cotton Appx. xxi*. 3 vols. Suffolk Charters, vols. 4–6. Woodbridge, 1982–4.

Hart, William Henry, and Ponsonby A. Lyons, eds. *Cartularium Monasterii de Rameseia*. 3 vols. Rolls Series. London, 1884–93.

Henry of Huntingdon. *Historia Anglorum: The History of the English People*, edited by Greenway, Diana E. Oxford, 1996.

Henry of Huntingdon. *Anglicanus Ortus: A Verse Herbal of the Twelfth Century*, edited by Winston Black. Toronto, 2012.

Holden, A. J., ed. *Le Roman de Waldef.* Geneva, 1984.

Holden, Anthony J., Stewart Gregory, and David Crouch, eds. *History of William Marshal.* 3 vols. London, 2002–6.

Holdsworth, C. J., ed. *Rufford Charters.* 4 vols. Thoroton Society Record Series, vols. 29, 30, 32, 34. Nottingham, 1972–81.

Holland, T. E. "The University of Oxford in the Twelfth Century." In *Collectanea II*, edited by Montague Burrows, 137–92. Oxford, 1890.

Hollings, Marjory, ed. *The Red Book of Worcester.* 4 vols. London, 1934–50.

Holt, N. R., ed. *The Pipe Roll of the Bishopric of Winchester, 1210–1211.* Manchester, 1964.

Holtzmann, Walther, ed. *Papsturkunden in England.* 3 vols. Berlin, 1930–52.

Holtzmann, Walther, Stanley Chodorow, and Charles Duggan, eds. *Decretales Ineditae Saeculi XII*, Monumenta Iuris Canonici. Series B, Corpus Collectionum, vol. 4. Vatican City, 1982.

Holtzmann, Walther, and Eric Waldram Kemp, eds. *Papal Decretals Relating to the Diocese of Lincoln in the Twelfth Century*, Publications of the Lincoln Record Society, vol. 47. Hereford, 1954.

Honorius. *Magistri Honorii Summa "De Iure Canonico Tractaturus,"* edited by Rudolf Weigand, Peter Landau, and Waltraud Kozur. Vatican City, 2004.

Houts, Elisabeth M. C. van, ed. *The Gesta Normannorum Ducum of William of Jumièges, Orderic Vitalis, and Robert of Torigni.* 2 vols. Oxford, 1992–5.

Hudson, John, ed. *Historia Ecclesie Abbendonensis: The History of the Church of Abingdon.* 2 vols. Oxford, 2002–7.

Hue de Rotelande. *Ipomedon: poème de Hue de Rotelande, fin du XIIe siècle*, edited by A. J. Holden. Paris, 1979.

Hue de Rotelande. *Protheslaus*, edited by A. J. Holden. 3 vols. Anglo-Norman Texts, vols. 47–9. London, 1991–3.

Hugh the Chanter. *The History of the Church of York, 1066–1127*, edited by Charles Johnson, M. Brett, C. N. L. Brooke, and M. Winterbottom. Oxford, 1990.

Iohannes, Blund. *Tractatus de Anima*, edited by D. A. Callus, R. W. Hunt, and Michael W. Dunne. 2nd edn. London, 2013.

Jaffé, Philipp, ed. *Regesta Pontificum Romanorum.* 2nd edn. 2 vols. Leipzig, 1885–8.

James, M. R. "Magister Gregorius de Mirabilibus Urbis Romae." *English Historical Review* 32 (1917), 531–54.

Jocelin of Brakelond. *The Chronicle of Jocelin of Brakelond*, edited by H. E. Butler. London, 1949.

John of Ford. *Wulfric of Haselbury*, edited by Maurice Bell. Somerset Record Society, vol. 47 Frome, 1933.

John of Salisbury. *Policraticus sive de Nugis Curialium et de Vestigiis Philosophorum*, edited by Clement C. J. Webb. 2 vols. Oxford, 1909.

John of Salisbury. *The Letters of John of Salisbury*, edited by W. J. Millor, H. E. Butler, and C. N. L. Brooke. 2 vols. Oxford, 1979–86.

John of Salisbury. *The Historia Pontificalis of John of Salisbury*, edited by Marjorie Chibnall. Oxford, 1986.

John of Salisbury. *Ioannis Saresberiensis Metalogicon*, edited by J. B. Hall and K. S. B. Keats-Rohan. Corpus Christianorum, Continuatio Mediaevalis, vol. 98. Turnhout, 1991.

John of Worcester. *The Chronicle of John of Worcester*, edited by Reginald R. Darlington and P. McGurk. 3 vols. Oxford, 1995–8.

Johnson, D. P., ed. *English Episcopal Acta. 26, London, 1189–1228*. Oxford, 2003.

Johnson South, Ted. *Historia de Sancto Cuthberto: A History of Saint Cuthbert and a Record of his Patrimony*. Cambridge, 2002.

Jones, W. H. Rich, ed. *The Register of S. Osmund*. 2 vols. Rolls Series. London, 1883.

Jordan Fantosme. *Jordan Fantosme's Chronicle*, edited by R. C. Johnston. Oxford, 1981.

Joseph Iscanus. *Werke und Briefe*, edited by Ludwig Gompf. Leiden, 1970.

Karn, Nicholas, ed. *English Episcopal Acta. 31, Ely, 1109–1197*. Oxford, 2005.

Karn, Nicholas, ed. *English Episcopal Acta. 42, Ely, 1198–1256*. Oxford, 2013.

Karpinski, Louis Charles, ed. *Robert of Chester's Latin Translation of the Algebra of al-Khwarizmi*. New York, 1915.

Kemp, B. R., ed. *Reading Abbey Cartularies: British Library Manuscripts, Egerton 3031, Harley 1708, and Cotton Vespasian E XXV*. 2 vols., Camden Society, 4th series, vols. 31, 33. London, 1986–7.

Kemp, B. R., ed. *English Episcopal Acta. 18, Salisbury, 1078–1217*. Oxford, 1999.

Kemp, B. R., ed. *Twelfth-Century English Archidiaconal and Vice-Archidiaconal Acta*. The Canterbury and York Society, vol. 92. Woodbridge, 2001.

Kemp, B. R. "The Acta of English Rural Deans in the Later Twelfth and Early Thirteenth Centuries." In *The Foundations of Medieval English Ecclesiastical History: Studies Presented to David Smith*, edited by Philippa M. Hoskin, Christopher Brooke, and Barry Dobson, 139–58. Woodbridge, 2005.

Lawn, Brian, ed. *The Prose Salernitan Questions*. London, 1979.

Laȝamon. *Laȝamon: Brut*, edited by G. L. Brook and R. F. Leslie. 2 vols. Early English Text Society, vols. 250, 277. London, 1963–78.

Lees, Beatrice A., ed. *Records of the Templars in England in the Twelfth Century*. London, 1935.

Liverani, Francesco, ed. *Spicilegium Liberianum*. Florence, 1863.

Long, R. James. "Alfred of Sareshel's Commentary on the Pseudo-Aristotelian *De Plantis*: A Critical Edition." *Mediaeval Studies* 47 (1985), 125–67.

Lovatt, Marie, ed. *English Episcopal Acta. 20, York, 1154–1181*. Oxford, 2000.

Lovatt, Marie, ed. *English Episcopal Acta. 27, York, 1189–1212*. Oxford, 2004.

Luard, Henry Richards, ed. *Annales Monastici*. 5 vols. London, 1864–9.

Lucentini, Paolo, and V. Perrone Compagni. *I testi e i codici di Ermete nel Medioevo*. Firenze, 2001.

Lucian of Chester. *Extracts from the Liber Luciani De Laude Cestrie*, edited by M. V. Taylor. Lancashire and Cheshire Record Society, vol. 64, part 1. [London], 1912.

Lunt, William E. "The Text of the Ordinance of 1184 Concerning an Aid for the Holy Land." *English Historical Review* 37 (1922), 235–42.

Lunt, William E., ed. *The Valuation of Norwich*. Oxford, 1926.

Maitland, Frederic William, ed. *Three Rolls of the King's Court in the Reign of King Richard the First, A. D. 1194–1195*, Publications of the Pipe Roll Society, vol. 14. London, 1891.

Major, Kathleen, ed. *Acta Stephani Langton Cantuariensis Archiepiscopi A. D. 1207–1228*. Canterbury and York Record Series, vol. 50. Oxford, 1950.

Malden, A. R. *The Canonization of Saint Osmund*. Salisbury, 1901.

Mason, Emma, ed. *The Beauchamp Cartulary Charters, 1100–1268*. Publications of the Pipe Roll Society, n.s. vol. 43. London, 1980.

Mason, Emma, ed. *Westminster Abbey Charters, 1066–c.1214*. London Record Society Publications, vol. 25. London, 1988.

Maurach, Gregor. "Daniel von Morley 'Philosophia'." *Mittellateinisches Jahrbuch* 14 (1979), 204–55.

Mayr-Harting, Henry, ed. *The Acta of the Bishops of Chichester, 1075–1207.* Canterbury and York Record Series, vol. 130. Oxford, 1964.

Meyer, P. "Melior et Ydoine." *Romania* 37 (1908), 235–44.

Meyer, P. "Notice du MS. 25970 de la bibliothèque Phillipps (Cheltenham)." *Romania* 37 (1908), 209–35.

Minio-Paluello, L., ed. *Twelfth Century Logic; Texts and Studies. Vol. 1. Adam Balsamiensis Parvipontani Ars Disserendi.* Rome, 1956.

Moore, Norman, ed. *The Book of the Foundation of St. Bartholomew's Church in London.* Early English Text Society, vol. 163. London, 1923.

Moore, Stuart A., ed. *Cartularium Monasterii Sancti Johannis Baptiste de Colecestria.* 2 vols. Roxburgh Club. London, 1897.

Morris, R., ed. *Old English Homilies of the Twelfth Century.* Early English Text Society, vol. 53. London, 1873.

Mullally, Evelyn, ed. *The Deeds of the Normans in Ireland. La geste des engleis en Yrlande.* Dublin, 2002.

Narducci, Enrico. "Intorno a due trattati inediti d'abaco." *Bullettino di bibliografica e di storia delle scienze matematiche e fisiche* 15 (1882), 111–62.

Neininger, Falko, ed. *English Episcopal Acta. 15, London, 1076–1187.* Oxford, 1999.

Nigel of Whiteacre. *Nigellus de Longchamp dit Wireker. Vol. 1 Introduction, Tractatus Contra Curiales et Officiales Clericos,* edited by André Boutemy. Paris, 1959.

Nigel of Whiteacre. *Nigel de Longchamps: Speculum Stultorum,* edited by John H. Mozley and Robert R. Raymo. Berkeley, 1960.

Ninth Report of the Royal Commission of Historical Manuscripts, Appendix, London, 1883.

Öberg, Jan, ed. *Serlon de Wilton: Poèmes Latins.* Stockholm, 1965.

Orderic Vitalis. *The Ecclesiastical History of Orderic Vitalis,* edited by Marjorie Chibnall. 6 vols. Oxford, 1969–80.

Oschinsky, Dorothea, ed. *Walter of Henley and other Treatises on Estate Management and Accounting.* Oxford, 1971.

Palgrave, Francis, ed. *Rotuli Curiæ Regis. Rolls and Records of the Court Held Before the King's Justiciars or Justices.* 2 vols. London, 1835.

Paris, Gaston. "Le donnei des amants." *Romania* 25 (1896), 497–541.

Pascal, Paul, ed. *Concilium Romarici Montis,* Bryn Mawr Latin Commentaries. Bryn Mawr, 1993.

Patterson, Robert B., ed. *Earldom of Gloucester Charters; The Charters and Scribes of the Earls and Countesses of Gloucester to A.D. 1217.* Oxford, 1973.

Peckham, W. D., ed. *The Chartulary of the High Church of Chichester.* Sussex Record Society, vol. 46. Lewes, 1946.

Peter of Blois. *Opera,* edited by, J. P. Migne. *Patrologia Latina,* vol. 207. Paris, 1855.

Peter of Blois . *The Later Letters of Peter of Blois,* edited by Elizabeth Revell. Oxford, 1993.

Peter of Blois. *Petri Blesensis Tractatus Duo: "Passio Raginaldi, Principis Antiochie," "Conquestio de Dilatione Vie Ierusolimitane,"* edited by R. B. C. Huygens. Corpus Christianorum, Continuatio Mediaevalis 194. Turnhout, 2002.

Peter of Waltham. *Remediarium Conversorum: A Synthesis in Latin of Moralia in Job by Gregory the Great,* edited by Joseph Gildea. Villanova, 1984.

Philippe de Thaon. *Le Bestiaire de Philippe de Thaün,* edited by Emmanuel Walberg. Lund, 1900.

Philippe de Thaon. *Le livre de Sibile,* edited by Hugh Shields. Anglo-Norman Texts, vol. 37. London, 1979.

Philippe de Thaon. *Comput (MS BL Cotton Nero A. V),* edited by Ian Short. London, 1984.

Pipe Rolls. *The Great Rolls of the Pipe*, Pipe Roll Society, 1884–present.

Powicke, F. M., and C. R. Cheney, eds. *Councils and Synods: With Other Documents Relating to the English Church. Vol. 2, Part 1, 1205–1265*. Oxford, 1964.

Raine, James. *Catalogi Veteres Librorum Ecclesiae Cathedralis Dunelmensis*. Surtees Society, vol. 7. London, 1838.

Raine, James. "Vita Oswini Regis." In *Miscellanea Biographica*, 1–59. Surtees Society, vol. 8. London, 1838.

Raine, James, ed. *The Historians of the Church of York and its Archbishops*. 3 vols. Rolls Series. London, 1879–94.

Ralph Niger. *De Re Militari et Triplici Via Peregrinationis Ierosolimitane (1187/88)*, edited by Ludwig Schmugge. Berlin, 1977.

Ralph of Coggeshall. *Radulphi de Coggeshall Chronicon Anglicanum*, edited by Joseph Stevenson. Rolls Series. London, 1875.

Ralph of Diceto. *Radulfi de Diceto Decani Lundoniensis Opera Historica*, edited by William Stubbs. 2 vols. Rolls Series. London, 1876.

Ramsey, Frances M. R., ed. *English Episcopal Acta. 10, Bath and Wells, 1061–1205*. Oxford, 1995.

Ransford, Rosalind, ed. *The Early Charters of the Augustinian Canons of Waltham Abbey, Essex, 1062–1230*. Woodbridge, 1989.

Reedy, William T., ed. *Basset Charters, c.1120 to 1250*. Publications of the Pipe Roll Society, n.s. vol. 50. London, 1995.

Reginald of Durham. *Libellus de Admirandis Beati Cuthberti Virtutibus*, Surtees Society, vol. 1. London, 1835.

Reginald of Durham. *Libellus de Vita et Miraculis Sancti Godrici, Heremitae de Finchale*, edited by Joseph Stevenson. Surtees Society, vol. 20. London, 1847.

Richard fitzNigel. *Dialogus de Scaccario and Constitutio Domus Regis*, edited by Emilie Amt and S. D. Church. Oxford, 2007.

Richard of Devizes. *The Chronicle of Richard of Devizes of the Time of King Richard the First*, edited by John T. Appleby. London, 1963.

Richard of Hexham. "The History of the Founding of the Church of Hexham." In *The Priory of Hexham*, edited by James Raine, 1–62. Surtees Society, vol. 44. Durham, 1864.

Rigg, A. G. "Henry of Huntingdon's Herbal." *Mediaeval Studies* 65 (2003), 213–92.

Robert Pullen. "Sententiarum Libri Octo." In *Patrologia Latina*, edited by J.-P. Migne, vol. 186, 639–1010. Paris, 1854.

Roberts, Phyllis. "Master Stephen Langton Preaches to the People and Clergy: Sermon Texts from Twelfth-Century Paris." *Traditio* 36 (1980), 237–68.

Robertson, James Craigie, and J. B. Sheppard, eds. *Materials for the History of Thomas Becket, Archbishop of Canterbury*. 7 vols. Rolls Series. London, 1875–85.

[Roger of Howden]. *Gesta Regis Henrici Secundi Benedicti Abbatis*, edited by William Stubbs. 2 vols. Rolls Series. London, 1867.

Roger of Howden. *Chronica Magistri Rogeri de Houedene*, edited by William Stubbs. 4 vols. Rolls Series. London, 1868–71.

Roger of Wendover. *Liber qui Dicitur Flores Historiarum*, edited by Henry G. Hewlett. 3 vols. Rolls Series. London, 1886–9.

Ross, C. D., and Mary Devine, eds. *The Cartulary of Cirencester Abbey, Gloucestershire*. 3 vols. London, 1964–77.

Round, John Horace, ed. *Ancient Charters, Royal and Private, prior to A. D. 1200*, Publications of the Pipe Roll Society, vol. 10. London, 1888.

Royce, David, ed. *Landboc sive Registrum Monasterii Beatae Mariae Virginis et Sancti Cenhelmi de Winchelcumba.* 2 vols. Exeter, 1892–1903.

Salter, H. E., ed. *Eynsham Cartulary.* 2 vols. Oxford Historical Society Record Series, vols. 49, 51. Oxford, 1907–8.

Salter, H. E., ed. *A Cartulary of the Hospital of St John the Baptist.* 3 vols. Oxford Historical Society Record Series, vols. 66, 68–9. Oxford, 1914–17.

Salter, H. E., ed. *Newington Longeville Charters*, Oxfordshire Record Society Record Series, vol. 3. Oxford, 1921.

Salter, H. E., ed. *Cartulary of Oseney Abbey.* 6 vols. Oxford Historical Society Record Series, vols. 89–91, 97–8, 101. Oxford, 1929–36.

Sanson de Nantuil. *Les proverbes de Salemon by Sanson de Nantuil*, edited by Claire Isoz. 3 vols. Anglo-Norman Texts, vols. 44–5, 50. London, 1988–94.

Savage, H. E., ed. *The Great Register of Lichfield Cathedral known as Magnum Registrum Album.* William Salt Archaeological Society Collections. Kendal, 1926.

Schlyter, Börje, ed. *La vie de Thomas Becket par Beneit.* Lund, 1941.

Schneider, Herbert, ed. *Die Konzilsordines des Früh- und Hochmittelalters.* Monumenta Germaniae Historica. Hannover, 1996.

Searle, Eleanor, ed. *The Chronicle of Battle Abbey.* Oxford, 1980.

Simpson, W. Sparrow. "Two Inventories of the Cathedral Church of St. Paul, London." *Archaeologia* 50 (1887), 439–524.

Simund de Freine. *Les œuvres de Simund de Freine*, edited by John E. Matzke. Paris, 1909.

Smith, David M., ed. *English Episcopal Acta. 1, Lincoln, 1067–1185.* Oxford, 1980.

Smith, David M., ed. *English Episcopal Acta. 4, Lincoln, 1186–1206.* Oxford, 1986.

Smith, David M., ed. *The Acta of Hugh of Wells, Bishop of Lincoln, 1209–1235.* Publications of the Lincoln Record Society, vol. 88. Woodbridge, 2000.

Smith, David M., ed. *English Episcopal Acta. 30, Carlisle, 1133–1292.* Oxford, 2005.

Snape, M. G., ed. *English Episcopal Acta. 24, Durham, 1153–1195.* Oxford, 2002.

Snape, M. G., ed. *English Episcopal Acta. 25, Durham, 1196–1237.* Oxford, 2002.

Stacy, N. E., ed. *Surveys of the Estates of Glastonbury Abbey c.1135–1201.* Oxford, 2001.

Stacy, N. E., ed. *Charters and Custumals of Shaftesbury Abbey, 1089–1216.* Oxford, 2006.

Stenton, Doris M., ed. *The Earliest Lincolnshire Assize Rolls, A. D. 1202–1209.* Publications of the Lincoln Record Society, vol. 22. Lincoln, 1926.

Stenton, Doris M., ed. *The Earliest Northamptonshire Assize Rolls, A.D. 1202 and 1203.* Publications of the Northamptonshire Record Society, vol. 5. Lincoln 1930.

Stenton, Doris M., ed. *Pleas before the King or his Justices.* 4 vols. Publications of the Selden Society, vols. 67–8, 83–4. London, 1953–67.

Stenton, F. M., ed. *Documents Illustrative of the Social and Economic History of the Danelaw.* London, 1920.

Stimming, Albert, ed. *Der anglonormannische Boeve de Haumtone.* Halle, 1899.

Stubbs, William, ed. *Itinerarium Peregrinorum et Gesta Regis Ricardi.* Rolls Series. London, 1864.

Stubbs, William, ed. *Epistolæ Cantuarienses, the Letters of the Prior and Convent of Christ Church, Canterbury.* Rolls Series. London, 1865.

Studer, Paul, and Joan Evans, eds. *Anglo-Norman Lapidaries.* Paris, 1924.

Talbot, C. H., ed. *The Life of Christina of Markyate: A Twelfth Century Recluse.* Repr. edn. Oxford, 1987.

Theobald of Étampes. "Epistola ad Roscelinum." In *Patrologia Latina*, vol. 163, edited by J.-P. Migne, 767–70. Paris, 1854.

Thomas de Burton. *Chronica Monasterii de Melsa*, edited by Edward Augustus Bond. 3 vols. Rolls Series. London, 1866–68.

Thomas, Master. *The Romance of Horn*, edited by Mildred K. Pope and T. B. W. Reid. 2 vols. Anglo-Norman Texts, vols. 9–10, 12–13. Oxford, 1955–64.

Thomas of Chobham. *Thomae de Chobham Summa Confessorum*, edited by F. Broomfield. Louvain, 1968.

Thomas of Chobham. *Summa de Arte Praedicandi*, edited by Franco Morenzoni. Corpus Christianorum, Continuatio Mediaevalis vol. 82. Turnhout, 1988.

Thomas of Chobham. *Sermones*, edited by Franco Morenzoni. Corpus Christianorum, Continuatio Mediaevalis, vol. 82A. Turnhout, 1993.

Thomas of Kent. *The Anglo-Norman Alexander (Le roman de toute chevalerie)*, edited by Brian Foster and Ian Short. 2 vols. Anglo-Norman Texts, vols. 29–33. London, 1976–7.

Thomas of Marlborough. *History of the Abbey of Evesham*, edited by Jane E. Sayers and Leslie Watkiss. Oxford, 2003.

Thomas of Monmouth. *The Life and Miracles of St William of Norwich*, edited by Augustus Jessopp and M. R. James. Cambridge, 1896.

Thomas Walsingham. *Gesta Abbatum Monasterii Sancti Albani*, edited by Henry T. Riley. 2 vols. Rolls Series. London, 1867–9.

Thomson, Rodney M., ed. *Chronicle of the Election of Hugh, Abbot of Bury St. Edmunds and Later Bishop of Ely*. Oxford, 1974.

Timson, Reginald Thomas, ed. *The Cartulary of Blyth Priory*. 2 vols. Thoroton Society Record Series, nos. 27–8. London, 1973.

Vacarius. *The* Liber Pauperum *of Vacarius*, edited by Francis de Zulueta. Publications of the Selden Society, vol. 44. London, 1927.

Vincent, Nicholas, ed. *English Episcopal Acta. 9, Winchester, 1205–1238*. Oxford, 1994.

Vincent, Nicholas, ed. *The Letters and Charters of Cardinal Guala Bicchieri, Papal Legate in England, 1216–1218*. The Canterbury and York Society, vol. 83. Woodbridge, 1996.

Wace. *The Roman de Rou*, edited by A. J. Holden, Glyn S. Burgess, and Elisabeth van Houts. St Helier, 2002.

Wace. *Wace's Roman de Brut: A History of the British, Text and Translation*, edited by Judith Weiss. Rev. ed. Exeter, 2002.

Walsh, P. G., ed. *Andreas Capellanus on Love*. London, 1982.

Walsh, P. G., ed. *Love Lyrics from the Carmina Burana*. Chapel Hill, 1993.

Walter Map. *De Nugis Curialium: Courtiers' Trifles*, edited by M. R. James, C. N. L. Brooke, and R. A. B. Mynors. Oxford, 1983.

Watkiss, Leslie, and Marjorie Chibnall, eds. *The Waltham Chronicle*. Oxford, 1994.

West, J. R., ed. *St. Benet of Holme, 1020–1210*. 2 vols. Norfolk Record Society, vols. 2–3. Norwich, 1932.

Whatley, E. Gordon, ed. *The Saint of London: The Life and Miracles of St. Erkenwald*. Binghamton, 1989.

Whitelock, D., M. Brett, and C. N. L. Brooke, eds. *Councils and Synods: With Other Documents Relating to the English Church. Vol. 1, Part 1, 871–1066*. Oxford, 1981.

Whitelock, D., M. Brett, and C. N. L. Brooke, eds. *Councils and Synods: With Other Documents Relating to the English Church. Vol. 1, Part 2, 1066–1204*. Oxford, 1981.

Wigram, Spencer Robert, ed. *The Cartulary of the Monastery of St. Frideswide at Oxford*. 2 vols. Oxford Historical Society Record Series, vols. 28, 31. Oxford, 1895–6.

William de Briane. *The Anglo-Norman* Pseudo-Turpin Chronicle *of William de Briane*, edited by Ian Short. Anglo-Norman Texts, vol. 25. Oxford, 1973.

William of Malmesbury. *Gesta Regum Anglorum. The History of the English Kings*, edited by
R. A. B. Mynors, Rodney M. Thomson, and Michael Winterbottom. 2 vols. Oxford, 1998–9.

William of Malmesbury. *William of Malmesbury, Saints' Lives: Lives of SS. Wulfstan, Dunstan, Patrick, Benignus and Indract*, edited by Michael Winterbottom and Rodney
M. Thomson, Oxford, 2002.

William of Malmesbury. *Gesta Pontificum Anglorum. The History of the English Bishops*,
edited by Michael Winterbottom and Rodney M. Thomson. 2 vols. Oxford, 2007.

William of Newburgh. *Historia Rerum Anglicarum* In *Chronicles of the Reigns of Stephen,
Henry II and Richard I*, vols. 1–2, edited by Richard Howlett. London, 1884–5.

Wollin, C., ed. *Petri Blesensis Carmina*, Corpus Christianorum, Continuatio Mediaevalis
128. Turnhout, 1998.

Woolgar, C. M., ed. *Household Accounts from Medieval England*. 2 vols. Oxford, 1992.

Wright, Thomas, ed. *The Latin Poems Commonly Attributed to Walter Mapes*. Camden
Society, vol. 16. London, 1841.

Wright, Thomas. "On Antiquarian Excavations and Researches in the Middle Ages."
Archaeologia 30 (1844), 438–57.

Wright, Thomas, ed. *The Anglo-Latin Satirical Poets and Epigrammatists of the Twelfth
Century*. 2 vols. London, 1872.

Wrottesley, George. "Staffordshire Suits, Extracted from the Plea Rolls temp. Richard I and
King John." *William Salt Archaeological Society Collections for a History of Staffordshire*
3 (1882), 1–163.

SECONDARY SOURCES

Adams, Tracy. "'Make me Chaste and Continent, but not yet': A Model for Clerical
Masculinity?" In *Masculinities and Femininities in the Middle Ages and Renaissance*, edited
by Frederick Kiefer, 1–29. Turnhout, 2009.

Aird, William M. *St Cuthbert and the Normans: The Church of Durham, 1071–1153*.
Woodbridge, 1998.

Allaria, A. "English Scholars at Bologna during the Middle Ages." *Dublin Review* 112
(1893), 66–83.

Althoff, Gerd. "Friendship and Political Order." In *Friendship in Medieval Europe*, edited by
Julian Haseldine, 91–105. Stroud, 1999.

Amos, Thomas L. "Preaching and the Sermon in the Carolingian World." In *De Ore
Domini: Preacher and Word in the Middle Ages*, edited by Thomas L. Amos, Eugene
Green, and Beverly Mayne Kienzle, 41–60. Kalamazoo, 1989.

Amt, Emilie. *The Accession of Henry II in England: Royal Government Restored, 1149–1159*,
Woodbridge, 1993.

Armstrong-Partida, Michelle. "Priestly Marriage: The Tradition of Clerical Concubinage
in the Spanish Church." *Viator* 40 (2009), 221–53.

Arnold, John H. "The Labour of Continence: Masculinity and Clerical Virginity." In *Medieval
Virginities*, edited by Anke Bernau, Ruth Evans, and Sarah Salih, 102–18. Toronto, 2003.

Arnold, John H. *Belief and Unbelief in Medieval Europe*. London, 2005.

Ashe, Laura. *Fiction and History in England, 1066–1200*. Cambridge, 2007.

Aurell, Martin. *The Plantagenet Empire, 1154–1224*. Translated by David Crouch. Harlow,
2007.

Aurell, Martin. *Le chevalier lettré: savoir et conduite de l'aristocratie aux XIIe et XIIIe siècles*.
Paris, 2011.

d'Avray, David L. *The Preaching of the Friars: Sermons Diffused from Paris before 1300.* Oxford, 1985.

d'Avray, David L. *Medieval Marriage: Symbolism and Society.* Oxford, 2005.

d'Avray, David L. *Medieval Religious Rationalities: A Weberian Analysis*, Cambridge, 2010.

d'Avray, David L. "Printing, Mass Communication, and Religious Reformation: The Middle Ages and After." In *The History of the Book in the West: Volume I, 400 AD–1455*, edited by Jane Annette Roberts and Pamela Robinson, 301–21. Farnham, 2010.

Avril, J. "L'Évolution du synode diocésain principalement dans la France du nord du Xe au XIIIe siècles." In *Proceedings of the Seventh International Congress of Medieval Canon Law*, edited by Peter Linehan, 302–35. Vatican City, 1988.

Bailey, Derrick Sherwin. *The Canonical Houses of Wells.* Gloucester, 1982.

Bakhtin, M. M. *Rabelais and his World.* Cambridge, MA, 1968.

Baldwin, John W. "A Campaign to Reduce Clerical Celibacy at the Turn of the 12th and 13th Centuries." In *Études d'histoire du droit canonique dediées à Gabriel le Bras*, 2: 1041–53. Paris, 1965.

Baldwin, John W. *Masters, Princes, and Merchants: The Social Views of Peter the Chanter and his Circle.* Princeton, 1970.

Baldwin, John W. "'Studium et Regnum': The Penetration of University Personnel into French and English Administration at the Turn of the Twelfth and Thirteenth Centuries." *Revue des Études Islamiques* 44 (1976), 199–215.

Baldwin, John W. "Masters at Paris from 1179 to 1215: A Social Perspective." In *Renaissance and Renewal in the Twelfth Century*, edited by Robert Louis Benson and Giles Constable, 138–72. Cambridge, MA, 1982.

Baldwin, John W. *The Language of Sex: Five Voices from Northern France around 1200.* Chicago, 1994.

Baldwin, John W. "The Image of the Jongleur in Northern France around 1200." *Speculum* 72 (1997), 635–63.

Balzaretti, Ross. "Men and Sex in Tenth-Century Italy." In *Masculinity in Medieval Europe*, edited by D. M. Hadley, 143–59. London, 1999.

Barker-Benfield, B. C. *St Augustine's Abbey, Canterbury*, 3 vols. London, 2008.

Barlow, Frank. *The English Church, 1066–1154: A History of the Anglo-Norman Church.* London, 1979.

Barlow, Frank. *Thomas Becket.* London, 1986.

Barlow, Frank, Kathleen M. Dexter, Audrey M. Erskine, and J. L. Lloyd, eds. *Leofric of Exeter.* Exeter, 1972.

Barrell, A. D. M. "Abuse or Expediency? Pluralism and Non-residence in Northern England in the Late Middle Ages." In *Government, Religion, and Society in Northern England, 1000–1700*, edited by John T. Appleby and Paul Dalton, 117–30. Stroud, 1997.

Barron, Caroline M., and Matthew Davies, eds. *The Religious Houses of London and Middlesex.* London, 2007.

Barrow, Julia. "Gerald of Wales's Great-nephews." *Cambridge Medieval Celtic Studies* 8 (1984), 101–6.

Barrow, Julia. "Cathedrals, Provosts, and Prebends: A Comparison of Twelfth-Century German and English Practice." *Journal of Ecclesiastical History* 37 (1986), 536–64.

Barrow, Julia. "Hereford Bishops and Married Clergy, c.1130–1240." *Historical Research* 60 (1987), 1–8.

Barrow, Julia. "Education and the Recruitment of Cathedral Canons in England and Germany, 1100–1225." *Viator* 20 (1989), 117–38.

Barrow, Julia. "Vicars Choral and Chaplains in Northern European Cathedrals, 1100–1250." In *The Ministry: Clerical and Lay*, edited by W. J. Sheils and Diana Wood, 87–97. Oxford, 1989.

Barrow, Julia. "A Lotharingian in Hereford: Bishop Robert's Reorganisation of the Church of Hereford 1079–95." In *Medieval Art, Architecture, and Archaeology at Hereford*, edited by David Whitehead, 29–49. [London], 1995.

Barrow, Julia. "The Canons and Citizens of Hereford, *c.*1160–*c.*1240." *Midland History* 24 (1999), 1–23.

Barrow, Julia. "Origins and Careers of Cathedral Clergy in Twelfth-Century England." *Medieval Prosopography* 21 (2000), 23–40.

Barrow, Julia. *Fasti Ecclesiae Anglicanae, 1066–1300. 8. Hereford*, London, 2002.

Barrow, Julia. "The Clergy in English Dioceses *c.*900–*c.*1066." In *Pastoral Care in Late Anglo-Saxon England*, edited by Francesca Tinti, 17–26. Woodbridge, 2005.

Barrow, Julia. "Grades of Ordination and Clerical Careers, *c.*900–*c.*1200." *Anglo-Norman Studies* 30 (2007), 41–61.

Barrow, Julia. "Ideas and Applications of Reform." In *The Cambridge History of Christianity. Vol. 3, Early Medieval Christianities, c.600–c.1100*, edited by Thomas F. X. Noble and Julia M. H. Smith, 345–62. Cambridge, 2008.

Barrow, Julia. *Who Served the Altar at Brixworth?: Clergy in English Minsters c.800–c.1100*. Brixworth, 2013.

Barstow, Anne Llewellyn. *Married Priests and the Reforming Papacy: The Eleventh-Century Debates*. New York, 1982.

Bartlett, Robert. *Gerald of Wales, 1146–1223*. Oxford, 1982.

Bartlett, Robert. *The Making of Europe: Conquest, Colonization and Cultural Change 950–1350*. Princeton, 1993.

Bartlett, Robert. *England under the Norman and Angevin Kings, 1075–1225*. Oxford, 2000.

Barton, Richard E. "'Zealous Anger' and the Renegotiation of Aristocratic Relationships in Eleventh- and Twelfth-Century France." In *Anger's Past: The Social Uses of an Emotion in the Middle Ages*, edited by Barbara H. Rosenwein, 153–70. Ithaca, 1998.

Baswell, Christopher. *Virgil in Medieval England: Figuring the Aeneid from the Twelfth Century to Chaucer*. Cambridge, 1995.

Bataillon, Louis J., Nicole Bériou, Gilbert Dahan, and Riccardo Quinto, eds. *Étienne Langton: prédicateur, bibliste, théologien*. Turnhout, 2010.

Bate, A. K. "Joseph of Exeter, Religious Poet." *Medium Aevum* 40 (1971), 222–9.

Bate, A. K. "Walter Map and Giraldus Cambrensis." *Latomus* 31 (1972), 860–75.

Bennett, Nicholas. "Pastors and Masters: The Beneficed Clergy of North-East Lincolnshire, 1290–1340." In *The Foundations of Medieval English Ecclesiastical History: Studies Presented to David Smith*, edited by Philippa M. Hoskin, Christopher Brooke, and Barry Dobson, 40–62. Woodbridge, 2005.

Benson, Robert Louis, and Giles Constable, eds. *Renaissance and Renewal in the Twelfth Century*. Cambridge, MA, 1982.

Bent, Ian. "The English Royal Chapel before 1300." *Proceedings of the Royal Musical Association* 90 (1963–4), 77–95.

Bériou, Nicole. "La prédication synodale au XIIIe siècle d'après l'exemple cambrésien." In *Le clerc séculier au moyen âge*, 229–47. Paris, 1993.

Bériou, Nicole. "Les sermons latins après 1200." In *The Sermon*, edited by Beverly Mayne Kienzle, 363–447. Turnhout, 2000.

Bezzola, Reto R. *Les origines et la formation de la littérature courtoise en Occident (500–1200)*. 3 vols. Paris, 1968.

Binski, Paul. *Becket's Crown: Art and Imagination in Gothic England, 1170–1300*. New Haven, 2004.

Bishop, T. A. M. *Scriptores Regis*. Oxford, 1961.

Bisson, Thomas N. *The Crisis of the Twelfth Century: Power, Lordship, and the Origins of European Government*. Princeton, 2009.

Blair, John. "Secular Minster Churches in Domesday Book." In *Domesday Book: A Reassessment*, edited by Peter Sawyer, 104–42. London, 1985.

Blair, John. *Early Medieval Surrey: Landholding, Church, and Settlement before 1300*. Stroud, 1991.

Blair, John. *The Church in Anglo-Saxon Society*. Oxford, 2005.

Blake, David. "The Development of the Chapter of the Diocese of Exeter, 1050–1161." *Journal of Medieval History* 8 (1982), 1–11.

Blakely, Ruth M. *The Brus Family in England and Scotland, 1100–1295*. Woodbridge, 2005.

Bloch, Herbert. "The New Fascination with Ancient Rome." In *Renaissance and Renewal in the Twelfth Century*, edited by Robert Louis Benson and Giles Constable, 615–36. Cambridge, MA, 1982.

Blumenthal, Uta-Renate. *The Investiture Controversy: Church and Monarchy from the Ninth to the Twelfth Century*. Philadelphia, 1988.

Bolton, Brenda, and Anne Duggan, eds. *Adrian IV, the English Pope, 1154–1159: Studies and Texts*. Aldershot, 2003.

Bolton, J. L. "The English Economy in the Early Thirteenth Century." In *King John: New Interpretations*, edited by S. D. Church, 27–40. Woodbridge, 1999.

Bond, C. J. "Church and Parish in Norman Worcestershire." In *Minsters and Parish Churches: The Local Church in Transition, 950–1200*, edited by John Blair, 119–58. Oxford, 1988.

Bond, Gerald A. *The Loving Subject: Desire, Eloquence, and Power in Romanesque France*. Philadelphia, 1995.

Bornstein, Daniel. "Parish Priests in Late Medieval Cortona: The Urban and Rural Clergy." In *Preti nel medioevo*, edited by Maurizio Zangarini, 165–93. Verona, 1997.

Boswell, John. *Christianity, Social Tolerance, and Homosexuality: Gay People in Western Europe from the Beginning of the Christian Era to the Fourteenth Century*. Chicago, 1980.

Boudet, Jean-Patrice. *Entre science et nigromance: astrologie, divination et magie dans l'occident médiéval, XIIe–XVe siècle*. Paris, 2006.

Boureau, Alain. "Hypothèses sur l'émergence lexicale et théorique de la catégorie de séculier au XIIe siècle." In *Le clerc séculier au moyen âge*, 35–43. Paris, 1993.

Bowker, Margaret. *The Secular Clergy in the Diocese of Lincoln, 1495–1520*. Cambridge, 1968.

Boyle, Leonard. "The Beginnings of Legal Studies at Oxford." *Viator* 14 (1983), 107–31.

Boyle, Leonard. "The Inter-Conciliar Period 1179–1215 and the Beginnings of Pastoral Manuals." In *Miscellanea Rolando Bandinelli, Papa Alessandro III*, edited by Filippo Liotta, 43–56. Siena, 1986.

Bozzolo, Carla, and Ezio Ornato. *Pour une histoire du livre manuscrit au Moyen Âge: trois essais de codicologie quantitative*. Paris, 1983.

Bremond, Claude, Jacques Le Goff, and Jean Claude Schmitt. *L'"Exemplum."* Turnhout, 1996.

Brett, M. *The English Church under Henry I*. London, 1975.

Britnell, Richard H. *The Commercialisation of English Society, 1000–1500*. 2nd edn. Manchester, 1996.

Britnell, Richard H., ed. *The Winchester Pipe Rolls and Medieval English Society*. Woodbridge, 2003.

Brooke, C. N. L. "The Composition of the Chapter of St. Paul's, 1086–1163." *Cambridge Historical Journal* 10 (1951), 111–32.

Brooke, C. N. L. "Gregorian Reform in Action: Clerical Marriage in England, 1050–1200." In *Medieval Church and Society: Collected Essays*, 69–99. London, 1971.

Brooke, C. N. L. "John of Salisbury and his World." In *The World of John of Salisbury*, edited by Michael Wilks, 1–20. Oxford, 1984.

Brooke, C. N. L. "The Archdeacon and the Norman Conquest." In *Tradition and Change: Essays in Honour of Marjorie Chibnall*, edited by Diana Greenway, Christopher Holdsworth, and Jane Sayers, 1–19. Cambridge, 1985.

Brooke, C. N. L. *The Medieval Idea of Marriage*. Oxford, 1989.

Brooke, Z. N. "The Register of Master David of London, and the Part he Played in the Becket Crisis." In *Essays in History Presented to Reginald Lane Poole*, edited by H. W. C. Davis, 227–45. Oxford, 1927.

Brooks, F. W. "William de Wrotham and the Office of Keeper of the King's Ports and Galleys." *English Historical Review* 40 (1925), 570–9.

Brown, Peter. *The Body and Society: Men, Women, and Sexual Renunciation in Early Christianity*. New York, 1988.

Brundage, James A. "Marriage and Sexuality in the Decretals of Pope Alexander III." In *Miscellanea Rolando Bandinelli, Papa Alessandro III*, edited by Liotta Filippo, 57–83. Siena, 1986.

Brundage, James A. *Law, Sex, and Christian Society in Medieval Europe*. Chicago, 1987.

Brundage, James A. "Sin, Crime, and the Pleasures of the Flesh: The Medieval Church Judges Sexual Offences." In *The Medieval World*, edited by Peter Linehan, and Janet L. Nelson, 294–307. London, 2001.

Burger, Michael. "The Date and Authorship of Robert Grosseteste's *Rules for Household and Estate Management*." *Historical Research* 74 (2001), 106–16.

Burger, Michael. *Bishops, Clerks, and Diocesan Governance in Thirteenth-Century England: Reward and Punishment*. Cambridge, 2012.

Burgess, Clive, and Martin Heale, eds. *The Late Medieval English College and its Context*. Woodbridge, 2008.

Burgwinkle, William E. *Sodomy, Masculinity, and Law in Medieval Literature: France and England, 1050–1230*. Cambridge, 2004.

Buringh, Eltjo. *Medieval Manuscript Production in the Latin West: Explorations with a Global Database*. Leiden, 2011.

Burman, Thomas E. *Reading the Qur'ān in Latin Christendom, 1140–1560*. Philadelphia, 2007.

Burnett, Charles. "A Note on the Origins of the Third Vatican Mythographer." *Journal of the Warburg and Courtauld Institutes* 44 (1981), 160–6.

Burnett, Charles. "Adelard, Music and the Quadrivium." In *Adelard of Bath: An English Scientist and Arabist of the Early Twelfth Century*, edited by Charles Burnett, 69–86. London, 1987.

Burnett, Charles, ed. *Adelard of Bath: An English Scientist and Arabist of the Early Twelfth Century*. London, 1987.

Burnett, Charles. "Give Him the White Cow: Notes and Note-Taking in the Universities in the Twelfth and Thirteenth Centuries." *History of Universities* 14 (1995–6), 1–30.

Burnett, Charles. "The Institutional Context of Arabic–Latin Translations of the Middle Ages: A Reassessment of the 'School of Toledo'." In *Vocabulary of Teaching and Research Between Middle Ages and Renaissance*, edited by Olga Weijers, 214–35. Turnhout, 1995.

Burnett, Charles. "Mathematics and Astronomy in Hereford and its Region in the Twelfth Century." In *Medieval Art, Architecture, and Archaeology at Hereford*, edited by David Whitehead, 50–9. [London], 1995.

Burnett, Charles. "Talismans: Magic as Science? Necromancy among the Seven Liberal Arts." In *Magic and Divination in the Middle Ages: Texts and Techniques in the Islamic and Christian Worlds*, 1–15. Aldershot, 1996.

Burnett, Charles. "The Translating Activity in Medieval Spain." In *Magic and Divination in the Middle Ages: Texts and Techniques in the Islamic and Christian Worlds*, 1036–58. Aldershot, 1996.

Burnett, Charles. *The Introduction of Arabic Learning into England*. London, 1997.

Burnett, Charles. "The Establishment of Medieval Hermeticism." In *The Medieval World*, edited by Peter Linehan and Janet L. Nelson, 111–30. London, 2001.

Burnett, Charles. "Communities of Learning in Twelfth-Century Toledo." In *Communities of Learning: Networks and the Shaping of Intellectual Identity in Europe, 1100–1500*, edited by Constant J. Mews and John N. Crossley, 9–18. Turnhout, 2011.

Burton, Janet E. "Monasteries and Parish Churches in Eleventh- and Twelfth-Century Yorkshire." *Northern History* 23 (1987), 39–50.

Burton, Janet E. *Monastic and Religious Orders in Britain, 1000–1300*. Cambridge, 1994.

Burton, Janet E. *The Monastic Order in Yorkshire, 1069–1215*. Cambridge, 1999.

Burton, Janet E., and Karen Stöber, eds. *Monasteries and Society in the British Isles in the Later Middle Ages*. Woodbridge, 2008.

Butler, L. A. S. "'The Haunted Tanglewood': Aspects of Late Twelfth-Century Sculpture in Yorkshire." *Proceedings of the Leeds Philosophical and Literary Society* 18 (1982), 79–95.

Bynum, Caroline Walker. *Docere Verbo et Exemplo: An Aspect of Twelfth-Century Spirituality*. Missoula, 1979.

Bynum, Caroline Walker. *Jesus as Mother: Studies in the Spirituality of the High Middle Ages*. Berkeley, 1982.

Bynum, Caroline Walker. *Wonderful Blood: Theology and Practice in Late Medieval Northern Germany and Beyond*. Philadelphia, 2007.

Callus, Daniel A. "The Introduction of Aristotelian Learning to Oxford." *Proceedings of the British Academy* 29 (1943), 229–81.

Carey, Hilary M. *Courting Disaster: Astrology at the English Court and University in the Later Middle Ages*. London, 1992.

Cartlidge, Neil. "An Intruder at the Feast? Anxiety and Debate in the Letters of Peter of Blois." In *Writers of the Reign of Henry II: Twelve Essays*, edited by Ruth Kennedy and Simon Meecham-Jones, 79–108. New York, 2006.

Casagrande, Carla, and Silvana Vecchio. "Clers et jongleurs dans la société médiévale (XIIe–XIIIe siècles)." *Annales* 34 (1979), 913–28.

Catto, J. I. *The History of the University of Oxford. Vol. 1. The Early Oxford Schools*. Oxford, 1984.

Chance, Jane. *Medieval Mythography: From Roman North Africa to the School of Chartres, A.D. 433–1177*. 2 vols. Gainesville, 1994.

Cheney, C. R. *English Bishops' Chanceries, 1100–1250*. Manchester, 1950.

Cheney, C. R. "Harrold Priory: A Twelfth-Century Dispute." *Bedfordshire Historical Record Society* 32 (1952), 1–26.

Cheney, C. R. *From Becket to Langton*. Manchester, 1956.

Cheney, C. R. *Hubert Walter*. London, 1967.

Cheney, C. R. *Medieval Texts and Studies*. Oxford, 1973.

Cheney, Mary G. "Master Geoffrey de Lucy, an Early Chancellor of the University of Oxford." *English Historical Review* 82 (1967), 750–63.

Cheney, Mary G. *Roger, Bishop of Worcester, 1164–1179: An English Bishop of the Age of Becket*. Oxford, 1980.

Christelow, Stephanie Mooers. "Chancellors and Curial Bishops: Ecclesiastical Promotions and Power in Anglo-Norman England." *Anglo-Norman Studies* 22 (2000), 49–69.

Church, S. D. *The Household Knights of King John.* Cambridge, 1999.

Clanchy, M. T. "*Moderni* in Education and Government in England." *Speculum* 50 (1975), 671–88.

Clanchy, M. T. *From Memory to Written Record, England 1066–1307.* 2nd edn. Oxford, 1993.

Clanchy, M. T. *Abelard: A Medieval Life.* Oxford, 1997.

Clay, Charles T. "Master Aristotle." *English Historical Review* 76 (1961), 303–8.

Coates, Alan. *English Medieval Books: The Reading Abbey Collections from Foundation to Dispersal.* Oxford, 1999.

Cochrane, Louise. *Adelard of Bath: The First English Scientist.* London, 1994.

Cohen, Jeffrey J. "The Flow of Blood in Medieval Norwich." *Speculum* 79 (2004), 26–65.

Colish, Marcia L. *Peter Lombard.* Leiden, 1994.

Colish, Marcia L. "Haskins's *Renaissance* Seventy Years Later: Beyond Anti-Burckhardtianism." *Haskins Society Journal* 11 (2003), 1–15.

Colvin, Howard. "The Origin of Chantries." *Journal of Medieval History* 26 (2000), 163–73.

Constable, Giles. *Monastic Tithes from their Origins to the Twelfth Century.* Cambridge, 1964.

Constable, Giles. *Letters and Letter-Collections.* Turnhout, 1976.

Constable, Giles. "The Structure of Medieval Society According to the *Dictatores* of the Twelfth Century." In *Law, Church, and Society: Essays in Honor of Stephan Kuttner*, edited by Kenneth Pennington and Robert Somerville, 253–67. Philadelphia, 1977.

Constable, Giles. "Aelred of Rievaulx and the Nun of Watton: An Episode in the Early History of the Gilbertine Order." In *Medieval Women*, edited by Derek Baker, 205–26. Oxford, 1978.

Constable, Giles. "The Language of Preaching in the Twelfth Century." *Viator* 25 (1994), 131–52.

Constable, Giles. "The Interpretation of Mary and Martha." In *Three Studies in Medieval Religious and Social Thought*, 1–141. Cambridge, 1995.

Constable, Giles. "Dictators and Diplomats in the Eleventh and Twelfth Centuries: Medieval Epistolography and the Birth of Modern Bureaucracy." In *Culture and Spirituality in Medieval Europe*, 37–46. Aldershot, 1996.

Constable, Giles. "The Diversity of Religious Life and Acceptance of Social Pluralism in the Twelfth Century." In *Culture and Spirituality in Medieval Europe*, 29–47. Aldershot, 1996.

Constable, Giles. *The Reformation of the Twelfth Century.* Cambridge, 1996.

Coss, Peter R. *The Knight in Medieval England, 1000–1400.* Stroud, 1993.

Cotts, John D. *The Clerical Dilemma: Peter of Blois and Literate Culture in the Twelfth Century.* Washington, D.C., 2009.

Cotts, John D. *Europe's Long Twelfth Century: Order, Anxiety and Adaptation, 1095–1229.* Basingstoke, 2013.

Courtney, F. *Cardinal Robert Pullen: An English Theologian of the Twelfth Century.* Rome, 1954.

Cowdrey, H. E. J. "Pope Gregory VII and the Chastity of the Clergy." In *Medieval Purity and Piety: Essays on Medieval Clerical Celibacy and Religious Reform*, edited by Michael Frassetto, 269–302. New York, 1998.

Cowdrey, H. E. J. *Lanfranc: Scholar, Monk, and Archbishop.* Oxford, 2003.

Cownie, Emma. *Religious Patronage in Anglo-Norman England, 1066–1135*. Woodbridge, 1998.

Cragoe, Carol Davidson. "The Custom of the English Church: Parish Church Maintenance in England before 1300." *Journal of Medieval History* 36 (2010), 20–38.

Crane, Susan. *Insular Romance: Politics, Faith, and Culture in Anglo-Norman and Middle English Literature*. Berkeley, 1986.

Crane, Susan. "Anglo-Norman Cultures in England, 1066–1460." In *The Cambridge History of Medieval English Literature*, edited by David Wallace, 35–60. Cambridge, 1999.

Crick, Julia C. *The* Historia Regum Britanniae *of Geoffrey of Monmouth: III. A Summary Catalogue of the Manuscripts*. Cambridge, 1989.

Crick, Julia C. *The* Historia Regum Britanniae *of Geoffrey of Monmouth: IV. Dissemination and Reception in the Later Middle Ages*. Cambridge, 1991.

Crosby, Everett U. *Bishop and Chapter in Twelfth-Century England: A Study of the* Mensa Episcopalis. Cambridge, 1994.

Crouch, David. *The Beaumont Twins: The Roots and Branches of Power in the Twelfth Century*. Cambridge, 1986.

Crouch, David. *The Image of Aristocracy in Britain 1000–1300*. London, 1993.

Crouch, David. "The Origin of Chantries: Some Further Anglo-Norman Evidence." *Journal of Medieval History* 27 (2001), 159–80.

Crouch, David. *William Marshal: Knighthood, War and Chivalry, 1147–1219*. 2nd edn. London, 2002.

Crouch, David. *The Birth of Nobility: Constructing Aristocracy in England and France, 900–1300*. Harlow, 2005.

Crouch, David. *The English Aristocracy, 1070–1272: A Social Transformation*. New Haven, 2011.

Crouch, David, and Claire de Trafford. "The Forgotten Family in Twelfth-Century England." *Haskins Society Journal* 13 (2004), 41–63.

Cubitt, Catherine. "Images of St Peter: The Clergy and the Religious Life in Anglo-Saxon England." In *The Christian Tradition in Anglo-Saxon England: Approaches to Current Scholarship and Teaching*, edited by Paul Cavill, 41–54. Cambridge, 2004.

Cubitt, Catherine. "The Clergy in Early Anglo-Saxon England." *Historical Research* 78 (2005), 273–87.

Cuffel, Alexandra. *Gendering Disgust in Medieval Religious Polemic*. Notre Dame, 2007.

Cullum, P. H. "Clergy, Masculinity and Transgression in Late Medieval England." In *Masculinity in Medieval Europe*, edited by D. M. Hadley, 178–96. London, 1999.

Cullum, P. H. "Learning to Be a Man, Learning to Be a Priest in Late Medieval England." In *Learning and Literacy in Medieval England and Abroad*, edited by Sarah Rees Jones, 135–53. Turnhout, 2003.

Curley, Michael J. *Geoffrey of Monmouth*. New York, 1994.

Cushing, Kathleen G. *Reform and the Papacy in the Eleventh Century: Spirituality and Social Change*. Manchester, 2005.

Cuttino, G. P. "King's Clerks and the Community of the Realm." *Speculum* 29 (1954), 395–409.

Darby, H. C. *Domesday England*. Cambridge, 1977.

Davies, Wendy. *Wales in the Early Middle Ages*. Leicester, 1982.

Davis, Adam J. *The Holy Bureaucrat: Eudes Rigaud and Religious Reform in Thirteenth-Century Normandy*. Ithaca, 2006.

Denton, Jeffrey H. *English Royal Free Chapels, 1100–1300: A Constitutional Study*. Manchester, 1970.

Denton, Jeffrey H. "The Competence of the Parish Clergy in Thirteenth-Century England." In *The Church and Learning in Later Medieval Society: Essays in Honour of R. B. Dobson*, edited by Caroline Barron and Jenny Stratford, 273–85. Donington, 2002.

Desborough, D. E. "Politics and Prelacy in the Late Twelfth Century: The Career of Hugh de Nonant, Bishop of Coventry, 1188–98." *Historical Research* 64 (1991), 1–14.

Dickinson, J. C. *The Origins of the Austin Canons and their Introduction into England*. London, 1950.

Douglas, Mary. *Purity and Danger: An Analysis of the Concepts of Pollution and Taboo*. Repr. edn. London, 1984.

Draper, Peter. *The Formation of English Gothic: Architecture and Identity*. New Haven, 2006.

Dronke, Peter. *Medieval Latin and the Rise of European Love-Lyric*. 2nd edn. 2 vols. Oxford, 1968.

Dronke, Peter. "Peter of Blois and Poetry at the Court of Henry II." *Mediaeval Studies* 38 (1976), 185–235.

Duggan, Anne. "Classical Quotations and Allusions in the Correspondence of Thomas Becket: An Investigation of their Sources." *Viator* 32 (2001), 1–22.

Duggan, Anne. *Thomas Becket*. London, 2004.

Duggan, Anne. "The Price of Loyalty: The Fate of Thomas Becket's Learned Household." In *Thomas Becket: Friends, Networks, Texts, and Cult*, edited by Anne Duggan, 1–18. Aldershot, 2007.

Duggan, Anne. "Thomas Becket's Italian Network." In *Thomas Becket: Friends, Networks, Texts, and Cult*, edited by Anne Duggan, 1–21. Aldershot, 2007.

Duggan, Anne. "Conciliar Law, 1123–1215: The Legislation of the Four Lateran Councils." In *The History of Medieval Canon Law in the Classical Period, 1140–1234: From Gratian to the Decretals of Pope Gregory IX*, edited by Wilfried Hartmann and Kenneth Pennington, 318–66. Washington, D.C., 2008.

Duggan, Charles. *Twelfth-Century Decretal Collections and their Importance in English History*. London, 1963.

Duggan, Charles. "The Becket Dispute and the Criminous Clerks." In *Canon Law in Medieval England: The Becket Dispute and Decretal Collections*, 1–28. London, 1982.

Duggan, Charles. "The Reception of Canon Law in England in the Later-Twelfth Century." In *Canon Law in Medieval England: The Becket Dispute and Decretal Collections*, 359–90. London, 1982.

Duggan, Charles. "Richard of Ilchester, Royal Servant and Bishop." In *Canon Law in Medieval England: The Becket Dispute and Decretal Collections*, 1–21. London, 1982.

Duggan, Charles. "Papal Judges Delegate and the Making of the 'New Law' in the Twelfth Century." In *Cultures of Power: Lordship, Status, and Process in Twelfth-Century Europe*, edited by Thomas N. Bisson, 172–99. Philadelphia, 1995.

Duggan, Charles. "Decretal Collections from Gratian's *Decretum* to the *Compilationes Antiquae*: The Making of the New Case Law." In *The History of Medieval Canon Law in the Classical Period, 1140–1234: From Gratian to the Decretals of Pope Gregory IX*, edited by Wilfried Hartmann and Kenneth Pennington, 246–92. Washington, D.C., 2008.

Dunbabin, Jean. "From Clerk to Knight: Changing Orders." In *The Ideals and Practice of Medieval Knighthood, II: Papers from the Third Strawberry Hill Conference*, edited by Christopher Harper-Bill and Ruth Harvey, 26–39. Woodbridge, 1988.

Dyer, Christopher. *Standards of Living in the Later Middle Ages: Social Change in England, c.1200–1500*. Cambridge, 1989.

Edwards, Kathleen. *The English Secular Cathedrals in the Middle Ages.* 2nd edn. Manchester, 1967.

Ehlers, Joachim. "Deutsche Scholaren in Frankreich wärend des 12. Jarhhunderts." In *Schulen und Studium im sozialen Wandel des hohen und späten Mittelalters*, edited by Johannes Fried, 97–120. Sigmaringen, 1986.

Elias, Norbert. *The Civilizing Process.* New York, 1978.

Elias, Norbert. *Power & Civility. The Civilizing Process: Volume II.* New York, 1982.

Elkins, Sharon K. *Holy Women of Twelfth-Century England.* Chapel Hill, 1988.

Elliott, Dyan. *Fallen Bodies: Pollution, Sexuality, and Demonology in the Middle Ages.* Philadelphia, 1999.

Evans, Joan. *Magical Jewels of the Middle Ages and the Renaissance, Particularly in England.* Oxford, 1922.

Everist, Mark. "Anglo-French Interaction in Music, *c.*1170–*c.*1300." *Revue Belge de Musicologie* 46 (1992), 5–22.

Falck, Robert. *The Notre Dame Conductus: A Study of the Repertory.* Henryville, 1981.

Faulkner, Kathryn. "The Transformation of Knighthood in Early Thirteenth-Century England." *English Historical Review* 111 (1996), 1–23.

Fenton, Kirsten A. *Gender, Nation and Conquest in the Works of William of Malmesbury.* Woodbridge, 2008.

Ferruolo, Stephen C. *The Origins of the University: The Schools of Paris and their Critics, 1100–1215.* Stanford, 1985.

Ferruolo, Stephen C. "The Paris Statutes of 1215 Reconsidered." *History of Universities* 5 (1985), 1–14.

Figueira, Robert C. "Ricardus de Mores and his *Casus Decretalium*: The Birth of a Canonistic Genre." In *Proceedings of the Eighth International Congress of Medieval Canon Law*, edited by Stanley Chodorow, 169–87. Vatican City, 1992.

Flahiff, G. B. "Ralph Niger—An Introduction to His Life and Works." *Mediaeval Studies* 2 (1940), 104–26.

Flanagan, Sabina. *Doubt in an Age of Faith: Uncertainty in the Long Twelfth Century.* Turnhout, 2008.

Fonge, C. R. "Patriarchy and Patrimony: Investing in the Medieval College." In *The Foundations of Medieval English Ecclesiastical History: Studies Presented to David Smith*, edited by Philippa M. Hoskin, Christopher Brooke, and Barry Dobson, 77–93. Woodbridge, 2005.

Foulon, Jean-Hervé "Le clerc et son image dans le prédication synodale de Geoffroy Babion, archevêque de Bourdeaux (1135–1158)." In *Le clerc séculier au moyen âge*, 45–60. Paris, 1993.

Fraher, R. M. "The Becket Dispute and Two Decretist Traditions: The Bolognese Masters Revisited and Some New Anglo-Norman Texts." *Journal of Medieval History* 4 (1978), 347–68.

Frassetto, Michael. "Heresy, Celibacy, and Reform in the Sermons of Ademar of Chabannes." In *Medieval Purity and Piety: Essays on Medieval Clerical Celibacy and Religious Reform*, edited by Michael Frassetto, 131–48. New York, 1998.

Frassetto, Michael, ed. *Medieval Purity and Piety: Essays on Medieval Clerical Celibacy and Religious Reform.* New York, 1998.

Frauenknecht, Erwin. *Die Verteidigung der Priesterehe in der Reformzeit.* Hannover, 1997.

Frazee, C. A. "The Origins of Clerical Celibacy in the Western Church." *Church History* 41 (1972), 149–67.

French, Roger. "Foretelling the Future: Arabic Astrology and English Medicine in the Late Twelfth Century." *Isis* 87 (1996), 453–80.

Gabel, Leona C. *Benefit of Clergy in England in the Later Middle Ages*. 2nd edn. New York, 1969.

Gabriel, Astrik L. *Garlandia. Studies in the History of the Mediaeval University*. Frankfurt, 1969.

Gaudemet, Jean. "Le celibate ecclésiastique." *Zeitshcrift der Savigny Stiftung für Rechtsgeschichte, Kanonistische Abteilung* 68 (1982), 1–31.

Genevois, A. M., J.-F. Genest, and A. Chalandon. *Bibliothèques de manuscrits médiévaux en France: relevé des inventaires du VIIIe au XVIIIe siècle*. Paris, 1987.

Gervers, Michael, and Nicole Hamonic. "Scribes and Notaries in Twelfth- and Thirteenth-Century Hospitaller Charters from England." In *The Hospitallers, the Mediterranean and Europe: Festschrift for Anthony Luttrell*, edited by Karl Borchardt, Nikolas Jaspert, and Helen J. Nicholson, 181–92. Aldershot, 2007.

Getz, Faye. *Medicine in the English Middle Ages*. Princeton, 1998.

Giandrea, Mary Frances. *Episcopal Culture in Late Anglo-Saxon England*. Woodbridge, 2007.

Gillingham, John. "The Context and Purpose of Geoffrey of Monmouth's *History of the Kings of Britain*." In *The English in the Twelfth Century: Imperialism, National Identity, and Political Values*, 19–39. Woodbridge, 2000.

Gillingham, John. "From *Civilitas* to Civility: Codes of Manners in Medieval and Early Modern England." *Transactions of the Royal Historical Society*, 6th series, 12 (2002), 267–89.

Gillingham, John. "A Historian of the Twelfth-Century Renaissance and the Transformation of English Society, 1066–ca. 1200." In *European Transformations: The Long Twelfth Century*, edited by Thomas F. X. Noble and John H. Van Engen, 45–74. Notre Dame, 2012.

Godman, Peter. *The Silent Masters: Latin Literature and its Censors in the High Middle Ages*. Princeton, 2000.

Goering, Joseph. "The Changing Face of the Village Parish II: The Thirteenth Century." In *Pathways to Medieval Peasants*, edited by J. A. Raftis, 323–33. Toronto, 1981.

Goering, Joseph . "The *Summa de Penitentia* of John of Kent." *Bulletin of Medieval Canon Law* n. s., 18 (1988), 13–31.

Goering, Joseph. *William de Montibus (c.1140–1213): The Schools and the Literature of Pastoral Care*. Toronto, 1992.

Goering, Joseph. "The Summa *Qui Bene Presunt* and its Author." In *Literature and Religion in the Later Middle Ages: Philological Studies in Honor of Siegfried Wenzel*, edited by Richard Newhauser and John A. Alford, 143–59. Binghamton, 1995.

Golding, Brian. "Gerald of Wales and the Monks." *Thirteenth-Century England* 5 (1995), 53–64.

Golding, Brian. *Gilbert of Sempringham and the Gilbertine Order, c.1130–c.1300*. Oxford, 1995.

Goodwin, Deborah L. *Take Hold of the Robe of a Jew: Herbert of Bosham's Christian Hebraism*. Leiden, 2006.

Gransden, Antonia. *Historical Writing in England c.550–c.1307*. London, 1996.

Gransden, Antonia. *A History of the Abbey of Bury St Edmunds, 1182–1256: Samson of Tottington to Edmund of Walpole*. Woodbridge, 2007.

Green, Judith A. *The Government of England under Henry I*. Cambridge, 1986.

Green, Judith A. *The Aristocracy of Norman England*. Cambridge, 1997.

Green, Judith A. *Henry I: King of England and Duke of Normandy*. Cambridge, 2006.

Green, Monica. "Rethinking the Manuscript Basis of Salvatore de Renzi's *Collectio Salernitana*. The Corpus of Medical Writings in the 'Long' Twelfth Century." In *La* Collectio Salernitana *di Salvatore de Renzi*, edited by Danielle Jacquart and Agostino Paravicini Bagliani, 15–60. Florence, 2008.

Greenway, Diana E. *Fasti Ecclesiae Anglicanae, 1066–1300. 1. St Paul's, London*. London, 1968.

Greenway, Diana E. *Fasti Ecclesiae Anglicanae, 1066–1300. 3. Lincoln*. London, 1977.

Greenway, Diana E. "The False *Institutio* of St Osmund." In *Tradition and Change: Essays in Honour of Marjorie Chibnall*, edited by Diana Greenway, Christopher Holdsworth, and Jane Sayers, 77–101. Cambridge, 1985.

Greenway, Diana E. *Fasti Ecclesiae Anglicanae, 1066–1300. 4. Salisbury*. London, 1991.

Greenway, Diana E. "Authority, Convention and Observation in Henry of Huntingdon's *Historia Anglorum*." *Anglo-Norman Studies* 18 (1996), 105–21.

Greenway, Diana E. *Fasti Ecclesiae Anglicanae, 1066–1300. 5. Chichester*. London, 1996.

Greenway, Diana E. *Fasti Ecclesiae Anglicanae, 1066–1300. 6. York*. London, 1999.

Greenway, Diana E. *Fasti Ecclesiae Anglicanae, 1066–1300. 7. Bath and Wells*. London, 2001.

Greenway, Diana E. *Fasti Ecclesiae Anglicanae, 1066–1300. 10. Exeter*. London, 2005.

Greenway, Diana E. "Jocelin of Wells and his Cathedral Chapter." In *Jocelin of Wells: Bishop, Builder, Courtier*, edited by Robert W. Dunning, 53–66. Woodbridge, 2010.

Hackett, M. B. "The University as a Corporate Body." In *The History of the University of Oxford. Vol. 1. The Early Oxford Schools*, edited by J. I. Catto, 37–95. Oxford, 1984.

Haines, Roy Martin. *Ecclesia Anglicana: Studies in the English Church of the Later Middle Ages*. Toronto, 1989.

Hamel, Christopher de. *Glossed Books of the Bible and the Origins of the Paris Booktrade*. Woodbridge, 1984.

Hamel, Christopher de. *A History of Illuminated Manuscripts*. 2nd edn. London, 1994.

Harper-Bill, Christopher. "Bishop William Turbe and the Diocese of Norwich, 1146–1174." *Anglo-Norman Studies* 7 (1985), 142–60.

Harper-Bill, Christopher. "Battle Abbey and its East Anglian Churches." In *Studies in Medieval History Presented to R. Allen Brown*, edited by Christopher Harper-Bill, Christopher J. Holdsworth, and Janet L. Nelson, 159–72. Woodbridge, 1989.

Harper-Bill, Christopher. "The Struggle for Benefices in Twelfth-Century East Anglia." *Anglo-Norman Studies* 11 (1989), 113–32.

Harper-Bill, Christopher. "The Anglo-Norman Church." In *A Companion to the Anglo-Norman World*, edited by Christopher Harper-Bill and Elisabeth M. C. van Houts, 165–90. Woodbridge, 2003.

Harris, Max. *Sacred Folly: A New History of the Feast of Fools*. Ithaca, 2011.

Hartridge, R. A. R. *A History of Vicarages in the Middle Ages*. Cambridge, 1930.

Hartzell, K. D. *Catalogue of Manuscripts Written or Owned in England up to 1200 Containing Music*. Woodbridge, 2006.

Harvey, Barbara F. *Living and Dying in England, 1100–1540: The Monastic Experience*. Oxford, 1993.

Harvey, P. D. A. "The English Inflation of 1180–1220." *Past and Present* 61 (1973), 3–30.

Harvey, P. D. A. "The Pipe Rolls and the Adoption of Demesne Farming in England." *Economic History Review*, 2nd series, 27 (1974), 345–59.

Harvey, Sally. "The Knight and the Knight's Fee in England." *Past and Present* 49 (1970), 3–43.

Haseldine, Julian. "Understanding the Language of *Amicitia*. The Friendship Circle of Peter of Celle (*c.*1115–1183)." *Journal of Medieval History* 20 (1994), 237–60.

Haseldine, Julian, ed. *Friendship in Medieval Europe.* Stroud, 1999.

Haseldine, Julian. "Love, Separation and Male Friendship: Words and Actions in Saint Anselm's Letters to his Friends." In *Masculinity in Medieval Europe*, edited by D. M. Hadley, 238–55. London, 1999.

Haseldine, Julian. "Thomas Becket: Martyr, Saint—and Friend?" In *Belief and Culture in the Middle Ages: Studies Presented to Henry Mayr-Harting*, edited by Richard Gameson and Henrietta Leyser, 305–17. Oxford, 2001.

Haskins, Charles Homer. *Studies in the History of Mediaeval Science.* Cambridge, 1924.

Haskins, Charles Homer. *The Renaissance of the Twelfth Century.* Cambridge, MA, 1927.

Hastings, Adrian. *Elias of Dereham: Architect of Salisbury Cathedral.* Much Wenlock, 1997.

Heath, Peter. *The English Parish Clergy on the Eve of the Reformation.* London, 1969.

Heimpel, Hermann. "Reformatio Sigismundi, Priesterehe und Bernhard von Chartres." *Deutsches archiv für Erforschung des Mittelalters* 17 (1961), 526–37.

Helmholz, R. H. *The Canon Law and Ecclesiastical Jurisdiction from 597 to the 1640s.* Oxford, 2004.

Henig, Martin. "The Re-use and Copying of Ancient Intaglios set in Medieval Personal Seals, Mainly Found in England: An Aspect of the Renaissance of the 12th Century." In *Good Impressions: Image and Authority in Medieval Seals*, edited by Noël Adams, John Cherry, and James Robinson, 25–34. London, 2008.

Heslop, T. A. "Late Twelfth-Century Writing about Art, and Aesthetic Relativity." In *Medieval Art: Recent Perspectives*, edited by Gale R. Owen-Crocker and Timothy Graham, 129–41. Manchester, 1998.

Hirata, Yoko. "John of Salisbury, Gerard Pucelle and *Amicitia*." In *Friendship in Medieval Europe*, edited by Julian Haseldine, 153–65. Stroud, 1999.

Hosler, John D. "The Brief Military Career of Thomas Becket." *Haskins Society Journal* 15 (2006), 88–100.

Houts, Elisabeth van. "The Fate of Priests' Sons in Normandy with Special Reference to Serlo of Bayeux." *Haskins Society Journal* 25 (2013), forthcoming.

Howell, Margaret. *Regalian Right in Medieval England.* London, 1962.

Hudson, John. *The Formation of the English Common Law: Law and Society in England from the Norman Conquest to Magna Carta.* London, 1996.

Hughes, Andrew. "British Rhymed Offices: A Catalogue and Commentary." In *Music in the Medieval English Liturgy*, edited by Susan Rankin and David Hiley, 239–84. Oxford, 1993.

Hughes, Paul. "Roger of Howden's Sailing Directions for the English Coast." *Historical Research* 85 (2012), 576–96.

Humphrey, Chris. *The Politics of Carnival: Festive Misrule in Medieval England.* Manchester, 2001.

Hunt, R. W. "English Learning in the Late Twelfth Century." *Transactions of the Royal Historical Society*, 4th series, 19 (1936), 19–42.

Hunt, R. W., and Margaret T. Gibson. *The Schools and the Cloister: The Life and Writings of Alexander Nequam (1157–1217).* Oxford, 1984.

Hyams, Paul R. *Rancor and Reconciliation in Medieval England.* Ithaca, 2003.

Hyatte, Reginald. *The Arts of Friendship: The Idealization of Friendship in Medieval and Early Renaissance Literature.* Leiden, 1994.

Jaeger, C. Stephen. *The Origins of Courtliness: Civilizing Trends and the Formation of Courtly Ideals, 939–1210.* Philadelphia, 1985.

Jaeger, C. Stephen. *The Envy of Angels: Cathedral Schools and Social Ideals in Medieval Europe, 950–1200*. Philadelphia, 1994.

Jaeger, C. Stephen. "Pessimism in the Twelfth-Century 'Renaissance'." *Speculum* 78 (2003), 1151–83.

James, Montague Rhodes. *The Ancient Libraries of Canterbury and Dover*. Cambridge, 1903.

Jestice, Phyllis G. "Why Celibacy? Odo of Cluny and the Development of a New Sexual Morality." In *Medieval Purity and Piety: Essays on Medieval Clerical Celibacy and Religious Reform*, edited by Michael Frassetto, 81–115. New York, 1998.

Jolliffe, J. E. A. *Angevin Kingship*. London, 1955.

Jones, W. R. "Patronage and Administration: The King's Free Chapels in Medieval England." *Journal of British Studies* 9 (1969), 1–23.

Jong, Mayke de. "*Imitatio Morum*. The Cloister and Clerical Purity in the Carolingian World." In *Medieval Purity and Piety: Essays on Medieval Clerical Celibacy and Religious Reform*, edited by Michael Frassetto, 49–80. New York, 1998.

Jong, Mayke de. "Charlemagne's Church." In *Charlemagne: Empire and Society*, edited by Joanna Story, 103–35. Manchester, 2005.

Jordan, Mark D. *The Invention of Sodomy in Christian Theology*. Chicago, 1997.

Karn, Nicholas. "Robert de Sigillo: An Unruly Head of the Royal Scriptorium in the 1120s and 1130s." *English Historical Review* 123 (2008), 539–53.

Karras, Ruth Mazo. *From Boys to Men: Formations of Masculinity in Late Medieval Europe*. Philadelphia, 2003.

Karras, Ruth Mazo. *Sexuality in Medieval Europe: Doing unto Others*. New York, 2005.

Karras, Ruth Mazo. "Thomas Aquinas's Chastity Belt: Clerical Masculinity in Medieval Europe." In *Gender and Christianity in Medieval Europe: New Perspectives*, edited by Lisa M. Bitel and Felice Lifshitz, 52–67. Philadelphia, 2008.

Karras, Ruth Mazo. *Unmarriages: Women, Men, and Sexual Unions in the Middle Ages*. Philadelphia, 2012.

Kealey, Edward J. *Roger of Salisbury, Viceroy of England*. Berkeley, 1972.

Kealey, Edward J. *Medieval Medicus: A Social History of Anglo-Norman Medicine*. Baltimore, 1981.

Kealey, Edward J. *Harvesting the Air: Windmill Pioneers in Twelfth-Century England*. Berkeley, 1987.

Keats-Rohan, K. S. B. "John of Salisbury and Education in Twelfth Century Paris from the Account of his Metalogicon." *History of Universities* 6 (1986–7), 1–45.

Kelleher, M. A. "'Like Man and Wife': Clerics' Concubines in the Diocese of Barcelona." *Journal of Medieval History* 28 (2002), 349–60.

Kemp, B. R. "Hereditary Benefices in the Medieval English Church: A Herefordshire Example." *Bulletin of the Institute of Historical Research* 43 (1970), 1–15.

Kemp, B. R. "Monastic Possession of Parish Churches in England in the Twelfth Century." *Journal of Ecclesiastical History* 31 (1980), 133–60.

Kemp, B. R. "Towards Admission and Institution: English Episcopal Formulae for the Appointment of Parochial Incumbents in the Twelfth Century." *Anglo-Norman Studies* 16 (1994), 155–76.

Kemp, B. R. "Informing the Archdeacon on Ecclesastical Matters in Twelfth-Century England." In *Medieval Ecclesiastical Studies in Honour of Dorothy M. Owen*, edited by M. J. Franklin and Christopher Harper-Bill, 131–49. Woodbridge, 1995.

Ker, N. R. *Catalogue of Manuscripts Containing Anglo-Saxon*. Oxford, 1957.

Ker, N. R. *Medieval Libraries of Great Britain: A List of Surviving Books*. 2nd edn. London, 1964.

Ker, N. R. "Books at St Paul's Cathedral before 1313." In *Books, Collectors, and Libraries: Studies in the Medieval Heritage*, edited by Andrew G. Watson, 209–42. London, 1985.

Kerr, Julie. "Food, Drink and Lodging: Hospitality in Twelfth-Century England." *Haskins Society Journal* 18 (2006), 72–92.

Kerr, Julie. "Welcome the Coming and Speed the Parting Guest: Hospitality in Twelfth-Century England." *Journal of Medieval History* 33 (2007), 130–46.

Kerr, Julie. *Monastic Hospitality: The Benedictines in England, c.1070–c.1250.* Woodbridge, 2007.

Keynes, Simon. "Regenbald the Chancellor (*sic*)." *Anglo-Norman Studies* 10 (1988), 185–222.

Kibre, Pearl. *The Nations in the Mediaeval Universities.* Cambridge, MA, 1948.

Kieckhefer, Richard. *Magic in the Middle Ages.* Cambridge, 1989.

Knorr, Wilbur R. "John of Tynemouth alias John of London: Emerging Portrait of a Singular Medieval Mathematician." *British Journal for the History of Science* 23 (1990), 290–323.

Knowles, David. *The Monastic Order in England: A History of its Development from the Times of St. Dunstan to the Fourth Lateran Council, 940–1216.* 2nd edn. Cambridge, 1963.

Knowles, David. *Thomas Becket.* Stanford, 1971.

Köhn, Rolf. "'Militia Curialis'. Die Kritik der Geistlichen Hofdienst bei Peter von Blois in der Lateinischen Literatur des 9–12 Jahrhunderts." In *Soziale Ordnungen im Selbsverständnis des Mittelalters*, edited by Albert Zimmerman, 227–57. Berlin, 1979.

Köhn, Rolf. "Schulbildung und Trivium im lateinischen Hochmittelalter und ihr möglicher praktischer Nutzen." In *Schulen und Studium im sozialen Wandel des hohen und späten Mittelalters*, edited by Johannes Fried, 203–84. Sigmaringen, 1986.

Kuefler, Mathew. *The Manly Eunuch: Masculinity, Gender Ambiguity, and Christian Ideology in Late Antiquity.* Chicago, 2001.

Kuttner, Stephan, and Eleanor Rathbone. "Anglo-Norman Canonists of the Twelfth Century." *Traditio* 7 (1949–51), 279–358.

Lachaud, Frédérique. "L'enseignement des bonnes manières en milieu de cour en Angleterre d'après l'*Urbanus magnus* attribué à Daniel de Beccles." In *Erziehung und Bildung bei Hofe*, edited by Werner Paravicini and Jörg Wettlaufer, 43–53. Stuttgart, 2002.

Lachaud, Frédérique. "Littérature de civilité et 'processus de civilisation' à la fin de XIIe siècle: le cas anglais d'après l'*Urbanus magnus*." In *Les Échanges culturels au Moyen Âge: XXXIIe congrès de la SHMES*, 227–39. Paris, 2002.

Lachaud, Frédérique. "L'idée de noblesse dans le *Policraticus* de Jean de Salisbury (1159)." *Cahiers de recherches médiévales et humanistes* 13 (2006), 3–19.

Lachaud, Frédérique. *L'éthique du pouvoir au Moyen Âge: l'office dans la culture politique (Angleterre, vers 1150–vers 1330).* Paris, 2010.

Lachaud, Frédérique. "La figure du clerc curial dans l'oeuvre de Jean de Salisbury." In *La cour du prince: cour de France, cours d'Europe XIIe–XVe siècle*, edited by Murielle Gaude-Ferragu, Bruno Laurioux, and Jacques Paviot, 301–20. Paris, 2011.

Langdon, John, and James Masschaele. "Commercial Activity and Population Growth in Medieval England." *Past and Present* 190 (2006), 35–81.

Langmuir, Gavin I. "Thomas of Monmouth: Detector of Ritual Murder." *Speculum* 59 (1984), 820–46.

Latimer, Paul. "Early Thirteenth-Century Prices." In *King John: New Interpretations*, edited by S. D. Church, 41–73. Woodbridge, 1999.

Latimer, Paul. "Wages in Late Twelfth- and Early Thirteenth-Century England." *The Haskins Society Journal* 9 (2001), 185–205.

Laudage, Johannes. *Priesterbild und Reformpapsttum im 11. Jahrhundert*. Cologne, 1984.

Lawrence, C. H. "The English Parish and its Clergy in the Thirteenth Century." In *The Medieval World*, edited by Peter Linehan and Janet L. Nelson, 648–70. London, 2001.

Le Goff, Jacques. "What did the Twelfth-Century Renaissance Mean?" In *The Medieval World*, edited by Peter Linehan and Janet L. Nelson, 635–47. London, 2001.

Le Saux, Françoise H. M. *Layamon's Brut: The Poem and its Sources*. Cambridge, 1989.

Leader, Damian Riehl. *A History of the University of Cambridge: Volume 1, The University to 1546*, edited by C. N. L. Brooke. Cambridge, 1988.

Leclercq, Jean. *The Love of Learning and the Desire for God: A Study of Monastic Culture*. New York, 1961.

Legge, M. Dominica. *Anglo-Norman in the Cloisters: The Influence of the Orders upon Anglo-Norman Literature*. Edinburgh, 1950.

Legge, M. Dominica. *Anglo-Norman Literature and its Background*. Oxford, 1963.

Lehmann, Paul. *Die Parodie im Mittelalter*. 2nd ed. Stuttgart, 1963.

Lemay, R. "L'authenticité de la préface de Robert de Chester à sa traduction du Morienus (1144)." *Chrysopœia* 4 (1991), 3–32.

Lennard, Reginald. *Rural England, 1086–1135: A Study of Social and Agrarian Conditions*, Oxford, 1959.

Lepine, David. *A Brotherhood of Canons Serving God: English Secular Cathedrals in the Later Middle Ages*. Woodbridge, 1995.

Levine, Robert. "How to read Walter Map." *Mittellateinisches Jahrbuch* 23 (1991), 91–105.

Leyser, Conrad. "Custom, Truth, and Gender in Eleventh-Century Reform." In *Gender and Christian Religion*, edited by R. N. Swanson, 75–91. Woodbridge, 1998.

Liere, Frans van. "The Study of Canon Law and the Eclipse of the Lincoln Schools, 1172–1225." *History of Universities* 18 (2003), 1–13.

Little, Lester K. *Religious Poverty and the Profit Economy in Medieval Europe*. Ithaca, 1978.

Losseff, Nicky. *The Best Concords: Polyphonic Music in Thirteenth-Century Britain*. New York, 1994.

Loud, G. A. *The Latin Church in Norman Italy*. Cambridge, 2007.

Loyn, H. R. *The English Church, 940–1154*. Harlow, 2000.

Luscombe, D. E. *The School of Peter Abelard: The Influence of Abelard's Thought in the Early Scholastic Period*. Cambridge, 1969.

MacDonald, Iain. "The Chronicle of Jordan Fantosme." In *Studies in Medieval French Presented to Alfred Ewert*, 242–58. Oxford, 1961.

Macy, Gary. *The Hidden History of Women's Ordination: Female Clergy in the Medieval West*. Oxford, 2008.

Mahrt, William Peter. "The Role of Old Sarum in the Processions of Salisbury Cathedral." In *The Study of Medieval Manuscripts of England: Festschrift in Honor of Richard W. Pfaff*, edited by George Hardin Brown and Linda E. Voigts, 129–41. Tempe, 2010.

Maitland, Frederic William. "Henry II and the Criminous Clerks." In *The Collected Papers of Frederic William Maitland*, edited by H. A. L. Fisher, 232–50. Cambridge, 1911.

Major, Kathleen. "The 'Familia' of Archbishop Stephen Langton." *English Historical Review* 48 (1933), 529–53.

Marritt, Stephen. "Secular Cathedrals and the Anglo-Norman Aristocracy." In *Cathedrals, Communities and Conflict in the Anglo-Norman World*, edited by Paul Dalton, Charles Insley, and Louise J. Wilkinson, 151–67. Woodbridge, 2011.

Martin, Janet. "Classicism and Style in Latin Literature." In *Renaissance and Renewal in the Twelfth Century*, edited by Robert Louis Benson and Giles Constable, 537–68. Cambridge, MA, 1982.

Martin, Janet. "John of Salisbury as Classical Scholar." In *The World of John of Salisbury*, edited by Michael Wilks, 179–201. Oxford, 1984.

Mason, Emma. *Saint Wulfstan of Worcester, c.1008–1095*. Oxford, 1990.

Mason, Emma. *Westminster Abbey and its People, c.1050–c.1216*. Woodbridge, 1996.

Mason, J. F. A. "The Officers and Clerks of the Norman Earls of Shropshire." *Transactions of the Shropshire Archaeological Society* 56 (1957–60), 244–57.

Masschaele, James. *Peasants, Merchants, and Markets: Inland Trade in Medieval England, 1150–1350*. Basingstoke, 1997.

Matthew, Donald. *Britain and the Continent, 1000–1300*. London, 2005.

Mayr-Harting, Henry. "The Role of Benedictine Abbeys in the Development of Oxford as a Centre of Legal Learning." In *Benedictines in Oxford*, edited by Henry Wansbrough and Anthony Marett-Crosby, 11–19. London, 1997.

Mayr-Harting, Henry. *Religion, Politics and Society in Britain, 1066–1272*. Harlow, 2011.

McCulloch, John W. "Jewish Ritual Murder: William of Norwich, Thomas of Monmouth, and the Early Dissemination of the Myth." *Speculum* 72 (1997), 698–740.

McHardy, A. K. "Careers and Disappointments in the Late-Medieval Church: Some English Evidence." In *The Ministry: Clerical and Lay*, edited by W. J. Sheils and Diana Wood, 111–30. Oxford, 1989.

McKitterick, Rosamond. *The Frankish Church and the Carolingian Reforms, 789–895*. London, 1977.

McKitterick, Rosamond. *The Carolingians and the Written Word*. Cambridge, 1989.

McLaughlin, Megan. *Sex, Gender, and Episcopal Authority in an Age of Reform, 1000–1122*. Cambridge, 2010.

McLoughlin, John. "*Amicitia* in Practice: John of Salisbury (*c.*1120–1180) and his Circle." In *England in the Twelfth Century: Proceedings of the 1988 Harlaxton Symposium*, edited by Daniel Williams, 165–81. Woodbridge, 1990.

McNamara, Jo Ann. "Chaste Marriage and Clerical Celibacy." In *Sexual Practices and the Medieval Church*, edited by Vern L. Bullough and James A. Brundage, 22–33. Buffalo, 1982.

McNamara, Jo Ann. "An Unresolved Syllogism: The Search for a Christian Gender System." In *Conflicted Identities and Multiple Masculinities: Men in the Medieval West*, edited by Jacqueline Murray, 1–24. New York, 1999.

McVaugh, Michael. "Who Was Gilbert the Englishman?" In *The Study of Medieval Manuscripts of England: Festschrift in Honor of Richard W. Pfaff*, edited by George Hardin Brown and Linda E. Voigts, 295–324. Tempe, 2010.

Meijns, Brigitte. "Opposition to Clerical Continence and the Gregorian Celibacy Legislation in the Diocese of Thérouanne: *Tractatus pro Clericorum Conubio* (*c.*1077–1078)." *Sacris Erudiri* 47 (2008), 223–90.

Melve, Leidulf. "'The Revolt of the Medievalists.' Directions in Recent Research on the Twelfth-Century Renaissance." *Journal of Medieval History* 32 (2006), 231–52.

Melve, Leidulf. "The Public Debate on Clerical Marriage in the Late Eleventh Century." *Journal of Ecclesiastical History* 61 (2010), 688–706.

Mews, Constant J., and Neville Chiavaroli. "The Latin West." In *Friendship: A History*, edited by Barbara Caine, 73–110. London, 2009.

Michael, M. A. "English Illuminators *c.*1190–1450: A Survey from Documentary Sources." *English Manuscript Studies 1100–1700* 4 (1993), 62–113.

Michael, M. A. "Urban Production of Manuscript Books and the Role of the University Towns." In *The Cambridge History of the Book in Britain. Vol. 2, 1100–1400*, edited by Nigel J. Morgan and Rodney M. Thomson, 168–94. Cambridge, 2008.

Miller, Edward. "England in the 12th and 13th Century: An Economic Contrast?" *Economic History Review*, 2nd series, 24 (1971), 1–14.

Miller, Maureen. "Religion Makes a Difference: Clerical and Lay Cultures in the Courts of Northern Italy, 1000–1300." *American Historical Review* 105 (2000), 1095–130.

Miller, Maureen. "Masculinity, Reform, and Clerical Culture: Narratives of Episcopal Holiness in the Gregorian Era." *Church History* 72 (2003), 25–52.

Minio-Paluello, L. "The *Ars Disserendi* of Adam of Balsham 'Parvipontanus'." *Mediaeval and Renaissance Studies* 3 (1954), 116–69.

Mitchell, Sydney Knox. *Taxation in Medieval England.* New Haven, 1951.

Monson, Don Alfred. *Andreas Capellanus, Scholasticism, and the Courtly Tradition.* Washington, D.C., 2005.

Moore, R. I. "Family, Community and Cult on the Eve of the Gregorian Reform." *Transactions of the Royal Historical Society*, 5th series, 30 (1980), 49–69.

Moore, R. I. "Property, Marriage, and the Eleventh-Century Revolution: A Context for Early Medieval Communism." In *Medieval Purity and Piety: Essays on Medieval Clerical Celibacy and Religious Reform*, edited by Michael Frassetto, 179–208. New York, 1998.

Moore, R. I. *The First European Revolution, c.970–1215.* Oxford, 2000.

Moore, R. I. *The Formation of a Persecuting Society: Authority and Deviance in Western Europe, 950–1250.* 2nd edn. Oxford, 2007.

Moorman, John R. H. *Church Life in England in the Thirteenth Century.* Cambridge, 1946.

Morenzoni, Franco. *Des écoles aux paroisses: Thomas de Chobham et la promotion de la prédication au début du XIIIe siècle.* Paris, 1995.

Morenzoni, Franco. "Pastorale et ecclésiologie dans la prédication d'Étienne Langton." In *Étienne Langton: prédicateur, bibliste, théologien*, edited by Louis J. Bataillon, Nicole Bériou, Gilbert Dahan, and Riccardo Quinto, 449–66. Turnhout, 2010.

Moreton, Jennifer. "Before Grosseteste: Roger of Hereford and Calendar Reform in Eleventh- and Twelfth-Century England." *Isis* 86 (1995), 562–86.

Morey, Adrian. *Bartholomew of Exeter, Bishop and Canonist: A Study in the Twelfth Century.* Cambridge, 1937.

Morgan, Nigel J. "Books for the Liturgy and Private Prayer." In *The Cambridge History of the Book in Britain. Vol. 2, 1100–1400*, edited by Nigel J. Morgan and Rodney M. Thomson, 291–316. Cambridge, 2008.

Morris, Richard. *Churches in the Landscape* London, 1989.

Moser, Thomas C. *A Cosmos of Desire: The Medieval Latin Erotic Lyric in English Manuscripts.* Ann Arbor, 2004.

Moulinier-Brogi, Laurence. "Jean de Salisbury: un réseau d'amitiés continentales." In *Culture politique des Plantagenêt, 1154–1224*, edited by Martin Aurell, 341–61. Poitiers, 2003.

Muratova, Xenia. "Bestiaries: An Aspect of Medieval Patronage." In *Art and Patronage in the English Romanesque*, edited by Sarah Macready and F. H. Thompson, 118–44. London, 1986.

Murray, Alexander. *Reason and Society in the Middle Ages.* Oxford, 1978.

Murray, Jacqueline. "Masculinizing Religious Life: Sexual Prowess, the Battle for Chastity and Monastic Identity." In *Holiness and Masculinity in the Middle Ages*, edited by P. H. Cullum and Katherine J. Lewis, 24–42. Cardiff, 2004.

Mynors, R. A. B. *Durham Cathedral Manuscripts to the End of the Twelfth Century.* Durham, 1939.

Mynors, R. A. B., and Rodney M. Thomson. *Catalogue of the Manuscripts of Hereford Cathedral Library.* Cambridge, 1993.

Neal, Derek G. *The Masculine Self in Late Medieval England*. Chicago, 2008.

Nederman, Cary J. *John of Salisbury*. Tempe, 2005.

Nederman, Cary J. "Friendship in Public Life during the Twelfth Century: Theory and Practice in the Writings of John of Salisbury." *Viator* 38 (2007), 385–97.

Nederman, Cary J. "Textual Communities of Learning and Friendship Circles in the Twelfth Century: An Examination of John of Salisbury's Correspondence." In *Communities of Learning: Networks and the Shaping of Intellectual Identity in Europe, 1100–1500*, edited by Constant J. Mews and John N. Crossley, 73–83. Turnhout, 2011.

Nederman, Cary J., and Karen Bollermann. "'The Extravagance of the Senses': Epicureanism, Priestly Tyranny, and the Becket Problem in John of Salisbury's *Policraticus*." *Studies in Medieval and Renaissance History*, 3rd series, 8 (2011), 1–25.

Nicholls, Jonathan. *The Matter of Courtesy: Medieval Courtesy Books and the Gawain-Poet*. Woodbridge, 1985.

Nilgen, Ursula. "Intellectuality and Splendour: Thomas Becket as a Patron of the Arts." In *Art and Patronage in the English Romanesque*, edited by Sarah Macready and F. H. Thompson, 144–58. London, 1986.

Noble, Thomas F. X. "Introduction." In *European Transformations: The Long Twelfth Century*, edited by Thomas F. X. Noble and John H. Van Engen, 1–16. Notre Dame, 2012.

North, John. "Some Norman Horoscopes." In *Adelard of Bath: An English Scientist and Arabist of the Early Twelfth Century*, edited by Charles Burnett, 147–61. London, 1987.

Norton, Christopher. *St. William of York*. Woodbridge, 2006.

O'Brien, Bruce R. *God's Peace and King's Peace: The Laws of Edward the Confessor*. Philadelphia, 1999.

Oggins, Virginia Darrow, and Robin S. Oggins. "Richard of Ilchester's Inheritance: An Extended Family in Twelfth-Century England." *Medieval Prosopography* 12 (1991), 57–128.

Oliver, George. *Lives of the Bishops of Exeter and a History of the Cathedral*. Exeter, 1861.

O'Malley, John W. "Introduction: Medieval Preaching." In *De Ore Domini: Preacher and Word in the Middle Ages*, edited by Thomas L. Amos, Eugene Green, and Beverly Mayne Kienzle, 1–11. Kalamazoo, 1989.

Orme, Nicholas. "Lay Literacy in England, 1100-1300." In *England and Germany in the High Middle Ages*, edited by Alfred Haverkamp and Hanna Vollrath, 35–56. Oxford, 1996.

Orme, Nicholas. *Medieval Schools: From Roman Britain to Renaissance England*. New Haven, 2006.

Orme, Nicholas, and Margaret Webster. *The English Hospital, 1070–1570*. New Haven, 1995.

Otte, James K. "The Life and Writings of Alfredus Anglicus." *Viator* 3 (1972), 275–91.

Owen, Dorothy M. "Historical Survey, 1091–1450." In *A History of Lincoln Minster*, 112–63. Cambridge, 1994.

Owst, Gerald Robert. *Preaching in Medieval England: An Introduction to Sermon Manuscripts of the Period, c.1350–1450*. Cambridge, 1926.

Page, Christopher. *The Owl and the Nightingale: Musical Life and Ideas in France, 1100–1300*. London, 1989.

Page, Christopher. "Music and the Origins of Courtliness." In *Courtly Arts and the Art of Courtliness*, edited by Keith Busby and Christopher Kleinhenz, 29–48. Cambridge, 2006.

Painter, Sidney. *Studies in the History of the English Feudal Barony*. Baltimore, 1943.

Painter, Sidney. *The Reign of King John*. Baltimore, 1949.

Palmer, Robert C. *Selling the Church: The English Parish in Law, Commerce, and Religion, 1350–1550*. Chapel Hill, 2002.

Panayotova, Stella. "Tutorial in Images for Thomas Becket." In *The Cambridge Illuminations: The Conference Papers*, edited by Stella Panayotova, 76–86. London, 2007.

Panofsky, Erwin. *Renaissance and Renascences in Western Art*. New York, 1972.

Parish, Helen L. *Clerical Celibacy in the West, c.1100–1700*. Farnham, 2009.

Parkes, M. B. *Their Hands before our Eyes: A Closer Look at Scribes*. Aldershot, 2008.

Partner, Nancy F. *Serious Entertainments: The Writing of History in Twelfth-Century England*. Chicago, 1977.

Patterson, Robert B. "Robert Fitz Harding of Bristol: Profile of an Early Angevin Burgess-Baron Patrician and his Family's Urban Involvement." *Haskins Society Journal* 1 (1989), 109–22.

Patterson, Robert B. *The Scriptorium of Margam Abbey and the Scribes of Early Angevin Glamorgan: Secretarial Administration in a Welsh Marcher Barony, c.1150–c.1225*. Woodbridge, 2002.

Pennington, Kenneth. *Pope and Bishops: The Papal Monarchy in the Twelfth and Thirteenth Centuries*. Philadelphia, 1984.

Pennington, Kenneth. "Decretal Collections 1190–1234." In *The History of Medieval Canon Law in the Classical Period, 1140–1234: From Gratian to the Decretals of Pope Gregory IX*, edited by Wilfried Hartmann and Kenneth Pennington, 293–317. Washington, D.C., 2008.

Pennington, Kenneth. "The Decretalists 1190–1234." In *The History of Medieval Canon Law in the Classical Period, 1140–1234: From Gratian to the Decretals of Pope Gregory IX*, edited by Wilfried Hartmann and Kenneth Pennington, 211–45. Washington, D.C., 2008.

Peters, Edward. *The Magician, the Witch, and the Law*. Philadelphia, 1978.

Pevsner, Nikolaus. *South and West Somerset*. Harmondsworth, 1958.

Pevsner, Nikolaus. *Staffordshire*. Harmondsworth, 1974.

Pevsner, Nikolaus, and Ian Nairn. *Sussex*. Harmondsworth, 1965.

Pevsner, Nikolaus, and Elizabeth Williamson. *Derbyshire*. 2nd edn. Harmondsworth, 1978.

Pevsner, Nikolaus, and Elizabeth Williamson. *Nottinghamshire*. 2d edn. Harmondsworth, 1979.

Pfaff, Richard W. *The Liturgy in Medieval England: A History*. Cambridge, 2009.

Pixton, Paul B. *The German Episcopacy and the Implementation of the Decrees of the Fourth Lateran Council, 1216–1245: Watchmen on the Tower*. Leiden, 1995.

Postles, David. "County *Clerici* and the Composition of English Twelfth- and Thirteenth-Century Private Charters." In *Charters and the Use of the Written Word in Medieval Society*, edited by Karl Heidecker, 27–42. Turnhout, 2000.

Poulle, Emmanuel. "Le traité de l'astrolabe d'Adélard de Bath." In *Adelard of Bath: An English Scientist and Arabist of the Early Twelfth Century*, edited by Charles Burnett, 119–32. London, 1987.

Powell, W. R. "The Administration of the Navy and the Stannaries, 1189–1216." *English Historical Review* 71 (1956), 177–88.

Powicke, F. M. *Stephen Langton*. Oxford, 1928.

Powicke, Michael R. "Distraint of Knighthood and Military Obligation under Henry III." *Speculum* 25 (1950), 457–70.

Prestwich, Michael. *Armies and Warfare in the Middle Ages: The English Experience*. New Haven, 1996.

Prestwich, Michael. *Plantagenet England, 1225–1360*. Oxford, 2005.

Quinto, Riccardo. "Stephen Langton: Theology and Literature of the Pastoral Care." In *In principio erat verbum: mélanges offerts en hommage à Paul Tombeur*, edited by B.-M. Tock, 301–55. Turnhout, Belgium, 2005.

Ramseyer, Valerie. *The Transformation of a Religious Landscape: Medieval Southern Italy, 850–1150.* Ithaca, 2006.

Rapp, Francis "Rapport introductif." In *Le clerc séculier au moyen âge*, 9–25. Paris, 1993.

Rasche, Ulrich. "The Early Phase of Appropriation of Parish Churches in Medieval England." *Journal of Medieval History* 26 (2000), 213–37.

Rathbone, Eleanor. "Master Alberic of London, 'Mythographus Tertius Vaticanus'." *Mediaeval and Renaissance Studies* 1 (1941–43), 35–8.

Rathbone, Eleanor. "John of Cornwall: A Brief Biography." *Recherches de théologie ancienne et médiévale* 17 (1950), 46–60.

Remensnyder, Amy G. "Pollution, Purity, and Peace: An Aspect of Social Reform between the Late Tenth Century and 1076." In *The Peace of God: Social Violence and Religious Response around the Year 1000*, edited by Thomas Head and Richard Landes, 280–307. Ithaca, 1992.

Reynolds, Susan. "Social Mentalities and the Cases of Medieval Scepticism." *Transactions of the Royal Historical Society*, 6th series, 1 (1991), 21–41.

Rhijn, Carine van. *Shepherds of the Lord: Priests and Episcopal Statutes in the Carolingian Period.* Turnhout, 2007.

Richards, Jeffrey. *Sex, Dissidence, and Damnation: Minority Groups in the Middle Ages*, London, 1990.

Richards, Mary P. *Texts and their Traditions in the Medieval Library of Rochester Cathedral Priory*, Transactions of the American Philosophical Society, n. s., vol. 78 Philadelphia, 1988.

Richardson, H. G. "William of Ely, the King's Treasurer (? 1195–1215)." *Transactions of the Royal Historical Society*, 4th series, 15 (1932), 45–90.

Richardson, H. G., and G. O. Sayles. *The Governance of Mediaeval England from the Conquest to Magna Carta.* Edinburgh, 1963.

Richter, Michael. *Giraldus Cambrensis: The Growth of the Welsh Nation.* Aberystwyth, 1972.

Ridder-Symoens, Hilde de, ed. *Universities in the Middle Ages.* Cambridge, 1992.

Rigg, A. G. *A History of Anglo-Latin Literature, 1066–1422.* Cambridge, 1992.

Roberts, Phyllis. *Studies in the Sermons of Stephen Langton.* Toronto, 1968.

Roberts, Phyllis. "The *Ars Praedicandi* and the Medieval Sermon." In *Preaching, Sermon, and Audience in the Middle Ages*, edited by Carolyn Muessig 41–62. Leiden, 2002.

Rocke, Michael. *Forbidden Friendships: Homosexuality and Male Culture in Renaissance Florence.* New York, 1996.

Rose, Valentin. "Ars Notaria: tironische Noten und Stenographie im 12. Jahrhundert." *Hermes* 8 (1874), 303–26.

Rothwell, W. "The Role of French in Thirteenth-Century England." *Bulletin of the John Rylands Society* 58 (1976), 445–66.

Round, J. H. "Bernard, the King's Scribe." *English Historical Review* 14 (1899), 417–30.

Rouse, Richard H., and Mary A. Rouse. "'Potens in Opere et Sermone': Philip, Bishop of Bayeux, and his Books." In *The Classics in the Middle Ages*, edited by Aldo S. Bernardo and Saul Levin, 315–41. Binghamton, 1990.

Rouse, Richard H., and Mary A. Rouse. *Illiterati et Uxorati: Manuscripts and their Makers: Commercial Book Producers in Medieval Paris, 1200–1500.* 2 vols. Turnhout, 2000.

Rousseau, Marie-Hélène. *Saving the Souls of Medieval London: Perpetual Chantries at St. Paul's Cathedral, c.1200–1548.* Farnham, 2011.

Rubin, Miri. *Corpus Christi: The Eucharist in Late Medieval Culture*. Cambridge, 1991.

Ruggiero, Guido. *The Boundaries of Eros: Sex Crime and Sexuality in Renaissance Venice*. New York, 1985.

Ruggiero, Guido. *Machiavelli in Love: Sex, Self, and Society in the Italian Renaissance*. Baltimore, 2007.

Saenger, Paul. "The British Isles and the Origin of the Modern Mode of Biblical Citation." *Syntagma: Revista de Historia del Libro y de la Lectura* 1 (2005), 77–123.

Saenger, Paul, and Laura Bruck. "The Anglo-Hebraic Origins of the Modern Chapter Division of the Latin Bible." In *La fractura historiográfica: las investigaciones de Edad Media y Renacimiento desde el tercer milenio*, edited by Javier San José Lera, Francisco Javier Burguillo López, and Laura Mier Pérez, 177–202. Salamanca, 2008.

Saltman, Avrom. *Theobald, Archbishop of Canterbury*. London, 1956.

Sayers, Jane E. *Papal Judges Delegate in the Province of Canterbury, 1198–1254: A Study in Ecclesiastical Jurisdiction and Administration*. Oxford, 1971.

Scaglione, Aldo D. *Knights at Court: Courtliness, Chivalry, and Courtesy from Ottonian Germany to the Italian Renaissance*. Berkeley, 1991.

Scammell, G. V. *Hugh du Puiset, Bishop of Durham*. Cambridge, 1956.

Scattergood, John. "Misrepresenting the City: Genre, Intertextuality and William Fitz-Stephen's *Description of London* (*c*.1173)." In *Reading the Past: Essays on Medieval and Renaissance Literature*, 15–36. Dublin, 1996.

Schimmelpfennig, Bernhard. "*Ex Fornicatione Nati*: Studies on the Position of Priests' Sons from the Twelfth to Fourteenth Century." *Studies in Medieval and Renaissance History*, n.s. 2 (1979), 3–50.

Schmugge, Ludwig. *Kirche, Kinder, Karrieren: Päpstliche Dispense von der unehelichen Geburt im Spätmittelalter*. Zürich, 1995.

Sharpe, R., J. P. Carley, R. M. Thomson, and A. G. Watson. *English Benedictine Libraries: The Shorter Catalogues*. London, 1996.

Sharpe, Richard. "Richard Barre's *Compendium Veteris et Novi Testamenti*." *The Journal of Medieval Latin* 14 (2004), 128–46.

Sheppard, Jennifer M. *The Buildwas Books: Book Production, Acquisition and Use at an English Cistercian Monastery, 1165–c.1400*. Oxford, 1997.

Sherman, Richard Mylius. "Robert de Gant (*c*.1086–*c*.1158): Dean of York and King's Chancellor." *Haskins Society Journal* 13 (2004), 99–110.

Short, Ian. "On Bilingualism in Anglo-Norman England." *Romance Philology* 33 (1980), 467–79.

Short, Ian. "Patrons and Polyglots: French Literature in Twelfth-Century England." *Anglo-Norman Studies* 14 (1992), 229–49.

Silverstein, Theodore. "Daniel Morley, English Cosmogonist and Student of Arabic Science." *Mediaeval Studies* 10 (1948), 179–96.

Smalley, Beryl. *The Study of the Bible in the Middle Ages*. 2nd edn. Oxford, 1952.

Smalley, Beryl. *The Becket Conflict and the Schools: A Study of Intellectuals in Politics*. Totowa, 1973.

Smith, David M. "Hugh's Administration of the Diocese of Lincoln." In *St. Hugh of Lincoln*, edited by Henry Mayr-Harting, 19–47. Oxford, 1987.

Smith, David M. "The 'Officialis' of the Bishop in Twelfth- and Thirteenth-Century England: Problems of Terminology." In *Medieval Ecclesiastical Studies in Honour of Dorothy M. Owen*, edited by M. J. Franklin and Christopher Harper-Bill, 201–20. Woodbridge, 1995.

Smith, Lesley. *The* Glossa Ordinaria*: The Making of a Medieval Bible Commentary*. Leiden, 2009.

Solopova, Elizabeth. "English Poetry of the Reign of Henry II." In *Writers of the Reign of Henry II: Twelve Essays*, edited by Ruth Kennedy and Simon Meecham-Jones, 187–204. New York, 2006.

Southern, R. W. *Medieval Humanism and Other Studies*. Oxford, 1970.

Southern, R. W. "From Schools to University." In *The History of the University of Oxford. Vol. 1. The Early Oxford Schools*, edited by J. I. Catto, 1–36. Oxford, 1984.

Southern, R. W. *Robert Grosseteste: The Growth of an English Mind in Medieval Europe*. Oxford, 1986.

Southern, R. W. "The Necessity of Two Peters of Blois." In *Intellectual Life in the Middle Ages: Essays Presented to Margaret Gibson*, edited by Lesley M. Smith and Benedicta Ward, 103–18. London, 1992.

Southern, R. W. *Scholastic Humanism and the Unification of Europe*. 2 vols. Oxford, 1995–2001.

Spear, David. "Power, Patronage and Personality in the Norman Cathedral Chapters, 911–1204." *Anglo-Norman Studies* 20 (1998), 205–21.

Spear, David. *The Personnel of the Norman Cathedrals during the Ducal Period, 911–1204*. London, 2006.

Spencer, H. Leith. *English Preaching in the Late Middle Ages*. Oxford, 1993.

Stacey, Robert C. *Politics, Policy, and Finance under Henry III, 1216–1245*. Oxford, 1987.

Stafford, Pauline. "Queens, Nunneries, and Reforming Churchmen: Gender, Religious States and Reform in Tenth- and Eleventh-Century England." *Past and Present* 163 (1999), 3–35.

Staunton, Michael. *Thomas Becket and his Biographers*. Woodbridge, 2006.

Stehling, Thomas. *Medieval Latin Poems of Male Love and Friendship*. New York, 1984.

Stenton, F. M. *The First Century of English Feudalism, 1066–1166*. 2nd edn. Oxford, 1961.

Stollberg, Gunnar. *Die soziale Stellung der intellektuellen Oberschicht im England des 12. Jahrhunderts*. Lubeck, 1973.

Stratford, Neil, Pamela Tudor-Craig, and Anna Marie Muthesius. "Archbishop Hubert Walter's Tomb and the Furnishings." In *Medieval Art and Architecture at Canterbury before 1220*, edited by Nicola Coldstream and Peter Draper, 71–93. London, 1982.

Stringer, K. J. *Earl David of Huntingdon, 1152–1219: A Study in Anglo-Scottish History*. Edinburgh, 1985.

Struve, Tilman. "The Importance of the Organism in the Political Theory of John of Salisbury." In *The World of John of Salisbury*, edited by Michael Wilks, 303–17. Oxford, 1984.

Swan, Mary. "Old English Textual Activity in the Reign of Henry II." In *Writers of the Reign of Henry II: Twelve Essays*, edited by Ruth Kennedy and Simon Meecham-Jones, 151–68. New York, 2006.

Swan, Mary, and Elaine M. Treharne, eds. *Rewriting Old English in the Twelfth Century*. Cambridge, 2000.

Swanson, R. N. *Church and Society in Late Medieval England*. Oxford, 1989.

Swanson, R. N. "Problems of the Priesthood in Pre-Reformation England." *English Historical Review* 105 (1990), 845–69.

Swanson, R. N. "Angels Incarnate: Clergy and Reform from Gregorian Reform to Reformation." In *Masculinity in Medieval Europe*, edited by D. M. Hadley, 160–77. London, 1999.

Swanson, R. N. *The Twelfth-Century Renaissance*. Manchester, 1999.

Symes, Carol. "The Performance and Preservation of Medieval Latin Comedy." *European Medieval Drama* 7 (2003), 29–50.

Symes, Carol. *A Common Stage: Theater and Public Life in Medieval Arras*. Ithaca, 2007.

Taglia, Kathryn Ann. "'On Account of Scandal . . .': Priests, their Children, and the Ecclesiastical Demand for Celibacy." *Florilegium* 14 (1995–6), 57–70.

Talbot, C. H., and E. A. Hammond. *The Medical Practitioners in Medieval England: A Biographical Register*. London, 1965.

Taliadoros, Jason. *Law and Theology in Twelfth-Century England: The Works of Master Vacarius (c.1115/1120–c.1200)*. Turnhout, 2006.

Taliadoros, Jason. "Communities of Learning in Law and Theology: The Later Letters of Peter of Blois (1125/30–1212)." In *Communities of Learning: Networks and the Shaping of Intellectual Identity in Europe, 1100–1500*, edited by Constant J. Mews and John N. Crossley, 85–107. Turnhout, 2011.

Tanner, Norman P. *The Church in Late Medieval Norwich, 1370–1532*. Toronto, 1984.

Tatlock, John S. P. *The Legendary History of Britain: Geoffrey of Monmouth's* Historia Regum Britanniae *and its Early Vernacular Versions*. Berkeley, 1950.

Tester, S. J. *A History of Western Astrology*. Woodbridge, 1987.

Thibodeaux, Jennifer D. "Man of the Church, or Man of the Village? Gender and the Parish Clergy in Medieval Normandy." *Gender and History* 18 (2006), 380–99.

Thibodeaux, Jennifer D. "The Sexual Lives of Medieval Norman Clerics: A New Perspective on Clerical Sexuality." In *Sexuality in the Middle Ages and Early Modern Times: New Approaches to a Fundamental Cultural-Historical and Literary-Anthropological Theme*, edited by Albrecht Classen, 471–83. Berlin, 2008.

Thibodeaux, Jennifer D., ed. *Negotiating Clerical Identities: Priests, Monks and Masculinity in the Middle Ages*. Basingstoke, 2010.

Thibodeaux, Jennifer D. *The Manly Priest*. Philadelphia, 2015.

Thomas, Hugh M. *Vassals, Heiresses, Crusaders, and Thugs: The Gentry of Angevin Yorkshire, 1154–1216*. Philadelphia, 1993.

Thomas, Hugh M. *The English and the Normans: Ethnic Hostility, Assimilation, and Identity, 1066–c.1220*. Oxford, 2003.

Thomas, Hugh M. "Lay Piety in England from 1066 to 1215." *Anglo-Norman Studies* 29 (2007), 179–92.

Thomas, Hugh M. "Violent Disorder in King Stephen's England: A Maximum Argument." In *King Stephen's Reign (1135–1154)*, edited by Paul Dalton and Graeme J. White, 139–70. Woodbridge, 2008.

Thomas, Hugh M. "Shame, Masculinity, and the Death of Thomas Becket." *Speculum* 87 (2012), 1050–88.

Thompson, A. Hamilton. "The Deans and Canons of Bridgnorth." *Archaeological Journal* 84 (1927), 24–87.

Thompson, A. Hamilton. *The English Clergy and their Organization in the Later Middle Ages*. Oxford, 1947.

Thompson, Edward Maunde, and S. M. Lakin. *A Catalogue of the Library of the Cathedral Church of Salisbury*. London, 1880.

Thompson, Sally. *Women Religious: The Founding of English Nunneries after the Norman Conquest*. Oxford, 1991.

Thompson, Victoria. *Dying and Death in Later Anglo-Saxon England*. Woodbridge, 2004.

Thompson, Victoria. "The Pastoral Contract in Late Anglo-Saxon England: Priest and Parishioner in Oxford, Bodleian Library, MS Laud Miscellaneous 482." In *Pastoral Care in Late Anglo-Saxon England*, edited by Francesca Tinti, 106–20. Woodbridge, 2005.

Thomson, Rodney M. *Manuscripts from St. Albans Abbey, 1066–1235.* 2 vols. Woodbridge, 1982.

Thomson, Rodney M. "England and the Twelfth-Century Renaissance." *Past and Present* 101 (1983), 3–21.

Thomson, Rodney M. *Catalogue of the Manuscripts of Lincoln Cathedral Chapter Library.* Woodbridge, 1989.

Thomson, Rodney M. "Robert Amiclas: A Twelfth-Century Parisian Master and his Books." In *England and the Twelfth-Century Renaissance*, 238–43. Aldershot, 1998.

Thomson, Rodney M. "Where were the Latin Classics in Twelfth-Century England?" In *England and the Twelfth-Century Renaissance*, 25–40. Aldershot, 1998.

Thomson, Rodney M. "Serlo of Wilton and the Schools of Oxford." *Medium Aevum* 68 (1999), 1–12.

Thomson, Rodney M. *William of Malmesbury.* Rev. edn. Woodbridge, 2003.

Thomson, Rodney M. *Books and Learning in Twelfth-Century England: The Ending of "Alter Orbis."* Walkern, 2006.

Thomson, Rodney M. "The Place of Germany in the Twelfth-Century Renaissance." In *Manuscripts and Monastic Culture: Reform and Renewal in Twelfth-Century Germany*, edited by Alison I. Beach, 19–42. Turnhout, 2007.

Thomson, Rodney M. "Monastic and Cathedral Book Production." In *The Cambridge History of the Book in Britain. Vol. 2, 1100–1400*, edited by Nigel J. Morgan and Rodney M. Thomson, 136–67. Cambridge, 2008.

Thorndike, Lynn. *A History of Magic and Experimental Science*, vol. 2. New York, 1923.

Tinti, Francesca. *Sustaining Belief: The Church of Worcester from c.870 to c.1100.* Farnham, 2010.

Townley, Simon. "Unbeneficed Clergy in the Thirteenth Century: Two English Dioceses." In *Studies in Clergy and Ministry in Medieval England*, edited by David M. Smith, 38–64. York, 1991.

Treharne, Elaine. "The Life of English in the Mid-Twelfth Century: Ralph D'Escure's Homily on the Virgin Mary." In *Writers of the Reign of Henry II: Twelve Essays*, edited by Ruth Kennedy and Simon Meecham-Jones, 169–86. New York, 2006.

Treharne, Elaine. *Living through Conquest: The Politics of Early English, 1020–1220.* Oxford, 2012.

Tristram, Ernest William. *English Medieval Wall Painting: The Twelfth Century.* London, 1944.

Türk, Egbert. *Nugae curialium: Le règne d'Henri II Plantegenêt (1154–1189) et l'éthique politique.* Geneva, 1977.

Turner, Ralph V. *The English Judiciary in the Age of Glanvill and Bracton, c.1176–1239.* Cambridge, 1985.

Turner, Ralph V. *Men Raised from the Dust: Administrative Service and Upward Mobility in Angevin England.* Philadelphia, 1988.

Turner, Ralph V. *Judges, Administrators and the Common Law in Angevin England.* London, 1994.

Turner, Ralph V. *King John.* London, 1994.

Tydeman, William. *The Theatre in the Middle Ages: Western European Stage Conditions, c.800–1576.* Cambridge, 1978.

Van Engen, John H. "The Twelfth-Century: Reading, Reason, and Revolt in a World of Custom." In *European Transformations: The Long Twelfth Century*, edited by Thomas F. X. Noble and John H. Van Engen, 17–44. Notre Dame, 2012.

Vincent, Nicholas. "New Light on Master Alexander of Swerford (d. 1246): The Career and Connections of an Oxfordshire Civil Servant." *Oxoniensia* 61 (1996), 297–309.

Vincent, Nicholas. *Peter des Roches: An Alien in English Politics, 1205–1238*. Cambridge, 1996.

Vincent, Nicholas. "Warin and Henry fitz Gerald, the King's Chamberlains: The Origins of the FitzGeralds Revisited." *Anglo-Norman Studies* 21 (1999), 233–60.

Vincent, Nicholas. "William Marshal, King Henry II and the Honour of Châteauroux." *Archives* 25 (2000), 1–15.

Vincent, Nicholas. *The Holy Blood: King Henry III and the Westminster Blood Relic*. Cambridge, 2001.

Vincent, Nicholas. "Master Elias of Dereham (d. 1245): A Reassessment." In *The Church and Learning in Later Medieval Society: Essays in Honour of R. B. Dobson*, edited by Caroline M. Barron and Jenny Stratford, 128–59. Donington, 2002.

Vincent, Nicholas. "The Court of Henry II." In *Henry II: New Interpretations*, edited by Christopher Harper-Bill and Nicholas Vincent, 278–334. Woodbridge, 2007.

Vincent, Nicholas. "Jocelin of Wells: The Making of a Bishop in the Reign of King John." In *Jocelin of Wells: Bishop, Builder, Courtier*, edited by Robert W. Dunning, 9–33. Woodbridge, 2010.

Vleeschouwers-Van Melkebeek, Monique. "Mandatory Celibacy and Priestly Ministry in the Diocese of Tournai at the End of the Middle Ages." In *Peasants & Townsmen in Medieval Europe*, edited by Jean Marie Duvosquel and Erik Thoen, 681–92. Ghent, 1995.

Vollrath, Hanna. *Thomas Becket: Höfling und Heiliger*. Göttingen, 2004.

Vollrath, Hanna. "Was Thomas Becket Chaste? Understanding Episodes in the Becket Lives." *Anglo-Norman Studies* 27 (2005), 198–209.

Walsh, Martin W. "*Babio*: Toward a Performance Reconstruction of Secular Farce in Twelfth-Century England." In *England in the Twelfth Century: Proceedings of the 1988 Harlaxton Symposium*, edited by Daniel Williams, 219–40. Woodbridge, 1990.

Warren, W. L. *King John*, Berkeley, 1961.

Warren, W. L. *Henry II*, Berkeley, 1973.

Waters, Claire M. *Angels and Earthly Creatures: Preaching, Performance, and Gender in the Later Middle Ages*. Philadelphia, 2004.

Watkins, C. S. *History and the Supernatural in Medieval England*. Cambridge, 2007.

Webb, Clement C. J. *John of Salisbury*. London, 1932.

Webber, Teresa. "The Scribes and Handwriting of the Original Charters." *Journal of the Chester Archaeological Society* 71 (1991), 137–51.

Webber, Teresa. *Scribes and Scholars at Salisbury Cathedral, c.1075–c.1125*. Oxford, 1992.

Webber, Teresa. "Monastic and Cathedral Book Collections in the Late Eleventh and Twelfth Centuries." In *The Cambridge History of Libraries in Britain and Ireland. Volume 1, To 1640*, edited by E. S. Leedham-Green and Teresa Webber, 109–25. Cambridge, 2006.

Webber, Teresa, and Andrew G. Watson. *The Libraries of the Augustinian Canons*. London, 1998.

Weber, Max. *Economy and Society: An Outline of Interpretive Sociology*. 3 vols. New York, 1968.

Weigand, Rudolf. "The Transmontane Decretists." In *The History of Medieval Canon Law in the Classical Period, 1140–1234: From Gratian to the Decretals of Pope Gregory IX*, edited by Wilfried Hartmann and Kenneth Pennington, 174–210. Washington, D.C., 2008.

Weisheipl, J. A. "Science in the Thirteenth Century." In *The History of the University of Oxford. Vol. 1. The Early Oxford Schools*, edited by J. I. Catto, 435–69. Oxford, 1984.

Weiss, Judith. "*Mestre* and Son: The Role of Sabaoth and Terri in *Boeve de Haumtone*." In *Sir Bevis of Hampton in Literary Tradition*, edited by Jennifer Fellows and Ivana Djordjević, 25–36. Woodbridge, 2008.

Wenzel, Siegfried. *Latin Sermon Collections from Later Medieval England: Orthodox Preaching in the Age of Wyclif*. Cambridge, 2005.

Werner, Janelle. "Promiscuous Priests and Vicarage Children: Clerical Sexuality and Masculinity in Late Medieval England." In *Negotiating Clerical Identities: Priests, Monks and Masculinity in the Middle Ages*, edited by Jennifer D. Thibodeaux, 159–81. Basingstoke, 2010.

Wertheimer, Laura. "Illegitimate Birth and the English Clergy, 1198–1348." *Journal of Medieval History* 31 (2005), 211–29.

Wertheimer, Laura. "Children of Disorder: Clerical Parentage, Illegitimacy, and Reform in the Middle Ages." *Journal of the History of Sexuality* 15 (2006), 382–407.

White, Stephen D. "The Politics of Anger." In *Anger's Past: The Social Uses of an Emotion in the Middle Ages*, edited by Barbara H. Rosenwein, 127–52. Ithaca, 1998.

Wilson, R. M. "English and French in England, 1100–1300." *History* 28 (1943), 37–60.

Wilson, Susan E. *The Life and After-life of St. John of Beverley: The Evolution of the Cult of an Anglo-Saxon Saint*. Aldershot, 2006.

Wolverton, Lisa. *Hastening toward Prague: Power and Society in the Medieval Czech Lands*. Philadelphia, 2001.

Wood, Susan. *The Proprietary Church in the Medieval West*. Oxford, 2006.

Wood-Legh, K. L. *Perpetual Chantries in Britain*. Cambridge, 1965.

Woods, Marjorie Curry. *Classroom Commentaries: Teaching the Poetria Nova across Medieval and Renaissance Europe*. Columbus, 2010.

Woolley, Reginald Maxwell. *Catalogue of the Manuscripts of Lincoln Cathedral Chapter Library*. London, 1927.

Wormald, Patrick. *The Making of English Law: King Alfred to the Twelfth Century. Volume 1: Legislation and its Limits*. Oxford, 1999.

Wright, Craig M. *Music and Ceremony at Notre Dame of Paris, 500–1550*. Cambridge, 1989.

Young, Charles R. *Hubert Walter, Lord of Canterbury and Lord of England*. Durham, N.C., 1968.

Ysebaert, Walter. "Medieval Letter-Collections as a Mirror of Circles of Friendship? The Example of Stephen of Tournai, 1128–1203." *Revue Belge* 83 (2005), 285–300.

Zarnecki, George, Janet Holt, and Tristram Holland, eds. *English Romanesque Art, 1066–1200*. London, 1984.

Zieman, Katherine. *Singing the New Song: Literacy and Liturgy in Late Medieval England*. Philadelphia, 2008.

Zier, Mark A. "Sermons of the Twelfth Century Schoolmasters and Canons." In *The Sermon*, edited by Beverly Mayne Kienzle, 325–62. Turnhout, 2000.

Zimmermann, Erich, and Kurt H. Staub. *Buchkunst des Mittelalters: Zimelien der Hessischen Landes- und Hochschulbibliothek Darmstadt*. Wiesbaden, 1980.

Zulueta, Francis de, and Peter Stein, eds. *The Teaching of Roman Law in England around 1200*. Selden Society supplementary series, vol. 8. London, 1990.

Index

Aaron of Lincoln 80
abbots and abbesses:
   clerical retinues of 101, 119, 130, 349–50
Abingdon Abbey 76–7, 108
absenteeism 26
Abū Ma'šar 287–8
Adam, bishop of St. Asaph 204
Adam of Balsham 232, 236, 238–9, 269, 290
Adam of Bromfield 149
Adam de Brus 89
Adam of Eynsham 66, 111, 137, 300, 309
Adam of Petit Pont, see Adam of Balsham
Adam of Tilney 114
Adelard of Bath 340
   and Arabic learning and science 235, 280–1,
     283–4, 292–4
   and music 281, 303, 306
Adgar 41, 44
Adrian IV 176, 231
Aelfric of Eynsham 156
Agace, daughter of Peter of Thorner 184
Agnes, daughter of Richard of Corney 184
Agnes, daughter of Warin de Burgh 176
Ailred of Rievaulx 168, 201, 205, 300
Alain of Lille 301
Alan Anglicus 233
Alard of Burnham 255 n 40, 314, 336
Alberic of London 41, 270, 285, 302
Albertus Magnus 292
alchemy 281, 283
Alexander III 68, 79, 93, 223–4, 347
   and appointments to benefices 82–3, 88–9,
     93–4, 101–2, 108
   on sex and celibacy 172, 174–5
Alexander, bishop of Lincoln 94
Alexander, dean of Wells 191, 280
Alexander, rector of Braybrooke 223
Alexander of Ashby 23–4, 31, 229, 253
Alexander of Dorset 315
Alexander Neckam 179, 234, 300
   and classical learning 271, 292, 294
   intellectual work of 267, 269
   on proper record keeping 131
   and the regular clergy 244, 346, 358
   and the religious status of the clergy 17,
     20–22
   and the royal court 136, 143
   sermons of 271, 292, 325–7
Alexander Romance 275, 285
Alfred, bishop of Worcester 107, 206
Alfred of Chard 259
Alfred of Hemel Hempstead 255
Alfred of Shareshill 235, 282, 340

Alne church 316
Alured, chaplain 166
Alured, master 249, 258
Ambrose, master 137
Andreas Capellanus 42
Anselm, archbishop of Canterbury 119, 186,
   255, 345
   and clerical celibacy 156, 158–60,
     172–3, 182
Anselm, cleric of John de Lacy 125, 128
Anselm, master 296
anti-Semitism 66, 179, 340–1, 344
Arabic learning 235–6, 240, 257, 259, 280–4,
   286–8
archdeacons 59–60
   corruption of 148–50, 173, 199
   duties of 118–19, 328
architecture 313–19
Arcoid, canon of St. Paul's 50
Arez, canon 302
Aristotelian learning 235, 257, 270, 282
Aristotle, master 75
Arnulf of Lisieux 145, 195, 202
art:
   attitudes toward 299
   see also architecture; gemstones and intaglios;
     manuscript illumination; metalwork;
     sculpture; textiles and vestments
astrology/astronomy 259, 266, 271, 281–8,
   292–4
Athelard, rector 316
avarice 25–8, 84–6, 148, 291, 356

Bartholomew, bishop of Exeter 21, 29, 108,
   110–11, 165–6, 175
Baldwin of Bethune 139
Baldwin of Ford, archbishop of Canterbury 17,
   22–3, 137
   and astrology 284, 286
   and the monks of Canterbury 40, 65,
     119–20, 286, 350–3, 356
Baldwin Tirell 123
Bartholomew of St. David's 248–9, 251–2,
   255–7, 259–60
Beleasez of Oxford 340
Belmeis family 94–6
benefices:
   acquisition of 25–6, 90–114
   competition for 87–90
   inheritance of 91–3, 161–3
   promises of 89, 105
Bernard of Clairvaux 343, 346, 358
Bernard the Scribe 131

Beverley Minster 45, 304–5
Bible:
  glossed 254–5, 262–3
  study of 267–9
bishops 15, 231, 317–18, 328
  and monks 349–53, 358, 360
  clerical retinues of 99–101, 119–20, 124–7,
    139–41, 143–5, 349–53
  incomes of 57
  recruitment of *magistri* by 112
Bologna, schools of 80, 136–7, 227–31, 233–4,
    237–8, 242
books:
  circulation and dissemination of 261–3
  clerical ownership of 246–63
  costs of 260–1
  numbers of, in clerical hands 246–54
  production of 263–5
Brictric, priest of Haselbury 69, 169, 323,
    329, 333
Bridgnorth, collegiate church of 317
Broadwater church 315
business, clerical involvement in 26–7

Cambridge University 227, 237–8, 262
canon law, study and practice of 136–8, 233–4,
    278–9
Canterbury Cathedral 319
  disputes between the monks and archbishops
    of 40–1, 65, 203, 345, 350–6, 359
  monks of 40, 42, 162, 345–6
cathedrals, construction of 317–19
cathedral chapters 57–9, 112–13, 317–18,
    349–50
Cecilia, countess of Hereford 19
celibacy, clerical 10, 47, 368–9
  campaign for 155–64
  degree of success of campaign for 183–6
  exhortation for 30–4, 178–83
  lenient enforcement of 174–7
  opposition to 154, 157–9, 164–74
  see also benefices, inheritance of; courtly love
centers of learning, international 227–39; *see also*
    Bologna, Paris, Salerno, Toledo
chantries and chantry priests 69, 333–4
charity 337–8
charters, production of 126–30
Chichester Cathedral, chapter and clergy
    of 113, 184
Christina of Markyate 182
Cistercians 84, 305–6, 343–4, 356–7
  and tithe disputes 223–4, 348–9
Clarembald, physician 255 n. 40
class conflict 48–51
Classical Latin learning and literature 44,
    257–8, 262, 270–2
  ambivalence and concern about 291–2,
    294–5
Clement III 88
clerical courtiers, criticism of 117–18, 139–53
clerics, *see* secular clerics

collegiate churches 60–1, 104–5, 250, 317,
    346–7, 350–3
commercialization 27–8, 73, 77–81, 264–5
common law 121–2, 136, 138, 279
concubines 49 n. 59, 175–7; *see also* wives,
    clerical
  criticism of priests for having 32–4, 253, 302,
    315, 355
  degradation of 180–2
  and drive for clerical celibacy 154, 157–61,
    184–5
  tolerant or favorable view of 166–70,
Conrad, archbishop of Mainz 204–5
conversation, art of 305–6
courtliness 47–8
courtly love 42–6, 51
Coventry Cathedral 313, 350–3, 360
criminous clerks, *see* violence
crusades 213–14
cultic purity 22, 31–2, 35, 173–4, 177, 180, 182

Daniel of Beccles 37, 127, 131, 287–8
Daniel of Morley 236, 259, 279, 282–3
darrein presentment 108–9
David, archdeacon of Buckingham 311
David, earl of Huntingdon 134
David of London 131–2, 230, 256 n. 41,
    261, 273
  and friendship and enmity 206–7
  and the patronage system 101, 110, 144–5
Dover, collegiate church of 61
drama 271–2, 304–5
drunkenness 24, 29–30, 344, 355–7
Durham cathedral, clergy of 347

Eadmer of Canterbury 158–60
ecclesiastical administration:
  corruption in 148–51, 173–4
  expansion of 118–20, 368–9
ecclesiastical courts 119, 121–2, 127, 137,
    162–4
  and clerical violence 209, 215–16, 218–19
economic development 75–81
Edith-Matilda 302
Edmund Rich 282
education, *see* learning and education
Edward Grim 319
Edwin, vicar 316
Eleanor of Aquitaine 45, 284
Elias, dean of Nottingham 161
Elias of Dereham 318
Elviva, mother of William of Norwich 168
Ely, archdeaconry of 62
English, writing in 277, 326
enmity 143–4, 205–8
entertainers 299–301, 305–6; *see also* liturgy;
    music
estate management 75–8
Etienne de Fougères 19, 126, 149, 192
  on sex and celibacy 173, 182
  on simony 25, 111

Eucharist 20–2, 27–9, 32, 331–2
exchequer 121, 130, 135
Exeter Cathedral 243, 250, 272, 301
  chapter of 12 n. 22, 58, 140, 170, 309
Eynsham, vision of monk of 178, 187, 323

falconry, *see* hunting
families, *see* secular clerics, families of
farmers, clerical 73–4, 78–9
feasting 29–30, 41, 356–7
Foliot family 94
French language 274–6
friars 8, 244, 327, 342–3, 364
friendship 106–7, 190, 199–208

gemstones and intaglios 285, 298, 308–9
Geoffrey, cleric of Fordham 176
Geoffrey, schoolmaster 304
Geoffrey de Bosco 316
Geoffrey of Buckland 223
Geoffrey de Lucy 176
Geoffrey of Monmouth 273–5, 277, 286, 372
Geoffrey fitz Peter 98, 103
Geoffrey Plantagenet, archbishop of
  York 112, 276
Geoffrey Ridel 179, 196
Geoffrey of St. Edmund 203
Geoffrey Trocrope 272
Geoffrey of Vinsauf 136, 228, 269, 271, 366
Gerald of Avranches 125
Gerald of Wales 17, 110–11, 213, 230,
  276, 334
  and art and architecture 299, 301, 309, 314
  and books 245, 253, 259, 261, 264
  and clerical households 196–8
  criticism of clergy by 27–30, 292, 301, 328–9
  criticism of monks by 343–5, 347–9, 351,
    353–4, 356–7, 361–2
  on ecclesiastical corruption 149, 199
  and friendship and enmity 201–5, 208
  as an intellectual 233, 237, 241, 278,
    288–90, 296
  intellectual works of 8, 43–4, 272–4, 277,
    291, 324, 331
  and patronage system 108, 114–15, 142, 277
  record keeping by 132
  relations of, with his nephew Gerald 93,
    193–8
  and royal service 55, 109, 136, 140,
    142–4, 237
  on sex and celibacy 33, 166, 172–4, 177–81,
    183–4, 187–9
  on skeptical priests 338–9
  on Walter Map's conversational skills 305–6
  wealth and benefices of 55, 65–6, 74, 84
Gerard, archbishop of York 158, 172–3, 279
Gerard, canon of Lincoln 258
Gerard, son of Lewin 258 n. 58
Gerard of Cremona 235, 282, 284

Gerard la Pucelle 108, 261
  and Eleanor of Aquitaine 46
  and friendship and enmity 203, 205–7
  teaching career of 231, 238, 278
Gerbert of Aurillac 286–7, 293
Gervase, archdeacon of Gloucester 191
Gervase of Canterbury 286, 347, 350,
  352–3, 355
Gervase of Chichester 34, 192, 268
  criticism of clerics by 21–3, 25, 29, 179, 253
  on the exalted status of the clergy 17, 20
Gervase of Tilbury 45, 231, 234, 266, 273, 285
gifts, *see* offerings and gifts
Gilbert Anglicus 233
Gilbert Foliot 343
  and friendship and enmity 107, 203, 206
  and the patronage system 88, 95, 107,
    109–12
  and his relatives 88, 95, 107, 111–12, 227,
    229–30
  and sex and celibacy 163, 174–5
  and Thomas Becket 49, 84
Gilbert Marshal 41, 46
Gilbert de la Porrée 46, 232, 290
Gilbert of Sempringham 109
Giles de Braose 103
glebes 27, 61
gluttony 24, 29, 148, 345, 356–7
Gnossall, collegiate church of 317
Godfrey de Lucy 279, 337
  as bishop of Winchester 139–40
  and Battle Abbey 107–8, 112, 203
  benefices and income of 66
  and his family 94, 108, 161, 17
  at the schools 112
Godric of Finchale 13, 338
Godwin, precentor of Salisbury 268, 309
  and clerical status 12, 21
  on clerical wealth 84–5, 355, 359, 362
  on marriage 171–2
greed, *see* avarice
Gregorian Reform 8, 18, 211, 369
  and clerical celibacy 156, 159, 184–5
Gregory, cleric 294–5, 299
Guibert, abbot of Fleury 201

habitus, Christian 334–5, 369–70
Hackington, planned collegiate church 313,
  350–3
hagiography, works of 256, 274
Hamelin, earl of Warenne 96, 112
Hamo, chancellor of Lincoln 256–7, 311
Hamo of Rochester 248, 256–7, 259–60
Hastings, collegiate church of 103, 106
Hawise, countess of Aumale 123
Hebrew learning 240–1, 267, 288–9, 339–40
Henry I, king of England 133, 159–60, 163
Henry II, king of England 104, 146, 347, 355
  assizes of 56, 89–90

Henry II, king of England (*cont.*)
  and criminous clerks 209, 214–17,
    220–1, 224
  on ecclesiastical corruption 59, 148–50
  and Herbert of Bosham 180, 309
  and Thomas Becket 3, 49, 99, 209
Henry, king of England, the Young
    King 151–2, 231
Henry, precentor of Chichester 300
Henry, son of Geoffrey fitz Peter 98
Henry of Blois 49, 317
Henry of Hereford 106
Henry of Huntingdon 25, 73
  and clerical celibacy 158, 160, 171–2, 175–6
  and contempt for the world 86
  and the court 139–40, 142
  descendants of 75, 92–3
  intellectual work of 43, 270, 272, 274, 285
Henry of London 65–6
Henry Marshal 69, 97
Henry of Northampton 298–9, 301, 308, 313,
    336, 338
Henry Pigun 352
Henry de Pomeray 123
Henry de Ver 122
Henry of Warwick 308
Herbert of Antioch 314
Herbert of Bosham 237, 309, 328
  as an intellectual 240–1, 267
  manuscripts of 312, 318–19
  as the son of a priest 180, 183
  on Thomas Becket 22, 152, 215–16
Herbert the Chamberlain 72
Herbert Losinga 158–9, 345, 357–8, 361
Herbert Medicus 248, 257–60, 262
Herbert Poore 68, 85, 95, 183, 326
Hereford Cathedral 237, 264, 279–80,
    284, 313
  chapter and clergy of 94, 97, 112, 165,
    229–30
  library of 248, 250–1, 261–2
heresy 23, 45, 290, 339–41
Hermann of Dalmatia 236
Heytesbury, collegiate church of 250
Hilary, bishop of Chichester 346
Hilary the Englishman 188
Hildegard of Bingen 261
history, works of 259, 274
histriones, *see* entertainers
homosexuality, *see* same-sex relationships
Honorius, canonist 175, 204, 230, 278, 292
  on forms of simony 28, 150
hospitality 198–9
  abuse of rights of 40, 199
households, clerical 40, 70, 81, 132, 196–8
Hubert Walter 97
  as archbishop of Canterbury 68, 127, 328
  clerical retinue of 136–7, 143–4, 204, 208,
    237, 352

  limited learning of 14, 136, 290
  and the monks of Canterbury 40, 350–2, 355
  as royal cleric 98, 120, 136
  wealth of 58, 73–4
Hue de Roteland 44–5, 134, 275–6, 306
Hugh, archdeacon of Leicester 256 n. 49, 258
Hugh, brother of Hugh de Taunay 106
Hugh of Avalon, bishop of Lincoln 79, 150,
    300, 309, 328
  and patronage 93, 104, 108, 110–11,
    137, 205
  relatives of 93, 191
  retinue of 51, 137
  on sex and celibacy 164–5, 175
Hugh Barre 72
Hugh Bigod 222
Hugh of Buckland 135
Hugh the Chanter 75, 345
Hugh the Chaplain 132
Hugh Foliot 110
Hugh de Hungrie 44
Hugh Malus Clericus 220
Hugh de Mapenor, 103, 165, 194, 235
Hugh de la Mare 211
Hugh Mortimer 96
Hugh Nunant 195, 308, 350–3, 360–1
Hugh of Reculver 336
Hugh de Santalla 236
Hugh Sottovagina 272
Hugh of Wells 68–9, 74, 316
hunting 30, 41–2

Ingelric 72
inheritance, *see* benefices, inheritance of
Innocent III 15, 147
  and appointments to benefices 71, 82, 89,
    91, 102
  and clerical celibacy 154, 164, 175
  and clerical violence 210, 214
intaglios, *see* gemstones and intaglios
intercession 332–4
interdict (1208–14) 102, 105–6, 146–7, 161
intolerance 339–41
Isaac of Skeftlynge 336

Jacob of Lincoln 340
Jacob of the Temple 106
Jews, *see* anti-Semitism; Hebrew learning
Jocelin de Bohun 173–4
Jocelin of Brakelond 88, 94, 107
joculatores, *see* entertainers
John, king of England 102, 146–7, 176
  and clerical concubines 161, 184
  patronage of, to clerics 66–7, 74, 103–6, 110
John, rector of Kirkby Lonsdale 199
John, son of Gervase 253
John Blund 276, 282
John of Brancaster 338
John Burgensis 165

John of Canterbury 107, 341
John of Cornwall 256, 267, 278, 287, 290
John of Ford 168–9
John de Lacy, constable of Chester 125, 128, 284
John of Leicester 272
John of Oxford 197, 283
John Planeta 343
John of Salisbury 12, 47, 49, 64, 140, 234
  on astrology and magic 284–5, 287, 292–3
  and books 261–2
  criticism of clerical courtiers by 140, 148–52
  and debates over education 290
  early education of 330
  on ecclesiastical corruption 148–51
  on friendship and enmity 107, 190,
    199–204, 206–7
  as intellectual 238–40, 270, 288
  intellectual works of 268, 273–4, 278, 297
  and the metaphor of the body politic 20–1
  and monks 345, 348–9, 357–8, 366
  on patronage and the patronage system 25,
    89, 107, 110–11, 148
  and the royal court 109, 237
  on sex and clerical celibacy 167, 169, 172,
    182, 186–7
  on supporting one's kin 190, 195
John of Tilbury 140, 288
John of Tynemouth 144, 204, 208, 278, 281
Jordan, treasurer of Lincoln 311
Jordan Fantosme 134, 232, 275
Jordan de Ros 207
Joseph of Exeter 201, 272
judges delegate 119, 137, 161–2, 223, 234, 279
Julian, rhetorician 270
justices, royal 122, 126, 138, 150–1

kinship 190–6; *see also* nepotism; priests,
    children of; secular clerics, families of
knights 37–9, 43, 50, 56–7, 59

Lambert, chaplain of the countess of Clare 125
Lambeth, planned collegiate church 350–3
Lanfranc, archbishop of Canterbury 20, 156–7
Latin language 241, 269
  clerics and 10, 137, 290, 330, 333
  laypeople and 132–5, 244, 263
  translations from 41, 275
  see also Classical Latin literature; literature,
    works of
law, *see* canon law; common law; Roman law
Lawrence, abbot of Westminster 346
Lawrence, archdeacon of Bedford 311
lay literacy 132–5
lay piety 28–9, 338
Laȝamon 277
learning and education:
  and acquisition of benefices 109–14
  controversies over 289–96
  expectation that clerics would acquire 23–4

at international centers of learning 227–38
  quality of, among the parish clergy 329–31
  and the royal government 135–9
  and social mobility 49
Leicester, archdeaconry of 62
Leofric, bishop of Exeter 243
letter collections 273
liberal arts 231, 269–70, 275, 277, 281
libraries 246–7, 250–1, 260–2
Lincoln Cathedral 79, 237, 272, 334, 360
  cathedral clergy of 41, 66, 68, 112, 175,
    316, 337
  deans of 83, 313, 316
  library of 250–1, 256, 258, 261–2, 311–12
literacy:
  administration and 78, 125–35, 367
  the definition of the clergy and 10, 14, 133–4
literature, works of 258–9, 271–7; *see also*
    Classical Latin literature
  carnivalesque aspects of 295–6
liturgy 301–4, 333
logic 138, 232, 291–2
Lucian of Chester 148, 212, 302, 332, 345, 358
Lucius III 83, 91, 230
Luke, monk of Combermere 130

magic and divination 267, 280, 283–7, 292–4
magistri 112–13, 135–9, 242–3
manuscript illumination 298–9, 310–12
manuscripts, *see* books
Margam Abbey, scribes of 130
marriage, clerical 30–34, 97, 154–60, 164, 168,
    170–2
masculinity 50, 165–6, 178–9, 222–3
mathematics 136, 280–1, 283, 287; *see also*
    numeracy and administration
Matilda, empress 71, 82, 222
Matthew, master 234
Matthew of Bigstrup 46–7
Matthew de Cigogné 64
Matthew Paris 318
Meaux Abbey 63–4, 108–9, 139, 223, 336, 359
medicine 165
  practice of 137, 279–80
  study of 113, 234
  textbooks in 256–7, 259
Merlin 286–7
metalwork 298–9, 307–9
misogyny 180–2
monks, *see* regular clergy
music 302–4

nephews 193–6
nepotism 88, 93–8, 191–3, 195
Nicholas, archdeacon of Huntingdon 172, 311
Nicholas de Sigillo 149, 151
Nigel, bishop of Ely 94, 135, 350
Nigel d'Aubigny 65
Nigel of Whiteacre 35, 199, 306

Nigel of Whiteacre (*cont.*)
  and clerical illiteracy 329–30
  and clerical scholars 232, 290
  on nepotism 191–2
  on the patronage system 25, 87–8, 97,
    113, 145
  on pluralism 26, 65
  and the rivalry between monks and clerics 12,
    353–4, 357
  on sex and celibacy 172, 180
North Newbald church 316
numeracy and administration 135
nuns 182, 221, 274, 314, 344

Odo, abbot of Battle 88, 107–9, 203, 323
Odo of Dover 278
offerings and gifts 28, 61–2, 79–80
Oliver de Merlimont 96
Orderic Vitalis 49, 122, 145, 346
  on clerics in comital households 120, 125
  education of 330
  Ordelarius his father 336
ordinary intellectuals 240–2, 265–6, 268
ordination 10–11, 13, 70–1, 328, 331–2
Osbern, priest of Haselbury 69, 169, 323
Osbert, sheriff of Yorkshire and
  Lincolnshire 164
Osbert de Camera 307–8, 336
Oxford University 227, 237–9, 262,
  264–5, 278

Palladius 77–8
papal provisions 101–2
Paris, schools of 227–33, 237–9, 296,
  325, 346
parish churches 75, 79, 349
  appropriation of 63, 348
  books in 253–4
  building and repair of 314–17
  incomes of 61–4
  leasing of 79–80
  ornaments in 307, 309–10
  patronage of 101, 104–5
parish clergy 15, 159
  attempts to improve 324–6
  incomes of 62–4, 67–70
  performance of duties by 328–35
  responsibility to flock of 23–4
  social status of 41–2, 70–1
Paschal II 158, 160
pastoral care 20–21, 23, 34, 323–33, 362–4
  treatises on 324
Patrick, cleric of Burgate
patristic texts 255
patronage 87–116
  and dependency 144–5, 143–4
Peche family 94
pensions 64–5
Peter, bishop of Périgord 192

Peter, cleric of Earl Ranulf III of Chester 74, 128
  Patrick, his son 102
Peter, rector of Thorner 184
Peter Abelard 38, 111, 231–2, 240, 343,
  346, 358
Peter of Blois 47, 80, 110, 214, 348
  as archdeacon 338
  and books 257, 261, 264
  and Canterbury dispute
  career of 98, 115, 127, 236
  and controversies over learning 290–1
  criticism of clergy by 21, 26–7, 36–8
  criticism of the court and courtiers
    by 117–20, 136, 139–46, 148, 151, 153
  criticism of knights and aristocrats by 48–50
  desire for fame of 289
  on the exalted status of the clergy 17, 21
  on excessive retinues 197–9
  on friendship and enmity 200–1, 203–7
  intolerance of 340–1
  medical interests of 234, 257
  and monks 119–20, 352, 359, 362–3
  and his nephews 194–5
  on nepotism 192
  as polymath 288
  and the royal court 109, 136, 143–4, 237
  on sex and celibacy 92, 173, 182, 187
  on the status of clerics 17, 37
  vestments of 66, 308–9
  on wealth 85–6
  wealth and benefices of 66, 82–4, 115
  works of 43, 268, 272–4, 297, 326, 366
Peter the Chanter 172, 233, 299–301
Peter Comestor 172, 256, 263–4
Peter of Cornwall 139–40, 184
Peter Damian 31, 186
Peter Lombard 231–3, 240–1, 256, 260
Peter Maude 20–1, 23, 271
Peter de Melida 268
Peter of Paxton 256, 263
Peter des Roches 105–6
Peter of Waltham 77–8, 138, 241–2, 258–9,
  314, 318
Petrus Alfonsus 45, 258, 271
Philip, cleric of William Marshal 48
Philip, son of Earl Patrick of Salisbury 96, 112
Philip Apostolorum 255 n. 40, 259, 312
Philip de Broi 209, 217
Philip of Fordham 176
Philip de Harcourt 251, 255, 260, 262
Philip of Manorbier 193
Philip Rufus of Cornwall 165
Philip of St. Edward 263, 337
Philippa Gulafre 129
Philippe de Thaon 41, 275 n. 47, 285
Pipewell Abbey 223
pluralism 26, 65–7, 82–4
poetry 43–5, 136, 188, 241, 272
preaching 23, 325–9; *see also* sermons

pride 85, 148, 187, 198, 289–91
priests, children of 176–7, 183–6, 194, 198
    attitudes toward 33–4, 166–73, 179–80
    inheritance of benefices by 91–3, 159–60,
        163–4, 173–6

Ralph, master 241–2
Ralph, priest of Whitchurch 257, 263
Ralph, vicar of Salford Priors 68
Ralph Basset 124
Ralph of Coggeshall 45, 302
Ralph of Diceto 42, 57, 110–11, 202, 333, 347
    on the Belmeis family 95
    on clerical service in royal government 146
    and St. Paul's Cathedral 78, 254, 309–10,
        313, 336, 338
    on sex and celibacy 160–1, 172, 181–2
    works of 259, 274
Ralph Foliot 248, 256 n. 41
Ralph de Hauterive 213
Ralph Medicus 311
Ralph Neville 110
Ralph Niger 186, 213–14, 279
    as composer 303
    intellectual work of 259, 267, 288–9
Ralph of Sarre 203, 359
    books of 251–2, 255–6, 259–60, 264
Ralph of Tamworth 108
Ranulf, cleric of Abbot Samson 101, 345
Ranulf, earl of Chester 74
Ranulf, son of Erchemar 107
Ranulf Flambard 48–9, 161, 182
    and the royal government 120, 136, 146
Ranulf de Glanville 49, 77, 111, 115, 279
record-keeping, *see* literacy, administration and
Regenbald the Priest 65, 99
Reginald de Bohun 143, 205, 207, 341
    as the son of a priest 173–4, 179–80
Reginald of Durham 29, 41, 337
Reginald Foliot 188
Reginald de Omine 165
reform 18–19, 34–6, 328–9, 369–70
regular canons 11–12, 23, 60, 344, 346; *see also*
    regular clergy
regular clergy 11–12, 119, 130, 369
    conflict of, with the secular clergy 84–5, 171,
        223–4, 343–64
    and English intellectual life 243–5
    and the incomes of the secular clergy 60, 62–4
    and intercession 332
    support of, by secular clerics 262–3, 314,
        336–7, 358–8
    and violence 221
Richard, chaplain of Windsor 310
Richard, dean of Wells 314
Richard I, king of England 55, 74, 97, 211,
    302–4
Richard, rural dean of Worcester 252
Richard, son of Segar 263

Richard, student of Serlo of Wilton 289
Richard Albericanus 339
Richard de Almaria 202, 255 n. 40
Richard Barre 72
    books of 256 n. 41, 256–7 n. 49, 259
    and the royal government 136, 138, 151–2
Richard Briger 105
Richard Belmeis I 95, 103, 163
Richard Belmeis II 95–6, 109–10
Richard of Clifford 311, 336
Richard of Devizes 313, 353
Richard of Dover, archbishop of Canterbury 75,
    88, 108, 127
Richard fitz Nigel:
    as bishop of London 94, 237
    and the deanery of Lincoln 313
    and the royal government 135, 146–7,
        151, 278
Richard of Ilchester 73, 95, 136
    power and influence of 108, 121, 139, 163
    and the royal government 121, 131, 135, 139
Richard of Leicester 120
Richard Marsh 122, 147
Richard de Morins 233
Richard Peche 175
Richard Poore 95, 175, 183
Richard Ruffus 183
Richard of Stortford 308, 336
Richard of Wetheringsett 324
Ripon Minster 60
ritual purity, *see* cultic purity
Robert, bishop of Bath and Wells 58
Robert, count of Meulan 120
Robert Amiclas 238, 268
    books of 248, 251–2, 255 n. 40, 257, 259
Robert of Arden 73
Robert Banastre 227, 229, 242
Robert de Bello Fago 201–2, 256 n. 41, 272
Robert de Béthune 73
Robert Bloet 139, 142
Robert Blund 269
Robert Bonn 263–4
Robert Butevilain 97
Robert Chesney 95, 107
Robert of Chester 281, 283–4
Robert de Courson 82, 232–3
Robert of Edington 248, 251–2, 254–6,
    258–60
Robert fitz Gille 169, 256–7 n. 49, 259, 314
Robert fitz Hamo 65, 102
Robert fitz Harding 111
Robert Foliot 95, 174
Robert de Gant 97–8
Robert Grosseteste 78, 111, 281–2
Robert de Hanc 312
Robert of Inglesham 72–3, 75, 202
Robert of Ketton 236, 240, 281
Robert of Melun 233, 238–9, 267, 290
Robert de Neville 263

Robert Pullen 324
  as cardinal 102, 236
  on correct clerical behavior 27, 30–1, 292
  and the rivalry between secular clerics and
    monks 346, 357–8, 362
  as theologian and teacher 230, 233, 239, 267
Robert of Salerno 234
Robert of Salisbury 192
Robert of Scottow 84
Robert de Sigillo 126 n. 57
Roger, archbishop of York 61, 107, 187–8
Roger, bishop of Worcester 49, 125, 206
Roger, earl of Warwick 91
Roger Arundel 72–3
Roger d'Aubigny 65, 163
Roger the chaplain, canon of London 337
Roger of Hereford 281, 283–4
Roger of Howden 42, 64–6, 123, 333
  intellectual work of 274, 288
  as the son of a priest 175
Roger of Rolleston 203
Roger of Tanton 352
Roger of Salisbury 94, 120, 135, 163, 171
Roger of Wendover 161, 184
Roman law 279
royal administration 74–7, 237, 278
  clerics and 103–6, 113, 120–6, 367, 372
  corruption in 148–51
  debate over clerical service in 139–53
  education and 135–9
  pluralism by clerics of 66–7
royal courts:
  clerics as justices in 121–2, 213
  clerics as defendants in 217–21
rural deans 59–60, 118, 148–50, 173, 196, 199

sacraments 10, 21–2, 27–8, 35, 331–3
St. Benet of Holme 73, 101, 176
St. Martin-le-Grand, London 60–1, 104–5,
    230, 317
St. Paul's 302, 338
  chapter and clergy of 12, 81, 95, 112,
    333–4, 336
  concubines of clerics of 160–1, 181–2
  inheritance of prebends at 91, 93, 118, 183
  management of estates of 73, 76, 78
  gifts of clerics to 66, 254, 298, 304,
    308–11, 313
saints and saints' cults 125, 331, 337, 361
Salerno, schools of 227–8, 234–5, 280
Salisbury Cathedral 57, 295, 301, 313–14,
    317–18
  chapter and clergy of 66, 69, 112
  gifts to 263, 308–10
  learning at 237, 268,
  library of 250
  parish churches connected to 253–4, 307,
    309–10, 330
  value of prebends of 58

same-sex relationships 186–9
Samson, abbot of Bury St Edmunds 66, 207
  clerical retinue of 101, 119, 137, 345–6
  and patronage 88, 94, 96,10, 107
Samson, cleric of William de Redvers 222–3
Samson d'Aubigny 65, 163
Savaric, bishop of Bath and Wells 69
schools 77, 204, 272, 296, 365
  abroad 227–39, 244, 276
  and credentialing 112–13
  in England 229, 269
  and monasteries 346, 362
  and the royal government 135–40
  writings of 260, 262, 324, 327
  see also learning and education
science 235–6, 259–60, 280–3; *see also*
    astrology/astronomy, magic
scribes 126–31
sculpture 299, 309, 316–17
secular aristocrats 56, 96–8, 114–15
  clerical retinues of 102–3, 113, 120, 123,
    125, 127–9
secular clergy:
  aristocratic lifestyles of 30, 38–48,
    50–51, 367
  as authors, 267–82
  commercialization and 27–8, 73, 77–81,
    264–5
  conflict of, with the regular clergy 84–5, 171,
    223–4, 343–64
  conflict of, with the secular aristocracy 48, 50
  criticism of 17, 21–36, 82–4, 140–53,
    178–80, 214–16, 354–5
  as cultural and artistic patrons 298–300,
    307–17
  definition of 9–14
  economic development and 75–81
  exalted religious status of 18, 20–1, 368
  families of 32–4, 91–8, 154–89, 191–6;
    see also priests, children of; concubines,
    clerical; wives, clerical
  as farmers of land 73–4, 78–9
  geographic mobility of 230–1, 236
  households of 196–8
  incomes of 56–75
  as inferior to regular clergy 360–4
  intellectual activities of 232–6, 240–5,
    266–89, 318–19, 365–6
  at international centers of learning 227–38
  kin groups among 93–5, 190–6
  landholding by 70–3
  managerial expertise of 76–8
  networks of influence and 107–9
  numbers of 219
  as owners of books 246–63
  as performers 301–7
  pious activities of 335–8
  ritual performances by 20–2, 27–8, 331–5,
    339, 362–3

service of, in royal administration 74, 76–7, 103–6, 120–6, 139–53
service of, to prelates 99–101, 119–20, 124–7, 130, 139–41, 143–5
service of, to secular magnates 74, 102–3, 120, 123, 125, 127–9
social status of 37–42, 46–7, 52, 70, 367
support of regular clergy by 262–3, 314, 336–7, 358–9
unbeneficed 70–1
Segar, confessor of Wulfric of Haselbury 168–8, 263
Serlo of Bayeux 170
Serlo of Wilton 43–4, 188, 289, 291–2
sermons 19, 256, 269, 271, 325–7
service books 253–4
sheriffs, clerics of 121
Sigar, priest of Newbald 330
Simon, bishop of Worcester 316
Simon of Sywell 204, 278
simony 25–6, 90–1, 111, 150
Simund de Freine 142, 201, 284
skepticism 338–9
social mobility 48–9, 71, 97–9, 115
sodomy, *see* same-sex relationships
Solomon, master 107, 206
Solomon Avenraza 340
Southwell Minster 60
Stephen, king of England 95, 160–1, 284, 286
Stephen Langton 114, 233, 267, 346, 362
Stephen of Segrave 13–14
Sylvester, master 125, 352
synods, attendance at 325–6

textiles and vestments 298, 307, 309–10
Theobald, archbishop of Canterbury 95, 98, 107, 137, 182, 207
Theobald of Étampes 229, 332
debate with monk by 345, 353–4, 362
and priests' sons 171–2
theology 233, 267–9
books of 255–6
Thomas II, archbishop of York 94
Thomas, master 276
Thomas, rector of Bungay 222
Thomas Agnellus 89, 271, 325, 340, 355
criticism of the clergy by 24, 28, 300
and the exalted status of the clergy 17, 20–1, 23–4
on sex and celibacy 32–4, 166, 179
Thomas Becket 110–11, 285, 343, 346, 361
aristocratic lifestyle of 3, 39–40, 42
hunting, 51–2, 300
benefices and income of 59, 84
as churchman 22, 150
and criminous clerks 209, 214–17, 220
and friendship 190, 195
and international centers of learning 137, 230, 232–3

learned entourage of 237
and patronage networks 95, 107, 144
as royal administrator 3, 39–40, 76, 121, 131, 152–3
seal of 308
service in war by 40, 47, 213
and sex and celibacy 175–5, 178–80
and social mobility 49, 98–9
Thomas of Britain 276
Thomas Brown 135
Thomas of Chobham 22, 49, 75, 205, 233, 337
on clerics and commerce 26–8, 79, 131
on clerics and violence 210–13
criticism of the clergy by 26–9, 144, 334
on entertainers 299–300
on magic 292
on nepotism 193
and pastoral care 269, 324, 328
on the results of poor teaching 70, 222
on sex and celibacy 165, 172, 177, 186–7
Thomas of Etton 166
Thomas of Hurstbourne 76–8, 138, 314
Thomas of Kent 275, 285
Thomas of Ludham 101, 176
Thomas of Marlborough 100–1, 204, 248–9, 255–8, 350
Thomas of Monmouth 168, 264, 340
Thomas de Neville 42
Thomas of Walton 101, 176
Thurstan, archbishop of York 303
Thurstin, cleric of Winchester 72
Tickhill, chapelry of 63
tithes 22–3, 27, 61–2, 79–80, 327, 348–9
disputes with the regular clergy over 223–4
misuse of 28–9, 32–3, 300
Toledo 227–8, 235–7
tonsure 11–13, 21
trivium, 228, 257–8, 266; *see also* liberal arts
Turbe family 94
Turchil 41, 135, 287
Twelfth-Century Renaissance 6–7, 265–7, 298, 372
England and 228, 238–40, 366–7

universities 227, 230, 237–9, 244–5, 365, 372; *see also* schools

Vacarius, master 35, 137, 236, 268, 279
vernacular writing 274–7
vestments, *see* textiles and vestments
vicarages 68–9
vicars choral 69, 303
violence:
ban against clerical use of 210–14
and dispute over criminous clerks 34, 209, 214–17, 220–1
motives for 222–4

violence: (*cont.*)
  protection of clerics against 210, 212
  use of, by clerics 209, 217–24
Virgil 257–8, 266, 271, 285

Wace 275, 277–8
Walcher, prior of Malvern 280
Waldric, bishop of Laon 122
Walter, archdeacon of Cornwall 73
Walter of Coutance 202
Walter de Grey 106, 136
Walter of Haselton 73
Walter de Insula 203
Walter of London 327
Walter Map 173–4, 201, 238, 276, 340
  benefices and income of 64, 104, 348
  conversational abilities of 305–6
  criticism of monks by 305–6, 343–5, 348–9,
    356–7
  household of 197–9
  as intellectual 273, 291
  on love and women 45, 182
  on nephews 195–6
  and the royal court 140, 143
  on social mobility 49, 111, 115
Waltham, collegiate church at 60–1, 92, 250,
    333, 347
Westminster Abbey 73, 101
warfare, clerics and 40–1, 47, 122, 213–14
Warin fitz Gerald 263
Warwick, collegiate church of 91, 93
Wedmore church 316
Wells Cathedral 15, 57–8, 89, 301,
    316–17
  chapter and clergy of 112
William, astrologer of John, Constable of Chester
William, bishop of Norwich 84
William, chaplain 184
William, dean of Lichfield 336
William, rector of Broadwater 314–15
William of Anfonia 188–9
William Anglicus 233
William Barbedavril 102, 128, 308
William de Briane 263
William of Briwerre 106
William of Canterbury 166–8
William de Capella 197–8
William of Chers 165
William of Chichester 258
William of Corbeil 346
William of Cornhill 123–4

William de Curzon 139
William of Ely 76, 79, 94, 183
William de Fauconberg 304
William of London 233
William Longchamp 136, 179, 188–9, 192,
    302, 354
William of Malmesbury 146, 157–8, 286–7,
    293, 302–3, 347
William de Mandeville 103
William Marshal 71, 97, 124, 127, 133
  clerical retinue of 48, 113
William de Montibus 20, 291, 348
  criticism of clergy by 17, 26–7, 315
  and pastoral care 324, 326–8
  works of 268, 324, 326
William of Newburgh 217, 220, 353
William of Norwich 168, 340
William of Potterne 311
William of Rule 63–4, 314
William of St. Faith 352
William de Sainte-Mère-Eglise 74, 76, 108,
    191, 201
William of Stafford 235
William of Stradsett 248, 255–6, 258–9
William fitz Stephen 59, 217, 319
  classical learning of 270
  on Thomas Becket 39–40, 51, 76, 95, 107
William of Tonbridge 262
William Turbe 174
William of Verdun 350
William of Wrotham 113, 310
  background of 98
  clerical status of 15
  and royal government 74, 76, 105–6,
    122–4, 136
William of York 166–7
Wimer the chaplain 83, 222–3
Wimund, rural dean 166
Wives, clerical 32–4, 154–60, 168–73, 176–7,
    181–2, 185
Wlward, priest 168
Wolverhampton, collegiate church of 66, 82,
    92, 98, 173, 359
written word, *see* literacy
Wulfric of Haselbury 41, 69, 168–9, 263, 330
Wulfstan, archbishop of York 156
Wulfstan II, bishop of Worcester 119, 157–8

York Minster 57, 65, 243, 272, 334
  chapter and clergy of 75, 97, 102, 112–13,
    316, 345